Poetry for Students

**Presenting Analysis, Context, and Criticism on
Commonly Studied Poetry**

Volume 11

Elizabeth Thomason, Editor

Foreword by David Kelly, College of Lake County

GALE GROUP

**Detroit
New York
San Francisco
London
Boston
Woodbridge, CT**

Poetry for Students

Staff

Editor: Elizabeth Thomason.

Contributing Editors: Anne Marie Hacht, Michael L. LaBlanc, Mark Milne, Jennifer Smith.

Managing Editor: Dwayne D. Hayes.

Research: Victoria B. Cariappa, *Research Manager*. Cheryl Warnock, *Research Specialist*. Tamara Nott, Tracie A. Richardson, *Research Associates*. Nicodemus Ford, Sarah Genik, Timothy Lehnerer, Ron Morelli, *Research Assistants*.

Permissions: Maria Franklin, *Permissions Manager*. Jacqueline Jones, Julie Juengling, *Permissions Assistants*.

Manufacturing: Mary Beth Trimper, *Manager, Composition and Electronic Prepress*. Evi Seoud, *Assistant Manager, Composition Purchasing and Electronic Prepress*. Stacy Melson, *Buyer*.

Imaging and Multimedia Content Team: Barbara Yarrow, *Manager*. Randy Bassett, *Imaging Supervisor*. Robert Duncan, Dan Newell, *Imaging Specialists*. Pamela A. Reed, *Imaging Coordinator*. Leitha Etheridge-Sims, Mary Grimes, David G. Oblender, *Image Catalogers*. Robyn V. Young, *Project Manager*. Dean Dauphinais, *Senior Image Editor*. Kelly A. Quin, *Image Editor*.

Product Design Team: Kenn Zorn, *Product Design Manager*. Pamela A. E. Galbreath, *Senior Art Director*. Michael Logusz, *Graphic Artist*.

Copyright Notice

ISBN 0-7876-4689-X
ISSN 1094-7019
Printed in the United States of America.

10 9 8 7 6 5 4 3 2 1

National Advisory Board

Table of Contents

Just a Few Lines on a Page

I have often thought that poets have the easiest job in the world. A poem, after all, is just a few lines on a page, usually not even extending margin to margin—how long would that take to write, about five minutes? Maybe ten at the most, if you wanted it to rhyme or have a repeating meter. Why, I could start in the morning and produce a book of poetry by dinnertime. But we all know that it isn't that easy. Anyone can come up with enough words, but the poet's job is about writing the *right* ones. The right words will change lives, making people see the world somewhat differently than they saw it just a few minutes earlier. The right words can make a reader who relies on the dictionary for meanings take a greater responsibility for his or her own personal understanding. A poem that is put on the page correctly can bear any amount of analysis, probing, defining, explaining, and interrogating, and something about it will still feel new the next time you read it.

It would be fine with me if I could talk about poetry without using the word "magical," because that word is overused these days to imply "a really good time," often with a certain sweetness about it, and a lot of poetry is neither of these. But if you stop and think about magic—whether it brings to mind sorcery, witchcraft, or bunnies pulled from top hats—it always seems to involve stretching reality to produce a result greater than the sum of its parts and pulling unexpected results out of thin air. This book provides ample cases where a few simple words conjure up whole worlds. We do not ac-

tually travel to different times and different cultures, but the poems get into our minds, they find what little we know about the places they are talking about, and then they make that little bit blossom into a bouquet of someone else's life. Poets make us think we are following simple, specific events, but then they leave ideas in our heads that cannot be found on the printed page. Abracadabra.

Sometimes when you finish a poem it doesn't feel as if it has left any supernatural effect on you, like it did not have any more to say beyond the actual words that it used. This happens to everybody, but most often to inexperienced readers: regardless of what is often said about young people's infinite capacity to be amazed, you have to understand what usually does happen, and what could have happened instead, if you are going to be moved by what someone has accomplished. In those cases in which you finish a poem with a "So what?" attitude, the information provided in *Poetry for Students* comes in handy. Readers can feel assured that the poems included here actually are potent magic, not just because a few (or a hundred or ten thousand) professors of literature say they are: they're significant because they can withstand close inspection and still amaze the very same people who have just finished taking them apart and seeing how they work. Turn them inside out, and they will still be able to come alive, again and again. *Poetry for Students* gives readers of any age good practice in feeling the ways poems relate to both the reality of the time and place the poet lived in and the reality of our emotions. Practice is just another word for being a student. The information given here helps you understand the way to read poetry; what to look for, what to expect.

With all of this in mind, I really don't think I would actually like to have a poet's job at all. There are too many skills involved, including precision, honesty, taste, courage, linguistics, passion, compassion, and the ability to keep all sorts of people entertained at once. And that is just what they do with one hand, while the other hand pulls some sort of trick that most of us will never fully understand. I can't even pack all that I need for a weekend into one suitcase, so what would be my chances of stuffing so much life into a few lines? With all that *Poetry for Students* tells us about each poem, I am impressed that any poet can finish three or four poems a year. Read the inside stories of these poems, and you won't be able to approach any poem in the same way you did before.

David J. Kelly
College of Lake County

Introduction

Purpose of the Book

The purpose of *Poetry for Students* (*PfS*) is to provide readers with a guide to understanding, enjoying, and studying poems by giving them easy access to information about the work. Part of Gale's "For Students" Literature line, *PfS* is specifically designed to meet the curricular needs of high school and undergraduate college students and their teachers, as well as the interests of general readers and researchers considering specific poems. While each volume contains entries on "classic" poems frequently studied in classrooms, there are also entries containing hard-to-find information on contemporary poems, including works by multicultural, international, and women poets.

The information covered in each entry includes an introduction to the poem and the poem's author; the actual poem text; a poem summary, to help readers unravel and understand the meaning of the poem; analysis of important themes in the poem; and an explanation of important literary techniques and movements as they are demonstrated in the poem.

In addition to this material, which helps the readers analyze the poem itself, students are also provided with important information on the literary and historical background informing each work. This includes a historical context essay, a box comparing the time or place the poem was written to modern Western culture, a critical overview essay, and excerpts from critical essays on the poem, when available. A unique feature of *PfS* is a specially commissioned overview essay on each poem by an academic expert, targeted toward the student reader.

To further aid the student in studying and enjoying each poem, information on media adaptations is provided when available, as well as reading suggestions for works of fiction and nonfiction on similar themes and topics. Classroom aids include ideas for research papers and lists of critical sources that provide additional material on the poem.

Selection Criteria

The titles for each volume of *PfS* were selected by surveying numerous sources on teaching literature and analyzing course curricula for various school districts. Some of the sources surveyed included: literature anthologies; *Reading Lists for College-Bound Students: The Books Most Recommended by America's Top Colleges;* textbooks on teaching the poem; a College Board survey of poems commonly studied in high schools; and a National Council of Teachers of English (NCTE) survey of poems commonly studied in high schools.

Input was also solicited from our expert advisory board, as well as educators from various areas. From these discussions, it was determined that each volume should have a mix of "classic" poems (those works commonly taught in literature classes) and contemporary poems for which information is often hard to find. Because of the interest in expanding the canon of literature, an emphasis was also placed on including works by international, multicultural, and women authors. Our advisory board members—current high school and college teachers—helped pare down the list for each volume. If a work was not selected for the present volume, it was often noted as a possibility for a future volume. As always, the editor welcomes suggestions for titles to be included in future volumes.

How Each Entry Is Organized

Each entry, or chapter, in *PfS* focuses on one poem. Each entry heading lists the full name of the poem, the author's name, and the date of the poem's publication. The following elements are contained in each entry:

- **Introduction:** a brief overview of the poem which provides information about its first appearance, its literary standing, any controversies surrounding the work, and major conflicts or themes within the work.

- **Author Biography:** this section includes basic facts about the poet's life, and focuses on events and times in the author's life that inspired the poem in question.

- **Poem Text:** when permission has been granted, the poem is reprinted, allowing for quick reference when reading the explication of the following section.

- **Poem Summary:** a description of the major events in the poem, with interpretation of how these events help articulate the poem's themes. Summaries are broken down with subheads that indicate the lines being discussed.

- **Themes:** a thorough overview of how the major topics, themes, and issues are addressed within the poem. Each theme discussed appears in a separate subhead and is easily accessed through the boldface entries in the Subject/ Theme Index.

- **Style:** this section addresses important style elements of the poem, such as form, meter, and rhyme scheme; important literary devices used, such as imagery, foreshadowing, and symbolism; and, if applicable, genres to which the work might have belonged, such as Gothicism or Romanticism. Literary terms are explained within the entry, but can also be found in the Glossary.

- **Historical and Cultural Context:** This section outlines the social, political, and cultural climate *in which the author lived and the poem was created.* This section may include descriptions of

related historical events, pertinent aspects of daily life in the culture, and the artistic and literary sensibilities of the time in which the work was written. If the poem is a historical work, information regarding the time in which the poem is set is also included. Each section is broken down with helpful subheads. (Works written after the late 1970s may not have this section.)

- **Critical Overview:** this section provides background on the critical reputation of the poem, including bannings or any other public controversies surrounding the work. For older works, this section includes a history of how poem was first received and how perceptions of it may have changed over the years; for more recent poems, direct quotes from early reviews may also be included.

- **Sources:** an alphabetical list of critical material quoted in the entry, with full bibliographical information.

- **For Further Study:** an alphabetical list of other critical sources which may prove useful for the student. Includes full bibliographical information and a brief annotation.

- **Criticism:** at least one essay commissioned by *PfS* which specifically deals with the poem and is written specifically for the student audience, as well as excerpts from previously published criticism on the work, when available.

In addition, most entries contain the following highlighted sections, set separately from the main text:

- **Media Adaptations:** a list of audio recordings as well as any film or television adaptations of the poem, including source information.

- **Compare and Contrast Box:** an "at-a-glance" comparison of the cultural and historical differences between the author's time and culture and late twentieth-century Western culture. This box includes pertinent parallels between the major scientific, political, and cultural movements of the time or place the poem was written, the time or place the poem was set (if a historical work), and modern Western culture. Works written after the mid-1970s may not have this box.

- **What Do I Read Next?:** a list of works that might complement the featured poem or serve as a contrast to it. This includes works by the same author and others, works of fiction and nonfiction, and works from various genres, cultures, and eras.

- **Study Questions:** a list of potential study questions or research topics dealing with the poem. This section includes questions related to other disciplines the student may be studying, such as American history, world history, science, math, government, business, geography, economics, psychology, etc.

Other Features

PfS includes a foreword by David J. Kelly, an instructor and cofounder of the creative writing periodical of Oakton Community College. This essay provides a straightforward, unpretentious explanation of why poetry should be marveled at and how *Poetry for Students* can help teachers show students how to enrich their own reading experiences.

A Cumulative Author/Title Index lists the authors and titles covered in each volume of the *PfS* series.

A Cumulative Nationality/Ethnicity Index breaks down the authors and titles covered in each volume of the *PfS* series by nationality and ethnicity.

A Subject/Theme Index, specific to each volume, provides easy reference for users who may be studying a particular subject or theme rather than a single work. Significant subjects from events to broad themes are included, and the entries pointing to the specific theme discussions in each entry are indicated in **boldface.**

Illustrations are included with entries when available, including photos of the author and other graphics related to the poem.

Citing Poetry for Students

When writing papers, students who quote directly from any volume of *Poetry for Students* may use the following general forms. These examples are based on MLA style; teachers may request that students adhere to a different style, so the following examples may be adapted as needed.

When citing text from *PfS* that is not attributed to a particular author (i.e., the Themes, Style,

Historical Context sections, etc.), the following format should be used in the bibliography section:

"Angle of Geese." *Poetry for Students.* Eds. Marie Napierkowski and Mary Ruby. Vol. 1. Detroit: Gale, 1997. 8–9.

When quoting the specially commissioned essay from *PfS* (usually the first piece under the "Criticism" subhead), the following format should be used:

Velie, Alan. Essay on "Angle of Geese."*Poetry for Students.* Eds. Marie Napierkowski and Mary Ruby. Vol. 1. Detroit: Gale, 1997. 8–9.

When quoting a journal or newspaper essay that is reprinted in a volume of *PfS,* the following form may be used:

Luscher, Robert M. "An Emersonian Context of Dickinson's 'The Soul Selects Her Own Society.'" *ESQ: A Journal of American Renaissance* 30, No. 2 (Second Quarterl, 1984), 111–16; excerpted and reprinted in *Poetry for Students,* Vol. 2, eds. Marie Napierkowski and Mary Ruby (Detroit: Gale, 1997), pp. 120–34.

When quoting material reprinted from a book that appears in a volume of *PfS,* the following form may be used:

Mootry, Maria K. "'Tell It Slant': Disguise and Discovery as Revisionist Poetic Discourse in 'The Bean Eaters,'" in *A Life Distilled: Gwendolyn Brroks, Her Poetry and Fiction,* edited by Maria K. Mootry and Gary Smith (University of Illinois Press, 1987, 177–80; excerpted and reprinted in *Poetry for Students,* Vol. 1, Eds. Marie Napierkowski and Mary Ruby (Detroit: Gale, 1997), pp. 59–61.

We Welcome Your Suggestions

The editors of *Poetry for Students* welcome your comments and ideas. Readers who wish to suggest poems to appear in future volumes, or who have other suggestions, are cordially invited to contact the editor. You may contact the editors via e-mail at: **ForStudentsEditors@galegroup.com.** Or write to the editor at:

Editor, *Poetry for Students*
Gale Group
27500 Drake Rd.
Farmington Hills, MI 48331–3535

Literary Chronology

1572: John Donne is born in London.

1615: Donne is ordained an Anglican minister.

1631: Donne dies.

1633: "A Valediction: Forbidding Mourning" is published, two years after Donne's death, in a collection of his poems called *Songs and Sonnets*.

1809: Alfred, Lord Tennyson is born in Somersby, Lincolnshire.

1830: Emily Dickinson is born in Amherst, Massachusetts.

1832: Lewis Carroll is born Charles Lutwidge Dodgson in Daresbury, Cheshire.

1851: "The Eagle: A Fragment" is published in the seventh edition of Tennyson's *Poems*, which had been published first in 1842.

1856: Carroll meets Alice Liddell who later serves as the model for the protagonist in *Alice's Adventures in Wonderland*.

1866: Dickinson's poem "A Narrow Fellow in the Grass" is published anonymously under the title "The Snake" in a journal called the *Springfield Republican*.

1872: Carroll's "Jabberwocky" is published in *Through the Looking-Glass*. It is the first of many nonsense poems set into the text of the beloved English novel.

1883: William Carlos Williams is born on September 17 in Rutherford, New Jersey.

1886: Dickinson is diagnosed with Bright's disease and dies in May.

1892: Tennyson dies.

1898: Carroll dies on January 14, in Guildford, Surrey, England.

1904: Pablo Neruda is born Ricardo Eliezer Neftali Reyes y Basoalto on July 12 in Parral, Chile.

1905: Stanley Kunitz is born in Worcester, Massachusetts.

1916: Williams writes "Overture to a Dance of Locomotives"; it is published in 1921 in his collection of poems *Sour Grapes*.

1921: Richard Wilbur is born in New York City on March 1.

1923: Louis Simpson is born in Kingston, Jamaica, West Indies.

1923: James Dickey is born in Buckhead, Georgia.

1924: "Tonight I Can Write" is published in a collection of poems by Neruda titled *Veinte poemas de amor y una cancion desesperada*. The collection is translated into English in 1969 by W. S. Merwin as *Twenty Love Poems and a Song of Despair*.

1927: John Ashbery is born in Rochester, New York.

1934: N. Scott Momaday is born in Lawton, Oklahoma.

1945: Neruda elected to Chilean Senate as a Communist.

1949: James Fenton is born in Lincoln, England.

1950: "Beowulf" appears in Wilbur's second volume of poetry, *Ceremony and Other Poems*.

1952: Alberto Rios is born in Nogales, Arizona.

1957: Wilbur wins the Pulitzer Prize and National Book Award for *Things of This World*.

1957: Li-Young Lee is born in Jakarta, Indonesia.

1958: "The War Against the Trees" is included in Kunitz's third volume of poetry *Selected Poems, 1928–1958*.

1959: Kunitz wins the Pulitzer Prize for *Selected Poems*.

1962: Dickey's poem "The Hospital Window" is published in the collection *Drowning With Others*.

1963: Williams dies in March.

1963: Williams is posthumously awarded the Pulitzer Prize for *Pictures from Brueghel*.

1964: Simpson wins the Pulitzer Prize for the collection *At the End of the Open Road*.

1968: Fenton, in his first year at Oxford, is awarded the Newdigate Prize for the best poem by an undergraduate.

1969: Momaday wins the Pulitzer Prize for *House Made of Dawn*.

1971: Neruda wins the Nobel Prize in Literature.

1973: Neruda dies from heart failure on September 23.

1976: Ashbery wins the Pulitzer Prize for *Self-Portrait in a Convex Mirror*.

1976: Momaday's poem "To a Child Running with Outstretched Arms in Canyon de Chelly" is first published in the collection *The Gourd Dancer*.

1980: "Chocolates" appears in Simpson's collection of poetry *Caviare at the Funeral*.

1981: "Paradoxes and Oxymorons" is published in Ashbery's collection of poems *Shadow Train* after previously appearing in the *Times Literary Supplement*.

1985: Ríos' poem "Island of the Three Marias" appears in the second section of his collection *Five Indiscretions*.

1986: Lee's poem "The Weight of Sweetness" is published in his first collection of poems *Rose*.

1987: Wilbur is named Poet Laureate of the United States.

1989: Wilbur wins the Pulitzer Prize for *New and Collected Poems*.

1994: "The Milkfish Gatherers" appears in Fenton's collection *Out of Danger*.

1997: Dickey dies on January 19.

Acknowledgments

The editors wish to thank the copyright holders of the excerpted criticism included in this volume and the permissions managers of many book and magazine publishing companies for assisting us in securing reproduction rights. We are also grateful to the staffs of the Detroit Public Library, the Library of Congress, the University of Detroit Mercy Library, Wayne State University Purdy/Kresge Library Complex, and the University of Michigan Libraries for making their resources available to us. Following is a list of the copyright holders who have granted us permission to reproduce material in this volume of *Poetry for Students* (*PfS*). Every effort has been made to trace copyright, but if omissions have been made, please let us know.

COPYRIGHTED MATERIAL IN *PFS*, VOLUME 11, WERE REPRODUCED FROM THE FOLLOWING BOOKS:

Ashbery, John. From *Shadow Train: Poems*. Penguin Books, 1981. Reproduced by permission Georges Borchardt, Inc., on behalf of the author.—Dickey, James. For "The Hospital Window" from *Drowning with Others; Poems*. Wesleyan University Press, 1962. Reproduced by permission.—Dickinson, Emily. From *The Complete Poems of Emily Dickinson*. Little, Brown, and Co., 1976. Copyright © 1976 by the President and Fellows of Harvard College. All rights reserved. Reproduced by permission of Harvard University Press.—Fenton, James. From *Out of Danger*. Farrar, Straus and Giroux, 1994. Reproduced by permission of Far-

rar, Straus, and Giroux. In the UK by permission of Sterling Lord Literistic, Inc.—Kunitz, Stanley. From *The Terrible Threshold: Selected Poems, 1940–1970*. Secker and Warburg, 1958. Reproduced by permission of Reed Books.—Lee, Li-Young. From *Leaning House Poetry, Volume 1*. Leaning House Press, 1996. Reproduced by permission.—Momaday, N. Scott. For "To a Child Running with Outstreched Arms in Canyon de Chelly" in *Carriers of the Dream Wheel*. Copyright © 1975 by N. Scott Momaday. Reproduced by permission of the author.—Neruda, Pablo. From *Twenty Love Poems: And a Song of Despair*. Translated by W. S. Merwin. Penguin Books, 1993. Copyright © 1993 by W. S. Merwin. No changes shall be made to the text of the above work without the express written consent of The Wylie Agency, Inc.—Rios, Alberto. From *Five Indiscretions*. Sheep Meadow Press, 1985. Reproduced by permission of the author.—Simpson, Louis. From *Caviare at the Funeral*. Franklin Watts, 1980. Reproduced by permission.—Wilbur, Richard. From *New and Selected Poems*. Harcourt Brace & Company. Reproduced by permission.

PHOTOGRAPHS AND ILLUSTRATIONS APPEARING IN *PFS*, VOLUME 11, WERE RECEIVED FROM THE FOLLOWING SOURCES:

Ashbery, John, photograph. AP/Wide World Photos. Reproduced by permission.—Dickey, James, photograph. AP/Wide World Photos. Reproduced by permission.—Dodgson, Charles L.

(Lewis Carroll), photograph. AP/Wide World Photos. Reproduced by permission.—Donne, John, engraving by W. Skelton Sculp. The Bettmann Archive/Newsphotos, Inc. Reproduced by permission.—Fenton, James, photograph by Jerry Bauer. Reproduced by permission.—Kunitz, Stanley, photograph by Jerry Bauer. © Jerry Bauer. Reproduced by permission.—Map; showing the Routes of the Underground Railroad, illustration. Gale Group. Momaday, N. Scott, photograph. UPI/Corbis-Bettmann. Reproduced by permission.—Neruda, Pablo, photograph by Jerry Bauer. © Jerry Bauer. Reproduced by permission.—Rios, Alberto (Alvaro), photograph. Reproduced by permission of Alvaro Rios.—Wilbur, Richard, 1954, photograph by Walter R. Fleischer, AP/Wide World Photos. Reproduced by permission.—Williams, William Carlos, photograph. Archive Photos, Inc. Reproduced by permission.

Contributors

Jonathan N. Barron: Barron is associate professor of English at the University of Southern Mississippi. Beginning in 2001, he will be the editor-in-chief of *The Robert Frost Review*. Original essays on *Hospital Window, Overture to a Dance of Locomotives* and *The War Against the Trees*.

Adrian Blevins: Blevins, a poet and essayist who has taught at Hollins University, Sweet Briar College, and in the Virginia Community College system, is the author of *The Man Who Went Out for Cigarettes*, a chapbook of poems, and has published poems, stories, and essays in many magazines, journals, and anthologies. Original essay on *Hospital Window*.

Jennifer Bussey: Bussey holds a master's degree in interdisciplinary studies and a bachelor's degree in English literature. She is an independent writer specializing in literature. Original essays on *A Narrow Fellow in the Grass* and *Valediction: Forbidding Mourning*.

Michele Drohan: Drohan is a professional editor and writer who specializes in classic and contemporary literature. Original essays on *Go Down, Moses* and *Jabberwocky*.

Joyce Hart: Hart, a former college professor, has lived with Native Americans and studied their traditional ceremonies. Original essay on *To a Child Running in Canyon de Chelly*.

David Kelly: Kelly is an instructor of creative writing at several community colleges in Illinois,

as well as a fiction writer and playwright. Entries on *To a Child Running in Canyon de Chelly* and *The Eagle*. Original essays on *To a Child Running in Canyon de Chelly* and *The Eagle*.

Judi Ketteler: Ketteler has taught Literature and English composition and is currently a freelance writer based in Cincinnati, Ohio. Entry on *A Narrow Fellow in the Grass*. Original essay on *A Narrow Fellow in the Grass*.

Sharon Kraus: Kraus' book of poems, *Generation*, was published by Alice James Books in 1997; individual poems have appeared in *The Georgia Review, TriQuarterly*, and elsewhere. She teaches creative writing, literature, and other courses at Queens College, CUNY (Flushing, NY). Original essay on *The Weight of Sweetness*.

Caroline M. Levchuk: Levchuck, a writer and editor, has published articles on literature along with nonfiction essays and children's books. Entry on *Valediction: Forbidding Mourning*. Original essays on *A Narrow Fellow in the Grass* and *Valediction: Forbidding Mourning*.

Mary Mahony: Mahony earned an M.A. in English from the University of Detroit and a M.L.S. from Wayne State University. She is an instructor of English at Wayne County Community College in Detroit, Michigan. Entry on *Go Down, Moses*. Original essay on *Go Down, Moses*.

Tyrus Miller: Miller is an assistant professor of comparative literature and English at Yale University, where he teaches twentieth-century literature and visual culture. His book *Late Modernism: Politics, Fiction, and the Arts Between the World Wars* is forthcoming. Original essay on *Beowulf*.

Katrinka Moore: Moore teaches writing at Long Island University in Brooklyn, New York, and is a poet whose work appears in anthologies and literary journals. Entry on *Beowulf*. Original essay on *The Weight of Sweetness*.

Carl Mowery: Mowery has a Ph.D. in writing and literature from Southern Illinois University, Carbondale, IL. Original essays on *Beowulf*, *Island of the Three Marias*, and *The War Against the Trees*.

Marisa Anne Pagnattaro: Pagnattaro has a J.D. and Ph.D. in English, and is a freelance writer and a Terry Teaching Fellow in the Terry College of Business at the University of Georgia. Original essay on *Tonight I Can Write*.

Wendy Perkins: Perkins, an Associate Professor of English at Prince George's Community College in Maryland, has published articles on several twentieth-century authors. Entry on *Tonight I Can Write*. Original essay on *Tonight I Can Write*.

John Pipkin: Pipkin is a scholar in the fields of British and American Literature. Original essays on *Paradoxes and Oxymorons* and *Valediction: Forbidding Mourning*.

Dean Rader: Rader is Assistant Professor of English at Texas Lutheran University in Seguin, Texas. Entry on *Overture to a Dance of Locomotives*. Original essays on *Overture to a Dance of Locomotives* and *Tonight I Can Write*.

Morton Rich: Rich, an associate professor of English at Montclair State University, is the author of *The Dynamics of Tonal Shift in the Sonnet*. Original essay on *Hospital Window*.

Sean K. Robisch: Robisch is an assistant professor of ecological and American literature at Purdue University. Original essay on *The Eagle*.

Cliff Saunders: Saunders teaches writing and literature in the Myrtle Beach, South Carolina, area and has published six chapbooks of poetry. Entry on *Jabberwocky*. Original essays on *Jabberwocky* and *Tonight I Can Write*.

Chris Semansky: Chris Semansky holds a Ph.D. in English from Stony Brook University and teaches writing and literature at Portland Community College in Portland, Oregon. His collection of poems *Death, But at a Good Price* received the Nicholas Roerich Poetry Prize for 1991 and was published by Story Line Press and the Nicholas Roerich Museum. Semansky's most recent collection, *Blindsided*, has been published by 26 Books of Portland, Oregon. Entries on *Chocolates*, *Island of the Three Marias*, *Paradoxes and Oxymorons*, *The War Against the Trees*, and *The Weight of Sweetness*. Original essays on *Chocolates*, *Island of the Three Marias*, *Paradoxes and Oxymorons*, *The War Against the Trees*, and *The Weight of Sweetness*.

Erica Smith: Smith is a writer and editor. Original essays on *Go Down, Moses*, *The Milk Fish Gatherers*, and *Overture to a Dance of Locomotives*.

Pamela Steed Hill: Hill has had poems published in over 100 journals and has been nominated for a Pushcart Prize three times. Her first collection, *In Praise of Motels*, was published in 1999 by Blair Mountain Press. She is an associate editor for University Communications at Ohio State University. Entry on *Hospital Window*. Original essay on *Hospital Window*.

Erika Taibl: Taibl has a master's degree in English writing and writes for a variety of educational publishers. Entry on *The Milk Fish Gatherers*. Original essays on *Chocolates* and *The Milk Fish Gatherers*.

Paul Witcover: Witcover is a novelist and editor in New York City with an M.A. in Creative Writing and Literature from the City University of New York. Original essay on *Jabberwocky*.

Beowulf

Richard Wilbur
1950

"Beowulf" appeared in Richard Wilbur's second volume of poetry, *Ceremony and Other Poems* (1950), the book that established him as one of the preeminent American poets of his generation. In this poem, Wilbur retells part of an Old English epic, or long narrative poem, also called "Beowulf." He describes the hero of the ancient poem from a mid-twentieth century point of view.

The epic "Beowulf" was written between the mid-seventh and the late tenth centuries A.D. It tells the story of a Scandinavian hero, Beowulf, who comes to save a kingdom from a monster named Grendel who attacks the castle each night. The hero fights and kills the monster; soon Grendel's mother appears, and Beowulf must defeat her as well. The Danes give Beowulf many gifts in thanks, and he returns home, where he is king of the Geats for fifty years. He eventually dies in a battle against a dragon.

Wilbur shows Beowulf as a melancholy hero. He bravely promises to fight the monster, but he also is aware that being a hero can be a lonely job. Despite his courageous deeds, he is isolated from other people, who cannot really understand him. Even the Danes, whom he saves, are remote from him. While the epic poem celebrates the heroic ideal, Wilbur's poem reveals the hero as a human being living in a less than perfect world.

Wilbur is often seen as a poet of affirmation, one who has a bright and witty view of the world. "Beowulf," then, is somewhat different from the

Richard Wilbur

Attending Amherst College in Massachusetts from 1938 to 1942, Wilbur studied literature in the then-popular method of New Criticism. New Critics encouraged poets to write in traditional forms while expressing the discord of modern life. Wilbur served as the editor of the student newspaper and published some poems, stories, and editorials in college publications. During the summers, he traveled around the country, hitchhiking and "riding the rails"—catching free rides on freight trains.

In 1942 Wilbur married Charlotte Hayes Ward, then joined the U.S. Army to serve in Europe in World War II. He began to write poems more frequently while in the army. Writing helped him, he said, make order out of the chaos he was experiencing. He sent poems to his wife and a few friends; at the end of the war these were published in his first book, *The Beautiful Changes.* Upon returning home, Wilbur went to graduate school at Harvard, and embarked on a university teaching career that lasted nearly forty years. In addition to teaching at Harvard, Wellesley College, Wesleyan University, and Smith College, Wilbur served as Poet Laureate of the United States from 1987 to 1988.

poet's other work in its tone and subject matter, though it is similar in its formal structure and musical rhythm. The power of this poem may come from Wilbur's exploration of a dark side of existence, in spite of his natural inclination to celebrate the details that make life worthwhile.

Author Biography

Richard Wilbur was born in New York City on March 1, 1921, to Lawrence L. Wilbur, a portrait painter, and Helen Purdy Wilbur, whose father and grandfather had been newspaper editors. Wilbur felt influences from both sides of his family. He enjoyed drawing and creating cartoons when he was young, but he also had a passion for words. His interests were combined when he began writing poems, since he uses vivid visual images in his poetry.

When he was two, Wilbur moved with his family to rural New Jersey. They rented a pre-Revolutionary War stone house on a four-hundred-acre estate owned by an English millionaire. Growing up in this environment, Wilbur developed his awareness of and appreciation for nature, which is evident in many of his poems.

Poem Text

The land was overmuch like scenery,
The flowers attentive, the grass to garrulous green;
In the lake like a dropped kerchief could be seen
The lark's reflection after the lark was gone;
The Roman road lay paved too shiningly   5
For a road so many men had traveled on.

Also the people were strange, were strangely
          warm.
The king recalled the father of his guest,
The queen brought mead in a studded cup, the rest
Were kind, but in all was a vagueness and a strain,   10
Because they lived in a land of daily harm.
And they said the same things again and again.

It was a childish country; and a child,
Grown monstrous. So besieged them in the night
That all their daytimes were a dream of fright   15
That it would come and own them to the bone.
The hero, to his battle reconciled,
Promised to meet that monster all alone.

So then the people wandered to their sleep
And left him standing in the echoed hall.   20
They heard the rafters rattle fit to fall,
The child departing with a broken groan,
And found their champion in a rest so deep
His head lay harder sealed than any stone.

The land was overmuch like scenery,   25
The lake gave up the lark, but now its song
Fell to no ear, the flowers too were wrong,

The day was fresh and pale and swiftly old,
The night put out no smiles upon the sea;
And the people were strange, the people strangely   30
    cold.

They gave him horse and harness, helmet and mail,
A jeweled shield, and ancient battle-sword,
Such gifts as are the hero's hard reward
And bid him do again what he has done.
These things he stowed beneath his parting sail,   35
And wept that he could share them with no son.

He died in his own country a kinless king,
A name heavy with deeds, and mourned as one
Will mourn for the frozen year when it is done.
They buried him next to sea on a thrust of land: 40
Twelve men rode round his barrow all in a ring,
Singing of him what they could understand.

Poem Summary

Stanza 1:

The poem opens with a description of the country that Beowulf has come to save. The speaker of the poem seems to be an unseen narrator who is describing this scene from the hero's point of view. There is something too perfect about the natural world; the land is like artificial scenery on a stage. The flowers and the grass seem to have human characteristics; they appear "attentive," or overly polite, and "garrulous," or too talkative. The lake is so still that the reflection of a bird remains after the bird has flown away. The road, built during the days of the now-fallen Roman Empire, seems untraveled. These images of the physical world have an unreal quality, creating a sense of mystery about this country.

Stanza 2:

Here the speaker introduces the people of the country. Like their land, they are strange, though they are hospitable to Beowulf. The king says that he had known Beowulf's father. Offering thanks for his help, the queen serves the hero mead, a wine made from honey, in a cup decorated with jewels. These details are similar to ones that appear in the original epic poem.

The other people have a "vagueness," which may mean that they don't think very clearly, or that they cannot be clearly seen, like shadows. They live in fear of "daily harm," which refers to the nightly attacks by the monster Grendel. This fear causes the people to repeat themselves when they speak. The strangeness of the residents adds to the atmosphere of mystery about this country.

Media Adaptations

- *A Conversation with Poet Laureate Richard Wilbur* is an interview with the poet by Grace Cavalieri, the host of the national radio series "The Poet and the Poem." This videotape is available in libraries or from the Library of Congress in Washington, D.C.

- The videotape *Richard Wilbur,* produced by Lannan Foundation in Los Angeles, CA, includes a reading by the poet at the University of Southern California in 1990, as well as an interview with Wilbur by poet David St. John.

- A 1997 audio recording of "Beowulf," translated by Francis B. Gummere and narrated by George Guidall, is available from Recorded Books Productions in New York.

Stanza 3:

At the beginning of this stanza, the "childish country" appears to refer to the childlike nature of the people. However, the "child / Grown monstrous" describes Grendel, who is a giant monster but also the child of a monster. Since he attacks the castle each night, the people are always afraid. In addition, because Grendel eats those he kills, people fear that he will "own them to the bone." Beowulf determines that he will fight the monster alone, so that others will not risk death.

The poet may have more than one meaning here. The people spend their days afraid of what will happen when night comes. Grendel, according to the Old English poem, lives in the wilderness outside the borders of the kingdom. Wilbur may be implying that the people's "dream of fright" is fear of the unknown. The hero, however, is willing to confront the mystery symbolized by the monster.

Stanza 4:

Wilbur condenses much of the action from the original poem in this stanza. In lines 19–20, he describes how the Danes go off to bed, leaving Beowulf alone to face the monster. The hall is "echoed" because it is a large, high-ceilinged room in the castle. When a crowd is feasting and celebrating there, the noise is very loud. When the hall is empty, it may echo with the slightest sound. Beowulf is a lonely figure standing in this great hall by himself, waiting for the monster. In addition, according to the epic poem, the sounds of human happiness in this hall first attract Grendel's anger, causing him to come and kill those in the castle.

Lines 21–22 describe the fight between Beowulf and Grendel. The fierce battle shakes the beams supporting the roof. Beowulf is so strong he defeats Grendel without using weapons; instead, he pulls the monster's arm completely off his body. The "child"—Grendel—leaves, groaning and dying.

When the fight is over, the Danes find Beowulf in an exhausted sleep. His head is "sealed" because he does not wake up for a long time, and no one knows what he is thinking or feeling. In the original poem, Beowulf fights not only Grendel, but Grendel's mother, who comes to avenge her child's death. Then the hero falls into a deep sleep.

Stanza 5:

The speaker returns to a description of the landscape. However, the country is apparently changed by the monster's death. It is still "overmuch like scenery," as in the first stanza, but now it is not friendly. The lark is free of the lake, but its song is silent. The day passes too quickly and the night offers no welcome. Line 30 echoes line 7, describing the people as strange. Here, though, they are cold instead of warm. It may be that now that they feel safe, they do not care about the hero as much as before.

The country seems to have lost its childishness when its child monster dies. In the first stanza, the land seemed too new, like the road "paved too shiningly" in line 5. In this fifth stanza, the day is "swiftly old." The people may have lost their innocence. While they had their monster, they could blame all their problems on an outside element. Now they have to look inside themselves to find out why the lark's song is not heard, or why the flowers are wrong.

However, since the speaker seems to be describing the adventure from Beowulf's point of view, this change in the land and its inhabitants may come from the hero's own feelings. Perhaps he is so tired from the battle that the country seems unfriendly. Perhaps he believes his effort was so great that the people cannot truly appreciate what

he has gone through. Or, he may feel that since his task is over, he is no longer welcome and should leave.

Stanza 6:

The people are not unappreciative, as this stanza shows. They shower Beowulf with valuable presents as a reward for his rescue of their kingdom. All of these gifts are needed by a warrior-hero—a horse, armor, and weapons. The speaker hints that by giving Beowulf these things, the people are encouraging him to fight other battles, to "do again what he has done." This may imply that the hero would prefer to rest after his great deed, but cannot because everyone expects him to do more great deeds. He may also have these expectations of himself.

Beowulf takes his presents and sails home. He is lonely despite his victory, because he has no son to leave his treasure to. The hero believes in the tradition of children carrying on the name of the father and honoring his accomplishments after his death. Beowulf may weep because he fears no one will remember him after he dies, since he has no son.

Stanza 7:

In this stanza the speaker most reveals Beowulf's isolation from the world. He becomes king of the Geats, but when he dies he has no family members left. He is famous for his brave deeds, and he is mourned, but his is a lonely death. He is buried at the edge of the sea, which is an in-between place, suitable for someone who lived outside the mainstream of the community. Although some of his followers ride around his barrow, or burial mound, and sing at his funeral, they do not fully understand him. Wilbur may be saying that a hero—or anyone who does great deeds—is never completely understood by the people around him.

Themes

Alienation and Loneliness

In describing the adventures of the legendary Beowulf, Wilbur provides him with the sensibilities of a mid-twentieth century person: the hero feels alienated from the rest of society. Beowulf does brave deeds and is appreciated for his courage, but he is isolated from his fellow human beings. He is not an ordinary member of the community, and he has no close family member or friend with whom he can share his feelings. This isolation makes him feel alienated and lonely, even though—

or because—he is a hero and king. Whereas the Old English hero is a member of his community, because the society of that time included warrior bands and small kingdoms often at war, the modern Beowulf may be an outsider in a world that wants to view peace as normal and war as an aberration.

Beowulf risks his life fighting the monster, but this very act sets him apart from those he saves. He must meet the "monster all alone," because everyone else is too afraid. After the battle, Beowulf falls into a deep sleep, his head "harder sealed than any stone." Since he has had an experience no one else has had, he cannot share his feelings with anyone. This situation alienates him from other people. The loneliness apparently continues for his entire life, for when he dies he is still not understood by those who mourn him.

The hero's alienation can be further illustrated by examining other themes. Each of the following themes reveals how Beowulf is alienated from society, whether he feels lonely because of the situation or because of his own perception of the situation.

Duty and Responsibility

Wilbur suggests that Beowulf does not question his duties and responsibilities as a hero. However, the poet implies that the hero's assumption of these responsibilities causes his feeling of alienation.

Beowulf is "to his battle reconciled"; that is, he accepts the duty of fighting the monster whether or not doing so may lead to his own death. He takes the responsibility of fighting the monster alone, without help, so that no one else may be harmed. The people are willing to let him take this responsibility; they go to bed and leave him alone to his fate. When he has saved them, they give him many gifts in thanks. However, even these presents are evidence of his continued duty and responsibility. He is given a horse, armor, and weapons, objects that will help him to take on further duties and responsibilities as a hero. He is expected—and expects of himself—to go fight more monsters. As the last stanza shows, he becomes a king and continues to achieve great heroic deeds, though always somewhat separated from other people. His acceptance of his responsibility to other people also makes him alienated from these same people.

Appearances and Reality

The speaker of the poem appears to interpret the events from Beowulf's point of view. There-

Topics for Further Study

- Explore how the rhymed lines affect the feeling of the poem. Read "Beowulf" aloud and determine how the rhyme scheme helps to create a certain atmosphere in the poem. Describe the atmosphere and explain how the rhyme contributes to it.

- Research the sixth century A.D. in Europe, the period of history in which Beowulf would have existed. How did people live? What weapons and methods were used in war? Why do you think this was a time of upheaval?

- Beasts and monsters have appeared in legends and literature throughout human existence. Is there any scientific basis for the idea of a monster? Trace the sources of such creatures as trolls, ogres, and dragons and try to determine how these monsters originated.

- Richard Wilbur wrote a short poem, retelling the epic of Beowulf from his own point of view. Choose a novel or movie that has made an impression on you. Write a poem in which you retell the story in your own way.

fore, it may be hard for the reader to distinguish whether a description is objective or colored by Beowulf's feelings. For example, do the people really change their behavior after the monster is killed? The second stanza describes them as "strangely warm," while the fifth stanza calls them "strangely cold." Do they change, or is Beowulf himself changed by the experience? Do the people keep themselves apart from him, or does he just believe that they do? Wilbur does not tell us directly whether this version of events is realistic or is based on Beowulf or the speaker's interpretation of events.

Likewise, the idea of childishness reflects the theme of appearances and reality. The speaker says that it is a "childish country." This may mean that the people are childish in their fear of the monster. There may not even be a real monster; it may be only a symbol of the people's fear of the dark, since it only attacks at night. In addition, the monster it-self is described as a child, though a huge and mean child. When Beowulf destroys the child/monster, the country loses its childishness as well.

Wilbur is exploring a theme that goes beyond Beowulf's story. He is asking how we can distinguish appearances from reality. He indicates that any story may be told from each observer's or participant's point of view, and the point of view will determine how the story is told.

Nature and Its Meaning

Wilbur uses nature imagery to reflect undercurrents in the events of the poem. The first stanza shows Beowulf's first impression of the land. It is too perfect and has an unreal quality. The old Roman road seems untraveled, perhaps because no one comes to this country out of fear of the monster. The "attentive" flowers and "garrulous" grass reveal how the country needs Beowulf's help. The oddness of the land is the result of the monster's presence.

The nature imagery in the fifth stanza has a different purpose. Here it may be revealing the hero's alienation or the shift in the country's perception of the hero. While it still has an unreal quality, the landscape has changed. The day is "swiftly old," and the flowers are "wrong." The reader might expect that the natural world would show happiness, or relief, but instead it is a depressing place, unwelcoming.

Style

"Beowulf" consists of seven six-line stanzas. Each stanza describes one part of the narrative, following chronological order. The tone is formal, in keeping with the account of a hero. However, Wilbur is not writing a story so much as a character study of Beowulf, or of all heroes. The most dramatic event—the battle with the monster—takes only two lines of the poem. The stanzas reveal the atmosphere of the hero's experience, but they do not provide much detail about the actual adventures.

The rhyme scheme is the same for each stanza. Using the letters a, b, and c to denote the end rhyme of each line, the rhyme scheme is a, b, b, c, a, c. For example, in the last stanza the final words of each line are king, one, done, land, ring, and understand. This consistent pattern of rhyming helps create the formal effect of the poem. It also makes some language in the poem sound inevitable. For instance, in the fifth stanza the last line ends in "cold," rhyming with the fourth line's "old."

The meter, or rhythm, of the poem is not quite as consistent as the rhyme scheme. A line of poetry can be divided into feet. Each foot has a pattern of light and heavy stresses, according to the way the words are read. In "Beowulf," most of the lines are iambic pentameter; each foot has one light stress followed by a heavy stress, and there are five feet in each line. Line 17 is iambic pentameter: The_ he_ ro_, to_ his_ bat_ tle_ rec_ on_ ciled_. [NOTE: the scanning symbols follow the syllables they should be directly over.] However, other lines break out of this meter. Line 30, for example, has two almost-equal parts: "And the people were strange, the people strangely cold." Here the rhythm is similar to the rhythm common in Old English poems, in which there is a pause in the middle of the line. The reader pauses between "strange" and "the." Wilbur is paying tribute to the original poem in constructing some of the lines in this way.

Historical Context

One way to study Wilbur's "Beowulf" is by comparing the poet's time with that of the epic hero's period. Wilbur published "Beowulf" in 1950, just a few years after the end of World War II. During the war, he served as an Army cryptographer and soldier. His infantry division fought in Europe, and Wilbur was in active combat in bloody campaigns for three years. It is interesting to note that he has written few poems directly about the war, although he has said that the experience of battle caused him to become serious about writing poetry.

Americans in 1950 wanted to put the war behind them. Many people had lived through World War I (1914–1918), the Great Depression (from 1929 into the late 1930s), and World War II (1939–1945). Many young couples, including Wilbur and his wife, were having families. America was victorious and prosperous, helping to finance the rebuilding of Europe and Japan after the war. However, tensions arose between the United States and the communist Soviet Union, the two dominant world powers, causing the Cold War, which lasted nearly fifty years.

The epic *Beowulf* takes place during a period in Europe known as the Migration Age. After the

Compare & Contrast

- **Sixth Century** A.D.: Throughout this period warrior bands and small kingdoms battle in northern Europe and Scandinavia. This is the time during which the legendary Beowulf would have lived.

  1941–1945: American involvement in World War II begins after the Japanese bombing of Pearl Harbor in December, 1941. The U.S. military fights in Asia, North Africa, and Europe in an effort to defeat German and Japanese hegemony.

  1950–1953: Americans fight along with other United Nations troops in the Korean War, a "hot" war resulting from the Cold War, which was caused by tensions between the United States and the communist nations, China and the Soviet Union.

  1961–1973: More than three million Americans serve in Vietnam during the U.S. involvement in that country's civil war. This war, also a result of the Cold War, creates bitter domestic conflict within the United States and ends in the defeat of American forces.

  1991: U.S. forces lead a multinational military alliance in the Persian Gulf War against Iraqi dictator Saddam Hussein.

- **1942:** Richard Wilbur experiences some effects of the American government's suspicion of anyone with leftist and communist sympathies. His training as a cryptographer is cut short when the FBI reports that he has "leftist views," and his service record is stamped "Suspected of Disloyalty." Despite this, Wilbur continues to serve in World War II as an army sergeant.

  1950: Senator Joseph McCarthy announces that he has a list of names of highly-placed U.S. officials who are members of the Communist Party. For the next four years, McCarthy uses his power to accuse many leading citizens of being communists, effectively adding to an atmosphere of distrust and fear throughout the country.

  1989: The Cold War comes to an end as countries in Eastern Europe renounce communism, the Berlin Wall is torn down, and the Soviet Union disintegrates.

Roman Empire fell, around 500 A.D., Germanic people of northern and central Europe moved south and west, creating new kingdoms. These migrating people included Germans, the Anglo-Saxons who settled in England, and Scandinavians, or residents of Sweden, Denmark, Norway, and Iceland. Since these Germanic groups were connected culturally, they held similar attitudes toward warfare and the ideal of the heroic figure. Thus Beowulf, although a Scandinavian hero, was recognized as heroic by the Anglo-Saxons as well. Based on historical persons who appear as characters in the epic poem, scholars have determined that the events took place in the sixth century A.D. While Beowulf himself is legendary, the world of warrior bands and small kingdoms throughout northern Europe that is the background of the poem is accurate.

A Modern Response to "Beowulf"

The epic *Beowulf,* written between the mid-seventh and the late tenth centuries A.D., tells of the adventures of a high-ranking warrior of the Geats, a tribe located in Sweden. Hearing of a kingdom in Denmark that is threatened by a monster, Beowulf sails across the sea to rescue the people. He fights and kills two monsters, then returns to the land of the Geats.

Wilbur's response to the epic is to change the Anglo-Saxon attitude toward heroes into a world-weary postwar sensibility. While he retains the original setting, he incorporates modern feelings into his lyric retelling. The critic Bruce Michelson sees the dreaminess of the landscape and its inhabitants as "dreams which have turned toward nightmare"—a possible reference to events of

World War II. According to critic Rodney Edge-combe, Wilbur takes the repetition of language that is common in epic poetry and conceives of it as the failure of language to capture inscrutable ideas. This view reflects the disorder and lack of harmony in modern life.

Critical Overview

When *Ceremony and Other Poems,* the book in which "Beowulf" first appeared, was published, the critic Joseph Bennett called Wilbur the "strongest poetic talent" of his generation. He singled out "Beowulf," calling it a "curious and disturbing vision which partakes of the nature of a poetic charm." Others acknowledge Wilbur's poetic workmanship; poet-critic Louise Bogan writes that he had proved himself a "subtle lyricist of the first order." Writing in the *New York Times Book Review,* Babette Deutsch notes his "musicianly skill." In further analysis, she describes the poems as "alive with light," yet "apt to close upon a somber chord, to admit an intrusive shadow."

Without denying Wilbur's ability, some critics feel he was too cautious in his writing. Randall Jarrell, reviewing the book in the *Partisan Review,* remarks that the "poems are all Scenes, none of them dramatic." He states that Wilbur "never goes too far, but he never goes far enough." This perception of Wilbur as a master of meter and rhyme who is too subdued in expressing the dark side of existence has persisted throughout his career.

However, more in-depth criticism over time has revealed fuller dimensions of Wilbur's work. Critic Stephen Stepanchev, writing in 1965, explores the poet's celebration of the "individual imagination, the power of mind that creates the world," seeing it as Wilbur's speculation on the nature of reality. Stepanchev also suggests that while this view of human as creator makes people appear "heroic," Wilbur has the twentieth-century writer's awareness of man's "roles as killer and victim." This tension, between ideal and actual, reality and dream, is very apparent in "Beowulf," as critic Donald Hill explains in his 1967 study of Wilbur.

In the years since the publication of *Ceremony and Other Poems,* American poetry has undergone radical changes. Many poets began writing in free verse, moving away from traditional forms. It became more common to write on personal and political subjects. Since Wilbur seemed somewhat

apart from this movement, few extended critical commentaries have been written on his work of late. In the 1980s and 1990s, however, Wendy Salinger, Bruce Michelson, and Rodney Edgecombe have reexamined Wilbur's poetry, finding it more relevant to the turbulence of the times than earlier reviewers had realized. Michelson called him a "serious artist for an anxious century," and claims his poetry "is many-faceted, personal, and intense in ways that have not been recognized." As Deutsch comments, Wilbur's apparent sunny view of the world has subtly realized shadows.

Criticism

Carl Mowery

Mowery has a Ph.D. in literature and composition from Southern Illinois University. He has written many essays for Gale. In the following essay, he examines imagery and Wilbur's use of Old English poetic techniques in the poem "Beowulf."

In his poem "Ars poetica," Archibald MacLeish said that "a poem should not mean but be." Richard Wilbur believes that a poem is not a vehicle for communicating a message but that it is an object with "its own life" and "individual identity." Wilbur's poetry is often intellectually taxing, and he expects the reader to be involved in the poem, its imagery and substance. He does not intend to communicate a message, but rather to create an interesting piece of writing. He believes that art ought to "spring from the imagination" and create a "condition of spontaneous psychic unity." That unity depends on the relationship of the inner parts of the poem, one to the other, and the involvement of the reader in the poem itself. He expects the reader to engage his or her intellect to understand and enjoy his poetry. As a result, a balance between the intellect and the imagination will be achieved, as in his poem "Beowulf."

Wilbur's way of maintaining the reader's involvement in the poem is by creating intense images out of routine images. For example, in the second line of "Beowulf," the routine images of flowers and grass are intensified by association with incongruous words. The flowers are "attentive"; the grass is "garrulous green." By personifying (giving human traits to a non-human object) these plants, he has created more intense images of flowers standing tall, seemingly listening for some sound, and then the talkative green grass supplying that sound. Additionally, the combination of these two new images creates one of a meadow (the scenery) with all its parts interacting with each other, fulfilling the image of the first line "overmuch like scenery." Here is a place of more than just vegetation in a landscape.

The lark image in the first stanza is only a reflection in the lake. The lake retains the reflection of the lark as though it were a tangible object that could be held and released at will. At the second lark image, the lake now gives up the reflection. But the lark's call goes unheard, the flowers are "wrong," the day was "swiftly old," and "the night put out no smiles." These now create an atmosphere of desolation and emptiness. The contrast between these two scenes is important: the first with its hopefulness and the second with its silence and foreboding.

This approach is like that of the imagist poets: Ezra Pound, William Carlos Williams, Wallace Stevens, and others. These poets reduced the number of words in their poems to a minimum and intensified the meanings by artful juxtaposition. An important aspect of the imagist approach to poetry is the creation of a concrete image that "presents an intellectual and emotional complex at one moment in time," according to the editors of *Modernism in Literature*. An example of this is Ezra Pound's poem "In the Station of the Metro." The entire poem reads:

> The apparition of these faces in the crowd;
> Petals on a wet black bough.

The immediate imagery is straightforward, but after a moment of reflection, these images combine in the mind of the reader to create a more intense one of people crowded into the subway station melding with the image of petals on a wet tree branch. The final purpose of the poem is the amalgamation of the two disparate images into one. Though Wilbur's poem is not an imagist poem, there are many similar aspects present in it.

Admittedly, some of the poetry of the imagists is difficult to fathom, but this is not the case with Wilbur's work. He does not give up the basic notion that poetry should be intellectually taxing, but he also feels that it should not be obscure. In the specific case of this poem, apparent obscurity may be the result of unfamiliarity with the original *Beowulf*, but such knowledge is not required to appreciate the story Wilbur is telling. It is his task to retell the tale in his own manner with enough detail to make it a complete story. It must conform to Wilbur's belief that a poem should be an "indi-

> " ... the 'strictness of form' in a poem is its strength and its advantage.... the 'strength of the genie comes of his being confined in a bottle.'"

vidual entity," even though it is far shorter than the original epic. Additionally, for the poem to succeed it must engage "the strict attention of the serious reader" say the editors of *American Tradition in Literature*.

Wilbur believed that the "strictness of form" in a poem is its strength and its advantage. He said that the "strength of the genie comes of his being confined in a bottle." As a result, what seems like a constriction becomes a strength. For this poem, he has selected the formal structure of seven six-line stanzas divided into two parts of four and three stanzas each. It uses the unique rhyme scheme: *abbcac*. The original *Beowulf* is a long poem (at least 3,182 lines exist and many more were likely lost over time) and for Wilbur to retell it might have taken many more stanzas. But he chose to limit it to just seven, requiring him to condense every part of the tale to fit his poetic form. The process of reduction and condensing, in combination with (what the editors of the *Anthology of American Literature* call) "the freshness of his imagery," created the intensely brief poem.

Beowulf is found in only one manuscript, which was probably written down in the tenth century. It is one of the best examples of Old English poetry extant. (Old English, the linguistic forebear of modern English, is derived from older forms of German and northern European languages from the middle of the first millennium.) These kinds of poems were recited or sung in public by a poet, called a scop. Many were tales of gallantry in battles (*The Battle of Maldon*), the lives of kings, religious poems (*The Dream of the Rood*), and tales of mythical beings. *Beowulf* is a combination of both historical kings and the mythical beasts that Beowulf fought to save the kings from annihilation.

What Do I Read Next?

- Richard Wilbur has translated poems and plays from the French, Russian, Spanish, and Italian. His translations of Old English include parts of the epic *Beowulf.* One Russian poet whose work Wilbur has translated into English is Joseph Brodsky, and Brodsky, in turn, has translated Wilbur's work into Russian. These two poets are similar in their use of rhyme and meter—aspects of poetry that are difficult to translate. Wilbur's translation of Brodsky's "The Funeral of Bob" appears in both *New and Collected Poems* and Brodsky's *A Part of Speech.*

- Robert Frost (1874–1963) was a major influence on Wilbur. Like Wilbur, Frost was from a New England family and drew inspiration from that area of the country. The poets share an attention to detail in nature and the use of formal rhyme and meter. Frost has many books; one to start with is his *Selected Poems.*

- Another poet who has retold a well-known narrative in a shorter poem is Denise Levertov (1923–1998), whose "A Tree Telling of Orpheus" describes a scene from the ancient Greek myth. Orpheus played such enchanting music on his lyre that, according to the legend, trees pulled up their roots in order to follow him and listen. In this poem, one of the trees tells what happened. "A Tree Telling of Orpheus" appears in Levertov's *Relearning the Alphabet,* first published by New Directions in 1966.

- Wilbur also wrote books for children, including *Opposites: Poems and Drawings,* which he illustrated himself. These riddle-like poems, based on a wordplay game he played with his children when they were young, are in the form of question and response, such as: "What's the opposite of two? A lonely me, a lonely you." Wilbur went on to write *More Opposites* and *Runaway Opposites,* which has collage illustrations by Henrik Drescher.

- As a young man teaching at Harvard after World War II, Richard Wilbur knew many of the prominent poets of his generation. Among his contemporaries, Wilbur says it was Elizabeth Bishop who most influenced him—by teaching him "the joy of putting a poem together." The critic M. L. Rosenthal notes the shared qualities of Wilbur and Bishop, describing their poems as having "elegance, grace, precision, quiet intensity of phrasing." Bishop's poetry is widely anthologized, but all her work can be found in *The Complete Poems, 1927–1979.*

Wilbur, a scholar of the ancient poets, adopted two important Old English poetic techniques for his poem of 1950. These are: the scansion or line structure of the poem and the alliterative nature of the poems. The scansion (metrical analysis) of the Old English poems consists of a two-part line, with each part having at least two stressed syllables. This can be seen in the following example from the epic *Beowulf.* The first lines (in Old English) are:

Hwæt, we gardena in geardagum,
theodcyninga   thrym gefrunon.

The metrical notation for these lines is:

/ _ _ / _ / _ / _
/ _ / _ _ / _ / _

The important aspects to note are the break in the middle of each line, called *ceasura,* and the two stressed syllables in each half line.

The poems of the time did not use rhyming sounds at the ends of lines. Instead, the Old English poems used alliteration (the repetition of consonant sounds) within the lines as the unifying "rhyming" formula. In the first line, the important sound is "g"; in the second line, the important sound is "th" (which is the "th" sound in Modern English). In both cases, this sound occurs at least once in each half line. A more striking use of this alliterative scheme occurs in line four of *Beowulf,* in which case the repeated sound is "s."

ing that sound. Additionally, the combination of these two new images creates one of a meadow (the scenery) with all its parts interacting with each other, fulfilling the image of the first line "overmuch like scenery." Here is a place of more than just vegetation in a landscape.

The lark image in the first stanza is only a reflection in the lake. The lake retains the reflection of the lark as though it were a tangible object that could be held and released at will. At the second lark image, the lake now gives up the reflection. But the lark's call goes unheard, the flowers are "wrong," the day was "swiftly old," and "the night put out no smiles." These now create an atmosphere of desolation and emptiness. The contrast between these two scenes is important: the first with its hopefulness and the second with its silence and foreboding.

This approach is like that of the imagist poets: Ezra Pound, William Carlos Williams, Wallace Stevens, and others. These poets reduced the number of words in their poems to a minimum and intensified the meanings by artful juxtaposition. An important aspect of the imagist approach to poetry is the creation of a concrete image that "presents an intellectual and emotional complex at one moment in time," according to the editors of *Modernism in Literature*. An example of this is Ezra Pound's poem "In the Station of the Metro." The entire poem reads:

> The apparition of these faces in the crowd;
> Petals on a wet black bough.

The immediate imagery is straightforward, but after a moment of reflection, these images combine in the mind of the reader to create a more intense one of people crowded into the subway station melding with the image of petals on a wet tree branch. The final purpose of the poem is the amalgamation of the two disparate images into one. Though Wilbur's poem is not an imagist poem, there are many similar aspects present in it.

Admittedly, some of the poetry of the imagists is difficult to fathom, but this is not the case with Wilbur's work. He does not give up the basic notion that poetry should be intellectually taxing, but he also feels that it should not be obscure. In the specific case of this poem, apparent obscurity may be the result of unfamiliarity with the original *Beowulf,* but such knowledge is not required to appreciate the story Wilbur is telling. It is his task to retell the tale in his own manner with enough detail to make it a complete story. It must conform to Wilbur's belief that a poem should be an "indi-

> *... the 'strictness of form' in a poem is its strength and its advantage.... the 'strength of the genie comes of his being confined in a bottle.'*"

vidual entity," even though it is far shorter than the original epic. Additionally, for the poem to succeed it must engage "the strict attention of the serious reader" say the editors of *American Tradition in Literature*.

Wilbur believed that the "strictness of form" in a poem is its strength and its advantage. He said that the "strength of the genie comes of his being confined in a bottle." As a result, what seems like a constriction becomes a strength. For this poem, he has selected the formal structure of seven six-line stanzas divided into two parts of four and three stanzas each. It uses the unique rhyme scheme: *abbcac*. The original *Beowulf* is a long poem (at least 3,182 lines exist and many more were likely lost over time) and for Wilbur to retell it might have taken many more stanzas. But he chose to limit it to just seven, requiring him to condense every part of the tale to fit his poetic form. The process of reduction and condensing, in combination with (what the editors of the *Anthology of American Literature* call) "the freshness of his imagery," created the intensely brief poem.

Beowulf is found in only one manuscript, which was probably written down in the tenth century. It is one of the best examples of Old English poetry extant. (Old English, the linguistic forebear of modern English, is derived from older forms of German and northern European languages from the middle of the first millennium.) These kinds of poems were recited or sung in public by a poet, called a scop. Many were tales of gallantry in battles (*The Battle of Maldon*), the lives of kings, religious poems (*The Dream of the Rood*), and tales of mythical beings. *Beowulf* is a combination of both historical kings and the mythical beasts that Beowulf fought to save the kings from annihilation.

What Do I Read Next?

- Richard Wilbur has translated poems and plays from the French, Russian, Spanish, and Italian. His translations of Old English include parts of the epic *Beowulf.* One Russian poet whose work Wilbur has translated into English is Joseph Brodsky, and Brodsky, in turn, has translated Wilbur's work into Russian. These two poets are similar in their use of rhyme and meter—aspects of poetry that are difficult to translate. Wilbur's translation of Brodsky's "The Funeral of Bob" appears in both *New and Collected Poems* and Brodsky's *A Part of Speech.*

- Robert Frost (1874–1963) was a major influence on Wilbur. Like Wilbur, Frost was from a New England family and drew inspiration from that area of the country. The poets share an attention to detail in nature and the use of formal rhyme and meter. Frost has many books; one to start with is his *Selected Poems.*

- Another poet who has retold a well-known narrative in a shorter poem is Denise Levertov (1923–1998), whose "A Tree Telling of Orpheus" describes a scene from the ancient Greek myth. Orpheus played such enchanting music on his lyre that, according to the legend, trees pulled up their roots in order to follow him and listen. In this poem, one of the trees tells what happened. "A Tree Telling of Orpheus" appears in Levertov's *Relearning the Alphabet,* first published by New Directions in 1966.

- Wilbur also wrote books for children, including *Opposites: Poems and Drawings,* which he illustrated himself. These riddle-like poems, based on a wordplay game he played with his children when they were young, are in the form of question and response, such as: "What's the opposite of two? A lonely me, a lonely you." Wilbur went on to write *More Opposites* and *Runaway Opposites,* which has collage illustrations by Henrik Drescher.

- As a young man teaching at Harvard after World War II, Richard Wilbur knew many of the prominent poets of his generation. Among his contemporaries, Wilbur says it was Elizabeth Bishop who most influenced him—by teaching him "the joy of putting a poem together." The critic M. L. Rosenthal notes the shared qualities of Wilbur and Bishop, describing their poems as having "elegance, grace, precision, quiet intensity of phrasing." Bishop's poetry is widely anthologized, but all her work can be found in *The Complete Poems, 1927–1979.*

Wilbur, a scholar of the ancient poets, adopted two important Old English poetic techniques for his poem of 1950. These are: the scansion or line structure of the poem and the alliterative nature of the poems. The scansion (metrical analysis) of the Old English poems consists of a two-part line, with each part having at least two stressed syllables. This can be seen in the following example from the epic *Beowulf.* The first lines (in Old English) are:

Hwæt, we gardena in geardagum,
theodcyninga   thrym gefrunon.

The metrical notation for these lines is:

/ _ _ / _ / _ / _
/ _ / _ _ / _ / _

The important aspects to note are the break in the middle of each line, called *ceasura,* and the two stressed syllables in each half line.

The poems of the time did not use rhyming sounds at the ends of lines. Instead, the Old English poems used alliteration (the repetition of consonant sounds) within the lines as the unifying "rhyming" formula. In the first line, the important sound is "g"; in the second line, the important sound is "th" (which is the "th" sound in Modern English). In both cases, this sound occurs at least once in each half line. A more striking use of this alliterative scheme occurs in line four of *Beowulf,* in which case the repeated sound is "s."

Oft Scyld Scefing sceathena threatum.

The use of alliteration by more modern poets is not a new occurrence. One of the most beautifully alliterative lines in American poetry comes at the end of the first stanza of the poem "To Helen" by Edgar Allan Poe:

The weary, way-worn wanderer bore
To his own native shore.

The special beauty of this line is that it combines both alliteration (the letter "w") and assonance (the repetition of a vowel sound, in this case the letter "o").

Wilbur's poetic vision for his poem did not stop at the modern schemes available to him. He has used these Old English techniques, adding their ancient strengths to his own poetic creativeness to write this poem. Each line is readily divisible into two parts, and each of those parts contains two stressed syllables. Additionally, most of the half lines have an alliterative relationship with the other half line. In some there are two sounds repeated, as in line one of stanza two: "Also the people were strange, were strangely warm." The repeated letters are "s" and "w."

The final measure of the success of a poem, according to Wilbur, is its sound. Just as the epic *Beowulf* was meant for public recitation, so too is the poem "Beowulf" intended to be read aloud. His "concern for structure coincides with his evident response to sensory impressions," according to the editors of *American Tradition in Literature*. He intended for the meaning of the poem to be carried "by the sound," as the reader is able to add dramatic emphasis to the poem. To feel the full beauty of the example by Poe, it must be spoken aloud. The process of saying these words will give the speaker an added enjoyment, too. For the listener to an Old English poem, the sound creates the atmosphere of the ancient scop. Wilbur's combination of the old alliteration and the new rhyme scheme creates a special set of sounds capturing the atmosphere of the old poem and pattern of the modern poem. As a result, the aural experience adds to the understanding of the poem.

Richard Wilbur said, "I like it when the ideas of a poem seem to be necessary aspects of the things or actions which it presents." For him, a poem is not just a series of techniques and words that create clever imagery. It is a total experience that combines all aspects of the poem into one moment. He once said that a poem is an effort to express knowledge and to discover patterns in the world. By reversing this process and joining two

established patterns, not only has he created a new one, but he has found a new way to stretch the imagination and intellectual engagement of his readers.

Source: Carl Mowery, in an essay for *Poetry for Students,* Gale Group, 2001.

Tyrus Miller

Tyrus Miller is an assistant professor of comparative literature and English at Yale University, where he teaches twentieth-century literature and visual culture. His book Late Modernism: Politics, Fiction, and the Arts Between the World Wars *is forthcoming. In the following essay, Miller examines how Wilbur echoes the strangeness and enigmatic nature of his poem's predecessor.*

Richard Wilbur's "Beowulf" provides an ironically truncated and lyrically simplified version of the Old English epic poem of the same name, which may date from eighth-century England. The original Old English poem, one of the most extended and powerful works of Anglo-Saxon to have survived, has several unresolved puzzles about it that lend it an air of mystery and strangeness. Its archaic and poetically stylized language, its origin in oral tradition predating its transcription, the loss of parts of its manuscript to fire in the eighteenth century, the reference of the poem to a still earlier time than that of the poet, its complex set of peoples and tribes, its supernatural figures of monsters and dragons, and its peculiar mixture of pagan rituals and Christian beliefs all contribute to the foreignness of this major early work of the English poetic tradition. Wilbur, indeed, finds in the original *Beowulf* a paradoxical quality. It is monumental and inescapably present for the poet as part of his literary legacy, and yet it is something he can only feebly understand. It stands like a heap of stones on a hillside or the stone blocks carved with serpentine patterns that can be found in the English, Irish, and Scandinavian countryside: testimony to an archaic past to which the present is connected, yet a testimony spoken in a language nearly incomprehensible to modern eyes and ears.

In Wilbur's version of "Beowulf," the character of Beowulf is viewed as possessing some of the same qualities of strangeness that the poem *Beowulf* has in the English literary tradition. Wilbur alludes to the fact that the character Beowulf, as a warrior coming from the Geats, is a stranger to the people with whom the poem is primarily concerned, the Danes. Furthermore, he is also a foreigner to the Beowulf poet, who may have been

> *For far from revealing an original intimacy with its heroic center, Wilbur suggests, the Anglo-Saxon poem also communicates strangeness, distance, and failure to comprehend its hero."*

from Mercia, in what is now the Midlands of England. Beowulf travels from abroad, coming unexpectedly to the Danes to fight the monster Grendel, who has invaded their lands and terrorized them, brutally killing off many of King Hrothgar's best warriors and weakening his kingdom. Beowulf succeeds in killing Grendel and the monster's vengeful mother as well. In later years, he kills a dragon and seizes its treasure for his people but is mortally wounded in the attempt. He is buried in a lavish funeral ceremony along with the treasure for which he died.

Wilbur emphasizes the inscrutable nature of Beowulf's motivations for taking on these deadly challenges. One day the stranger shows up from beyond the sea, boasting that he can kill the monster that no one has been able to touch for years. He performs the deed, gains the praise and glory of the Danes, and goes home. For Wilbur, this inscrutability of Beowulf as a character is matched by the enigma of the poem that bears his name. An Old English poem about ancient Germanic societies, it arrives in the English tradition like a stranger without a name. As modern readers, we know only external details: those partial and fragmentary clues to its meaning given to us by archeological study, other poems in the Anglo-Saxon language, and the few elements of the archaic traditions passed down to later times. We are forced to strain our minds to imagine what it might mean. Like the Danes who have heard of the warrior but to whom the man Beowulf was and remained a stranger, we can only say that we know "of" and "about" the poem "Beowulf," but cannot say that we really know and understand it. In the end, our attempts to read and interpret "Beowulf" are akin to the funeral rituals of Beowulf's people after he

has killed the dragon and been killed by it. Reading it, marking its place in the literary tradition, and writing poems based on it as Wilbur has done, one does honor to something that is nevertheless understood only to a limited extent.

Rather than representing the setting and story of "Beowulf" in a realistic mode, Wilbur underscores the artifice with which the poet crafted his tale by projecting a stiff and stylized aspect onto the scene itself: "The land was overmuch like scenery, / The flowers attentive, the grass too garrulous green; / In the lake like a dropped kerchief could be seen / The lark's reflection after the lark was gone." This landscape has been rendered artificially still, like a painting; even the reflection is not subject to change, but endures after the reflected object is gone. Similarly, the "road" in the fifth and sixth lines is hardly a real place where vehicles, animals, and people are moving. It is more like a glossy strip of paint receding into a painted backdrop: "The Roman road lay paved too shiningly / For a road so many men had traveled on." Similarly, in the next stanza, Wilbur self-consciously comments on a quality of the poetic language of the Old English epic: "And they said the same things again and again." Like the Greek classical poets coming out of an oral tradition, Anglo-Saxon poets depended on stock formula and epithets, generic scenes and ritual enumeration of genealogies and of objects, around which the poet would improvise and embroider new variations. As one of the oldest poems of the Anglo-Saxon tradition, *Beowulf* is strongly marked by the ritualized, formulaic nature of its poetic diction. It says "the same things again and again."

Moreover, it is characterized by another form of repetition typical of Anglo-Saxon poet, in its use of alliterations within the basic four-stress line. Usually, three out of four of the stressed words in a line would begin with the same consonant sound. Wilbur formally alludes to this metrical practice in such lines as the fourth, which alliterates the "g" sound ("The flowers attentive, the grass too garrulous green"); the thirteenth, with its repeated "c" ("It was a childish country; and a child"); the thirty-first, with its insistent "h" ("They gave him horse and harness, helmet and mail"); and the thirty-seventh, which introduces a variant with the hard "c" paired to two "k" sounds ("He died in his own country a kinless king"). In this way, he signals that his poem represents less a narration of a real scene than a revisiting of a fictional site made up of words: the foreign Anglo-Saxon words of the anonymous *Beowulf* poet.

Wilbur touches very cursorily on the most exciting plot event of the source poem, Beowulf's unarmed battle with and slaying of the bloody monster Grendel. Speaking of Grendel, he writes, "It was a childish country; and a child, / Grown monstrous, so besieged them in the night / That all their daytimes were a dream of fright / That it would come and own them to the bone." Wilbur treats the monster as if it were the anthropological equivalent of a childhood phobia, which in turn implies that the triumphant hero Beowulf is likewise less a real person than an imaginative expedient invented by the collective mind to keep such fears at bay. "The hero," Wilbur continues, "to his battle reconciled, / Promised to meet that monster all alone." Through the fictive invention of their poets, who have imaginatively brought the heroic stranger to their shores to save them, the people can leave the task of fighting monsters to the hero himself, who will face Grendel alone. Wilbur thus suggests the ways in which the poet's inventions are necessary to the people, yet serve their purpose precisely insofar as they remain different from everyday life, insofar as they remain irreducibly strange to those for whom they render fictive aid.

The battle with Grendel is similarly distanced. The long and grim struggle of the hero with the monster, which ends with Beowulf's tearing off Grendel's arm at the shoulder and displaying it to the relieved Danes, is passed over in a single sentence, followed by a strange calm: "They heard the rafters rattle fit to fall, / The child departing with a broken groan, / And found their champion in a rest so deep / His head lay harder sealed than any stone." It is as if the mighty Beowulf, having fulfilled his sole task of banishing the childish fear that had been materialized as a monster, has become a mere statue of himself, "the hero" carved in granite.

The fifth stanza reprises the setting of the first, even repeating the opening line: "The land was overmuch like scenery." Yet if in the opening stanza, the landscape appeared artificially luminous and still, in this later stanza, the hero's victory over Grendel seems to have drained any life from the scene. "The lake gave up the lark, but now its song / Fell to no ear, the flowers too were wrong," Wilbur writes. "The day was fresh and pale and swiftly old / … / And the people were strange, the people strangely cold." Having performed his single task, the hero departs, loaded with the gifts granted a warrior and the glory of his deeds. But Wilbur suggests that the hero is doomed to the tragic repetition of his entry and departure as a

stranger. He takes the spoils and sets sail, but as the last line of the sixth stanza reveals, he laments even in his triumph: "These things he stowed beneath his parting sail, / And wept that he could share them with no son."

The last stanza draws together the enigma of Beowulf as a hero and *Beowulf* as a paradoxical starting-point of the English poetic tradition. Having fought against the dragon and been mortally wounded in this last great deed, Wilbur writes, Beowulf "died in his own country a kinless king, / A name heavy with deeds." Yet even in death he has remained a stranger to his people, his tragic self-sacrifice and confrontation of threatening monsters being only partially comprehensible to those under his protection. Wilbur alludes in his last lines to the enigmatic ending of the Old English poem, in which the fallen Beowulf is buried with the dragon's treasure that he lost in life in capturing: "They buried him next the sea on a thrust of land: / Twelve men rode round his barrow all in a ring, / Singing of him what they could understand." The final line, which connects Beowulf's death to poetry and song, suggests that where the mystery of the hero Beowulf left off, the poem "Beowulf" began.

The Anglo-Saxon *Beowulf,* Wilbur is suggesting, pays homage to and immortalizes that limited fraction of the man that the community could understand, making more familiar what had been irreducibly strange and archaic about him. Wilbur's own poem entitled "Beowulf," however, stands in a similarly fragmentary, summary, and reductive relation to the mysteries of understanding posed by the long Anglo-Saxon poem. Condensing into forty-two lines the hundreds of lines of the original poem, Wilbur signals his own relation to this "stranger" of the tradition; within the restricted ambit of his ability to grasp Beowulf, he too is "singing of him." In a final irony, however, his last lines suggest that, despite all the centuries that have passed, he is entirely in tune with the tradition, even at its earliest moment. For far from revealing an original intimacy with its heroic center, Wilbur suggests, the Anglo-Saxon poem also communicates strangeness, distance, and failure to comprehend its hero. It is from this strangeness and failure that poetry takes its point of departure. Once again experiencing the impossibility of grasping "Beowulf," both the poetic hero and the enigmatic poem that bears his name, Wilbur affirms his repetition of the Anglo-Saxon's predicament as he makes anew the earlier poet's troubled "song."

Source: Tyrus Miller, in an essay for *Poetry for Students,* Gale Group, 2001.

Sources

Bender, Todd K., et al., *Modernism in Literature,* Holt, Rinehart and Winston, 1977, p. 246.

Bennett, Joseph, *Hudson Review 4,* Spring 1951, pp. 131–145.

Bly, Robert, ed., *The Best American Poetry 1999,* Scribner, 1999, p. 213.

Bogan, Louise, *Achievement in American Poetry 1900–1950,* Henry Regnery, 1951.

Bradley, Sculley, Richmond Croom Beatty, and E. Hudson Long, eds., *American Tradition in Literature,* W. W. Norton and Co., Inc., 1967, pp. 1659–1660.

Crossley-Holland, Kevin and Bruce Mitchell, *Beowulf,* Farrar, Straus & Giroux, 1968.

Deutsch, Babette, *New York Times Book Review,* February 11, 1951, p. 12.

Edgecombe, Rodney Stenning, *A Reader's Guide to the Poetry of Richard Wilbur,* University of Alabama Press, 1995.

Evans, Harold, *The American Century,* Alfred A. Knopf, 1998.

Hill, Donald, *Richard Wilbur,* Twayne Publishers, 1967.

Hollander, John, ed., *The Best American Poetry 1998,* Scribner, 1998, p. 324.

Jarrell, Randall, *The Third Book of Criticism* Farrar, Straus & Giroux, 1965.

McMichael, George, ed., *Anthology of American Literature,* Macmillan Publishing Co., Inc., 1974, p. 1678.

Michelson, Bruce, *Wilbur's Poetry: Music in a Scattering Time,* University of Massachusetts Press, 1991.

Rosenthal, M. L., *The Modern Poets,* Oxford University Press, 1960.

Sacks, Peter, "Richard Wilbur," in *American Writers,* edited by Lea Baechler and A. Walton Litz, Charles Scribner's Sons, 1991.

Salinger, Wendy, ed., *Richard Wilbur's Creation,* University of Michigan Press, 1983.

Stepanchev, Stephen, *American Poetry Since 1945,* Harper & Row, 1965.

Stern, Carol Simpson, "Richard Wilbur," in *Contemporary Poets,* edited by Tracy Chevalier, St. James Press, 1991.

Swanton, Michael, *Beowulf,* Manchester University Press, 1997.

Wilbur, Richard, *New and Collected Poems,* Harcourt Brace Jovanich, 1988.

For Further Reading

Butts, William, ed., *Conversations with Richard Wilbur,* University Press of Mississippi, 1990.

In these nineteen interviews and conversations with Richard Wilbur, ranging from 1962 to 1988, the reader has the opportunity to hear Wilbur's "disarmingly open" voice and his views on poetry. A chronology of the poet's life and Butts' introduction trace changes in Wilbur's poetry over his long career.

Edgecombe, Rodney Stenning, *A Reader's Guide to the Poetry of Richard Wilbur,* University of Alabama Press, 1995.

This book is meant to be perused with a copy of Wilbur's *New and Collected Poems* at hand. Edgecombe discusses each poem in this collection, and gives his comments on Wilbur's recurring themes over his years of writing.

Heaney, Seamus, *Beowulf,* Farrar, Straus & Giroux, 2000.

The Noble Laureate Seamus Heaney translates the original epic, using the four-stress line and heavy alliteration common to Anglo-Saxon poetry, in this Whitbread Prize-winning book. In *The New York Times Book Review,* James Shapiro writes that "generations of readers will be grateful" for Heaney's accomplishment in translating this poem.

Salinger, Wendy, ed., *Richard Wilbur's Creation,* University of Michigan Press, 1983.

Salinger explores the critical reaction to Wilbur's work throughout the changing literary views in the post-World War II years. While in the introduction Salinger makes clear her own bias in favor of Wilbur's genius, she provides a balanced selection of reviews and essays by critics, incorporating dissenting voices along with more sympathetic ones.

Wilbur, Richard, *New and Collected Poems,* Harcourt Brace Jovanich, 1988.

This volume contains all seven of Wilbur's books of poetry published before 1988, including *Ceremony and Other Poems,* in which "Beowulf" first appeared. In addition, this book contains the text of the cantata "On Freedom's Ground," which Wilbur wrote in honor of the centennial of the Statue of Liberty and which was performed in New York City in 1986.

Chocolates

Louis Simpson
1980

"Chocolates" appears in Louis Simpson's collection of poetry *Caviare at the Funeral* in Section Three, directly after the title poem. Both the title poem, "Caviare at the Funeral," and "Chocolates," reference or feature Russian writer Anton Chekhov, the nineteenth-century playwright and fiction writer known for his realistic portrayals of Russian life. Simpson's idea of poetry as primarily a narrative act that details the real lives of people matches Chekhov's own idea of what makes effective writing. "Chocolates" is a narrative poem that recounts a true story about people who go to visit Chekhov. After struggling to make conversation, the group livens after Chekhov asks them if they like chocolates.

In his essay "Chocolates" from his *Selected Prose,* Simpson writes that he was at a friend's house reading the daily newspaper when something sparked his memory of hearing about the incident on which the poem is based. Simpson says that he picked up a notepad and wrote the poem in a few minutes. With the exception of a few minor revisions, the poem was published as is. Simpson notes two changes he made from the original story. The first is that in the poem the speaker describes the visitors as "some people," whereas in the actual incident the visitors were women. Simpson says he made this change to avoid the appearance that either he or Chekhov was condescending to women. The second change is the detail of Chekhov taking his visitors' hands as they left. This is something that Simpson says he imagines that Chekhov would have done.

This poem conveys the idea that human life consists of material events and things. Poetry itself should also consist of these events and things, and not metaphysical questions which can never be answered. Chekhov, though widely considered a genius, was uncomfortable talking about himself. In this poem his genius was in his ability to coax others to talk about subjects which really mattered to them, such as their preferences for different kinds of chocolates.

A number of the poems in *Caviare at the Funeral* take Russia or people associated with Russia as their subject. Simpson's mother's family was from Russia, and in his poem "Why Do You Write about Russia?", also included in this collection, the speaker remembers the voices of his mother and grandmother, who would tell him stories of life in Russia.

> When I think about Russia
> it's not that area of the earth's surface
> with Leningrad to the West and Siberia
> to the East—I don't know anything
> about the continental mass.
>
> It's a sound, such as you hear
> in a sea breaking along a shore
>
> My people came from Russia,
> bringing with them nothing
> but that sound.

For Simpson, the sound of the storytelling voice is the most human element of stories, more compelling than the story itself. He attempts to embody that voice in "Chocolates" and his other poems.

Author Biography

As the son of a mother of Russian ancestry and a celebrated writer himself, Louis Simpson is well qualified to write about the popular Russian writer Anton Chekhov. Simpson was born in Kingston, Jamaica, West Indies, in 1923, to Aston Simpson, a lawyer, and Rosalind Marantz Simpson, a World War I émigré and actress. His father was successful, and the Simpsons led a privileged life, with a large house, and maids, cooks, chauffeurs, and assorted other servants. In Simpson's own words they lived as "well-to-do colonials." His mother's storytelling was an early influence on Simpson's writing. She told stories about growing up in Poland and she told fairytales. Simpson's childhood desire, in fact, was not to be a poet but to write stories.

Educated at Munro College, referred to by islanders as the "Eton of Jamaica," the young Simp-

Louis Simpson

son read English literature and English history, and cultivated the taste of an Englishman. But he was not English; he was Jamaican. In his book of autobiographical essays *The King My Father's Wreck,* Simpson said that many Jamaicans had an inferiority complex because of this discrepancy. Simpson's eight years at Munro (from the age of nine to seventeen) were difficult. The poet has written that some of the teachers were sadists and that bullying, both by teachers and other students, was the norm. Aston Simpson and Rosalind divorced when Simpson was a teenager, and when his father died, Simpson discovered that he had been almost nothing of the estate, which his father had willed to his second wife. Simpson left soon after for America and New York City to visit his mother.

In New York, Simpson studied literature at Columbia University and, after a three-year stint in the military during World War II, returned to Columbia to complete his Ph.D. After working as a book editor and reporter, Simpson settled down to a career in academia. From 1959 to 1967 he was a Professor of English at the University of California at Berkeley, and from 1967 until his retirement in 1993, he was a Professor of English at the State University of New York at Stony Brook.

Although Simpson's literary style has evolved over his career, he has always believed that poetry is about the emotions, and that successful poetry should make people feel. Much of his early poetry, especially, *The Arrivistes* and *Good News of Death and Other Poems,* was written in conventionally ordered meter and rhyme, although it addressed contemporary subject matter. This changed in his Pulitzer Prize-winning collection *At the End of the Open Road.* In this collection, Simpson deviates somewhat from his tight forms and experiments more with imagery to shoulder the emotional weight of his poems. Whereas his earlier work was more realistic in its depiction of character and event, his middle period explored what critics came to call "deep imagery" or "emotive imagination" to give resonance to his words. In the third phase of Simpson's career, his poems reveal a heightened sensitivity to the feelings, thoughts, and experiences of other people. This is particularly evident in poems like "Chocolates" in *Caviare at the Funeral.* In the last few decades he has been associated with a group of writers who are attempting to bring narrative back to poetry, specifically poets and writers associated with Story Line Press, which has published much of the poet's recent work. Simpson is also a critic, having published a number of books on other poets, including *Three on the Tower,* a study of Ezra Pound, T. S. Eliot, and William Carlos Williams, and *A Revolution in Taste: Studies of Dylan Thomas, Allen Ginsberg, Sylvia Plath, and Robert Lowell.* In addition he translates poetry from the French. His *Modern Poets of France: A Bilingual Anthology* won the Academy of American Poets 1998 Harold Morton Landon Translation Award.

Poem Text

Once some people were visiting Chekhov.
While they made remarks about his genius
the Master fidgeted. Finally
he said, "Do you like chocolates?"

They were astonished, and silent.   5
He repeated the question,
whereupon one lady plucked up her courage
and murmured shyly, "Yes."

"Tell me," he said, leaning forward,   10
light glinting from his spectacles,
"what kind? The light, sweet chocolate
or the dark, bitter kind?"

The conversation became general.   15
They spoke of cherry centers,
of almonds and Brazil nuts.

Losing their inhibitions
they interrupted one another.   20
For people may not know what they think
about politics in the Balkans,
or the vexed question of men and women,

but everyone has a definite opinion   25
about the flavor of shredded coconut.
Finally someone spoke of chocolates filled with
        liqueur,
and everyone, even the author of *Uncle Vanya,*
was at a loss for words.

As they were leaving he stood by the door   30
and took their hands.
In the coach returning to Petersburg
they agreed that it had been a most
unusual conversation.   35

Poem Summary

Stanza 1:

The opening stanza of "Chocolates" begins by recounting a story about the Russian writer and physician, Anton Chekhov. Anton Pavlovich Chekhov (1860–1904) wrote plays and stories known for their detailed characterizations of men and women who were frequently frustrated in their desires to live good and meaningful lives. His sympathy for his characters and his ability to present the comedy, tragedy, and pathos of a story all at once mark him as one of the most admired storytellers of the nineteenth century. Some of his best-known short stories include "My Life" (1896), "About Love" (1898), and "The Lady with the Little Dog" (1899). His plays include *The Seagull* (1895), *Uncle Vanya* (1901), *Three Sisters* (1901), and *The Cherry Orchard* (1904). The success of Simpson's poem, in no small part, depends on readers' familiarity with either Chekhov's life or his plays and stories, or both. Chekhov frequently had visitors, and by referring to Chekhov as "the Master" the speaker underscores his own attitude towards Chekhov, which is one of respect, even reverence. Being spoken to *as* a genius makes Chekhov uncomfortable, and he changes the topic to the seemingly mundane subject of chocolates.

Stanza 2:

This stanza continues the scene initiated in the first stanza. From the visitors' surprised responses, readers understand that they did not expect the great Chekhov to broach such a question as "Do you like chocolates?" Though Simpson does not physically

Media Adaptations

- Watershed Tapes has put out a cassette of Simpson reading his poems. The cassette is titled *Louis Simpson: Physical Universe*.

- More than 200 Chekhov stories can be read on-line at http://eldred.ne.mediaone.net/ac/chekhov.html

- The Academy of American Poets sponsors a website on Louis Simpson's poetry and prose: http://www.poets.org/lit/poet/lsimpfst.htm

- In 1983 New Letters on the Air recorded and published a cassette of Simpson reading his poems on public radio.

depict any of the visitors, his description of their reactions enables readers to imagine people with a rather formal demeanor. Using words such as "astonished," and "whereupon," also highlight the speaker's own formality. It is obvious that he is comfortable describing the interactions of these characters.

Stanza 3:

Whereas the second stanza focused on the visitors, this stanza focuses on Chekhov. Simpson provides just the right details to allow readers to visualize the scene. Combined with Chekhov's "leaning forward" when he speaks to the lady, the image of the "light glinting from his spectacles" suggests almost a mischievous and seductive quality to the writer's actions. A simple question such as that asked in lines three and four takes on added significance. Light and dark chocolate suggest ways of describing the world or one's desires without actually being symbols of either.

Stanzas 4 and 5:

Chekhov's seemingly innocuous and strange question has occasioned a burst of talk, as the conversation about chocolates is now in high gear, with everyone contributing. The formerly staid and reserved visitors are now alive and expressive, not

worrying about how they are perceived. Implicit in this description is not only the importance of the material and sensuous world in human beings' lives, but of the small, often overlooked things such as chocolates. The speaker begins to draw the distinction between weighty topics such as politics and men and women, and shredded coconut (an ingredient in some chocolates) in the final three lines of stanza four and then runs the sentence over into the next stanza. This break between stanzas anticipates a break in the action of the story itself, as someone's comment about "chocolates filled with liqueur" stops the heated conversation cold. These lines are humorous because they are presented as sounding almost scandalous. Simpson has written that during poetry readings these lines also receive the most laughs.

The speaker pokes a little fun at Chekhov himself in the last few lines of stanza five. *Uncle Vanya* is one of Chekhov's most popular and often staged plays, full of witty and droll dialogue. It would be hard to imagine one of the characters in the play being at a "loss for words."

Stanza 6:

In this stanza the scene changes, leaving readers to imagine what occurred after the conversation ended. Two images end the poem: the first is of Chekhov himself, presented as the gracious host he has been, taking his visitors' hands in a gesture of friendship and good will. The final image is of the visitors returning to Petersburg. That the visitors live in Petersburg—the second largest city in Russia and a place of great architectural and natural beauty—tells readers that they are probably sophisticated and cultured. During its history, Petersburg changed its name three times. Initially it was named after the fortress St. Petersburg, so called in honor of Peter the Great's patron saint, St. Peter. At the start of the twentieth century the name was changed to Petrograd, translated from the Russian as "the City of Peter." After Lenin died in 1924, the city's name was changed again, this time to Leningrad, which means "the city of Lenin." Its original name was reinstated in 1991. From 1712 to 1917, St. Petersburg was the capital of the Russian empire.

The understatement of the last line is in keeping with the understated tone throughout the poem and highlights the formal quality of the characters' social relationships. That the subject they discuss is chocolates as opposed to, for example, baseball games or beer, also highlights the social class of the visitors and of Chekhov.

Themes

Artists and Society

While initially appearing to undermine the notion that artists are geniuses, "Chocolates" ultimately reinforces it. The idea of genius has been associated with writers since the seventeenth century, and generally has meant a person with exceptional ability that often possesses a kind of rarified knowledge. The speaker presents Chekhov as a "Master," highlighting his own belief in the writer's genius, but he also questions the notion that genius exists on a plane separate from ordinary life and ordinary people. The genius of Chekhov, Simpson suggests, resides precisely in his connection to ordinary life, in his ability to empathize with regular people. Chekhov's ability to change an uncomfortable and tense situation into one where everyone is relaxed underscores this "ordinary genius" because it shows his concern for others. He "fidgets" when asked about his genius. He does not have to be nor does he want to be the center of attention, and is content that the conversation has taken on a life of its own.

When the conversation becomes tense in the fifth stanza, even Chekhov is "at a loss for words," once again demonstrating his "ordinariness," and the power of such a seemingly ordinary topic. His "ordinariness" shows his social genius in the manner in which he graciously says goodbye to his guests, taking their hands in a gesture of affection. This final gesture reinforces the idea that a true genius is someone who belongs to the people, not someone who sets himself apart from them.

Art and Experience

"Chocolates" is an example of mimetic verse, whose chief aim is to imitate reality and give pleasure to the reader. Aristotle defined poetry as an imitation of human actions, but historically critics have argued over what actions were worth representing, with earlier critics claiming that only the actions of "great men" were worthy of poetry. With the nineteenth century, however, and the advent of Romantic poetry, the poet's feelings and imagination became the stuff of representation, and language a tool by which human beings could more deeply experience the world.

Simpson grabs the reader's attention and interest in the first stanza by mentioning Chekhov, a well-known writer, and by implicitly asking readers to imagine themselves at his house in the nineteenth century. Human beings love gossip and this poem is one form of gossip, as it recounts an ac-

Topics for Further Study

- Write the dialogue that you think might have occurred between the fifth and sixth stanzas.

- Compose a poem about the most unusual conversation in which you have ever participated, then describe why it was unusual.

- Re-write "Chocolates" as prose. Does reading the poem as prose change its meaning or effect? How?

- Think of a famous writer that you would like to visit. What would you talk to him or her about? Write a dialogue of your conversation.

- After reading a few chapters from Simpson's autobiography *The King My Father's Wreck* and completing biographical research on Chekhov, write a poem in which Chekhov visits Simpson.

- Simpson himself has written that "Chocolates" is a poem about happiness, specifically "the delight we feel when we are able to express our happiness to another person." After defining what happiness means to you, locate the points in the poem that you believe contribute to the notion that the characters are happy.

- Discuss how "Chocolates" can be read as a poem about social class.

tual experience between a popular person and his admirers. The poem sustains a readers' interest because it is a narrative, and human beings have an almost genetic need for stories, to "find out what happens next." By providing details such as dialogue and descriptions of the characters' gestures, Simpson successfully persuades readers that they too are in the room during the event. Representational, or mimetic, literature is successful when it works at the level of emotion and perception. Readers empathize with both Chekhov and the visitors as they, no doubt, have been in similar social situations. Readers need not understand the poem so long as they *experience* what it represents. They experience the poem through imagining themselves in the place of the characters.

It is important that the poem carries no explicit moral, simply an ending, with which readers can take as they see fit. Simpson accomplishes this by not psychologizing the actions of his characters, but simply describing them. In his essay "To Make Words Disappear," included in his *Selected Prose,* Simpson writes "I would like to write poems that make people laugh or make them want to cry, without their thinking that they were reading poetry. The poem would be an experience—not just talking about life—but life itself. I think that the object of writing is to make words disappear."

Style

Narrative

"Chocolates" is a narrative poem composed of six free-verse stanzas and told from the point of view of an omniscient narrator. An omniscient narrator has access to actions everywhere in the story. Narratives are stories and constitute a sub-genre of poetry whose basic elements are plot, character, atmosphere, and theme. "Chocolates" is constructed primarily of dialogue and description. Most of the action in the poem takes place in the reported speech. However, Simpson makes use of ellipsis in his transition from one scene to the next. Ellipsis literally means omission. In narrative, it refers to leaving out action, leaving readers to infer what happened through using their imagination. For example, readers have to imagine what happened after the abrupt end of the conversation in stanza five, for the next thing that occurs is the guests leaving.

Characterization

Simpson characterizes the people in his poem through their actions. Rather than tell readers what Chekhov and the visitors are like, he shows them. The narrator himself is also a character in the poem. Readers can tell, through the details he chooses to include and omit, and the vocabulary that he uses, that he admires Chekhov.

Tone

The tone, or atmosphere, of "Chocolates" is relatively formal, and comic. This is in keeping with the setting, the house of an intellectual and a cultural icon, Anton Chekhov, and the discrepancy between what readers imagine conversations in such a setting are about and what they actually are about. The language of the poem is restrained, the sentences simple and declarative, making the comic effect subtle.

Historical Context

"Chocolates" takes place in the late nineteenth or early twentieth century in the house of Russian writer Anton Chekhov. Simpson often writes about historical people and events, and sometimes fictionalizes or embellishes events to get closer to the emotional truth of his subject. But he is by no means a confessional poet, as Peter Stitt wrote: "Although Louis Simpson writes a poetry of personality, and although the most important unifying feature of his work is the sensibility that lies at its heart, he is not a confessional poet. In fact, Simpson has been very hard on this type of poetry, which he sees as part of the "cult of sincerity." Confessional poetry is personal because it takes for its subject matter the literal details of the poet's life and feelings, the truth of that life as lived in the real world; Simpson's poetry is personal because it emerges from and expresses a single, central, perceiving sensibility." Simpson has written a number of poems about Chekhov, and *Caviare at the Funeral* itself contains a number of poems about Russia and a few which feature or address Chekhov in some way. His interest in Russia and Chekhov is partly personal—Simpson's mother is of Russian ancestry—and partly aesthetic—Simpson admires Chekhov's approach towards writing.

Many critics consider Anton Pavlovich Chekhov the father of the modern short story and of the modern play. Born in 1860 in the Russian coastal town of Taganrog, near the Black Sea, Chekhov was the son of a grocer and the grandson of a serf; his knowledge of the working classes was deep. Like Simpson's mother, Chekhov's mother was a first-rate storyteller and a chief influence on the writer's own narrative art. Chekhov's early adolescence was traumatic. After his father's business failed and the family lost their home, the family moved to Moscow, leaving Chekhov behind to finish school. Chekhov made ends meet by tutoring younger schoolboys and selling off family goods bit by bit. Later he began selling satirical stories to comic magazines. In both his plays and his stories Chekhov aimed for economy of language and for presenting people as they were without psychologizing their actions. Often, Chekhov ignored plot and focused on the atmosphere or mood of a story, showing character through a combination of external detail and psychic projection. Chekhovian themes include the meaninglessness of human endeavors, disillusionment, poverty, inscrutable state bureaucracy, and the difficulties inherent in human communication.

Compare & Contrast

- **1972:** The United Soviet Socialist Republic celebrates its fiftieth anniversary.

  1979: Soviets invade Afghanistan.

  1980: The United States begins a grain embargo against the Soviet Union to protest their invasion of Afghanistan. The United States and sixty-four other countries boycott the Moscow Summer Olympics to protest the invasion.

  1982: Leonoid Brezhnev dies; Yuri Andropov becomes general secretary of USSR.

  1984: Andropov dies; Konstantin Chernenko becomes general secretary. The Soviets withdraw from the Summer Olympics in Los Angeles.

  1985: Konstantin Chernenko dies; Mikhail Gorbachev becomes general secretary and calls for economic reforms, popularly known as *Perestroika.*

  1987: Russian-born poet Joseph Brodsky is awarded the Nobel Prize for literature. Brodsky, who wrote in English as well as Russian, came to the United States in 1972.

  1987: *Doctor Zhivago* is first published in Russia.

  1989: The first multi-candidate elections are held in the Soviet Union, and several uncontested candidates are defeated.

  1989: The Berlin Wall comes down.

  1990: Mikhail Gorbachev is awarded the Nobel Prize for peace.

  1999–2000: Vladimir Putin, former head of the Federal Security Service (FSB), one of the successor bodies of the Soviet-era KGB, is named Russian prime minister and elected president.

In 1980 when "Chocolates" was published in *Caviare at the Funeral,* a group of poets were arguing against the ubiquity of lyric poetry in the United States, and against the overuse of the confessional "I," claiming that, among other things, it suggested isolation of the self from the larger human community. In the 1980s this loose group of poets were considered part of the Expansive Movement in poetry, which called for a return to narrative and formalism. In his essay "Poetry and Politics" included in the anthology *Poetry After Modernism,* poet and critic Frederick Pollack claimed that after modernism "Poetry seems not to be a *public* discourse at all, or to be only incidentally or vestigially public." Pollack uses Simpson's poem "In the Suburbs" to underscore the lemming-like attitude of writers who ignore the possibility that language in general, and poetry in particular, can represent a world outside of itself. Pollack denounces the tendencies of groups such as those aligned with the L=a=n=g=u=a=g=e poets, some of whom hold that language and poetry refer only to themselves. Like other writers in the anthology, Pollack wants poetry to be "about something" other

than the petty travails of the self. The editor of *Poetry After Modernism,* Robert McDowell, himself a leading critic of much contemporary poetry, has argued that poetry has become largely the domain of academic critics and the privileged few. Poets such as John Ashbery, McDowell has written, do poetry a disservice because their language is often abstract and difficult. McDowell's Story Line Press, founded in 1985, has attempted to cultivate a popular audience for poetry by publishing writers who embrace the possibilities of storytelling in their art. Other poets besides Simpson who are considered to be part of the Expansive Movement in poetry include Frederick Turner, John Gery, Mark Jarman, Rita Dove, Dick Allen, and Dana Gioia.

1980 also marked the beginning of the "Reagan Revolution." Former actor and ex-governor of California Ronald Reagan was elected to his first term as United States President in a landslide victory over Jimmy Carter. Reagan's promise of tax cuts, reduced social welfare, and government deregulation appealed both to traditional Republican and conservative voters as well as to many De-

---

mocrats, who increasingly blamed the government for the depressed economy and what they perceived as America's diminished role in world affairs. In foreign policy, Reagan was an unabashed and at times vocal opponent of détente with the Soviet Union.

The Economic Recovery Act of 1982 reduced individual income taxes by twenty-three percent over three years. However, that could not stop the country from a deepening recession. In 1982, unemployment stood at 10.8 percent, and budget deficits increased. The country recovered from the recession in the mid-80s but more than half of the nine million new jobs that were created were low-paying jobs in the service sector with salaries of less than $7,000 a year.

Critical Overview

"Chocolates" is one of Simpson's more popular later poems. He has written an essay on how he composed the poem and what reactions to it have been, which initially appeared in *Forty-Five Contemporary Poets: The Creative Process,* edited by Alberta Turner. The essay has subsequently been reprinted in a few anthologies and in Simpson's own *Selected Prose.* In the essay Simpson notes that the poem has had favorable reactions from the public. The poet writes "I recall a letter in the London *Times* praising 'Chocolates' because, the letter-writer said, it showed that poetry could be understood."

In the introduction to *On Louis Simpson: Depths Beyond Happiness,* editor and critic Hank Lazer wrote that with *Caviare at the Funeral,* the collection in which "Chocolates" appears, "Simpson achieved consistent mastery of his new narrative style." Lazer pointed out that from this collection on, Simpson received renewed attention from critics. Paul Breslin noted in the *New York Times Book Review* that "[Simpson] has learned, from his heroes, Chekhov and Proust, the significance of the seemingly trivial detail and the importance of memory." Peter Makuck, in his review of *Caviare at the Funeral* in *Tar River Poetry* also praises the collection, writing that "[h]is new book, perhaps his richest yet, is vintage Simpson and provides the reading we have come to relish: freshness of sensation, telling detail, an ability to accommodate the humorous, the terrible, and the lyrical almost simultaneously." G. E. Murray complimented Simpson's storytelling voice in his article in the

Hudson Review, stating that "Chocolates" is one of "his most compelling" poems in the *Caviare at the Funeral.* Douglas Dunn agreed, writing in the *Times Literary Supplement* that "Chocolates" "is an amusing account of an incident from Chekhov's life," and observing that "The Chekhovian atmosphere on which Simpson's imagination seems to thrive is peculiarly adaptable to American settings. His storytelling also reminded me of a remark made by one of Chekhov's characters—'Keep it brief and skip the psychology.'"

On the dust jacket of *Caviare at the Funeral* poet William Matthews wrote "If Chekhov were an American poet alive now, his gentle and heart-breaking poems would read like these, and like these would release slowly, almost reluctantly, but certainly their fierce and balanced compassion."

Criticism

Chris Semansky

Semansky publishes widely on twentieth-century poetry and culture. In the following essay, Semansky considers "Chocolates" in relation to Simpson's poems on the art of poetry and as an example of narrative poetry.

Much of the poetry written in the latter half of the twentieth century has been lyric poetry. Lyric poetry, by its very definition, is short and focuses on the subjective thoughts and emotions of the speaker. For lyric poetry, the "I" is at the center of the universe, and the imagination helps to shape the speaker's thoughts and emotion. Louis Simpson's poetry, especially the poetry written in the latter part of his career, has aimed at bringing poetry back to its narrative, or storytelling roots. His poetry tells stories about other people, not himself. "Chocolates" is one such example of Simpson's narrative poetry.

In the same collection in which "Chocolates" appears, Simpson includes poems that describe his theory of how he writes. These poems can help readers appreciate poems such as "Chocolates." "The Art of Storytelling" recounts a story about a kosher butcher (a *shocket*) who one day was accosted, verbally abused and, eventually, conscripted into the navy by three sailors. The speaker summarizes the story of the butcher's life, his acceptance of his fate and his adventures on the high seas, and states: "It wasn't a bad life—nothing is." This line highlights Simpson's belief that anyone's life is suitable material for poetry. The mundane, the spectacular, the ordinary are all roughly parallel in Simpson's universe. All lives have stories, and all are worthy of poetry.

The last few stanzas of "The Art of Storytelling" provide additional evidence for what Simpson believes is important in poetry. After the speaker of the poem finishes the story of the butcher, he draws attention to the fact that the story he is telling about the butcher is in fact a story he had been told. The poem, then, is a recounting of a recounting. Simpson writes:

> At this point, the person telling the story
> would say, "This shocket-sailor
> was one of our relatives, a distant cousin."

> It was always so, they knew they could depend on it.
> Even if the story made no sense,
> the one in the story would be a relative—
> a definite connection with the family.

Although the smallest life is worth writing about, Simpson points out that human beings are most interested in stories about their own families, people who have some connection to them. Stories need not have morals, nor do the actions of the characters need to be explained, justified, or psychologized in any way. The story itself, and the audience's connection to and trust in the storyteller are what is important.

Anton Chekhov, the subject of "Chocolates" is, like Simpson's mother's family, Russian, and Chekhov has been a muse of sorts for Simpson's own writing, often appearing in his prose and poetry. In fact, the title of the collection in which "Chocolates" appears, *Caviare at the Funeral,* comes from Chekhov's story "In the Ravine." And the anecdote about Chekhov that makes up "Chocolates" is fittingly Chekhovian, that is, it is written in the narrative style that Chekhov himself used.

Traditionally, narratives consist of theme, atmosphere or tone, character, and plot. The focus of "Chocolates," like the focus of many of Chekhov's stories, is on mood and atmosphere, and the speaker's voice accounts for much of that mood. Voice and atmosphere are often difficult concepts to grasp. Voice, or as some critics say, tone, reflects the *attitude* of the speaker towards the subject or towards the reader. Think of the phrase "tone of voice" in this respect. Atmosphere, on the other hand, is the *effect* of the writer's voice *on* the reader. Both of these elements can be hard to pin down, especially the latter, as any given work can have a number of effects on its readers depending on the era and culture in which the work is read,

> *Although the smallest life is worth writing about, Simpson points out that human beings are most interested in stories about ... people who have some connection to them."*

and the readers' own sensibilities, age, gender, race, ethnicity, class, and awareness of literary traditions.

The voice in "Chocolates" is matter-of-fact, yet somewhat formal and understated. The speaker refers to Chekhov as "the Master," a name commonly used for the Russian writer, but still one that shows Simpson's respectful, even reverential attitude towards Chekhov. The combination of conversational phrasing (e.g., "Once some people were visiting Chekhov") and reportage makes for a realistic poem, for a desire to show things as they really happened. Readers are persuaded to believe that the poem is a true account of an event. The event itself, of course, is fairly ordinary: some people are making a visit. That they are visiting someone of Chekhov's stature piques readers' interest. In an essay he wrote about "Chocolates," Simpson has this to say about the visit:

> Superficially it may appear that I am poking fun at the kind of people who would go to see a famous author, but readers who feel superior to these visitors are missing the point. In real life I might find such people absurd but I would not hold them up to ridicule in a poem—I am more intelligent when I write than I am in person. The desire to see and speak to a great man or woman is not something to poke fun at. Only snobs, who are usually people of no talent, look down on those who have a sincere wish to better themselves.

Although readers aren't bound to experience the poem the way in which Simpson wants us to, his claim that he is not "ridiculing" the visitors at least helps us to understand his intention that "Chocolates" is not necessarily a comic poem, even though the situation described is comic. It's comic because of the importance the group attaches to its preferences for certain kinds of chocolate, and the

What Do I Read Next?

- A fine introductory book on Anton Chekhov's stories and plays is Donald Rayfield's *Understanding Chekhov: A Critical Study of Chekhov's Prose and Drama,* published in 1999 by the University of Wisconsin Press. Rayfield's study is geared towards the beginning Chekhov student. He provides close readings of stories and plays, and draws connections between them and European literature of the time.

- For an understanding of what Simpson thinks should be important to poetry readers, read his 1967 textbook, *An Introduction to Poetry,* published by St. Martin's Press.

- Ronald Moran's 1972 study of Simpson, *Louis Simpson,* published by Twayne, offers a fine introduction to Simpson's early work. Moran's study, however, ends with Simpson's 1971 collection *Adventures of the Letter I,* published by Oxford University Press.

- Simpson's poems are included in the 1986 anthology of formal verse, *Strong Measures,* edited by David Jauss, and published by Harper and Row.

- Simpson's *Selected Prose,* published in 1989 by Paragon House, includes an essay on his poem, "Chocolates," and other previously uncollected essays.

---

passion with which they discuss their preferences. But as Simpson himself says, "It didn't have to be chocolates—anything they liked would have done … birthdays, for instance, or picnics … but chocolates were a happy choice. The visitors were relieved—like the audience at a poetry reading when the solemnity is broken." What readers remember most about this poem, however, isn't necessarily what happened, the plot of the story, but rather its voice, its levelness and sincerity. We trust the storyteller. Simpson writes about the importance of voice in storytelling in his poem "Why Do You Write About Russia?" Here he recounts stories his mother used to tell him about life in the "old country" when he visited her in New York:

> These stories were told,
> against a background of tropical night …
> a sea breeze stirring the flowers
> that open at dusk, smelling like perfume.
> The voice that spoke of freezing cold
> itself was warm and infinitely comforting.
>
> So it is with poetry: whatever numbing horrors
> it may speak of, the voice itself
> tells of love and infinite wonder.

What stories or poems say about their subjects is usually referred to as their theme, and themes can be multiple. A significant theme of "Chocolates" is the idea that given the opportunity most people would rather talk about the world as it is rather than the world as they want it to be. The visitors are relieved that they don't have to discuss "politics in the Balkans, / or the vexed question of men and women," which are perhaps the subjects they felt they'd have to discuss at the house of a great thinker like Chekhov. This theme runs throughout Simpson's poetry and underscores the importance he places in the universe of things, rather than ideas *per se.* Simpson has always considered himself a realist, that is, someone who unflinchingly looks at the world and says what he sees.

Who are "most people," though? Simpson creates his characters through imagination, but his imagination is itself based on his experience in the material world. Rendering drawing-room characters who come to visit a great writer wasn't difficult for Simpson, as he himself has led a relatively privileged life, first in Jamaica as a member of a prominent and successful family, then in the United States as a university professor. In the section called "Profession of Faith" from his poem "Unfinished Life," Simpson describes how he develops characters:

> As a writer I imagine characters,
> giving them definite features
> and bodies, a color of hair.
> I imagine what they feel
> and, finally make them speak.
>
> Increasingly I have come to believe
> that the things we imagine
> are not amusements, they are real.

Reality, then, for the poet has as much to do with the poet's capacity to empathize with others as it does with his ability to choose the right word. This feature of Simpson's poetry distinguishes it from other poetry that is more focused on getting the external details of narrative right. Simpson, however, injects his stories with a lyric sensibility, as he works as much at trying to inhabit the minds and bodies of those he describes as he does at depicting their actions. Using his imagination like this puts Simpson squarely in the romantic camp of poets such as William Wordsworth, who described poetry as "emotion recollected in tranquility." But the imagination itself is part of life, part of the physical world for Simpson. Again, in "Profession of Faith," he writes:

> The things we see and the things we imagine,
> afterwards, when you think about them,
> are equally composed of words.

> It is the words we use, finally,
> that matter, if anything does.

It is also these words that Simpson attempts to make as transparent as possible, for in storytelling the voice should act as a camera throwing up images on the screen of the reader's imagination. The final lines of "Chocolates" leaves us with just such images. Imagine the last stanza as a scene: first a shot of Chekhov standing near the door, graciously taking the hands of his guests, then a shot of the guests themselves in the carriage heading home, recounting their experience. The effect of cutting from the first to the second image leaves readers with a sense of Chekhov's magnanimity and a feeling for the odd and various events that make up human lives. Readers share this feeling because rather than telling us directly that the experience was strange, Simpson makes it part of the conversation reported by the poem's speaker. We hear it and see it, and make sense of it on our own. In his essay "To Make Words Disappear" from his *Selected Prose* Simpson writes "I don't care about writing that merely tells me that the writer is having a feeling. I want to be able to experience the feeling. I want lyric or narrative poetry."

Source: Chris Semansky, in an essay for *Poetry for Students*, Gale Group, 2001.

Erika Taibl

Taibl has published most frequently in fields of nineteenth- and twentieth-century poetry. In the following essay, she discusses binaries and their meanings in "Chocolates."

"Chocolates" is a poem about meeting places; the point where the individual sees himself as a part of the community and where the foreign and exotic appear in the common, elevating the ordinary to the extraordinary. The poem uses opposites, or binaries, to explore how perceived extremes are found within one another. Louis Simpson has explored style binaries, journeying from the structure of traditional English verse to a new kind of nonmetrical verse that captures a distinct quality of be-

> *This discovery of one element in the other, the poet in the people and the people in poet, is what makes the poem's realization extraordinary."*

ing American. Simpson uses this nonmetrical verse to polish common scenes to an extraordinary sheen. In "Chocolates," which is a part of the 1980 collection *Caviare at the Funeral,* a fictionalized Chekhov, the great Russian writer and playwright, is portrayed as an individual with a common passion for chocolate. This passion is a meeting point, something that is shared between the genius and his visitors, a nameless, common lot. Chekhov, "the Master," set aside by his genius, connects with his visitors and they with him, and an ordinary meeting is elevated to an extraordinary event. The visit inspires boundaries in class and chasms in knowledge to disintegrate like a chocolate melting on the tongue.

Simpson uses narrative, or a poem in the mode of storytelling, as a kind of trope, or figure of speech. Figurative language in poetry is a kind of pleasant literary manipulation. It is using words to evoke some deeper meaning, elevating them beyond their commonness. It is saying one thing and meaning another. Simpson shies away from traditional figures and conceits and relies on the narrative to do this work. Simpson pits the life of the mind against the vulgarity of the middle-class, their ignorance of current affairs and shallowness of spirit. The poem shames people who, as the poem states, "may not know what they think about politics in the Balkans, or the vexed question of men and women," just as it celebrates the fact that "everyone has a definite opinion about the flavor of shredded coconut." Simpson pokes fun at the discrepancies in the perceived importance of these topics, but seems also to say that to have any kind of conviction is a beautiful thing; it brings people together, even if it is about shredded coconut. Opposites are nothing if not designed to define this middle ground. In the meeting place between binaries, or opposites, Simpson defines a place for the reader as well.

Simpson uses a third person point of view in the poem, which is telltale of his work. He has been likened to the poet Robert Browning, who also put a unique spin on this point of view. Yohma Gray in his article, "Poets in Progress: The Poetry of Louis Simpson" in *Poets in Progress* writes, "Although he [Simpson] sometimes writes in the third person, the reader senses a subjective 'I' in the poem, just as Browning often writes in the first person but conveys the sense of an objective 'he.'" This unique third person point of view that hints of the "I" allows Simpson to welcome his readers into the lives of his drama. His is a sympathizing voice, without being self-indulgent, to invite the reader to sympathize with his characters. In "Chocolates," the learned reader stoops to the role of the visitor faced with the genius of Chekhov. The reader is also Chekhov, the one set aside, estranged by his own persona, a source of magic and exile. In his autobiography, *The King My Father's Wreck,* Simpson writes about discovering the great Russian playwright exclaiming that "He [Chekhov] knew how to tell a story about ordinary people who turned out to be extraordinary." This is exactly what Simpson provides the reader in "Chocolates," a place for ordinary people to be extraordinary, even if it is only in the space of one small visit, and even if it is only in a conversation about chocolates. Simpson makes the visitors' commonness something extraordinary by placing it on Chekhov's plane.

Sympathizing with the realm of an ordinary society comes late in Simpson's poetic career. Its strict metrical form colors his earlier work. It is tight and generally unyielding to the subject. As Simpson changed his form to a more free flowing verse, his personality as a poet was birthed. The critic and writer Peter Stitt wrote about the phases of Simpson's poetic career in his article "Louis Simpson: In Search of the American Self," in *The World's Hieroglyphic Beauty: Five American Poets.* He divides Simpson's career into three phases, the first marked by traditional English verse detached from the society in which the poet lived, the second marked by a departure from the formal structured verse to a more free verse and the third, which begins in the mid-1970s, as a melding of literary skill with the humanity of which it speaks. Stitt wrote about the transition from the second to the third phase, "through a dual interest in the work of Chekhov and in his [Simpson's] own Jewish Russian ancestors, the sensibility of these poems recognizes his inherent kinship with the ordinary citizens of the society he had been hating." This kinship is exemplified in "Chocolates" as two disparate characters, that of the learned

genius, set apart by his knowledge, and that of his visitors, ordinary citizens of the society, who discover a shared love and interest in a common thing.

The dualisms presented in "Chocolates," the individual against the society and the learned versus the generally ignorant, are true for Simpson as a poet as well, as he shares a commonality with the fictionalized Chekhov. The poet is, in general, as Stitt described, "seen as different from most people, one of the 'strange kind.' This strangeness results from a commitment not just to poetry but to a life of the mind generally." This strangeness of the poet and of a life of learning appears again and again in Simpson's work, yet the poet overcomes and unites with society. The poet is Chekhov seeing himself in his visitors. He is living the life of the mind as the writer, yet seeing himself, indeed, reading himself in the reader, who is the ordinary citizen of the society. This discovery of one element in the other, the poet in the people and the people in poet, is what makes the poem's realization extraordinary.

Simpson's characters help illuminate the extraordinary as they are painted in their stark reality. In *The King My Father's Wreck,* Simpson talks about the trend in American writing to dumb down characters, make them easily digestible, easy in every way to read and forget. He says, "there's a tradition in the States that puts down any kind of learning. Writers are supposed to be naïve, and the characters in American fiction don't think about books." In "Chocolates," this unique piece of American fiction, the visitors also appear quite ignorant and shallow. In this way, the narrative does nothing for the idea of being American. Yet, even in their ignorance, they come to voice their opinions and state their preferences. The poem gives them a self as it is defined through each other and their opposite. As the poem elevates the visitors to Chekhov's plane, it also brings the genius down to touching level as Chekhov the man becomes real. In portraying his characters in this way, Simpson makes a special invitation to readers, to meet themselves at the place between the fictional Chekhov and his visitors, to know themselves at the meeting place, to know for the sake of knowing.

To know for the sake of knowing which chocolates are delicious, to have preferences, to have an opinion about the flavor of shredded coconut, to interrupt the flow of a conversation to voice an idea; all are scenes of empowerment in "Chocolates" and in many of Simpson's later works. Yohma Gray said, "There is a value simply in knowing, and Louis Simpson's poetry reflects and refines that value." This is a great compliment to the poet who is dissuaded from entering his poetry in the first person, in preaching, or being the all-knowing voice in his lines. Simpson's goal, as he states it, is "to render the thing itself exactly as it happened." In doing so, the narrative becomes a trope, injecting the common with the extraordinary, commenting on a middle-class vulgarity that lacks opinion and is poorly educated, yet celebrating in that commonness, that an opinion can be achieved.

By rendering the scene exactly as it appears, Simpson refines the notion begun by the imagist movement. Imagism was a movement that flourished in England in the early twentieth century. It was begun as a revolt against what Ezra Pound, an imagist by name, called the "rather blurry, messy … sentimentalistic mannerish" poetry at the turn of the century. The imagists, among them such names as Pound, Amy Lowell, Hilda Doolittle, and William Carlos Williams, undertook to render as exactly and tersely as possible, without comment or generalization, the writer's response to a visual object or scene. Simpson, an inheritor of their ideas, portrays the scene without metaphor, without the masks of figurative language. He creates the scene's depth by utilizing the narrative and bending it to his goal. Simpson simply tells us about the visit between Chekhov and his guests. The narrative details lead readers to ruminate over the individual in community, the foreign and the common, and the learned and the ignorant. This type of imagism, sympathetic and true, gives Simpson a name in modern poetry. Yohma Gray wrote, "He [Simpson] sees reality through particulars; he is a kind of 'responsible vagrant' who finds meaning in any situation." The scene, the image, is rendered exactly as it is, and it speaks.

The image, or in Simpson's case, the whole scene, is heavy with its own baggage. Meaning is found in the interaction of the image with the readers' understanding and feeling of the image. This pregnancy of the image recalls T. S. Eliot's objective correlative. Eliot argued that each emotion composing the image has its own recipe. An author knows the ingredients to this recipe and when he mixes the ingredients, he knows what response he will elicit. By using certain images and details, the response is certain. As Peter Stitt wrote, "if the image is properly prepared for and invested with appropriate suggestions, it should call up in the reader the same emotions it evokes in the author or in the character he is writing." Simpson does this in "Chocolates," as he writes the details of the scene, the "Brazil nuts," and the "sweet chocolate" or the

"dark and bitter kind." He relies on our own feelings and opinions about chocolates. The scene is rendered exactly, with just enough detail to invest it with the ingredients of the readers' own emotional life.

Simpson connects intimately with the reader. In an article he wrote for *Harper's* magazine in 1965 called "What's In It For Me," Simpson wrote, "We are still waiting for the poetry of feeling, words as common as a loaf of bread, which yet give off vibrations." This is what Simpson gives us, words and scenes as common as loaves of bread, but giving off vibrations. Part of this narrative's vibration stems from the fact that it remains lyrical, or song-like, at its base. The ebb and flow of the poem, the rhythms and incantations make the narrative sing. This is an act of creative intimacy by the poet. As Stitt wrote, "the work is defined most centrally by the personality of the poet himself." Simpson identifies with the characters in his narrative. He is Chekhov finding himself in his visitors. He is the visitor encountering the "unusual." He is judging and celebrating the extraordinary in the common.

Even in intimacy, Simpson stays away from the confessional. Though he shares crucial material about his life and beliefs as a poet, he avoids delving into the tradition of psychic biography. He does not claim the confessional "I" as Robert Lowell, Anne Sexton, or Sylvia Plath do. Simpson's third person narrative with a subjective "I" relates elements of his life to the reader, but avoids what he has called "the cult of sincerity." Simpson describes his relationship with the poem, "I have a very funny sense of myself in the poem—I'm not talking about me, I'm talking about how the poem makes a self for me." Perhaps this is the ground he shares most intimately with his reader. The poem makes selves for them too. They are Chekhov feeling the strangeness of their minds' life. They are the visitors without opinions. They are Chekhov finding himself in his visitors. They are the visitors finding opinions. They are the individual finding the community of the poem, finding the self in the poem, and discovering that the poem is a meeting place.

Source: Erika Taibl, in an essay for *Poetry for Students,* Gale Group, 2001.

Sources

Breslin, Paul, "Three Poets," in *New York Times Book Review,* November 2, 1980, p. 12.

Dunn, Douglass, "Review of *Caviare at the Funeral*," in *Times Literary Supplement,* June 5, 1981, p. 645.

Ellman, Richard, and Robert O'Clair, eds., *The Norton Anthology Of Modern Poetry,* 2d edition, Norton, 1983.

Gray, Yohma, "The Poetry of Louis Simpson," in *Poet in Progress,* Northwestern University Press, 1967, pp. 227–243.

Horowitz, David A., Peter N. Carroll, and David D. Lee, eds., *On the Edge: A New History of Twentieth-Century America,* West Publishing Co., 1990.

Howard, Richard, "Alone with America," in *Atheneum,* 1961, pp. 451–470.

Hungerford, Edward, ed., *Poets in Progress: Critical Prefaces to Thirteen Modern American Poets,* Northwestern University Press, 1967.

Jarman, Mark, "On Either Side of the Water," in *Hudson Review,* 1996, pp. 513–520.

Klinkowitz, Jerome, *The American 1960s: Imaginative Acts in a Decade of Change,* Iowa State University Press, 1980.

Lazer, Hank, ed., *On Louis Simpson: Depths Beyond Happiness,* University of Michigan Press, 1988.

Lensing, George S., and Ronald Moran, *Four Poets and the Emotive Imagination,* Louisiana State University Press, 1976.

Macuck, Peter, "Review of *Caviare at the Funeral*," *Tar River Poetry,* Fall, 1981, pp. 48–53.

McDowell, Robert, ed., *Poetry After Modernism,* Story Line Press, 1991.

Moran, Ronald, *Louis Simpson,* Twayne, 1972.

Murray, G. E., "Review of *Caviare at the Funeral*," in *Hudson Review,* 1981.

———, "Seven Poets," in *Hudson Review,* 1981.

Rosenthal, M. L., *The New Poets: American & British Poetry Since World War II,* Oxford, 1967, pp. 323–24.

Simpson, Louis, *"Baruch,"* in *The King My Father's Wreck,* Story Line Press, 1995, pp. 80–83.

———, *"Moody Colonials,"* in *The King My Father's Wreck,* Story Line Press, 1995, pp. 32–35.

———, *North of Jamaica,* Harper, 1972.

———, *"Notes of the Old Boys' Association,"* in *The King My Father's Wreck,* Story Line Press, 1995, pp. 24–25.

———, *Selected Prose,* Paragon House, 1989.

———, *Ships Going into the Blue: Essays and Notes on Poetry,* University of Michigan Press, 1994.

———, *"The Vigil,"* in *The King My Father's Wreck,* Story Line Press, 1995, pp. 140–141.

———, *"Waterloo, The Story of an Obsession,"* in *The King My Father's Wreck,* Story Line Press, 1995, pp. 10–11.

———, *"What's In It for Me?"* in *Harper's,* 1965, p. 173.

Stitt, Peter, "Louis Simpson: In Search of the American Self," in *The World's Hieroglyphic Beauty: Five American Poets,* 1985, pp. 109–139.

Wojahn, David, "On Louis Simpson," in *Tar River Poetry,* 1984, pp. 41–51.

For Further Reading

Simpson, Louis, *Caviare at the Funeral,* Franklin Watts, 1980.

> In poems which closely resemble anecdotes and vignettes, *Caviare at the Funeral* reports on the lives of people and places which have had an impact on Simpson. He writes about America, Russia, and the Australian Outback with an equal degree of passion and insight. This is a very accessible collection of poems.

———, *The Character of the Poet,* University of Michigan Press, 1986.

> Simpson's collection of short and occasional pieces provides a glimpse into his motivations for writing and his attitudes towards other modern and contemporary poets.

Stepanchev, Stephen, *American Poetry Since 1945,* Harper, 1965.

> Stepanchev's literary history is a highly readable account of the aesthetic and ideological movements in American poetry after World War II.

The Eagle

Alfred, Lord Tennyson
1851

"The Eagle: A Fragment" was first published in 1851, when it was added to the seventh edition of Tennyson's *Poems,* which had itself been published first in 1842. As with the best of the poet's works, this short poem displays a strong musical sense; the words chosen, such as "crag," "azure," and "thunderbolt" not only fit the meaning of the poem but also fit the slow musical sensibility which gives the poem its thoughtful, almost worshipful, tone.

Since the title of the poem identifies it as "a fragment," the reader may be led to wonder if it represents a completed work and a completed idea. This uncertainty is enhanced by the question of what actually happens to the eagle at the end of the poem: does he become ill, somehow lose his ability to fly, and tumble helplessly into the sea, or is the poet using the term "he falls" figuratively, to portray the quick action of a powerful bird diving to scoop up its prey? The poem is too short, and offers too little background for us to tell if the sudden reversal in the last line is meant to be ironic (the frailty of the mighty eagle) or if it continues to indicate the eagle's harmony with his surroundings, so that his dive is phrased in terms of gravity. Because neither explanation seems more likely than the other, and we can assume that a powerful poet like Tennyson could have leaned his audience toward one interpretation if he had wanted to, it is fair to say that "The Eagle: A Fragment" is purposely constructed so that both interpretations apply. Tennyson wants us to see the eagle as both a swift predator and a powerful bird who is nonethe-

Alfred, Lord Tennyson

The wrinkled sea beneath him crawls:
He watches from his mountain walls,   5
And like a thunderbolt he falls.

Poem Summary

Line 1:

The words "clasps," "crag," and "crooked" associate the eagle with age: "craggy," for instance, is still used to describe a lined, age-weathered face. The hard "c" sound that begins each of these words also establishes a hard, sharp tenor to this poem's tone that fits in with the idea of the eagle's similarly hard, sharp life. The repetition of first sounds is called alliteration, and Tennyson uses it in this short "fragment" to convey a sense of the eagle's situation.

If there is any question in the reader's mind about why we should care to read about the habits of an eagle in the wild, Tennyson settles it at the end of the line, where he uses the poetic technique of personification in talking about the eagle's "hands." When Tennyson makes the association of the eagle's claws with human hands, he lets us know that the story of the eagle is not just a study of an animal in its natural environment, but that, symbolically, he is telling us about human beings. Because of the implications of the descriptions mentioned above, we can assume that the eagle represents an elderly person.

Line 2:

The idea that is presented to the reader in the phrase "close to the sun" could be expressed more directly, but in using these words Tennyson accomplishes two goals. First, by bringing the sun in to describe how high up in the air the eagle is, he uses hyperbole, or exaggeration, to associate the eagle with a sense of grand majesty. Tennyson lived during the Enlightenment, a time when scientific curiosity and learning were greatly valued, and as an educated man he would not have believed that an eagle's altitude could reach anywhere near the sun's, but this association makes the eagle seem, like the sun, more powerful than anything of this earth. Placing the eagle near the sun also alludes to the myth of Icarus. An allusion is a reference to something else, specifically another literary work, so that readers can use knowledge of that other work to sharpen their understanding. In Greek mythology, Icarus and his father Daedalus escaped from imprisonment on the Isle of Crete by making

less susceptible to defeat by other forces (quite possibly human).

Author Biography

Tennyson was born in 1809 in Somersby, Lincolnshire. The fourth of twelve children, he was the son of a clergyman who maintained his office grudgingly after his younger brother had been named heir to their father's wealthy estate. According to biographers, Tennyson's father, a man of violent temper, responded to his virtual disinheritance by indulging in drugs and alcohol. Each of the Tennyson children later suffered through some period of drug addiction or mental and physical illness, prompting the family's grim speculation on the "black blood" of the Tennysons. Biographers surmise that the general melancholy expressed in much of Tennyson's verse is rooted in the unhappy environment at Somersby. He died in 1892.

Poem Text

He clasps the crag with crooked hands;
Close to the sun in lonely lands,
Ringed with the azure world, he stands.

wings out of wax and feathers and flying away, but Icarus became too ambitious and flew close to the sun; the wax melted, and Icarus fell into the sea and drowned. By placing the winged eagle near the sun, Tennyson seems to be implying that it may be too confident of its own ability, just as Icarus was. This connection is made complete in the last line of the poem, when the eagle falls.

Line 3:

The image in this line points backward, to the ancient notion that the sky consisted of a series of spheres that circled the earth, as well as forward to modern science's understanding of the earth's atmosphere. The "azure sphere" brings to mind not just a blue (azure) sky reaching from horizon to horizon; it also alludes to a sense of confinement. Being "ringed" traps the eagle, keeps him surrounded, so that, in spite of what line 2 says about the eagle being close to the sun, he is still bound to this earth. If we take into account the fact that this poem, by using words to describe the eagle that are usually used for humans, makes a connection between eagle and human lives, we can assume that Tennyson is telling us something about the human condition in the way the eagle has the power to approach the sun but is held down by the earth. The idea of the majesty of the intellect or spirit being weighed down by the body's weakness is a common idea in Tennyson's works.

Line 3 provides a perspective from which the poem is being told. If the eagle were being viewed from above, the background that "rings" him would not be the blue sky but the ground. There is not much revealed about the speaker of the poem, but this detail divulges that the speaker, and by association the reader, "looks up" to the eagle.

Line 4:

The two strongest words used to describe the sea, "wrinkled" and "crawls," reflect the images of old age that were associated with the eagle in line 1. Unlike the eagle, though, the sea is not being shown as proud and strong in its old age, but as decrepit—crawling like a drunkard. Here, Tennyson may be implying that the things of the earth are more vulnerable, more susceptible to decay, than things of the sky like the eagle. Since the perspective in this line is obviously the eagle's (the sea would only look "wrinkled" from a great height), the poem seems to be implying that it is the eagle, and not necessarily the speaker of the poem, who views the sea as weak. This fits with the myth of Icarus whose thoughts of his own power and im-

Media Adaptations

- A group named Techno has a short clip of music incorporating Tennyson's poem into what they call "a groovin' ramble," available at http://artists.mp3s.com/artists/26/interval.html for download from MP3.

- The Teaching Company, of Springfield, VA, includes an audiocassette lecture titled "Alfred, Lord Tennyson, England's National Treasure," as Lecture Twelve in a lecture series by John B. Fisher titled *Great Writers: Their Lives and Works*.

- Robert Speaight and Arthur Luce Klein read poems from Tennyson on a cassette recording from Spoken Arts called *A Treasury of Alfred Lord Tennyson* from 1963. Included are selections from *The Princess* and *In Memoriam*.

- A 1997 collection on audiocassette called *The Victorians* features poems by Tennyson, as well as Robert Browning, Lewis Carroll, Matthew Arnold, and others. Tennyson's poems are on Tape One of a six-tape set from Recorded Books.

- Center for the Humanities presents a 1986 videocassette named *The Victorian Age,* which presents excerpts from the writings of Dickens, Browning, Arnold, Tennyson, Carlyle, and Ruskin.

portance led him further and further away from the earth.

Line 5:

The dominant image in this line is one of a stone barrier: "mountain walls." Although nesting and perching on the sides of mountains could be seen as simply an accurate description of eagle behavior, a reader has to wonder why Tennyson took the time and space to mention it in this short poem, when so many other eagle behaviors have been left out. The most apparent explanation would be that the poet not only wants to give a fact about eagles' lifestyles, but that he also wants to mention "walls" for the symbolic associations it brings. The implication is that there is something restraining the eagle, setting a limit to his abilities, the way a stone wall would. Earlier lines indicate a contrast between the glory of flight, height, and the sun and the weakness of the earth, the sea and the eagle's own body: if there is something holding him back, it is that the eagle, although he can fly, is still a creature of earth.

Line 5 also uses a strangely passive verb to describe the eagle's action. "He watches." The reader, naturally, must wonder what he is watching, since watching would have to be focused on a specific thing. What do eagles watch? It is this verb that justifies interpreting the "fall" in the last line as a dive into the sea to pluck a fish from the water, because eagles and animals in general watch mainly for food. In this interpretation the eagle is mighty and supreme through to the end, and is so much a part of the natural world that attacking his prey is described as an act of gravity.

Line 6:

Although line 5 raised a question about what was going through the eagle's mind, what he was watching, just before he fell, the most common interpretation of line 6 is that the eagle really did fall unintentionally, the victim of illness or decay. This is a sudden, shocking end for the strong and proud creature portrayed in the first five lines, but it is not unanticipated in the rest of the poem. Line 2, for instance, alludes to the myth of Icarus, who ended up falling into the sea and drowning. Line 5 ends with a mention of "walls," which increases the reader's awareness of this strong creature's limitations. If Tennyson actually did structure this poem around reversing the reader's expectations, we can see why he left it "a fragment," rather than expanding it: the balance between the first five lines and the sixth would have to be exact. If the eagle, the proud bird, can drop dead off of the face of a mountain, Tennyson seems to be warning us that people, no matter what heights they reach, can fall in the end.

Themes

Freedom

The bird soaring in the sky has always been used as an example of freedom from the bonds of gravity, which anchors plants, people, and most an-

imals to the earth. The eagle in this poem is pictured "close to the sun"—another symbol of high-flying freedom that is not controlled by the limitations of the earth's atmosphere. This area of the sky, just inside of and barely contained by the "azure world" of outer space, is what is meant by "lonely lands." Loneliness implies detachment or a lack of responsibility to any other thing, while referring to the eagle's perch as a different land once more enforces the idea that it is free of the rules and constraints that govern the lands of the earth.

He is not, however, completely detached: as the poem's first words put it, the eagle "clasps" onto the side of a mountain. This verb usage implies a sense of desperation. In a poem this short, using so few words, the words that the author chooses to include must be chosen with precision for their broadest implications. Tennyson's use of the word "wall" suggests more than the simple description of the side of a mountain and can be taken as a reminder of the limitations that a wall usually implies. The eagle is free to roam the skies but is also attached to a stone wall. It hangs on tightly to the wall instead of soaring freely, and when it lets go of its grasp, it does not move freely but falls to earth like a rock. Even if the action at the end is not just the eagle succumbing to gravity but is in fact a dive toward a prey that it has seen, the thunderbolt-like speed of its descent still implies a compulsion beyond its free will.

Flesh versus Spirit

Readers are not told anything directly about the eagle's spirit in this poem. It is written from the point of view of an observer down on the ground, who sees the bird high above, with the sky as a backdrop. The eagle's spirit is implied in the words that were chosen by Tennyson. There is strength implied by the hard *k* sounds repeated, early on, in the words "clasps," "crag," and "crooked." Other words stir up emotional associations of power in the reader because they are commonly used to describe powerful things. These words, used for their connotative effect, include "clasps," "sun," "ringed," "stands," "mountain," and especially "thunderbolt." All of these images of strength are associated with the eagle, implying that he has a powerful spirit. Readers get a sense that this is a noble creature that reigns over the world beneath him.

On the other hand, there is plenty of evidence that this eagle is old, that its body is weak. In the first line, its claws are called "crooked hands"— this image brings to mind the look of a bird's claws, but it also implies an old, arthritic human. "Wrinkled" is not used to describe the bird but refers instead to the rippling waves on the sea, but the very mention of age in this poem, which is so brief, reflects on the eagle. The sea is a crucial part of the bird's environment. It is wrinkled and crawling, establishing a mood of weakness in this poem.

The eagle's physical weakness is shown most emphatically in the poem's last word. Tennyson could have chosen a more forceful, proactive word if he meant to show the eagle to be as physically powerful in body as it is in spirit. To say that he "falls" implies that the bird has lost its ability to hold on or to fly. The powerful spirit that is implied by other forceful words in the poem is turned inside-out by this evidence that it is a doddering, weak, incapable, old thing that is not in control of its own body, much less its world.

Permanence

Most of the imagery used in "The Eagle" is used to show things of a lasting, geological scale absorbing the eagle into an unchanging landscape of stone and sky. The crag in line one and the mountain walls in line five are permanent fixtures that will not change within the course of centuries. The eagle's crooked hand fits into the crag in both an audible sense ("clasp" and "crag" have matching sounds) and in a visual sense. The poem's use of these images implies that the eagle is just as permanent as the stone wall. The reference to the "azure world" of the sky also implies a sense of permanence, with celestial bodies appearing in the same places overhead consistently each year regardless of what changes are taking place on the earth in the ensuing time. Even the sea, which is constantly in motion, is presented here as unchanging, because the small, always-moving waves are described as stationary wrinkles.

One more clue that subtly makes readers believe that the scene presented here is unchanging is the poem's strict rhyme scheme. There is a sense of concreteness in the fact that all of the lines are of the same length and that they all end with similar sounds. This poem is built like a block of granite, raising expectations that the same tone that has been established in the first five lines must necessarily be carried on into the last.

By showing the eagle's environment to be still and unchanging, Tennyson leads readers to view the bird as permanent, an unchanging part of an unchanging setting. In the end, though, he turns expectation on its head and exchanges the stillness for sudden, lightning-fast motion. The last line comes as a surprise because the abrupt, almost vi-

Topics for Further Study

- Write a brief descriptive poem about an animal, making people look at it in a way they never have before. In the last line, include a surprise action.

- Compare this poem to Ted Hughes's "Hawk Roosting." Why do you think both birds are portrayed with such nobility? Which poem do you think contradicts that noble appearance most? How?

- This poem has references to the ancient Greek myth of Icarus. Study that story, and explain how you think knowing it helps a reader interpret what Tennyson is saying here.

olent activity that it describes shatters the poem's stillness. This abrupt reversal of expectations reminds readers of the ever-changing nature of living things more effectively than the poem could have done had it not reversed directions.

Style

"The Eagle: A Fragment" is written in two stanzas of three lines each and utilizes the iambic-tetrameter form of meter. Iambic meter is structured in units of two syllables where the first syllable is unstressed and the second is stressed. If the stresses are identified, the first line appears as follows:

Heclasps / thecrag / withcrook / edhands;

"Tetrameter" ("tetra" meaning four) indicates that there are four iambic units, or feet, in each line. It should be noted, however, that Tennyson varies the iambic pattern in two places. In both lines 2 and 3, the first two syllables do not form an iamb (an unstressed syllable followed by a stressed syllable), but rather a trochee, meaning that the first syllable is stressed and the second unstressed. After these first two syllables, the lines revert to iambic construction.

The rhyme scheme in the poem is *aaa bbb*, meaning that the last words in the three lines of the first stanza rhyme with one another and the same is true of the last words in the lines of the second stanza.

Another device employed by Tennyson in "The Eagle: A Fragment" is alliteration, which is the repetition of the first sounds in words. This is most noticeable in the line 1, with the repetition of the hard "c" sound: "clasps," "crag," and "crooked." "Lonely lords" in line 2 and "watches" and "walls" in line 5 also use this technique to heighten the musical sound of the poem.

Historical Context

Tennyson was appointed by Queen Victoria to be England's Poet Laureate in 1850, a year before "The Eagle" was first published, and he served in that position until his death in 1892. He is considered to be one of the most influential voices in the long period of British prosperity during Victoria's reign, which is broadly referred to as the Victorian Age.

Queen Victoria was born at Kensington Palace on May 24, 1819. She ascended to the throne of England and Ireland in 1837, when her uncle, William IV, died without any children. For sixty-four years she ruled Great Britain, which was the most powerful country in the world. At first, the eighteen-year-old queen upheld liberal sentiments. The early part of the nineteenth century was still marked by liberalism, which was a belief in equality and individual rights. The height of liberalism had occurred earlier marked by the American Revolution in 1776 and the French Revolution in 1789. In both cases, the old, hereditary, aristocratic order was overturned in favor of the ability of the people to govern their own affairs. Victoria's early liberalism is considered to have been influenced by a number of things, including her own youthful idealism and the world's lingering enthusiasm with liberal ideals.

The nineteenth century was a time of great social transformation, and the queen's sympathies altered as both she and England changed. One of the most profound influences on her thinking came when she married Albert, her first cousin, in 1840. For the next twenty years, Victoria and Albert ruled Great Britain closely. His conservative attitude came to be hers. Albert was formal, straight-laced, and it is his prudish attitude toward public behavior that has left the Victorian Age with the reputation for being repressed about matters of social behavior.

At the same time, the Industrial Revolution was reorganizing the structure of society and raising doubts about the effectiveness of liberalism. Because mechanical efficiency was creating larger and more successful cities, there was a shift in population in Western countries (meaning, mainly, England and the Americas) away from farms and toward cities. Machines that were powered by steam that was created by burning coal were able to turn out products at a rate many times what had been possible before. Society was redefined by such technological developments as the telegraph (1844), which made long-distance communication possible; the daguerreotype (1837), which was the first workable method of photography; and the first development of the electric lamp in 1808, which eventually led to Edison's light bulb in 1879. At the same time that these technological marvels were being introduced, though, the problems associated with the rapid growth of cities made life miserable for large masses of people.

Cities, unprepared to absorb the rapid growth that they were faced with, became crowded, squalid, dirty pockets of poverty. London, the main city of the world at that time, quadrupled in population in forty years from 598,000 in 1801 to 2.42 million in 1841. The resulting population density led to overworked and inefficient waste disposal methods, which hastened the spread of disease, particularly tuberculosis and cholera. Early industrial methods created the dense pollution that readers are most familiar with from the novels of Charles Dickens such as *Bleak House* or *Great Expectations*. In one of Dickens' most familiar descriptions, based on an actual situation, the streetlights of London had to be lit at midday because the pollution from coal-burning industries had blocked out the sun. The liberal ideal of having government run by common people gave way quickly when faced with the increasing perception of the "common people" being a grubby crowd fighting for survival among squalid conditions, living like rats among rats. The mood among the educated toward aristocrats keeping tight control of the political process coincided with Victoria's political views, as influenced by her Prince Consort, Albert.

In the second half of the century, the plight of the urban poor could not be ignored, and the government set about passing reform measures that regulated their exploitation. Work days were shortened to ten hours for women and children, health inspectors began closing down the worst boarding houses, and mission houses were opened to try to help the poor rather than just throwing them into

Compare & Contrast

- **1851:** The Crystal Palace is commissioned for the first World's Fair, London Great Exposition. Made of glass walls, it is the largest structure in the world, four times the size of St. Peter's Basilica in Rome.

  Today: World's Fairs seldom attract attention, because communications advances have allowed new wonders to be shown to the world in books and on the Internet.

- **1851:** Slavery is legal in the United States, and opponents of the practice struggle with slave holders to tip the balance of power. The 1850 Fugitive Slave Act, providing stiff federal penalties against anyone who helped a slave escape, is part of a compromise made for admitting California to the Union as a non-slave, "free" state.

  Today: Federal laws are designed to prevent discrimination on the basis of race, although many Americans identify racial tension as one of the country's greatest problems.

- **1851:** A telegraph cable is laid across the English Channel, connecting France and England with telegraph communications for the first time.

  Today: Cell phones are inexpensive and enable anyone anywhere to call anyone else who has a phone.

- **1851:** The largest city in the world is London, with a population of 2.37 million people.

  Today: The largest city in the world, Tokyo, has almost 27 million people.

- **1851:** Ireland continues to suffer from the potato famine that began in 1846, causing thousands to starve and even more to move to other countries.

  Today: Modern shipping methods make it possible to transport food to famine-stricken nations, but government bureaucracies and corruption often make it difficult to distribute donated food.

---

jails. Labor organizations were formed, and they fought for better working conditions, while Karl Marx's *Communist Manifesto* redefined the relationship between laborers and the owners of the means of production.

After Prince Albert died in 1861, Queen Victoria never remarried but tried to stay true to his memory for the forty years that she continued to live. As the upper social classes continued to recognize and accept the "vulgar" behaviors of the lower classes, the court of the Queen became more insistent on what was considered proper behavior, leaving the Victorian era with a dual legacy of oversentimentalization and hypocrisy. The age included the very earliest experiments in artistic photography and the rise of the impressionist movement elsewhere in Europe, but the image that the phrase Victorian Art conjures up today is an idealized, ornate style with swirls of pastel and flower petals filling in the borders of every scene. Likewise, pub-

lic behavior was, in keeping with the queen's tastes, based in hypocrisy. The modern concept of polite social manners comes from the Victorian tastes regarding public behavior, and books outlining the rules of those manners defined the elements of "class" for the new aristocracy who had not been born to the upper class, but who had risen into it as the old social rules came apart and wealth became the deciding factor of one's social position.

Tennyson's death in 1892 and Victoria's death in 1901 coincided with the birth of a new century. They had both lived long and been in the public eye for decades, and were seen as relics of the past by a world that was ready for change. The Victorian manner, which developed as a response to the country's industrialization and its uneasy adjustment to the passing of the strictly hereditary social class system, was no longer practical. Attempts to hold onto the image of a gentler and politer time stopped being charming as Great Britain began los-

---

ing its economic edge to other countries, especially America, and the codes of the Victorian Era became an embarrassing sign of faded greatness.

Critical Overview

Novelist Henry James once made a comment that was meant to address Tennyson's work in general, but is especially true of "The Eagle: A Fragment": "a man has always the qualities of his defects, and if Tennyson is … a static poet, he at least represents repose and stillness and fixedness of things with a splendour that no poet has surpassed." In general, critics tend to praise Tennyson's skills more highly when he writes about inactivity than when he writes about activity, because his weakness is in describing what motivates action. Since the eagle in this poem clasps, stands, and watches, and his only motion, in the poem's last word, is passive, Tennyson avoids his weakness and shifts the focus to his stronger descriptive abilities.

In delineating a situation, Tennyson's style often implies concepts beyond the state at hand, shedding light on the interaction between humans, nature, and God. Critic Herbert F. Tucker referred to such unexplained inferences as "naked lyrical address." In his essay "Tennyson and the Measure of Doom," Tucker notes that "The Eagle" is one of several Tennyson poems that uses this technique lightly. Nonetheless, writes Tucker, in these works "Tennyson's theme and imagery gravitate toward some inevitable ground on the power of God, the drift of nature, or the obsessions of human nature."

Criticism

David Kelly

Kelly teaches creative writing at Oakton Community College and College of Lake County in Illinois. In this essay, he explores the anomalous nature of "The Eagle" among Tennyson's works of the early 1850s.

The fact that Alfred Lord Tennyson's poem "The Eagle" is still studied along with the rest of his poetry is an oddity unto itself, testimony to the simple, clean package that the poem presents, to its unique power. The poem has hardly any large-scale significance in the history of literature, it just happens to be a powerful, solid piece of work. It certainly does not have the pointed mythological references, the historical significance or the biographical elements that stir modern curiosity about some of Tennyson's other works.

"The Eagle" deserves attention not for where it came from but for what it is, which is a poem that makes use of all of the tools at its disposal. It makes optimum use of poetic devices, such as the rhyming tercets, the alliteration, and the elevated language that all work to raise its natural subject to a position of nobility. At the same time, the poem is modern enough to avoid the pretense that it can give its readers a complete picture of what is going on with only this fragment. Its honesty comes from provoking readers to think about the scene described, as opposed to the sentimental manipulation that critics have accused Tennyson of stooping to at his worst.

The poem was first published in 1851, the year after Tennyson achieved the triple blessings of marrying his longtime lover, publishing an immensely popular book, and winning the Poet Laureateship of England, succeeding William Wordsworth. Most critics have considered it a period of transition in the poet's life from his humble struggle out of poverty to almost universal fame, taking the most prominent government literary position in a country that values its literary heritage. The year 1850 is considered the crease in the center of Tennyson's life and literary career, and his style took a subsequent change of direction. "The Eagle," at the division, shows signs of both his old style and his new.

The way that the poem was released does not match what might be expected of what would grow to become one of this much-studied writer's most-studied works. It was not brought out in a triumphant volume of new poetry by the new Poet Laureate but slipped into the latest edition of his *Poems,* which had first been published nine years earlier and was then on its seventh edition. It might be thought that, in a sense, Tennyson published this incomplete fragment to burn off old material that he did not intend to develop further. It certainly is a better fit for his earlier persona as a struggling artist than as his new one, in which he had the moral responsibility, as a member of the government, for recording the public mood. It seems to be an example of nothing else that occurred in Tennyson's life or in his work, but examining the works that surround it, "The Eagle" can be seen as fitting perfectly into the situation of its publication.

Tennyson was always a writer with a wide range of abilities. The 1842 collection, which has survived to be his most critically acclaimed, shows off his diversity. That book gave the world such classic Tennyson pieces as "The Lady of Shallott," a long narrative about one of the knights of Camelot (a subject he also explored in *Idylls of the King,* which was started around this time but published more than a decade later); "The Lotos-Eaters," which was also a long narrative with a mythical theme, in this case concerning sailors who travel to an enchanted land and eat lotus flowers, which make them too lethargic and content to return to their homes any more; and "Break, break, break," a short piece of four quatrains that calls upon the sea to act out the speaker's violent anguish by smashing against the shore. The first two of these were completely revamped versions of poems that had appeared in his last published collection, ten years earlier, and are the versions that readers study today. These and others from the 1842 *Poems* were proof of Tennyson's power in handling short and long forms and in envisioning complete stories and his proclivity toward natural and human heroics. Even though these examples each has a sense of completeness that he was unable to achieve with "The Eagle," they also show a sense of storytelling that this short fragment only hints at. Although all of the action is reserved for the last line, when the eagle plummets down into the sea, this fall is made meaningful by the sense of drama that is built up in the five lines preceding it.

One of the finest examples from the 1842 book and one that seems to capture the wealth of most of Tennyson's other work is "Ulysses," his version of the myth handed down since antiquity in Homer's *The Odyssey.* In Tennyson's version, Ulysses is back from his thirty-year-adventure in the Trojan War and is ruling Ithaca once more. He is, in his own words, an "idle king" grown lazy and bored with ruling people that he does not know any more because of his long absence. He can see that his son Telemachus is more suited for the job of leading a government than he is, and so, in the end, he decides to sail off with his aging crew, once more, to find new adventures. In this poem are the classical allusions of much of Tennyson's most imaginative work as well as the roiling angst of a great man whose emotions are held in check, which is a point that is alluded to in many of his shorter, non-narrative works. Ulysses seems to be a better-defined, human version of the eagle, standing tall at great heights and then growing tired, drooping under the weight of sheer existence despite the grandeur that surrounds him. Like "The Eagle," "Ulysses" is allowed to leave matters unsettled and

> *The year 1850 is considered the crease in the center of Tennyson's life and literary career, and his style took a subsequent change of direction."*

to respect the intelligence of readers, who are allowed to draw their own conclusions. It is a poem that can reveal the nature of power and frailty, but only if one is willing to read those elements into it.

Between the 1842 volume and 1850, the pivotal year that changed his life so drastically, Tennyson published *The Princess* in 1847. It was his first full-length narrative poem, and its success was mixed. The poem was meant to address the issue of education for women and the establishment of women's colleges, which was controversial at the time. The critical response tended to divide Tennyson's talents into two parts, the better to assess them. His story has central male and female characters that are destined for ruin until they start acting out the traditional gender roles, with the man becoming more masculine and the female turning feminine and both finding their fulfillment by parenting a new generation. Critics found the story forced, but they could not easily dismiss it because it was laden with fine, short poems, such as "Crossing the Bar," which has come to be one of Tennyson's most lasting poems. The lyrical poems each worked fine by themselves, and if the poet could have stayed with short lyric expressions or even the sort of lengthy emotional ruminations of his next book, *In Memoriam,* he may have turned out a different sort of writer. The best examples of Tennyson's writings are these poems, taken out of the book and left to stand as fragments, giving them the missing context and the internal energy that powers "The Eagle."

The Princess was enthusiastically accepted by the reading public and continually required republication over the next generation. *In Memoriam,* a powerful evocation of the psychology of grief, established him as one of the greatest poetic voices of his generation, and, as if that needed official government verification, Queen Victoria found Tennyson to be a personal favorite, which finalized his

What Do I Read Next?

- One of Tennyson's most respected biographers, Norman O. Page, wrote the text accompanying a book of pictures illustrating the poet's life and works called *Tennyson: An Illustrated Life.*

- Replica Books has recently reissued the book *Alfred Lord Tennyson: A Memoir by His Son,* by Hallam Tennyson. For over a hundred years, this has been an important primary source for students studying Tennyson.

- Robert Browning was the poet whose career most closely paralleled Tennyson's. A good collection of Browning's poetry is found in the Penguin Poetry Library's *Robert Browning: Selected Poems.*

- Harold Bloom's volume *Alfred Lord Tennyson* for Chelsea House's *Modern Critical Views* series collects some of the most insightful, short essays available about the poet, including works by T. S. Eliot, Marshall McLuhan, and Cleanth Brooks.

- *Tennyson: The Growth of a Poet,* by Jerome Hamilton Buckley, is a well-considered, psychological biography. It was published by Harvard University Press in 1960.

- Ekbert Faas' book *Retreat into the Mind: Victorian Poetry and the Rise of Psychiatry* traces how the poetry of Tennyson and his contemporaries led almost directly to the science of the mind.

---

appointment to the post of Poet Laureate. He was no longer a poet who was at liberty to scribble off his thoughts and develop them wherever they might lead him any more. Although his new post and fame gave him a degree of economic freedom, they carried with them a responsibility to his fans and to his country.

It is particularly understandable, given the circumstances, that "The Eagle" would remain a fragment. The time of his life that this poem appeared seems to have been the last time when he could let a good idea to stand on its own without being developed or explained. Of course there were critics who complained that fame and success had spoiled Tennyson, as there might be such critics, today, who complain of a poet who rises so far and so fast. This attitude represents an overgeneralization: Tennyson's ability as a poet in no way became weaker when he took over his new position, nor did his instincts become in any way muted or deluded. He still showed the same lyric brilliance that he always had, and his weakness was still in telling stories and in trying to directly advocate any particular morality. The difference was that he no longer had the market forces to consider or to hold him back from his own worst instincts.

Possibly his best known work today, "The Charge of the Light Brigade" offers an illustration. This poem, about a failed military charge during the Battle of Balaclava in 1854, was reputedly written out by Tennyson in a matter of hours, polished in a matter of days, and eventually acclaimed as something of a national treasure. In some ways it is the opposite of "The Eagle," in that it tells a long, heroic narrative with little verbal grace and almost no sense of mystery. In other ways, it is the opposite of "Ulysses": while the earlier poem expressed pity for the successful military figure in peacetime, "The Charge of the Light Brigade" celebrated a military failure, churning up nationalistic emotions about an episode that would hardly be worth dwelling on if not for the heroic lilt given by the poet's skill with words. "Into the valley of Death / rode the six hundred," the poem proclaims with thundering language, and readers of several generations have thundered along with them, feeling the uplifting cadence of Tennyson's rhythm carry them like the roll of galloping horses. Like Tennyson's other narratives, this poem was more popular with the general public than with critics, who found little subtlety here.

It is a bit unfair to generalize about all of Tennyson's work between 1850, when he was made Laureate, and 1892, when he died, on the basis of one popular poem. Still, it is not a judgement, only a fact, that most of the poet's work after that date was done in the long, epic form. *Idylls of the King* was begun in 1859 and put into final form in 1885. *Maud,* which was published the year after "The Charge of the Light Brigade," was a long epic built of self-contained quatrains. The isolated fragment such as "The Eagle" was certainly worth writing, as any one who has read it can attest, but it probably would not have been written once Tennyson reached a position of comfort. It is only fitting that the poet would turn his attention to lengthier material once he had the comfort to do so. It is the poetry of a struggling poet who does not have answers to the questions he raises and is not willing to pretend that he does; society rightfully expects more assurance from those raised to honored positions.

Source: David Kelly, in an essay for *Poetry for Students,* Gale Group, 2001.

S. K. Robisch

Robisch is an assistant professor of ecological and American literature at Purdue University. In the following essay, he focuses on the mythic eagle versus the physical eagle in Tennyson's poetic fragment.

Birds have long been known as the representatives of the flight of the soul and as mediators between heaven and earth. They have been characterized according to the traits that seem most dominant to the writers who watch them; the crow's blackness, the lark's song, the peacock's plumage. In poetry as a whole—but very often in poems about birds, it seems—readers learn about the poet's own preferences, about some personal condition, or a general human condition, that the poet wishes to symbolize through the bird. The real characteristics of the bird are limited to the ones most useful for the poem, and so what readers finally envision in the writing is sometimes less the actual bird than a character that serves the writer's purpose. Edgar Allen Poe's raven is mysterious and tormenting; Howard Nemerov's phoenix is fearsome and religious; Ted Hughes' hawk in "Hawk Roosting" is arrogant and godlike. Unlike Hughes, who gives his raptor careful attention in several stanzas, Alfred Tennyson gives readers a great bird in a small poem, "The Eagle," a brief glimpse at his raptor, and, ultimately, at his own preferences for the craft of a formalist poem.

Tennyson wrote epic poems and lyrics about grand literary moments, most of which were more fictional than historical. "The Eagle" fits into this mode and, more generally, into the mode of the mid-nineteenth century, when the romantic vision of the world experienced its resurgence at the end of the Enlightenment. Tennyson has sometimes been called an Enlightenment poet, but although he did exhibit some interest in the sciences, his poetry hardly exhibited a scientific mind. The work is quintessentially romantic, and "The Eagle" has only been read as an ambiguous tribute rather than as a treatise on the nature of eagles. In *Tennyson*

> *So the mythic force of the eagle ... generates in the reader of the poem opportunities for investing long conversation over history, mythology, other poems, and Tennyson himself.*

as a Student and Poet of Nature, printed not long after Tennyson's death, Sir Norman and Winnifred Lockyear make a case for Tennyson's interest in and knowledge of the natural world. But the Lockyears leave "The Eagle" out of their analysis, perhaps because the poem is too thin for readers to make any judgment about Tennyson's education regarding eagles. On the one hand, Tennyson holds the poem to plausible actions and stays out of the eagle's head, unlike Ted Hughes, who regularly imagines the thoughts of his animal subjects and uses them to present messages to humans. On the other hand, Tennyson is writing in the bardic tradition of having the eagle represent some condition of the world around it; the catch is that the condition is left for the reader to figure out.

This trick of ambiguity in poetry is now a cliché, unwelcome in contemporary craft because it absolves the poet of responsibility for the work. Leaving readers with too little to go on does not necessarily empower them. But Tennyson labeled the poem "a fragment," so that the reader knows that he intended it to be a kind of detail from a painting, or a *partita* in music—a piece intended to imply a larger work that could function according to the rules of the piece. Fragments were common in Tennyson's time—he had published several himself—and served the arts community as conversation pieces. What lay behind the fragment was open to the speculation of the reader, which made finding reference points and comparisons for the piece a great preoccupation. So the mythic force of the eagle as indicated in a mere six lines generates in the reader of the poem opportunities for investing long conversation over history, mythology, other poems, and Tennyson himself. So has the project of literary criticism always been; to treat a work as the tip of an iceberg of thought. The project of literary criticism has always been to treat a written work as the tip of an iceberg of thought, and all the volumes about his poetry serve as proof that Tennyson's thought ran very deep and soared very high.

Besides "The Blackbird," which is a lyrical poem of observation, Tennyson's other "bird poems" are equally metaphoric. For example, the three-act, comedic play called *The Falcon* depicts the bird as a symbol of the royal court; "The Goose" is the symbol of relative wealth or poverty (yes, it lays a golden egg); and his "Song: The Owl" shows a white owl in a belfry watching over the passing of days. This last mention is closest to what Tennyson may be doing in "The Eagle," which is to depict the bird as a measure of time, a representative of the passage of one era and the coming of another (as at least one critic has observed through the language of withering age, such as "crag" and "wrinkle").

This focus on the end of an era was a popular sentiment during Tennyson's life. In America, where Tennyson was widely respected, such painters as Thomas Cole of the Hudson River School were depicting the ruins of great civilizations overgrown by nature, by the deep green of a new Eden, a return to the splendor of a natural world unbound. At the same time, many romantics, especially during times of war, tried to invoke, in their storybooks, the chivalry and mythic heroism of the Arthurian age with its forests and green fields. This was certainly a trait of Tennyson (well known for "The Charge of the Light Brigade"), and readers may easily see the eagle of his poem as Arthurian not only in its majestic position against the sky (and its being the representative bird of the high king in the courtly practice of falconry) but in its age and its fall at the poem's end.

Tennyson composed "The Eagle" in Cauteretz, France, during a trip through the French Pyrenees in 1831, but the poem did not appear until twenty years later, in the seventh edition of his *Poems*. Literally, then, the poem might refer to a French eagle, a raptor of the Pyrenees that Tennyson encountered. Or it could be that the eagle is a vision in Tennyson's mind, a bird he never actually saw while trekking. Perhaps he imagined it in the mountains around him near the Mediterranean. Perhaps he imagined it back in Britain by the Atlantic. Perhaps he was thinking, as he often did, of the mythic stories he would rewrite in his poetry, and saw an eagle from an epic or a great romance, the regal bird from the mews of a great king. Whatever

process he used is unknown, so the reader must turn to the form of the poem and the words he uses to depict the eagle in order to find out what sort of bird to imagine, to speculate about what sort of bird he was imagining.

But any poem about an animal deserves careful consideration of the animal as well as of the poet, which is why the reader might speculate about the role a real eagle plays in a poem about a mythic eagle. Even the mythic nature may be overstated, far-reaching as it is. Many critics, for instance, have cited "The Eagle" as being a reference to the story of Icarus, who constructed a set of wax wings and flew too close to the sun, then fell when the wax melted. The images in the poem that look directly to this myth are few and vague; a number of sun myths, sky myths, and bird legends could be invoked by the right reader with a long reach for stories. More likely is the possibility that critics assume the Icarus myth because Tennyson probably assumed it; he loved Greek mythology, often incorporated into his poems, and lived in a time when schools included Greek and Latin as part of their curriculum. The widespread familiarity with Icarus may have prompted interpretations of the poem, just as the widespread belief in eagles as especially majestic birds prompts poets to write about them—instead of, say, starlings or blue jays—as mythic figures.

All of this talk about the mythic figure and the eagle as a symbol of however many things (time, age, the human condition, the romantic era, Arthurian majesty, the flight of Icarus) is really about the way readers—particularly critics—takes the language Tennyson chose and interprets it based on Tennyson's other works, the period during which he wrote, and, certainly, their own dispositions. For instance, some critics have found the line "The wrinkled sea beneath him crawls" to be an ingenious and beautiful depiction of the sea in motion, while others consider it to represent decrepitude or drunkenness. Here again the reader has what may be a strength of ambiguity, but what is more likely the poem's tremendous weakness.

Taken as is, the poem is a brief glimpse at an eagle, and perhaps the reader shouldn't require the poet to provide some better reason to look at a bird than simply to do so. The bird has its own value, the moment has its intrinsic merit. We might consider that Tennyson, while hiking in the Pyrenees, saw above him on a crag, literally closer to the sun than he was, an eagle. Maybe he uses "hands" in place of "claws" or "talons" because he likes the sound, because the talons are the eagle's hands in terms of their use; it is anthropomorphic (presenting animals with human qualities), but there is not doubt that this is still an eagle. Maybe Tennyson himself is holding onto a lower crag, pulling himself along the mountain trail. He imagines the bird over "lonely lands"—perhaps because he felt lonely at the time (although his trip was a good one, and he was with his closest friend, so this is less likely), or because for the poem's sake he imagined a wasteland, or because by "lonely" he may have simply meant unpopulated and rough country in southern France. Whether or not the poet can see the ocean from the mountains, he would know where it was, and could speculate that the eagle, with its keen vision and higher vantage point, could spot the sea. The wrinkles on the sea are simply a means for the reader to imagine wind on water, the notice of wind is very likely when one is in a high place, and the Pyrenees are in a windy region. That the eagle falls like a thunderbolt is no more metaphoric than is a thunderbolt (that is, lightning) striking like an eagle. The simile is a means of showing us the speed of the drop, which, in the depiction of a bird of prey, is no great surprise even if it is still impressive. That the poem ends with the eagle's fall may only prove that the poet could not see where the eagle went when it left the crag— hunting, flying, simply falling to the ground. Mountainous terrain could interfere with the point of view. And there is the fragment, just as readers experience many such fragments in their encounters with other species when out on their excursions. The bird is present, then it is gone. The reader is merely trekking in its region.

Poets and critics alike, in any century, may sometimes be prone to favor the poet over the poem, the narrator over the subject matter. It is often assumed that what is important in a poem is what it says about humans, about the poet who wrote it, or about the act of reading. All of these are important, of course, and contribute to what makes poetry great. But the reader must also always pay attention to certain facts that provide them with poetry—facts they did not create, conditions of the world that make such poems about majestic birds possible. Tennyson chose an eagle for the same reason that Sir Edmund Hillary climbed Mount Everest—because it was there. "The Eagle" is, finally, a poem about an eagle, and that brief bit of awareness may be important enough all by itself.

Source: S. K. Robisch, in an essay for *Poetry for Students,* Gale Group, 2001.

Sources

Amis, Kingsley, "Introduction," in *Tennyson,* Penguin Books, 1973, pp. 7–19.

"Explanations: The Eagle," GaleNet, "Exploring Poetry," Gale Group, 2000.

James, Henry, quoted in *Nineteenth-Century Literature Criticism,* Volume 30, Gale, 1991, p. 203.

Kissane, James, *Alfred Tennyson,* Twayne Publishers, Inc., 1970.

Lockyear, Sir Norman, *Tennyson as a Student and Poet of Nature,* Russell and Russell, 1910.

Lucas, F. L., *Tennyson,* Longman Green & Co., 1957.

Priestly, J. B., *Victoria's Heyday,* Harper & Row, 1972.

Tennyson's Poetical Works: Student's Cambridge Edition, Houghton Mifflin Company, 1898.

Thorn, Michael, *Tennyson,* St. Martin's, 1992.

Tucker, Herbert, Jr., "Tennyson and the Measure of Doom," in *PMLA,* Vol. 98, No. 1, January, 1983, pp. 8–20.

For Further Reading

Carr, Arthur J., "Tennyson as a Modern Poet," from *Critical Essays on the Poetry of Tennyson,* edited by John Killham, Routledge and Paul, 1960, pp. 41–66.
    Examines themes and styles used in Tennyson's works that anticipated the twentieth-century rise of modernism.

Culler, A. Dwight, *The Poetry of Tennyson,* Yale University Press, 1977.
    Culler looks at "The Eagle" as both an example of Victorian poetry and as an example of Tennyson's balance of nature with spirit.

Madden, Lionel, "Tennyson: A Reader's Guide," in *Writers and their Background: Tennyson,* D. J. Palmer, Editor, Ohio University Press, 1973, pp. 1–22.
    Gives an overview of the poet's life. Directs readers to many other significant works about Tennyson.

Mustard, Wilfred P., *Classical Echoes in Tennyson,* The Folcroft Press, Inc., 1970.
    Traces similarities between "The Eagle" and Virgil's *The Aeneid.*

Pinion, F. B., *A Tennyson Chronology,* G. K. Hall & Co., 1990.
    Provides a detailed accounting of Tennyson's life, month-by-month in some parts. An invaluable tool for students of Tennyson.

Go Down, Moses

Anonymous

1800

"Go Down, Moses" is an African-American spiritual, a type of lyric that is also referred to as a Negro folk song. As a folk song, it is thought of as having been created by a community rather than an individual, in this case the community of African-American slaves who lived in the South prior to the Civil War. An early reference to it places it in Maryland in the late eighteenth century. It was a popular slave song and was sung throughout the South by slaves while they worked and during their occasional times of rest and prayer. "Go Down, Moses" is also said to have been sung by abolitionists to signal escape or rebellion. The lyrics use biblical imagery expressing the desire for a release from bondage. The song is marked by its strong tone of determination in the struggle for freedom. To this day, "Go Down, Moses" has remained popular and is performed by gospel singers throughout the world.

Poem Text

Go down, Moses
'Way down in Egypt land,
Tell ole Pharaoh,
To let my people go.

When Israel was in Egypt's land;   5
Let my people go,
Oppressed so hard they could not stand,
Let my people go.

"Thus spoke the Lord," bold Moses said;
Let my people go,   10

If not I'll smite your first born dead,
Let my people go.

Poem Summary

Lines 1–2:

The opening lines tell Moses, leader of the Jews who were held as slaves by the Egyptians, to go deep into Egypt, the land of the oppressors. In the Old Testament book of *Exodus,* God chooses Moses to lead his people out of slavery. In this song, Egypt may stand for the "slave states" in the American South. This assumption is reinforced by use of the word "down" since slave-holding states were referred to as being "down south." In this interpretation, Moses would be thought of as an abolitionist, one who helps slaves escape from the South, or as a political leader who fights for the abolition of slavery altogether.

Lines 3–4:

The lyrics instruct Moses to speak to the Egyptian Pharaoh, demanding freedom for the Jews. In *Exodus* God commanded Moses to say "Let my people go" to the Pharaoh. God also told Moses to warn the Pharaoh ten times of ten different plagues that were sent by God to force the Egyptians to grant the Jews freedom. Because the Pharaoh failed to release the Jews from slavery after each plague except the last, Moses had to return to him repeatedly with the message, "Let my people go." In this first stanza, the assonance of long *o* and the *o* sounds *ow* and *oo* that occur in the words "go," "Moses," "ole," "Pharaoh," "down," and "to" creates a sustained melodic effect.

Lines 5–8:

Lines five and seven elaborate on the story of Moses by describing the condition of the Jews. "Israel" refers to the Jews who are destined to live in the promised land of Israel, but are instead being kept as slaves by the Egyptian Pharaoh. They are oppressed, that is, burdened, to such an extent that they cannot stand, a condition that implies more than literally being on the point of collapse; it may also refer to the inability to stand up for one's rights. Both the physical exhaustion and political subjection of the Jews reflect the conditions of African-American slaves. Forced to work from daybreak to sunset, underfed, and physically brutalized, slaves often found themselves physically

Media Adaptations

- The 1998 PBS series *Africans in America* traces the history of Africans from the early 1600s to the period just before the Civil War.

- *Roots,* the saga of an African-American family based on the best selling novel by Alex Haley, was re-released by Warner Home Video in 1992.

- A 1997 production by Films for the Humanities, *Too Close to Heaven, Part I,* discusses spirituals and their origins, including the early performances by the Fiske Jubilee Singers.

- "Go Down, Moses" is included on a CD released by Pavilion Records in 1995 entitled *Marian Anderson Sings Spirituals.*

- *Flight to Freedom: The Underground Railroad,* a 1995 release by Films for the Humanities, discusses how spirituals were used as a code on the Underground Railroad.

unable to stand. If they tried to stand up for their rights, their actions were punished by whipping and sometimes by death. In addition to the description of the condition of the slaves, this stanza contains two repetitions of the chorus "Let my people go," which creates the effect of a determined group of voices united in the struggle for freedom.

Lines 9–10:

Each time he warned the Egyptians that they would suffer at the hands of God, Moses always said that he spoke the words of the Lord as God told him to do. Although Moses could have easily been put to death by the Pharaoh, he went as God's messenger and identified himself each time as speaking God's will. This took great courage, since he was addressing the Pharaoh, who was not only the most powerful man in Egypt, but who was also considered a god himself. Furthermore, the Egyptians did not include Moses's God among the other deities that they worshipped besides the Pharaoh. Therefore, Moses would be considered extraordinarily rebellious by the Pharaoh. In light of this, the song rightly calls Moses "bold." If the song is taken to be a metaphor for the African Americans quest for freedom, then the reference to a "bold Moses" reminds the listener that African-American slaves also needed great courage to escape from their captivity. If a slave were caught trying to escape or helping others escape, the punishment frequently was death. Line twelve repeats the chorus, creating a further feeling of brave rebellion.

Lines 11–12:

Line eleven refers to the last plague sent by God to free the Jews. After nine attempts to convince the Pharaoh to free the Jewish slaves, God told Moses to warn the Pharaoh that every first-born child in Egypt would be killed as a sign of God's power and his displeasure that his chosen people were in bondage. When this plague causes the death of every first-born Egyptian child, including the Pharaoh's son, the Pharaoh grants the Jews their freedom. The Pharaoh would not relent until he had suffered drastic punishment. Reference to this extreme measure may be read as a strong threat that slavery in America would not be tolerated forever; with the help of abolitionists, slavery would end, even if bloodshed were necessary to bring about justice. In the concluding chorus, "Let my people go," the forceful demand for freedom again rings out.

Topics for Further Study

- Investigate the history of the Underground Railroad, focusing on the role that spirituals played in communicating messages.

- There are a number of connections between spirituals and the protest songs of the Civil Rights movement. Compare and contrast some of these songs.

- Write a report on the role of the griot or storyteller in African tribal culture.

- Choose a famous tale from history, the Bible, folk or fairy tales, even current events. Retell it in song or poetry.

- Spirituals connect the Hebrews of the Old Testament with the slaves in the United States. Over the past several decades, however, prominent African-American leaders such as Louis Farrakhan have been accused of anti-Semitism. Investigate these charges and write a report on your findings.

Themes

Freedom

"Go Down, Moses," a spiritual with its origins in the slave community of the southern United States, adopts the Biblical story of Moses from the book of *Exodus* to express the unquenchable desire for freedom felt by the African Americans held in captivity. Any study of the body of spirituals will reveal that this hunger is the clear and overriding theme of the genre. In his detailed study of the origins and meanings of the African-American spirituals, *Black Song: The Forge and the Flame,* John Lovell, Jr. states that "There is hardly a better way to nail down the Afro-American spiritual than to describe the central passion of it and its creators— a thing called freedom."

While Lovell indicates that freedom is the theme of every spiritual, in many songs it is obscured in some way. Too obvious an expression of this longing could frequently be dangerous; therefore, many slave songs utilized a code that

was transparent to insiders, but easily overlooked by others. Thus several religious songs, such as "Swing Low, Sweet Chariot" and "New Jerusalem," were interpreted by the white listeners as possessing only a theological meaning. Even some twentieth-century scholars felt that the creators of these songs hoped for a better life only in the hereafter, rather than the here and now. This is certainly not the case with "Go Down, Moses." It draws a direct parallel between the situation of the Jews in Egypt and the Africans who had been taken to the Americas. Both were slaves forced to endure abominable treatment. Families were torn apart. Biblical Hebrews and Africans in America alike were beaten, exploited as labor, killed at the whim of an overseer. Although the song does not specifically mention any of these facts, it effectively sums up all the hardship in the simple phrase, "Oppressed so hard they could not stand."

Moses is the spokesman for the oppressed, both in front of the Pharaoh and in defiance of the American system of slavery. In the song, as in the

Bible, the message is clear and direct. It appears both in the verse and the refrain as well: "Let my people go." Over and over it is repeated, giving voice to the longing of a people for freedom. In the introduction to *The Books of American Negro Spirituals,* James Weldon Johnson describes how this song was traditionally performed, using the lead and response style traditional in African music. A chorus opens with the first verse, harmonizing its last line, which states for the first time the phrase, "Let my people go." A leader sings, "Thus saith the Lord, bold Moses said." The chorus responds again, "Let my people go." This pattern is followed throughout the song. It is almost impossible to interpret this as anything other than an impassioned cry for freedom. In fact, because of its message, "Go Down, Moses" was outlawed in many communities throughout the South.

Indictment of Slavery

Like many other spirituals, "Go Down, Moses" includes a forceful indictment of the entire system of slavery. The Pharaoh represents the earthly power of the oppressor. He symbolizes the authority that upholds slavery, both in Egypt and the Americas. Owners, overseers, traders, auctioneers—all function under his protection. Thus, at first, he seems to represent an almost undefeatable enemy for the slave who has neither the law nor weapons on his side.

However, while the Pharaoh may seem invincible because of his physical strength, he is vulnerable on a moral level. The wickedness of the governmental policies he upholds must demand some type of retribution. This is clearly a key theme in the biblical tale of Moses, and it is carried out in the spiritual as well. Every time the Pharaoh denies Moses' request to free his people a new plague is placed upon his people. "Go Down, Moses" only mentions the last and most terrible of the punishments, the killing of the first born sons. Yet the message is clear: God will not allow such evil to go unpunished forever. Moses and the Israelites had the power of a just God to protect them from the Pharaoh and his armies. Spirituals such as "Go Down, Moses" extended that protection to the African Americans in bondage.

Several critics, such as Johnson and Lovell, have compared African religious practices with the Christianity practiced in the southern part of the United States during the centuries of slavery. While African religion was an intrinsic part of daily life, many slaves were puzzled by the fact that Christianity seemed to be a Sunday event, whose principles were unrelated to day-to-day existence.

Courage and Community

The southern spirituals that came out of the slave community exhibit an astonishing degree of unity, dignity, and courage. Given the fact that the slaves had been torn from their families and language, were forced to live in often appalling conditions and were given no opportunity to group together in a social environment, the thematic consistency of the spiritual demonstrates the enormous desire for freedom which stretched throughout the entire slave community. "Go Down, Moses" is one of the boldest statements of this longing, and therefore one of the most courageous. It stands as a direct attack on the slave system. It contains an almost mocking view of the Pharaoh. He is always described as "ole Pharaoh," a phrase which holds a subtle connotation of weakness. When this is compared with "bold Moses" who stands up to him and defeats him, the scorn becomes even clearer. "Go Down, Moses" emphasizes the courage and dignity of the oppressed. In "The Negro Spiritual," David Simms discusses the affirmative power of the spirituals that "consistently hold to the view that every human being is a child of God and that all men are therefore brothers ... This is the greatest theme of the Negro Spirituals."

Style

As noted by John Wesley Work in his book *American Negro Songs and Spirituals,* African-American songs often retain forms that originated in African tribal customs. "Go Down, Moses" belongs to the largest group, a class of spirituals that use the African "call-and-response chant form." Mr. Work describes it as "interesting as well as distinctive. Its feature is a melodic fragment sung repeatedly by the chorus as an answer to the challenging lines of the leader which usually change." In this version the chorus, "Let my people go," repeats every second and fourth line in stanzas two and three and as the last line in stanza one. It is meant to be sung by a group in answer to an individual voice that sings the first and third lines of each stanza. This repetition not only provides structure for the song, it also enables the lyrics to be easily remembered. Another aid to memory exists in the rhymes that occur at the end of the first and third lines in stanzas two and three: "land" with "stand," and "said" with "dead." The last two lines of stanza one also end with rhymes: "Pharaoh" and "go."

Historical Context

In many American history books, 1620 is singled out as an important date. That was the year when the Mayflower landed at Plymouth colony, bringing a shipload of Pilgrims who had left their homes and set sail for a new world hoping to find the religious freedom which had been denied them in Europe. Those same books seldom record an equally momentous event which occurred one year earlier: in 1619, a Dutch man-of-war arrived in Jamestown, bringing the first African slaves to the land which would become the United States. These two events prefigure a divisive split in our nation's history: between those who settled the land looking for freedom, gain, or adventure and those who were violently ripped from their own country and forced into bondage to suffer for another's dream.

In the decades immediately following 1619, there was little increase in the slave trade in the English colonies. The small towns and farms did not require intensive labor, and thus did not provide a profitable market for the traders. Work was frequently performed by indentured servants, workers who committed themselves to serve a master for a period of several years, after which they received their freedom. In addition, many settlers hoped to enforce the native Indian population into either indentured servitude or slavery. Thus, the slave trade in the Americas first flourished in the West Indies and the Caribbean where large sugar plantations were established.

Gradually, however, slavery was extended throughout North America. At first, slaves in these English colonies were considered the same as indentured servants. Eleven Angolans who had been brought to work as slave laborers in New Amsterdam in 1626 were released from their servitude by the governor of the colony in 1644. However, this attitude quickly changed. By the later part of the seventeenth century, codes were established which legalized a system of slavery allowing a slave to be considered as chattel or property. As the large plantations of the southern United States developed, so did the increased demand for slaves. Soon a triangular trade route flourished. Ships would leave England loaded with goods and sail to Africa. There the goods were traded for slaves. Ships then made the infamous Middle Passage to the West Indies or the colonies. Slaves were exchanged for sugar and other commodities, after which the ships returned to England to begin the process again. Such continual trade meant the number of slaves increased by the thousands almost every year. In *Africans in America,* the authors state: "By the mid-1750s, one in every five Americans was a slave— nearly 300,000 out of a total population of a million and a half. And five thousand new captives arrived from Africa or the Caribbean each year."

Thus, from 1619 until the slave trade ended, almost 15,000,000 Africans were wrenched from their homes and brought to the New World under appalling conditions. Many died en route. Those who survived found themselves totally ripped from family and tradition, often without even the presence of someone who spoke the same language. Nevertheless, slaves formed communities with common dreams and goals. They adapted aspects of Christianity which allowed them to retain many African religious overtones. They struggled against their oppressors, mentally and physically. In *The Black Spirituals and Black Experience,* James Cone proclaims that "Black slaves were not passive, and black history is the record of their resistance against the condition of human bondage."

Many slaves struggled against the harsh conditions. Several stories have been passed down about slaves who threw themselves off the ships if possible, preferring death to life in captivity. During the 230 years when slavery flourished in North America, there were many slave rebellions. Over sixty-five have been documented. One of the first occurred in the north, in New York City in 1711, when a group of runaway African slaves burned several buildings. In 1739, a man named Jeremy, a recent arrival from Angola, led over twenty slaves in a rebellion in Stony River, South Carolina. Word of a large-scale slave rebellion in Haiti in 1791 reached the United States, inspiring fear in slave-owners and hope in many slaves. One man who was encouraged by this example was Gabriel. He hoped to force the white slave-owners of Richmond Virginia, to negotiate with him. Both poor weather and a traitor in his ranks helped to defeat his troops, but not before his rebellion received national attention, including that of the president-elect, Thomas Jefferson.

However, armed rebellion was not the only method of seeking freedom for slaves. Many fled North, either on their own or aided by the Underground Railroad, a loose connection of individuals who provided guidance and shelter for runaway slaves. One of the best known figures of the system was a former slave, Harriet Tubman. After reaching the relative safety of the northern states, she decided to help others escape. Her role was that

Compare & Contrast

- **1800:** Gabriel's revolt, an attempt by several slaves to call attention to the injustice of slavery, takes place in Richmond, Virginia.

  1963: Martin Luther King delivers his "I Have a Dream" speech in Washington, D.C., calling for civil rights for all citizens.

  1995: Louis Farrakhan and Benjamin Chavis organize the Million Man March to combat negative stereotyping of black men, attacks on affirmative action, and hostile practices by governmental authorities.

- **1800:** Thomas Jefferson is elected third president of the United States.

  1998: DNA evidence confirms that Jefferson was the father of at least one of the children of his slave, Sally Hemings.

  2000: The Jefferson Memorial Foundation, which runs the tours of Jefferson's home, Monticello, decides to include information about Hemings and the DNA tests in its literature.

---

of a conductor on the railroad. She ventured into the South, escorting groups of fleeing slaves back North with her. Her passion and success were so overwhelming that she became known as Moses, or at times the Black Moses. Spirituals were a prime means of communication on the Underground Railroad, and she would frequently signal her presence by singing, "Go Down, Moses." Word then spread through the slave cabins that Moses had arrived to make the words of the spiritual a reality. Thus the spirituals held out the hope of freedom, not just in the afterlife, but in the present also.

The importance of such songs in providing hope is vividly demonstrated in *The Music of Black Americans* by Eileen Southern. She describes a meeting of black men held on December 31, 1862, in Washington, D.C. As they waited for the stroke of midnight, when the Emancipation Proclamation would "bring freedom to the slaves in the secessionist states … the assembled blacks sang over and over again: *"Go Down, Moses … Let my people go."*

Critical Overview

Discussion about "Go Down, Moses" often centers on the degree to which the song should be considered as a metaphor for the escape from slavery. Some historians believe that "Moses" in the song refers to Harriet Tubman, one of the leaders of the Underground Railroad, a group of abolitionists, both black and white, who formed a network of transportation and safe houses that assisted slaves in their escape from Southern plantations. This interpretation receives full treatment in *Harriet Tubman, The Moses of Her People* by Sarah Bradford. In this reading, Egypt and the Pharaoh represent the plantation and the slave owner, and of course, the Israelites represent the African-American slaves themselves. Among those who agree with this interpretation are Bernard Katz, John Lovell, Irwin Silber, Russell Ames, and Earl Conrad. Conrad writes, "Negro slaves chanted thinly-disguised songs of protest set to the meter of spirituals [such as] 'Go Down, Moses,' the fighting song of Harriet Tubman who came like Moses to redeem her black kinsman from the 'Egypt-land of the South.'" In *Black Song* Lovell reports that Denmark Vesey, who lead an attempted slave uprising in Charleston in 1822, used this song as a signal for fugitive slaves. Lovell credits "Go Down, Moses" with "filling every listener with a pervasive contempt for oppression and a resounding enthusiasm for freedom." He speaks of the importance of Moses to the slaves: "they lavished great attention upon Moses. He was no legendary figure, he had actually lived. Through him a very bitter slavery had been overthrown. If it could happen once, it could happen again." And he calls "Go Down, Moses" a song

Harriet Tubman and the slaves she brought to freedom on the underground railroad.

"intended to chide Americans, South and North, about permitting slavery and to issue a solemn warning that slavery will not be indefinitely tolerated."

Another interpretation of the song casts it as a tribute to Bishop Francis Asbury, who in the 1790s as leader of the Methodist church spoke out strongly against slavery. Miles Mark Fisher describes the love and gratitude that the slaves felt for this white religious leader and suggests that they "immortalized him in a great spiritual. He was their Moses."

Criticism

Mary Mahony

Mahony is an English instructor at Wayne County Community College in Detroit, Michigan. In this essay, Mahony discusses West African influences and multiple levels of meaning in African-American spirituals.

Folk song is the voice of a people, of a community. It tells of the sorrows, triumphs, and yearnings—not of the individual but of the collective. Folk songs are attributed not to a single composer or poet, but to a nation, a tribe or a race. This helps

to explain the power and the beauty, as well as the miracle, of the African-American spiritual. In the introduction to *The Books of American Negro Spirituals,* the poet James Weldon Johnson marvels at the creation of this powerful music: "These people came from various localities in Africa. They did not speak the same language. Here they were, cut off from the moorings of their native culture, scattered without regard to their old tribal relations, having to adjust themselves to a completely alien civilization, having to learn a strange language, and moreover, held under an increasingly harsh system of slavery; yet it was from these people this mass of noble music sprang; this music that is America's only folk music and, up to this time, the finest distinctive artistic contribution she has to offer the world. It is strange!"

Because of the amazing difficulties that the slaves faced, some early evaluators of the spiritual, such as E. Franklin Frazier and George Pullen Jackson, decided that it would have been impossible for slaves to have originated such works. Frazier argued that the African roots of the slaves had been almost completely eradicated so that any music they composed had to come from their contacts in America. Jackson began to trace the development of the white spiritual, comparing these songs to the black spirituals. He then theorized that the white spiritual had come first. Therefore, Frazier and Jackson concluded that songs like "Go Down, Moses" were simply born of the slaves' introduction to the Christian religion, and were merely primitive adaptations of stories or music they had heard.

These theories were soon challenged by many critics who conducted research into the African origins and background of the songs. One of the most extensive works, *Black Song: The Forge and the Flame: The Story of How the Afro-American Spiritual Was Hammered Out* by John Lovell, Jr., evaluated the spiritual as both song and folklore, first considering the musicality and then the subjects or themes of the spirituals. After an examination of over 3,000 references, he concluded that "It was and is an independent folk song, born of the union of African tradition and American socio-religious elements."

To understand the influence of West African tradition and music on the spiritual, it is necessary to understand the role of music in that culture. In most West African tribal societies, music played an intrinsic role in the day-to-day lives of the people. Almost every occasion was accompanied by song. This included not only special events like weddings, births, or funerals, but many of the daily rituals were also celebrated in music and dance. Doing chores, hunting and fishing, building structures—all were frequently performed to music. Thus, drama, music, and dance became a way of communicating what happened in the lives of individuals and the tribe.

These musical performances were centered around the community rather than the individual. Therefore, when everyday or even special events like these were reenacted, they took place in group performances. The main singer or drummer might hold a role as song leader, but usually the entire community would participate. In *Black American Music,* Hal Roach notes that the community would create a performance, for example of a typical hunting or harvesting experience. These occasions were based on real events; thus, the words and actions would change, depending on what had actually taken place. Initially, the master drummer would begin, setting the theme and mood. His music would spur onlookers to join in, creating songs and performing dances reflecting their own and the communal experiences. The theme of the performance was set, but the community itself developed the individual content.

Almost every occasion was accompanied by song.... Thus, drama, music, and dance became a way of communicating what happened in the lives of individuals and the tribe."

Another important West African musical technique that inspired community involvement was the "call and response." The leader would state a theme that would be taken up by a chorus. Many spirituals, including "Go Down, Moses" use this form. Because of these elements, music became a vital, fluid changeable part of community life, which both celebrated and recorded community history.

These same characteristics are true of African-American spirituals where the songs reflect the lives and longings of the people. The participatory style of West African music was a central ingredient of spirituals before the Civil War. Roach demonstrates this with a quotation from E. A. McIlhenny, who had frequently listened to slave songs when he was a child. "It is impossible to get the exact wording of spirituals for even the same singer never sings one twice the same ... Stanzas never occur twice in the same order, but are sung as they come to the mind of the singer, and as the singer will improvise ... the number of stanzas ... is unlimited."

Another important role of music in African life was to convey history and tradition. These were not written down in books, but passed on to successive generations in music and stories. Griots, who were expert musicians and tale-tellers, traveled from place to place serving as a sort of portable library, dispensing the chronicles and the wisdom of the tribe. However, griots were not the only communicators of tribal wisdom. Every community established its own rituals for conveying community history to subsequent generations. Frequently, this information was passed on in secret meetings, a sort of initiation ritual where the men of the tribe used song and dance to prepare the youth for the day when they would accept the mantle of adulthood and leadership. A similar ceremony was held for

What Do I Read Next?

- The biblical story of Moses is joined with black folklore in Zora Neale Hurston's *Moses, Man of the Mountain,* which was reprinted in 1999 by Econo-Clad Books.

- *The Souls of Black Folk* by W. E. B. DuBois contains the essay "Of the Sorrow Songs," one of the earliest and most insightful discussions of the role of the spiritual in portraying the sufferings and hopes of slaves.

- Slavery is graphically portrayed, including the role of the spiritual, in the first person narrative *The Life and Times of Frederick Douglass.*

- William Faulkner's novel, *Go Down, Moses,* deals with racism and the lingering effects of slavery in the South.

- *The Shaping of Black America* by Lerone Bennett provides a gripping historical account of realities of life for African Americans in the United States.

- Toni Morrison's 1998 novel *Beloved* is a powerful and tragic story of the far-reaching effects of slavery.

girls approaching womanhood. Such secret ceremonies were an intrinsic part of tribal culture.

Partly because of these centuries-old traditions, Africans who were sold into slavery managed to retain many elements of their past. The role of music as a central focus of their lives and history was ingrained into their thought and behavior, so that despite the fact that an individual had been ripped from his old community, he or she retained many basic beliefs. Even when faced with linguistic differences, the language of music remained a common medium, and this tradition helped in the formation of new slave communities, composed of peoples from different tribes or areas. Many of the first slave songs in America were simple—calls, cries, hollers or shouts. Later, they developed into the more complex musicality of the spirituals.

As these spirituals developed, many retained West African patterns. The use of call and response between the leader and the chorus helped to create a new sense of community. The same was true for the dramatic or performance aspect of song. When drums or other musical instruments were unavailable or forbidden, the human body served as an instrument, preserving many of the rhythms of African music. Since African culture, music, religion, and history were all interwoven, the songs had an intensely personal quality reflecting identity and heritage. This quality was also transferred to the spirituals where the use of personal pronoun was common. One of the most evident transferences, however, is the use of song to convey wisdom, information, and history. Ironically, the fact that much of this type of information was originally shared in secret meetings in Africa became essential to survival in this new environment. The fear of rebellion and insurrection permeated much of the South. Therefore, most states enacted laws forbidding slaves to gather together. Slave owners hired men to patrol the countryside making sure no gatherings took place. However, slaves were still allowed to communicate freely through the use of religion and religious songs.

Thus both the themes and frequently individual phrases in spirituals such as "Go Down, Moses" were crafted to convey a variety of meanings. In the United States, several spirituals operated on numerous different levels of communication. The first level, designed for the ears of the slave owner, held a simple religious message. In "Go Down, Moses," it was the retelling of Exodus. In "Swing Low, Sweet Chariot" and "Steal Away to Jesus," the surface message discussed the longing for heaven. The secondary meaning dealt with themes such as the longing for freedom. Here words contained a double meaning. Bondage referred to slavery. The suffering of the Hebrew people was equated with the sufferings of the slaves. Moses was a liberator. However, several songs had a third level that dealt with specific practical advice for attaining that freedom. Code words and phrases permeated these songs. Moses was the name for Harriet Tubman, who frequently used the song, "Go Down, Moses" to announce her presence in an area. Slaves who had been waiting for her would gather their bundles to set out on the journey north when she signaled her presence. Many other songs, too, used codes. Canaan and Heaven both were frequently synonymous with Canada. The song "Follow the Drinking Gourd" contained directions for traveling north. "Wade in the Water," which slave owners thought spoke of baptism, made a very pragmatic suggestion. Don't directly cross a stream; instead you must walk a distance in the water so as not to leave a trail for slave catchers to follow.

Johnson has called the spirituals America's only true folk music. Certainly, they are one of the most permanent types of folk music in this country. The spiritual has never fallen into disuse. It remains alive today in churches and in gospel choirs. Songs like "Go Down, Moses" are performed by orchestras and choruses across the world. Along with many other spirituals, "Go Down, Moses" remains viable on its many levels. It is still a dramatic and powerful folk version of the story of Moses and the Israelites. It is still a poignant plea for freedom. And finally, it still recreates the history of the slave community in both its struggles and its triumphs.

Source: Mary Mahony, in an essay for *Poetry for Students,* Gale Group, 2001.

Michele Drohan

Drohan is a professional editor and writer who specializes in classic and contemporary literature. In the following essay, she explores the history of "Go Down, Moses" and the connection the poem makes between the struggle of the enslaved Jews escaping Egypt and the struggles of African-American slaves in pre-Civil War America.

"Go Down, Moses" is an old African-American spiritual, or folk song, that has remained popular for hundreds of years. Many historians believe it originated in the late eighteenth century among the slaves in the southern states. Prior to the civil war, African Americans were held captive as slaves on southern plantations, forced to work long hours and to endure tremendous physical and emotional brutality. Because plantation owners feared an uprising of the slaves, any sign of rebellion was met with severe punishment, such as whipping, branding, dismembering, or castrating. In fact, it was completely legal to kill a slave who had tried to escape. It also became illegal for the slaves to assemble or learn how to read or write. This left the slaves with little privacy or ability to communicate. To protect themselves and communicate with one another without fear of punishment, the slaves often sang while working in the fields.

According to musicologist Horace Clarence Boyer, the Negro spiritual was created for a specific purpose or need. As a result, the song was only used when it was needed. In addition, there are two types of spirituals—liberation and sorrow.

> *Just as the Jews were severely oppressed by the Pharaoh, so did the plantation owners oppress the African-American slaves."*

Boyer identifies "Go Down, Moses" as a song of sorrow. Thus, it gave the slaves an outlet for their suffering. However, because the song discussed Moses and the Jews, it let the slaves disguise their desire for freedom without the threat of punishment.

The first four lines of the song, "Go down, Moses / Way down in Egypt land, / Tell ole Pharaoh / To let my people go," introduce the concept of slaves in Egypt. As related in the Old Testament, Moses was chosen by God to free the Jews from slavery. The Pharaoh had enslaved the Jews living in Egypt because he and the people of Egypt feared and resented them—a testament that easily translates to the plight of the African-American slaves. Moses was instructed by God to go "way down in Egypt land," and speak to the Pharaoh, who was holding the slaves captive. The idea that Moses should go "down" refers to the fact that slavery was rampant in the southern colonial states of America, and Egypt represents those slave states. The song then becomes a call to abolitionists to take up the slaves' cause and go south to help end slavery.

In the same way that Moses was chosen by God, the slaves hoped for a "chosen" leader who could lead them from bondage. Moses was not a mythical figure. Rather, he was a real person who lived and succeeded in freeing his people. Because Moses is firmly grounded in reality, some historians, such as Sarah Bradford, Bernard Katz, John Lovell, and Russell Ames, agree that Moses was symbolic of Harriet Tubman, who ran the Underground Railroad and, with her network of abolitionists, helped to free thousands of slaves. However, there is another interpretation that connects Moses with Bishop Francis Asbury, a church leader who outwardly expressed his opinions against slavery. Still most agree with the Harriet Tubman theory, some going so far as to name her Harriet "Moses" Tubman.

THE ROUTES OF THE UNDERGROUND RAILROAD

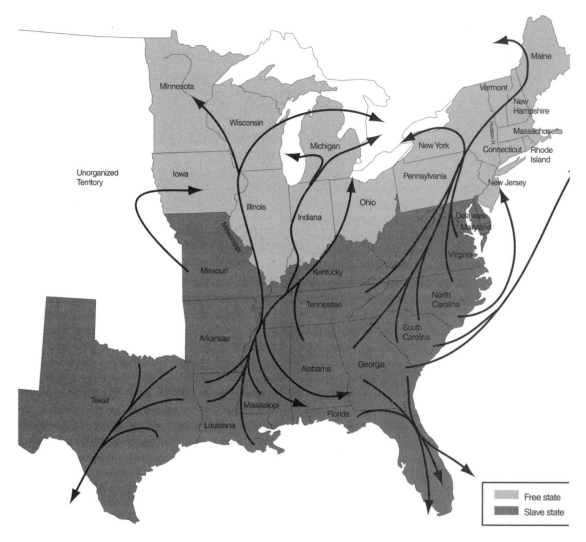

Map of the Underground Railroad.

The lines in the second stanza of the song, "When Israel was in Egypt's land; / Let my people go, / Oppressed so hard they could not stand, / Let my people go," further connect the slaves of Egypt with the African-American slaves. Just as the Jews were severely oppressed by the Pharaoh, so did the plantation owners oppress the African-American slaves. The oppression in both cases was crippling, and the backbreaking work they both did was so harsh, the slaves were physically exhausted to the point "they could not stand." That last line has a deeper meaning, however, meaning that the slaves could not stand up for their rights for fear of punishment. Again, any sign of uprising usually resulted in a severe beating or death.

In the Old Testament, God told Moses not only to implore the Pharaoh to let his people go, but also to warn the Pharaoh, because, if the Pharaoh did not heed God's warning, he would set a plague upon the people of Egypt. The line "Let my people go" is repeated at the end of the second stanza. This repetition refers to the fact that Moses warned the Pharaoh several times to heed God's wishes. God inflicted a series of ten different plagues upon the people of Egypt, but nothing happened and the slaves were not freed. Each time Moses said, "Let my people go," the Pharaoh ignored him, refusing to let the Jews return to the land of Israel. The repetition also serves to shed light on the construction of African-American spirituals. Because the songs were used to communicate, the slaves traded lines back and forth, which is referred to as "call-and-response chant form." The slaves repeated verses to feel united and to acknowledge the determination they all felt in their struggle. However, because "Go Down, Moses" is considered a song of sorrow, the repetition also indicates a feeling of resignation. This feeling is perhaps in part because the slaves themselves could not fight for their freedom, but rather depended on another to fight for them.

The last stanza of the song indicates just how brave a freedom fighter would have to be to secure the slaves' freedom. The line, "Thus spoke the Lord, bold Moses said," indicates that Moses could have easily been killed for his rebellion. He was "bold" and stood up against the most powerful man in Egypt, the Pharaoh, who may have only spared Moses' life because he claimed to speak God's will. However, the God of Moses was not even acknowledged in the land of Egypt, which made his actions much more courageous. By acknowledging Moses' bravado, "Go Down, Moses" seems to say that anyone willing to secure the freedom of the African-American slaves would have to find the same kind of courage.

It is common knowledge that Harriet Tubman took enormous risk in travelling to the South to transport over 100,000 slaves to safety in the North. In addition, the slaves who took that journey to freedom risked being caught and killed if discovered. They often traveled great distances in difficult and often hazardous conditions to make their way to freedom. If Harriet Tubman or anyone else aiding a slave to freedom had been caught, they would have been immediately executed for their so-called crimes. In addition, the fact that the song says Moses spoke God's will seems to be saying that the African-American slaves need to fight their cause using a higher law. Since slavery was legal, the only way to argue the injustice of the times was to argue God's law.

The eleventh line of the song speaks to the lengths that God would go to free his people. Through Moses, he said, "Let my people go, / If not I'll smite your first born dead." It was the tenth, and final, plague that God sent upon the people of Egypt that finally convinced the Pharaoh to let the Jews go. God decided that the first-born son of every Egyptian would be slain, including the Pharaoh's child. Moses protected the Jews from the plague by painting their doors red to indicate they were not to be harmed. When the Pharaoh discovered his dead son, he was so devastated by his loss that he finally agreed to let Moses' people go.

> *Just as the Jews were severely oppressed by the Pharaoh, so did the plantation owners oppress the African-American slaves."*

This drastic measure indicates how far the slaves needed to go to secure their freedom. Even if it meant bloodshed, slavery could no longer be tolerated. As the chosen one for her people, Harriet Tubman carried a gun with her on her missions to protect herself and the people she was transporting. She was willing to achieve her goals by any means necessary. Even though the Civil War had yet to occur, this idea of necessary bloodshed can be applied to the war. Abolitionists, like Moses, tried to secure the slaves' freedom through other means, but it wasn't until real bloodshed and a war that tore the country apart emerged that the African Americans became free.

Finally, the song ends with the line, "Let my people go." Again, this closes the call-and-response chant form. This line is repeated five times throughout the short song, in the last line of the first stanza, and the second and fourth lines of the last two stanzas. An individual would usually sing the other lines so that a group could respond with "Let my people go." By ending the song with this line, which is sung by the group, it becomes a powerful, united cry for freedom that resonates with the plight of many enslaved Africans throughout the American South.

Source: Michele Drohan, in an essay for *Poetry for Students,* Gale Group, 2001.

Erica Smith

Erica Smith is a writer and editor. In this essay she discusses the history, imagery, and cultural impact of the spiritual "Go Down, Moses."

"Go Down, Moses" is a spiritual, a kind of African-American religious folk song. Spirituals were first sung in early America by African-American slaves. These songs were related to Christian hymns—songs based on the Bible and sung in the churches of white Americans. But spirituals also

Although sung for years by plantation slaves, spirituals did not gain widespread notoriety in American culture until the outbreak of the Civil War. The war brought plantation slaves into contact with Northerners who, hearing these songs for the first time, were deeply affected by them."

had the unique features of African music, including call-and-response singing (in which one person sings a phrase and others respond) and improvisation (in which verses are made up on the spot, often commenting on an issue or conflict of the present moment).

"Go Down, Moses" recounts the incident in the Old Testament of the Bible in which Moses led the Jews out of Egypt. Because these Jews had been slaves, African-American slaves felt a strong connection with their plight. They too yearned for freedom, and with the commencement of the Civil War (1861–65), many of them believed that it was coming. The chorus of the song is both direct and elegant: "O go down, Moses / Away down to Egypt's land, / And tell King Pharaoh / To let my people go!" In this case, "Pharaoh" was thought of as the slaves' overseer. The Moses figure ultimately came to be affiliated with Abraham Lincoln, who was president during the Civil War. (In 1863 Lincoln signed the Emancipation Proclamation which did, in fact, free the slaves in the rebellious Southern states.)

As scholar John Lovell, Jr., notes in *Black Song: The Forge and the Flame,* part of the song's appeal is that it is powerful and clear:

> "Go Down, Moses" is a direct statement all the way. It does not employ … undercurrent symbolism…. It says flatly that Moses freed these Egyptian slaves boldly and justly because slavery is wrong. It clearly

projects the principles of this experience to all the world: Wherever men are held in bondage, they shall be freed.

The "Let my people go!" refrain is thunderous. It does not argue economic, sociological, historical, and racial points. It does not concern itself with what the Pharaohs shall do for substitute labor. It is one of the great freedom declarations of literature and history.

Although sung for years by plantation slaves, spirituals did not gain widespread notoriety in American culture until the outbreak of the Civil War. The war brought plantation slaves into contact with Northerners who, hearing these songs for the first time, were deeply affected by them. Soldiers commented on these stirring songs in their letters home, and newspaper reporters began to write about them. Of these spirituals, "Go Down, Moses" was the first to gain distinction.

It is unclear exactly how long this song had been in existence prior to these accounts. In his assessment of "Go Down, Moses" Lovell draws attention to the description given by Russell Ames and others—that this spiritual had been sung by Harriet Tubman to summon those whom she was helping travel to freedom. (She used the song "Wade in the Water" for a similar purpose: instructing runaway slaves how to throw bloodhounds off the trail of their scent.) The first white people to make a written record of the song claimed that it had been in existence nine or ten years, but due to the slow and evolving nature of the oral tradition, the song is likely older than that.

In *Sinful Tunes and Spirituals: Black Folk Music to the Civil War* scholar Dena J. Epstein recounts the pivotal episode in bringing slave music into contact with white Northerners. It was also the incident that set in motion the Civil War: the surrender of Fort Sumter to the Confederacy on April 14, 1861. After the surrender, refugee slaves entered Fortress Monroe in Virginia. General Benjamin Butler of the Union forces refused to return the slaves to their masters, instead, citing them as "contraband of war." (This phrase, or simply "contraband," became a popular synonym for slave, and "Go Down, Moses" was called a "song of the contrabands" in its earliest versions.)

Reverend Louis C. Lockwood, an employee of the YMCA, was sent to Fortress Monroe as a missionary to aid the refugees. According to the chaplain of the First Regiment of New York State Volunteers, the contrabands were "destitute and desolate," deeply in need of clothing, shelter, and social services. While helping out at Fortress Monroe, Lockwood heard slave music for the first time. He was so deeply moved that he wrote of his experiences in the October 12, 1861, *National Anti-Slavery Standard*—the first accounts of "Go Down, Moses" to appear in print:

> I overheard music.... I found a number of colored people assembled for a prayer-meeting. The brother who led in the concluding prayer had a sing-song manner, but his sentiments were very scriptural and impressive. He prayed that He who brought Israel out of Egypt, Jonah out of the mouth of the whale, and Daniel out of the den of lions, might bring them out into full deliverance, spiritually and temporally.

> I told my mission in few words.... They assured me that this is what they had been praying for; and now that "the good Lord" had answered their prayers, they felt assured that some great thing was in store for them and their people. There are some peculiarities in their prayer-meetings. Their responses are not boisterous; but in the gentle, chanted style ... The themes are generally devotional ...: "Go down to Egypt—Tell Pharaoh / Thus saith my servant, Moses—Let my people go."

According to Epstein, newspaper accounts of contrabands and their music became common during the Civil War, interspersed with military reports and descriptions of camp life.

The publication of sheet music for "Go Down, Moses" was announced in December, 1861. It was the first spiritual to be published with its music, and publication occurred not even two weeks after the text of the song was sent to the *New York Tribune*. The song did not gain a great deal of popularity as a direct result of its publication, for the arrangement (for piano and harp, by Thomas Baker) was weak and did not reflect the original song's power. However, the original version, as sung by African Americans, did prevail through the years.

The song unfolds as a vivid and poetic story. The stanzas are structured so that the first and third lines comprise the narrative, and the second and fourth lines deliver the refrain "[O] Let my people go!" The first stanza, for example, begins—"When Israel was in Egypt's land, / Let my people go! / Oppressed so hard they could not stand, / Let my people go!"—and each stanza is followed by a chorus. The song was sung by a group, with a song leader delivering the first and third lines, a group singing the refrain, and a collaboration of all singers coming in at the chorus. This powerful delivery of the song dramatizes the events within it.

The singers could deeply identify with the feeling of oppression related in the first stanza.

The scene is further described as a "dark and dismal night"—this can be read literally as well as figuratively, as a dark night of sorrow and fear within the soul. Some of the stanzas that follow convey direct action ("The Lord told Moses what to do / to lead the children of Israel through") while others convey poignant images ("O Moses, the cloud shall cleave the way / A fire by night, a shade by day") and philosophy ("We need not always weep and mourn / And wear these Slavery chains forlorn.")

For the duration of the song Moses is, by turns, reassured, praised, and shouted onward. The singers cajole him to "come along, Moses, you'll not get lost" and later implore him to hold a lighted candle so as not to lose his way in the wilderness. Knowing the triumph to come at the end of the song, the singers can adopt an attitude of wisdom, encouraging him to be brave. In this way, the song is helping the singers to muster their own bravery and faith. As the story unfolds, the waters of the Red Sea are parted for Moses and the freed slaves to pass safely through, but converge again to drown the Pharaoh and his army. The jubilant singers declare to Moses: "Your foe shall not before you stand / And you'll possess fair Canaan's land."

This assuredness of the singers also mingles with a sorrowful insight: the world is described as a "wilderness of woe," but the singers still vow to press onward to Canaan and put their faith in Christ. At the end of the song, the singers declare "what a beautiful morning that will be! / When time breaks up in eternity!" They have found their deliverance, and it is eternal.

"Go Down, Moses" has survived and flourished. After the end of the Civil War, the song continued to find new listeners. It was sung by the popular Fisk Jubilee Singers, a singing group of African-American singers from Fisk University who toured the United States and Europe, as well as the Tuskegee Choir; popular twentieth-century singers such as Paul Robeson and Harry Belafonte adapted the song; and Antonin Dvorak was influenced by it while composing his *American Symphony*. In other forms of media, the song is alluded to in the movie *Gone with the Wind* and inspired William Faulkner's novel *Go Down, Moses*.

"Go Down, Moses" is a spiritual of roaring power and tender feeling, unforgettable for its historical meaning as well as its enduring poetry.

Source: Erica Smith, in an essay for *Poetry for Students*, Gale Group, 2001.

Sources

Ames, Russell, *The Story of the American Folk Song,* Grosset Dunlap, 1955.

Boyer, Horace Clarence, "The Negro Spiritual," in *The American Experience: Jubilee Singers: Sacrifice and Glory,* PBS Online.

Bradford, Sarah, *The Moses of Her People,* Peter Smith, 1981.

Cone, James H., *The Spirituals and the Blues,* Orbis Books, 1991.

Conrad, Earl, *General Harriet Tubman,* Associated Publishers, 1943.

Epstein, Dena J., *Sinful Tunes and Spirituals: Black Folk Music to the Civil War,* University of Illinois Press, 1977.

Fisher, Miles Mark, *Negro Slave Songs in the United States,* Russell and Russell, 1968.

Johnson, Charles, Patricia Smith and the WGBH Series Research Team, *Africans in America,* Harcourt Brace, 1998.

Johnson, James Weldon and J. Rosamund Johnson, *The Books of American Negro Spirituals,* DaCapo Press, 1969.

Jones, LeRoi [Amiri Baraka], *Blues People,* Morrow Quill Paperbacks, 1963.

Katz, Bernard, *The Social Implications of Early Negro Music in the United States,* Arno Press, 1969.

Locke, Alain, Ph.D., *The Negro and His Music,* Kennikat Press, 1936.

Lovell, John Jr., *Black Song: The Forge and the Flame,* Macmillan, 1972.

———, "The Social Implications of the Negro Spiritual," in *The Social Implications of Early Negro Music in the United States,* Arno Press, 1969, pp. 128–37.

Roach, Hildred, *Black American Music: Past and Present,* 2d edition, Krieger Publishing, 1992.

Silber, Irwin, *Songs of the Civil War,* Columbia Press, 1960.

Simms, David McD., "The Negro Spiritual: Origins and Themes," in *The Journal of Negro Education,* Winter, 1996, pp. 35–41.

Southern, Eileen, *The Music of Black Americans,* 2d edition., W. W. Norton, 1983.

Work, John Wesley, *American Negro Songs and Spirituals,* Crown Publishers, 1940.

For Further Reading

Ajayi, J. F. A. and Michael Crowder, eds., *The History of West Africa,* Columbia University Press, 1972.
    This collection of scholarly essays provides a West African view on the history of the area, including an article on the slave trade.

Allen, William Francis, Charles Pickard Ware, and Lucy McKim Garrison, *Slave Songs in the United States,* Peter Smith Publications, 1951.
    This volume, which was originally copyrighted in 1867, is one of the oldest collections of spirituals. The introductory commentary provides insight into the attitudes towards spirituals at that time.

Lawrence-McIntyre, Charshee Charlotte, "The Double Meaning of the Spirituals," in *Journal of Black Studies,* June, 1987, pp. 379–401.
    A fascinating article which points out many of the double and triple meanings in spirituals.

Peters, Erskine, "The Poetics of the Afro-American Spiritual," in *Black American Literature Forum,* Fall, 1989, pp. 559–578.
    Peters discusses the categories and characteristics of spirituals, focusing on rhetorical devices and use of language.

Petry, Ann, *Harriet Tubman: Conductor on the Underground Railroad,* Archway, 1955.
    This clearly written story provides a good introduction for both adult and young adult readers to the amazing accomplishments of Harriet Tubman.

Spencer, John Michael, *Protest and Praise: Sacred Music of Black Religion,* Fortress Press, 1990.
    Spencer includes an extensive analysis of the story of Moses as it is retold through spirituals.

The Hospital Window

James Dickey

1962

The strength of James Dickey's poetry lies in this southern writer's ability to turn a commonplace event into a moment of personal transcendence. His poems never simply lie flat on a page; instead, they shout with intense—sometimes shocking—imagery and action. Dickey's poems and his novels (most notably *Deliverance,* which became a major film in 1973) often present common people doing common things. But there is always a twist or a rise to an unexpected level that moves the persona and the themes into a realm far beyond what the simple action may imply.

In "The Hospital Window," the speaker has been visiting his gravely ill father in the hospital, and, as he leaves the building, he turns to wave toward the window that he believes is in his father's room. This is something that anyone might do in a similar situation. Once outside, however, the son experiences a rapturous moment of true understanding—both of his father's impending death and of his own resignation to mortality. So strong is this sudden transcendence beyond grief and pain that he stands in the middle of the street continuing to wave while traffic backs up and angry drivers begin blowing their horns. Even the honking horns become a part of the speaker's rising spirit and sense of euphoria, and he incorporates them into his dreamlike state, imagining that the loud noises can "blow down the walls of the world" and set the souls of the dying free. In this poem, the hospital window is much more than a pane of glass, and Dickey once again manages to turn a simple gesture into personal revelation.

James Dickey

Author Biography

Anyone who assumes that the biography of a poet is bound to be filled with a list of mundane academic positions and descriptions of a lofty, mostly sedentary lifestyle has not read a biography of James Dickey. This poet was a high school and college football player, a track star at Vanderbilt University, a bow hunter, a guitarist, and a fighter pilot in both World War II and the Korean War. He was an advertising copywriter, novelist, actor, and teacher. And, of course, he was a poet—one whose adventurous, often daring, outdoorsman practices provided much fuel for his richly image-laden poems and prose.

James Dickey was born in 1923 in Buckhead, Georgia, a suburb of Atlanta. He entered Clemson College in 1942 but enlisted in the Army Air Corps before completing his education. After the war, he transferred to Vanderbilt University in Nashville, earning his undergraduate degree in 1949 and his master's in 1950. Working at advertising firms in both Atlanta and New York, Dickey began to fill his idle time with poetry writing, and, after meeting and developing a friendship with Ezra Pound, he began to work more seriously on his poetry. Within a few years, his poems were appearing in top American literary journals, and he was awarded

a Guggenheim Fellowship to study in Europe. This was the beginning of his long literary career, and he would go on to hold teaching and writer-in-residence positions at Rice University, the University of Wisconsin, George Mason University, and the University of South Carolina, among others. James Dickey was still at the lectern in the English Department at South Carolina until five days before his death on January 19, 1997.

Poem Text

I have just come down from my father.
Higher and higher he lies
Above me in a blue light
Shed by a tinted window.
I drop through six white floors   5
And then step out onto the pavement.

Still feeling my father ascend,
I start to cross the firm street,
My shoulder blades shining with all
The glass the huge building can raise.   10
Now I must turn round and face it,
And know his one pane from the others.

Each window possesses the sun
As though it burned there on a wick.
I wave, like a man catching fire.   15
All the deep-dyed windowpanes flash,
And, behind them, all the white rooms
They turn to the color of Heaven.

Ceremoniously, gravely, and weakly,
Dozens of pale hands are waving   20
Back, from inside their flames.
Yet one pure pane among these
Is the bright, erased blankness of nothing.
I know that my father is there,

In the shape of his death still living.   25
The traffic increases around me
Like a madness called down on my head.
The horns blast at me like shotguns,
And drivers lean out, driven crazy—
But now my propped-up father   30

Lifts his arm out of stillness at last.
The light from the window strikes me
And I turn as blue as a soul,
As the moment when I was born.
I am not afraid for my father—   35
Look! He is grinning; he is not

Afraid for my life, either,
As the wild engines stand at my knees
Shredding their gears and roaring,
And I hold each car in its place   40
For miles, inciting its horn
To blow down the walls of the world

That the dying may float without fear
In the bold blue gaze of my father.
Slowly I move to the sidewalk   45
With my pin-tingling hand half dead
At the end of my bloodless arm.
I carry it off in amazement,

High, still higher, still waving,
My recognized face fully mortal,   50
Yet not; not at all, in the pale,
Drained, otherwordly, stricken,
Created hue of stained glass.
I have just come down from my father.

Poem Summary

Line 1:

The first line in "The Hospital Window" may
be singled out for attention because it is used for
both the beginning and the ending of the poem. The
fact that the same line opens and closes this work
gives it a circular motion, one that is very apt in a
poem addressing living and dying, father and son,
and the sense of roundness in human life—"ashes
to ashes, dust to dust," so to speak. Literally, the
speaker simply means he has just returned to street
level after visiting his ill father on the sixth floor
of the hospital. However, the son has also just
"come down" from his father in the metaphorical
sense, for he believes the dying man is starting to
ascend into the heavens, far out of range of being
reached.

Lines 2–6:

The lines that make up the rest of the first
stanza introduce color and light into the poem, references that will be repeated throughout. The father lies "higher and higher" above the speaker,
indicating a movement upward, and he appears to
be ascending in a blue light, perhaps implying a
soul floating through the sky. There is a mixture
of the physical and the metaphysical in this stanza.
Even though the words "higher" and "blue" may
be used as metaphors, the last three lines simply
tell the reader that the windows of the hospital are
tinted blue and that the speaker has taken an elevator down six floors to reach the pavement. The
language the poet uses, however, implies something more than a simple elevator ride, for the
speaker claims to "drop" through the floors, and
the floors are "white." It is as though the son has
fallen from the purity and the sterility that surround the dying as they transcend earthly matters
and physical objects.

Media Adaptations

- An audio version of Christopher Dickey's biography of his father, entitled *Summer of Deliverance: A Memoir of Father and Son,* is now
  available. The tape runs 600 minutes and is performed by Alexander Adams.

- In 1986 James Dickey released a recording of
  his best-selling novel *Deliverance.* The book has
  been recorded by other readers as well, but none
  compares to the author's own version.

Lines 7–10:

Line seven continues the son's perception of
his father's movement toward heaven, or his drawing closer to death. Not only is there a sense of the
dying man's upward motion, but the poem itself
seems to ascend as well. This will become clearer
as the speaker moves readers through his physical
actions and his emotions as they rise toward the final stanza. He emphasizes his father's light, ethereal existence by contrasting it to his own on the
"firm street." But as he crosses the roadway, he
feels his "shoulder blades shining with all / the
glass the huge building can raise." Here, an obvious question may be, why shoulder blades as opposed to just shoulders or back or head? The reason is most likely that shoulder blades imply angel
imagery, for the wings of angels are depicted as attached to what would be human shoulder blades.
With this description, Dickey continues to mix reality and metaphor, as well as compare the "concrete" world of the living to the spiritual, divine
presence of those near death. While the realistic indication is that the speaker can feel sunlight reflecting as heat on his back as he crosses the street,
the angel imagery implies an otherworldly essence
to the bright day.

Lines 11–12:

These two lines are rich with double meaning.
On one hand—the literal hand—the speaker is saying that, as he crosses the street, he knows he is
obligated to turn around and wave toward a win-

dow of the hospital that is in the vicinity of his father's room. It is a gesture of both love and duty, even though the son realizes that all the windows look alike, and chances are he cannot locate the exact one. Figuratively, though, there is much more going on. The word "must" is very strong, indicating a greater urge than dutiful obligation. Instead, the speaker is compelled to turn around, whether by his own accord or by some force that lies beyond him. The phrase "face it" refers to looking at the hospital, or "huge building" as described in the previous line, but "it" may be a much greater, more difficult object to face than a building. What the son must also turn around and face is his father's death and the fact that the ill parent will never emerge alive from the hospital that looms so large in his son's vision.

The twelfth line means, literally, that the son must find his father's window out of all the others, but the key word in the line is "pane." Spelled as is, it refers to a sheet of glass, or simply the hospital window, but, spelled *pain*, the meaning is just as valid and even more revealing. The speaker needs to attempt to separate his father's pain from all that is suffered by hundreds of other patients. But he understands that this endeavor is just as futile as trying to pinpoint one single window on the sixth floor out of all the others on the building's façade.

Lines 13–15:

The sun's reflection on windows is a common sight, but the windows in Dickey's poem are exceptional for each one "possesses the sun." This strong verb is in keeping with the poem's rising passion, a fervor that is echoed in much of the language and emotion. The windows also play a prominent role in the imagery of whiteness and light that runs throughout the poem, acting as vehicles that reflect purity and allow transcendence to occur. The sun is like a candle flame for it seems to burn "on a wick" in each pane of glass. Line 15 is arguably the most vital one in the poem, for it marks the beginning of the revelation that the speaker will experience later on, and it indicates his first wave toward his father. But it is not just an ordinary wave, for he does it "like a man catching fire"—a simile reflecting the speaker's urgency, passion, and need. Note that he doesn't wave like a man on fire—which may connote pain or hopelessness—but like a man catching fire, a phrase that is used to describe something exciting, finally getting underway.

Lines 16–18:

These lines continue the flame-in-the-window metaphor, as well as the references to color. The windowpanes are "deep-dyed" with their blue tint and they "flash" with the sun's reflection. Behind the windows, all the hospital rooms are white, but they begin to "turn to the color of Heaven." The color of heaven, in this case, is blue, like the skies above, and the white walls of the rooms appear to turn azure as the sunlight falls upon them through blue-tinted windows. Physically, these concepts are accurate—hospital rooms are typically white and colored glass makes other objects appear colored when light passes through it. But, figuratively, the white rooms turn to the color of heaven because many of the ill people within them are closer to dying.

Lines 19–21:

The three adverbs that make up line nineteen (along with the conjunction "and") describe the patients in the hospital. They are physically weak and emotionally grim, but they return the wave "ceremoniously" even though they don't know the person waving from the street, or, perhaps, because that person could be one of their own relatives. The signal of friendliness is automatic even after sincerity has been lost. The speaker sees dozens of waving hands, but he cannot recognize faces for they are hidden "inside their flames," or behind the sun's reflection on the glass. The word "flames" here most likely represents each dying person's own luminosity and passion as he or she approaches the final moments of life.

Lines 22–25:

Line 22 picks up on the same word-play as line twelve with the use of the word "pane." In the earlier line, the son needed to know his father's "one pane from the others," and in line twenty-two he notices that "one pure pane among" all the others is bright with reflected sun, but there is no hand waving behind it. Instead, he envisions only the "erased blankness of nothing." Recognizing how close his father is to dying, the speaker assumes that the window from which no one waves is his parent's, for he claims, "I know that my father is there." After this line, there is a stanza break, indicating the possibility that the man has already passed away. This ambiguity is intentional, but it is quickly explained in the following line that begins the fifth stanza: "In the shape of his death still living." Now it is clear that the father is alive, but the son acknowledges that he is in "the shape of his death."

Lines 26–29:

Not since line eight has there been any mention of the speaker's actual whereabouts, and, when last noted, he had started to cross the street. It is not unlikely for readers to get caught up in the rich imagery of the windows, the light, the flames, and the colors and forget all about where the son is waving from. Dickey works his poem like a well-crafted novel, complete with rising action and asides that pull readers away from the immediate placement of the speaker. Line 26 brings back reality. The speaker has stopped in the middle of the street to turn and wave to his father. He stands there waving as cars slow down to get around him, and he thinks of the traffic as a "madness called down" on his head. The meaning of madness may be twofold here. On one hand, the scene in the street is chaotic, with horns blowing "like shotguns" and drivers leaning out of their windows to yell, "driven crazy." On the other hand, madness is what the speaker is beginning to feel within himself as he moves toward both an acceptance and an understanding of human mortality.

Lines 30–34:

Line 30 shifts the action back to the hospital room where the dying man, propped up in his bed, "lifts his arm out of stillness at last." The scene becomes surreal as the son, still standing among heavy traffic and angry drivers, is struck by the light from the window in his father's room. While much of the poem incorporates spiritual themes and imagery, lines 30 through 34 reveal an unquestionable religious experience on the part of the speaker. He is truly touched by the light—in the biblical sense—and he feels as though he has turned "as blue as a soul." Recall that the white rooms in the hospital had turned "the color of Heaven" (or blue), and now the speaker, too, is brilliantly azure like the heavenly skies. He believes that he is as immaculate and untarnished as he was at birth and that the light from his father's window has cleansed him of his human impurities. These lines play a vital role in the rising action of the poem, for they act as the culmination of the speaker's hold on reality before he tips over into the surreal frenzy of transcendence.

Lines 35–37:

Although the specifics of the son's metaphysical revelation are not spelled out, his sudden elation seems to stem from what many human beings consider a religious experience. Whether it is a feeling of having contact with a divine presence or an unexpected and swift comprehension of something mysterious (the proverbial light bulb going off in the mind), the speaker in Dickey's poem responds euphorically to it. He says, in all honesty, "I am not afraid for my father." It is as though he has witnessed life after death and knows his father has no reason to fear dying—that there is indeed a better place to go after leaving earth. There is now a stronger bond between the father and son than has ever existed, for the older man has apparently experienced the same revelation: "Look! He is grinning." But before we are allowed to celebrate the dying man's new-found happiness, Dickey once again throws up a road block at the end of the stanza: the phrase "he is not" seems to contradict the words preceding it that tell the reader that the father is smiling. The he is/he isn't confusion is again quickly cleared up with the first line in the seventh stanza, which turns out to be the conclusion of the thought begun at the end of the sixth. Now it is clear that the father is grinning and that "he is not / afraid for" his son's life, either.

Lines 38–41:

In these lines, the tension increases as the speaker emphasizes the dangerous situation he has put himself in, and yet neither he nor his father expresses any fear. The scene is chaotic as drivers come to a halt because of an apparent madman standing in the middle of the road waving his hand frantically toward the hospital. As the son continues his transcendence to a higher level of awareness, he begins to envision the physical objects around him in a new way. Drivers gun their engines and threaten him, but he continues to "hold each car in its place." Instead of finding their loud horns frightening, he decides he is "inciting" them for good reason.

Lines 42–44:

These lines explain why the son is provoking the angry drivers into blowing their car horns. He believes the noise can "blow down the walls of the world" and release the souls of the dying into the heavens. Dickey again refers to the color blue, describing his father's gaze as "bold blue." The meaning of this phrase can be taken two different ways— either the dying man's gaze is both blue and bold or the color has become a very bold shade of blue. Both possibilities work in the poem, for the notion of something becoming "bold" is consistent with the intensified action and heightened emotion.

Lines 45–49:

The movement of the speaker in these lines is very visible to the reader. His slow retreat to the sidewalk is in keeping with the oblivion he has experienced since walking into a busy street and stopping traffic. It is as though he is now dazed by all that has happened and feels only the tingling sensation that comes with a limb that has "gone to sleep." His waving arm has become like a detached object, something so odd and separate that he must "carry it off in amazement." Even though the strange limb aches and is "half dead," it continues to wave "high, still higher."

Lines 50–53:

With the climax of the action now over, the speaker (and the language of the poem) slows down and unwinds. He acknowledges that his face is "recognized," possibly meaning that he thinks his father has spotted him from the window, but, considering the religious transcendence he has just experienced, he could also mean that his face is now recognized by God. His thoughts are still in flux, for he first describes his face as "fully mortal," then immediately contradicts the description with "Yet not; not at all." The next string of adjectives— "pale, / drained, otherworldly, stricken, / created"—depicts the hospital window's blue tint with words that directly oppose its previous description. What was before "deep-dyed" and "the color of Heaven," reflecting the sun as though "it burned there on a wick," is now weakened, nearly exhausted. The poem's language, as well as its persona, has gone through a frenzied euphoria and now exhibits the typical down-spiraling after-effect. The glass is now "stained" instead of "tinted," insinuating the religious experience again, since stained glass is often associated with houses of worship.

Line 54:

As noted earlier, "The Hospital Window" ends the same way it begins. This line brings the speaker, his father, and the poem full circle. But these words forming the last line carry more metaphorical weight than they did as the first line. It is very unlikely that an elevator ride down to street level has anything to do with the ending. Instead, the sense of spiritual awakening and transcendence beyond mortality fill this line with meaning. The "father" mentioned may certainly refer to the speaker's own parent who is nearing death, but it may also imply a heavenly father with whom the speaker has just had an intimate encounter.

Themes

Objective Observer

One recurring theme in James Dickey's poetry is the idea of the main persona as an objective ob-

server. At first, it may appear absurd to include "The Hospital Window" in this category, for this poem's general premise—a son and his dying father—would speak of anything but objectivity. And yet, Dickey is a poet who can make the ironic seem natural and who can take his speaker to extremes without getting him helplessly tangled in a bizarre setting or in the emotional plot of the work.

In "The Hospital Window," the glass itself is a barrier between the speaker and his father. Not only is it a physical separation, but the window also serves to take the son mentally further away from the dying man and the crowd of angry drivers as well. Within the glass, he sees "blue light," the sun that seems to burn there "on a wick," the "bright, erased blankness of nothing," and a "pale, / drained, otherworldly, stricken, created hue." As each of these appearances evolves, so do the emotions of the speaker, and he describes each thought as though he were the only one who needed to understand its significance. At no point does he express grief over the fact that his father is dying. Instead, he very objectively gives an account of the events that take place after he has visited the patient, and these events depict a speaker who is in his own world commenting from the narrow perspective of that world. He reports on his transcendence from its beginning ("Now I must turn round and face it") to its end ("Slowly I move to the sidewalk") and does so with great intensity and clarity, but without falling into a subjective, distorted lamentation of his father's or his own sorrow. Although the dying man seems to experience a parallel spiritual uplift along with his son in the street, the two men remain distinctively apart throughout the revelation.

Solitary Experience

Closely related to the theme of the objective observer is the recurring idea of solitary experience by the personae in Dickey's poetry. This means that the speaker often goes through life-changing moments without sharing the occurrence with other characters in the poem and without trying to make anyone else feel what he/she is feeling. In "The Hospital Window" the persona, or the son of the dying man, reaches an emotional and spiritual epiphany in his life while standing among hundreds of other people—people who are in their cars trying to get around him and who are angry at his presence in the street. But instead of reacting rationally to their feelings of hostility and amazement, the speaker responds as though he is completely alone with his own euphoria.

For the first half of the poem, the speaker does not even acknowledge that there is a public present, other than the pathetic patients in the hospital who wave feebly as a reply to his own fervent salute from the street. Not until the fifth stanza does he mention that the "traffic increases" around him, and at that point it comes as a surprise to the reader that he is actually in the middle of a busy roadway. The son is so caught up in the mounting tension of his own experience that he ignores the reality of everyday existence—horns blasting "like shotguns" and drivers leaning out, "driven crazy." Throughout the second half of the poem, the speaker fluctuates between his transcendence to a higher realm of understanding and the lowliness of life on the street, but he uses the lowliness to further his move into the metaphysical. He declares that "the wild engines stand at my knees" and that "I hold each car in its place" while their horns "blow down the walls of the world" as though they, too, play a part in the revelation taking place.

This aloneness or solitary experience on the part of the speaker serves to heighten the strangeness of the situation as well as the intensity of the son's mind-set. If he were as typically concerned as anyone may be while standing in the middle of a busy street with cars piling all around him, the poem could not deliver the strong sense of otherworldly understanding and personal excitement that it does. The point is made in the lines, "Slowly I move to the sidewalk / With my pin-tingling hand half dead / At the end of my bloodless arm. / I carry it off in amazement," which describe the emotional state of the speaker. He is truly alone, in spite of the crowd, and makes his own experience more visible by not recognizing the presence of those who exist in reality.

Religious Transcendence

While the theme of religious transcendence is interwoven with the poem's other themes, a brief, separate mention of it is not undue, considering the weight it carries in Dickey's work. Whether it stems from the poet's southern upbringing, or any particular church affiliation, or even a need for personal enlightenment, the fact is that many of his personae go through a spiritual crisis and/or revelation. In "The Hospital Window," the son's transcendence of normal responses (grief, pain, sorrow, etc.) is evident in his easy ability to overcome fear in the midst of what should be a frightening situation. The point Dickey makes is that a moment of otherworldly recognition and understanding can supercede any mortal hindrances that normally crop

Topics for Further Study

- Write an essay detailing any "otherworldly" or transcending experience that you or someone you know may have had. Describe what you think its significance was and whether there may be more than one way of interpreting it.

- Write a poem about the death of someone dear to you (real or imagined) and consider how you as the persona in the poem may react to the inevitability of the event.

- Choose any color and take time to consider all the ways that color may be used or how it affects objects and people around it. Think about all the interesting ways the color may be described and all the ways it can describe other things. Then write an essay on how and why the hue you have selected is significant.

- How do you think you would respond if you were a driver caught up in a traffic jam caused by someone standing nonchalantly in the middle of the street, waving toward a hospital? What if the person were waving toward an office building or toward an empty meadow? Write an essay on how your response may or may not change, based on the situation.

up during times of strange occurrences and hopeless longing. The speaker in this poem knows that both he and his father are mortal, and, yet, religious transcendence allows him to proclaim that "I am not afraid for my father / he is not / afraid for my life either."

Style

Free Verse

"The Hospital Window" is a free verse poem with elements of meter and rhythm dispersed throughout. Dickey's early poetry—primarily the first three collections, *Into the Stone, Drowning With Others,* and *Helmets*—are actually less free than his later work, but still avoid heavy rhyming and overdone alliteration. He was, however, fond of the anapest, or a metrical unit containing two short syllables followed by a long one. One example of this form of meter in "The Hospital Window" is in the first line: "I have just—." Read the phrase aloud and note how the word "just" seems longer, how the voice tends to stretch it out more than the words "I have," which are pronounced more quickly. Try it with other anapests from the poem, such as "six white floors," "the firm street," "In the shape," "Lifts his arm," and "And I turn."

In his preface to *The Early Motion,* a volume published in 1981 containing the poems from *Drowning With Others* and *Helmets,* Dickey had this to say about how these early works came about: "These poems emerged from what I call a night-rhythm, something felt in pulse, not word. How this anapestic sound was engendered by other poetry, good or bad … I cannot say, except … I have always liked heavy recurrence of stress." He went on to say about the collection containing "The Hospital Window": "In the poems of *Drowning With Others* I edged toward the end of sound over sense, toward the foreordained hammering of ultra-rhythmical English, and tried to make the concepts, images, and themes of my life conform to what the night-rhythm had caused to come through me." This so-called night-rhythm is evident in lines that are not only rhythmical but that use alliteration (like-sounding consonants and vowels) as well. Examples from "The Hospital Window" include, "Still feeling my father ascend," "my shoulder blades shining," "the bright erased blankness of nothing," and "To blow down the walls of the world / That the dying may float without fear."

The general construction of this poem is methodical in that it consists of nine stanzas, each with six lines of similar length. While it is officially composed in free verse, the poetic style incorporated by Dickey (the anapests, alliteration, and rhythm) is subtle. As is the case here, many poems would be weaker if their structure was more obvious, and Dickey was a poet who did not let the structure intrude.

Historical Context

The 1960s will long be remembered as one of the most tumultuous times in the history of the United States, as well as in many places throughout the world. Drastic changes in lifestyles, cultural expectations, personal views on drugs and sexual freedom, and a host of other revolutionary ideals served to create both excitement and tension in Americans, young and old. By the late 1950s and early 1960s, when James Dickey was back from the Korean War and writing the poems that would appear in his first volumes of work, everything from music and clothing to civil rights and economics was in flux. Young Americans were not the only ones celebrating new-found freedom and an anything-goes means of expression. So too were the middle-aged and older members of the creative set—artists, musicians, dancers, writers, Hollywood producers, and poets. In an article entitled "James Dickey: The Whole Motion," originally published in the *Southern Review* (1992) and later included in a collection of essays edited by Robert Kirschten called *"Struggling for Wings": The Art of James Dickey,* critic and poet Richard Tillinghast describes the culture in which Dickey began writing:

> Dickey came of age during a cultural moment when poets' reputations were often founded as much on the excesses of their personal lives as on the quality of their work. When one surveys the lives of Robert Lowell, Sylvia Plath, John Berryman, Allen Ginsberg, Randall Jarrell, Elizabeth Bishop, Theodore Roethke, and Anne Sexton, one gets the impression that mid-century American poetry somehow, with great difficulty, managed to get written between gin-fueled one-night stands in motel rooms and recovery periods in mental hospitals and drying-out spas, in an atmosphere of extreme emotional and mental states and strikingly unconventional behavior.

Dickey himself was no stranger to unconventional behavior, and colleagues could tell stories of his antics, from motel room parties to bow-hunting trips throughout Georgia without having to think too hard. But the decade of the 1960s was not all revelry and come-what-may. It was also a time of great sorrow and violence. A year after the publication of *Drowning With Others,* President John F. Kennedy was assassinated, and, in 1968, both Robert Kennedy and Martin Luther King, Jr., lost their lives to gunmen. In 1962, the Cuban Missile Crisis nearly caused nuclear war between the Soviet Union and the United States, and American involvement was intensifying in Vietnam. In 1963, four black Alabama schoolchildren were killed when a bomb exploded during Sunday services at a Baptist church in Birmingham, and race riots became commonplace in cities throughout the country. As the war in Southeast Asia escalated, antiwar protests grew stronger and more violent on college campuses across the country, and, in 1969, hundreds of thousands of demonstrators showed up in Washington,

Compare & Contrast

- **1960:** William L. Shirer's twelve-hundred-page history of *The Rise and Fall of the Third Reich* becomes a bestseller despite its length and weighty subject, encompassing the world wars.

  1995: Former U.S. Secretary of Defense Robert S. McNamara is criticized for bringing up controversial and disturbing subjects when he publishes *In Retrospect: The Tragedy and Lessons of Vietnam.*

- **1965:** The International Society for Krishna Consciousness becomes a popular alternative to conventional western religion. It promotes a mental transcendence over social ills and drugs.

  1995: The "Million Man March on Washington," led by the controversial leader of the Nation of Islam, Louis Farrakhan, attracts nearly half a million African-American men to listen to speeches urging them to take responsibility for raising their families. Many people disregard the march because of Farrakhan's publicized racist, sexist, and homophobic remarks.

D.C. as a part of the "New Mobilization Committee to End the War in Vietnam." American involvement, however, would continue another six years. The last year of the decade brought some positives to the public's attention. Neil Armstrong placed the first human footsteps on the moon, the Woodstock Music Festival in New York brought thousands of people together to enjoy peace and love (often translated into drugs and sex), and a booming American economy employed a record number of workers. In the end, one can only look back on the 1960s as a time when stability gave way to revolution and change often happened for the sake of change, when no better reason was evident.

"The Hospital Window" is not necessarily set in the 1960s, for its exact place and time are indeterminate. The only fact about its setting is that it is some time after the development of elevators, automobiles, and high-rise hospitals. The events of the poem could have taken place at anytime, anywhere. Sons have always suffered the loss of fathers, and spiritual transcendence has always been a possibility for human beings. The poem itself transcends a need for specific time and place, for it would have made no difference if Dickey had mentioned the name of a city or the year in which his father died. Not all his poems are ambiguous in this way, and some depend on a reader's knowledge of certain historical dates and events—especially regarding World War II—for greater understanding. But "The Hospital Window" carries themes that are universal, and to reach for some cultural influence or specific historical motivation in its creation would be too long a stretch.

Critical Overview

James Dickey was an American poet fortunate enough to realize his popularity with the public and high regard from his colleagues while he was still living. From the publication of his early volumes of poetry to the best-selling novel and movie, *Deliverance,* to the collections of more recent poetry and the novel he was working on when he died—all were well received by most critics, fellow poets, and scholars over the years. Dickey's use of intense language, his unique perspectives on common events, and his willingness to take on controversial subjects in his work made him one of the most talked about writers in contemporary literature. Critic Benjamin DeMott, writing for the *Saturday Review,* stated that Dickey's poetry has a "feeling for the generative power at the core of existence. A first-rate Dickey poem breathes the energy of the world, and testifies to the poet's capacity for rising out of tranced dailiness—habitual, half-lived life—into a more intense physicality.... " Not surprisingly, Dickey was a recipient of numerous awards for his works, including a Guggenheim Fellowship, a National Book Award, and a National Institute of Arts and Letters Award.

Of course, every popular figure has his or her detractors, and Dickey was no exception. Those who criticized his poetry and prose most often called attention to the abundance of violence it contained and the tendency toward taboo or "uncomfortable" topics. Because so many of his poems and novels dealt with "man in a natural state," many critics translated that into the writer's own uncivilized, primitive endeavors and accused Dickey of romanticizing violence. But these voices were not nearly as loud as those of his fans, and most readers accepted the subject matter as an exploration of all sides of human nature as opposed to just a shielded glance at what most people would rather not see.

"The Hospital Window" itself has not been singled out very often for critical attention, but the collection that contains it, *Drowning With Others,* is a part of the body of work that many scholars consider Dickey's strongest. The early books and the later volumes that compiled the poems from them tend to be signature pieces, containing the works most often found in anthologies and taught in literature classes. And while some writers may lose readers when they switch from one genre to another, Dickey simply picked up more with the publication of *Deliverance*—perhaps the strongest testament to his ability as a writer in any form.

Criticism

Pamela Steed Hill

Hill has published widely in poetry journals and is the author of a collection entitled In Praise of Motels. *In the following essay, she contends that the speaker of "The Hospital Window" has no choice but to be alone in his experience with spiritual transcendence.*

"The Hospital Window" is a poem that takes readers inside the mind of a man trying to deal with the impending death of his father. This scenario may conjure up several typical images that accurately describe what he must be feeling—grief, great sorrow, even fear and anger. But this poem goes a step further in the realm of human response to a tragic event. The persona here experiences a sudden and overwhelming happiness, and he does so in a very unlikely place—the middle of a busy street. The oddity of his unforeseen euphoria, however, is not the main idea behind Dickey's poem. What is even more noteworthy is that the speaker

is alone with his feeling even though he stands among a throng of angry drivers blowing their horns at him. To achieve the type of metaphysical or religious transcendence that overpowers his emotions, he has no choice but to experience it completely within his own mind.

The first two stanzas of the poem do not indicate anything unusual about the son's attitude or behavior after visiting his dying father in the hospital. He seems melancholy and resigned to the fact that he must "turn round and face" all that the hospital itself represents—sadness, pain, helplessness, and, ultimately, death. Perhaps the only hint that the speaker has not given himself totally over to grief is his belief that his father is ascending. Using this word to describe someone close to dying implies faith in an afterlife, or in a heaven above, to which souls rise after the death of the body. It may also be an allusion to the Christian belief in the ascension of Christ into heaven after his crucifixion and resurrection. With this in mind, the son is able to turn around and try to distinguish his father's "one pane from the others."

The act of turning and waving is not strange, but doing it in the middle of the road certainly is. This peculiar behavior is the beginning of the son's shift into a solitary state, and, as the poem moves along, it appears as though he cannot help doing it. Like a man daydreaming, he turns his attention inward, focusing intently on his own thoughts and seeming oblivious to events around him. He may not be sure what is happening to him, but he knows it is undeniable, and that is why he begins to wave "like a man catching fire." What is really catching fire is the possibility to go beyond or to transcend the sorrow that mortality brings. In his mind, the son experiences a revelation—a vision perhaps—that shows him life beyond death. At the moment when he begins to wonder if his father is too weak even to respond to his waving, the dying man "Lifts his arm out of stillness at last." This gesture is like a miracle to the son, and it is at this point that the light from the hospital window strikes him, and he turns "as blue as a soul." The father's wave is, presumably, only in the speaker's imagination. It is unlikely that the father can even see the street from his bed on the sixth floor of the hospital and even more unlikely that anyone standing down there could choose the right window and see any movement behind it. Nonetheless, the act is very real to the son, and he remains in a trance-like state feeling the euphoria of knowing his father is going to heaven, even while he himself is being told by angry drivers to go elsewhere.

The father's wave is not the only sign that the son envisions. At the peak of the speaker's transcendence—when he says, "I am not afraid for my father"—he also sees the old man "grinning" and has managed to get inside his thoughts, claiming that "he is not / Afraid for my life, either." This acknowledgement strengthens the idea of faith in the poem. If ever a father would fear for his son's life, it would be when the child is doing something as dangerous as standing in the middle of a heavily traveled street. And, yet, because the son has experienced a revelation of Heaven (and imagines that his father has had the same experience), he no longer sees a reason to fear death. He goes so far as to tempt the fates by holding "each car in its place" while the "wild engines" roar and he incites the drivers to blow their horns at him. In his mind, he does not recognize the loud honking as anger directed toward himself. Instead he imagines that the horns can "blow down the walls of the world" so that souls, such as his father's, can make it to heaven unimpeded.

As the son finally makes his way to the sidewalk, he still appears to move as though in a trance. Completely occupied by his own thoughts, he walks slowly and keeps waving his hand although it has gone to sleep at the end of his "bloodless arm." Some sense of clarity seems to return to him as he acknowledges his "mortal" face, but then he quickly discounts mortality. Going through such a startling mental transformation has made him able to see beyond life on earth and to know that physical death is not the end.

Why is this necessarily a solitary experience? Why does the speaker keep all his thoughts, visions, and unexplainable happiness to himself? The answer is just that—it's unexplainable. There is no evidence in the poem that implies a rational understanding on the part of the son as to what has happened to him. In the beginning, he seems "normal," but as he is overcome with emotion, he does not appear to be able to control his behavior. This type of religious and metaphysical happening is too personal to relate to others who are not feeling it. After all, if he does not even comprehend it himself, how could he make others do so? Imagine what the already angry drivers would do if the man blocking the roadway tried to explain why he was there. Think of their reactions to a man telling them his father was dying and that he had never been happier, and, furthermore, that he needed them to keep honking their horns to help his father's soul get to heaven!

> *Like a man daydreaming, he turns his attention inward, focusing intently on his own thoughts and seeming oblivious to events around him. He may not be sure what is happening to him, but he knows it is undeniable. . . ."*

For obvious reasons, then, the speaker in "The Hospital Window" finds himself completely alone in a crowd. But there is a more subtle reason that transcendence over the fear of death must be experienced on a solitary basis. A feeling so strong and so enlightening that it allows an individual to overcome common mortal fears would be diminished if it were shared among hundreds of strangers or even among friends and family. In this poem, the son is already facing a traumatic event in the inevitable loss of his father. He needs to find a way to deal with it on his own, for no matter how much sympathy—or how much misunderstanding—he receives from other people, he will not achieve true peace of mind until he can reconcile the event for himself. Although the speaker claims that he can see the dying man waving and grinning, this vision, too, is a part of the son's imagination. He thinks that he and his father have reached the same level of spiritual understanding and that is a solace to him. Regardless that the old man is probably oblivious to most everything around him, his son is comforted by creating an emotional connection with him whether he knows it or not. But the connection is not real, and, therefore, the son is still alone with his experience.

"The Hospital Window" may be a poem concerning emotional effects—transcendence, religious awakening, metaphysical and mystical revelations, etc.—but it is full of physical descriptions and metaphors relating to the senses. The speaker imagines his "shoulder blades shining with all / the glass the huge building can raise" and that "each window possesses the sun / as though it burned

What Do I Read Next?

- Many readers who do not know James Dickey the poet are very familiar with James Dickey the novelist. Published in 1970, *Deliverance* became a bestseller and was turned into a full-length feature film in 1973. Dickey himself played a backwoods southern sheriff in the movie.

- In 1999, A. J. Conyers published *The Eclipse of Heaven: The Loss of Transcendence and Its Effect on Modern Life*. In this book, Conyers argues that people in the modern world have lost a belief in the power of transcending mortality and, as a result, have only a depressing, shallow view of life and death.

- Robert Kirschten's *Approaching Prayer: Ritual and the Shape of Myth in A. R. Ammons and James Dickey* (published in 1998) is a good look at these two southern poets' use of myth, mysticism, and "word-magic" in their poems. It includes commentary on later collections by Ammons and Dickey.

- Editors Jeffrey J. Folks and James A. Perkins published a collection of essays on contemporary southern writers in 1997 called *Southern Writers at Century's End*. The essays highlight twenty-one writers whose work reflects the confusion and violence of American culture since 1975.

---

there on a wick." He hears the car horns blast "like shotguns" and the engines "shredding their gears and roaring." And in the last stanza, he describes the color of the "stained" hospital windows as "pale, / drained, otherworldly, stricken, / created." This use of physical imagery to illuminate and expound upon mental phenomena serves to make the inaccessible more accessible. It has already been noted that the son's experience with transcendence is unexplainable, but at least the reader is helped to understand as much as is possible through language that is very graphic and detailed.

In an article titled "Things, Voices, Minds: A Review of *Drowning With Others* by James Dickey," originally published in the *Yale Review* (1962) and later included in a collection of essays edited by Robert Kirschten called *"Struggling for Wings": The Art of James Dickey,* critic and poet Thom Gunn notes that the poet, "builds fantasy on a basis of solid physical detail ... His is, by choice, an almost entirely sensuous imagination." Gunn goes on to say that the nature of Dickey's fantasy "is an effort to make [it] meaningful, to turn it into vision." The speaker in "The Hospital Window" makes his fantastic spiritual encounter meaningful by giving it very lucid, physical characteristics. His vision—or what he sees exactly—is not possible to relate. But its essence and its life-changing qualities are both real and evident in the son.

Source: Pamela Steed Hill, in an essay for *Poetry for Students,* Gale Group, 2001.

Adrian Blevins

Adrian Blevins is a poet and essayist who has taught at Hollins University, Sweet Briar College, and in the Virginia Community College System. She also is the author of The Man Who Went Out for Cigarettes, *a chapbook of poems. In this essay, Blevins explores the ways in which James Dickey's "The Hospital Window" articulates and makes accessible an experience that is, in the end, of a highly spiritual and even metaphysical nature.*

In his introduction to *The Best American Poetry 1991,* the American poet Mark Strand tells an especially illuminating story about his mother's fear and bewilderment in the face of his decision, as a college student, to become a poet. "But then you'll never be able to earn a living," his mother said. Strand, after a commendable discussion on the differences between the language of poetry and the language of nonfiction prose—generally fact-bound news—that his parents read, says that it wasn't until after his mother's death that his father came to understand the purpose and value of poetry:

> It is 1965. My mother has died. My first book of poems has been published. My father, who, like my mother, has never been a reader of poems, reads my book.... The [poems] that mean most are those that speak for his sense of loss following my mother's death. They seem to tell him what he knows but cannot say. Their power is almost magical. They tell him in so many words what he is feeling.

A poet's highest goal is or should be to put inexpressible feelings (sometimes of loss, sometimes of mystification, sometimes of elation and wonder) into expressible terms, and Strand's story is especially poignant because it narrates, in clear-eyed terms, poetry's power to "formalize emotion difficult to articulate." James Dickey's "The Hospital Window," which we take from Dickey's second volume, *Drowning with Others,* is also about a moment between a father and son during a time of crisis. It illuminates in a representative way a transcendent moment between two people who are unable to articulate the power and significance of their own feelings. Thus it attributes meaning and significance to an experience fraught with silence and suffering, and thereby illustrates, like Strand's story, how important poetry is or should be to everyone.

James Dickey is, without question, among the best known of the poets of his generation, in part because of his ability, as poet and critic Neal Bowers says in *James Dickey: The Poet As Pitchman,* to sell himself. Bowers says that "no poet in this century, with the possible exceptions of Dylan Thomas and Vachel Lindsay, has publicized himself and promoted his work more actively than James Dickey." Yet one of the advantages of Dickey's (sometimes shameless) self-promotion is the fact that it helped him bring poetry to a more comprehensive audience. If the consequence of a poet's need for celebrity status acts, in the end, to service an often misunderstood medium in a culture too often distracted by the temptations of the external world, so be it.

As Bowers says in "Selling the Poem," "The Hospital Window" "draws as near to the straightforward, confessional style that Dickey gets." For this reason "The Hospital Window" is among the best of Dickey's poems as an introduction to some of his themes and devices. It is also a good poem for the study of Dickey's ability to contain the spiritual or metaphysical within the confines of a narrative—his facility for moving a narrative poem beyond the boundaries of its characters and plot lines. It's this facility, coupled with his willingness to marry a colloquial and plain-spoken speech to a more mystic and surreal sense of diction and rhythm, that makes James Dickey a poet worthy of our continued attention.

"The Hospital Window" begins and ends with a very direct, prosaic statement. "I have just come down from my father," the speaker says twice. These twin lines locate both the poet, as a protagonist in his own poem, and his subject matter, which concerns a notably ethereal experience and vision, in a solid place and time. Dickey's decision to firmly place himself at the beginning and ending of "The Hospital Window" frees him to explore

> *The poem's value and power comes from both the poet's willingness to describe his own experience with his father ... and from his aptitude for knowing which poetic devices would best help him invent a still life, describing a transcendent moment firmly in praise of even the darkest or most frightening of human processes."*

the more mystical moment inevitably inherent in a poem about the nature of death and dying, and, as Dickey himself says in *Self Interviews,* about the experience of trying and failing "to say to his father that unsayable thing that one hopes to be able to say, but which nobody since the beginning of time has ever been able to say."

One of the ways "The Hospital Window" transcends its narrative base can be seen in how its architecture seems to duplicate, in a recognizably contemporary landscape, the Christian cosmology of heaven and hell. The entire hospital, from the poet's perspective on the street, becomes a symbol of heaven. At first, Dickey makes this allusion in the most direct way imaginable. As the speaker of the poem waves from the street, trying to determine behind which window his father lies "in the shape of his death still living," he says that "all the white rooms / ... turn the color of Heaven." Dickey then associates the hospital with heaven by using a reoccurring color motif. Early in the poem, the poet talks about his father as "he lies / above me in a blue light." He then repeats this reference to the color blue throughout the entire poem, saying, for example, that he turns—as he stands paralyzed in the middle of the street (while "The horns blast at me like shotguns, / and drivers lean out, driven crazy)—"as blue as a soul." Later on in the poem, he expresses his wish "that the dying may float without fear / in the bold blue gaze of my father." The hospital also has "six white floors" and "dozens of pale hands" within "the bright, erased blankness of nothing." Although Dickey has said time and time again that he is not a Christian poet, these images fully evoke the spirit-centered architecture and color scheme of a traditional Christian cosmos.

In contrast to the father in his heavenly blue hospital, the son, down below in the middle of the street, nearly goes blind from the sun glaring on the hospital windows. He says that "each window possesses the sun / as though it burned there on a wick" and that he waves "like a man catching fire." This conflict between the calming white/blue hospital and the frantic noise down below on the street, with its "wild engines / … shredding their gears and roaring," implies that the son is either in a kind of hell or, with his "shoulder blades shining with all / the glass the huge building can raise" is standing in the pre-dawn of a Christ-like ascension. Either reading works to set the reader up for the poem's greatest moment, which is when the speaker transcends his place in the street, with his "pin-tingling hand half dead / at the end of [his] bloodless arm" to connect, perhaps for the last time, with his father.

This turn is what makes "The Hospital Window" more than just a documentary about a man's feelings regarding the inevitability of his father's death and his inability to say anything about it. The turning point in the poem comes when the father finally raises his hand to wave back to his son. He "lifts his arm out of stillness at last," the speaker tells the reader. At this point, "The light from the window strikes" the speaker, removing him from his place among the crowd, and he turns, as was shown, "as blue as a soul." This is the moment in the poem when the speaker begins to share fully in his father's experience. Dickey then likens this moment to "the moment when I was born," linking birth to death in a way that suggests his appreciation for the natural order of the universe. (This appreciation or theme can be seen throughout all of Dickey's work.) The speaker then describes himself as moving "high, still higher, still waving," going on to say that he is both "fully mortal, / and yet not … in the pale, / drained, otherworldly, stricken / created hue of stained glass."

A second refrain in "The Hospital Window" further reinforces this idea of the son transcending, for a moment, his place and time on earth. At the beginning of the poem, Dickey describes his father as lying "higher and higher … above me in a blue

light." Then, at the end of the poem, the poet describes himself as moving "high, still higher." This refrain works beside the refrain of the twin beginning and ending lines to tie the poem into a coherent frame. It also helps to fully unite father and son in an experience that is often described in much more singular or exclusive terms.

There's no dogma in "The Hospital Window" —no sermon about how readers should live their lives or explication for why a belief in the afterlife could help them send their dying parents away from them in a kind of life-affirming flash of blessing. "The Hospital Window" is in this sense not a poem with an agenda. The poem's value and power comes from both the poet's willingness to describe his own experience with his father as clearly as possible and from his aptitude for knowing which poetic devices would best help him invent a still life describing a transcendent moment firmly in praise of even the darkest or most frightening of human processes. These devices—the poet's refrains, his willingness to combine plain-spoken lines ("And then step out onto pavement"; "I know that my father is there") to more figurative lines in which the sun burns glass windows on a wick, and the speaker becomes "drained, otherworldly, and stricken"— all work to help Dickey articulate and make accessible an experience that is, in the end, of a highly spiritual and even metaphysical nature.

Although James Dickey worked all his life to produce an accessible poetry that could be read and understood by all people, he was always, in nature and inclination, a metaphysical poet striving toward a coherent expression of the mythological realms, moving step by step in many poems from the everyday into unseen (or imaginary) realms of human experience, expressing his own various transformations into and toward the *other* in the hopes, as he said often, that his readers would move, too, beyond and past and above their own daily experiences.

Mark Strand's remarks about his father's gradual understanding of the power of poetry may also express, in some strange way, Dickey's vision in "The Hospital Window." Most of Dickey's poems strive, as Howard Nemerov says, to express a kind of "salvation … apprehending the continuousness of forms, the flowing of energy through everything." "The Hospital Window," as the reader has just seen, is no exception. Strand says:

> It may be, therefore, that reading poetry is often a search for the unknown, something that lies at the heart of experience but cannot be pointed out or de-

scribed without being altered or diminished—something that nevertheless can be contained so that it is not so terrifying. It is not knowledge, at least as I conceive of knowledge, but rather some occasion for belief, some reason for assent, some avowal of being.

Source: Adrian Blevins, in an essay for *Poetry for Students*, Gale Group, 2001.

Jonathan N. Barron

Jonathan N. Barron is an associate professor of English at the University of Southern Mississippi. Beginning in 2001, he will be the editor in chief of The Robert Frost Review. *In the following essay, Barron discusses how the elegy, as an ancient poetic genre, explains the principle theme of "The Hospital Window."*

Elegy, one of the most ancient and important poetic genres, has, in the past 150 years, undergone such a shift that recent scholars now distinguish between the elegy, on the one hand, and a new "modern elegy" on the other hand. One scholar, a professor of English at the University of Virginia, Jahan Ramazani, has done the most work on this distinction. According to him, the modern elegy does not conform to its traditional three-part mission: consolation, lamentation, praise. Instead, the modern elegy, as he says, "rebel[s] against generic norms but reclaims them through rebellion." This means that the modern poet writing an elegy is unwilling to accept death and will often refuse such typically comforting devices as praising the dead, lamenting the dead one's absence, or seeking consolation for the death. Yet even though the modern elegy refuses to engage in these comforting strategies it does, nonetheless, find a rather crooked, off-beat way of achieving consolation, lamentation, and even praise. In the modern elegy, the old strategies are re-packaged in irony, bitterness, and experimental poetic technique. It is true that, sometimes, the modern elegy will even go so far as to refuse to lament, to ask for consolation, or to praise the dead but, more often, according to Ramazani, such wholesale rebellions are rare. Instead, the modern elegy usually continues the work of mourning by establishing a distance from the traditional task of compensating for the loss. It does find some kind of healing but not in the language of either praise or lamentation. What makes the modern elegy's continuation of the traditional task "modern," then, is the presence of anger, irony, bitterness often in the company of experimental poetic forms and techniques. As Professor Ramazani says, the modern elegy is "anti-consolatory and ... anti-Ro-

> *The son's drop is not a descent into hell, nor is it a fall. Despite what it is not, the allusions and the language remind readers ... of the language of faith."*

mantic ... and anti-conventional." He adds, "If the traditional art of elegy was an art of saving, the modern elegy is what Elizabeth Bishop calls an 'art of losing.'" Since this "art of losing" is more art than anything else it does not give up on the tradition to which it belongs. Despite its attempt to reject the traditional function of the elegy it often incorporates, as Ramazani says, "the traditional elegy within the modern."

To understand how this tension works between the old way of mourning through a willingness to accept death and the more modern experience of mourning as anger, resentment, and bitterness one need only turn to James Dickey's "The Hospital Window." Happily, Professor Ramaziani, himself, discusses this poem. Sadly, he hardly discusses the poem at all. This is not a surprise since his book is devoted literally to hundreds of poets and poems. Although a widely read and well-known poem, "Hospital Window" is surprisingly under-studied. This is a shame since the poem's elegaic qualities manifest a most interesting, moving, and complex attitude towards grief.

In nine stanzas, the poem works through a son's grief for his father. Distancing is the poem's most immediately notable strategy. From afar, the son describes his father's death. This adds an objective quality to what is otherwise an intensely personal event. The son, one notices, only watches his father from afar seeing him through a dark window. This image is particularly important since it conjures up the biblical reference to seeing as "through a glass darkly." In the Bible, the image reminds people of their limitations, particularly with regard to matters of faith and religion. This is a particularly nice allusion here because it establishes the poem's principle theme as a tense dance between the language of faith and religion and the language of science and technology. In his brief comment on the poem, Professor Ramazani notes that the poem is interesting precisely because it contrasts the ascent to heaven of the father with the descent of the son in the elevator. But one might add that this contrast is not as clean as it appears to be. Yes, the poet keeps the Christian language of the soul's ascension to heaven but, at the same time, he deflates that language by referring not to the ascent to heaven and the descent to hell but rather to simple elevators. This deflation of what ought to be a serious Christian idea about death is part of the larger contest between religion and science: a conflict central to the poem's principle theme.

Looking more closely at the first stanza will make some of this more clear:

> I have just come down from my father.
> Higher and higher he lies
> Above me in a blue light
> Shed by a tinted window.
> I drop through six white floors
> And then step out onto the pavement.

In this stanza, the father rises only because the son descends. But rather than the have the father journey to the blue light of heaven, Dickey has the father "lie" in the antiseptic "blue light" of a "tinted window" in the hospital. The son's drop is not a descent into hell, nor is it a fall. Despite what it is not, the allusions and the language reminds readers, who are assumed to be familiar with Christian ideas of the afterlife, of the language of faith. The language makes readers think of the soul, and of heaven, even though this is not the plot of the poem. The first stanza plays Christian motifs—ascent, fall, descent—against technological reality. In terms of strictly realistic facts, however, there is no contest between heaven and hell. The stanza merely describes a simple trip in a hospital elevator.

This double strategy, saying two things at once, also applies to the second stanza. Here, Dickey uses the language of geometry and technology to play with the idea that the father is really ascending to a better place. In so doing, this stanza revives two of the major functions of the elegy: consolation and praise. The idea of heaven will console the son; he will be able to feel better about this death if he can believe that his father will be in heaven. Also, by suggesting that his father is in heaven, he implicitly praises his father's good name: the father is a man who deserves to go there. Here is that stanza:

> Still feeling my father ascend,
> I start to cross the firm street,

> My shoulder blades shining with all
> The glass the huge building can raise.
> Now I must turn round and face it,
> And know his one pane from the others.

In this stanza, the father's ascent is, in terms of strict logic, merely a technological illusion. It is simply the fact that the son has left the building by going down, which therefore makes the father appear to go up. This trick of geometry allows the son and the readers to make the Christian association with heaven. And, as if to underline that point, the building itself casts what would, in a religious context, be a divine glow of holiness on the son's shoulders (the place where one finds an angel's wings). As if called by some divine light, the son turns to face his father. But when he turns to his father, he is already twice distanced. First, he is physically removed: he is outside many floors below; and second, while he appears to be speaking the language of faith, he is really quite distanced from that language: the facts are just the neutral reality of architecture, and twentieth-century technology.

In the third stanza, the clash between realistic, technological facts, and the spiritual interpretation of death increases. The son waves to the building, saying that the sunlight glowing on him makes him "like a man catching fire." What is really happening? The son is grieving. He wants to lament; he wants to lash out and scream with anger. He wants to declare that this death is unfair. But the fact that he only says this in metaphors tells readers that he is even distanced from his own grief. The tradition of lamentation, of public weeping so common to the history of elegy, is masked here. Rather than weep openly, as so many elegiac poems do, Dickey's poem makes use of metaphors and similes. The son burns, but this fire is just an image cast by the sun on his body. He at once welcomes the need for lamentation and refuses to do it. Similarly, the traditional language of solace that would comfort him is also refused. Rather than insist that his father is now in a "better place," Dickey refuses such religious sentiments and says only that "all the white rooms / they turn to the color of Heaven." On the one hand, he says that he is one fire, below in hell, a great sinner. On the other hand, the fire is just a trick of light catching the descent of the sun on a hospital.

The fourth stanza is the most modern stanza of all and is the very heart of the poem. Here, the poet imagines that he has received a response from his father. Having waved to the window, he imagines a response. What kind of response? "[T]he bright, erased blankness of nothing." In the space of the window, the son does not find the conventional, feel-good conclusion to his elegy. Instead, he finds nothingness, a void where praise, lamentation, consolation, and solace are impossible. There is only a great emptiness, a vacuum. Dickey's speaker merely reports: "I know that my father is there."

The enjambment here, the place where Dickey breaks the line, is especially interesting. The stanza and the line end, but the sentence continues over the stanza break. The rest of the sentence, the second modifying clause in the next stanza, tells readers only that his father is in a place—"In the shape of his death still living." This is the most mysterious line of the poem. What does it mean? How can one's death still be living? One interpretation is that this is the moment of death. The son who is removed below, far from the body, somehow senses the moment of his father's death, and, having sensed this, the son refuses the traditional language of grief. Neither the Romantic poetic tradition of solace, nor the Christian tradition is suitable here. Although one does not know why they are not suitable, one does know for sure that this speaker will not and does not invoke them. Instead he merely reports that he cannot know what death means. Or, if he knows what it means, the line that explains the death is, itself, meaningless. It cancels out its own meaning: "the shape of his death still living."

This mysterious line, which really has no understandable meaning, is also the first line of the fifth stanza. Oddly, it has no logical relationship to the self-contained image of that stanza: it has nothing to do with what follows. Dickey here yokes the image of his father's body in the hospital room to a new scene of traffic on the street below. The fifth stanza describes the son, evidently lost in grief, standing in the street. The stanza tells readers that he is nearly run down by passing cars. The effect of combining the line about his father's death with this traffic scene is to make the world itself, the technological fact of the modern city, somehow speak to and for the son. The traffic honking and screaming articulates the son's grief. Since he can't do it, the traffic will "blast" like "shotguns" for him; it will sound his lamentation since he cannot. In another strange juxtaposition or radical jump cut the final line of this stanza returns to the father's body back in the hospital room. The most modern, disconnected, and strange stanza of the poem, it is also the moment when grief is sounded. How thoroughly modern! Rather than have the son grieve as in a typical elegy, this modern elegy lets the traf-

fic sounds be the traditional lamentaion, the wail of sorrow. Taken as a whole, then, this fifth stanza links two places and two people together: a father in the hospital room and a son on the street. It associates one with heaven and one with hell. It jumps between them both. Notice, too, that the speaker, the son, never cries. He is in public, but there is no public lament. The traffic does it for him. In the contest between faith and technology, the technological world appears to win. It becomes a substitute language. The poem implies that, for a variety of reasons, no language can satisfy the needs of the poet in despair. He would rather be silent.

As if to underline this point, the sixth stanza decidedly turns its attention on the speaker and away from the newly dead father:

> The light from the window strikes me
> And I turn as blue as a soul,
> As the moment when I was born.
> I am not afraid for my father—
> Look! He is grinning …

This stanza, like the previous one, also accents the enjambment. The new vision of the father "grinning" suggests that, at this point in the poem, the atmosphere and tone have begun to change and become more positive. From the low point of "blank nothingness," the poem now gestures toward some equivalent for the traditional language of Christianity, of a soul's journey toward redemption and grace.

In a weird vision, the father is said to look at the son standing in the traffic. Just as the son is trying to find a way to cope with the father's death (to worry no more for him), the father, so the speaker tells his readers, decides not to worry about the son. In the plot of the poem, the son, standing in the middle of a busy street lost in his grief and confusion and waving at the hospital window becomes the object of his father's concern. It should have been the other way around! The joke here is that the father, even though he is dead, still watches out for the son. The son reports that he is not "afraid for my life, either." As if newly energized by this realization, the son also says that he holds "each car in its place." From a low point of despair, the son now has gained a new sense of power and positive energy. Once more the sound of grief is heard. Once more the traffic speaks his grief: "[I]nciting its horn/to blow down the walls of the world." This time, however, the son commands such speech: a slight but significant advance from his silence in the previous stanza.

The poem's final stanza is the most enjambed of them all. Its sentences are continuations of sentences begun in the eighth stanza. Like the previous two stanzas, they also accent the fragmented, disconnected, and discontinuous theme of the poem. But, by this point in the poem, neither the language of technology, nor that of religion has been able to console the son. A new source of consolation is required. It does arrive. Notice that the language that had associated the son's location on the ground with hellfire and damnation now associates his same position with the height that one usually assigns to heaven. By the concluding stanza, the son although still on earth is said to be "high, still higher, still waving." These metaphors of height traditionally refer to happiness, to ascent, to heaven, to a glorious and better world after life. The poem gestures to a heavenly redemptive, Christian consolation even as it deflates such religious imagery by referring only to a man waving his arms and hands. After all, the high thing depicted here is just his "bloodless arm" still raised, still waving. What matters, though, is that the son has decided, through his imagination, that his father did express concern for him. No matter how distanced he is from his father's death and his own ability to grieve, he has through his imagination, found a connection, an emotional bond with his father. This bond allows the poet to turn once more to himself:

> My recognized face fully mortal,
> Yet not; not at all, in the pale,
> Drained, otherworldly, stricken,
> Created hue of stained glass.
> I have just come down from my father.

One way to interpret these lines is to ask: whose face does he carry off here? If it is his own, then he has just distinguished himself from his father and, in so doing, has found a way to accept his father's death. He must accept the fact that he is alive. He must accept his own life and, in so doing, will be able to cope better with his father's death. This, of course, is not a traditional elegy's conclusion. Typically, an elegy focuses strictly on the dead. But this conclusion is modern. For by turning to himself at the end, to his own imagination, the son finds a source of comfort that is neither strictly Christian nor entirely cold, bloodless, and logical. On the other hand, the face he carries might also be understood as the image of his father's face and not his own. If that is the reading one finds, then, the poem must be read as dark and despondent.

In the end, though, whatever image the son "carries," the final line, which repeats the first line exactly, does conclude the poem. It does tell readers that the son has come down. At the same time, it leaves open the question of whether or not that descent is a fall into sin, a spiral to hell, or any kind of religious journey at all. Readers can only be certain that from the heights of grief, the son has come down to an earth of pavement, traffic, and blazing sun. The only compensation he will receive for his father's life will have to come from him. Readers will differ if it does come from the son in the end. When this elegy turns to the speaker and not to the corpse in its search for solace, it becomes distinctly modern. It refuses to side entirely with the realistic facts of science and technology or with the Christian idea of heaven. Neither are able to offer Dickey what his own "amazement" delivers.

Source: Jonathan N. Barron, in an essay for *Poetry for Students,* Gale Group, 2001

Morton D. Rich

Rich, an associate professor of English at Montclair State University is the author of The Dynamics of Tonal Shift in the Sonnet. *In the following essay, he discusses the key roles that structure and plot play in "The Hospital Window."*

The line "I have just come down from my father" both begins and ends a poem that on the surface seems to be about a speaker who is in the street below, looking up at his father's hospital window after visiting him. He is trying to see his father behind the sun-glare reflected in the window. Upon seeing him, the speaker experiences a complex epiphany that is anticipated stanza by stanza through careful plotting. Using puns, syntactic structure, and references to movement, color, and light imagery, Dickey provides four simultaneous levels of plot—the means by which the poem gets from its beginning to its end and closure—that inform a reader's experience. The surface content of the poem would seem ordinary or banal without the dense complexity of the plot maneuvers that Dickey interweaves so seamlessly that they can escape a casual reading. Indeed, critic Neal Bowers mistakenly offers that the poem "adheres to the commonplace," that the opening and closing lines are "flat, unemotional statements," and that "this poem draws as near to the straightforward, confessional style as Dickey gets." On the contrary, the imagery of movement and color, the puns and allusions, and the syntax combine to create a mythic presentation of a seemingly ordinary event. Critic James Applewhite is closer to the mark when he writes that "Dickey's tendency to use sensory illusion … seems related to his sense of awakening to

the world and its curiousness." Through examining plot devices, the reader will see how the epiphany is anticipated and brought to light.

The poem is presented with brackets marking main and subordinate clauses. When two or more brackets appear together pointing in the same direction, two or more clauses are beginning or ending. A subordinate clause (a dependent clause within a main clause) is said to be embedded. In "The Hospital Window," the greatest and most significant amount of embedding occurs within the seventh and eighth stanzas, beginning with the line, "As the wild engines stand at my knees" and concluding with, "In the bold blue gaze of my father," where four clauses are brought to closure. Poet and critic John Ciardi would call this the fulcrum or point of balance of the poem. It is after this line that the speaker's epiphany occurs, signaled most clearly by the word "amazement." While forty-four lines precede the fulcrum and only ten follow it, the poem balances, not mechanically, but emotionally. The content preceding the fulcrum leads to the revelations of the last ten lines, the speaker's sense of experiencing heaven and hell simultaneously. When the first line reappears as the last, the speaker and the reader experience closure, just as listeners do at the end of a musical composition that restates its opening theme at the end. This phenomenon is fully explored by critic Barbara Herrnstein Smith in her book *Poetic Closure: A Study of How Poems End.*

Within the stanzas of the poem, directional words name movements of the speaker and his father. The father is "higher and higher," "above," and "propped up"; his father "lifts," and the speaker feels him "ascend." The speaker has just "come down," and says "I drop," "step out," "cross," "turn round," "wave," "slowly I move," "I have just come down." All the movements of the father are upward, while all of the movements of the speaker are downward or lateral until the final two stanzas, when the speaker says of his

hand half dead
At the end of my bloodless arm
I carry it off in amazement
High, still higher.

The characters are in counter-motion relative to each other except for this moment when the speaker symbolically joins his father with the upward motion of his arm. Note also that the "wild engines stand" and the "dying ... float." They do not have upward, downward, or lateral motion, and are thus contrasted to the father moving toward

heaven, and the speaker existing in the hell of his mortality, reprised in the final line, "I have just come down from my father." The meaning of the last line has layers and weight far greater than its twin, the first line of the poem.

While blue and white are named in the poem, and other colors are implied by the phrases "tinted window," "deep-dyed," "hue of stained glass," "sun ... burned ... on a wick," "flames," and "color of heaven." The implied colors are simultaneously abstract and intense, suggesting a church setting, heaven or hell, or all combined. The references to white—"six white floors," "all the white rooms"—seem to name aspects of a hospital, but imply more. Similarly, references to blue—"he lies / Above me in a blue light," "And I turn as blue as a soul," "In the bold blue gaze of my father"—seem literal, but expand beyond direct reference, contributing to the epiphany of the speaker. The qualities of light and color either reflected off glass surfaces of the hospital or transmitted through them create an atmosphere of otherworldliness that deeply affects the speaker. In a sense, by visiting his father, the speaker has become a martyr—

My recognized face fully mortal,
Yet not; not at all, in the pale,
Drained, otherworldly, stricken,
Created hue of stained glass."

While remaining "fully mortal," he has also become a figure in a stained glass window, implying that he is a martyr, dead and sainted.

Poets use puns, ambiguity, and allusions frequently, and Dickey is no exception. Starting with the first line, words and phrases in this poem resonate with multiple meanings. "I have just come down from my father" can be read literally—the speaker has just descended from an upper floor of a hospital building—and, in current parlance, he has experienced an emotional letdown. In the second line, "he lies" places the father in a bed, and also implies a question about truth telling, an issue common to the hospital experiences of patients, their families, and doctors. "I drop," in line five, refers to the action of an elevator descending and also implies the emotional state of the speaker, underlining "come down." In the last line of the stanza, "step out" is literal, and suggests the speaker removing himself psychologically from his father.

In the second stanza, first line, "ascend" is the speaker's feeling first, then hints at the father's death and ascent to heaven, leading to the speaker's "cross[ing]" both himself and the street. The street is "firm" because it is on earth, not in heaven.

Again, there is a doubling of meaning. In the third line, the "shining" of his shoulder blades may be from reflected light or from the image of angel's wings. When he turns round to "face it," he is facing both the building and his father's coming death. And of course "his one pane" has an obvious double meaning.

The words "burned there on a wick" of line two of the third stanza indicates a candle flame; candles burn out, just as his father's life will burn out. When he writes, "I wave," which could be read as, I waver or I move unsteadily, and when the son catches fire, both could be interpreted as the son too will expire or will be in Dante's hell. The rest of the lines in this stanza offer images of heaven and hell that move away from the literalness of the hospital building seen from outside. The people inside are within flames, grave (double meaning) and weak, but the father is not seen because he has become a shadow "In the shape of his death still living."

The light in the sixth stanza—"light from the window strikes me"—is both reflected sunlight and the light of heaven that turns the speaker "as blue as a soul, / as the moment when I was born." And the father "is grinning" like the proud parent of a newborn, confident, "not afraid for my life, either." The word "either" points to both father and son. The father is not afraid of the traffic, the drivers driven crazy, their wild engines, shredding gears, or roaring. Why not? Because "the bold blue gaze of my father," reminiscent of Renaissance paintings of blue-eyed Jesus among clouds, has given the speaker more power than the mere cars stretching for miles. Their horns are like trumpets announcing a royal arrival—the rebirth of the speaker in his father's gaze. This line, "In the bold blue gaze of my father," with its four clauses coming to closure, marks the fulcrum of the poem and the beginning of the speaker's epiphany.

Like a mythic hero, he carries off his "pin-tingling hand half dead / at the end of my bloodless arm / … in amazement." On the literal level, his arm is bloodless and his hand is tingling from holding them up for so long, but more significantly, he is participating in the coming death of his father by experiencing the partial death of part of his body. He carries it off "in amazement / high, still higher, still waving" as if his arm were ascending toward his father's window or heaven, pointing the way. Because his father has seen him, the speaker's "recognized face [is] fully mortal," but at the same time "not at all, in the pale, / drained, otherworldly, stricken, / created hue of stained glass." He has

awakened to his mortality, to his coming death foreshadowed by visiting the hospital where his father lies above him.

When the first line of the poem reappears as the last, it has added weight and gravity. The speaker is in spiritual crisis, having felt his own rise and fall, the tension and balance between life and death. He has "just come down from my father," but by the end of the poem the father of the last line feels more like god than a mortal father. He is a father who offers the possibility of redemption. Thus the son is held in the grace of an epiphany.

The accomplishment of Dickey's poem lies in its transformation of the seemingly ordinary into a spiritually significant moment that results from his careful manipulation of syntax, imagery, puns, and allusions.

Source: Morton D. Rich, in an essay for *Poetry for Students,* Gale Group, 2001.

Sources

Amazon, www.amazon.com (June 9, 2000).

Applewhite, James, "Reflection on Puella," in *Modern Critical Views: James Dickey,* Harold Bloom, editor, Chelsea House, 1987.

Bowers, Neal, *James Dickey, The Poet as Pitchman,* University of Missouri Press, 1985, p. 1.

Bowers, Neal, "Selling the Poem," in *Modern Critical Views: James Dickey,* Harold Bloom, editor, Chelsea House, 1987.

Ciardi, John, *How Does A Poem Mean?,* Houghton Mifflin, 1960.

Dickey, James, *Drowning With Others,* Wesleyan University Press, 1962.

———, "Preface to *The Early Motion,*" in *Night Hurdling,* Bruccoli Clark, 1983.

———, *Self-Interviews,* Louisiana State University Press, 1970, p. 117.

DISCovering U.S. History, Gale Group, 1999.

Gunn, Thom, "Things, Voices, Minds: A Review of *Drowning With Others,* by James Dickey," in *"Struggling for Wings:" The Art of James Dickey,* edited by Robert Kirschten, University of South Carolina Press, 1997.

Nemerov, Howard, *Reflections on Poetry and Poetics,* Rutgers University Press, 1972.

Ramazani, Jahan, *Poetry of Mourning,* University of Chicago Press, 1994.

Rich, Morton D., *The Dynamics of Tonal Shift in the Sonnet,* Edwin Mellen Press, 2000.

Smith, Barbara Herrnstein, *Poetic Closure: A Study of How Poems End,* University of Chicago Press, 1968.

Strand, Mark, ed., *Best American Poetry 1991,* Macmillian, 1991, pp. xiii–xvii.

Tillinghast, Richard, "James Dickey: *The Whole Motion,*" in *"Struggling for Wings:" The Art of James Dickey,* edited by Robert Kirschten, University of South Carolina Press, 1997.

For Further Reading

Dickey, James, *The Whole Motion: Collected Poems, 1945–1992,* Wesleyan University Press, 1992.

> As the title suggests, this is a definitive James Dickey collection of poetry, including some of his most recognized works alongside other less anthologized material that readers find just as intriguing. This book provides a very comprehensive look at Dickey's unique perspective on nature, family, war, guilt, and love.

Hart, Henry, *James Dickey: The World as a Lie,* Picador USA, 2000.

> This recent biography of James Dickey is lengthy (over six hundred pages) but well worth the time and effort. Hart's account of the poet's extraordinary life and works is fair, factual, and very detailed.

———, *The James Dickey Reader,* Touchstone Books, 1999.

> This is a collection of selected poems and prose, including excerpts from Dickey's unfinished novel, *Crux,* and some early, previously unpublished poems. The book is organized chronologically and by genre and is an excellent representation of the poet's entire body of work.

Kirschten, Robert, *James Dickey and the Gentle Ecstasy of Earth,* Louisiana State University Press, 1988.

> As one of James Dickey's most important critics and advocates, Robert Kirschten presents in this book a comprehensive look at Dickey's poetry up to that time. He highlights the motion in Dickey's poetry, whether it is in the themes, the subject matter, or the language.

Island of the Three Marias

Alberto Ríos

1985

Although "Island of the Three Marias" refers to a real geographic place, the poem draws on the literary tradition of islands as locales of the exotic and the fantastic. Umberto Eco's *Island of the Day Before* and H. G. Wells' *Island of Dr. Moreau* are two well-known examples in this tradition. Ríos' poem appears in the second section of his 1985 collection, *Five Indiscretions*. The collection as a whole addresses themes of gender, sexuality, and desire, and the section in which "Island of the Three Marias" appears deals with representations of masculinity and martyrdom. The poem, consisting of six free verse stanzas—alternating quatrains and longer stanzas—presents brief descriptions about three men who live on one of *Las Islas Marias* (The Mary Islands), a group of four islands that are ninety miles off the southwestern coast of Mazatlán, Mexico. Although readers are not explicitly told, the men are either convicts or employees of Islas Marias Federal Prison, which was established on the largest island, Maria Madre, in 1905.

Ríos hones in on a detail of each of the men's lives, letting that detail serve as a symbol for the life as a whole. Even though the poem refers to a real place, like many of Ríos' poems, it has a fantastic and fabulous feel about it and an elegiac tone. Other poems in the section, such as "A Man Walks as if Trapped," "A Man Then Suddenly Stops Moving," "The Carlos Who Died and Left Only This," and "On January 5, 1984, El Santo the Wrestler Died, Possibly," have a similar tone, and all make attempts to symbolically sum up the essence of a

particular man's life. Ríos' style is often described as magical realism, a term made popular by Latin American authors such as Gabriel García Márquez and Jorge Luis Borges. Magical realism combines the dreamlike elements of myth and fairy tale with the sharply etched description of everyday events.

Author Biography

Born in 1952 in the border town of Nogales, Arizona, to a British mother, Agnes Fogg Ríos, and a Mexican father, Álvaro Alberto Ríos, Alberto Ríos grew up between two worlds. It is no surprise, then, that his poetry and stories negotiate the borders between fantasy and reality, between the seen and the unseen. In his essay "West Real," Ríos describes his childhood: "I grew up around my father's family, but I look like my mother—which means I got to see two worlds from the beginning, and could even physically experience the difference growing up where I did: I could put, every day of my life, one foot in Mexico and one foot in the United States, at the same time." A daydreamer in school, Ríos learned quickly about what kind of language was valued when his teachers forced him and other Chicano students to give up Spanish. As a result of this Ríos developed a third language, one rooted in the imagination that drew on cartoon imagery, family lore, and his grandmother's recipes. He cultivated this language by scribbling poems on the back of notebooks and continuing to dream about the places he read about but had never seen. Ríos' reading during his high school years included comic books, science fiction, fairytales, and the *World Book Encyclopedia.*

A high school teacher encouraged him to pursue his interest in literature by introducing him to the poetry of Lawrence Ferlinghetti, the San Francisco Beat poet. Ríos enrolled at the University of Arizona, where he graduated with degrees in English and creative writing. After a year at law school, Ríos entered Arizona's M.F.A. program, from which he graduated in 1979. Since joining the creative writing faculty at Arizona State University in 1982, Ríos has produced a steady output of poetry and short-story collections, winning critical and popular acclaim. His poetry titles include *Whispering to Fool the Wind* (1982), *Five Indiscretions* (1985), *The Lime Orchard Woman* (1988), and *Teodoro Luna's Two Kisses* (1990). His story collections include *The Iguana Killer: Twelve Stories of the Heart, Pig Cookies and Other Stories* (1995), and *The Curtain of Trees: Stories* (1999). Ríos has

Alberto Ríos

also published *Capirotada: A Nogales Memoir,* a memoir about growing up on the Mexican border. Ríos has been awarded fellowships by the Guggenheim Foundation and the National Endowment for the Arts and has won a number of other state and national grants and prizes.

Ríos' motivation to write can perhaps best be summed up in the words of Chilean poet Pablo Neruda, which Ríos uses as the epigraph for his first full-length poetry collection, *Whispering to Fool the Wind:* "You see, there are in our countries rivers which have no names, trees which nobody knows, and birds which nobody has described…. Our duty, then, as we understand it, is to express what is unheard of." In all of his writing Ríos attempts to do just that.

Poem Text

The pale nuns of St. Joseph are here
    in groups, on the island of the just
    arrived from having been somewhere else
    and will be leaving soon without scars.

There are really four islands here   5
    but the others are simply ignored.
    No one has thought to ask why,
    not Faustino, his wife, the children
    the others, or even these white nuns

    10

not in a Christian place, prison islands
inherited from the lepers who decomposed.
On this particular island the family makes
a living, and this is their punishment.
A burden placed in the hands of Faustino
the poor man who kills.   15

This place is the physical moment
for which the nuns are Easter lilies.
White is the frayed habits of the young
women who will not be women here.

He is too young, never married   20
who feels the two pains:
north, he could have no woman,
here he could, and had none.
He erased the laughing, his own
laughing that echoed—he said came—   25
from the mouths of those around him
with the needle in his leg
sometimes even though his pants
when he felt that way he felt,
crying pain he called *wife,*   30
Because of his soft noises then
he sometimes was loaned Mrs. Marez.
Faustino let him, thank you Faustino,
and when she left, whore! to Mrs. Marez.
He knew the truth which was dreaming   35
to leave this place to do again
what made his father proud
who, carefully, had shown him now.

White is the coldest color handed down
from old to new like one photograph,   40
like the story of the child martyrs
or the stale candies said to be blessed.

The man in the suit did not care.
His wife who did not come here
suffered from the embarrassment   45
of marriage with the one
too formal for this frivolous place
because he could be nothing else,
too important to have liked his name,
to have liked the boys   50
who were everywhere smiling at him.
Fresco Peach, the name he invented.
It reminded him of something
American western, Frisco Pete,
something tough but not quite   55
and that is better. He stayed inside
so no one would laugh here, and never
told his name to a woman.
A man is ugly, he says to himself,
a man then suddenly stops running.   60

Poem Summary

Stanza 1

The island of the Three Marias to which the
title refers is Maria Madre, the largest of the four
islands ninety miles off the coast of Mazatlán in
Mexico, and the home of Islas Marias Federal

Prison. The prison is unusual in that convicts live
in communities, not behind bars. Those who have
earned the privilege have been allowed to bring
their families to live with them. Historically, the
Catholic church has ministered to the prisoners.
The first stanza introduces the "pale nuns of St.
Joseph," workers for the church. The description of
Maria Madre as "the island of the just / arrived from
having been somewhere else / and will be leaving
soon without scars" refers to the missionaries themselves, who have the freedom to come and go as
they please, as opposed to the prisoners, who must
remain and who will be scarred by their experience
on the island. Ríos uses line breaks effectively in
this stanza, enjambing the second line to ironically
play on the meaning of "just." This long description of the island also makes humorous use of understatement.

Stanza 2

In addition to Maria Madre, the names of the
other three islands are San Juanito, Maria Maga-
lena, and Maria Cleophas. They are ignored because
the prisoners are confined to the one island. Ríos
might also be humorously observing that both Mary
Cleophas (the Virgin Mary's sister-in-law) and
Mary Magdalene (former prostitute turned saint)
have historically been ignored in favor of Mother
Mary. All the characters are represented as accepting their lot "even these white nuns / not in a Christian place." Ríos alludes to the use of the island as
a leper colony before it became a federal prison in
1905. Historically, leper colonies were established
and run by Christian missionaries. The word
"white," which appears throughout the poem, in this
instance highlights the nuns' racial difference from
the Mexican prisoners, who are brown-skinned.

Ríos presents the first named character,
Faustino, as a family man whose family's "punishment" is similar to any family's not in prison.
Given Ríos' penchant for convoluted sentence
structure, the last two lines are ambiguous. Faustino
is either himself "the poor man who kills," (alluding perhaps to the crime that put him behind bars)
or he is the guard of "the poor man who kills," and
that is his burden. In either case he is drawn as a
sympathetic character. Faustino is the Spanish
name for Faustus, which in Latin means fortunate.
Ríos uses the name ironically.

Stanza 3

Preceding each longer stanza Ríos uses a
shorter stanza, a quatrain, as a kind of refrain.
Whereas the longer stanzas each describe the par-

ticularity of a given man, the shorter stanzas provide generic comments on the place. Easter lilies are white and symbols of Christ's resurrection, and Ríos' comparison of the nuns to the lilies underscores their innocence and virginal status. He also puns on the word "habit," which refers both to their dress and to a ritualized action or, in the nuns' case, a ritualized non-action (i.e., remaining celibate). That they "will not be women here" tells readers that the speaker considers romantic or sexual relations with a man to be a marker of "womanness."

Stanza 4

This stanza describes another man, unnamed, on the island who obviously has a history of troubled relationships with women. His "two pains" are that he could never have a relationship with another woman while on the mainland ("north"), and that even though he could have a relationship on Maria Madre, he has not. The speaker suggests that the man is mentally ill, as he is described as confusing the voices of others with his own: "He erased the laughing, his own / laughing that echoed—he said came— / from the mouths of those around him / with the needle in his leg." The needle suggests that the man is on medication or perhaps addicted to narcotics. Faustino, the man in the second stanza, acts as a pimp of sorts, "loaning" the man to Mrs. Marez, most likely the wife of another inmate. The young man verbally assaults her when she leaves, calling her a "whore." The stanza ends with the young man "dreaming" of doing what his father had taught him. What this is, is left unsaid. Most likely it has to do with the kind of life the man would have led had he not wound up in prison. Whatever it is, the man longs for it, and it is part of his "truth," what he lives for.

Stanza 5

This stanza, like the previous quatrain, uses the symbol of white. This time, however, instead of innocence, white represents a range of ideas, including memory, sacrifice, and mystery, corresponding to a photograph, the story of child martyrs, and state candies respectively. White is "handed down / from old to new," in the same way that the young man's father had handed down to his son what he knew in the previous stanza. All of the objects that are referred to as being white function as evidence of some sort. A photograph preserves memory and is evidence of an event; "the story of the child martyrs" is evidence of sacrifice, of martyrdom; and the "state candies said to be blessed" are evidence of superstition, and symbolize mystery and the unknown.

Media Adaptations

- The Academy of American Poets sponsors a page on Ríos at http://www.poets.org/poets/poets.cfm?prmID=51.

- Arizona State University's online magazine carries a story on Ríos at http://researchmag.asu.edu/articles/alphabet.html. Ríos teaches at Arizona State University.

- Ríos' poem "Chileñno Boys" from *Five Indiscretions* has been set to reggae music by David Broza for CBS Records.

- *Las Islas Marias,* a Mexican movie about a revolutionary fighter who ends up in Las Islas Marias was released in 1951. It is in Spanish and stars Pedro Infante and Tito Junco.

Stanza 6

This stanza introduces another unnamed man, possibly an official of the prison, as he is dressed in a suit. Or he may be a white collar criminal or an eccentric one. The speaker represents him as a man who is on Maria Madre because he has failed at other things in his life. The speaker presents this indirectly, though, by describing the man's wife's opinion of him. Readers can infer from the description that the man is arrogant and self-important. The name he chooses for himself, Fresco Peach (fresh peach), and the fact that he "never / told his name to a woman" suggests an ambiguous sexuality. Ríos ends the poem with this man's thought of self-loathing mixed also with self-acceptance or resignation. The poem can be read as a triptych, that is, as a trio of portraits of men who inhabit Maria Madre, and the effect that the island has had on them.

Themes

Sexism

"Island of the Three Marias" presents the male desire for the opposite sex as an inherently destructive drive which often results in contempt for

Topics for Further Study

- In a team of at least two other students, research the history of penal colonies. Then, assuming that your group will be responsible for founding a new penal colony, draw up a document detailing how you would govern it. Back up any policies or rules you might have with reasons.

females. This expression of this contempt is sometimes referred to as misogyny, which means hatred of women. Each of the three men described displays either implicit or overt loathing for females. Faustino pimps for Mrs. Marez, securing the "too young man" for her pleasure; the "too young man," who tellingly calls his pain "wife," calls Mrs. Marez a "whore" after she leaves; and the man in the suit, who takes the (to him) macho name Fresco Peach, never tells his name to a woman. Apart from Mrs. Marez, the other women in the poem are "the pale nuns of St. Joseph," who the speaker says "will not be women" on the island, presumably because they will not have relations with men. Such a conventional notion of what makes a woman a woman, while not misogynistic, per se, nevertheless perpetuates a stereotypical image of female identity, an image based on what women can do for men.

Atonement

"Island of the Three Marias," a poem about the desires of men who live in a penal colony, questions the idea that prisons can be places of rehabilitation where criminals can atone for their mistakes and remake themselves. Ríos presents the missionaries as largely ineffectual, saying that "they will be leaving soon without scars," underscoring the scarring that occurs to those who stay on the island. The fact that no one, not even the nuns, asks why the other islands are ignored suggests that those on the island are resigned to their fates, even the "white nuns / not in a Christian place."

Echoing the idea of scarring, Ríos draws attention to the history of the islands, writing that they are "inherited from the lepers who decom-

posed." Christian missionaries have a tradition of working with lepers whom society has shunned. Leprosy, primarily a tropical disease, is chronic but it is not easily transmitted, as is the popular belief. Nor does the disease cause the skin to fall off. Ríos, however, plays off both of these images to suggest the similarity between lepers and criminals. In the Old Testament of the Bible lepers are the unclean whom God is punishing for their sins. Similarly, the inhabitants of Maria Madre are being punished for their wrongs, but not by God. By focusing on details or events which show how the men have not changed, Ríos explicitly questions the usefulness of religion in the prisoners' lives.

Alienation and Loneliness

"Island of the Three Marias" uses the setting of a Mexican federal prison to explore the idea of humanity's alienation, one of the primary features of modern society. Ríos does this by presenting a contradiction at the heart of Western legal systems: although people are imprisoned ostensibly to "pay back" society for their wrongs, they very often become more alienated from society and themselves as a result of their time in prison. Ríos emphasizes the futility of prison as a place for rehabilitation in his description of Faustino, whose "punishment" is his family making a living. The Islas Marias Federal Prison is unique in that prisoners do not live behind bars but in eleven communities throughout the island and work regular jobs. Prisoners on good behavior are allowed to bring their families to live with them during their incarceration.

The young man described in the third stanza is the most manifestly alienated, even from himself, showing signs of mental illness when he cannot distinguish the source of his own laughter. The "man in the suit" simply "does not care" and has given up trying to be a part of society, even on the prison island. Ríos makes plain the symbol of the island as a place of alienation and loneliness by linking it historically to lepers, "who decomposed." The unremitting bleakness of the men's lives and the fact that even the nuns cannot offer solace emphasize the failure of the prison to change the men.

Style

Metaphor and Symbol

"Island of the Three Marias" employs metaphor and symbol in its three quatrains to comment on the description in the three longer stanzas.

Compare & Contrast

- **1988:** Carlos Salinas de Gortari is elected president of Mexico amidst charges of widespread election fraud. Salinas signs the North American Free Trade Agreement, clamps down on unions, and privatizes many state enterprises.

  2000: Mexico signs a free trade treaty with El Salvador, Guatemala, and Honduras. The treaty lifts tariffs on many agricultural and manufactured goods within twelve years.

  2000: Opposition candidate and former Coca-Cola executive Vicente Fox of the National Action Party wins Mexico's presidential elections, ending the ruling party's seventy-one-year lock on the presidency. Fox promises to improve education, fight corruption, and help the poor.

The "scars" in the first quatrain are suggestive of the scars of Christ on the cross; the "Easter lilies" in the second quatrain suggest Christ's resurrection; and the "story of the child martyrs" and the "stale candies said to be blessed" in the last quatrain attest to the ongoing presence and importance of belief, however conceived, and how it is passed down from one generation to the next.

Paleness is used in the first stanza and white in the second and third to symbolize naivete, innocence, purity, rebirth, and hope. All of these images together resonate with both hope and a kind of naivete and are juxtaposed with descriptions of men who are, essentially, hopeless. The most important symbol in the poem is the island itself, Maria Madre, which Ríos refers to as "Island of the Three Marias." Mother Mary is the mother of Jesus Christ.

Historical Context

Ríos frequently draws upon real places, people, and events in creating his fabular poems, but he injects his writing with a sense of the fantastic and strange. Critics often mention Ríos' affinity with the magical realist writers of Latin America such as Gabriel García Márquez, Jorge Luis Borges, Mario Vargas Llosa, and Manuel Puig to name but a few who have helped to popularize Latin-American fiction in the last thirty years. A term with a long and complicated history, magic realism, when used to describe literature, refers to a mixture of familiarity and strangeness. Critics often describe Latin-American magic realism as an attempt to liberate the facts and things that stories describe from historical reality and to place them in a setting that more closely resembles that of a fairy tale, where characters and plot take on allegorical and mythical meaning. Márquez, a Colombian who received the Nobel Prize in Literature in 1982, is often cited as the central figure of this style of writing. Propelled by the popularity of magic realists of the 1960s and 70s, and helped by the booming population of Hispanics in the United States in the 1980s and 90s, Mexican-American writers produced a raft of novels, poems, short stories, and essays which met with both critical and popular success. Chicano and Chicana writers such as Ríos, Ron Arias, Juan Felipe Herrera, Francisco X. Alarcon, Ray Gonzales, Rudolpho Anaya, Lucha Corpi, Sandra Cisneros, and Alma Luz Villanueva all give voices to the Mexican-American experience and validate the important contributions of Mexican culture to the United States.

In the early 1980s when "Island of the Three Marias" was published, Ronald Reagan was President of the United States and his administration was heavily involved in attempting to alter the political direction of Central America. One of Reagan's first acts after assuming office was to suspend economic aid to Nicaragua, claiming that the Sandinista government under Daniel Ortega was a puppet state of Cuba and the Soviet Union and that a communist country to the south of the United

States threatened national security. Reagan authorized the CIA to help rebel forces overthrow the Nicaraguan government. During the mid-1980s, in violation of the Boland Amendment passed by Congress which prohibited CIA activity in helping the Contras, the CIA continued to interfere in the domestic affairs of Nicaragua. After American pilot Eugene Hasenfus was shot down on a covert mission over Nicaragua and confessed to his spying activities, the Iran-Contra Affair began to unfold. During a lengthy process which included televised House and Senate committee hearings and a presidential commission investigation, Lieutenant Colonel Oliver North, a former marine and consultant to the White House National Security Council, testified that he had helped to divert funds from thirty-eight million dollars in Iranian arm sales to the "freedom fighters" in Nicaragua in 1985. North was dismissed from his White House National Security Council position and national security adviser John Poindexter resigned his post. Reagan, though admonished by a bi-partisan House investigation committee for letting these events happen under his watch, was never indicted.

Critical Overview

"Island of the Three Marias" appears in *Five Indiscretions*. Although the poem itself hasn't received much critical attention, a few publications reviewed the collection. José David Saldívar writes that "most of the poems achieve a level of excellence not far below the peak moments in his earlier poetry." Lawrence Joseph notes that "*Five Indiscretions* displays the breadth and richness of the American language—a language which requires and will require complex techniques." Rochelle Ratner claims that Ríos "offers the insights into the lives of women seldom found in the work of a male writer." Adrián Pérez Melgosa praises the book, writing that "[*Five Indiscretions*] traces a genealogy of the seemingly capricious or irrational behavior of human beings by exploring how this behavior develops as a result of the experiences each person goes through in the secrecy of his or her most intimate moments…. [The poems] focus on processes of discovery, of learning from the experiences and stories of people, a learning that is not calculated according to a goal that has to be achieved but that is driven by a mixture of desire and chance." Melgosa claims that "No Chicano poet writing today is a more exquisite—a more fas-

tidiously deliberate—technician than Ríos. His poetry is always lavishly textured."

Criticism

Chris Semansky

A widely published poet and fiction writer, Semansky teaches literature at Portland Community College. In the following essay, Semansky examines how "Island of the Three Marias" explores non-Christian ideas of suffering and martyrdom.

"Island of the Three Marias" is a mysterious poem resonant with Christian imagery and symbolism. It is effective because it leaves out more than it says. Ríos plays with prominent Judeo-Christian ideas about redemption and suffering, using the Island of the Three Marias, home to a Mexican federal prison, as his setting, but he gives the poem its air of mystery, of magic, by leaving much to the reader's imagination.

As a poet who mines the real world of places, things, and events for stories he can imbue with an otherworldly feel and mythic significance, Ríos belongs to that group of writers sometimes referred to as magical realists. Taking their lead from Latin American writers Gabriel García Márquez and Jorge Luis Borges, magical realists seek the extraordinary in the mundane, find the fantastic in the everyday. For example, "On January 5, 1984, El Santo the Wrestler Died, Possibly," a poem included in *Five Indiscretions,* the collection in which "Island of the Three Marias" appears, concerns the funeral of a famous wrestler named *El Santo* (the Saint). Ríos takes the event of the wrestler's death and creates a surreal landscape in which the pallbearers all wear sequined masks in honor of their dead friend. Weaving mourners' superstitions about the dead into the fabric of his story, Ríos uses the idea that the dead can hear what the living say about them as a means to imagine the wrestler's past, how he came to be the feared yet loved person he was. In "Island of the Three Marias," Ríos imagines the lives of men who are part of the Islas Marias Federal Prison. This isn't literal reportage; by imagining what happens in a little-known real place, Ríos can create a dreamworld far more strange than one made up about a place with no basis in physical reality. It is precisely the familiarity of the descriptions that give the poem its mysterious atmosphere. Ríos critic Adrián Pérez Melgosa notes that the poet creates beauty out of conflict by "convert[ing] the day-to-day lives of individuals living on the borderlines created between cultures, languages, genders, and geographies into lyric sites where fate dances hand in hand with political resistance, and magic becomes the origin of common sense."

The first borderline that Ríos negotiates in transforming this prison island into a magical place is the one between imagination and reality. Rather than naming the poem "The Maria Islands" (the actual geographic name of the islands), Ríos calls it "Island of the Three Marias," echoing the structure of the holy trinity. In Christian theology, the holy trinity refers to the doctrine that God exists as three persons—Father, Son, and Holy Spirit—who are united in one substance or being. "Island of the Three Marias" suggests, then, that three entities reside in one place. Ríos takes the three islands—named after the three biblical Mary's (the Virgin Mary, Maria Cleophas, Maria Magdalene)—and compresses them into one. In Latin America, a country heavily influenced by the Roman Catholic Church, the image of Mary is revered as much if not more than the image of Christ himself. The shift from calling Jesus' mother the Virgin Mary to calling her the Mother of God occurred around the second century and primarily was a way of emphasizing the divinity of Christ himself. In Mexico, it is Mary's status as mother that is so pronounced. It is telling—although the poem does not tell readers—that the island that houses the prison is Maria Madre (Mother Mary). Rather than describing the place itself, Ríos describes the men who live on the island, emphasizing that a place is more than simply a geographic entry; it also includes the people who live there and the way that the place is expressed in their behavior.

Faustino is the first person named in the poem. The second stanza presents him as a hapless sort, whose life is all suffering.

> There are really four islands here
> But the others are simply ignored.
> No one has thought to ask why,
> Not Faustino, his wife, the children
> The others, or even these white nuns
> Not in a Christian place, prison islands
> Inherited from the lepers who decomposed.
> On this particular island the family makes
> A living, and this is their punishment.
> A burden placed in the hands of Faustino
> The poor man who kills.

He is presented as one of the people on the island who has grown inured to curiosity about life outside the island. The details Ríos uses to describe Faustino underscore his normality. He has a wife

... by imagining what happens in a little-known real place, Ríos can create a dream world far more strange than one made up about a place with no basis in physical reality."

and a family, and they suffer to make ends meet, "this is their punishment." Ríos depicts Faustino as an everyman whose life, perhaps, hasn't turned out the way he thought it would. Readers do not, however, know Faustino's status on the island. The ambiguity of the last two lines suggests that he could be either a convict (i.e., Faustino is "the poor man who kills") or a prison guard (Faustino's burden is guarding "the poor man who kills.") To understand how a convict's family can make a living, it's important to know that Islas Marias Federal Prison is unique in that prisoners live and work in community settings and, in some cases, are allowed to bring their families to live with them. Whether he is a convict or a guard, Faustino is drawn as a sympathetic and long-suffering character in a non-Christian place. It's ironic that Faustino's name in Latin means "fortunate."

The second man described is no doubt a convict. Like Faustino, he also suffers on the island: his emotional and mental torment is salved only by a "needle in his leg," most likely medication. His disabilities prevent him from establishing relationships with women. But Faustino, exercising authority and compassion, arranges for the young man to sleep with Mrs. Marez. This is a decidedly different kind of compassion than might be exercised by someone of conventional Christian faith. Also in contradiction to Christianity is the young man's idea of truth. For Christians, the truth is that Jesus Christ died for humanity's sins and that it is only through him that one can be saved; for the young man, however, it is "dreaming / to leave this place to do again / what made his father proud / who, carefully, had shown him how."

The description of the last man, "the man in the suit," suggests that he is an administrator for the prison. Abandoned by his wife, who was

What Do I Read Next?

- Ríos' collection of stories, *The Iguana Killer: Twelve Stories of the Heart,* published in 1984, is considered by some critics to be a classic of Chicano literature.

- Ríos' first collection, *Whispering to Fool the Wind,* is the poet's first full-length collection of poems. It won the Walt Whitman Prize of the Poetry Society of America in 1982. Readers can see in these poems the style that Ríos would develop in later collections.

- In 1995, Cambridge University Press published Rafael Perez-Torres' study *Movements in Chicano Poetry.* This book challenges the perception that all Chicano poetry deals with the same subject matter and in a similar manner.

- *Beyond Bounds: Cross-Cultural Essays on Anglo, American Indian, and Chicano Literature,* a 1996 anthology edited by Alberto Franklin Gish, examines the inter-relationships of literature by these three groups.

- Matt S. Meier and Feliciano Rivera's 1972 book *The Chicanos: A History of Mexican-Americans* offers a progressive historical reading of Mexican migration into the United States.

---

ashamed of him, the man suffers from his own arrogance and inability to be someone other than the uptight pretender he has become, "the one / too formal for this frivolous place," the one who takes the name "Fresco Peach" (fresh peach) because "it reminded him of something / American western." His suffering has led to self-loathing and resignation about the future as evidenced in the last two lines of the poem.

All of these men's sufferings, compassions, hopes, and dreams are described in very secular ways. The descriptions of their lives are juxtaposed with the description of the nuns, who are innocent and "without scars"; and unlike the men who have suffered in their relationships with women, the nuns are described as "women who will not be women

here," precisely because they will not have romantic relationships. Their appearance in the poem symbolically underlines the idea of the island as a prison of desire where the religious and the secular suffer alike. The recurring symbol "white" in the three quatrains further highlights distinctions between the men and the nuns. The nuns are "in groups," whereas the men are always alone. The nuns' whiteness, suggestive not only of their goodness but of their skin color as well, contrasts with the brown-skinned Mexicans on the island.

"Island of the Three Marias" is not a description of good versus evil or even a comment on the silliness of missionaries on a prison island. By describing the suffering of three men and the hopes of the nuns to bring religion to their lives, Ríos is saying something deeper about human nature: that is, suffering, whether it be in the name of faith or as a result of an act over which humans may or may not have control, is the lot of human beings. For Christians, martyrs are those who suffered and died for their belief in Christ. For those in the secular world, martyrs might be those who died for a particular belief or cause, for example, the Irish Republican Army's Bobby Sands, who died during a lengthy hunger strike protesting Great Britain's rule of Northern Ireland. But what kind of martyrs can prisoners be, who have broken society's laws and who are meant to suffer to atone for their transgressions? Ríos seems to suggest that belief isn't a necessary criterion for martyrdom. The only thing necessary is being human. He suggests that human desire itself is often inscrutable and that men, especially, suffer for their desires.

Source: Chris Semansky, in an essay for *Poetry for Students,* Gale Group, 2001.

Carl Mowery

Mowery has written extensively for the Gale Group. In the following essay, he considers the existential philosophy present in Ríos' poem "Island of the Three Marias."

The Chilean poet Pablo Neruda once said, "Our duty, then, as we understand it, is to express what is unheard of." By this he meant that the poet's task is to investigate, examine, and explore the world from new and different angles. Alberto Ríos used this quotation as the epigraph for his first book, *Whispering to Fool the Wind* (1982). By doing so, he has adopted it as his writing philosophy. The consequence of this for him is that he must come to grips with the fact that some of the characters he will reveal will not be the beautiful people, but rather they will be the down-trodden or the unsavory members of society. The editors of the *Norton Anthology of Modern Poetry* have remarked that Alberto Ríos populates his writings with "grotesques," people who are by their very nature unappealing while at the same time interesting, haunting characters. These same editors also say that Ríos' careful and sympathetic characterizations of these kinds of people make his readers "accept and take friendly pleasure" in them.

An interesting example of this is the character Madre Sophía in Ríos' short story "Eyes Like They Say the Devil Has." A young boy, the narrator, is taken by his mother to see Sophía to get his fortune told. She is described in various unflattering ways. As she enters the room the boy says her head is "like a loose jar top on plum jam." Later, he says her head looks "fake." As she sits reading his fortune, her ample bosoms seems to jump out at him and he describes them as "horse nuzzles." Despite these unflattering descriptions and the boy's expressed fear of her, the reader develops a sympathetic feeling about the fortune teller.

Even though the characters in the poem "Island of the Three Marias" are unsavory, they are sympathetic characters whose plight is understandable because their behaviors are often similar to those experienced by many people. Readers do not come away from this poem with any deeply felt rejection of the characters. But though they might be willing to forgive bad behavior, they are not likely to forget the serious consequences of those acts.

Ríos' use of contrasts in his poem reflects his family background. He was born in Arizona, his father was from southern Mexico, and his mother was from England. He once remarked that his family life gave him a "language–rich, story–fat upbringing." The combination of these cultural heritages, which heightened his perception of society, and his linguistic background helped him define his writer's voice. His language is clear, crisp, and direct; it is the language of the people who populate his poetry and fiction.

The poem is divided into three main parts, each with two stanzas. The sections open with a short introductory stanza of four lines that leads directly into a longer stanza that examines an individual character in detail. The longer stanzas are freely constructed without a rhyme scheme and are of varying lengths.

Ríos knew both the Mexican-American and the Mexican societies. When he looked at them, he saw an insidious disintegration of several important as-

> *Even though the characters in the poem 'Island of the Three Marias' are unsavory, they are sympathetic characters whose plight is understandable because their behaviors are often similar to those experienced by many people."*

pects upon which they were built. The church and the governmental institutions charged with caring for the incarcerated, either prisoners or mentally ill patients, were not meeting their responsibilities to the whole society. Additionally, he found the disintegration of strong personal value structures to be as threatening to society as was each of these failing institutions. In his poem, Ríos shows these parts of society combined in a negative synergy of destruction that none of them seems capable of nor interested in reversing. The nuns and the government, which oversees "the man in the suit," are just as responsible for the deterioration of personal morality as Faustino, the youth in the second set and the man in the third set are. The wife who would not visit her husband in the institution is as complicit in creating his mental instability as is the institution that keeps him "in the suit." Their combined failure to accept responsibility is the chief cause of the disintegration of the society that is represented in the poem. Ríos indicates that the interconnected responsibility of individual behavior and corporate behavior is necessary for a strong society.

In Latin America, the roles of men and women are much more rigidly established than they are in mainstream society in the United States. The Latino man is often the dominant force in a relationship with the woman as the submissive one. Despite the fact that these roles are changing, deep seated expectations still exist. Women are expected to be the care-givers and the nurturing members of society. The women in the poem are the nuns, representing the Roman Catholic Church, the whore in the second set, representing the loss of personal morality, and the woman who does not come to the island in the third set, representing the institution of marriage. Each stands for a specific facet of the society that Ríos believes is failing to meet its responsibility.

These women seem selfish and unconcerned about the people they meet. The nuns, who are expected to be compassionate and involved with the prisoners on the island, "will be leaving soon without scars." The internal and/or emotional scars they hope to avoid come from ministering to those in need. Rather than serving those who need them, they are more interested in getting away as fast as they can.

Ríos uses colors symbolically to indicate the nuns' declining role in the service to the Church. He calls the nuns "pale," indicating that they lack the conviction and purpose that is expected from representatives of the Catholic Church. Their paleness stands in stark contrast to the black and white habits often worn by nuns, black and white indicating the strong contrasts between right and wrong, truth and falsehood.

Their habits are also "frayed," another symbol of their declining stature. "The white nuns not in a Christian place" are in such a place of their own making. Their failure to maintain a strong position in the life of the Church's ministry is their own creation. They "will not be women" on the island who meet the expectations of nurturing and comforting representatives of the Church. They also "will not be women" who meet the physical needs of the men on the Island.

The striking contrast between the nuns and Mrs. Marez is not as great as it might seem. In both cases, the women are located in a "physical moment." The physicality for Mrs. Marez is her sexual perfidy, allowing herself to be "loaned" for the purpose of satisfying someone else's sexual needs. The nuns' "physical moment" is likened to "Easter lilies," flowers with religious meaning, but they are static, potted emblems. Since the nuns "will not be women here" they are seen only as the visual image of the lily. But these women have abdicated their personal responsibility for their own behavior. The nuns fail to provide comfort to the prisoners; the whore fails to protect herself but offers the men a false comfort instead.

The failure of individual responsibility also exists in the role the wives play in the lives of their husbands. In the second and third sets, the wife is associated with uncomfortable feelings. In the third set, at line 45, the wife "suffered from the embarrassment of marriage" to a man who is inside an institution. She displays the same attitude as the nuns from stanza one by wanting to be "somewhere else" and "without scars." In her refusal to become involved with her husband, she takes one more step: she does not come to the "frivolous place." Just as the nuns have abdicated their role as spiritual comforter, the wife abdicates her role as emotional comforter to her husband.

The role of the wife in stanza four is figurative. Here the man seeks to soothe his hurt feelings from being laughed at by "those around him." He finds solace in drugs, which, from the needle in his leg "through his pants," calm the "pain he called wife." Ironically, the man personifies his pain and discomfort as a wife, turning the expected role of comforter into a pain-giving role.

Since the Latin-American man is very often the dominant person in a relationship between a man and a woman, he expects to be taken care of and comforted by the woman. The man then is a "taker" not a "giver." The first man in the poem is Faustino, Little Faust. In the well-known story by Goethe, Faust sells his soul to the Devil in exchange for earthly gratification. But by the end of the tale he loses everything. In Ríos's poem, Faustino is "the poor man who kills" and is sent to the island where he serves his punishment and where his family also lives and serves "their punishment." In this way, the family lives out the biblical lesson that the sins of the father are visited upon the son.

Later, Faustino "lends" the woman, Mrs. Marez, to the drug-taking youth to satisfy the youth's sexual needs. The youth has left a place where he could not have sexual contact with a woman, and now he is in a place where he could have contact but does not. As a result of his sexual ineptitude, he becomes the object of laughter "from the mouths of those around him." Because of his inability to secure sexual release, he seeks Faustino's help. The youth tries to rid himself of the echoing laughter by making "soft noises," the muted begging for Faustino's aid in acquiring the services of Mrs. Marez. In an ironic perversion of the polite ritual of saying thanks to someone, the youth thanks Faustino for the woman, and then calls the woman a "whore" even though she has given him the sexual gratification he desired.

Ríos uses white as a transition color into the last set, the sterile, cold white of government institutions and the detached and uninvolved "white nuns" from stanza two. "The man in the suit" from line 43 is a ward of the government and the institution where he is housed. Ríos shows the unsympathetic nature of the government through "the boys who were everywhere smiling at him." The man tries to hide from these people by inventing a name, "Fresco Peach," which he will not tell "to a woman." His emotional walls are as confining as the walls of the institution where he stays. He is isolated from his wife by his walls and by his wife's walls of embarrassment. In the last lines, he makes a final recognition of himself and his situation saying, "A man is ugly." With this acceptance of his condition, he "stops running." This man from the "frivolous place" acknowledges and accepts his status. Once that has been done, he no longer needs to run away from anything.

In the society in this poem, Ríos connects individual members with corporate members, demonstrating that even the slightest shortcoming has broad consequences for the whole community. No matter how insignificant a behavior pattern is, others will share in the fallout. Individual failures by themselves may seem less threatening and thereby more acceptable, but they are nonetheless devastating to the society as a whole. The French philosopher Jean-Paul Sartre said it best when he wrote that it is necessary "to make every man aware of what he is and to make the full responsibility of his existence rest on him. And when we say that a man is responsible for himself, we do not only mean that he is responsible for his own individuality, but that he is responsible for all men." Thus the interconnectedness Ríos exposes in his poem is a phenomenon that everyone must recognize or else suffer the consequences.

Source: Carl Mowery, in an essay for *Poetry for Students,* Gale Group, 2001.

Sources

Bruce-Novoa, Juan, *Chicano Poetry: A Response to Chaos,* University of Texas Press, 1982.

Ellman, Richard, and Robert O'Clair, eds., *The Norton Anthology Of Modern Poetry,* 2d edition, Norton, 1988.

Jenks, Deneen, "The Breathless Patience of Alberto Ríos," in *Hayden's Ferry Review,* Fall/Winter, 1992, pp. 115–23.

Joseph, Lawrence, Review in *American Book Review,* May–June/July–August, 1987.

Melgosa, Adrián Pérez, "Alberto Alvaro Ríos," in *American Writers Supplement,* Charles Scribner's Sons, 1996, pp. 537–56.

Muske, Caro, "Disc Jockeys, Eggplants and Desaparecidos: Five Indiscretions," *New York Times Book Review,* February 9, 1986, p. 28.

Ratner, Rochelle, Review in *Library Journal,* May 1, 1985, p. 64.

Ríos, Alberto, *Five Indiscretions,* The Sheep Meadow Press, 1985.

———, "West Real," *Ploughshares,* Spring, 1992, pp. 1–5.

Saldívar, José David, "Alberto Alvaro Ríos" in *Dictionary of Literary Biography,* edited by Francisco A. Lomeli and Carl R. Shirley, Vol. 122: Chicano Writers: Second Series: Gale Research, 1992, pp. 20–24.

Saldívar, Ramon, *Chicano Narrative: The Dialectics of Difference,* University of Wisconsin Press, 1990.

Sartre, Jean Paul, "Existentialism," in *Classic Philosophic Questions,* 6th edition, edited by James A. Gould, Merrill Publishing Co., 1989.

Stuttarford, Genevieve, Review in *Publishers Weekly,* April 12, 1985. p. 97.

For Further Reading

Lopez, Tiffany Ana, ed., *Growing Up Chicana/o,* Avon Books, 1995.
    A collection of coming-of-age stories in America from Chicana/o writers such as Rudolfo Anaya, Denise Chavez, Alberto Alvaro Ríos, Marta Salinas, Gary Soto, and others. These stories celebrate the tremendous diversity of Chicana/o life through the universal themes of boundaries, family, education, and rites of passage.

Martinez, Julio A., and Francisco A. Lomeli, eds., *Chicano Literature,* Greenwood Publishing Group, 1985.
    The book is arranged alphabetically with comprehensive coverage of the individual authors' lives and examination of their works by more than forty critics of Chicano literature. The selected bibliography provides access both to the authors' works and to secondary sources.

Ríos, Alberto, *Capirotada: A Nogales Memoir,* University of New Mexico Press, 1999.
    Ríos' memoir of his childhood in Nogales, Arizona, and Nogales, Mexico, is well worth reading. He weaves together memories of family and friends to create a vivid portrait of growing up Chicano in the 1950s.

Soto, Gary, ed., *Pieces of the Heart: New Chicano Fiction,* Chronicle Books, 1993.
    Introduced by Soto, this collection of Chicano fiction includes stories from well-known writers such as Sandra Cisneros, Helena Viramontes, Alberto Ríos, and Dagoberto Gilb.

Jabberwocky

Lewis Carroll

1872

"Jabberwocky" is probably Carroll's most well-known poem. It is the first of many nonsense poems set into the text of the beloved English novel *Through the Looking-Glass,* published in 1872, six years after the more commonly known *Alice's Adventures in Wonderland.* Because the poem employs conventional structures of grammar and many familiar words, however, it is not "pure nonsense." In fact, while both books were composed for the ten-year-old Alice Liddell, it is generally accepted that Carroll's studies in logic firmly ground the thought beneath the imaginative works, so that adults find as much to appreciate in the novels and poetry as children. The importance of "Jabberwocky" as a central focus of meaning for the novel is indicated by Carroll's intention that the drawing of the Jabberwock should appear as the title-page illustration for *Through the Looking-Glass.*

In the novel, Alice goes through a mirror into a room and world where things are peculiarly backward. She finds a book in a language she doesn't know, and when she holds the book up to a mirror, or looking-glass, she is able to read "Jabberwocky," a mock-heroic ballad in which the identical first and last four lines enclose five stanzas charting the progress of the hero: warning, setting off, meditation and preparation, conquest, and triumphant return. The four lines that open and close the poem were published originally in 1855 as *Stanza of Anglo-Saxon Poetry.* It is this stanza that Humpty Dumpty, whom Alice meets shortly after

reading the poem, takes pains to explicate. While the meaning of the poem is obscured by its nonsense elements, and general interpretations widely vary, Humpty Dumpty's explication is certainly much less helpful in discovering meaning in "Jabberwocky" than Alice's initial response:

"Somehow it fills my head with ideas—only I don't exactly know what they are! However, *somebody* killed *something:* that's clear, at any rate—"

Author Biography

Lewis Carroll was born Charles Lutwidge Dodgson on January 27, 1832, in Daresbury, Cheshire; he was the eldest son of a clergyman in the Church of England. At a young age, Dodgson began writing humorous poetry and demonstrated an aptitude for mathematics. After completing his education at home and at schools in Richmond and Rugby, he began studies at Oxford at the age of 18. Two and a half years later Dodgson was made a fellow of Christ Church, Oxford, and assumed a position as lecturer in mathematics. In 1856 he began writing humorous pieces for journals under the pen name Lewis Carroll, which was based on Latin translations of his first and second names. 1856 was also the year Dodgson met Alice Liddell, the daughter of the dean of Christ Church, who later served as the model for the protagonist of *Alice's Adventures in Wonderland* and the other "Alice" books. Four years later Dodgson's first mathematical treatise was published. He remained at Oxford for the rest of his life, lecturing until 1881 and writing a variety of scholarly works on mathematics and logic as well as his poetry, fiction, and essays. He died in Guildford, Surrey, England on January 14, 1898.

Lewis Carroll

And, as in uffish thought he stood,
The Jabberwock, with eyes of flame,
Came whiffling through the tulgey wood,   15
And burbled as it came!

One, two! One, two! And through and through
The vorpal blade went snicker-snack!
He left it dead, and with its head
He went galumphing back.   20

"And, hast thou slain the Jabberwock?
Come to my arms, my beamish boy!
O frabjous day! Callooh! Callay!"
He chortled in his joy.

'Twas brillig, and the slithy toves   25
Did gyre and gimble in the wabe:
All mimsy were the borogoves,
And the mome raths outgrabe.

Poem Summary

Lines 1–4:

Carroll explicitly defined certain words when the first stanza of this poem was published as a poem in its own right as "Stanza of Anglo-Saxon Poetry." He provided a glossary, or list of meanings, for some of the unfamiliar words; this list was later incorporated into Humpty Dumpty's explica-

Poem Text

'Twas brillig, and the slithy toves
Did gyre and gimble in the wabe:
All mimsy were the borogoves,
And the mome raths outgrabe.

"Beware the Jabberwock, my son!   5
The jaws that bite, the claws that catch!
Beware the Jubjub bird, and shun
The frumious Bandersnatch!"

He took his vorpal sword in hand:
Long time the manxome foe he sought—   10
So rested he by the Tumtum tree,
And stood awhile in thought.

Media Adaptations

- In 1966, a television production called *Alice Through the Looking Glass* was aired. Those in the cast included the Smothers Brothers as Tweedledum and Tweedledee, Jimmy Durante as Humpty Dumpty, and Jack Palance as the Jabberwock.

- Jan Svankmajer has long been considered one of the world's most original and clever animators. His amusing (and somewhat disturbing) take on "Jabberwocky" was made in Czechoslovakia (now the Czech Republic), released in 1971, and runs thirteen minutes.

- Donovan, a British pop star who had several hits in the 1960s, has song versions of both "Jabberwocky" and "The Walrus and the Carpenter" on his album *H. M. S. Donovan*. The album was originally released in 1971 on the Dawn Records label and was re-released in 1998 on Beat Goes On Records.

- Another musical version of "Jabberwocky" appears on Marianne Faithfull's 1965 album *Come My Way,* released on the Decca label.

- A videocassette entitled *The Hunting of the Snark [and] Jabberwocky* was released in 1999 by First Run Features. Although sections of "Snark" have been omitted, "Jabberwocky" has been included in its entirety.

- A CD-Rom entitled *Lewis Carroll—Selected Writings with Illustrations and Readings* has been released by HarperCollins Publishers Ltd. It contains *Through the Looking-Glass* and other major works by Carroll, as well as biographical material and readings by Sir John Gielgud in full CD-audio.

- The Lewis Carroll Society of North America maintains the Lewis Carroll Home Page at http://www.lewiscarroll.org with links to other interesting sites.

- One of the links for lovers of "Jabberwocky" is the site www.jabberwocky.com, which has all kinds of interesting items related to Carroll's poem.

---

tion in *Alice in Wonderland.* The first line begins with the now archaic English contraction for "It was" and contains the noun "brillig" which Carroll says comes from the broiling or grilling done in the early evening (br + ill + i[n]g) in preparation for dinner. "Toves" are supposedly badger-like creatures, and the adjective "slithy" is a portmanteau made up of "lithe" and "slimy." The definition offered for "gyre" in the second line is "to scratch"; "gimble" is defined as "to bore holes." Carroll has directed us to pronounce these both with a hard "g." However, in American English "gyre" is pronounced with the soft sound of the "j" in "june." Furthermore, "gyre" as a noun in its own right means "to circle," so it makes sense that its use as a verb might have that same meaning. "Gimble" is said to be associated with the noun "gimlet," "a small tool for boring holes." "Wabe" is defined by Carroll as "the side of a hill," but the explanation proposed by Alice as a portmanteau of "way + be-

fore/behind" seems much more helpful. Thus, the line can be read, quite poetically, as "Did spin and spike in the way beyond." The second line ends with a semi-colon in some versions of the poem, but with a colon in the last version edited by Carroll. A semi-colon would indicate a lesser break than a period, establishing two independent thoughts connected into one sentence. A colon suggests a further amplification of, or elaboration on, what has already been said, and in fact in this case the colon might stand for a break plus the word "however": "It was evening and the toves were having a great time [; however,] the borogoves weren't very happy and the raths felt so bad they cried." "Mimsy" in line 3 is made up of "flimsy" and "miserable," and the "borogoves" which it describes are said to be parrots. The "raths" of line 4 are defined as turtles, and Carroll offers an interesting etymology, or word history, for the adjective "mome" as being related to "solemn," which he suggests comes from an earlier (imaginary) word "solemome." The verb that ends the stanza is said to derive from a word meaning "to shriek," although Humpty Dumpty is more explicit, indicating that it is something "between bellowing and whistling," which suggests a sobbing, crying kind of sound, and which coupled with the sound of "outgrabe," perhaps might come close to being a past tense form for "outgrieve," or "grieve out[loud]." Carroll's original intention of the alliteration of the hard "g" for "gyre" and "gimble" in line 2 is lost with the American pronunciation of the soft "j" beginning "gyre." However, the assonance between the vowel sounds in "slithy" and "gyre" in lines 1 and 2 remains to emphasize the musicality of the poem, as does the assonance of the short "i" in "brillig," "gimble," and "mimsy" in lines 1, 2, and 3, respectively, and the long "o" sounds in "borogoves" and "mome" in lines 3 and 4. The stanza containing lines 1–4 establishes the setting for the story about to be told. Carroll has offered a literal English translation of the passage:

> It was evening, and the smooth active badgers were scratching and boring holes in the hill-side: all unhappy were the parrots; and the grave turtles squeaked out. There were probably sun-dials on the top of the hill, and the "borogoves" were afraid that their nests would be undermined. The hill was probably full of the nests of "raths," which ran out, squeaking with fear, on hearing the "toves" scratching outside. This is an obscure, but deeply-affecting, relic of ancient Poetry.

The first two lines set a scene of lighthearted happiness in which all seems well, but the last two hint at impending doom.

Lines 5–8:

The first proper noun in this stanza is related to the title of the poem itself, and so bears some serious consideration in both its form as the thing, the "Jabberwock," and the activity of the thing, "Jabberwocky." The first part of either word is "jabber," and a synonym for this is "babble," a word that brings up immediately an association with the biblical tower erected in the city of Babel. "Babble" thus refers to the sounds that resulted from God's confusion of the supposed one original human language into many so that people could no longer understand each other and cooperate to build the tower to heaven. "-Wock" or "-wocky" may refer to an old Scottish word for "voice." Hence, the "Jabberwock" could be called a "Babble-Voice," and "Jabberwocky" might be "Babblement." The central idea is that a father is warning his son against a creature whose sounds are without meaning.

The father's warning becomes explicit in the sixth line about the dangers inherent in the Jabberwock's jaws and claws. In the seventh line he extends the warning to include a second important creature: the Jubjub bird. Since sound is such a significant feature of this poem, it seems justified to take the sound of "jubjub" as being close to the word "jujube," a candy named for a fruit tree, and to assume an association with the sticky sweetness of the fruit the bird eats. Furthermore, in Carroll's later book-length poem *The Hunting of the Snark* it is made clear that the Jubjub bird sings songs that are attractive to the Jabberwock, so that one would likely find the Jabberwock in close proximity to the Jubjub bird.

"Frumious" in the eighth line is a portmanteau explained at length in Carroll's preface to *The Hunting of the Snark* (which he says "is to some extent connected with "Jabberwocky"). In short, to simply have two words packed together as, for example, "fuming-furious," does not have the poetic effect of "frumious," for it stresses the one over the other. Thus, "if you have … a perfectly balanced mind, you will say 'frumious.'" This gives the full effect of both meanings in a familiar-sounding adjective structure that is much more efficient than a hyphenated word.

Also in the eighth line, the third proper noun, "Bandersnatch," has two parts, which appear readily comprehensible: "Bander-" and "-snatch." The "snatch" would of course refer to something which "snatches" or takes, as a "snitch" is one who "snitches." "Bander" might feasibly be a combination of "band" and "banter," a kind of portmanteau. There is a specialized meaning of the word "band" which is in keeping with Carroll's pursuits in logic, wherein "band" refers to the link between the subject and predicate of a sentence that helps them make sense together. "Banter" is a light verbal exchange between people. Thus it might be that the father is warning the son against this creature who pretends to exchange conventional pleasantries (for example, "Have a nice day!") while actually stealing the meaning or sense from the words.

The sound of the poem is enhanced in this stanza by the use of alliteration of the "j" in the words "Jabberwock," "jaws," and "Jubjub," and of the "b" in "Beware," "Jabberwock," "bite," "Jubjub," and "Bandersnatch."

The basic sense of lines 5–8 is clear. The grammatical structure here, as with all the stanzas, is familiar and not nonsensical in itself. In addition, Carroll's use of nonsense words follows what we know and expect of nouns, adjectives, and verbs, and in fact most of the nonsense words are adjectives and nouns.

A plausible "translation," or interpretation, of the stanza might be: "Be careful of the Babble-Voice, my son, because it will either bite you or scratch and tear you. And take care around the bird that eats those sticky-sweet fruits, for the Babble-Voice is attracted to its song, and where you hear the one you will often find the other. And for Heaven's sake, stay away from the fuming and furious creature that robs sentences of their meaning!"

Lines 9-12:

In line 9 of this stanza "sword" has assonance with the adjective "vorpal." This is a portmanteau which might imply the joining of the words "verbal" and "voracious," given the emphasis in the previous stanza on words (the "jabber" of the Jabberwock) and jaws. Thus it would seem reasonable to imagine that the son takes up his "voracious word-sword" to go out and do battle with a thing that misuses or abuses words: the "Babbler" or "Babble-Voice." The colon at the end of this line implies that the act of taking the sword in hand entails more than simply picking it up; it means engagement in the task, so that the sword is "in hand" while seeking the foe, and even while resting and thinking.

The adjective "manxome" in line 10, which is in assonance with the long "o" of "foe" could be interpreted as having something to do with "Manx," such as an enemy coming from the Isle of Man. Interestingly, "Manx" also refers to the ancient Celtic language once spoken on this island. Now hardly ever heard and no longer taught, the Celtic languages are characterized by their musicality. Thus, once again, there is an emphasis on the sound of language, rather than its sense. This is further picked up by mention of the "Tumtum tree," for "tum" is an onomatopoeic imitation of the sound made by plucking a tense string, accentuated by the alliteration of "t" sounds. With this understanding of the three nonsense adjectives "vorpal," "manxome," and "Tumtum," we can see the son or knight-figure armed with his word-sword against an enemy who uses words for sound, waiting and thinking by a singing tree that might attract such an enemy.

It is in lines 9–12 of this stanza that the ballad of the Jabberwock can be established as an allegory about language itself. Carroll's background supports this because of his studies in logic and the concern for language that naturally goes along with that. This is further established by the associations of the sense and sound of language in the portmanteau words. Keep in mind that Carroll has "verified" the identical first and last stanzas as ancient Anglo-Saxon poetry, and that the "foe" to be dealt with is recognized in the third stanza as "manxome" or of a Celtic language-speaking race. Historically, the Anglo-Saxon language displaced the Celtic languages indigenous to the British Isles and became the precursor to the English language.

Lines 9–12 could be read thus: "The boy took up his hungry word-sword and went off on a long search for the foe who speaks the lyrical Celtic language, but eventually came to rest under the tree that makes a musical sound in the wind, thinking that the Babble-Voice might come this way, attracted by the sound."

Lines 13–16:

"Uffish" in line 13 is a likely combination of the word "huffy" meaning "arrogant," the word "offish" meaning "aloof," and perhaps the word "oafish," meaning "like a simpleton." In the following line the Jabberwock is described in stark contrast to the removed distance and coolness of the boy's attitude: "with eyes of flame" carries the connotation, or hint, of fire and passion.

"Whiffling" in line 15 is the first of two seemingly nonsense words, associated with things the Jabberwock does, which are in fact actual verbs. "Whiffling" means "to blow or drive with puffs of air"; it may be used as a figure of speech meaning "to speak evasively."

Presumably the boy is aware of the Jabberwock's imminent arrival as it comes noisily through the wood, which is described in line 15 as "tulgey." This is an adjective perhaps compounded of the word "turgid" meaning "swollen" (but also often used to describe language that is "grandiloquent" or "overblown") and the word "fulgent," which means "glittering" or "of a showy splendor."

"Burbled" in line 16 sounds like a portmanteau made up of "bubbled" and "gurgled," but is in fact a word that is onomatopoeic for "bubbled"; in addition, it is used figuratively as "to confound or confuse," as well as for its alliteration with the "b" and "r" sounds in "Jabberwock."

Lines 13–16 might be explained as saying: "The boy was aloof, thinking, when he heard the fiery and passionate Babble-Voice, as if blown by puffs of wind, come through the overblown and showy woods of its natural habitat; as it came, it made sounds without any possible sense or meaning."

Lines 17–20:

The double two-counts at the beginning of this line suggest that it is with two back-and-forth slashes of the sword that the boy slays the Jabberwock "through and through." The quickness of the action is further suggested by the internal rhyme of "two" and "through," as well as by the onomatopoeia of "snicker-snack." This is a portmanteau made up of "snickersnee," a word for "a large knife," and "snack," meaning "bite, snap," but also "a sharp remark."

Lines 17–18 could be paraphrased as: "The ancient Anglo-Saxon language met the even more ancient Celtic languages and very quickly and thoroughly, as if with a hungry word-sword and the force of incisive observation, displaced them. Thus the Celtic languages were no longer used and so did not grow and change, or *live;* the work of the world went on in Anglo-Saxon, which ultimately developed into the English language."

In lines 19–20 the boy has proved successful in the battle and takes the Jabberwock's head as a proof. He goes "galumphing" back, a verb made up by Carroll to mean "galloping in triumph." Note how the "uffish" of line 13 combines with "galumphing" to give a connotation of clumsiness, perhaps of an individual not particularly subtle or sensitive.

Lines 21–24:

The father asks the question in Archaic English, a reminder from Carroll that this is supposedly an ancient Anglo-Saxon legend. The question is presumably answered by the presence of the Jabberwock's head, and he calls his son to his arms for a welcoming hug, using the adjective "beamish" for its alliteration of the "b" sound. Carroll very likely intended the play on the word "son" in line 5 with "sun," making this word for "radiant" even more precise in its usage in this particular instance.

Line 23 contains joyful exclamations at the success of the boy. "Frabjous" is a portmanteau feasibly combining "fabulous" (in both the sense of "beyond belief" and "relating to fable") and "rapturous" (in both the sense of "ecstatic" and "being taken away"). Again, the musicality characteristic of a ballad is accentuated by the internal rhyme of "O frabjous day!" with "Callooh! Callay!" as well as by the alliteration with the hard "c" and "l" sounds. "Callooh! Callay!" at first glance appear to

be two of what are perhaps four of the only true nonsense words in the poem (along with "Jubjub" and "Tumtum"). However, again taking into consideration the emphasis on sound in this poem and the emphasis on echo words in its composition, it would make sense to find something that sounds like these syllables (as with "Jubjub" and "jujube"). In this case, it might be suggested that the words are actually a type of portmanteau made up of "collocate" and "colloquy," so that the father's joy is at having things once again "put in proper order" ("collocated") by the death of the Jabberwock, and at having the Jabberwock's demise and his son's return make "dialogue" ("colloquy") between him and his son possible.

The word "chortle" in line 24 to describe the father's wordless joy at his son's return is made up of "chuckle" and "snort." Along with "galumphing" it is one of two portmanteaus in this poem which have come into the English language for valid use.

The sense of lines 21–24 could credibly be rendered: "The father welcomes his son on this 'fabulous' day—a day that will live in legend, a 'rapturous' day that will forever mark when the life was taken from the Celtic languages. The father welcomes the boy to 'properly ordered dialogue.'"

It is interesting to note that the father's joy, however, is expressed with "chortling"—a nonsense word that has now become a valid verb. In contrast, the verbs used for the Jabberwock in the fourth stanza that seemed to be nonsense were in fact valid words at the time Carroll was writing.

Lines 25–28:

See lines 1–4 above. The sense of these lines, repeated, might carry this idea: "In the world there is still, as always, the mix of joy and sorrow which it is possible for animals without language to express."

Themes

The Heroic Quest

Despite its seeming playfulness, "Jabberwocky" contains a very serious theme as old as literature itself (as seen in such ancient texts as *The Odyssey* and *Beowulf*). This theme is the heroic quest, in which a (usually) young male will strike out for parts unknown, encounter some horrific beast, and either triumph over this force of dark-

Topics for Further Study

- Compare "Jabberwocky" with Robert Burns' "To a Mouse, on Turning up Her Nest with the Plough, November, 1785." Discuss how reading the made-up language in Carroll's poem can help you read the unfamiliar Scottish dialect that Burns uses.

- How does this poem's structure—the *abab* rhyme scheme, the repetition of the first stanza at the end—make you accept it as a poem? Does anything with a poetic form qualify as a "poem"? What if, like "Jabberwocky," it tells a story from beginning to end. What is poetry?

---

ness or be consumed by it. The roots of the literary heroic quest reach as far back as Greek, Roman, and early Christian mythology, and examples include Jason and the Argonauts encountering all types of fantastical beasts in their quest for the golden fleece, Oedipus' victory over the vicious Sphinx to rescue the city of Thebes, and David's encounter with Goliath. The tradition of the heroic quest is prevalent in poetry as well as in drama and fiction, and this theme has long appealed to young boys (remember Jack, the Giant Killer?), who are expected to eventually strike out on their own and conquer their demons (personal or otherwise) in order to "prove" their manhood. Along with Carroll's memorable fabrication of imaginative new words in "Jabberwocky," the heroic quest recounted in the poem is a key reason why it remains one of the most popular (if not the *most* popular) examples of nonsense verse ever penned.

Indeed, once past the disorienting yet fanciful description of the opening stanza, the reader encounters a number of elements that are the heroic quest's stock-in-trade. These include fantastical and menacing creatures (the Jabberwock, the Jubjub bird, the Bandersnatch), ancient weaponry (the "vorpal sword"), the long journey into a dark forest where the hero's encounter with "the manxome foe" is to take place, and the mandatory return of the vanquished creature's head as proof of the heroic deed. In composing "Jabberwocky," Carroll clearly wanted to evoke mythical battles of long ago, in the knowledge that such action-packed episodes appeal deeply to the youthful audience he so cultivated.

Carroll is known for having directed much of his literary output specifically at young girls, whose company he is well-known to have preferred over that of young boys. "Jabberwocky," however, is clearly aimed more at young male readers, dealing as it does with the gender-specific theme of the heroic quest. The power of such archetypal material, of course, has by no means diminished in this day and age; one only has to look at the immense popularity of the *Star Wars* movies among male youngsters for proof of this fact. Yet it is important to note that at the time of the publication of "Jabberwocky," during the height of Victorian England, young men, more so then than now, were expected (and even pressured by their fathers) to undertake some type of heroic quest, whether it be for queen or country or for personal or familial gain. Back then, there weren't many people who questioned the ostensible validity of war and aggression under sanctioned circumstances, and such endeavors were even encouraged by most fathers of their sons. The pressure to be a hero, therefore, was very much in the Victorian public mind, and the greater the menace (i.e., the Jabberwock with its "jaws that bite" and "claws that catch"), the greater the glory and paternal pride for the son.

Fantasy versus Reality

One of the remarkable things about "Jabberwocky" is how deftly Carroll synthesizes the worlds of fantasy and reality. Both worlds remain closely balanced throughout the poem, and readers can thank Carroll's close attention to poetic form for this clever balancing act. The danger with fantasy, of course, is that meaning and sense can get lost if the author creates a "wonderland" without any worldly touchstones or uses nonsense words in such a way that the overall effect baffles rather than enlightens. By mixing unfamiliar words such as "borogoves" and "frabjous" with familiar ones like "sword" and "wood," Carroll is able to kill two Jubjub birds with one stone. On the one hand, he can appeal to children's fascination with verbal sounds as well as their sense of playfulness, and on the other, he can transmit warnings to his youthful readers about the all-too-real dangers of the world around them.

Another key point to make with regard to this theme is how the poem's fantasy elements cast an unsettling, even threatening, shadow on terra firma ("terror" firma?). Ever the logician and champion of rational, civilized society, Carroll may be suggesting in "Jabberwocky" that anything irrational (i.e., "uncivilized") is to be feared and avoided. Of course, concrete representations of the irrational abound in "Jabberwocky": the Jabberwock, the Jubjub bird, the Bandersnatch. Such agents of chaos presumably dwell far from the safe confines of civilization, given that the hero must journey a long way to encounter the dreaded Jabberwock, and the fact that Carroll doesn't describe these creatures in much detail makes them even more mysterious and potentially terrifying to young readers. Indeed, to members of Victorian society, with its obsessive adherence to order and manners, anything that couldn't be categorized and thus "controlled" would be considered a threat to the desired social order.

Hence the poem's supreme irony. By giving the uncontrollable forces of nature names (e.g., Jabberwock and Bandersnatch), Carroll is attempting to gain a measure of control and order over an ostensibly irrational universe. Yet the names of these creatures are nonsense words that are themselves expressions of the irrational. Could Carroll be implying that the human mind, with its capacity for irrational acts such as the creation of nonsense words, is as much a threat to the order of things as any jaw-toothed, red-eyed denizen of the dark forest? Perhaps, perhaps not. Still, if the poet's mission is to use language to impose order on a seemingly chaotic world, Carroll appears to be carrying out this mission in "Jabberwocky," even if the world described in the poem is more fantastical than the one we're used to seeing in our waking lives.

Style

Any song that tells a story is a ballad. Originally intended for singing, ballads became "poetry" when the English poet Sir Walter Scott began collecting them to write down so they would not be forgotten. This is a typical form for stories about knights, which "Jabberwocky" purports to be, although it is considered a literary ballad, to be read rather than sung.

The ballad-stanza is usually four lines rhymed *abcb,* in which the lines have a syllable pattern of *8, 6, 8, 6.* Note how the third, fifth, and sixth stanzas of the poem follow this rhyme scheme, with the others rhyming *abab.*

Carroll also plays with the syllable pattern, with each of the first three lines of a stanza having eight syllables and the last line six, except in the third stanza, where it might be said that the third line "borrows" a syllable from the last line. The effect of the 8, 8, 8, 6 pattern is that the shortest last line gives a sense of separateness to each of the actions described in the stanza, whereas the typical ballad syllable pattern creates a sense of anticipation that carries through each stanza to the end of the ballad.

A further structural characteristic of "Jabberwocky" is the use of what Humpty Dumpty in his explication calls "portmanteau" words, which are two words "packed up into one." Examples of these are "slithy" and "mimsy" from the first four stanzas. The sound of words, rather than meaning, is thus accentuated.

Sound is a major structural concern of the poem, strongly established by the use of alliteration, assonance, and onomatopoeia. "Callooh! Callay!" in line 23 is an example of the consonant sounds characteristic of alliteration: the hard "c" is initial alliteration between the two words, and the repeated "l" sound is internal alliteration. "Jaws" and "claws" in line 6 exemplify the vowel sounds of assonance. Onomatopoeia occurs with the word "snicker-snack" in line 18 to describe the sound of the "vorpal blade." The utilization of sound in these ways centers attention on the musical quality of the words, an emphasis particularly well-suited to the ballad form. Further underplay of the content meaning of the words through the consistent use of portmanteaus, as well as use of words completely made up, also enhances the musicality of the poem.

Finally, the poem as a whole may be seen as an allegory, in which the characters and the story have meaning as concepts and acts on another level.

Historical Context

Universal Appeal

Surely one of the most appealing factors in Lewis Carroll's "Jabberwocky" is the sheer timelessness of the poem's setting. The boy's encounter with the mysterious Jabberwock beast has no specific reference point in history. This factor boosts the poem's universal appeal, for "Jabberwocky" is capable of captivating readers of any era—Elizabethan, Victorian, Industrial, Computer, or otherwise. Although the poem was written and published

Compare & Contrast

- **1871:** At the end of the Franco-Prussian War, Germany becomes newly unified under the Imperial Proclamation. King Wilhelm I of Prussia is crowned emperor of Germany, establishing the Second Reich. Germany's sudden emergence as a national power is perceived in Britain as a potential threat to that country's political and economic interests.

  1945: The Third Reich established under Adolf Hitler is crushed by the Allied Forces in World War II. Soon Germany is cleaved into two parts, with communist Russia dominating East Germany and Western democracies overseeing West Germany. This partition creates the so-called Cold War, which will last over forty years.

  1990: Forty-five years after the end of World War II, the two Germanies are finally reunited into one country. Under Chancellor Helmut Kohl, Germany establishes itself as a global economic power.

- **1903:** Just five years after Lewis Carroll's death, the first of many film versions of *Alice in Wonderland* is made by English film producer Cecil Hepworth. Primitive by today's standards, the ten-minute-long film is later preserved by The British Film Institute, though the film has noticeably faded in parts.

  1999: A lavish new version of *Alice in Wonderland* (with segments from *Through the Looking-Glass*) airs on television. The production features many stars and remarkable special effects, with Whoopi Goldberg as the Cheshire Cat and Ben Kingsley as the Caterpillar. The technique of "morphing" is used to great effect in the scenes involving Alice's shifts in size.

at the height of Victorian England, no special knowledge of that era is required in order to understand and enjoy the poem. Similarly, a reasonable facsimile of "Jabberwocky" could have been penned in any number of historical eras, given that the poem contains no noticeable references to Carroll, his life, or his times. A Roman scribe in Pompeii named Barnacus Frabjus could have written a "Jabberwocky"-like poem (and indeed, his readership, given its receptivity to the wildly fantastical creatures embedded in its mythology, would have eaten the thing up), as could have some beatnik bard given to opium-induced excursions on the page circa 1960. The point is, "Jabberwocky" transcends notions of time and history, and in having done so, the poem continues to increase its readership yearly by the thousands, if not millions.

Victorian England

Clearly, Carroll wanted his poem's narrative element (i.e., the boy's search for and encounter with the Jabberwock) to echo such mythological battles as Hercules' struggle with the Hydra, a ferocious beast with seven dragonlike heads. Carroll's main concern in the poem is the eternal battle between good and evil, and for many (if not most) readers, interpreting the poem on this level is enough. However, if readers look beneath the poem's surface, "Jabberwocky" *can* be interpreted in terms of the time in which it was written. Published as part of Carroll's *Through the Looking-Glass* (1872), the much anticipated sequel to *Alice's Adventures in Wonderland* (1865), "Jabberwocky" made its debut at the height of the Victorian Era (1834–1901), when England was undergoing tremendous expansion in terms of power, wealth, and cultural influence. In large measure, England called the shots around the world at that time, and for other countries, such as war-beaten France, envy with regard to England's global superiority must have been running high. Indeed, in 1872, England was enjoying a renaissance the likes of which it hadn't seen since Elizabethan times.

The Threat of Germany

However, "barbarians" were rapping at the gates, so to speak. To the English, the Prussians (Germanic peoples) had long been viewed as a worrisome threat to the "civilized" world, and in January 1871, less than a year before "Jabberwocky" was published, Germany became newly unified under the Imperial Proclamation, potentially tipping the balance of power in Europe and creating a sense of insecurity within Britain. To "defenders of the realm" like Carroll, the strengthening of Germany and its "barbaric" peoples would have, at the very least, created a certain uneasiness. This tangible fear at the time opens up an interesting potential subtext to the seemingly innocent "Jabberwocky." Could the Jabberwock, the Jubjub bird, and the Bandersnatch (notice how these names have a certain Germanic ring to them linguistically), all of which are portrayed as bestial, savage creatures in the poem, be the Germanic "barbarians" in disguise? Could the poem's hero (the boy out to prove his manhood) be a symbol of a Britain that needs to go out and tame the Jabberwock of a rising Germany? In light of the time's political environment, Carroll may have been subconsciously expressing a fear that many Britons would have felt in 1872.

It's important to emphasize, however, that interpretations such as the German and African connections to "Jabberwocky" discussed above may be thought-provoking but ultimately tenuous. Carroll, after all, was not the most politically active member of Victorian society, so viewing "Jabberwocky" in terms of the geopolitical machinations of the day may be reading too much into the poem. For instance, it has been well-documented that the first stanza of "Jabberwocky" was written in 1855, at a time when Germany wasn't seen by the English as such a big threat. Still, it may be naive and presumptuous to think that England's global chess game of colonialism in the Victorian era had no effect on Carroll, consciously or subconsciously. Concern *was* mounting in England over Germany in 1872, and ironically in the case of Carroll, such concern may have been warranted. As noted by author Anne Clark in *Lewis Carroll: A Biography,* Dr. Robert Scott, co-author of the *Greek Lexicon,* "wrote an excellent German translation" of "Jabberwocky" in February 1872, soon after the poem's initial appearance in *Through the Looking-Glass* around Christmas, 1871. Moreover, as Clark reports in her book, Scott claimed that his translation was the original and that Carroll's poem was the translation! Even then, it seems, England and Germany were girding themselves for a struggle—if not for control of Europe, then at least for control of the authorship of "Jabberwocky."

Colonial Africa

Germany wasn't the only source of concern for England in the 1870s, however. Along with other European states, Britain was deeply immersed in a chess game for control of strategic parts of Africa, and it wouldn't be long before the British and Afrikaners of Dutch descendency would battle over tracts of Africa in the first Boer War of 1880–81. Africa, interestingly enough, was a source of great wonderment for Britons around the time "Jabberwocky" was published, with new species of flora and fauna being discovered every year. British explorer Henry Morgan Stanley's highly publicized search for Dr. David Livingstone in the jungles of Africa was very much in the public imagination at the time. Stanley found Livingstone in 1871, the same year in which "Jabberwocky" first appeared in print, though the official publication date for *Through the Looking-Glass* is 1872. This popular fascination with the dark secrets of Africa may have influenced the verbal choices made by Carroll in "Jabberwocky." The Jubjub bird, the Bandersnatch, the Tumtum tree—are these descriptive, tonally captivating names all that different from the names of real-life African species, such as the bongo and the tsetse fly, being discovered at the time?

Conrad's Heart of Darkness

This African connection also seems relevant to the poem's theme of the heroic quest in the sense that the hero (in this case the boy searching for the Jabberwock) had to journey often to the darkest, farthest reaches of the known world to slay the dreaded incarnation of evil, whatever it may be. And during Carroll's lifetime, no place in the known world was viewed as darker, more mysterious, and more potentially life-threatening than Africa. In fact, it wouldn't be long before the theme of the journey into the center of evil and depravity, as set in Africa, would be captured unforgettably by novelist Joseph Conrad in *Heart of Darkness* (1899), which chronicles the journey of a character named Marlow down the Congo River in search of a madman named Kurtz, who has attained godhood status among certain tribespeople in the jungle. Kurtz and the Jabberwock are agents of evil and chaos whom Marlow and Carroll (in the guise of the boy) are trying to neutralize and thus control.

Critical Overview

"Jabberwocky," the central poem in *Through the Looking-Glass,* is typically categorized as a nonsense poem. It has, however, been taken seriously by writers, as well as by scholars of literature, logic, and language. For example, the portmanteaus in "Jabberwocky" are a primary element of composition adopted by the Irish writer James Joyce for his modernist novel *Finnegans Wake*. Indeed, Martin Gardner draws a compelling parallel between the poem and the abstraction of the modernist painting of Picasso; however, his conclusion that Carroll is concerned with the sound of words over the sense of words indicates a lighthearted play that many logicians and linguists would deny. What Patricia Meyer Spacks says about the seriousness of *Through the Looking-Glass* is typically categorized as a nonsense poem. It is specifically true of "Jabberwocky": that Carroll's singular gift is the ease with which he conceals the significance of the logic of his work, so that the amusing wordplay is simultaneously its profound logical center.

Carroll was himself a philosopher and logician. The prevailing opinion, nevertheless, is that his best logic appears in the *Alice* books. As the English critic Edmund Wilson has noted, the poetry and logic in Carroll's work are inextricably linked. Roger W. Holmes points out, further, that Carroll not only explores the very history of the English language in the nonsense word constructions of "Jabberwocky," but also examines how words come to have meaning. And in fact, English poet and critic William Empson has proposed that words may acquire meaning when, as in "Jabberwocky," they are so pleasurable to say and to listen to that they thus seem to make their own sense simply by their sounds.

John Ciardi, an American poet and critic, explores this phenomenon in *How Does a Poem Mean?*, declaring that words are not the only means by which we communicate; in fact, there is a musical force in language developed from the sounds of words. The most important of Ciardi's observations on "Jabberwocky" develops the notion that there is a dance to the music of the sounds of words going on beneath the meanings of words. This dance invokes image, mood, and gesture as a fundamental component of what he refers to as "the poetic performance" of a poem. For Ciardi the typical reading or "performance" of "Jabberwocky" as nonsense belies the meaningful comment it makes on a recognizable topic. He interprets Carroll's comic treatment of the hero and ballad in the poem as an allegory about the pretentious and stuffy Victorian times during which Carroll wrote. Clearly, there is validity in reading the poem as such a commentary, and in fact there have been several widely ranging allegorical explications offered for this poem. However, as Ciardi says, no poem is constructed of words by themselves, and individual associations of image, mood, and gesture will dance with the meanings of words to create varying interpretations of what any poem "means." Carroll's inventive wordplay in "Jabberwocky" has left room for interpretation of the poem along the spectrum from nonsense poem to highly specific allegory.

Criticism

Cliff Saunders

Saunders teaches writing and literature in the Myrtle Beach, South Carolina, area and has published six chapbooks of poetry. In the following essay, he examines Carroll's need to impose order on the chaotic characters and language in "Jabberwocky."

In the history of literature, no writer was apparently more "sane" than Lewis Carroll, one of the most beloved children's authors in the world. On the surface, at least, Carroll struck his contemporaries as the paradigm of the rational, "adjusted" gentleman, one who was prized for his unflagging support of—and contributions to—British society in the Victorian era. Indeed, the numerous biographies and critical studies on Carroll all agree that unlike many poets in literary history, who either directly challenged the social order of the day or at least sought to live outside the accepted order, Carroll was very much an "insider" who would have considered upsetting the established order a foolhardy venture and perhaps even a gross, punishable offense. Here was no literary rebel à la French symbolist poet Charles Baudelaire, American experimental poet e. e. cummings, or Marxist poet Pablo Neruda of Chile, but a committed acolyte of the status quo. To undermine the order and structure of Victorian society would have been unthinkable to Carroll. And yet, underneath that surface of manners and propriety, deep within the recesses of his subconscious mind, a repressed irrationality kept demanding expression, kept demanding to be let *out.* His great nonsense poem "Jabberwocky" reveals this to be true, as do such absurd Carroll creations as the Mad Hatter and the hookah-smoking Caterpillar from *Alice's Adventures in Wonderland* (1865). More than perhaps any writer in history, Carroll stands as a testament to the fact that things aren't always what they seem.

The theme of reality versus appearance has long been a staple of literature. Prime examples of works using this theme include *Oedipus the King* by Greek tragedy writer Sophocles, *Othello* by English playwright William Shakespeare, and *The Red Badge of Courage* by American novelist Stephen Crane. For a fantacist such as Carroll, this theme is essential grist for the creative mill. After all, a world in which *anything* is possible, such as Carroll's *Wonderland*, turns everything topsy-turvy in such a way that the visible world (appearance) seems merely a flimsy veil that, when lifted, uncovers the absolute truth of things (reality). Here's another way of "looking" at this idea: when you stare into a mirror, you are not seeing the truth or the reality of yourself, only how you *appear* on the outside to yourself and others. The mirror is like the skin of your body, revealing only that which can be seen (i.e., perceived), but if you could peer beneath your skin or through the mirror, thus piercing the veil of the visible world, you would see the absolute reality behind all things and know the truth. Is it any wonder, then, that Carroll chose a mirror in *Through the Looking-Glass* (1872) to return his Alice to that other, hidden world where the truth resides, where, as in dreams, we see things for what they really are?

Behind that mirror, behind that skin of glass, exists a land of infinite wonder, a world where the ordinary becomes wondrous and the extraordinary becomes commonplace. Like our dreams, this world seems chaotic and insane at first, but a certain logic almost always manifests itself, a symbolic logic that eventually takes control of the dream and demands allegiance from the dreamer. A dream will often present a jumble of images early on, but usually some type of pattern will emerge before the dreamer awakens. Similarly, in *Through the Looking-Glass,* Carroll imposes order upon the chaos in the form of a giant chessboard, bringing rules and regulations to a land where none seemingly exist. Rationality and orderliness were of paramount importance to Carroll (his complaints about the unruliness of his young male students at Christ Church in Oxford, where he was a mathematical lecturer for many years, are legendary), and time and again throughout his body of work, Carroll creates situations where things seem to be wildly irrational and disorderly and then tries to impose order on the chaos. "Jabberwocky"—which first appeared in *Through the Looking-Glass* (1872), the book in which Carroll most tried to bring order to an ostensibly insane world—is no exception.

> " *By slaying the Jabberwock, whose name itself connotes mindless disorder, the boy (and, by extension, Carroll himself) brings the 'chaos of reality' under control . . . .*"

As noted by scholar Richard Kelly in *Lewis Carroll,* Carroll possessed three "qualities of mind—meticulousness, logicality, and orderliness—that made him "the genius of nonsense." Kelly goes on to say that in his nonsense writing, Carroll "implicitly acknowledges the terrifying absurdity and chaos of reality and proceeds to deal with it as if it were capable of control." This strategy is executed symbolically in "Jabberwocky" when the boy slays the frightening Jabberwock, a wild beast that, like Grendel in *Beowulf,* represents the dark forces of chaos and irrationality. By slaying the Jabberwock, whose name itself connotes mindless disorder, the boy (and, by extension, Carroll himself) brings the "chaos of reality" under control in a fashion. Viewed on another level, Carroll attempts to bring the irrational side of language under control as well, for the Jabberwock (emphasis on "jabber"?) represents not only the disorderly side of life on Earth but also the capacity of words to create irrational associations. This is what makes Carroll's choice of the title "Jabberwocky" so appropriate for the poem. Broken down into its constituent parts, the word suggests both the ability to *jabber* (i.e., mindless chattering) and that which is *wacky,* establishing a provocative synthesis that equates language (or at least its capacity for creating confusion and disorder) with the irrational mind. Seen in this light, then, the Jabberwock represents more than just the "chaos of reality"; it also represents the inherent chaos of language, a chaos that Carroll—as do other poets in their poems, nonsense or otherwise—wants to bring under control, to fit into logical patterns. In a sense, Carroll slays the Jabberwock of language in his nonsense classic, ensuring that control wins out over chaos in the end. Or does it?

In his examination of "Jabberwocky" in *Lewis Carroll,* Kelly cogently points out that the

What Do I Read Next?

- Several of the characters in "Jabberwocky" make a return visit in Carroll's *The Hunting of the Snark: An Agony in Eight Fits* (1876). Like "Jabberwocky," *The Hunting of the Snark* is considered a masterpiece of nonsense verse.

- Published toward the end of his life, Carroll's *Sylvie and Bruno* (1889) and its sequel, *Sylvie and Bruno Concluded* (1893), have not enjoyed nearly the popularity that the two Alice books have. Still, these somewhat neglected books abound in fantasy and nonsense elements and offer some pleasurable reading.

- Carroll, a lecturer in Mathematics at Christ Church in Oxford for many years, was as fascinated with logic as he was with fantasy and nonsense verse. For a look into this side of the author of *Alice's Adventures in Wonderland,* his book *Symbolic Logic* (1896) makes for a thought-provoking read.

- Although Carroll and his great nonsense-verse contemporary, Edward Lear (1812–1888), never met, it is widely believed that Carroll was greatly influenced by Lear's nonsense verse. An excellent choice for encountering Lear's equally zany world is *The Book of Nonsense,* originally published in 1846.

- For a time, Carroll maintained a friendship and correspondence with the great English poet laureate Alfred Lord Tennyson (1809–1892). Carroll, an early buff in the dawning age of photography, even took some photos of Tennyson and his family. For a look at the kind of "serious" poetry being composed in Victorian England, the kind of poetry that Carroll was never able to master, Tennyson's poems are widely anthologized and published in a number of hefty collections. A particularly comprehensive collection is Tennyson's *Poems and Plays* (1973).

- While several anthologies of nonsense verse are available, a particularly choice one is *The Faber Book of Nonsense Verse* (1979), edited by Gregory Grisson. The book offers poems by such nonsense masters as Carroll, Lear, Christian Morgenstern, A. E. Housman, and Walter de la Mare.

---

poem's "central interest … is not in its story line but in its language." While the mock-heroic battle between good and evil is fun in its own right, this aspect of the poem deals with the *known,* with the familiar, and as such is unremarkable. Ultimately, it is the *unknown,* the unfamiliar, that really sparks the reader's imagination in "Jabberwocky" and that places this piece in the pantheon of nonsense verse. What it all boils down to is music, the universal language, and Carroll has not been given nearly enough credit over the decades for this component of his poetic writings. In the case of "Jabberwocky," almost all of the critical attention has been focused on Carroll's clever creation of so-called portmanteau words, in which two words are synthesized into a new one. The example from "Jabberwocky" used most often to illustrate this technique is *slithy,* which, according to no less a literary authority than Humpty Dumpty, is a synthesis of *lithe* and *slimy.* Another portmanteau word, as suggested earlier in this essay, is the poem's title, a synthesis of *jabber, wacky,* and perhaps a dash of *mock* thrown in for good measure. This is all eye-catching in its cleverness and playfulness, but it's the very *sounds* of the words themselves—along with the syntactical and metrical patterns in which Carroll places them—that truly make "Jabberwocky" a memorable reading experience. More likely than not, it isn't the boy's heroic quest for the Jabberwock that young readers most recall but that incredible first stanza, so perfect in its nonsensical power that Carroll couldn't help repeating it as the poem's final stanza:

> 'Twas brillig, and the slithy toves
> Did gyre and gimble in the wabe:
> All mimsy were the borogoves,
> And the mome raths outgrabe.

Aside from its loose iambic tetrameter structure (four beats of short-long stresses), this quatrain masterfully integrates a number of sonic and tonal elements crucial to good poetry. Among them are assonance (e.g., the soft "i" tone of "brillig," "Did," "gimble," and "mimsy"); consonance (e.g., the repeating "b" in "brillig," "gimble," "wabe," "borogoves," and "outgrabe" and the repeating "g" in "brillig," "gimble," "borogoves," and "outgrabe"); and alliteration (e.g., "'Twas" and "toves," "wabe" and "were," and "mimsy" and "mome"). Together, these elements create a highly kinetic fabric of sound and tonality, and without this most musical quatrain, it is difficult to imagine "Jabberwocky" gaining the popularity it has over time. True, "Jabberwocky" offers other memorable words and sound patterns, such as "burbled" and "O frabjous day!" However, they are nestled in a more understandable context (stanzas 2–6, where Carroll incorporates a greater number of common words to recount the boy's heroic quest) and thus lack the dense wallop of the first/last stanzas, which sacrifice nearly all meaning to pure sound. Today, as in the past, learning institutions encourage readers of poetry to look for meaning first and to subordinate all else to this investigation. In "Jabberwocky," Carroll playfully reminds us that, first and foremost, poetry is about the music—sound, rhythm, meter, tonality—of language and that meaning should always be a secondary consideration ("A poem should not mean / But be"—Archibald Macleish). After all, good poems have multiple meanings, and besides, if meaning were the be-all and end-all of poetry, how could nonsense verse even exist, let alone thrive?

And thrive it has, thanks in no small measure to Carroll. His influence can be seen in such twentieth-century poets as e. e. cummings (another master fabricator of new words), Gertrude Stein (who often stressed sound, rhythm, and repetition over meaning), and such committed Dadaists as Tristan Tzara who, in the years around World War I, wrote absurdist, nonsensical poems to reflect what they saw as the apparent meaninglessness of life on Planet Earth. Cummings, Tzara, and others like them saw themselves as literary rebels, questioning everything around them, from government and industry to the arts and religion. Frankly, these poets would have shocked Carroll, that standard-bearer of the status quo. Carroll would have undoubtedly seen their verbal attacks on the social order as "bad form." Of course, much transpired between 1872 (the year "Jabberwocky" was published and a relatively tranquil year for England)

and World War I, when all hell broke loose around the world, when the many transgressions of Western civilization at the time became too blatant to ignore. For Carroll, though, Western civilization, guided over by the then-powerful Britain, made all the "sense" in the world. Which makes a poem like "Jabberwocky" even more remarkable. In his poem, Carroll may have tried to bring the irrational Jabberwock under rational control, but at poem's end, those "slithy toves" are still gyrating and gimbling "in the wabe," suggesting that at least subconsciously, even Carroll knew that the irrational side of life is too strong and constant to be fully controlled. Perhaps he even secretly wished that it would never be.

Source: Cliff Saunders, in an essay for *Poetry for Students,* Gale Group, 2001.

Paul Witcover

Witcover's fiction and critical essays appear regularly in magazines and online. In the following essay, he examines the relationship between sense and nonsense in Lewis Carroll's poem, "Jabberwocky."

What is one to make of Carroll's "Jabberwocky"? As Alice herself remarks in *Through the Looking-Glass* after reading the poem for the first time, "It seems very pretty ... but it's *rather* hard to understand! ... Somehow it seems to fill my head with ideas—only I don't exactly know what they are!"

Anyone who has read this masterpiece of nonsense verse, which has mystified, amused, and inspired generations of children and adults, can sympathize with Alice's reaction. "Jabberwocky" rarely fails to inspire equal measures of puzzlement, anxiety, and delight in any but the dullest of readers. Indeed, these qualities seem to mutually reinforce each other, so that the less a reader understands exactly what the poem is about, in a traditional sense, the more he or she enjoys it. The more a reader enjoys it, the more he or she is driven to understand it, to devise (in the manner of Humpty Dumpty) rational explanations not only for its content but for its stimulating effect on the senses and the intellect. These explanations, however ingenious (or tedious), are always more or less failures, however, and the cycle begins anew. The result can be an enchantment that lasts a lifetime. Some of the greatest artists and writers of the twentieth century have acknowledged a debt to "Jabberwocky" and the other creative works of Carroll, among them James Joyce (whose masterpiece *Finnegans Wake* is rich in Car-

> " *Carroll playfully reminded his readers ... that at the very heart of sense lies nonsense, that order can tip into disorder at any time, and that sanity is very much in the eye, or mind, of the beholder.* "

rollian allusions) and Vladimir Nabokov (author of *Lolita,* who translated *Alice in Wonderland* into his native Russian). Carroll's influence is evident in the Surrealist and Dadaist movements of the 1920s and 30s and has even been detected in the Cubist style of painting developed by the artists Picasso and Braque. ("Now if you had the two eyes on the same side of the nose, for instance," Humpty Dumpty helpfully suggests to Alice in *Through the Looking-Glass.*) After World War II, writer and artist Theodore Geisel, better known as Dr. Seuss, brought the anarchic spirit of Carrollian nonsense back into the realm of children's books, and in the 1960s, *Alice in Wonderland* and *Through the Looking-Glass* became a kind of Bible—old testament and new—to elements of the counterculture. At present, Carroll's creative imagination has permeated every nook and cranny of popular culture, from music to movies to advertising. In fact, it has been estimated that only Shakespeare and the Bible are quoted more frequently than Charles Lutwidge Dodgson, the shy and stammering Oxford mathematician and logician who wrote under the pseudonym of Lewis Carroll.

If every explanation of "Jabberwocky" is doomed to be more or less a flop, then why bother to write (or, more to the point, read) an essay about it? While it's true that the poem cannot be fully explained or neatly pigeonholed (and few good poems *can* be), that needn't be the aim of an essay ... and it's certainly not the aim of this one. But how to talk about what writer and critic Joyce Carol Oates, in her essay "First Loves: From 'Jabberwocky' to 'After Apple-Picking,'" has called "the greatest nonsense poem in English"?

A logical place to start would seem to be the word "nonsense" itself. *The New Shorter Oxford English Dictionary* defines "nonsense" as "[t]hat which is not sense or which differs from sense; absurd or meaningless words or ideas ..." But this is not quite as helpful as might have been hoped; it seems that to understand what is meant by "nonsense," we must first understand what is meant by "sense." Another trip to the *Shorter Oxford* yields "[m]eaning, signification .... The meaning of a word or phrase; ... the way a word etc. is to be understood within a particular context ..." as well as "[t]he mental faculties in a state of sanity; one's reason or wits." Now we have something to work with. Sense has to do with meaning and signification—that is, with words, which signify or stand for things, and whose meanings coincide with the things they signify. Equally important for our purposes is the linguistic connection between sanity and the meaning and signification of words. Consider the word "chair," for instance. Everyone knows what a chair is and what the word signifies. Using the word "chair" to signify the object in which people sit is not only, as the saying goes, to talk sense, it's also preeminently sane; it reflects the speaker's acceptance of and participation in a cultural system in which certain rules are followed in speech and action to facilitate understanding between large numbers of people. What if, however, someone comes along who uses the word "chair" to refer to a different object, or to many different objects interchangeably, or as a verb or adjective instead of a noun, and calls the thing people sit in by another name entirely, such as "bathtub," or even a made-up word like "wubble"? Such an individual would be said to be "talking nonsense" and might even be labeled insane, perhaps with good reason. But setting such behavior and its unpleasant consequences aside, what if one were simply to repeat the word "chair" over and over again to oneself? What could be the harm in that? Try it and see. A curious phenomenon occurs in which the signifier (the word "chair") becomes separated from the signified (the object used by people to sit in), with an existentially dizzying and discomfiting result. A certain arbitrariness is revealed at the heart of language, which we normally use almost as thoughtlessly as we breathe air and take as much for granted as the earth beneath our feet. Viewed this way, the authority of a dictionary like the *Shorter Oxford* is undermined; this cornerstone of sensibility and rationality, on which the edifice of comprehensible language, and hence civilization itself, depends, seems not quite so firmly cemented in place as it once had. Indeed, the closer one looks, the more shaky the whole construction seems, as if the mere act of inquiring into the meaning and signification of words and language renders them increasingly unstable, and what we'd always comfortably assumed to be a fortress of sense turns out to be—to have always been—a Tower of Babble. Better, perhaps, not to look at all!

Carroll was not the first to discover (or rediscover, rather, for children instinctively know it) this strange and strangely alarming property of words not only to construct but to deconstruct reality, often simultaneously, but he was the first to apply the insight in literature in a systematic, consciously subversive (in other words, modern) way. This is what elevates Carroll's work above that of lesser but more prolific artists like Edward Lear; charming as Lear's nonsense verse (such as "The Owl and the Pussycat") undoubtedly can be, he is not in Carroll's league by a long shot. In "Jabberwocky" and other works, Carroll playfully reminded his readers (who, it should be remembered, were the children of the middle and upper classes of Victorian England, a society which enshrined concepts of good sense and rational order among its chief virtues) that at the very heart of sense lies nonsense, that order can tip into disorder at any time, and that sanity is very much in the eye, or mind, of the beholder. "You may call it 'nonsense' if you like," remarks the Red Queen to Alice in *Through the Looking-Glass,* "but *I've* heard nonsense, compared with which that would be as sensible as a dictionary!" Indeed. Or, as the Cheshire Cat laconically puts it in *Alice in Wonderland,* "[W]e're all mad here. I'm mad. You're mad."

In the best of Carroll's fiction and poetry, nonsense and madness (qualities as closely linked as Tweedledum and Tweedledee) are not characterized so much by an absence of sense and sanity as by their abundance, if not super-abundance. In his essay "What is a Boojum? Nonsense and Modernism," critic Michael Holquist observes that "nonsense, in the writings of Lewis Carroll, at any rate, does not mean gibberish; it is not chaos, but the opposite of chaos. It is a closed field of language in which the meaning of any unit is dependent on its relationship to the system of the other constituents." Critic Elizabeth Sewell expresses the idea more plainly, and less restrictively, in her essay "The Balance of Brillig": "Nonsense is a game with words." Few writers have played the nonsense game as skillfully as Lewis Carroll, and Carroll himself never played it as purely as he did in "Jabberwocky."

"Jabberwocky" appears in *Through the Looking-Glass,* first published in 1872, but its origins can be traced back to 1855. It was then that the twenty-three-year-old Charles Dodgson, in *Misch-Masch,* a magazine he wrote and illustrated for the amusement of his brothers and sisters, set down as a "curious fragment" of Anglo-Saxon poetry the opening stanza of what, seventeen years later, would become "Jabberwocky." The two versions are almost identical, with only small differences in spelling: "bryllyg" for the later "brillig," for example. As this essay will refer to the opening stanza of "Jabberwocky" in some detail, it seems a good idea to give it in its entirety:

> 'Twas brillig, and the slithy toves
> Did gyre and gimble in the wabe:
> All mimsy were the borogoves,
> And the mome raths outgrabe.

In that 1855 issue of *Misch-Masch,* Dodgson thoughtfully appended a glossary for the edification of his siblings, and the meanings elaborated therein are also nearly identical to the explanations put forward by Humpty Dumpty for Alice's edification in *Through the Looking Glass.* There are, however, some notable exceptions. The meaning of the verb "gyre," for example, is given by Dodgson as to scratch like a dog, while Humpty Dumpty's far more satisfying definition is to spin like a gyroscope. In the case of almost every difference, in fact, Humpty Dumpty's explanations are the more successful as pure, inspired nonsense. But even if the younger Dodgson did not yet possess the mature creative imagination of his older alter ego, Carroll, he was no slouch in the nonsense department, as his literal English translation of the mock Anglo-Saxon verse, with its absurd echo of *The Song of Solomon,* demonstrates: "It was evening, and the smooth active badgers were scratching and boring holes in the hill-side; all unhappy were the parrots; and the grave turtles squeaked out."

This is an attempt, however ridiculous and satirical, to link the nonsensical words of the "curious fragment" to the normal, everyday world inhabited by Dodgson and his siblings. Humpty Dumpty makes no such attempt. He offers Alice no literal translation, offers her no bridge back to the other side of the looking glass; he merely explains the meanings of individual words with little or no regard for the sense of the passage as a whole. Many but by no means all of his meanings are derived from the application of what might be called the portmanteau rule, a portmanteau being a kind of suitcase. Here is Humpty Dumpty explaining the adjective "slithy": "Well, *'slithy'* means 'lithe and slimy.' 'Lithe' is the same as active. You see, it's like a portmanteau—there are two meanings packed up into one word." Another example of a portmanteau word, according to Humpty Dumpty, is "mimsy," which he unpacks into "flimsy and miserable." There is a peculiar dreamlike logic to this system, which contains in a nutshell, as it were, the foundations of Freudian psychoanalysis. In fact, so reasonable is this method that two of Carroll's portmanteau words have entered into common usage and are now to be found in all English dictionaries: "chortle" and "galumph." (Even odder, and more confusing, words that seem to be portmanteaus invented by Carroll, like "burble" and "whiffle," have pedigrees long predating him.) Humpty Dumpty also derives meaning through the suggestiveness of sounds and/or spellings; thus, the already mentioned "gyre" / "gyroscope" explanation, and "mome," which he tentatively suggests as being "short for 'from home'—meaning that they'd lost their way, you know." Here, too, there is some recognizable system at work (as well as an entirely characteristic note of melancholy and anxious distress whose shadowy presence in the *Alice* books has led hard-hearted, soft-headed moralists to proclaim them inappropriate for children). Finally, as with the noun "rath," which Humpty Dumpty describes as "a sort of green pig," there seems to be no easily identifiable system at work at all, but rather pure, unadulterated fancy.

In the end, each of these systems of extracting meaning from words explains the poem equally well—which is to say, not at all. This is part of the game Carroll is playing with his readers, a game of nonsense that is also a practical joke (and like all practical jokes, a little bit cruel). He teases his readers with the perfectly sensible expectation that every puzzle has a solution, one which, when found, will explain everything, thus rewarding the effort made in searching it out in the first place. This expectation, sensible though may be, is also, as far as Carroll is concerned, dead wrong. The circumstances in which Alice first encounters the poem "Jabberwocky" are a perfect illustration of Carroll's sly method. Soon after passing through the mirror and entering the world on the other side, Alice discovers a book filled with strange writing in a language she doesn't know. It baffles her for a moment, "until at last a bright thought struck her. 'Why, it's a Looking-glass book, of course! And if I hold it up to a glass, the words will all go the right way again.'" Which of course is just what happens ("glass" being a synonym for "mirror"). *Voila!* The puzzle has been solved. Or has it? Although she

can now read the words of "Jabberwocky" perfectly well, poor Alice can no more understand them than when they'd been written (from her perspective) backwards. Another practical joke along these lines is Carroll's habit, already mentioned above, of mixing real words in with the made-up variety in such a way that they're indistinguishable from each other. In *Alice in Wonderland,* the Duchess expounds to Alice: "Take care of the sense, and the sounds will take care of themselves." On the other side of the looking glass, the opposite rule holds true: take care of the sounds, and the sense will take care of itself. As Alice says, "Somehow it seems to fill my head with ideas—only I don't exactly know what they are! However, *somebody* killed *something:* that's clear, at any rate." But *why* is it clear?

To answer that question, let's forget for a moment that "Jabberwocky" is part of a larger piece of fiction, *Through the Looking-Glass,* and consider it on its own, as a poem. It turns out that it's a meticulously structured poem; a lot of craziness may be going on at the surface, but below the surface order reigns. To begin with, although the number of syllables per line in each of the seven four-line stanzas varies slightly from the average of 8, 8, 8, 6, the number of feet or stresses are an unvarying 4, 4, 4, 3 (the metrical pattern is iambic; an unstressed followed by a stressed syllable). There is something inherently heroic and bestirring about this metre: it is the same used by the poet Samuel Taylor Coleridge to begin his visionary poetic fragment "Kubla Khan," for example (with the minor difference that Coleridge uses five lines—of rhyme scheme a, b, a, a, b—to Carroll's four). What else? The second and fourth lines of "Jabberwocky" invariably rhyme. The first and third lines rhyme as well in the first, second, fourth, and seventh stanzas, giving a rhyme scheme there of a, b, a, b. In the third, fifth, and sixth stanzas, the rhyme scheme is a, b, c, b; however, to make up for the missing rhyme between the first and third lines in these stanzas, Carroll has introduced an internal rhyme into the third line: "he" and "tree"; "dead" and "head"; "day" and "Calay!" The firm skeleton of "Jabberwocky" aids Alice's understanding, and the reader's, by providing the reassurance of an underlying structure that can be fleshed out with multiple meanings.

Equally if not more important is the careful balance of sense and nonsense words in the poem, and the use of nonsense words in ways that allow readers to ascribe to them if not meaning, then *function.* Even if we don't know what the various words might mean, we can identify what parts of speech they are. For example, returning to the first stanza we find the unfamiliar words "brillig," "slithy," "toves," "gyre," "gimble," "wabe," "mimsy," "borogoves," "mome," "raths," and "outgrabe." A lot of unfamiliar words to digest! But we know more valuable things about them than Humpty Dumpty can reveal with his various methodologies of meaning extraction. Because of the internal structure or grammar of the English language, we know that "brillig," following the word "'Twas," is a noun. Similarly, we know "slithy" is an adjective because of the "y" ending and because it is modifying "toves," another noun. "Gyre" is a verb because it follows "did," and so is "gimble," while "wabe" is another noun. And so on. Joyce Carol Oates describes the operation of this process on young readers in "From 'Jabberwocky' to 'After Apple-Picking'": "For young children, whose brains are struggling to comprehend language, words are magical in any case; the magic of adults, utterly mysterious; no child can distinguish between 'real' words and nonsensical or 'unreal' words, and verse like Lewis Carroll's brilliant 'Jabberwocky' has the effect of both arousing childish anxiety (what do these terrifying words mean?) and placating it (don't worry: you can decode the meaning by the context)."

All of which is true enough, but too serious, perhaps. After all, "Jabberwocky" wasn't written to educate children, but to amuse and entertain them. If anyone has been educated by "Jabberwocky," it's been the adults of the world, though one could certainly argue that not nearly enough of them have learned its uffish yet frabjous lessons.

Source: Paul Witcover, in an essay for *Poetry for Students,* Gale Group, 2001.

Caroline M. Levchuck

Levchuck, a writer and editor, has published articles on literature along with nonfiction essays and children's books. In this essay, she focuses on Carroll's "Jabberwocky" as the perfect portmanteau poem.

Lewis Carroll's poem "Jabberwocky" has long been categorized as a shining example of nonsense verse. Carroll employs what is called amphigory, which is, in essence, nonsense verse that appears to have meaning but in fact has none. This classification, however, should not be taken at face value to mean that the poem hasn't any meaning. In fact, "Jabberwocky" is rife with meaning (and meanings, because of Carroll's introduction of new

words). It conveys not only a tale but also offers a commentary of sorts not only on Anglo-Saxon poetry but on the literature of the Victorian era in which Carroll created. It is a poem that works on two distinct levels, conveying different ideas, making it a portmanteau poem. "Jabberwocky" works in two distinct manners, first as a stand-alone poem with rich imagery and a compelling narrative that comes full circle. Secondly, it serves as a commentary on the English language and literature, sometimes celebratory, at other times mocking their conventions.

The beginnings, literally, of "Jabberwocky" first appeared in the appropriately named periodical put out by Carroll's family, *Misch-Masch* in 1855 under the title "Stanza of Anglo-Saxon Poetry." Carroll wrote and illustrated the issues of *Misch-Masch* almost exclusively for the purpose of amusing his younger siblings. What would become the very first stanza, then, of "Jabberwocky" appeared in the periodical as such:

"Twas bryllg, and ye slythy toves / did gyre and gymble in ye wabe: / All mimsy were ye borogoves; / And ye mome raths outgrabe."

Carroll generously provided some interpretation of the lines for his relations. As the poem grew into its later incarnation of "Jabberwocky" as part of *Through the Looking-Glass,* he supplied readers with an interpretation by allowing Humpty Dumpty to explicate some of the more obscure words' meanings. Of course, it has been long pointed out that Humpty Dumpty is a rather unreliable source. However, because of the manner in which Carroll used these new words (some of which are actually old words or variations thereof) which Humpty Dumpty deemed "portmanteau" words, it allowed readers to come to their own conclusions as to the meanings of the terms.

When used in *Through the Looking-Glass,* young Alice comes across the poem "Jabberwocky" in a book and can only read it when viewing its reflection in a mirror, or looking glass. Upon first perusal of it, Alice proclaims, "Somehow it fills my head with ideas—only I don't exactly know what they are! However, *somebody* killed *something:* that's clear, at any rate—." When Humpty Dumpty offers his insight into the poem, he points out that the nonsensical words are "portmanteau" words; that is, two words placed together to form one word with a single meaning.

In its extended form, then, Carroll sets a rather idyllic scene, speaking of it being evening and talking of the creatures that inhabit the pastoral landscape. A father warns his young son of a mythical creature known as the Jabberwock, which possesses "jaws that bite" and "claws that catch!" He makes mention too of the other dangerous creatures that are associated with the Jabberwock. The son, perhaps in part out of his naiveté, embarks on a journey to locate the monster, stopping along the way to collect his thoughts. Before the boy can find the beast, it finds him. From the monster's noises, the boy realizes it is approaching and, using his sword, stabs and beheads the creature. He then returns home, triumphantly. The father is proud of his son's heroic efforts. The poem then repeats the first stanza, coming full circle to reinforce the fact that the earlier peace had returned and all was as it should have been.

The reason the poem is considered a nonsense poem, primarily, is its use of these so-called portmanteau words. For example, Carroll refers to the evening as "brillig" (changed from its initial spelling of "bryllg"), which is a reference, according to Carroll himself, of the time of broiling things, i.e., dinner. Other portmanteau words are slithy (first published as "slythy"—a combination of slimy and lithe), mimsy (the marriage of flimsy and miserable). Other words are not portmanteau words but rather hearken back to old English, such as borogoves (an extinct kind of parrot) and toves (a type of badger). It should also be noted that, when Carroll offered his explanation of his "Stanza of Anglo-Saxon Poetry," he referred to the entirety of the initial idyllic scene (in which the raths ran out of their nests in the hills, in particular) as "an obscure, but yet deeply-affecting relic of ancient Poetry."

In looking at the story that is unfolding underneath the surface of these nonsensical words that blur the overt meaning of the text, it is easy to understand why "Jabberwocky" might initially be dismissed as simply a jumble of nonsense itself as, the title implies, it will be gibberish about the Jabberwock. However, there is a clear and distinct narrative, as discussed above. Furthermore, the structure of the poem itself has its roots in some of the most classical forms of poetry. For example, because of the subject matter of the poem, it may be likened to an epic poem, also known as a heroic poem, similar to that of *Beowulf,* in which the main character journeys to slay uber-beast Grendl. "Jabberwocky" also possesses the characteristics of a ballad (which is usually a song) in that it tells a story, usually of heroic knights. In a sense, then, "Jabberwocky," with its sing-song words, may be considered as something of a ballad. Also, the poem possesses some of the same qualities of the ballad in that certain stanzas contain rhyme schemes particular to the ballad (only the third, fifth, and sixth stanzas do this). On top of these devices, though, Carroll has added the element of mockery. This is evident in the fact that he injects seemingly absurd content into several classic forms of poetry, thus ridiculing the form and style of these types of poetry. Present too, according to some critics, is the device of allegory. An allegory refers to when symbolism is used to point to other things, thus infusing the poem with meaning on another level. Specifically, the poet John Ciardi, in his *How Does a Poem Mean?* posits that "Jabberwocky" is Carroll's veiled commentary on the confinements of the standard style of writing during the Victorian era.

The second part of Carroll's portmanteau poem is that it functions as a teaching manual not only for poetry in its references to established forms of poetry but in its treatment of language. While Carroll offers up explanations for several of the nonsense words in the poem, many can be discerned by simply deconstructing each stanza and looking at each nonsense word in the context of the part of speech it represents. Clearly, brillig is a noun and slithy is modifying the plural noun toves, who "were gyre[ing] and gimble[ing]"—both verbs—"in the wabe," which, because of its placement must be a noun. "Jabberwocky," in fact, is so famous for possessing this quality that contemporary teachers will use this fun, multidimensional poem as a way to introduce their students to the parts of speech.

Other important lessons of literature that may be imparted by a careful study of "Jabberwocky" include alliteration, assonance, and onomatopoeia. Alliteration, which is the repetition of consonant sounds either in two (or more) words or syllables, is present in several ways. Carroll uses this device throughout the poem, specifically in referencing the "Tumtum tree," "snicker-snack," "beamish boy," "Callooh! Callay?" Onomatopoeia, a term that refers to the sound of a word reflecting its meaning, is also put to extremely effective use, particularly with the portmanteau words. Nearly all of these hybrid words belie their meaning simply by their sounds. Galumphing seems to imply a sort of triumphant galloping on a horse. Other examples of words whose sounds point to their context include burbled, uffish, and whiffling. Assonance, which refers to words having similar sounds, is present in the phrases "raths outgrabe," "vorpal sword," and "manxome foe."

"Jabberwocky," then, with all of its seemingly swirling confusion actually makes perfect sense. Its presentation in *Through the Looking Glass* —that it must be read by viewing its contents in a mirror (which is something that usually renders things illegible) and its nonsensical elements, may cause it to appear upon first glance to be a throwaway poem, something that Carroll rifled off with nary a thought. Upon closer examination, though, this multi-layered poem is a shining example of a portmanteau. Clearly, the fact that Carroll first introduced the work in 1855 and revisited it again in *Through the Looking Glass,* published in 1882, is evidence, together with the poem's complexities, that Carroll put much thought into constructing this famous verse. "Jabberwocky" works in two distinct manners, first as a stand-alone poem with rich imagery and a compelling narrative that comes full circle. Secondly, it serves as a commentary on the English language and literature, sometimes celebratory, at other times mocking their conventions. Elements and devices of literature are here aplenty and, thus, "Jabberwocky" can serve as a stand-alone entrée to poetry.

Source: Caroline M. Levchuck, in an essay for *Poetry for Students,* Gale Group 2001.

Sources

Alkalay-Gut, Karen, "Carroll's JABBERWOCKY," in *The Explicator,* Vol. 6, No. 1, Fall, 1987, pp. 27–31.

Bloom, Harold, ed., *Lewis Carroll,* Chelsea House Publishers, 1987.

Brown, Lesley, ed., *The New Shorter Oxford English Dictionary,* Clarendon Press, 1993.

Ciardi, John, ed., *How Does a Poem Mean?*, Houghton Mifflin, 1960; revised and enlarged by John Ciardi and Miller Williams, Houghton Mifflin, 1975.

Clark, Anne, *Lewis Carroll: A Biography,* Schocken Books, 1979.

Empson, William, "'Alice in Wonderland,'" in *Some Versions of Pastoral,* New Directions, 1935, pp. 253–94.

Goldfarb, Nancy, "Carroll's JABBERWOCKY," *in The Explicator,* Vol. 57, No. 2, Winter, 1999, pp. 86–88.

Holmes, Roger W., "The Philosopher's 'Alice in Wonderland,'" in *Aspects of Alice: Lewis Carroll's Dreamchild as Seen through the Critics' Looking-Glasses, 1865–1971,* edited by Robert Phillips, Vanguard, 1971, pp. 159–74.

Holquist, Michael, "What Is a Boojum? Nonsense and Modernism," in *Alice In Wonderland,* A Norton Critical Edition, 2d ed., edited by Donald Gray, W. W. Norton & Company, 1971, p. 390.

Hudson, Derek, *Lewis Carroll,* Greenwood Press, 1972.

Kelly, Richard, *Lewis Carroll: Revised Edition,* Twayne Publishers, 1990.

Oates, Joyce Carol, "First Loves: From 'Jabberwocky' to 'After Apple-Picking,'" in *American Poetry Review,* Vol. 28, Issue 6, p. 9.

Sewell, Elizabeth, "The Balance of Brillig," in *Alice in Wonderland,* Norton Critical Edition, 2d ed., edited by Donald Gray, W. W. Norton & Company, 1971, p. 387.

Spacks, Patricia Meyer, "Logic and Language in 'Through the Looking-Glass,'" in *Aspects of Alice: Lewis Carroll's Dreamchild as Seen through the Critics' Looking-Glasses, 1865–1971,* Vanguard, 1971, pp. 267–78.

Wilson, Edmund, "C. L. Dodgson: The Poet Logician," in *Aspects of Alice: Lewis Carroll's Dreamchild as Seen through the Critics' Looking-Glasses, 1865–1971,* edited by Robert Phillips, Vanguard, 1971, pp. 198–206.

For Further Reading

Cooke, John D., and Lionel Stevenson, *English Literature of the Victorian Period,* Russell & Russell, 1949.

This is a comprehensive overview of the Victorian era's politics, science, religion, and culture. It explores the era's top English poets and fiction writers, including Alfred Lord Tennyson, Matthew Arnold, Charles Dickens, George Eliot, and Carroll himself. The section on "Literature for Children" is somewhat threadbare, but overall, the book is a valuable resource.

Green, Roger Lancelyn, ed., *The Diaries of Lewis Carroll,* Cassell, 1953.

In 1854, Carroll began keeping a diary, which by the end of his life filled the equivalent of thirteen volumes. Nine of these thirteen volumes have been collected in Green's book, and they offer a probing look into the private life of Carroll.

Guiliano, Edward, ed., *Lewis Carroll Observed,* Clarkson N. Potter, Inc., 1976.

This is one of the most fascinating books about Carroll, his art, and his life. Edited by Guiliano for the Lewis Carroll Society of North America, the book contains unpublished photographs, drawings, and poems by Carroll as well as several essays about his varied artistic endeavors.

Guiliano, Edward, ed., *Lewis Carroll: A Celebration,* Clarkson N. Potter, Inc., 1982.

Guiliano does another fine job of pulling together fascinating material on Carroll and his art in this book. Among the many excellent essays in this collection are ones that explore Carroll's influence on the Surrealists and James Joyce's *Finnegan's Wake* and the importance of illustrator Sir John Tenniel in the success of the Alice books.

Tucker, Herbert F., ed., *A Companion to Victorian Literature & Culture,* Blackwell Publishers, 1999.

Offering a huge collection of essays, this book covers all aspects of Victorian society, from politics and economics to theology and literature. Of particular interest is Claudia Nelson's essay "Growing Up: Childhood," which examines the Victorians' obsession with childhood and the booming market in literature for children during that era.

The Milkfish Gatherers

James Fenton
1994

"The Milkfish Gatherers" appears in Fenton's 1994 collection *Out of Danger*. The poem is an example of New Formalism or poetry that has returned to the roots of more traditional English verse forms. Fenton, a British poet, takes W. H. Auden as a mentor for form but moves his own verse further into the realm of the social and political world. "The Milkfish Gatherers" is a more recent work, coming late in the poet's career. The poem makes use of Fenton's geographical wanderings and comments on the political and social history of the Philippines. On a metaphorical level, the poem is also a commentary on the state of contemporary poetry.

"The Milkfish Gatherers" tells the story of fishermen in Manila during the Philippines' century-long fight for political independence, which began when the country was ruled by Spain in the 1800s and continues to this day. The poem is about the revolutionary idea: how it is born, how it dwindles, and the hope of its return. At hopeful points, the poem anticipates a new future but settles at the end into the waiting time before the dormant revolution awakens. In the latter part of the poem, the Filipino story becomes a human story. The revolution becomes humanity's struggle to retain things of value, maintain dignity, and cultivate dreams of the future. The poem is also an example of an *ars poetica,* or a poem about the writing of poetry. In this way, the poem can be read as an extended metaphor. The fishermen are like poets, casting their lines, poetic lines, in an attempt to write some-

thing of value. The revolution, then, is one of language. The speaker muses about the current world of the contemporary poet; how the fish or the poems are milkfish or, in other words, nothing much.

Fenton's travels and experiences outside of his life as a poet give him a broad terrain in which to roam. This poem is representative of many of his works that take possession of alien subject matter—other cultures and the lives of people that encompass those cultures—and allow the alienation to be absorbed and formed into a more universal story.

Author Biography

Fenton was born in 1949 in Lincoln, England, to Mary Hamilton Ingoldby Fenton and John Charles Fenton, an Anglican priest. At the age of nine, Fenton was sent to musical preparatory school, then on to Repton Public School in Derbyshire, before entering Magdalen College in Oxford in 1967. Fenton began his stay at Oxford studying English with the poet John Fuller, who became his mentor and friend. But the life of a poet had little professional appeal to Fenton, who switched to a course of study of philosophy, psychology, and physiology—the three Ps. He believed he wanted to be an anthropologist. A school friend from those early days recalls that Fenton said he wanted a job like anyone else because one couldn't just be a poet. Fenton's pull to poetry began when he read "About this House," W. H. Auden's collection of verse. Fenton met Auden at a reading Auden gave at Fenton's school. A minor friendship between the two lasted until Auden's death in 1973.

When his mentor died in 1973, Fenton was already well on his way to establishing himself as a poet. In 1968, his first year at Oxford, he won the Newdigate Prize for the best poem by an undergraduate. The poem was a sonnet sequence called "Western Furniture," which chronicled the opening of Japan to Western culture. The poem was broadcast on British radio through the BBC and published in pamphlet form by his friend Fuller. As he was finishing "Western Furniture," Fenton had the urge to experiment with language and form. The resulting poems were interesting failures, but they contributed to Fenton's later vocabulary and tone.

In 1970, Fenton graduated Oxford and began his professional career as a freelance writer of literary reviews. By 1972, he had finished his first full-length collection of work titled *Terminal*

James Fenton

Moraine, which won the Gregory Award. Fenton used his prize money to travel to Cambodia and Vietnam, beginning a wanderlust that has lasted a lifetime. In the latter 1970s, Fenton's career spanned several journalistic pursuits, first as the political correspondent for *New Statesman,* then as the German correspondent for *The Guardian,* and, finally, as the theater critic for the *London Sunday Times,* a position he still holds.

Poem Text

The sea sounds insincere
Giving and taking with one hand.
It stopped a river here last month
Filling its mouth with sand.

They drag the shallows for the milkfish fry—   5
Two eyes on a glass noodle, nothing more.
Roused by his viligant young wife
The drowsy stevedore

Comes running barefoot past the swamp
To meet a load of wood.   10
The yellow peaked cap, the patched pink shorts
Seem to be all his worldly goods.

The nipa booths along the coast
Protect the milkfish gatherers' rights.

15

Nothing goes unobserved. My good custodian
Sprawls in the deckchair through the night.

Take care, he says, take care—
Not everybody is a friend.
And so he makes my life more private still—
A privacy on which he will attend.   20

But the dogs are sly with the garbage
And the cats ruthless, even with sliced bread,
As the terns are ruthless among the shoals.
Men watch the terns, then give the boat its head

Dragging a wide arc through the blue,   25
Trailing their lines,
Cutting the engine out
At the first sign.

A hundred feet away
Something of value struggles not to die.   30
It will sell for a dollar a kilo.
It weighs two kilos on the line—a prize.

And the hull fills with a fortune
And the improbable colours of the sea
But the spine lives when the brain dies   35
In a convulsive misery.

Rummagers of inlets, scourers of the deep,
Dynamite men, their bottles crammed with wicks,
They named the sea's inhabitants with style—
The slapped vagina fish, the horse's dick.   40

Polillo 'melts' means it is far away—
The smoking island plumed from slash and burn.
And from its shore, busy with hermit crabs,
Look to Luzon. Infanta melts in turn.

The setting sun behind the Sierra Madre   45
Projects a sharp blue line across the sky
And in the eastern glow beyond Polillo
It looks as if another sun might rise—

As if there were no night,
Only a brother evening and a dawn.   50
No night! No death! How could these people live?
How could the pressure lanterns lure the prawns?

Nothing of value has arrived all day—
No timber, no rattan. Now after dark,
The news comes from the sea. They crowd the   55
       beach
And prime a lantern, waiting for the shark.

The young receive the gills, which they will cook.
The massive liver wallows on the shore
And the shark's teeth look like a row of sharks
Advancing along a jaw.   60

Alone again by spirit light
I notice something happening on a post.
Something has burst its skin and now it hangs,
Hangs for dear life onto its fine brown ghost.

65

Clinging exhausted to its former self,
Its head flung back as if to watch the moon,
The blue-green veins pulsing along its wings,
The thing unwraps itself, but falls too soon.

The ants are tiny and their work is swift—
The insect-shark is washed up on their land—   70
While the sea sounds insincere,
Giving and taking with one hand.

At dawn along the seashore come
The milkfish gatherers, human fry.
A white polythene bowl   75
Is what you need to sort the milkfish by.

For a hatched fish is a pair of eyes—
There is nothing more to see.
But the spine lives when the brain dies
In a convulsive misery.   80

Poem Summary

Lines 1–4:

In this opening stanza, Fenton personifies the sea, allowing it to take on human characteristics. The sea "sounds insincere," sets an ominous tone for the poem. The word "insincere," coupled with its "giving" and "taking," prompts caution and distrust. It is a source of destruction, stopping the flow of the river. The physical setting of the poem is a place where the sea is unpredictable and unfriendly. If the poem is read as a metaphor for the writing and reception of poetry in contemporary times, the sea could be a raft of critics or a fickle audience giving and taking praise on a whim. This kind of sea stops a flow of descent literature, the "river," and fills the "mouth" of the poet "with sand." The sand prevents the art of poetry, reducing it to mediocrity.

Lines 5–8:

In this stanza, Fenton continues to build the scene. The reader is uncertain who "they" is. "They" might be fishermen or scroungers, dragging the sea for some gem of nourishment. They are trying to catch the milkfish, who lurk in the shallows. Milkfish are food fish found in the tropical Pacific and Indian Oceans. Fenton places the poem in the tropics. Later he will tell us that he is near Luzon, which is a city in the Philippines. The poem glosses the Filipino quest for independence, which has lasted from 1872 until the present time. In this quest, revolutionaries have been spied upon and killed. The fish that "they," the revolutionaries, are trying to catch are the different ideas of revolution. In this scenario, the revolutionary ideas available to "them" are toothless, bony fishes that look like "two eyes on a glass noodle," in other words, nothing much. If "they," the fisherman, were poets in the contemporary scene, they would be fishing for poems. The metaphor states that the poems being fished for are found in the shallows; they are a product of the shoals, toothless and bony. The current poems are, in other words, nothing much. At the end of the stanza, Fenton introduces people to this scene, a longshoreman and his wife. This "stevedore" is "drowsy" presumably from hard, thankless work, the work of the want-to-be revolutionary that doesn't know how to revolutionize.

Lines 9–12:

The stevedore, the want-to-be revolutionary/poet, is flushed out in this stanza. He is poor, running to "meet a load of wood," making a living. What he is wearing seems to be all "his worldly goods." Here, the speaker assesses him and almost seems to admire his poverty as an honest way to make a living in a political climate that does not breed integrity. Even in his oppressed state, there is something still bright about him in his hat and pink shorts, a subdued energy.

Lines 13–16:

In this stanza, the speaker becomes cynical. He talks about the "milkfish gatherers' rights," when, in fact, they seem to have no special rights but to scrounge and scurry in the shallows. The ominous tone returns to the poem with the acknowledgement that "nothing goes unobserved." There are no secrets on this shore. The speaker comments on the political scene in the Philippines, the putting down of the people during a century of struggle, the oppression of the "milkfish gatherers" who have nothing left to forfeit. The fact that nothing goes unobserved suggests that everyone is being watched and accused. The speaker has a watchdog, a political friend, who sits by him all night long during the darkest times. The "friend" is his protector. For the speaker as poet, nothing goes unobserved either. The poet is observed by history, a lineage of poets who have come before him. But who is the poet's guardian and protector? Fenton's guardians in the poetic world are his British forefathers, Auden and Philip Larkin. The poet's guardians are also his mentors, who can inadvertently hinder growth by protecting too much, dissuading the revolution of language with their safe and proven formulas.

Lines 17–20:

In this stanza, the guardian tells the speaker to "take care," that "not everyone is a friend." The speaker muses about this and becomes discouraged; by being cautious of everyone and everything, his life becomes lonelier. The political revolutionary has no friends and trusts no one. To take care is good advice for the poet as well, who is in danger of losing himself to the viciousness of the business of poetry, the past glories, and the push toward the commercial. To be set apart, for the poet, as well as for the revolutionary, is also the making of loneliness. The guardians, the poets with their big reputations and styles and voices are restrictive as well as protective to the poet. Their voices are the ones that will push the speaker into himself, into the private rather than the public world.

Lines 21–24:

This stanza transitions away from the people of the poem to a completely different scene. The conjunction "but" suggests that the animals in this stanza are connected to the previous stanzas, but how? The dogs, cats, and terns, each in their own turn act ruthlessly and slyly. It's as if they are spies wearing masks. The traits of the sea are now absorbed by these creatures. As the terns move among the shallows, they show the fishermen where to catch those easy milkfish. The men must calculate according to what the terns tell them to do if they are going to catch anything. The revolutionaries watch the big politicos much as the fishermen watch the terns. The fisherman is also the poet watching the turns (or "terns") of the audience, watching for anything that may point to some success. The terns as an audience tells the poet where to fish to get something that they, the audience, will eat. The audience, in other words, dictates the art. If the audience stays in the shallows, the art will too. The speaker eases up on the artist, seeing the artist as the one who is dictated to. If the art is shallow, it is because that is what the people want.

Lines 25–28:

Here the fishermen act out fishing. They drag their lines until there is some activity, then cut the engines when they see something move so as not to scare the fish away. They are cautious fishermen much as the revolutionaries must be cautious so as not to draw attention to themselves. The speaker implies that the contemporary poet also follows the fishermen's moves. The poet drags his poetic line, which can be quite beautiful as "a wide arch through the blue," but cuts the rhythm and momentum of the poem, its engine, when he sees the first sign that it may be eliciting some reaction from the public. The contemporary poet doesn't want to scare his audience away.

Media Adaptations

- An audiocassette called *Poets Night* features eleven poets, including Fenton, reading from their work and the work of their mentors, as they celebrate the contribution Farrar, Strauss, and Giroux has made to the publishing of poetry. The cassette was released in 1998 by Penguin audio books.

- A video recording on Fenton's translation of the Verdi opera *Rigoletto* was released by HBO Video in 1982.

Lines 29–32:

This stanza talks about the big fish, not the milkfish but the salmon that is caught in deep water; it is valuable and will fetch "a dollar a kilo," "a prize." The big fish is struggling not to die; but it will. The big fish for the Filipinos is the big revolutionary, the leader who carried within himself the big, valuable vision of a political future. In 1872, the idea of a revolution was first birthed. The revolution would die and come to life many times before being successful with the fall of Marcos. The poem implies that there is not a revolutionary capable of victory in the present circumstance. The big fish is also the vast, deep, and truly poetic poem. This rare and beautiful creature will fetch a lot, because there simply aren't a lot of rare and beautiful poems with big, epic, poetic visions. This kind of poem will flourish and die many times; it will die for lack of an audience and lack of poets who can write such poems.

Lines 33–36:

This stanza talks about making it big when the "improbable colours of the sea" fill up your boat and make you a fortune. For the revolutionary, it is going halfway, making a good show of revolution without committing all the way. For the poet, it means selling-out, shocking with language to make the big buck. The "improbable colours" for the poet are flashes in the pan, pretty trinkets without the gold—facades. This stanza marks the first time the poem's gutsy refrain appears. "The spine lives when the brain dies / In a convulsive misery."

The line implies that the thing of value that was struggling in the previous stanza has died. The revolutionary ideal and the new fresh poetic voice have expired. The will for revolution has not died, but the means by which to make the vision real have passed for now. The line suggests for poetry that the will to write well thrives in the contemporary world, but the intelligence by which to write the revolutionary poem has dissipated.

Lines 37–40:

In this stanza, the speaker introduces the Adams, the first namers of things, the people who took dares and risked danger to explore the world and name the things they found. These were magic people, "rummagers" who weren't afraid to get dirty, "scourers" who weren't afraid to get lost, and "dynamite men" who risked everything. Politically, these true historical revolutionaries are gone from the coast. There is only the stevedore and his wife running to fetch and carry. There are only people left to distrust. There are no risk takers or revolutionaries. This is suggestive of poetry as well. Here there are no Audens or poets like T. S. Eliot stretching the language, naming things through verse. The poet and the audience have become complacent, dictating each other's mediocrity. The magicians have vanished.

Lines 41–44:

The introduction of a foreign word into this stanza is the speaker's attempt to be a dynamite man, to stretch the language, to define and engage it. It is also a daring political act. The smoking island "plumed from slash and burn" connotes the mountain of garbage, Smokey Mountain, that burned in Manila during the reign of Marcos. The burning garbage is, indeed, a sign of the Marcos regime, a time and place of rot, death, and decay. Humanity's tendencies toward self-destruction are prevalent in this stanza. The little scavengers, the "hermit crabs," are left the scraps of this destruction, the fruits of the halfway revolution. The poet is also only left scraps. If art is a reflection of society, then humanity's various modes of self-destruction kill the poet as humanity kills itself.

Lines 45–48:

The poem shifts to Mexico, here, and the mountain ranges of the Sierre Madre. In the 1800s, the Philippines were ruled by Spain but governed from Mexico. By crossing the world geographically, the poem tells the history of the Philippines. This geographical disembodiment also makes the poem a more universal object. The setting sun suggests an end to the political regime and injects hope into the scene. The sun that "projects a sharp blue line" across the sky is vibrant and hints that something fresh and new is returning, the poet's blue lines from line 25. The other sun that might rise is also a sign of hope. It is a precarious hope framed in an "as if" statement but a hope nonetheless. For the poet, this suggests that poetry is not dead, but that a new voice is on the horizon, a revitalizing voice, a vibrant new vision.

Lines 49–52:

The cycle of death, destruction, and resurrection appears in this stanza. The speaker cannot imagine a world in which there was always light and no darkness. The speaker implies there is a time and place for both, that this is the cycle of life. The current time is still dark and full of destruction, but the light will come. This is also the speaker's rumination about the creative process, its low and high points. There can't always be sunlight. The "pressure lanterns luring the prawns" can only lure the delicacies of the deep. The light must come from the dark. The prawn, the thing of value, must be lured from darkness. The prawn is the successful revolution that must be birthed in the dark times and lured into the light. Translated to the realm of poetry; there can be no renaissance without the dark ages. A new, vital poetry is birthed in ruble. The sea can take, but at some point the tide will turn, and it will give again.

Lines 53–56:

The poem returns to the dark ages in this stanza. A glimpse was seen of the future world, but the current world is the one they live in, and in this world "nothing of value has arrived all day." For the stevedore, this is bad news. For the speaker, it is bad news. But this return to the bleakest of realities is short-lived. A shark is washed up on the shore. This something of value arrives, and the people rush to it and are hungry for it. It is lured by a lantern, which is a small light. For the revolutionary, a small victory begins the quest for the larger victory. Each small victory is a light illuminating the path to success. For the poet and the revolution, the dark ages are still real, but every once in a while something of value arrives on the scene— an idea or poetic vision that is worth looking at. That something of value is greeted warmly by an audience; that is also an act of hope. The poem is a small light in the dark world.

Lines 57–60:

In this stanza everyone is fed. Each person on the shore takes something home to eat. For the Fil-

ipino people, the small light was, perhaps, the beginning of the Cuban-American skirmish in 1898. It was this war that resulted in a short-lived Filipino freedom before the country was plunged into the darkness of dictatorship again. The people had a taste of what could be, and it was enough for everyone. This is true of a good poem as well. A good poem carries within it something for everyone. This shark, the good poem in a dark time, is aggressive; it has sharp teeth and foretells more sharp teeth. The "rows of sharks advancing along a jaw," predict a string of valuable poems, a string of mini-revolutions, and a gradual return to better literary and political times.

Lines 61–64:

In this stanza, the speaker is alone again. The brief gathering of community, the brief return of trust and value, has dissipated. The speaker is "alone by spirit light," alone in his own vast world. If the shark was a thing of value for the whole community, what the speaker witnesses in this stanza is a thing of value for himself. This "real" vision, this valuable thing is the impetus for living, a fragile and precarious living. The thing bursting its skin is the idea of the revolution, the glimpse of the new life. It is the private vision, one that must be in place before the public revolution can occur. For the poet, the thing bursting its skin is the poet's own voice being discovered. If the previous stanza was about poetry for all, this stanza is about poetry for one, the public versus the private.

Lines 65–68:

In this stanza, there is a birth of something rare, vital, and fragile. It is a revolution for the speaker, a feast of senses in the "blue-green veins pulsing." The creature has wings by which to fly, but "falls too soon." It is not its time. The stanza suggests that the revolution is a highbred creature that has come too soon into the world. The people are not ready to receive it. This is also true for poetry. The new voice of poetry comes too soon and fades away again before returning stronger. Getting rid of former, stagnant selves is not easy. The stanza suggests that sometimes that isn't all bad. If the world clings to a former self, then perhaps it is not time to give it up.

Lines 69–72:

In this stanza, the new thing, the insect-shark, the new poetry, the revolution is cleaned up and tossed out. Any evidence that the new creature existed is carried away by "ants." The alien being, the revolution, is too alien yet to be welcomed into the world of the human. The beginning line returns, the sea again sounding "insincere." The big politicos have sentenced the revolution to death. The critics have sentenced the "insect-shark," a new form and voice in poetry, to death.

Lines 73–76:

In this stanza, the milkfish gatherers become "human fry." It is ultimately up to them to sort the good fish from the bad. They are the worker bees, the ones left to sort out all the political fussing, the good political moves from the bad. The audience and the poet himself are also "human fry," left to sort the good poems from the bad poems. Only a few are worth all the effort, the revolutionary ones.

Lines 77–80:

In this final stanza, the milkfish is dissected and discovered to be just a pair of eyes, the current state of politics, just show, no substance. The contemporary poem is just a shocking image and nothing more. If we stretch the image of the eyes, we can speculate that the "eyes" are also *I*s and that the speaker is commenting on the trend of political leaders to serve for their own selfish reasons such as Marcos and his regime and the Spanish and Japanese that came before him. The *I*s also comment about current trends of confessional and self-indulgent poetry. These two *I*s or "eyes" carry out a shallow conversation with themselves. The refrain returns at the end to reiterate the will or the spine's determination to revolt and embrace the "insect-shark" or the new life. It is a life of poetry as well. The revolution of politics and the revolution of linguistics lack, at this point, the intelligence to execute the will's desire. This is the "convulsive misery," knowing what is missing in the world but not having the talent or tools to make it appear.

Themes

Alien Lands

In "The Milkfish Gatherers," the reader is tossed into an alien land. The placeholders, the "milkfish" and "Luzon," identify the setting as the Philippines at the time of political upheaval. Readers must know a bit about Filipino history or the poem is geographically disembodying, because when the readers are tossed to Mexico with the appearance of the Sierre Madre, they wonder where they are. Spain ruled the Philippines, but it was governed from Mexico until 1872, when the fight for Filipino independence began, a fight that continues to this day. Along the way, the zest and desire for revolution has died and been resurrected many times. The poet's own extraordinary travels and involvement with Filipino history allow the poem a broad terrain over which to roam. The confusion of setting also serves as a tool for universalizing the poem. Because every land has been privy to revolution at some time, and every person has felt the birth and death of the revolutionary idea, the place begins to matter very little as the scene of the action. Every person becomes a fisherman scouring the shallows, trying to survive and thrive in his or her own climate. The alien land becomes familiar. The alien territory of the poem becomes accessible.

Poetry as Revolution

The revolutionary setting of the poem, fraught with struggle and blooming and fading ideas of future lives after political victory, is a vast metaphor for the current and ongoing revolution of the poem. This poem is about war, but this poem is also about poetry's continual fight for metamorphosis. The creative process blooms and fades. Poetry's history has dark ages and ages of renaissance. Sometimes the "new" poetry arrives too soon, when the world is not yet ready to receive it. It becomes the insect-shark dying on the line having burst its skin too soon. And poetry goes through ages of history when the will to write is present but the intelligence and point of view is not. Fenton is actually the product of the end of one of these dark ages. In the eighties, the British lacked a poet laureate, a grandfather for the important British poetic tradition. Auden, who had died in 1973, left no worthy heir. Fenton was just coming through the ranks then, making small poems of light that have helped lead the current British poetic revolution. "The Milkfish Gatherers" then is a commentary on Fenton's knowledge of Filipino history on one level and the poem's history of revolution on another.

Private versus Public

"The Milkfish Gatherers" explores the realms of the public and private as it pertains to the making and absorption of poetry. The poem, ultimately, is a public thing. The only way it is a success is if it has an audience. "The Milkfish Gatherers" suggests that the successful poem thrives on many levels. It is the shark-insect or the valuable thing of the deep and private world: this is the poetic process. It is also the shark on the line, the thing dissected by the public, ravaged for its parts by the voracious reading masses.

This poem is a poem that is literally in the world, all over the world. It is public by function of language as well. The point of view, third person, creates a more universal aspect to the poem, which helps it avoid the confessional. A reader could easily miss the *ars poetica* all together. This poem could simply be a poem about the desire of Filipino revolution on the seashore of Manila, and how that translates to other revolutionary times for people all over the world. But the poem speaks on all kinds of levels. It speaks to the environmentalist who protests slash and burn agricultural practices. It speaks to advocates of the poor and hungry. It speaks to proponents of communal living. It divides itself out to the masses, hands out its liver and gills. The poem, though, is also a private thing. It is the "insect-shark" hanging from the fishing line observed by spirit light. It is vulnerable and inside the body with "blue-green veins." The act of making the poem, which is also a function of reading, is then also a very private endeavor.

Dark versus Light

Besides the obvious correlation of darkness with evil and light with good, the dark and light imagery in "The Milkfish Gatherers" offers many plays on these classic figures of language. The colors of the stevedore's clothes, the "yellow peaked cap" and "patched pink shorts," offer their own sense of light. The stevedore is the future revolutionary. These clothes may be all his worldly goods, but he has the light on his side. The light is also a destructive force. The island burns, and the "sharp blue line across the sky," which is a thing of light and future life, also connotes pain. New life cuts and stings.

As the old sun sets and a new sun rises, the reader feels the old cliché, an apt one for the death of an old regime and the rising of a new democratic agency. The dark is a time of destruction, the light of rebirth. The speaker states, "No night!— How could these people live?" Everyone is, as a part of humanity an equal shareholder in the darkness and the light. The "pressure lanterns lure the prawns." In other words, a small light is how the revolution begins. And the revolution is a prawn, something valuable and meaty that comes from dark times. The "spirit light" is another small light. Where the pressure lanterns lure many, it is by the spirit light that individuals find it in themselves to join the revolutionary masses. If the masses are not

Topics for Further Study

- Explain how the poem takes geography into consideration. How do the elements of geography contribute to the feeling and meaning of the poem?

- Revolutions require passionate people to fight as a cohesive whole. Report on what psychologists say are the traits of a revolutionary. Discuss the ways Fenton illuminates these traits in the poem.

- Linguists are concerned with how language evolves and changes. Research what it takes to have a linguistic revolution. In other words, what do experts say inspires changes in language?

ready, the premature idea of revolution dies by moonlight, a faint light. In the following dawn, life returns to normal as the people continue to sort through the "milkfish" or the political propaganda once again. A new and possible dawn of revolution is implied though never experienced in the poem. But one feels it is coming as the insect-shark, following the light, willing the sunrise to hurry.

Style

Rhyming Quatrains

"The Milkfish Gatherers" is written in quatrains, end-rhymed perfectly in lines two and four of each stanza. This verse form is the most popular in English poetry. Rhymes articulate a resonance among vowels or words that seem to echo previous vowels or words. This echoing results in a pattern of aural effects. The rhyming of lines two and four lulls the poem as if at sea. Later, the first line will repeat, heightening the wave effect. Rhyme probably began as a device to aid memory, hence, nursery rhymes or stories meant to teach children lessons by drilling them into their heads. In this same vein, rhyme used in chants and protests has the power to stick with people and aid revolution. This sentiment echoes the content of "The Milkfish Gatherers." The revolution needs a song.

Refrain

The repetition of the first line of the poem later in the narrative along with the line "But the spine lives when the brain dies / In a convulsive misery" is called a refrain. The word *refrain* is derived from the Latin *refrangere,* "to break." The refrain is a line that is broken off from the main part of the poem and keeps coming back. The refrain also breaks the way a wave breaks, echoing the idea of the sea once again.

Alliteration

Alliteration begins "The Milkfish Gatherers" with "The sea sounds insincere." The repetition of consonant sounds, the *s,* heightens the sinister sense of the poem. Alliteration is one of the principal devices of melopoeia, which is the aural and musical quality of language. The *s* is used most repetitively in "The Milkfish Gatherers" to draw attention to "the setting sun behind the Sierra Madre" and the insect-shark "bursting its skin." The *s* is the sizzle of the sun hitting dusk's dew and the blood sliding from the veins of the highbred creature. Alliteration adds texture to the text and is invaluable in setting the scene.

Historical Context

"The Snap Revolution," which appears in a 1986 edition of the journalistic magazine, *Granta,* chronicles Fenton's time in the Philippines as the Marcos regime fell from power. "The Milkfish Gatherers" was spawned during Fenton's time in the Philippines, but the poem tells a larger story than the fall of one regime. The Marcos regime was an oppressive dictatorship that was the last in a long line of oppressive dictatorships for the small country. "The Milkfish Gatherers" tells, in capsule, the entire history of Filipino revolution, which began as far back as 1872 and continues to this day as the country cleans up its political system and makes way for the highbred, the "insect-shark" of the poem, or the truly free and revolutionized democratic life.

In the 1800s, the Philippines were ruled by Spain, but governed from Mexico. The poem initially places the reader in the Philippines, near Luzon, which is not far from the capital city of the Philippines, Manila. The Sierre Madre of Mexico,

which appear in the second half of the poem, echo back to the 1800s when the Filipino people revolted against Spanish rule and a new, more hopeful sun of freedom rose. The "Infanta" or the daughters of Spanish royalty melted away. But the revolt of 1872 was just a taste of what was to come. The Filipino people would experience many small victories and dark times before gaining political freedom in 1986. One of the early Filipino revolutionaries was Doctor Jose Rizal. Rizal was a writer, a poet, and "dynamite man," who inspired many Filipinos to seek freedom. The poem intimates that he was a "rummager," a "scourer," and a "dynamite" man, the kind of revolutionary that was needed to make the revolution happen. In 1892, Rizal was captured and later killed. With Rizal's death, and the death of his revolutionary contemporaries, the push for revolution died as well.

The poem suggests that in the dark times, the revolution must be lured into the light. The dark times lasted a long time in the Philippines. From 1898 until 1986, the Philippines had a succession of oppressive rulers, ending in 1986 with the ouster of Ferdinand Marcos. The poem reminisces about the fall of the more contemporary regime. The smoking mountain in the latter half of the poem recalls a place in Manila, which Fenton recalls in "The Snap Election." The smoking mountain was a burning mountain of garbage, which came to represent the current state of politics under Marcos. Many people, scavengers, much like the hermit crabs of the poem, were killed on the smoking mountain. The status of the country prompted, finally, what Fenton calls, a "non-revolution" or the basically uneventful turnover of the Philippines to the inexperienced governing force of Corazon Aquino.

Whereas Rizal, the "dynamite" man and legendary revolutionary, is compared to the vibrant, highbred creature dying on the line, Corazon Aquino's government is compared to the milkfish. The poem and, indeed, Fenton suggest that the Philippines is not ready for another "dynamite" man. For now, the country is ruled by a governing power that has not banished corruption in the military and has not truly dealt with the deeper issues of political and social freedom. The current state, then, is not a risen sun but the returning dawn of an in-between revolution. In this dawn, people sort through the political rubbish like the milkfish gatherers looking for fish. Their will to revolutionize remains, but the means by which to achieve revolution still elude them.

Compare & Contrast

- **1972:** Richard Nixon is reelected President of the United States in a near-record landslide. Democrats win majorities in both houses.

  1980: Ronald Reagan becomes the fortieth President of the United States after a landslide victory over Jimmy Carter; Republicans control the Senate for the first time since 1964.

  1986: President Reagan admits secret arms deals with Iran in breach of the U.S. arms embargo (the "Irangate" scandal).

- **1972:** Philippines President Ferdinand Marcos declares martial law in response to what he calls a "communist rebellion"; Marcos assumes near-dictatorial powers.

  1986: In the Philippines' presidential election, Ferdinand Marcos retains the presidency by defeating Corazon Aquino, who alleges extensive ballot rigging; subsequently Marcos flees the Philippines, and Corazon Aquino becomes the new President.

Critical Overview

Fenton has made a name for himself as a journalistic poet. The poet as journalist is evident in the cinematic quality of his work. The critic Carol Rumens has analyzed his use of figurative language saying, "Metaphorical exuberance is out; the poet is par excellence a narrator, his metaphors a matter of action not image." Fenton is an ethnographer, historian, and anthropologist collecting images for the record.

Fenton's use of traditional English verse forms has placed him in the field of New Formalism, a sect that has returned to the roots of traditional poetry but makes use of contemporary themes and language. Because of his use of more traditional forms, Fenton has been compared to W. H. Auden, whose English standards are some of Britains most celebrated. Don Bogen, in a review of Fenton's latest collection *Out of Danger,* compares Fenton to Auden saying that the work is "grounded in speech but not self-dramatizing, at home with conventional forms, open to a range of tones including humor (but distrustful of high seriousness) and eminently sensible in its outlook." The same comments can be made of Fenton's work throughout his career. He has taken the traditional forms and modified them only enough to carve a niche for his own voice. His own voice involves an eclectic ensemble of subject and setting. In his most famous piece of literary criticism, "Of the Martian School," Fenton set out an idea for a new class or school of poetry, one that utilizes bizarre metaphors to illuminate every day objects. The poetry that came out of the Martian school is, as the famous poet Seamus Heaney said in a review in the *New Statesman,* "Highly self-conscious, anticonfessional, detached, laconic, and strangely popular considering their various devices for keeping the reader at arm's length." But, even so, there is something fresh about the voice, something that Fenton himself has coined, the "new recklessness," where "poets should yodel or write sonnet sequences as they see fit." The energy, not necessarily the ability to connect with the reader, is what draws the audience into the poem and intrigues them enough to stay.

The element of anticonfessinalism in Fenton's voice is balanced by the twists and turns of meter and subject. There is intrigue and mystery in Fenton's work. Stephen Spender, a critic writing for the *New Republic* says, "the poet has created within the poem a mysterious world with mysterious laws which work by their own logic. One feels there is a need of some ideological system of belief which would make everything clear." Fenton relies on his readers to make their own clarity in a world of chaos. His poetry is both of the world as well as acting in it. It is full of social commentary and critiques of politics, modern values, and the world of art. As critic Ian Parker, writing for the *New Yorker* says, Fenton "takes metre into new and marvelous places of public and private alarm while keeping an eye on Byron, W. H. Auden, Lewis Carroll, eighteenth century satire, and music hall." Critics generally celebrate Fenton's revitalization of form and his use of it to cross divides between tradition and modernity, academia and journalism, and humor and seriousness.

Criticism

Erika Taibl

Taibl has published most frequently in fields of nineteenth and twentieth-century poetry. In the following essay, she discusses revolution of the political and literary variety in "The Milkfish Gatherers."

"The Milkfish Gatherers" is a poem about revolution. In it, James Fenton uses the political history of the Filipino independence quest as an extended metaphor to illustrate literary revolution. Fenton crosses divides of form and subject matter, bringing contemporary ideas to a traditional verse form and foreign lands to universal assimilation. Fenton is a political poet whose first concern is language. In "The Milkfish Gatherers," he marries the political to the private, the form to chaos, and the past to a vital future.

Fenton's sense of past begins with the form of his poetry. Fenton has said, in an interview with the reviewer Ian Parker in an article for the *New Yorker,* that his feeling is "that poetry will wither on the vine if you don't regularly come back to the simplest fundamentals of the poem; rhythm, rhyme, simple subjects—love, death, war." "The Milkfish Gatherers," written in quatrains or stanzas with four lines, is perfectly rhymed every second and fourth line of each stanza. This rhythm allows for feelings of the sea, which is the subject of the first line, a repeated line, "The sea sounds insincere / giving and taking with one hand." The rhythm of the sea is evident and heightened by the rhyme scheme, as are Fenton's use of lines as refrains, lines that break like waves with the poem and return again and again, cresting to emphasize a point.

Fenton utilizes long standing poetic traditions to break new ground. Peter Stitt, a critic and writer, addresses Fenton's use of form in his article "Harnessing the Horse" saying, "A poet like Fenton, it may be, shows his conservatism by writing out of

the tradition handed down to him, changing it only enough to accommodate his own voice." Indeed, Fenton is considered a student of W. H. Auden's work, yet he alters the form and subject matter just enough to emphasize his own will. Dan Bogen, a critic writing for *The Nation,* suggests that Fenton's poetry "comes out of what may be called the Auden tradition in English verse; grounded in speech but not self-dramatizing, at home with conventional forms, open to a range of tones, including humor (but distrustful of high seriousness) and eminently sensible in its outlook." This is high praise for the poet who emulated Auden in his Oxford days. Yet Fenton reaches beyond Auden's subjects and embraces the world on political and social levels. Fenton has not thought of himself as a poet but as an archeologist and historian, a journalist and an ethnographer. His experiences, especially as a journalist, appear again and again in his poems and bring a certain life and vitality to his work.

"The Milkfish Gatherers" is a fine example of how Fenton marries his political schemes to his art. The poem handily drops place clues like "Luzon" and the catching of "milkfish" and emphasizes a tone of sinister doings. This establishes the place as the Philippines in an age of revolutionary struggle that began in the late 1800s as the Filipino people defined their desire for a revolution to free them from Spain's rule. The Filipino revolution began in 1872 as pockets of activists began to define the needs of people but did not reach maturity and victory until 1898. It was at this time that a short-lived freedom was established before the country was plunged into the darkness of dictatorship again, a darkness that slightly dissipated with the fall of the Marcos regime in 1986. The history of Filipino revolution is long and embittered. The poem chronicles the fear of the people and their pure will to survive, like the stevedore running to unload ships. The chief aim of the poem on a revolutionary level is to emphasize how the world must be ready to receive a revolution before it can truly occur. The beautiful insect-shark that has "burst its skin" is the premature revolution that has fallen "too soon" into the world. Bogen writes, "Like Auden, Fenton is a fundamentally social poet, working toward verse that is out in the world, significant and accessible to readers." The poetry is not simple by any means, indeed, the revolution is not simple, yet the poem provides clues to its meaning and allows for interpretation on many levels.

As a poet of the world, Fenton allows a sense of universality to enter his work. The revolution begun in "The Milkfish Gatherers" is a revolution in the traditional sense. It is concerned with change, it is full of fear and uncertainty, and it puts only a small amount of order on a larger chaos. Stitt writes, "there is that ironic power, the way the chaos of the described situation mercilessly undermines the pretension to harmony put forth by the form." The revolution suggests a chaos that Fenton plays with in form to heighten the tension between harmony and cacophony. The revolution can be read not just as a Filipino or even a political revolution; the lines the fishermen are casting could very well be poetic lines and the revolution that is occurring could very well be a revolution of poetic style and voice.

Fenton is fond of making waves. In his most celebrated piece of literary criticism, "Of the Martian School," Fenton discusses the need for a new school of poetry and calls for practitioners of "bizarre metaphors" to illuminate everyday objects. The milkfish is such a bizarre metaphor with its "two eyes on a glass noodle." The common, toothless fish of the Pacific is the revolutionary idea not fully hatched as well as the mediocre poem not fully flushed out. The ability of the extended metaphor to illuminate on different levels is part of Fenton's strength. Carol Rumens, a writer and critic writing for *Poetry Review,* says that "Fenton's purposeful eye trains itself over events and scenes from a distance; the vision has a cinematic quality in common with the scientist and the journalist telling us human interest stories, though his field is the macrocosm rather than the microcosm." Fenton's wide ranging eye coupled with his tendency toward the strange and illuminating metaphor makes "The Milkfish Gatherers" touchable by all. What the poem lacks in the realm of the confessional as a means to engage the reader, it makes up for in the use of the intriguing image and the vastness of the real world.

"The Milkfish Gatherers" travels from Luzon, a city in the Philippines, to Mexico's Sierre Madre, and then to the vast ocean. This geography speaks to the poem's political situation, but it also serves to disorient the reader and place the ideas of the poem in a more universal light. John Bayley, a critic writing for the *Times Literary Review,* says, "Fenton's strength is to get the external world of his travels and readings into his art, not to refine and enlarge upon a world of his own imagining." Though Fenton's imaginings are an intriguing riprap of unfinished cultural business, his strength lies in meeting the world on its own terms and using his skill with language to illuminate its truth. His travels as a journalist and figurehead for social

> *The chief aim of the poem on a revolutionary level is to emphasize how the world must be ready to receive a revolution before it can truly occur."*

justice contribute to the depth and vastness of his poems. Rumens writes, "Fenton's experience as a war correspondent in Indo-China is important not simply because it has given him a broader geographical and political terrain in which to operate, but because it has enabled him to take possession of an alien subject matter—other people's culture and wars—in a way that allows for and absorbs the alienation." Fenton makes the revolution everyone's revolution. He allows for the elasticity in the poem, defines it according to what he knows of language and human tendency, and he uses form to push at the chaos presented by the world.

For all of Fenton's leanings toward tradition, there are elements of his voice and style that speak to the goals of the revolution, a new and spirited voice. Fenton takes what he knows and loves of English verse and plays with it. Waves break in "The Milkfish Gatherers" as refrains ebb and flow, emphasizing the spirit of the line and the persistence of an idea. This kind of form in a long narrative creates what Fenton has called a "new recklessness." Parker describes Fenton as "a rap fogey, who is forever commuting across the divide—or showing that there was no divide in the first place— between ancient and modern, scholarship and journalism, journalism and poetry, poetry and song, sense and nonsense, socialism and luxury, self-mockery and high-seriousness." Fenton is pigeonholed, then, in what is called the New Formalism or a school of poetry in that he takes traditional verse forms and injects them with the verbiage and cultural baggage of contemporary times.

"The Milkfish Gatherers" chronicles a revolution, that has been on-going. It suggests, as most good poetry does, a universality of the revolutionary idea. Fenton makes it vital as he pays homage to his mentors, Lord Byron, W. H. Auden, and Lewis Carroll, without practicing the trend of con-

What Do I Read Next?

- The "Collected Poems" by W. H. Auden and edited by Edward Mendelson, offers a glimpse into the roots of contemporary British poetry. Auden was a mentor to many contemporary poets writing in English. The collected poems offer insight into the range, skill, and depth of his work.

- Besides being a political journalist and poet, Fenton has also spent many years as a theater critic for the London *Sunday Times*. His witty and entertaining drama reviews are collected in a book titled *You Were Marvellous,* offering yet another look at a truly renaissance, writing man.

- The Martian school, which Fenton brought into being with his critical article "Of the Martian School," includes many talented contemporary British poets. Craig Raine is among these contemporaries. His book, *A Martian Sends a Postcard Home,* introduces readers to another member of the Martian school of poetry.

- Fenton has been called a New Formalist or a practitioner of traditional verse forms in a contemporary atmosphere. He is not the only one embracing the old in new and exciting ways. *Rebel Angels: 25 Poets of the New Formalism,* brings together twenty five new formalists and allows them to strut their poetic skills and prove that English verse is not dead but alive and kicking.

- Seamus Heaney, Irish poet and winner of the 1995 Nobel prize for poetry, has been a vocal critic of Fenton and his school. Two of Heaney's collections of poetry, *Death of a Naturalist* and *Seeing Things,* offer a view of another celebrated and inspiring voice in contemporary poetry.

fessionalism embraced so viciously by Sylvia Plath, Robert Lowell, and Anne Sexton. Fenton does not follow trends, he creates new ones. After all, this is a man who has translated Verdi's opera "Rigoletto" into English, reviewed all our culture's best at the theater, and traveled the world. Parker

says, "Fenton has lived with a pet monkey in Phnom Penh, farmed prawns in the Philippines, eaten a bowl of live ants—that sort of thing" and given us a new spin on old rules much to the delight of readers. Fenton's revolution is an on-going one. It is grounded in what he knows, and it explores what he doesn't know. He pulls readers along for the ride proving, as Parker says, "Things do matter and on these issues, he [Fenton] keeps his readers posted."

Source: Erika Taibl, in an essay for *Poetry for Students,* Gale Group, 2001.

Erica Smith

Erica Smith is a writer and editor. In the following essay, she examines James Fenton's "The Milkfish Gatherers" from his 1994 volume Out of Danger. *Smith discusses how the poem's speaker brings forth images of violence that illustrate the dangers present in the Phillipines.*

The poem opens with a meditation on the sea: "The sea sounds insincere / Giving and taking with one hand." The speaker seems to be accusing the sea. Furthermore, in the following lines the speaker describes how the sea closed up a river the month before, "filling its mouth with sand." The brutality of this image intimates that the speaker's world is hazardous.

The speaker then turns his attention to those who are gathering the milkfish fry (young fish). He describes the tiny fish as "two eyes on a glass noodle, nothing more." The description is at once endearing and strange. The reader may be reminded of a polliwog, but the image also has a grotesque power. In the next few lines, the importance of the milkfish becomes apparent: the speaker notes that there is a stevedore keeping watch over the milkfish gatherers, together with his "vigilant" young wife. As the stevedore runs to meet a load of wood, the speaker notices that he is barefoot and wearing only shorts and a cap. Clearly the region is impoverished, and whatever business they do must be carefully guarded.

The following stanzas continue to emphasize this feeling of watchfulness. The speaker draws attention to nipa booths along the coast that protect the rights of the milkfish gatherers, commenting that "nothing goes unobserved." The stevedore, whom he calls "my good custodian," issues an ominous warning that "not everybody is a friend." The reader gains a sense that the speaker is an outsider, one who needs to be protected in an unfamiliar environment. This need for protection isolates the speaker; he comments that the stevedore "makes my life more private still."

The viciousness and danger to which the stevedore alludes is reflected in the speaker's portrait of his surroundings. He looks at the animals:

> But the dogs are sly with the garbage
> And the cats ruthless, even with sliced bread,
> As the terns [marine birds] are ruthless among the
>   shoals.

Coincidentally, the speaker chooses to single out two animals that are commonly considered beloved pets in Western culture. It is significant that they are presented here as wild—devious and competitive. The common perceptions and comforts of the Western world have no place in these surroundings, and the reader gains the sense that all the speaker's assumptions about the world have been turned upside-down.

It is interesting to note that although the speaker is writing in plain, clear language, he relies on the reader's powers of inference to discern the emotional climate. The facts of the omnipresent danger are conveyed as if from a distance; the speaker does not directly communicate his feelings, instead he reflects them off the stevedore and the animals. Seamus Heaney, writing in the *New York Review of Books,* also commented on this phenomenon in Fenton's work, calling Fenton's work "anticonfessional, detached, laconic." Others, such as Ellen Kreger Stark in *Critical Quarterly,* have argued that Fenton's work—and this volume in particular—is indeed confessional. The critical difference, according to Stark, is that Fenton's confessionalism does not rely on autobiographical detail; and the end result is that it serves to more clearly expose the primal violence of the world. With regard to this poem, the reader may resolve these opposing viewpoints by envisioning the speaker's descriptions as echoes he sounds out to his surroundings. In turn, the calls that come back are even more resonant and better understood than what was first issued forth.

In turn, the speaker moves his attention to the water. Men are out in boats,

> dragging a wide arc through the blue,
> trailing their lines,
> Cutting the engine out
> At the first sign.

The sign they are looking for, presumably, is of fish. The speaker sees one nearby: "Something of value struggles not to die. / It will sell for a dollar a kilo." Again, common assumptions about the world are being turned on their head: the value of a thing is not in its life, or preservation, but its

The common perceptions and comforts of the Western world have no place in these surroundings, and the reader gains the sense that all the speaker's assumptions about the world have been turned upside-down."

death. Here, one looks at a fish and sees money; the speaker notes that as the men gather fish "the hull fills with a fortune." The face of death, however, is quite clear and unsavory to the speaker. Looking at the fish, he comments that "the spine lives when the brain dies / In a convulsive misery."

While the fish are being collected into the boat, other men venture forth using another tactic. They are "Rummagers of inlets, scourers of the deep, / Dynamite men, their bottles crammed with wicks." Presumably they set off explosions in water to kill large quantities of fish, and then collect the bodies. The speaker points out that despite their grisly task, these men have a sense of humor; they "named the sea's inhabitants with style— / The slapped vagina fish, the horse's dick." This sexual innuendo is the first instance of levity in the poem.

The following stanzas also take the speaker away from the imminent realities of death and danger. The sun is setting, and the speaker's words capture its pure beauty:

> Polillo 'melts' means it is far away—
> The smoking island plumed from slash and burn.
> And from its shore, busy with hermit crabs,
> Look to Luzon. Infanta melts in turn.
>
> The setting sun behind the Sierra Madre
> Projects asharp blue line across the sky
> And in the eastern glow beyond Polillo
> It looks as if another sun might rise—

These lines are of staggering elegance, and the reader is left awestruck. Even the decimated island of Polillo is shrouded in metaphor. The scenery is bathed in light; the speaker bids the reader to "[l]ook to Luzon," the largest island in the Philippines, as well as to California's Sierra Madre. The effect of the light captures the speaker's imagination, to the point where he imagines another sun rising as this one goes down.

In the next lines, he considers that there would be no night. Yet he quickly rails against that thought: "No night! No death! How would these people live? / How could the pressure lanterns lure the prawns?" The irony of this statement is that the aura of fear that surrounds the area is, in effect, representative of night; and death abounds. Yet night is literally a necessity for these people in their work, as they use lanterns to lure fish.

The speaker then makes a statement of defeat: "Nothing of value has arrived all day— / No timber, no rattan." After the intoxicating quality of the sundown, this is a jarring snap back to reality. And when word comes that a shark is being brought in, and the animal arrives, its presence takes over:

> The young receive the gills, which they will cook.
> The massive liver wallows on the shore
> And the shark's teeth look like a row of sharks
> Advancing along a jaw.

The beast, even when in pieces, is still immense and awe-inspiring. One can imagine the speaker staring dumbfounded at the sight of it. Yet soon the speaker is transfixed by another sight. In a stark moment, "by spirit light," he sees that "something" is hanging from a post. It appears that whatever it is, it has burst its skin and is hanging on tenuously to life. The reader may presume that it is what remains of the shark, disemboweled but not yet dead. This is a truly terrifying state of existence, and the speaker describes it unflinchingly:

> Clinging exhausted to its former self,
> Its head flung back as if to watch the moon,
> The blue-green veins pulsing along its wings,
> The thing unwraps itself, but falls too soon.

This is a transcendent moment much like that of the setting sun, but unlike the earlier moment this one is both beautiful and grisly. It is abjectly interrupted as the dying animal falls to the ground and is soon covered by ants that will surely devour it.

Having witnessed these extraordinary instances of beauty and death, the speaker turns his attention to something else entirely: the milkfish, the image prevalent at the beginning of the poem. This time he notes the milkfish gatherers themselves, whom he calls "human fry." The speaker seems to be blurring the distinction between human being and fish, perhaps implying that humans are no more special than fish. Then he ends the stanza by mentioning that "a white polythene bowl / Is what you need to sort the milkfish by." Taken

together, these lines form a stanza that reads almost like a didactic nursery rhyme, retaining the *abcb* rhyme structure that has prevailed throughout the poem. These few lines, however, sound dreamy and singsongy, as if the speaker is lost in reflection.

The concluding stanza capitalizes on this eerie quality by being yet another refrain: the last two lines echo, "the spine lives when the brain dies / In a convulsive misery." In light of the death of the shark, these lines, when repeated, take on more meaning. The speaker has seen misery and has lived among death. The speaker is shaken, and, by extension, the reader is left jarred.

Source: Erica Smith, in an essay for *Poetry for Students,* Gale Group, 2001.

Sources

Bayley, John, "The Verse of Accomplishment," in *Times Literary Supplement,* August 27, 1982, p. 919.

Bogen, Don, "Out of Danger (book review)," in *The Nation,* October 24, 1994, pp. 464–69.

Gioia, Dana, "The Barrier of a Common Language: British Poetry in the Eighties," in *Hudson Review,* Spring, 1984, pp. 6–20.

Heaney, Seamus, "Making It New," in *New York Review of Books,* October 25, 1984, pp. 40–2.

Longley, Edna, "Seedy Menagerie," in *Poetry Review,* April, 1984, pp. 59–61.

Motion, Andrew, "An Interview with James Fenton," in *Poetry Review,* June, 1982, pp. 17–23.

Parker, Ian, "Auden's Heir," in *The New Yorker,* July 25, 1994, pp. 62–8.

Rumens, Carol, "War and Grief," in *Poetry Review,* January, 1983, pp. 51–2.

Spender, Stephen, "Politics and a Poet," in *New Republic,* May 14, 1984, pp. 31–3.

Stark, Ellen Krieger, "An American's Confession: On Reading James Fenton's 'Out of Danger,'" in *Critical Quarterly,* Summer, 1994, Vol. 36, p. 106.

Stitt, Peter, "Harnessing the Horse," in *The Georgia Review,* Spring, 1984, pp. 166–70.

For Further Reading

Espada, Martin, ed., *Poetry Like Bread: Poets of the Political Imagination from Curbstone Press,* Curbstone Press, 1994.

This is a unique anthology of thirty poets whose focus is writing about political topics. Settings range from Algeria and Vietnam, to Los Angeles and Philadelphia. This collection has something to offer anyone interested in how literature and poetry, in particular, have a political voice.

Fenton, James, *All the Wrong Places: Adrift in the Politics of the Pacific Rim,* Little, Brown Publishers, 1988.

Fenton offers what he knows and has experienced in the Philippines during the "snap revolution," as well as what he has learned and experienced in Vietnam and Korea. The book offers a keen understanding and a valuable perspective on the situation in the whole Pacific.

———, "The Snap Revolution: James Fenton in the Philippines," in *Granta,* 1986, pp. 34–155.

Fenton offers a unique account of the Marcos regime. His riveting and informed account of the revolution and fight for independence of the Filipino people is inspiring and highly intelligent. While fascinating for pure literary value, "The Snap Revolution" also offers savvy political commentary and a fresh perspective on the more contemporary story of the Philippines.

Thompson, Mark R., *The Anti-Marcos Struggle: Personalistic Rule and Democratic Transition in the Philippines,* Yale University Press, 1996.

This book intelligently explores the recent history of the Philippines and the fall of the Marcos rule. It explores issues of democracy and the challenges faced by a still developing democratic nation.

A Narrow Fellow in the Grass

Emily Dickinson

1866

"A Narrow Fellow in the Grass" is believed to have been written in 1865. A year later, it was published anonymously under the title "The Snake" in a journal called the *Springfield Republican*. The natural world is portrayed vividly throughout Dickinson's work, and this poem closely examines one of nature's most infamous creatures, the snake.

The poem begins with a description of the shock of encountering a snake. Although the poem's speaker never actually uses the word "snake," the scene is familiar enough for most readers to relate to it. The snake is almost magical as it moves, ghost-like, through the tall grass. The speaker sees only flashes of the snake's scaly skin, but there is evidence of its presence as the grass separates in its wake.

The poem goes on to illustrate how snakes can be deceptive. The word "barefoot" makes the speaker seem even more vulnerable to the serpent's potential threat. Mistaking a snake for the lash of a whip on the ground, the speaker reaches down to grab it and is startled to see it slither away.

The snake, one of the most notorious creatures in the natural world, has long been a symbol of treachery. Although the poem's speaker claims to be a lover of nature, it seems that the snake, while fascinating, is impossible to love. In fact, the speaker reacts to the snake as if it were a living manifestation of the terror of the unknown, for it is both startling and chilling.

Author Biography

Dickinson was born in Amherst, Massachusetts, in 1830 and lived there all her life. Her grandfather was the founder of Amherst College, and her father Edward Dickinson was a lawyer who served as the treasurer of the college. He also held various political offices. Her mother Emily Norcross Dickinson was a quiet and frail woman. Dickinson went to primary school for four years and then attended Amherst Academy from 1840 to 1847 before spending a year at Mount Holyoke Female Seminary. Her education was strongly influenced by Puritan religious beliefs, but Dickinson did not accept the teachings of the Unitarian church attended by her family and remained agnostic throughout her life. Following the completion of her education, Dickinson lived in the family home with her parents and younger sister Lavinia, while her elder brother Austin and his wife Susan lived next door. She began writing verse at an early age, practicing her craft by rewriting poems she found in books, magazines, and newspapers. During a trip to Philadelphia in the early 1850s, Dickinson fell in love with a married minister, the Reverend Charles Wadsworth; her disappointment in love may have brought about her subsequent withdrawal from society. Dickinson experienced an emotional crisis of an undetermined nature in the early 1860s. Her traumatized state of mind is believed to have inspired her to write prolifically: in 1862 alone she is thought to have composed over three hundred poems. In that same year, Dickinson initiated a correspondence with Thomas Wentworth Higginson, the literary editor of the *Atlantic Monthly* magazine. Over the years Dickinson sent nearly one hundred of her poems for his criticism, and he became a sympathetic adviser and confidant, but he never published any of her poems. Dickinson's isolation further increased when her father died unexpectedly in 1874 and her mother suffered a stroke that left her an invalid. Dickinson and her sister provided her constant care until her death in 1882. Dickinson was diagnosed in 1886 as having Bright's disease, a kidney dysfunction that resulted in her death in May of that year.

Emily Dickinson

The Grass divides as with a Comb—
A spotted shaft is seen—
And then it closes at your feet
And opens further on—

He likes a Boggy Acre
A Floor too cool for Corn—   10
Yet when a Boy, and Barefoot—
I more than once at Noon

Have passed, I thought, a Whip lash
Unbraiding in the Sun
When stooping to secure it   15
It wrinkled, and was gone—

Several of Nature's People
I know, and they know me—
I feel for them a transport
Of cordiality—   20

But never met this Fellow
Attended, or alone
Without a tighter breathing
And Zero at the Bone—

Poem Text

A narrow Fellow in the grass
Occasionally rides—
You may have met Him—did you not?
His notice sudden is—   5

Poem Summary

Lines 1–4:

In the opening quatrain, Dickinson cleverly disguises the subject of the poem, a snake. This

Media Adaptations

- Julie Harris reads selections by Dickinson in the audiocassette *Poems and Letters of Emily Dickinson.* Produced by Caedom, 1960.

- *Come Slowly Eden: A Portrait of Emily Dickinson* is a play by Norman Rosten. Produced by Dramatists Play Service, 1967.

- *Magic Prison* is a classical music adaptation, inspired by Emily Dickinson's poems and letters. Produced by the Louisville Orchestra, 1971.

- Glenda Jackson reads from Dickinson in the audiocassette *The Mind of Emily Dickinson.* Produced by Argo, 1977.

- Emily Dickinson is included in *Voices and Visions,* produced by the New York Center for Visual History, 1988 which details the lives and poetry of thirteen major American poets.

creature sounds harmless enough as it is introduced in line one. The term "narrow Fellow" is a nice use of colloquial language, "narrow," meaning small in width as compared to length, and "fellow" being a familiar term for a man or a boy, with an undertone that suggests commonness. The choice of the word "rides" is also interesting because it sounds like "glides" and "writhes" but gives the impression that the snake is being carried, or that it is floating along. In addition, the word can also mean torment, harass, or tease, and this definition fits the snake's reputation as a sly tempter. The speaker goes on to ask readers if they, too, have ever encountered snakes, noting that these "narrow fellows" always seem to take people by surprise.

Lines 5–8:

This second quatrain vividly describes the way a snake moves through tall grass. In line one, the grass is compared to hair and the snake to a comb moving through it. In line two, only part of the snake is seen, "a spotted shaft." The snake is long, slender, and marked with spots, and it is quickly glimpsed as it passes at the speaker's feet. After the flash of snake, the grass closes up and then is "combed" apart again as the snake moves on. There is something invisible, or ghost-like, in the way the snake slithers along, for the creature is mostly unseen but evidently there.

Lines 9–12:

The snake likes "boggy," or wet and marshy, land. Corn grows best in hot, dry soil, so the snake's favorite environment is not suitable for growing corn. The speaker goes on to reminisce about one of many childhood encounters with a snake during a morning walk. The speaker's detail about being barefooted is particularly provocative, for the thought of a snake slithering across one's naked extremities would make most people cringe.

Lines 13–16:

In these lines, the speaker continues the description of the childhood encounter. While walking along, the speaker sees something that appears to be a "Whip lash," or flexible part of a whip, "unbraiding," or coming apart. The lash of a whip is often made of braided pieces of leather, so the speaker might have thought that the Whip lash was disintegrating because it had sat so long in the harsh sunlight. The speaker recalls being well deceived by the snake. The speaker bends over the supposed "Whip lash" in order to pick it up, when it is suddenly metamorphosed in to a living creature that "wrinkled," or crumpled and folded, and then slithered away. Oddly enough, a colloquial definition of the noun form of "wrinkle" is "a clever trick." In a sense, the speaker was tricked by the snake, for it was not what it appeared to be.

Lines 17–20:

In this quatrain, the poem's speaker claims to be familiar with some of "Nature's People," or animals, and they with the speaker. The speaker seems to feel a real closeness to these creatures, referring to this connection as a "transport," or strong emotion, "of cordiality," or of warm friendliness.

Lines 21–24:

The snake appears to be the one exception to the opinion described in quatrain five. Every encounter with a snake, whether a shared or solitary experience, is a moment of shock and fear. "Tighter breathing" refers to an attack of panic, in which the heart races and breathing becomes strained. Most people who have ever been startled can relate to the sensations of this description. The final line contains a brilliant metaphor, for the term "Zero at the Bone" describes both bone-chilling terror and absolute nothingness. This final quatrain strongly suggests that the snake, who is casually referred to as a harmless, "narrow Fellow" in the first quatrain, might possibly be a manifestation of deception. The speaker, who loves all creatures, cannot love this treacherous trickster, the snake in the grass.

Themes

Appearances and Reality

"A Narrow Fellow in the Grass" is built around the contrast between what appears to be and what is. Dickinson wrote several "riddle" type poems, where she uses an extended metaphor to compare her subject to something, without coming right out and telling the reader what she is describing. Each stanza offers "clues" in the form of imagery, vivid word pictures such as the "spotted shaft" that divides the grass "as a comb."

Dickinson describes her object—in this case a snake—by hinting at what it resembles. The speaker falsely recognizes the object, taking it for something else. There is a split between what it appears to be and what it actually is. This theme of appearances versus reality comes through most strongly in the fourth stanza. The speaker is recalling time spent walking through the grass barefoot. The speaker—a young boy—spots the snake in the grass, but perceives it to be the lash of a whip: "I more than once at Noon / Have passed, I thought, a Whip lash / Unbraiding in the Sun." But just as the speaker reaches down to grab the Whip, he discovers it to be a snake, which slithers away: "It wrinkled, and was gone."

What makes Dickinson's poetic technique interesting is that she avoids words we would normally associate with snakes, such as "slither," "scaly," "slide," "coil," or the traditional descriptions of snakes as evil, demonic, or Satan-like. She chooses instead unlikely images, calling the snake a "fellow" who "rides" instead of slithers, who "wrinkles" away. She makes the reader conscious of language and forces him or her to imagine something in a way that one would not intuitively imagine it. In this way, she calls into question what reality is, and how much appearance plays a part in what we imagine to be real.

Fear

"A Narrow Fellow in the Grass" starts out with an image that seems to evoke the opposite of fear. The "fellow" in the first line hardly seems fearful, especially since the word "fellow" evokes a feel-

Topics for Further Study

- Dickinson describes a snake in this poem without ever calling it by name, but also without pretending that its identity is supposed to be a secret: this poem is not a guessing game. Write a poem in which you make your subject clear from the very start, so that there is no need to actually say what it is.

- Compare this poem with William Blake's "The Lamb." What do you think is the attitude of each author toward her or his subject? Which author do you think loves nature more? Which author do you think is a more talented poet ?

- Describe the setting of this poem—are there many or few of "nature's people" around for the speaker to be cordial with?

ing of familiarity and a sense of ease. By calling the snake a "fellow," Dickinson almost gives it a personality. It seems far from the imposing, fearful creature the snake has traditionally been thought to embody.

As the poem proceeds, the imagery continues to paint a picture of the snake as a harmless creature, one of "nature's people," with whom the speaker is well-acquainted. The snake is again called a "fellow" in the final stanza, but this time, the context is different. The speaker is revealing his fear of the snake. Meeting this creature, this "narrow fellow," either "attended or alone" causes "tighter breathing." It causes the speaker to feel "zero at the bone," or to be chilled to the bone. The final stanza describes an irrational fear. Literary critic Barbara Seib Ingold explains: "Irrational fears arise from what we do not understand; it is the many things one does not understand about a snake that add to one's fear of snakes."

Perhaps the speaker is thinking of the venomous bite of the snake, or of the mysterious habits of the snake. Often a creature associated with fear, and at times, evil, the snake has a curious place in history. We might say that "A Narrow Fellow in the Grass" is an exploration of fear, using the creature of the snake as a catalyst for that fear. This poem shows fear to be a complex emotion—an emotion that exists in balance with comfort, as is suggested by the characterization the fearful snake as a "fellow."

Style

Dickinson constructed the great majority of her poems around the short stanza forms and poetic rhyme schemes of familiar nursery rhymes and Protestant hymns. "A Narrow Fellow in the Grass," for instance, is written in six quatrains, or stanzas of four lines each, rhyming only in the second and fourth lines. Most, but not all, of the rhythms are iambic, meaning the poem has regularly recurring two-syllable segments, or feet, in which the first syllable is unstressed and the second syllable is stressed. The first two quatrains of the poem are laid out in the hymn meter called common meter, alternately eight and six syllables to the line. But Dickinson narrows the pattern thereafter to sevens and sixes, alternately seven and six syllables to the line.

Dickinson made many deviations from the conventional exact rhyme used by her poet contemporaries. "Alone/bone" in the final stanza is this poem's single exact rhyme, with similar sounds in the stressed vowels and in subsequent vowels and consonants, but not in the consonants immediately preceding the stressed vowels. "Me/cordiality" in stanza five is a vowel rhyme, and the other end rhymes are half rhymes, also called imperfect rhymes, off rhymes or slant rhymes, as in "rides/is" where the rhyming vowels are followed by different consonants, or in "seen/on" and "sun/gone" where the stressed vowels are different, but followed by identical consonants.

Dickinson often used alliteration and other repeated vowel and consonant sounds within lines and across lines and stanzas as alternatives to formal rhyme. In this poem, for example, the repetition of the sound "s" suggests the slithering of a snake. Alliteration is used effectively in "Attended or alone" and "breathing/bone" in the final stanza. Note, too, the echoing consonant and vowel sounds in stanza three's "A floor too cool for corn," and the prevalence of the long "o" sound in the concluding stanza underscoring the word "zero."

Historical Context

Born in 1830, poet Emily Dickinson lived during one of the most tumultuous and—at the same time—booming periods in American history. At once turbulent and idyllic, the mid-nineteenth century saw the flowering of literature, along with the push towards creating a unique American literary identity. But it also saw a society on the brink of violence with the increasing debates over slavery and the continued encroachment upon and displacement of Native Americans. Ultimately, the country became embroiled in a massive Civil War, tearing it apart and creating a legacy of strained race relations for future generations.

Because she was secluded in her Amherst, Massachusetts, home, readers often falsely assume Dickinson was disconnected from the events of the day. On the contrary, Dickinson was an active reader, followed current events and was very much aware of the world around her. Dickinson scholars Peggy McIntosh and Ellen Louise Hart state: "We know that Dickinson was a cosmopolitan and eclectic reader. Her letters indicate that she read newspapers and periodicals, following closely local and national events and reading contemporary poetry and fiction as soon as it came into print." Although very few of her poems were published during her lifetime, Dickinson was a committed poet, writing, revising, sending poems to friends, reading other poets' works as soon as they came into print.

The publishing world was booming during the nineteenth century, with an increase in both literacy and printed material. According to literary critic Paul Lauter, in the first third of the nineteenth century, the number of newspapers in the country increased from about 200 to over 1200. The number of novels in print also increased, with "popular" type novels leading the way, usually appearing serialized in weekly or monthly papers and magazines. Not only was the country expanding westward, more people were becoming literate. Lauter states: "It was in the early nineteenth century that writing first became an available profession, not only for white gentlemen, but for others." While Dickinson did not gain fame as a poet in her own lifetime as many of her contemporaries such as Whitman and Poe did, her poetic sensibilities and feelings of fragmentation were integral to nineteenth-century literature as it stood on the eve of the modern world.

America was still a very young country in the early part of the nineteenth century. As a relatively new nation, it was important for America to develop a sense of identity separate from England. Thomas Jefferson espoused an agrarian society, a nation of independent farmers; this was more plausible in eighteenth-century America. But the urban

Compare & Contrast

- **1800s:** In America, white women are not allowed to vote, own property or divorce their husbands, and until the Civil War, black women are held as chattel in slavery. The suffrage movement gains strength mid-century, especially after it joins with the anti-slavery movement. White and black women activists organize conventions—the most notable of which was the Seneca Falls Convention in 1849—where they deliver powerful speeches, drawing parallels between the enslavement of blacks and the domestic enslavement of white women. The ratification of the Fourteenth Amendment—which gives black men the right to vote—ultimately splits the civil rights movement from the women's movement.

  1920: The Nineteenth Amendment grants white and black women the right to vote.

  1960s and 1970s: The women's movement in the nineteenth century is known today as the first wave of feminism. In the 1960s and 70s, the second wave of feminism began, with such leaders as Gloria Steinem, Betty Friedan and U.S. Representative Shirley Chisholm. Women fought to end discrimination, earn equal pay for equal work, and end feminine stereotypes which dictated to women their place was in the home.

  Today: Many feminists argue we are experiencing a third wave of feminism, with many younger women involved (hence, the popular phrase "girl power"). While both the first and second waves of feminism saw tremendous gains for women, feminists today are still fighting many of the same issues, namely an end to gender discrimination, violence against women, and negative stereotypes of women.

- **1800s:** When Emily Dickinson was writing in the mid-nineteenth century, American literature was still in the formative stages. American writers were trying to create a tradition of their own, separate from the British literary tradition. The early part of the century saw an increase in the printed word, with an explosion in poetry. "The flowering of New England"—as it is often called—was a more high-brow movement, appealing to the growing class of educated, middle-income Americans. But there had always been a steady stream of popular, or "low-brow," literature in the form of stories published in periodicals and newspapers. As the century wore on, the division between high-brow and low-brow grew deeper. The best-selling novels and authors were not always the ones the majority of Americans were reading.

  Today: The divisions between high-brow and low-brow literature are still very much with us. We have an established "canon" of literary classics that appear on college syllabi and in grade school and high school curriculum. We also have a great deal of "popular" or best-selling literature (although some authors do manage to achieve best-seller status and a place in the canon). Still, popular types of literature such as Steven King, Danielle Steel, John Grisham, or the scores of romance, sci-fi, mystery or other novels are often looked down upon by more "serious" academic scholars. Much like in the nineteenth century, it is a flourishing market for popular writers, especially with the invention of the Web and the renewed interest in reading, with new bookstores and book groups popping up all the time.

---

population continued to grow in the 1800s as more and more immigrants came to the shores of America in search of a better life. America needed its own identity on the world stage.

While there were distinct literary and intellectual voices in the seventeenth and eighteenth centuries—poets Phillis Wheatley and Anne Bradstreet, the writings of Thomas Jefferson, Ben Franklin, Thomas Paine, and the stories of Hannah Webster Foster and Charles Brockden Brown, to name a few—America as of yet had no strong literary tradition it could truly call its own. Until, that is, the "flowering of literature," beginning in New England with poets William Cullen Bryant, Henry Wadsworth Longfellow, Oliver Wendell Holmes, and Walt Whitman. The topics they wrote about ranged from the celebration of American history to the praise of nature. Another important literary and intellectual movement of the nineteenth century was transcendentalism, with writers such as Ralph Waldo Emerson, Margaret Fuller, and Henry David Thoreau discoursing on nature and spirituality, on "transcending" the modern world by looking to nature. Emily Dickinson was very much aware of the literary boom; her style was shaped by the poetry of the day and, at the same time, was highly unique.

Literary energy was not limited to New England and intellectual circles of Harvard and Cambridge. There were many distinct voices and literary trends. The novel came into full force in the middle part of the century, with best-sellers such as Susan Warner's *Wide, Wide World* and Maria Cummins' *The Lamplighter*. Women's texts, often labeled "sentimental novels" were increasingly popular, and Nathaniel Hawthorne was quoted as referring to the "damn mob of scribbling women." Two interrelated issues, "the woman question" and the antislavery movement, achieved a great deal of momentum as white women and white and black anti-slavery activists teamed up to fight the dual oppressions of patriarchy and slavery. White and black women such as Elizabeth Cady Stanton, Lucy Stone, Frances Harper, Harriet Beecher Stowe, and Sojourner Truth fought for the liberation from women's domestic sphere, where women were not allowed to vote, own property, or divorce their husbands, as well as the liberation from slavery, where women were held as chattel, forced to submit to their white masters. The nineteenth century was full of powerful rhetoric that lit readers and audiences on fire.

The mid-nineteenth century was a unique era. Along with strides made by white women and blacks was the continuous shameful treatment of Native Americans. The economy boomed, new inventions surfaced, cities grew, the world became more modern as the country became divided. Daily life became increasingly more fragmented as America moved away from the organic ideal of an agrarian society and towards a more urban one. This was Emily Dickinson's world, and although we look to her as an eccentric of

her time, she was still very much a product of that time.

Critical Overview

Perhaps because it is one of only a few poems that Dickinson agreed to publish in her lifetime, "A Narrow Fellow in the Grass" has received a great deal of critical attention. The famous critical biographer George Frisbie Whicher, in his *This Was a Poet,* writes of the poem's first publication in 1866. According to Whicher, no readers in Dickinson's day appreciated the poem's "quaint wizardry of precision," nor did her contemporaries seem to recognize "that nothing at once so homely and so unexpected, so accurate in image and so unpredictable in its aptness, had yet appeared in American poetry." In fact, Whicher, who calls the poem a "tiny masterpiece," goes on to point out that the only notable comment made about the poem was a question concerning how Dickinson, a woman, could have known that a boggy field was bad for corn.

Another critic, Cynthia Griffin Wolff, writing in her literary biography *Emily Dickinson,* praises "A Narrow Fellow in the Grass" as "perhaps the most nearly perfect poem addressing a nature possessed of some compelling mystery." Wolff describes how the poem "moves the snake into some undefined psychological relationship with the speaker, a move away from simple realism toward a portent of danger." According to Wolff, the poem begins with the "civilized" experience of an adult describing the motion of a snake, "then moves beyond the boundaries of arable land, into the swamp where not even corn can grow." There, the speaker recalls the "more vulnerable" experience of encountering snakes as a frightened child. Wolff suggests that this terror of snakes formed during childhood experiences carries into adulthood, so that in the final stanzas the adult speaker is unable to see the snake as anything but "fearsome and chill."

A third critic, David Porter, writing in his *Dickinson: The Modern Idiom,* focuses his criticism of the poem upon the way that Dickinson uses language. According to Porter, Dickinson "shows us less the way a snake looks than how ingenuity can reanimate language and put it up to saying new things." Porter highlights Dickinson's peculiar use of the word "narrow," saying that it is an "unlikely quantification" for a snake, and goes on to point out how the whole poem is a "word performance" full of wonderfully surprising, unconventional language.

Criticism

Judi Ketteler

Ketteler has taught literature and composition, with a focus on nineteenth-century literature. This essay examines the poetic techniques Dickinson uses in "A Narrow Fellow in the Grass" and the various levels of meaning embedded in the imagery.

Emily Dickinson uses a medley of poetic techniques to craft her poem "A Narrow Fellow in the Grass." Throughout the poem, Dickinson balances the tension between the admiration of the object she describes—the snake—and the fear of it. "A Narrow Fellow" is in many ways a study in poetic technique, with carefully chosen images, instances of alliteration and rhyme, and the use of personification. Dickinson pays close attention to the look, shape, and sound of the words themselves, as well as the feeling created by the punctuation. "A Narrow Fellow" can be interpreted at several levels. First, it can be read on a literal level as a description of a snake. On a second level, however, Dickinson's imagery can be read as sexually nuanced. Reading the poem at these various levels creates ambiguity in the meaning. It also shows Dickinson to be ahead of her time in poetic technique, allowing "A Narrow Fellow" a more modern feel.

Very few of Dickinson's poems were published in her lifetime. "A Narrow Fellow" was one of about a dozen poems published in her lifetime, and scholars aren't sure if it was published with her permission or not, or even if she sought publication. The poem appeared on February 14, 1866, in the *Springfield Daily Republican,* originally titled "The Snake." "A Narrow Fellow" has received a good deal of critical attention, with literary critic Daniel Hoffman calling Dickinson's "Zero at the Bone" the finest image in American poetry (as quoted in George Monteiro's article). When reading this poem, it's important to look and listen closely to Dickinson's language, tone, images and use of punctuation. Dickinson was a poet who took risks. Biographer Paula Bennett explains: "Dickinson had to take risks—risks with her language and risks with her audience's willingness to play along. Reading her poem, we must think and see in new ways and entertain descriptions in wording, tone, subject and grammar for which conventional usage

> *Dickinson uses the device of sound throughout the poem; hearing this poem is as important as seeing the words. Dickinson creates both a visual and an auditory image of the snake with her language."*

provides few, if any, precedents." This essay examines Dickinson's unconventionality, as well as some of the risks she takes as a writer.

The old adage that poetry is meant to be read aloud is appropriate for this poem. Dickinson uses the device of sound throughout the poem; hearing this poem is as important as seeing the words. Dickinson creates both a visual and an auditory image of the snake with her language. This begins from the very first line: "A narrow Fellow." Literary critic George Monteiro has looked closely at the sound devices Dickinson uses in this poem. He argues that the phrase "narrow fellow" "recreates, in a sense, the very movement of the snake as it 'rides' along the ground. The very size of the letters—all letters of a small size in the first word and an organized sequence of letters of a small and a taller size in the second word—orchestrate the poet's perception of the way this creature makes its way around."

The phrase "narrow fellow"—in addition to replicating the movement of the snake—also creates a very soothing sound that rolls off the tongue. Too, the word "grass" has a flow and movement about it, and its "ss" ending could be said to mimic a snake's hissing sound. The "s" sound continues throughout the first stanza, with "occasionally rides" and "his notice sudden is." Even the look of the letter "s" itself is snakelike. Dickinson employs the technique of euphony, where the sound of words easily flows. Literary critic Barbara Seib Ingold, building on Monteiro's interpretation of the poem, writes: "The extensive use of long, resonant vowels and other soft, mellifluous consonants (l, m, n, r, v, f, w, th, and wh) throughout the poem gives it a euphonious sound." This euphonious

What Do I Read Next?

- Elizabeth Barrett Browning was one of Emily Dickinson's chief influences. The collection *Complete Works of Elizabeth Barrett Browning,* published in 1900 in six volumes and edited by Charlotte Porter and Helen Clarke, serves as a good introduction to Browning.

- An extensive anthology of women writers in English, *The Norton Anthology of Literature by Women: The Tradition in English,* edited by Sandra Gilbert and Susan Gubar, includes fiction, poetry and prose by more than 140 female authors, including a biographical essay about Dickinson. Published in 1985.

- A contemporary of Emily Dickinson, Walt Whitman is perhaps best known for his collection of poems entitled *Leaves of Grass,* first published in 1855.

- A popular novelist who made her living by writing, Fanny Fern (Sarah Willis Parton) was also a contemporary of Emily Dickinson. Her novel *Ruth Hall,* published in 1855, is about a woman succeeding in the male-dominated world of publishing.

- Francis Ellen Watkins Harper was a nineteenth-century African-American poet, active in the anti-slavery and women's movements. She published several collections of poetry, including *Poems on Miscellaneous Subjects* (1854) and *Poems* (1871).

---

sound no doubt sets the tone for the poem: calm, musical, almost Edenic. The speaker is comfortable with the subject, the "narrow fellow" that seems harmless and, in fact, graceful.

But the snake is elusive; it hides in the grass, flitting out of sight when the speaker spots it. The grass is conducive to the snake's movement; it "divides as with a Comb," creating an opening and closing movement. The fluid "s" sound continues throughout the second stanza, with such alliteration as "spotted shaft." Cynthia Griffin Wolff, a Dick-

inson scholar, writes about the snakelike quality of the letter "s" and the sound it creates in this poem: "Sinuous, serpentine movement is sustained for many lines by the insistent reiteration of the sounds." Also, the continuous dashes—an unconventional use of punctuation Dickinson is known for—keep the poem moving from one line to the next. The snake continues to move as well, coming into close proximity to the speaker: "And then it closes at your feet / And opens further on—." Throughout the poem, the speaker refers to the snake as "he." He starts out by calling it a fellow—a very familiar type of term. The snake begins to take on a personality as Dickinson uses personification to bring it to life. The personification is dependent upon the speaker feeling familiar and comfortable with the snake, which clearly he does. Dickinson also makes her speaker male, referring to him as a "boy" in the third stanza. These images of maleness will become important as we look at the poem in different ways later in this essay.

In the third stanza, we see another instance of alliteration, this time with the soft "oo" sound. Dickinson speaks of the boggy acre, or wet marshy land, that has a "floor too cool for corn." Again, the sound is fluid, and it is matched with the image of a cool, wet swampy floor and the snake "riding" through it. In this stanza, the speaker is recalling a childhood memory of watching the snake and not recognizing it. In the fourth stanza, he recalls a time he mistook the snake for a "Whip lash / Unbraiding in the Sun." The "s" sound continues as he tries "stopping to secure it," but it "wrinkled, and was gone—."

The image of a snake "wrinkling" suggests the snake was frightened by the approach of the speaker. "Wrinkle" hardly seems the graceful image of the grass dividing or the spotted shaft riding along the boggy acre. This characterization of the snake as a timid creature further develops the personification. In the next stanza, the speaker even refers to animals as "Nature's People," suggesting a kind of collective personification of animals. The speaker feels close to animals, feels for them a kind of "cordiality." The speaker makes this statement as a sort of caveat or disclaimer—this is understood in the final stanza when the speaker makes it clear that the snake, this "narrow fellow," is an exception to that safe feeling of comfort and cordiality.

In fact, the speaker's fear is exposed in the final stanza, leaving us with the final image of the speaker meeting the snake with a "tighter breathing" and a feeling of "Zero at the Bone." Ingold has remarked that this final image "vividly portrays the breathtaking, icy feeling that one experiences when faced with an irrational fear. When one reads these lines, the thought of being 'zero at the bone' causes one to feel coldness and to shiver." This immense feeling of fear contrasts with the rest of the poem; even the language changes. Dickinson moves from the soft "s" sounds and cool "oo" sounds with the hard sound of "z" in "Zero" and "b" in "Bone." This creates a cacophony, or harder, disjointed sounds. The fear of the speaker echoes through the final cacophonous sounds.

Cynthia Griffin Wolff has read this poem on a more symbolic level. She says: "Dickinson stipulates a man-and-boy for speaker, perhaps to emphasize the implications of male sexuality or even phallic brutality that the notions of a snake so often carries—implications that are reinforced here in part by the exposed feet and toes and in part by the 'whip lash' whose leather is quietly 'unbraiding in the sun' like a bundle of worms." Looking closely at some of the images in the poem, we can get an idea of what Wolff means by this. Snakes have long been phallic images associated with male sexuality; snakes have also been associated with danger, evil, and temptation. Even naming the snake a "narrow fellow" with a "spotted shaft" is sexually suggestive of male genitalia, just as the grass that divides, closing and then "opening further on" is suggestive of female genitalia. Wolff mentions the "phallic brutality" associated with the snake. Throughout the poem, the snake is referred to as a familiar "fellow." But suddenly, at the end, fear takes over and we're left with a sense of danger. Whether or not Dickinson was purposefully trying to link male sexuality to a sense of fear and danger, we'll never know, but the suggestion is there.

Writing about sexuality in the nineteenth century was not as taboo as we might think. Dialogs about sexuality were carried on in covert ways. Women, who were supposed to be pure and demure, couldn't be quite as open as men. After all, Walt Whitman, a contemporary of Dickinson, celebrated the body and wrote openly about sexuality—both heterosexual and homosexual longings—in his poetry. And the anti-slavery movement often spoke of the horrors of rape and sexual violations black women endured at the hands of their masters. To speak so openly as Whitman was not Dickinson's style. Her poems are much more controlled, nuanced, and often cryptic. It is this ambiguity that gives her poems their depth. Her language is playful, but it is also doing serious things. Paula Bennett explains: "In the unconventionality of her

grammar, as in the unconventionality of her thinking, Dickinson was striking at the foundations supporting Western phallocentric thought."

In other words, she was quietly challenging the values of her culture that prescribed certain roles for men and certain roles for women and little flexibility between them. This is not to say Dickinson was unhappy in her life, for there is much evidence to show that she was very happy and loved her home and her life in Amherst. But it is to say that Dickinson was a deep thinker, and she took risks with her poetry. Joyce Carol Oates, a writer and critic, sees Dickinson' poetry as exhibiting a kind of artistic tension. She says: "Art is tension, and poetry of the kind Emily Dickinson wrote is an art of strain, of nerves strung brilliantly tight. It is compact, dense, coiled in upon itself very nearly to the point of pain: like one of those stellar bodies whose gravity is so condensed it is on the point of disappearing altogether."

Dickinson's poetic technique was very much an art form she worked hard to refine and hone. The tension in her poetry is still, as Oates say, "strung brilliantly tight" over one hundred years later. The modern reader can glean so much from Dickinson—whether or not Dickinson absolutely intended her poems to be interpreted in certain ways or not—because she leaves so much unsaid, and yet, says so much with so little.

Source: Judi Ketteler, in an essay for *Poetry for Students,* Gale Group, 2001.

Jennifer Bussey

Bussey holds a Master's degree in Interdisciplinary Studies and a Bachelor's degree in English Literature. She is an independent writer specializing in literature. In the following essay, she analyzes Emily Dickinson's "A Narrow Fellow in the Grass" as a nature poem containing metaphors that bring the reader new insights.

Emily Dickinson was a reclusive and mysterious woman who spent half her life in seclusion. Dickinson had a strong sense of her own spirituality even as a young woman. Before she reached twenty years of age, she left Mount Holyoke Female Seminary because she refused to join the Congregationalist church, which was heavily influenced by Calvinism. Unwilling to live the restricted lifestyle required by the church (which included, among other things, disapproval of reading novels), Dickinson returned home to her family. She, like Henry David Thoreau, simplified her life in terms of objects and duties. Her poetry testifies

> *She believed that wisdom was accessible through sense perception, and that if she gave her attention to nature, it would reveal itself to her."*

to her attention to spiritual matters, and although she did not participate in church services, she was a Christian, a belief that is reflected in her poetry. Her simple life enabled her to turn inward, observe nature, and write poetry daily as she liked.

Among Dickinson's daily tasks was tending her beloved garden, and many of her poems reflect this interest. Dickinson's poetry often describes natural images that lead to deeper insight, and the sparse structure and simple lines frequently belie complex and profound messages. She believed that wisdom was accessible through sense perception, and that if she gave her attention to nature, it would reveal itself to her. Because she wrote little poetry intended for publication, the act of writing poetry may have been a means for her to clarify for herself or at least privately honor what she had learned. "A Narrow Fellow in the Grass" is a perfect example of a seemingly simple poem that contains many insights about the nature of life.

"A Narrow Fellow in the Grass" is typical of Dickinson's nature poetry because of its succinct presentation, by a detached observer, of the harmonious coexistence of different natural elements. In the first two quatrains (stanzas of four lines), the speaker describes the snake moving through the grass, neither apparently harming the other

> A narrow Fellow in the grass
> Occasionally rides—
> ….The Grass divides as with a Comb—
> A spotted shaft is seen—
> And then it closes at your feet
> And opens further on—

The snake is not hindered by the thick grass, nor is the grass permanently parted or flattened by the snake's movement through it. The middle stanza explains that the snake enjoys boggy areas, again illustrating the comfortable interaction of nature's creatures and environments. The snake also lies in the sun, a completely different environment

from a bog, yet this, too, suits the snake very well. Dickinson writes:

> I more than once at Noon
> Have passed, I thought, a Whip lash
> Unbraiding in the Sun …

The snake is disturbed only when a little boy reaches for him, suggesting that human interference disrupts the natural balance between the snake and his sunny environment ("It wrinkled, and was gone—").

Until the last stanza, the snake is depicted as a non-threatening creature. The speaker expresses thoughts with an almost childlike sensibility, which is another common feature in Dickinson's nature poems. The tone is one of discovery and delight, rather than fear and disgust, despite the subject being a snake. For Dickinson, creatures generally considered ugly or repulsive were deserving of poetry because they were part of the natural world. Subjects of her poems include a rat, a fly, a spider, a mushroom, a bat, and weeds. Dickinson's initial presentation of the snake as non-threatening is expressed by her reference to him as a "fellow," a congenial, light-hearted word often used to address a boy or man, or even a dog. In the middle stanza, the speaker says that the snake "likes" a bog, rather than using a more neutral term like "seeks out" or "prefers." By personifying the snake in this way, the speaker casts him as a creature with feelings, and feelings similar to our own.

The change of tone in the final quatrain can be accounted for in numerous ways, but two possibilities seem most worthy of consideration. One is that earlier in the poem the speaker seems to be reminiscing, but at the end the speaker moves into the present. The light-hearted tone and the mention of boyhood experiences in the middle stanza are consistent with the childlike sensibility of the poem. In the last stanza, the speaker uses the word "never," which includes not only boyhood, but also youth and adulthood. The fear of the snake expressed at the end of the poem may illustrate adult fears of things that seemed harmless in childhood. The loss of innocence educates a person and creates fear; in this case, fear of a snake. Dickinson writes:

> But never met this Fellow
> Attended, or alone
> Without a tighter breathing
> And Zero at the Bone—

Here the poem shows its underlying complexity, developing the image of the snake to show more than one aspect.

A second way to interpret the shift of tone in the last quatrain is that it refers to the dual nature of living things. Throughout most of the poem, the snake is described in friendly terms, but at the end the snake's threatening aspect is revealed; the speaker describes the tightening chest and icy chills upon seeing one. Of course, from the beginning, the reader may be thinking about the slithery or venomous qualities of snakes that bring dread to most people. At the end, then, the reader is able to understand the speaker's anxiety when confronted with a snake. Readers can readily identify with the speaker, who is both intrigued and repelled by the snake. It is both threatening and non-threatening, as are most living things. Wisdom comes from understanding both aspects of the snake and, by extension, the dual nature of all creatures. In fact, Dickinson hints at the dual nature of human beings by assuming a male voice when she writes in the middle stanza of her "boyhood."

Dickinson's use of the word "rides" in the second line also connotes duality. While the most obvious meaning of the word is emotionally neutral (the snake riding the grass in the same way a person would ride a horse), the word can also mean "harassing" or "irritating relentlessly." A careful reader may conclude that, although the grass is not harmed by the snake's presence, it is helpless under the snake's passing and is, in fact, temporarily ruffled. While not meaningful on a literal level, the grass's powerlessness to respond to the snake has implications on a metaphorical level.

Dickinson's nature poetry has retained its popularity because of its ability to use natural events and images to lead the reader to new insights. The snake's movement through the grass, which returns to its original state after the snake has passed, can be read as a metaphor for people's movements through life. People make decisions and carry out acts that make a difference or create a change, but such change is often temporary. Dickinson's point is not that life is futile, but rather that the snake gets what it needs from the grass without destroying it. Further, there is a lesson about the world's return to order. Although the snake parts the grass, the grass returns to its intended state afterwards. The use of the word "rides" to describe the snake's movement is intriguing because it is unusual, and because it conjures parallel images, such as a fish swimming through water or a bird flying across the sky. In each case, the medium through which the object moves is not destroyed. Dickinson's technique is subtle, but noteworthy. By introducing metaphorical language early in the poem, she en-courages the reader to look beyond the immediate image to a larger pattern.

Dickinson also makes her imagery universal by not naming her subject. The word "snake" does not appear in the poem; although the reader is certain of the subject's identity, every mention of the snake ("fellow," "spotted shaft," "it") is non-specific. The speaker seems to have taken an assortment of recalled images of the snake and generalized them before beginning the poem. Barbara Seib Ingold of *Explicator* especially admired Dickinson's descriptions of the snake's attributes ("narrow," "spotted shaft," like a "Whip lash / Unbraiding in the Sun,"), and use of "s" sounds ("Grass," "His notice sudden is," "The Grass divides as with a comb," "Have passed, I thought, a Whip lash," "When stooping to secure it"), to convey the snake's identity. The poem's language conveys that it is about something more than a single snake, and even about something more than snakes.

"A Narrow Fellow in the Grass" was written in about 1865, by which time poets had been writing about nature for a very long while. Although some nature poetry is trite and unoriginal, great poets, such as William Wordsworth, Ralph Waldo Emerson, and Emily Dickinson, were able to maintain the appropriate spirit, energy, and function of such poetry. By providing interesting, familiar, and well-written descriptions, these poets show their readers the wonders of nature, which is much more effective and memorable than simply telling about them.

Source: Jennifer Bussey, in an essay for *Poetry for Students,* Gale Group, 2001.

Michele Drohan

Drohan is a professional editor and writer who specializes in classic and contemporary literature. In the following essay, she explores Emily Dickinson's love of nature and her expression of its inherent contradictions and mysteries in "A Narrow Fellow in the Grass."

Dickinson composed over five hundred poems that examined the relationship between man and nature, a select few of which are categorized as anti-transcendentalist. This means a selection of her nature poems deals with ideas that are in direct opposition of transcendentalist poets, such as Ralph Waldo Emerson and David Thoreau, who believed one could achieve a spiritual connection with nature. Dickinson departed from what she thought to be a simplistic view of nature to show that nature will remain forever elusive from any real under-

> *'A Narrow Fellow in the Grass' asserts that while it is possible to be a part of nature, humans are inevitably outsiders who are allowed to observe it, but never understand its secrets.'*

standing or interpretation. Her unique ideas are represented most succinctly with "A Narrow Fellow in the Grass."

When the poem was published, Dickinson was tackling a well-worn literary subject. She certainly wasn't the first poet to explore nature in her work. By 1860, the subject of nature had been explored for hundreds of years. However, she succeeded in breathing new life into a tired concept. Ralph Waldo Emerson was a direct influence on Dickinson; however, she did not follow in his transcendental footsteps. Emerson put forth ideas and theories in his work *Nature* that proposed nature is not a mere commodity, but rather a path to divine truth. He truly believed he could uncover the real purpose and meaning of the natural world. Fellow friend and poet Thoreau also believed that by studying and exploring nature, one could find a moral illumination and discover divine truths. Together, they created the transcendental movement, which was exalted by some and criticized by others for its perceived criticisms of the Christian church.

While the transcendental poetry movement greatly affected the American literary world, Dickinson turned those ideas on its head by introducing a deep skepticism for the sentimentality that permeated the poetry in that movement. In addition, Dickinson lived an isolated life, surrounded by the natural world, giving her an opportunity to form her revolutionary perspective. Even though Dickinson did subscribe to a transcendental philosophy in some of her work, evidenced by poems that explored the mystical connection between man and nature, she took the idea one step further and created a doctrine that celebrated the unknowable mysteries of nature and therefore contradicted Emerson's theories.

"A Narrow Fellow in the Grass" asserts that while it is possible to be a part of nature, humans are inevitably outsiders who are allowed to observe it, but never understand its secrets. Dickinson did not randomly choose the snake as an emblem of nature. Rather, the snake, which is ripe with biblical references, is used to symbolize the idea that nature is capable of betrayal. The poem begins by placing the narrator in a field where he suddenly happens upon a snake making its way through the grass. The line, "You may have met Him—did you not?," implies that the sight of a snake will occasionally occur when one wishes to enjoy what nature has to offer. The snake rides on the ground with ease, highlighting its rightful place in the natural world. However, the snake moves quickly and divides the grass "as with a comb." The grass "closes at your feet / And opens further on," thus mirroring the elusive quality of nature. Just as a snake only allows a mere glimpse of itself as it makes its way through the grass, nature, too, only reveals a part of itself to those who wish to know it. The next lines, "He likes a Boggy Acre / A Floor to cool for Corn," also reveals that the snake has access to and even finds pleasure in places too barren for other forms of life. Dickinson is ascribing a certain amount of superiority to the snake by saying it inhabits places the narrator will never know or understand.

The narrator in the poem then recalls a time when he was just a boy who walked barefoot in the field. By walking barefoot, the boy makes himself closer to nature but also more vulnerable to it. Dickinson seems to be saying that no matter how close the boy in the poem gets to nature, he will never be admitted into its spiritual realm. This point hits home in the following lines: "I more than once at Noon / Have passed, I thought, a Whip lash / Unbraiding in the sun." Because the boy perceives the snake to be a type of toy, at first, he believes he can participate or play with nature. However, the boy learns quickly that the closer he gets to the snake and, consequently, to nature, the more it eludes his grasp. As the boy bends down to "secure it / It wrinkled, and was gone." The frustration that exists in the ability to capture or touch the snake alludes to nature's indifference toward humans. The snake's actions, like nature, are unpredictable. Nature exists in its own world. It's cyclical, persistent, and stops for no one. It does not care whether or not it reveals its secrets to man. In fact, it has a distinct lack of conscience, and it probably prefers to retain its mysteries because therein lies nature's power.

As the poem continues, the narrator announces, somewhat proudly, that he is a friend of nature: "Several of Nature's People / I know, and they know me." This is a naïve statement to make because, in reality, the narrator can never "know" nature. At this point in the work, the narrator seems to be in a state of denial, as if he is trying to convince nature that he is a friend that can be trusted with its secrets. This idea is also indicated in the title of the poem. Calling the snake a fellow is not only an attempt to reduce the snake to anthropomorphism, but it also implies a certain amount of familiarity with the creature when, in fact, nothing could be further from the truth. The narrator even goes so far as to say, "I feel for them [nature's creatures] a transport / Of cordiality." However, the narrator's generosity is a moot point as nature is clearly not interested in taking the time to accept his offer. In addition, the word "transport" is indicative of the constant change and mobility that is at the core of nature.

The last stanza of the poem further reveals the narrator's perspective. For the first time in the work, an element of fear is introduced. Up until this point, the narrator tried to capture or tame the spirit of the snake by turning it into a civilized, even friendly, creature. The tone of the poem also serves to startle the reader. Up until the last stanza, the work feels light and airy, as if Dickinson meant to celebrate the natural world. The abrupt change in tone at the end of the poem highlights how the narrator's instinctual feelings betray him, and the reader goes through an emotional transition as well. All of a sudden, the reader, like the narrator, senses great danger. While the narrator would like to be a friend to nature, he cannot help but fear the sight of the snake and acknowledge its potential evil. It is common knowledge that the snake has the potential to inflict harm with its poison. In addition, a snake, because of its physical structure, can make a quick, unanticipated attack at any time, thus destroying the narrator's life and permanently ending his relationship with nature.

The narrator is unable to deny his fear because of his body's intense physiological changes. His feelings of terror are represented by "a tighter breathing" and a chill to the bone. It is further revealed that the narrator has always had these feeling when he encounters a snake. This statement implies that the narrator has been plagued by nature's inconsistencies all his life. Even if the narrator is accompanied by one or more friends, he is not able to abate his feelings of terror upon meeting a snake. The consistency of fear insinuates that the narrator is in a constant struggle with the mysteries of nature. He desperately wishes to uncover nature's secrets and continues to attempt to do so but fails to succeed in his mission. The narrator must face the reality of his situation as he can no longer pretend to be one with nature. Ultimately, he's an outsider who must give up the fantasy and keep a certain distance from nature. Ironically, if the narrator were to succeed in capturing the snake, he might be bitten and meet his demise. This idea implies that the closer one gets to nature, the closer one gets to death. Dickinson further confirms her anti-transcendentalist feelings by addressing the issue of mortality. Paul Ferlazzo believes that while romantic poet Walt Whitman believed death signaled unity with nature because his body would be buried in the dirt and then renewed, Dickinson thought that death signaled a complete disconnection with nature and, therefore, the end of her relationship with it. However, by closing her struggle with its mysteries, Dickinson may finally achieve a kind of freedom that was unattainable in life.

Source: Michele Drohan, in an essay for *Poetry for Students,* Gale Group, 2001.

Sources

Bennett, Paula, *Emily Dickinson: Woman Poet,* University of Iowa Press, 1990.

Emerson, Ralph Waldo, *Nature: An Essay and Lectures on the Times,* H. G. Clarke, 1844.

Ferlazzo, Paul J., "Emily Dickinson," in *Twayne's United States Authors Series Online,* G. K. Hall & Co., 1999.

Ingold, Barbara Seib, "Dickinson's 'A Narrow Fellow,'" *The Explicator,* 1996, pp. 220–23.

Lauter, Paul, *The Heath Anthology of American Literature, Volume One, Second Edition,* edited by Paul Lauter, DC Heath and Company, 1994.

McIntosh, Peggy and Ellen Louise Hart, *The Heath Anthology of American Literature, Volume One, Second Edition,* edited by Paul Lauter, DC Heath and Company, 1994.

Monteiro, George, "Emily Dickinson's 'A Narrow Fellow in the Grass,'" *The Explicator,* 1992, 120–22.

Oates, Joyce Carol, "Dickinson Constructed Her Own Elusive Image," *Readings On Emily Dickinson,* edited by David Bender, et al., Greenhaven, 1997.

Porter, David, "The Puzzling Idiom," in *Dickinson: The Modern Idiom,* Harvard University Press, 1981, pp. 37–80.

Whicher, George Frisbie, "Literary Friends," in *This Was a Poet,* Shoe String Press, 1980, pp. 113–33.

Wolff, Cynthia Griffin, *Emily Dickinson,* Knopf, 1986.

For Further Reading

Bender, David, et al., *Readings on Emily Dickinson,* Greenhaven, 1997.

This collection offers various critical perspectives on Emily Dickinson's life and poetry. Includes twenty different essays by various authors.

Dickinson, Emily, *Final Harvest: Emily Dickinson's Poems,* edited by Thomas H. Johnson, Little, Brown, 1961.

An extensive collection of Emily Dickinson's poems. Also includes biographical information.

Krane, Paul, ed., *Poetry of the American Renaissance,* George Braziller Press, 1995.

This anthology contains a wide spectrum of nineteenth-century American poets, from lesser known authors such as Lydia Sigourney to well-known authors such as Edgar Allen Poe, Ralph Waldo Emerson, and Henry Wadsworth Longfellow.

Longsworth, Polly, *The World of Emily Dickinson: A Visual Biography,* W. W. Norton, 1990.

This visual biography is made up of an extensive collection of photographs and sketches from the life of Emily Dickinson, including pictures of Amherst, her home, her friends and family.

Overture to a Dance of Locomotives

William Carlos Williams

1916

Written at the end of 1916 and the beginning of 1917, "Overture to a Dance of Locomotives" remains one of Williams' most intriguing poems, as it signifies a number of different things to various readers. Although the poem did not appear in print until 1921 in his collection of poems *Sour Grapes,* the poem did make an appearance when Williams read it in New York City at the 1917 Independents Exhibition held by the Society of American Artists in the spring of that year.

The occasion of the poem is the hustle and bustle of people, porters, and passenger trains in Pennsylvania Station in New York City. Porters yell train numbers and times, passengers rush to the correct track to get on their trains, and the trains themselves smoke and churn in the station, anxious to put their modernist muscle to work. But rather than represent this scene as chaos, Williams suggests that the landscape before the reader is an artistic landscape, and the station is a kind of museum. His language in describing the station and the throngs of people is sympathetic, artistic, lyrical. He even arrests his narrative about porters and passengers to describe the light filtering through the windows, as if the station is some sort of cathedral to modern industry.

This sympathetic portrayal of the train station and the trains themselves has led many scholars to argue that this poem represents Williams' futurist leanings. Futurism championed aggression, typographical experimentation, language free of logical

William Carlos Williams

order, ameliorative possibilities of technology, and the beauty and symmetry of war. While the poem may contain some futuristic traces, it functions more like an anti-pastoral, a celebration of industry and travel, and the symmetry of people and machines moving in concert. Additionally, its myriad of voices has impressed many readers as an early experiment in collage (a work in which various images or ideas are juxtaposed with each other in no particular order) and pluralism (an approach that seeks to give expression to many views, not just one).

Author Biography

Williams was born on September 17, 1883, in Rutherford, New Jersey, to William George and Raquel Helene Hoheb Williams. From 1897 to 1899, he went to school in Switzerland and Paris but graduated from New York City's Horace Mann High School in 1902. From 1902 to 1906, he attended the school of dentistry and then the school of medicine at the University of Pennsylvania. These proved to be important years for young Williams as he later would enjoy a life-long career as a medical doctor. His time at the university

proved fruitful for his other career, that of a poet, as this was where he met fellow American poets Ezra Pound and H. D. (Hilda Doolittle) and fellow Pennsylvania painter Charles Demuth.

In 1909, after interning in New York City, he self-published his first collection of poems, adequately titled *Poems.* For the next few years, Williams lived overseas but returned to marry Florence Helman on December 12, 1912.

Through the influence of Pound, Williams began to enjoy some moderate success with his poetry. Pound persuaded a British press to publish Williams' collection of poems *The Tempers* in 1913, and then in 1914, Pound included Williams' "Postlude" in his collection of Imagist work. An influential approach to poetry advocated by Pound, Imagist poetry tried to evoke an image or picture using as few words and forms as possible. In 1917, Williams' first major book, *Al Que Quiere!,* appeared to critical acclaim. Other collections followed: *Kora in Hell* and *Improvisations* in 1920, *Sour Grapes* in 1921, and perhaps his most famous early book *Spring and All* in 1923. In 1925, Williams published what remains an American classic, *In the American Grain.* This book solidified his reputation as a major American literary voice, a reputation galvanized by the 1926 awarding of the Dial Prize for Poetry, Williams' first major award, but not his last.

Between the publication of *Spring and All* and *In the American Grain,* Williams traveled in Europe and met many great literary figures of the twentieth century, including James Joyce, Gertrude Stein, and Ford Maddox Ford. Williams' allegiances with painters, writers, and intellectuals would serve him well throughout his life. Williams was also a father by now, having two sons. This was a wildly busy time for him becasue he was raising children, maintaining his medical practice, and writing every day.

Even though Williams was quite prolific, he didn't produce a major literary contribution until 1946 when *Paterson, Book 1* appeared. This book, a long poem musing over Paterson, New Jersey, would reinvigorate Williams. He would go on to write five Paterson books in all, and, in so doing, he created one of the greatest long poems in American history. Though he suffered a heart attack in 1948, he recovered. In 1950, his *Collected Later Poems* appeared, and *Paterson, Book 3* won the first National Book Award for Poetry. Williams finally finished the Paterson project in 1958 when book 5 appeared. He died in 1963.

Poem Text

Men with picked voices chant the names
of cities in a huge gallery: promises
that pull through descending stairways
to a deep rumbling.

The rubbing feet   5
of those coming to be carried quicken a
grey pavement into soft light that rocks
to and fro, under the domed ceiling,
across and across from pale
earthcolored walls of bare limestone.   10

Covertly the hands of a great clock
go round and round! Were they to
move quickly and at once the whole
secret would be out and the shuffling
of all ants be done forever.   15

A leaning pyramid of sunlight, narrowing
out at a high window, moves by the clock;
discordant hands straining out from
a center: inevitable postures infinitely
repeated—   20
two—twofour—twoeight!
Porters in red hats run on narrow platforms.
This way ma'am!
—important not to take
the wrong train!   25
Lights from the concrete
ceiling hang crooked but—
Poised horizontal
on glittering parallels the dingy cylinders
packed with a warm glow—inviting entry—   30
pull against the hour. But brakes can
hold a fixed posture till—
The whistle!

Not twoeight. Not twofour. Two!

Gliding windows. Colored cooks sweating   35
in a small kitchen. Taillights—

In time: twofour!
In time: twoeight!

—rivers are tunneled; trestles
cross oozy swampland: wheels repeating   40
the same gesture remain relatively
stationary: rails forever parallel
return on themselves infinitely.
The dance is sure.

Poem Summary

Lines 1–4

The opening lines of the poem might be confusing for some readers, as it seems like Williams
is describing a man yelling in a museum. However,
upon further reading, it's clear that this is no ordinary museum, though it might still be unclear what
exactly the setting of the poem is. One clue might

be the fact that the men "with picked voices chant
the names of cities." The fact that they are yelling
the names of cities might lead the reader to believe
that the poem takes place somewhere where travel
is done. When one considers that the poem was
written in 1916 and 1917, there are very few other
locations this poem could have taken place but in
a railway station.

The reader might also notice the form of the
poem. Early on, the lines are unrhymed, but they
find formal use in Williams' tetrameter, a line containing four metrical feet. The first three lines of the
opening stanza feature end rhymes, but, overall, the
stanza feels less orchestrated and more random.

Some scholars have noted that the opening
stanza creates a dark, almost spooky, underground
world resembling T. S. Eliot's *The Wasteland,* or
worse, yet, hell.

Lines 5–10

Williams continues the disturbing description
here, noting the "rubbing feet of those coming to
be carried." For those readers familiar with Dante's
Inferno, this passage might sound like Dante's description of the thousands of souls being marched
through hell before being carried across the river
Styx. But just as it appears the poem will continue
on a downward spiral toward something doleful
and nefarious, the poet informs us that the feet of
the passengers transform the "grey pavement into
soft light that rocks to and fro." So rather than the
nameless, bodiless feet walking their way into the
underworld, these feet magically change the "pale
earthcolored walls of bare limestone" into something luminous. This magical transformation might
remind readers of some of Williams' other poems
like "This Is Just to Say" or "The Red Wheelbarrow" in which ordinary items are transfigured into
enchanted objects that reflect the hidden beauty of
the world.

Willliams does a fine job of setting the stage
of the poem here. Notice how these first two stanzas are rather slow and plodding. The reader is
given very little information. Because Williams
eases into the poem, the energy of the voices that
comes later seems all the more unexpected and
wonderful.

Lines 11–15

In this stanza, Williams diverts the gaze of the
reader away from the passengers and toward the
"great clock" in the station. But just as quickly, the
camera of the poem pans down on the masses of
bodies shuffling into the terminal, and, again, the

Media Adaptations

- A video that features brief clips of Williams, visual representations of his poems and commentary by leading scholars was released in 1988 through the PBS Voices and Visions series.

- Williams reads his own poems on an audiocassette entitled *William Carlos Williams Reads,* published by HarperCollins.

- There is a small website devoted to Williams, including a bibliography at http://www.charm. net/~brooklyn/People/WilliamCarlosWilliams. html (August 18, 2000).

- A page exploring Williams' connection between poetry and art is available at http://www.cwrl. utexas.edu/~slatin/20c_poetry/projects/relatproject/WCW.html (August 18, 2000).

- The best Williams web site is at http://www. poets.org/poets/poets.cfm?prmID=120 (August 18, 2000) and is maintained by the Academy of American poets. The page not only features text and images but also links to poems.

poem embraces an infernal landscape. Williams' image of "shuffling ants" being "done forever" predicts lines 60–68 of Eliot's *The Wasteland* in which Eliot, paraphrasing Dante, offers a description of the masses of people flowing over London Bridge. In both poems, the modern industrial landscape seems burdened, darkened by seas of mechanical bodies moving, not in time with their internal clock, but as slaves to the great clock overhead that determines their destinies.

Again, Williams is playing with the notion of an overture here. An overture is the prelude piece of music to an orchestra. Generally, it is slower, more understated than the rest of the composition. Williams is setting the reader up for the crescendo that awaits.

Lines 16–20

The last movement in the overture, stanza four, shifts from describing the shuffling ants of stanza three to a rarified portrait of light in the great station. Here, Williams asks the reader to consider the station itself as art. The "leaning pyramid of sunlight" that streams through the "high window" creates a myriad of associations. First and foremost, Williams implicitly draws subconscious comparisons with Egyptian pyramids and the modern railroad stations, certainly the grand architectural designs of Pennsylvania Station and Grand Central Station. Secondly, the image of light filtering through high windows probably makes the reader conjure up images of churches or cathedrals. The pyramid image is a favorite of Williams, also making appearances in the poems "March" and "History." Without question, Williams wants the reader to think of these stations as secular, modern equivalents to the great pyramids of Egypt and the great cathedrals of Europe. In so doing, Williams does sound a bit like a futurist, here, in that he suggests that the triumph of man's ingenuity in the modern era rivals the grace and mystery of past architectural structures.

Additionally, the description of light might recall the reference to a "gallery" in stanza one. Postures that are "indefinitely repeated" might be referring to a museum in which portrait after portrait lines the walls. Whether it is a museum or a modern day cathedral, Williams takes the reader out of the mundane and into an entirely new world.

Lines 21–24

Without warning, without introduction, the methodical rhythm of the overture surges into a cacophony of sounds and shouts. The tetrameter of the first four stanzas gives way to the fragmentation of human voices shouting out numbers, directions, suggestions. Here, the monotony of one voice narrating the poem becomes a symphony of human voices, each creating their own music.

The shift in tone is reflected in the poem's form. The first twenty lines of the poem, though unrhymed, look and sound relatively conventional. Many readers might be used to somber, earnest, poetic descriptions of interior spaces. But all of a sudden, lines like "two-twofour-twoeight!" make their way into this poem. Such fragmentary lines are uncommon in lyric poetry. What might Williams be thinking?

Notice also how the lines suddenly gain some space in between them, as if each is their own stanza. What's more, it seems like the voices of the porters demand their own stanzas, as if they are music themselves. In this sense, Williams is less a futurist and more a humanist. It is finally the human voice and only the human voice that can break the monotony of the overture. Like a symphony itself, the poem makes a wonderful shift from solo to orchestra. In other words, in these stanzas, the poem moves from monologue to dialogue.

Lines 25–26

This brief stanza marks a movement away from the voices in the previous stanzas and a return to the narrator, the omniscient voice, whose mission appears to be one of commentary. Once more, the speaker draws the reader's gaze upward toward the light. It's unclear what Williams' motive is in this stanza, but most likely, he wants the reader to be aware of movement and beauty, both above and below. The obvious action is the people rushing to make their trains, and that dance requires poetic attention. But there is a quieter dance going on; one in the ether of the station—the dance of light. So wonderful is the light that Williams describes it in artistic terms. It "hangs" like a painting that needs to be straightened, and like a painting, it demands and deserves the reader's sense of aesthetics.

This and previous descriptions of light suggest another poetic reference, the pastoral. A pastoral is, traditionally, a short, lyrical poem set in a natural setting. The poet, once he enters the setting, admires the beauty of nature and comes to some sort of realization about himself and the world about him. The repeated references to light in this poem recall hundreds of pastoral poems that laud sunlight sifting through the clouds and illuminating the leaves, the gentle brook, the dewy grass. Williams' poem reads like an anti-pastoral, a modernist version in which a man-made industrial building, not nature, provides insight and beauty.

Lines 27–31

Williams continues the pastoral language in this stanza. He describes the station in decidedly lush and overtly sexual language. Perhaps the most opaque and most complex stanza in the poem, the sexual overtones have raised a number of comments from scholars. One can hardly overlook the erotics of this section, and given their clarity, one begins to go back over the poem to see if equally sexual imagery appears elsewhere.

Perhaps the best way into this section is to pay close attention to the language Williams' employs. He repeatedly depicts the station in feminine terms. In fact, one critic goes so far as to suggest Williams' representation of the station is "womblike." Indeed,

Williams describes the light as "soft" and that it "rocks / to and fro." Conversely, the trains, classic phallic symbols, surge into the station, disseminating passengers into the tunnels of the station. However, it would appear that the trains also carry feminine characteristics, as they are "[p]oised horizontal" and possess a "warm glow-inviting entry." Always the iconoclast, Williams turns conventional sexual metaphors and archetypes on their heads here. For him, trains carry both masculine and feminine qualities, like people themselves, and, not surprisingly, like dances. To Williams, the entry and egress of trains and people remind him of human behavior: dances and sex. Thus, not even the most mechanized space can escape the most human of endeavors.

Lines 32–34

This short stanza returns to the dynamism of the trains. The sexuality of the last stanza continues here. The pause and anticipation of the "fixed posture" finds exuberant release in the whistle, an almost climactic discharge of sound and energy. Placing the two-lined stanza almost flush with the right margin in it's own stanza, provocatively recreates the surprise and anticipation of the signal that the train is about to leave the station, that the big machine is about to pull out, en route to another city and another station.

Again, the shouts of the porter are heard, giving a warning to avoid train 28 and train 24, and to go for train 2. This line interrupts the narrative flow of the poem just as the last interjection of voices did. This technique suggests that for Williams, the singular narrative of the poet will give way to the plurality of voices in the station.

Lines 35–38

In this stanza, the poet returns to his position as tour guide. He describes, for the reader, what he sees as the trains depart from the station. He sees windows glide past and African American cooks "sweating in small kitchens." Then, like that, nothing but "Taillights." After all that waiting, after all that anticipation and pent-up energy, the train is gone in seconds. Again the poet's monologue is interrupted by the porters informing the reader that trains "twofour" and "twoeight" will depart in time.

A point of interest in this stanza is Williams' bizarre observation of "colored cooks." One possible reading of this line cites Williams for racism by subtly reminding us that blacks are found sweating in tight kitchens, not as passengers on the trains themselves. This reading would suggest that Williams is both implicitly racist and classist, linking race with menial tasks. No other races or groups of people are mentioned, so why single out African Americans? Yet, another reading of the poem might argue that Williams' inclusion of blacks reveals an egalitarianism, a sense of equality. Very few other poets would have even considered incorporating a black person into their poems, whereas the only ethnic group warranting mention in Williams' text is African Americans. So an equally persuasive interpretation could argue that Williams is attempting to break down racial barriers in his poem. Most likely, it is a little bit of both.

Lines 39–43

Here, Williams drives home the idea of the modern pastoral. Williams brilliantly compares the underground tunnels, bridges, wheels, and rails to rivers and "oozy swampland." For Williams, man-made landscapes and so-called "natural" landscapes are equally beautiful and equally deserving of poetry. This tendency to link natural beauty with industrial efficacy stands as yet another futuristic characteristic of Williams. Note how nature seems plundered, transcended by technology, as if the great inventions of man triumph over the chaotic and brazen natural world.

The repetitions that seemed lifeless and monotonous at the beginning of the poem now appear not only exciting, but immanent. The promise of returning trains on parallel tracks functions as a constant, a reminder, a marking of the land. The earth will always wear the trace of railroad tracks, an inscription of the covenant between man and industry. Trains will always run. Like the great clock in the station, they are a permanent fixture on society's external and internal landscape.

Line 44

The final stanza in the poem is also the final line: "The dance is sure." The certainty of the railroad system drives home the point of the previous stanza. You can always count on railroads. However, this dance serves as a larger metaphor for America. The sureness of the railroads functions as a metonym, a kind of metaphor or stand-in, for the industrial power that was rebuilding America in the 1910s and 1920s. The promise of reliable travel, of conquering the landscape, of barreling like a train headlong into the glorious future are all ancillary meanings encoded in the final line.

What's more, the last line serves as the final movement in the symphony. The dance, which has taken the reader all over the station and all over the nation, has come to an end. But the reinforcement of this final line suggests a dance, a glorious, powerful dance, in which trains, people, and the modern metropolis all move together, in step, in time.

Themes

Technology and Modern America

The most obvious theme of "Overture to a Dance of Locomotives" lies in the poem's affectionate, even jingoistic stance on the promise of technology and an industrialized America. For instance, the title itself is evocative enough. That a poet would think of trains arriving and leaving a large, crowded metropolis in terms of a dance suggest an unflagging appreciation for the wonder of modern transportation and invention. Instead of seeing the trains as ugly, tedious prisons that separate humans from nature, the poet finds them utterly human, engaging in typical human behaviors. Furthermore, Williams seems to suggest that his poem is merely an overture, a prelude for the real artistic experience—the trains. Traditionally, poets and writers would think of their work as art, but, here, Williams wants his poem to function as a mere overture to the more impressive performance.

Without question, futuristic subtexts run beneath the poem like so many subways. Williams' uncritical ode to modern technology seems, on one level, as though it came right out of the Futurist Manifesto. Clearly, Williams sees modern America as teeming with energy, promise, and interaction, just like a train station. For him, technological innovations can offer as much for modern society as poetry, and according to this poem, they can work together to achieve common ends. What interests Williams is the sense of continuity the trains and their stations bring. They are something society can count on, something to look forward to, yet, unlike so much of history, they don't act oppressively. They help. They carry. In this sense, Williams does convert them into a hopeful metaphor for modern American society.

Poetry and the Mundane

More than any other American poet, Williams is best known for his ability to show the poetry in everyday life. In poems like "This Is Just to Say," in which he turns stealing plums into a mystical experience, and "The Red Wheelbarrow," in which he forces the reader to ask how much depends on how the reader sees the world, Williams suggests that the world is what the reader makes of it. His fiercest competitor on this front is Wallace Stevens, whose poems "Thirteen Ways of Looking at a Blackbird" and "Anything is Beautiful if You Say it Is" argue essentially the same thing. But Williams, the only poet daring enough to write an epic poem about Paterson, New Jersey, has made a life's work of forcing his readers to see art in what appears to be artless. In the very same exhibit in which Williams debuted his poem, Marcel Duchamp put on display his most famous and most controversial sculpture—a men's urinal. What Duchamp wanted to argue was that anything could be seen as art. Similarly, Williams would argue that anything, when looked at creatively, could become poetry.

In this poem, Williams enables the reader to see the majesty, the symmetry, and the beauty in a modern-day train station and, believe it or not, in the trains themselves. What is utterly remarkable about the poem is that Williams ultimately suggests that the real poem takes place in the station and on the tracks, not on the page. For him, one must look for poetry in order to find it. To alter how one sees the world is to alter the world.

Poetry and Art

Williams and Stevens are also best known for incorporating art and art theory into their poems. In fact, Williams once wrote an entire cycle of poems on the paintings of Peter Brueghel. While Stevens wanted to incorporate theories of art in his poems, Williams wanted his poems to do on paper what paintings do on canvas. In "Overture to a Dance of Locomotives," Williams creates a kind of painting by the way he uses language, typography, and metaphor.

First of all, Williams suggests, in the opening stanza, that the train station is itself a gallery. If that is the case, then the stage is already set to begin looking at items inside the gallery as art. Light caresses the walls, filtering in through the high windows and landing on the columns of the station. Is he describing the Lourve or Pennsylvania Station? It is designed to be unclear. Furthermore, Williams goes to great length to create a visual picture of the stations and the trains within it, as if he were painting a picture with words. Just as painters use light, color, and symbol to evoke emotions and associations so, too, does Williams use symbol, light, and shade to evoke a sense of what the station might look like. But, as is typical with modern art, he doesn't come right out and offer a representational version of reality. He distorts it. Thus, his poem re-

Topics for Further Study

- To what degree does the form of the poem mirror or complement the theme of the poem?

- Look at another poem by Williams, perhaps "March" or "History" and explain how and why the poems are similar. Are they similar only in form, or do they share some common thematic concerns?

- Imagine the poem as a painting. What would it look like? Try to describe it as best you can. Does it remind you of any other paintings or photographs?

- Do you agree with the critical interpretations of the poem? Does Williams succeed in transforming the station into a cathedral? Is the exchange of passengers and trains similar to a dance?

- What kind of dance would the poem suggest? A waltz? A cha cha? Hip Hop? Swing?

- Think of ways in which the poem resembles a musical composition. Does the form of the poem contribute to its musicality?

- Do you agree with Williams that trains and train stations are appropriate metaphors for American progress and democracy? Would something else serve as a better metaphor at this point in history?

sembles the modernist paintings of Charles Demuth, especially a painting like "End of the Parade," in which a modern industrial landscape reaches to the sky as light slashes across the canvas. Thematically, Williams' poem mirrors Demuth's "Incense of a New Church," whose title and figures suggest that the smoke emanating from a skyline is incense issuing from the new holy place, the modern city. Likewise, Williams suggests in "Overture to a Dance of Locomotives," that the train station rivals the great cathedrals of old, that it is as sacred to modern societies as churches were to past eras.

Style

Free Verse

Though the poem does not adhere to any conventional poetic form like a sonnet or a villanelle, it does possess a certain form. First of all, the opening stanzas are written in an uneven but effectively droll tetrameter. The lines do not intentionally rhyme, though an occasional end-rhyme sneaks into the poem. However, the steady rhythm of the first four stanzas is radically interrupted by the intrusion of outside voices, the shouts of the railway porters. Here, the lines become jagged and fragmentary, so that the narrative that was originally fairly symmetrical has now become asymmetrical. In keeping with the symphonic metaphor suggested by the title, the poem moves from harmony to discord, from consonance to dissonance. In poetic terms, the poem shifts from monologue to dialogue. The singular lyric voice has to give way to a collage of other voices, all of whom are competing for the reader's attention.

The monotonous rhythms of the opening stanzas, the juxtapositions of the voices, and the intermittent shifts from one voice to many voices and back again are not simply random. In the first few stanzas, the constancy of the beat mirrors the chug-chug-chug of the trains. Similarly, the frequent movements from one voice to many resembles the come-and-go movements of the trains rolling in and out of the station. Sounds in a train station are rarely constant; there are always shifts and changes. Williams recreates this sensation through the shifts in his poem.

Not only does Williams use poetic form to recreate the surging and stopping of trains, he also wants to recreate the symphony of sounds in the station. In a train station you hear trains, announcements, dialogue, and music, each overlapping the other. Such is the case in "Overture to a Dance of Locomotives." Williams presents various sounds, even if they interrupt the flow of the poem, in an attempt to show that, ultimately, the scene is not one of chaos but one of order, like the poem itself.

Historical Context

"Overture to a Dance of Locomotives" was written at a time of unparalleled cross-fertilization of the arts in both America and Europe. The 1910s were witness to some of the most important innovations in art, music, poetry, business, communication, photography and architecture. In the art world, figures like Pablo Picasso and Georges Braque were experimenting with what would become cubism, perhaps the most influential artistic movement of the century. In 1917, the same year Williams read this poem, Marcel Duchamp shocked the art world by exhibiting a men's urinal as a piece of sculpture. In America, artists like Georgia O'Keefe and Charles Demuth began painting large non-representational canvases that attempted to evoke emotions and reactions rather than replicate images. All of these people were transforming art from a kind of passive activity that beautified the world into an active, dynamic gesture that commented on modern society's tendency to disrupt convention and tradition.

Innovations in the arts were not limited to painting and sculpture. Music was also undergoing radical change. In classical music Gustav Mahler introduced assonance and dissonance into contemporary music, suggesting that the harmony and symmetry of the nineteenth century simply would not suffice in the twentieth century. American music put itself on the map through the popularization of jazz. The concept of jazz, that it relied on improvisation, that it did not require formal training, and that it became the purview of African Americans, seemed to symbolize a sea change in American culture. The predictability and conservatism of twentieth-century America was turned on its head by the wide spread acceptance of jazz and the lifestyle such energetic music engendered.

In other art forms, people like Man Ray were revolutionizing the way people took pictures; Charlie Chaplin and Sergei Eisenstein altered how movies were made; and soon, Virginia Woolf, William Faulkner, and James Joyce would alter the way novels would be conceived. But, perhaps, no changes were more dramatic than in the realm of poetry.

In 1916 and 1917, World War I was on everyone's minds. The world had not experienced death and destruction on such a grand scale. In this decade, people were moving from the country to the city; they were travelling by boat and train; they were listening to the radio and watching movies; they were living in large cities and large buildings where they may not know their neighbors; and young men were dying in battle. Poetry, more than any other written form, has always been mimetic, which is to say, it has always mirrored the world in which it was written. In the seventeenth, eighteenth, and nineteenth centuries, people saw the world as orderly, symmetrical, harmonious; hence,

Compare & Contrast

• **1917:** Wallace Stevens writes what some scholars consider his most Williamesque poem, *"Thirteen Ways of Looking at a Blackbird."*

1917: T. S. Eliot publishes one of his most famous poems, "The Love Song of J. Alfred Prufrock."

1917: Friend and supporter of Williams, Ezra Pound publishes the first of his famous and infamous "Cantos" in small magazines.

1917: In support of our allies in Western Europe, namely Great Britain, the United States enters World War I. For the first time, world wide newspapers carry stories and photographs of war.

1941: After the bombing of Pearl Harbor, the United States declares war on Japan and enters World War II. Newsreels offer glimpses of the casualties of modern-day warfare to eager moviegoers.

1989: When Iraqi leader Saddam Hussein invades Kuwait, the United States bombs Iraq, initiating the Gulf War. Much of the fighting is captured and broadcast on national television.

• **1913:** The Armory Show, an exhibit of European post-impressionism and cubism, takes place in New York. For the first time, many Americans see the work of Henri Matisse, Marcel Duchamp, Pablo Picasso, Paul Cezanne, and Georges Braque. Duchamp's cubist painting "Nude Descending the Staircase" causes much controversy.

1917: Planned by many of the same people involved in the Armory Show, the 1917 Independents Exhibition in New York takes place. Williams reads his poem *"Overture to a Dance of Locomotives."*

1999: At the "Sensations" exhibit at the Brooklyn Museum, a painting by African artist Chris Ofili enrages many people, including the mayor of New York, because Ofili's piece features a droplet of elephant dung on a representation of the Virgin Mary.

---

poetry was harmonious. It rhymed, it found expression in orderly forms like sonnets, villanelles and sestinas.

But after the writings of Darwin and Nietzsche, the horror of the first world war, and the alienating experiences of modern life, the world no longer held the same sense of harmony. So, neither did poetry. Writers like Williams, Stevens, Pound, Eliot, Hart Crane and others began writing a poetry that tried to capture the sense of anguish and angst of early twentieth century America. Thus, poets like e. e. cummings splayed their lines all over the page; Eliot and Pound resorted to collage; Stevens and Williams exploded traditional notions of form. Poems stopped rhyming. No longer were they written in lofty tones. Order was supplanted by disorder. Nature took a back seat to technology.

As dismal as this may sound, artists and writers saw this time as a glorious opportunity to create a new and exciting art. They believed that finally, art and literature could be wrested from the grasp of the elite and be made available to everyone. Above all, they saw the 1910s and 1920s as a time of innovation. Innovation was the spirit of the age. Ezra Pound's famous dictum, "Make it new" captured the zeitgeist of America and Europe as it entered its third decade. In their poetry, Williams and Wallace Stevens were constantly trying to make things new. They experimented with different forms, they imitated painters (both Stevens and Williams tried to replicate cubism and fauvism), they found inspiration in music, and they saw poetry as a means of social and political commentary.

Williams was friends with a number of poets, painters and musicians, so his work, including "Overture to a Dance of Locomotives," reflects his interest in other arts and in the industrial progress of America. For him, the railway station was a symbol for democracy—people coming together, travelling side by side, engaging in a hopeful, artistic dance that may usher them and him into a peaceful and progressive new era.

Critical Overview

"Overture to a Dance of Locomotives" is not one of Williams' better known poems. In fact, most of the authoritative critical studies of Williams either mention the poem only in passing or not at all. Generally, the poem seems to find favor with critics who see it as an example of Williams' zeal for burgeoning American industrialism.

Though neither critic follows up on his claim or offers a reading of the poem, both Peter Halter and Paul Mariani see the poem as endemic of Williams' interest in futurism.

Peter Schmidt probably offers the most thorough reading of the poem. In his study of Williams and other arts, he argues that the poem gains its strength from the shift in tones. According to Schmidt, Williams begins the poem "by writing a monologue in a single mood" but ends the poem "with a suite of contending voices." Schmidt also explores the thinly veiled sexuality in the poem, claiming that Williams links the entry and egress of trains with human sexuality. Ultimately, Schmidt sees the poem as Williams' celebration of the urban world.

Christopher MacGowan picks up on the gallery imagery in the poem and links this imagery with Williams' reading of the poem at the 1917 Independents Exhibition, which took place at the Grand Central Palace in New York, which had been constructed over the renovated Grand Central Station. MacGowan claims that the descriptions of light work like the "interlocking forms of a vorticist painting" that "captures both stillness and energy."

The most unique reading of the poem belongs to Barry Ahearn who claims that the poem unifies two utterly distinct eras. According to Ahearn, the chant of the porters at the beginning of the poem evokes Gregorian chants, especially when one considers the fact that Williams describes the train station as one might describe a cathedral. The second stanza functions as a dual narrative: it could be a description of people making their way to a train or a narrative about "pilgrims making their way through an immense temple."

Criticism

Dean Rader

Rader has published widely in the field of twentieth-century poetry. He is chair of the Department of English and Communication Studies at Texas Lutheran University. In the following essay, he looks at Williams' use of synthesis and his connection to Walt Whitman.

Without question, William Carlos Williams is, along with Wallace Stevens and Ezra Pound, one of the most important American poets of the twentieth century. He gained his reputation through a staggering series of relatively short poems that tend to explore a singular issue or image. Indeed, Williams is often linked to a group of poets called the Imagists, whose mission was to write poetry that did little else but evoke a picture. Pound's famous poem "In a Station at the Metro" lasts only two short lines, but creates a vivid picture of faces emerging from the Paris trains: "The apparition of these faces in the crowd; / Petals on a wet black bough." Williams, known for his short poem "This is Just to Say" and, in particular, the sixteen-word poem, "The Red Wheelbarrow," was an admirer and follower of Pound and often applied Imagistic ideals to his poetry. Thus, his poems possess a singular vision, a tight, reductive quality.

This is not the case for "Overture to a Dance of Locomotive." In this poem, Williams embraces a poetics of fusion, as he seems to be working throughout the piece to fuse disparate elements together. Because of his tendency in this poem to connect, or unite, and because of his celebratory tone and manner of depicting crowds of people, Williams sounds much less like Pound or Stevens, here, and much more like a different poetic father—Walt Whitman. By looking at these poetic gestures, it becomes clear that, like a locomotive himself, Williams seems to be departing from a distant station, the nineteenth-century hub of Whitman's poetry.

While Williams' poem does not directly mimic or copy any particular poem by Whitman, his eager, exuberant tone, his desire to unify otherwise unconnected items, and his interest in throngs of people does stem from Whitman. In an early poem from the "Children of Adam" section of *Leaves of Grass* titled "Once I Pass'd through a Populous City," Whitman sees the populated city as an opportunity. Something similar transpires in *Crossing Brooklyn Ferry,* in which Whitman admires and wonders about the seas of people getting on and off the ferry. For instance, in a poem like "Sparkles from the Wheel," Whitman observes a large crowd of people moving through the city: "Where the city's ceaseless crowd moves on the livelong day, / Withdrawn I join a group of children watching, I pause aside with them." Whitman, always the casual observer, takes a step away from the action and describes to the reader exactly how the masses of people before him form a kind of hub to the larger wheel that is America. Williams performs a similar task in "Overture to a Dance of Locomotives." Like Whitman's, Williams' narrator is not among the people scurrying into and out of the train station. He hangs back to observe and to comment. In fact, at one point he refers to the mob below as shuffling ants. But for him the movement of people forward and backward, their incessant rhythms and the pinpoint timing of the trains combines to create a glorious dance, just as for Whitman the people passing him combine to form a giant wheel. In Williams' poem and in these mentioned of Whitman, both poets are enlivened by the connection between large groups of people and transportation, because both men connect these things with the burgeoning energy and mass of the United States.

One of the great moments in American literature takes place at the beginning of canto XXI of Whitman's *Song of Myself.* Whitman writes:

> I am the poet of the Body and I am the poet of the
> Soul,
> The pleasures of heaven are with me and the pains
> of hell are with me,
> The first I graft and increase upon myself, the latter
> I translate into a new tongue.

> I am the poet of the woman the same as the man.

In this passage, Whitman connects three sets of opposites that have been a profound part of Anglo-American culture since white people arrived in North America in the seventeenth century. Whitman boldly fuses the binarisms, or set of opposites, of body and soul, heaven and hell, and man and woman. Later in the same canto, he offers a convincing yet tender example of his means of reuniting humans with the earth. Thus, for Whitman, opposites only drive a people apart. His poetic mission has always been to unite. Elsewhere in *Song of Myself* he seeks to heal racial separatism, class division, and the unhealed wound between the North and the South.

While Williams' poetic project lacks the overarching vision of Whitman's, in this particular poem, he seems to be channeling the spirit of the

> *Shouts from porters, warnings from conductors, voices over the loudspeakers, all contend with the persona's narration for the reader's attention. Thus, Williams is able to enact a synthesis of the singular voice outside the poem with the plurality of voices within it."*

great bard, for we find an unusual desire to connect. For example, Williams links the rather monotonous, ambling mob with the energy of the trains, suggesting in the final stanza that the two actually work together to form a kind of erotic relationship and, finally, a dance. Additionally, Williams sees railroad tracks as a viable and useful means of connecting the natural world with the mechanized world: "rivers are tunneled: trestles cross oozy swampland." Moreover, where Whitman seeks to connect details within his poem, Williams opts to link items appearing in the poem with ideas or concepts outside the text. For instance, his description of the railway station in the opening stanzas of the poem makes the station appear transfigured into something wholly otherworldly. According to Barry Ahearn, Williams deliberately draws comparisons between Pennsylvania Station, the great Egyptian pyramids, and European cathedrals. Through this comparison, Williams unites three utterly distinct eras' architectural designs and the purposes behind those designs. Also, in what is perhaps his most Whitmanesque gesture, Williams sees the trains as a uniter of all people, regardless of race, class, and gender. It seems clear that he sees the trains and the station as a metaphor for America—a grand space where people are brought together and bolstered by the promise of industry and innovation. Finally, Williams achieves another kind of unity in the poem that remains uniquely his. While the a synthesis of the singular voice outside the poem with the plurality of voices within it.

Both Williams and Whitman tend to write a celebratory poetry. This is particularly unusual given modernism's grave tenor of alienation and suffering. For instance, Eliot's poems are often mournful; Pound's are intellectual and often satirical; Stevens' alternate between giddy and meditative. However, Williams, more than any other modern American poet, opts for the poem of exuberance. In poems like "Danse Russe" and "This is Just to Say," Williams celebrates the simple pleasures in life. In "Danse Russe," the poet describes the luxurious moments when everyone in his family is gone or asleep and he can dance naked, ecstatic, in front of the mirror. Similarly, in "This is Just to Say," the poet walks the reader through the sensuous delights of eating frozen plums that someone else was saving for breakfast. Regarding "Overture to a Dance of Locomotives," Williams' celebratory mode turns from the personal to the public. Here he venerates modern American industry and technology. Without a doubt, he sees the trains as symbols of American progress and the stations themselves as their temples. So powerful and full of potential are the trains, they begin to acquire human qualities. Williams describes the trains as "[p]oised horizontal ... / packed with a warm glow—inviting entry." Peter Schmidt has commented on the implicit sexuality of these lines, but more importantly, Williams is so excited by the trains that he turns them into pulsing, glowing beings. In fact, he turns the entire exchange of passengers and trains into a dance, as suggested by the title.

As celebratory as Williams is, Whitman is even more so. His most famous poem, "Song of Myself" is exactly that—a song celebrating himself. In fact, *Song of Myself* honors all classes of people, all animals, all cities, and all nature. However, two poems in particular stand as possible sources, or influences, for Williams' poem. Whitman's poem "Years of the Modern" remains a classic panegyric of contemporary America. The poem begins: "Years of the modern! years of the unperform'd! / Your horizon rises, I see it parting away for more august dramas." Here, Whitman praises the modernity of America, even though the poem was written in the middle of the nineteenth century. The idea behind the poem is that present-day America, the America in which the poet lives, deserves and even demands veneration. Just as Whitman lauds the promise of the rising horizon, so does Williams laud the potential of America, as exemplified by the surging, capable locomotives. However, the locomotive

What Do I Read Next?

- The poet most often compared to Williams is the great American poet Wallace Stevens, who was Williams' longtime friend. Like Williams, Stevens held an interest in art and poetic form. Stevens' *Collected Poems,* published in 1954, collects most of his published poetry.

- The 1989 publication *William Carlos Williams and James Laughlin: Selected Letters* collects the fascinating correspondences between Williams and his editor at New Directions.

- William's *I Wanted to Write a Poem,* a 1958 autobiography features Williams talking about how he came to be a poet and how he thinks of his poetic career.

- Another poet commonly linked to Williams is Ezra Pound. His *Selected Poems* offers a survey of his poetic career, which takes a very different path than that of Williams'.

- *Many Loves and Other Plays* is a collection of all seven plays that Williams wrote.

- The catalogue *Pennsylvania Modern: Charles Demuth of Lancaster,* edited by Betsy Fahlman, offers some interesting illustrations of the modernist painter's work.

- Edward Fry's important book *Cubism* offers a detailed history of the important art movement. Some critics claim that many of Williams' poems, including "Overture," reflect cubist ideals.

- Albert Gelpi's comprehensive study of modern American poetry *A Coherent Splendor: The American Poetic Renaissance, 1910–1950* offers readings of Williams, Stevens, Pound, Eliot, and other important American poets.

---

poem begins in a typically earnest lyric voice, the linear progress is interrupted by the intrusion of a collage of voices. Shouts from porters, warnings from conductors, voices over the loudspeakers, all contend with the persona's narration for the reader's attention. Thus, Williams is able to enact as a symbol for progress and innovation does not lie with Williams alone. Whitman's poem "To a Locomotive in Winter" reads like a blueprint for Williams' text. Like Williams, Whitman personifies the train ("black cylindric body," "fire-throated beauty," "madly-whistled laughter") even to the point, like Williams, of allotting it passion ("thy measured dual throbbing" and "thy metrical, now swelling pant and roar"). But most intriguing of all is how Whitman, like Williams, sees the locomotive as a symbol of advancement and innovation. Whitman writes, "Type of the modern—emblem of motion and power—pulse of the continent, / For once come serve the Muse and merge in verse." One can imagine Walt Whitman watching with wonder as the train chugs and puffs and blows smoke into the winter air as it glides along the tracks. An impressive engineering achievement, it is no wonder Whitman would identify the locomotive as the emblem of modern America's promise of progress, an identification his poetic heir would make a generation later. And just as Whitman saw the train as a means of connection, of merging, so would Williams see the station as a grand terminal, an even larger type of the modern.

In the last few lines of his locomotive poem, Whitman links the train to music, so it is not surprising to remember that Williams engenders his poem with metaphors of dance. Dances and music always repeat, returning upon themselves, as do trains. For both Williams and Whitman, the music and dance of trains hold symbolic value for American culture, whether, the dance is "sure," as Williams would suggest, or whether, according to Whitman, the train remains "unpent and glad and strong."

Source: Dean Rader, in an essay for *Poetry for Students,* Gale Group, 2001.

Erica Smith

Smith is a writer and editor. In this essay, she discusses how William Carlos Williams' "Overture to a Dance of Locomotives" juxtaposes the modern world of locomotive travel with thoughts of the infinite.

In *William Carlos Williams and the American Poem,* critic Charles Doyle observed that Williams' undertaking was a process of distilling things to their essence:

Seeing clearly, for him, was the great virtue.... Throughout Williams's career we encounter the isolation of the moment of clear perception or experience as if it were hard won from the ever-encroach-

> *The first kind of mechanized travel, the locomotive contradicts traditional notions of how long it takes to get somewhere. In that way, it defies time, making it seem irrelevant."*

ing flux. In a constant state of alertness the artist makes his discoveries.... Genuine contact is made through concentration on the object with great intensity, to 'lift it' to the imagination. An object lifted to the imagination reveals its 'radiant gist.' Sometimes this is simply discovered, while at others ... the process is completed by the poet by means of invention or structuring.

In many of Williams' early poems, the poem itself is presented in a pure, distilled moment. "The Red Wheelbarrow," arguably his most famous poem, presents a poised and timeless image of "a red wheel / barrow / glazed with rain / water." Likewise, one can hear echoes of Japanese haiku in his "Poem":

As the cat
climbed over
the top of
the jamcloset
first the right
forefoot
carefully
then the hind
stepped down
into the pit of
the empty

flowerpot

In poems such as these, the poet fixates on a single image, or motion, and presents it as an unpretentious thing of beauty.

However, in William Carlos Williams' "Overture to a Dance of Locomotives," originally published in the volume *Sour Grapes* (1921), the poet achieves a feeling of stillness through a different process. He paints a whole spectrum of activity, drawing the reader's attention to various objects and sounds, and briefly and exquisitely focusing upon them. Thus, Williams is inviting the reader to go through the distillation process with him.

"Overture to a Dance of Locomotives" is set in a busy train station. Even the title of the poem prepares the reader for a grand scene—an overture usually refers to an instrumental composition intended as an opening piece to an extended musical work. Likewise, in the mind of the poet the locomotives are dancing—a surreal, almost psychedelic image. This coexistence of precise and swirling images is apparent even in the opening lines of the poem: "Men with picked voices chant the names / of cities in a huge gallery." The chanting and "huge"-ness imply that the reader is in the middle of a larger-than-life scene. However, some images have a striking clarity: the men have "picked voices," presumably clear and ringing. Likewise, they are chanting specific, recognizable things: names of cities, the trains' destinations.

The choice of the locomotive, as the dominant image of the poem, is significant in light of Williams' ideologies. Considered one of America's leading modernists, Williams relentlessly pursued the development of a distinctly American mode of verse, different from the English verse traditions used by his contemporaries Ezra Pound, T. S. Eliot, and Wallace Stevens. Fittingly, the locomotive is in many ways a distinctly American machine. Its development in the 1800s gave form and structure to the fulfillment of manifest destiny—the idea that the United States would reach the Pacific Ocean— by enabling more and more people to travel West.

Williams' American-ness can be compared to the uniquely American poet who preceded him, Walt Whitman. Whitman had a voice as vast and dramatic as the Western landscape. And although Williams' verse is exuberant, it is more along the lines of what critic Charles Tomlinson called a "cubist re-structuring of reality." (Cubism is an early twentieth-century school of painting and sculpture in which natural forms are presented through abstract, often geometric, fragments.) Williams' cubist-influenced consideration of the locomotives suggests an evolving American consciousness.

Certainly Williams' experience of the train station is different, ultimately darker, than what Whitman would have related. Williams calls echoes of the cities' names "promises / that pull through descending stairways / to a deep rumbling." Presumably, the stairways lead to the trains waiting on the tracks, but his description of them can be seen as ominous. However, in the following stanza Williams also shows compassion. He calls attention to "The rubbing feet / of those coming to be carried." Although the passengers are presented only as anonymous feet, the poet depicts them as coming to be carried, as if seeking deliverance.

Next, the poet turns his attention to the physical reality of the train station:

"soft light that rocks
to and fro, under the domed ceiling,
across and across from pale
earth-colored walls of bare limestone.

Suddenly, the reader is aware that the train station is grand, elegant, and still, despite the activity within its walls. The rocking of the light suggests meditation and comfort, as if one were in a cradle. Likewise, the limestone walls suggest the timelessness of rock, and a connection to the earth.

The feeling of timelessness is further developed in the next stanza. "Covertly the hands of a great clock / go round and round!" the poet declares. He seems not to notice, or care, that the clock operates according to well-defined increments of time. Instead, the hands of the clock are playful, like a merry-go-round. The poet's imagination thrives on this image, and he wonders what would happen if, in effect, time ceased:

Were [the clock hands] to move quickly and at
    once the whole
secret would be out and the shuffling
of all ants be done forever.

Now, instead of being playful, the poet's imagination is dark and cosmic. In effect, he is fantasizing about the end of time and the cessation of all life. Something about the frenzy inside the station has led him to feel a sense of doom.

As if to temper these disturbing thoughts, the poet shifts his attention again, this time to the light:

A leaning pyramid of sunlight, narrowing
out at a high window, moves by the clock:
discordant hands straining out from
a center.

The phrase "pyramid of sunlight," especially as related to a clock, evokes the structures of the ancient Egyptians: pyramids and sundials. The hands on the clock in the train station seem to be full of life. They strike poses—"inevitable postures infinitely repeated." They are anonymous, like the people whose feet shuffle through the station, and have, seemingly, been in effect since ancient times.

Through this scene comes a cry: "two— twofour—twoeight!" This sound, echoing the beat of the locomotive's wheels gaining momentum, sends a jolt through the frenzied dance within both the station and the poet's mind. The reader's focus shifts to the characters at hand: "Porters in red hats run on narrow platforms. / This way ma'am! / — important not to take the wrong train!" The poet's consideration of infinity has been replaced by a woman hurrying to catch a train. For now, considerations of the immediate have replaced the eternal

The poet briefly considers his larger surroundings again, noticing that "Lights from the concrete / ceiling hang crooked, but—" and his thoughts are cut off, interrupted again by the image of a train waiting on the tracks. The scene is comforting to him: train tracks are "glittering parallels;" the cylinders, though dingy, "invit[e] entry." The poet also notes that they "pull against the hour": a suggestion that the locomotive itself is in a complex relationship with time. The first kind of mechanized travel, the locomotive contradicts traditional notions of how long it takes to get somewhere. In that way, it defies time, making it seem irrelevant.

Again, though, the abstractions are interrupted, this time by a whistle. The churning of the locomotive wheels speeds up: "Not two eight. Not twofour. Two!" The poet watches the train pull out, seeing several realities pass by: "Gliding windows. Colored cooks sweating / In a small kitchen. Taillights—" and the train keeps going, according to a very strict rhythm: "In time: twofour! / In time: twoeight!"

In the final stanza the poet shifts perspective again, this time considering the path that the locomotive will take. He considers a landscape: "—rivers are tunnelled: trestles / cross oozy swampland." The ability of a locomotive to cross such difficult terrain is indeed a feat of the modern era. At the same time, though, the train has a quality of stillness: "wheels that repeat the same gesture remain relatively / stationary." Finally, the poet meditates on the rails; they too have a universal quality, "forever parallel / return on themselves infinitely." In this infiniteness the poet feels as if he has found certainty: "The dance is sure."

The world that Williams has distilled for the reader is both rarefied and frightening. He can look at things deeply, seeing the realities of the station, feeling the thrill of locomotive travel, while at the same time considering them alongside the eternal concepts of time and space. His suggestion of confusion and doom reflects his modern sensibility, but, ultimately, his faith in "the dance" prevails.

Source: Erica Smith, in an essay for *Poetry for Students,* Gale Group, 2001.

Jonathan N. Barron

Barron is an associate professor of English at the University of Southern Mississippi. Beginning

Let words on the page happen wherever they want ... Do not ... just print poems line after line in a logical order leading to a conclusion."

in 2001, he will be the editor-in-chief of The Robert Frost Review. *In the following essay, he considers the impact of the early 20th-century artistic movement, Italian Futurism, on "Overture to a Dance of Locomotives."*

In the history of twentieth-century art, Italian futurism was one of the first and most exciting new movements to include both poetry and painting. It began in 1909 when Italian poet and painter F. T. Marinetti published a manifesto. This dramatic full-page article, published in the staid, conservative Paris newspaper *Le Figaro,* announced the birth of a new idea for art. Among that paper's respectable readership, the manifesto caused a sensation, because it challenged and contested the readers' mostly traditional notions of poetry and painting. Soon the movement became notorious. By 1910, five Italian painters had joined with Marinetti. Together they announced, in another manifesto, the existence of futurist painting. Marinetti, meanwhile, had gone further still in his experimentation with language and declared the freedom of the word with the now famous, if not infamous, phrase "parole in liberta" (words in freedom). Marinetti's new poetic program of "word freedom" argued that words themselves needed to be free and so had to break from the rules of syntax (logical sentence order). He declared that poets should play with typeface and page arrangements. Let words on the page happen wherever they want, he demanded. He advocated the use of huge bold type, italics, tiny print, and giant print on the same page, even in the same sentence. He called on poets to play with every kind of typographical trick. Do not, he argued, just print poems line after line in a logical order leading to a conclusion.

By 1917, when William Carlos Williams first made his "Overture to a Dance of Locomotives" public, Italian futurism, particularly among poets and painters, had achieved international attention: exhibitions, performances, and what, today, would be called interventions—crazy, surprising, creative happenings in unexpected places—had occurred in London, Paris, and New York. Already in 1917, Williams was himself part of the avant-garde scene in Greenwich Village, New York. His closest friends were painters and poets in the futurist mold. So it was not surprising that he, too, should be a part of avant-garde festivals. In fact, it was at one of these festivals in New York, according to the scholars of Williams' poetry, A. Walton Litz and Christopher MacGowen, that William Carlos Williams first "read the 'futurist' poem" "Overture to a Dance of Locomotives." Specifically, they report that Williams read the poem at "the Independents exhibition of avant-garde art that opened at Grand Central Palace in April 1917." Eventually, this same poem was published in Williams' book of other futurist, and similarly experimental, avant-garde poetry, *Sour Grapes* (1921).

Given that the poem first came to public attention in a futurist artistic milieu, what does it mean to think of this poem as futurist? Before answering that question in detail, it will help to provide some more information about futurism itself. In a wonderful book detailing the connection between poets, composers, and painters in the early twentieth century, the English literary critic Christopher Butler explains that: "For the Futurist the city is the environment in which the museum-bound culture of the past can be subverted, and new boundaries between art and life evolved." What Butler means is that city things in the first part of the twentieth-century had been devalued and condemned as anti-human, alienating, even destructive to the soul and to happiness. The Italian futurists, by contrast, loved the city and the new kind of lifestyle it made possible. They loved the new facts of speed, machines, and action. They loved all the urban things that a romantic and agrarian art world thought of as mechanized death. What was to the romantic imagination the very source of destruction to the inner life of the feeling soul, was to the Italian futurist a source of invigorating joy and pleasure: the city. To the futurist, the city was the site of a new human being. Therefore, they wanted to abolish museums, because the museums contradicted the city's relentless drive toward new things. Everything devoted to the past, the futurist opposed. Futurists, as their name implies, only cared for the present—an eternal present leading to the future, but at constant war with the dead weight and burden of the past.

Butler adds that futurism "promised an urban subject-matter which was also to be stirred up and given a crudely dynamic quality." In other words, futurist painting and poetry accented motion, dynamism, and speed, and refused to work out of the traditions of art history and poetic history that privileged geometry, stability, and the still life. Futurism attempted to destroy the preceding history of art by making energy, speed, and action part of the painting and the poem itself. Butler even reports that one of the futurist painters, Umberto Boccioni, described just what was so new and exciting, so dynamic, about the city when he said: "we enter into the overwhelming vortex of modernity through its crowds, its automobiles, its telegraphs, its bare lower-class neighbourhoods (sic), its sounds, its shrieks, its violence, its cruelties, its cynicism." Boccioni and his friends wanted to depict, praise, even celebrate such things in their art. Their poet compatriots meant to do the same.

Another literary critic and a scholar of Italian futurism Peter Nicholls insists that its most important characteristic was a focus on time. To Nicholls, Italian futurism must be understood as an entirely, absolutely new artistic movement. He says it was "a moment of absolute rupture with what has gone before." Marinetti himself accented this pursuit of the new and this disdain for the past when he went so far as to demand that all museums be burned. To the Italian futurist, in other words, the new twentieth-century industrial city experience was the only human experience worth discussing precisely because it was so new. Inner life, the soul, they argued, could, given the fact of city life, now only be represented in terms of motion, speed, and machines. As Nicholls says, "time flows away, carrying with it experiences that cannot be lived again, though they can become present momentarily as memories."

The Italian futurist association of human experience with machines, speed, urban architecture, and time, as well as its focus on the new, is at the very heart of William Carlos Williams' poem. And while this poem is not as crazy in its typography, word order, or use of typeface as are some other futurist poems, it is, nonetheless, typically futurist through its use of fragments, jump-cuts from one scene to another, and urban imagery and themes.

Williams' poem is particularly futurist because it refuses to tell the romantic story of how one man feels in a particular place. There is no one human being in this poem. There is no one character. Instead of a character, the poem has city people, trains, a train station. Things and people seem to co-exist on the same field. Every item that Williams asks the reader to see—trains, stairs, light, feet, sidewalk, clock—shares equal prominence. This is not a poem about people in the city. Rather it is a poem about a city where all of its things, even people, are understood to be equivalent objects. Futurists loved to make such points in their art and poetry. They loved to say that people were not so special, and that they should be no more important than machines. They loved to make people and things equivalent. For doing such things, they were often called anti-humanists.

Specifically, Williams' poem takes place in New York City's Pennsylvania Station which, in 1917, was a cathedral to the modern city. Eventually destroyed, this railroad station, in its day, was a modern wonder. A huge vault of glass designed by the famous architectural firm of McKim, Mead, and White, it was, in the words of New York historian Elizabeth Hawes, the firm's "masterpiece." Inspired by the Baths of Caracalla in Rome, the station filled all those who entered it with a sense of awe. Eight years in the making, it covered eight acres of prime Manhattan real estate when it opened in 1910. As Hawes explains, the firm that built the station were the architects of choice for the city's wealthy elite. She tells readers that McKim, Mead, and White had "taught the aristocracy all they knew about Renaissance style": they had built "houses, clubs, and memorials" for the rich, and "[t]hey were doubtless the busiest, the most fashionable, the most eminent architects in America the high priests of classicism." This is especially relevant because Pennsylvania Station was one of their only public buildings. True, this was a time when passenger railroads, like the Pennsylvania line, were private companies, but they were also dependent on civic structures. Therefore, of all the places for Williams to choose for his poem, he chooses one of the fanciest, most amazing public and modern buildings in the most vibrant and largest city in America. In a poem about the glories of city life, industry, and machines, he uses, as his primary scene, the most glorious public building (only seven years old) in the city. The station itself, in other words, was already considered a futurist artwork by Williams and his friends just by being so beautiful, so new, and so colossal in scope.

Turning, now, directly to the poem, one sees that it presents a specifically futurist tension between stasis (standing still, things that do not move) and flux (motion, energy, movement). This tension between stasis and flux is also a common element in futurist painting. And in this poem, Williams, like a painter, creates images that will show how time itself might exist in a perpetual present as constant energy with no past.

Looking first at the title, one discovers that Williams challenges the static, non-moving quality of dead words on a page. By calling the poem an "Overture," he compares it to the musical opening, or introduction to a longer work, usually an opera. In this case, the overture, or musical introduction, will come before a dance. But this dance, it turns out, is a dance of trains, of locomotives. The city, thanks to this title, is already an artwork, a grand symphony and a grand ballet. Since music and dance are arts of movement, dependent on sequence in time and moment of performance, Williams has, with this title, taken the reader out of the poetry and, metaphorically, placed the reader right into the thick of the city; it is as if New York itself were an action, a performance work in progress. Given this title, then, one might also say that Williams is asking readers to think of the train station as a site where a symphony of sound becomes an overture to a dance of trains. Such a perspective can only be understood through the lens of Italian futurism.

To read the poem as a futurist work, one begins, then, with the musical metaphor of the titles. Like a futurist musical performance, which futurists called "the art of noise," the first stanza tells us that the music comes from the rhythmical chanting of the various cities to which the trains are headed. Echoing through the huge dome of Pennsylvania Station, the "picked voices chant the names" and so create a new, urban, modern music. Following the colon in line two, Williams explains what this new music does: the repeated names are "promises / that pull through descending stairways / to a deep rumbling." Every name becomes a lure that will send people down the stairs to the train platforms where more music, "a deep rumbling," awaits. The names from on high echo in the dome's air and lure the passengers to the stairs where the sound of the trains will add more notes to their journey, their own dance as they speed off to exotic temptations in other cities. This first stanza is distinctly futurist, then, because what would typically be a static scene—a huge room at the center of a train station—is depicted entirely through metaphors of energy and motion. Even the noise moves up and down the stairs.

In the second stanza, Williams changes his scene with a cut to an entirely new image. This, too, is a typical strategy of Italian futurism. The second stanza brings readers outside of the station.

Readers are asked to see people entering from the street. At the same time, Williams describes the light that, like the people, is also moving. Rather than focus on one, or even many, characters, Williams, instead, only lets readers see "rubbing feet." This is a poem of the masses, of the group. In this second stanza, then, two new instruments have joined the overture: feet and light have joined with train sounds and announcements. Notice that the feet "quicken a / grey pavement into soft light." The light, meanwhile, "rocks / to and fro, under the domed ceiling."

The third stanza, as was true of the first two, also changes the scene. Now back inside the station Williams focuses on the giant clock. He describes the clock's hands, and, in so doing, he makes time itself an issue for the poem. Because the Italian futurists expected their art to defeat the past and champion the present, Williams, in this stanza, tells his readers that "Covertly the hands of a great clock / go round and round!" In the actual experience of this train station, in other words, the clock's constant changing is not noticed. It is "covert." This is another way of saying that, to those hurrying to catch a train, the passage of time, the creation of a past, has to be covert: all that matters is the present moment, the future, and the hope that one will not miss one's train. In a real overture in a real symphony, the moment of the performance is also happening just then: it, too, is always present. In this stanza, Williams articulates a futurist vision. Describing the hands of the clock he says:

> Were they to
> move quickly and at once the whole
> secret would be out and the shuffling
> of all ants be done forever.

The "secret" Williams refers to, here, is the secret of "time." In this city, in the futurist vision of the world, time does not exist if time means the need to think of and depend on the burden of the past. In fact, says Williams, the city is so energized, so dependent on speed, that everything feels like it is moving "quickly and at once." Were the misguided "feet" hurrying to their trains and wishing to maintain their regulated commuter lives to know that all time happens "at once," they would no longer be ants but rather they would be men and women, fully attuned to the overture and dance of the continuous present.

As if to insist on the futurist need for an eternal now of constant, ever-present energy in the living moment, Williams plays the image of light against the image of the clock. In this dance, nature's time, sunlight, contrasts with human time, the mechanical clock. Williams describes the "pyramid of light" moving by the clock. When the geometrically precise natural light (a pyramid) hits the mechanical hands, it proves that the clock is just "disaccordant hands straining out from a center." In other words, the clock is just two points forced to travel round and round a surface: its real energy is too controlled, not liberated and natural like the sunlight. When he says this, Williams implicitly judges all those hurrying feet. He implies that if they would only liberate themselves from the clock, they would be even more free, more committed to the eternal present. He implies that movement, energy, speed ought not to be bound to two hands on a circle: that a clock always refers, if even covertly, to the past.

When Williams did finally publish this poem in his 1921 collection, he concluded the first section just after line twenty. Such a division, however, actually maintains the poem's futurist quality. By breaking the poem into two parts here, Williams suggests that after line twenty, the overture has concluded, and now the dance can begin. Following the music of time, Williams next represents the dance of the locomotives. In the concluding twenty lines of the poem, labeled in *Sour Grapes* with a roman numeral two, one finds far more choppy syntax, and a lot more interruptions and jump-cuts from scene to scene. The poem, as it were, speeds up. The final twenty-four lines (Part II) are constantly interrupted by voices. Even the words seem to dance on the page. Be that as it may, by the end of the poem, the trains begin to move, the dance has certainly begun as the trains become the focus of the poem. Ultimately, Williams even follows a train out of the station and along its way into the great country where, presumably, the dance will continue. Futurism, in this poem, is always now, never confined to any one place.

Source: Jonathan N. Barron, in an essay for *Poetry for Students,* Gale Group, 2001.

Sources

Ahearn, Barry, *William Carlos Williams and Alterity: The Early Poetry,* Cambridge University Press, 1994.

Butler, Christopher, *Early Modernism,* Oxford University Press, 1994.

Doyle, Charles, *William Carlos Williams and the American Poem,* St. Martin's Press, 1982.

Halter, Peter, *The Revolution in the Visual Arts and the Poetry of William Carlos Williams,* Cambridge University Press, 1994.

Litz, A. Walton and Christopher MacGowen, editors, *The Collected Poems of William Carlos Williams Vol. 1,* New Directions, 1986.

Marling, William, *William Carlos Williams and the Painters, 1909–1923,* Ohio University Press, 1982.

MacGowan, Christopher J., *William Carlos Williams's Early Poetry: The Visual Arts Background,* UMI Research Press, 1984.

Nicholls, Peter, *Modernisms: A Literary Guide,* University of California Press, 1995.

Schmidt, Peter, *William Carlos Williams, The Arts, And Literary Tradition,* Louisiana State University, 1988.

Williams, William Carlos, *Selected Poems,* edited by Charles Tomlinson, New Directions, 1985.

For Further Reading

Axelrod, Steven Gould and Helen Deese, *Critical Essays on William Carlos Williams,* G. K. Hall, 1988.
    This book collects both early and late reviews of Williams' books and offers a large menu of essays exploring the myriad of Williams' poetry

Duffey, Bernard, *A Poetry of Presence: The Writing of William Carlos Williams,* University of Wisconsin Press, 1986.
    Instead of focusing on either poetry or prose or drama, Duffey sees all of these as interrelated writings that help define Williams and his themes.

Mariani, Paul, *A New World Naked,* McGraw, 1981.
    A comprehensive critical biography of Williams placing his poems in both personal and cultural contexts. It is well-researched and contains some helpful pictures.

Mazzaro, Jerome, ed. *A Profile of William Carlos Williams,* C. E. Merrill, 1971.
    A valuable collection of essays by leading scholars and poets who comment on various aspects of Williams' poetry.

———, *William Carlos Williams: The Later Poems,* Cornell University Press, 1973.
    Since commentary on "Overture" usually falls in studies of Williams' early poetry, it is sometimes useful to look at studies of his later work. This book may prove useful because Mazzaro tries to show how the later poems fulfill the dreams of the younger poet.

Rosenthal, M. L., *A William Carlos Williams Reader,* New Directions, 1996.
    A very useful book that collects selected poems, "improvisations," fiction, drama and excerpts from Williams' autobiography. It is an excellent starting point for further reading of Williams' work.

Paradoxes and Oxymorons

John Ashbery

1981

"Paradoxes and Oxymorons" originally appeared in the *Times Literary Supplement* and was later published in John Ashbery's 1981 collection of poems *Shadow Train,* nominated for the American Book Award. A favorite both of the poet's and of editors', "Paradoxes and Oxymorons" has been widely anthologized. At one point Ashbery wanted the poem to be the title of the collection because he felt that it was the most accessible poem in the book. Written between March and mid-October 1979 in the poet's newly acquired Victorian-era house in upstate New York, *Shadow Train* contains fifty sixteen-line poems that some critics have likened to a sonnet sequence. Unlike sonnets, which consist of fourteen lines, Ashbery's poems have no set rhyme scheme, and Ashbery himself has said that he doesn't much like sonnets.

Typical of many of Ashbery's poems, and of much post-modern verse, it directs readers' attention to the words themselves, placing the language's materiality and the process of meaning-making in the foreground. The poem, its speaker, and its readers all take part in this process. Paradoxes are statements that contain often inexplicable or contradictory elements that nonetheless may still be true in some way. For example, in the third line the speaker says of the poem, "You have it but you don't have it." Oxymorons are rhetorical figures in which contradictory terms are combined in a phrase, such as "jumbo shrimp," or such as "A deeper outside thing" at the beginning of the ninth line in Ashbery's poem.

Also typical of Ashbery's poetry is the high level of abstraction and self-questioning. His lines often suggest or echo other lines or ideas that readers "think" they know, only to shift suddenly to something altogether different. This is why many critics and general readers are often at a loss to describe what Ashbery's poems are "about." In many ways he can be read as a poet with no "real" subjects. Because Ashbery's poems rely heavily on associative thinking and connections between and among lines, images, and ideas are often tenuous at best, and critical interpretations of individual poems may yield little in the way of insight. Readers interested in grasping Ashbery's work would be better served by reading a complete collection of his poems, treating them as part of the longer poem of Ashbery's life's work.

Author Biography

John Ashbery

Born in 1927 in Rochester, New York, to farmer Chester Frederick and Helen Lawrence Ashbery, John Ashbery grew up on a farm in western New York State near Lake Ontario. He attended Deerfield Academy before taking his B.A. from Harvard, where he was classmates with Frank O'Hara, James Schuyler, and Kenneth Koch, all of whom came to be associated with the New York School of poets. An informal group of writers with an interest in making poetry funnier, more colloquial, and more contemporary, the New York School poets also shared a love of popular culture, studding their poems with images and allusions to movie stars, music, and film. After graduating from Harvard, Ashbery completed an M.A. in English from Columbia University, writing his thesis on Henry Green, a minor English novelist.

Passionate about painting as a teenager, Ashbery cultivated a love for writing and literature at Harvard. After winning a scholarship to France, he began writing about art for the *New York Herald Tribune* in Paris, supporting himself for a decade through his art criticism and translation projects. In 1956 W. H. Auden selected his first collection of poems, *Some Trees,* for the Yale Younger Poets Prize. Since then, Ashbery's reputation has blossomed, and he is now considered by some critics to be the most influential American poet of the last half of the twentieth century. Ashbery is not, however, without his critics. Because of his intensely abstract style in which he often experiments with syntactical structure, associative thinking, point of view, and subject matter, many readers find his poems impossible to grasp, and some suspect that at root he is being deliberately elusive in his meanings. Such a stance is also precisely what appeals to many other readers, who see in Ashbery a poet whose interest in capturing the randomness of experience and the part that language plays in that randomness a fresh kind of realism more in tune with life in the late twentieth century. Ashbery's poems often evoke feelings and thoughts but rarely have a determinate meaning that more than a few readers would agree on. His desire to include as much of the world as possible in his poems gives his writing an expansiveness few other contemporary poets share. Yet his refusal to pin the things of the world down to a meaning or set of meanings makes for an obscurity that some consider so much verbal posturing.

Along with French surrealism, modern painting and music have been strong influences on Ashbery's poetry. Abstract expressionists, action painters, and collagists of the 1950s, such as Willem de Kooning and Robert Rauschenberg, focused on the process of composition and the surface of the canvas, creating works that were non-representational and open to a multitude of interpretations. Ashbery's own crosscutting, experiments with associative imagery, stream-of-consciousness, and improvisational methods create similar surfaces, though verbal. His incorporation of random thoughts and images also echo the compositional methods of composers such as John Cage. In one of his more lucid poems, "What is Poetry?", Ashbery "answers" the title's question in his typically elusive manner, by asking more questions:

> The medieval town, with frieze
> Of boy scouts from Nagoya? The snow
> That came when we wanted it to snow?
> Beautiful images? Trying to avoid
> Ideas, as in this poem? ...

Poem Text

This poem is concerned with language on a very
    plain level.
Look at it talking to you. You look out a window
Or pretend to fidget. You have it but you don't
    have it.
You miss it, it misses you. You miss each other.

The poem is sad because it wants to be yours, and   5
    cannot.
What's a plain level? It is that and other things,
Bringing a system of them into play. Play?
Well, actually, yes, but I consider play to be

A deeper outside thing, a dreamed role-pattern,
As in the division of grace these long August days   10
Without proof. Open-ended. And before you know
It gets lost in the stream and chatter of typewriters.

It has been played once more. I think you exist
    only
To tease me into doing it, on your level, and then
    you aren't there
Or have adopted a different attitude. And the poem   15
Has set me softly down beside you. The Poem is
    you.

Poem Summary

Stanza 1:

Paradoxes and oxymorons are rhetorical figures, and by naming the poem after them Ashbery is setting up readers' expectations to look for these figures. The first line is ironic, whether intentionally or not is unimportant. Any poem with the title "Paradoxes and Oxymorons" cannot be "concerned with language on a very plain level," as these figures of speech are themselves often difficult to understand. Ashbery's poems frequently contain a high degree of self-reflexivity, and this

poem is no different. A poem is self-reflexive when it is its own subject, when it describes and explains itself. The speaker, who is one with the poem, directs readers to witness the poem talking to them and "scripts" the reader's response: "You look out a window / Or pretend to fidget." The image of "fidgeting" speaks to the intense self-consciousness of the speaker and of human beings in general, especially those in romantic relationships. It echoes the kind of response someone might have in an awkward conversation with his or her lover. The next sentence, "You have it but you don't have it," is itself a paradox, that is, a statement that contains terms or ideas that on the surface appear to be irreconcilable. Ashbery here refers to the process of meaning-making in reading a poem. Readers, especially those unfamiliar with contemporary poetry, sometimes think they "get" the poem but then think they don't. On a different level, these lines also echo the ways in which human beings communicate with one another, the way they frequently "miss" each other's meanings and intentions.

Stanza 2:

The first line is silly and sentimental if readers think of poems as inanimate objects, which cannot feel or desire. More likely, Ashbery is poking fun at the idea of sentimentality. However, it also speaks, again, to the idea of meaning and comprehension, a reader's own struggle to "possess" language, and a lover's desire to possess another. The speaker refers back to his own statement in the first stanza when asking, "What's a plain level?" Such self-interviewing draws readers deeper into the poem, forcing them to pay closer attention to their own thinking processes. The "that" refers to "plain level" itself. By stating, in essence, that a plain level is a plain level, Ashbery is being tautological, that is, redundant. "Other things" is left undefined. Continuing with his method of making statements and then questioning those very statements, Ashbery introduces the notion of "play," again referring to the very thing that he is doing in the poem itself. The introduction of the "I" into the poem in the last line brings another element into play, the author. Ashbery builds meaning through suggestion and through asking questions, but he never answers them directly. The accumulation of statements and questions, of assertions and qualifications, of abstractions without referents, gives the poem texture, makes it dreamlike, surreal.

Stanza 3:

The "outside thing" in the first line might refer to the world outside the poem itself, the world from which the poem springs. "A dreamed role-pattern" suggests both structure *and* randomness, which the poet suggests is the stuff of "play." The second and third lines are enigmas, that is, Ashbery gives no clue as to how "a dreamed role-pattern" and "the division of grace these long August days / Without proof" are similar. One possibility is that Ashbery finished composing the poem during August. In his endnotes on *Shadow Train,* John Shoptaw lists the composition date of "Paradoxes and Oxymorons" as July 29, which is close enough to support this theory. August is also considered by many to be the slowest month of the year, when summer is at its height. This would account for the description of the month as "long." Ashbery underscores the poem's own sense of play by making "Open-ended" its own sentence and enclosing it in the middle of a line. "The steam and chatter of typewriters" is the most concrete image in the entire poem and throws the reader into the world of things, as opposed to ideas.

Stanza 4:

The poet, the poem, and the reader are all in play in this final stanza. The "it" in the first line is, presumably, the poem. Ashbery appears to liken it to a piece of music, which can also be "played." The "I" makes its second and final appearance in the first line of this stanza, thinking of "you," presumably the reader. It is important to note that "you" can also mean the speaker himself. The use of the second person to address another part of the speaker has a rich history in poetry, and Ashbery plays with this convention. The poet writes with the idea of the reader in mind ("I think you exist only / To tease me into doing it"), an idea that changes as he composes the poem. The poem mimics the dance of lovers, a dance that frequently includes indecision, playfulness, and evolving attitudes. In the final lines, poem, reader, and speaker conflate into one entity. The processes, both of composing the poem and of reading the poem, are included in the idea of the poem.

Themes

Language and Meaning

"Paradoxes and Oxymorons" questions the idea that language is an effective tool for communicating ideas about the physical, empirically verifiable world. The poem suggests that poetry, and by extension all language, is ultimately about itself and its inability to say anything definitive about the world. The first stanza underscores this idea, as the poem eludes the understanding of the reader: "You miss it, it misses you. You miss each other." These words also echo the way that lovers frequently misunderstand one another, showing how language is often at a distance from things. By making the poem into a lover of sorts, a lover who can never be fully understood or possessed by the reader, Ashbery shows how language also makes promises, promises that often go unfilled. The self-questioning in the second stanza dramatizes the notion that even the speaker is not in control of what he says. Language seems to have a mind of its own, separate from that of the speaker. After asking himself, "What's a plain level?", the speaker responds, "It is that and other things." The speaker's very inability (or unwillingness) to adequately define the term "plain level" underscores the impossibility of definitive meaning. Using pronouns such as "it" and "that"—which refer only back to themselves—underscores the self-reflexivity of language. This

Topics for Further Study

- Do you agree with the speaker's claim that "This poem is concerned with language on a very plain level"? Why or why not?

- Rewrite "Paradoxes and Oxymorons" using language that, to you, is on "a very plain level." Try to get at what you see as the meaning of the poem.

- Write a poem that contains at least five allusions to popular culture.

- Many modern and contemporary poets like Ashbery see poetry primarily as a form of play. After defining the term "play" to your satisfaction, discuss how you see "Paradoxes and Oxymorons" as an illustration (or not) of play.

- Ashbery is frequently linked by personal history and aesthetic affinity to the abstract expressionists, a group of painters who were more interested in the process of creation than in the product itself. After researching abstract expressionism, write a short essay arguing for the ways in which Ashbery might be called an abstract expressionist poet.

means that language can only point back to itself, and not to the world of things, which human beings often assume is what language does. Similarly, the "Steam and chatter of typewriters," highlights the material production of words for its own sake, without paying attention to the meaning of these words. In case the reader missed it during the first three stanzas, the final stanza hammers home the idea that the reader has quite literally been "played," that is, the poem, by hinting at meaning and then withdrawing further into muddy abstractions, toys with the reader's expectations and processes of meaning-making.

Appearances and Reality

"Paradoxes and Oxymorons" illustrates the idea that the world is never quite what it seems to be; appearances are deceptive. Greek philosopher Plato addresses this idea in *The Allegory of the Cave,* claiming that human beings live in the shadows of the real world. "Paradoxes and Oxymorons," a poem included in a collection titled *Shadow Train,* is in itself obscure and elusive in nature. One of the central paradoxes of the poem is its relationship to reality. After establishing that the poem is "concerned with language on a very plain level," the speaker complicates that level, ultimately suggesting, in the third stanza, that the poem, like reality itself, is "a dreamed role pattern." The poem, like reality, is a form of play "without proof." This last phrase calls attention to the idea that perception itself is unreliable. What happens in reality is like what happens in this poem: Both are unpredictable; both contain random events.

Rather than representing reality, language *is* reality. The way in which human beings use it determines the ways in which they will perceive and experience the world. The final stanza underscores how the poem, itself a rarified form of language, has manipulated the reader's expectations and desires. The poem, like reality, is ultimately embodied in the reader. It exists because someone exists to read it.

Style

Sonnet

"Paradoxes and Oxymorons" is not a sonnet, but it approximates one in form and subject matter, and critics reviewing *Shadow Train* regularly comment on the collection as a variation on a sonnet sequence. Historically, sonnets consist of fourteen lines. The Petrarchan sonnet, named after the fourteenth-century Italian poet Petrarch, has an octave (eight lines) that rhymes *abbaabba,* and a sestet (six lines) that rhymes *cdecde* or sometimes *cdccdc,* while the English, or Shakespearean sonnet consists of three quatrains (four lines) that rhyme *abab cdcd efef,* and a couplet (two lines) which rhymes *gg.* "Paradoxes and Oxymorons," like the other forty-nine poems in the collection, consists of four unrhymed quatrains. Ashbery's poem, however, like many sonnets, takes love (loosely) as its subject.

Address

"Paradoxes and Oxymorons" addresses the reader, which is unusual but not unheard of in contemporary poetry. The use of the second person "you" is more common when used by the speaker

Compare & Contrast

- **1981:** International Business Machines introduces its personal computer for the home market, and in the first year and a half 136,000 are sold. Shortly after an entire industry of "PC clones" begins.

1997: Deep Blue, a 32-node IBM supercomputer, defeats World Chess champion Gary Kasparov.

- **1981:** A number of near-miss nuclear accidents occur. The USS *George Washington,* a submarine carrying 160 nuclear warheads, collides with a Japanese freighter in the East China Sea, and an American *Posiedon* nuclear missile being removed from the USS *Holland* is caught by a safety mechanism just seconds before it would have hit the ship's hull.

1997: The United States breaks a five-year moratorium on nuclear testing and conducts an underground sub-critical nuclear weapons test at the Nevada Test Site.

1997: Alexander Lebed, Russian President Boris Yeltsin's former National Security Advisor, claims that 100 suitcase-sized nuclear bombs are missing in Russia.

1998: Both India and Pakistan conduct nuclear weapons tests. Tensions between the two countries run high.

2000: Officials announce that crucial data on United States' nuclear weapons is missing from a vault in Los Alamos, New Mexico.

to address another part of himself. Ashbery's poem complicates these two uses of "you." The reader can be both other people reading his poem *and* Ashbery himself as he reads along with it as he's composing. The conflation of "I," "you," and the poem at the end all contribute to the sense of playfulness and mystery in the poem's address.

Historical Context

The poems in *Shadow Train* were composed during an eight-month period between March and mid-October 1979. Ashbery, a New York City apartment dweller for his entire adult life, had just purchased a Victorian house in upstate New York. In his study of Ashbery's poetry, *On the Outside Looking Out,* John Shoptaw speculates that "With its multiple rooms, this house may have provided a blueprint for the many-chambered volume [i.e., *Shadow Train*]." In a *New York* magazine article, "Capital Gains," Ashbery likens the poems in *Shadow Train* to abstract art, saying, "These compositions go about their business as though dealing with the customary square or oblong containing

frame, yet they are unexpectedly truncated and finally liberated by the soaring and diminishing implications of the diamond shape."

Music and art play major roles in Ashbery's composing processes. His house boasts paintings and artwork from friends such as Fairfield Porter, Alex Katz, and Willem De Kooning, all internationally known artists, and Ashbery frequently composes his poems while listening to music. In his interview with Ashbery titled "A Blue Rinse for the Language," Michael Glover writes that "The language of his books is informed by his roving enthusiasms for particular composers." In the same interview Ashbery states, "I've always felt myself to be a rather frustrated composer who was trying to do with words what musicians are able to do with notes.... The importance of meaning that's beyond expression in words is what I've always been attracted to." Shoptaw claims that "Paradoxes and Oxymorons" is similar to experimental music, writing that "What deepens Ashbery's level playing field are his random [John] Cagean procedures, a hugely varied 'division of labor' between the poet and language." John Cage, who died in 1992, used chance operations in writing his music and, in general, was a proponent of non-intentionality in composition. Ashbery is well-known for saying that he has no desire to plumb the great metaphysical questions of existence but rather is interested in surface details and thoughts as they cross his mind. Ashbery, like many of the painters he admires and like Cage, is sometimes referred to as a postmodernist.

Postmodernism, a hotly debated term, refers to the radical experiments in the arts that took place after World War II. Some historians use the two world wars as markers for the beginnings of modernism and postmodernism. Some of the features commonly associated with postmodern literature and art include an attention to surface, as opposed to depth; a willingness to mix genres, mediums, and subject matter; a focus on the materiality of art, as opposed to the meaning of art; more attention paid to the process of composition than to the finished product; and an embrace of popular culture and forms of "low" art such as cartoons, popular music, and so forth. Like modernism, post-modernism often depicts human beings as alienated and often self-deluded and human life as having no inherent meaning. Artists, writers, and musicians often described as post-modernists include John Ashbery, Robert Rauschenberg, Thomas Pynchon, Kathy Acker, Merce Cunningham, Steve Reich, Jeff Koons, and Andy Warhol.

Critical Overview

Shadow Train (1981), the collection in which "Paradoxes and Oxymorons" appears, received mixed reviews. In his study of Ashbery's poetry *On the Outside Looking Out,* critic John Shoptaw calls "Paradoxes and Oxymorons" the most popular poem in *Shadow Train* and notes that at one point Ashbery considered making it the title poem of the collection but then thought better of it when he realized that many readers might not know what an oxymoron was. Shoptaw writes that "The poem itself voices Ashbery's populist impulse to reach the common reader, who thinks poems are constructed on many interpretive levels." In his essay on Ashbery for *American Writers,* Shoptaw says that "Although *Shadow Train* is dwarfed by earlier volumes such as *Three Poems* or *As We Know,* it may be the right place to begin for the reader who wants to learn Ashbery's alphabet." Vernon Shetley, on the other hand, cautions new Ashbery readers *not* to begin with *Shadow Train,* writing that "it occupies a curious position in the evolving body of his [Ashbery's] work. This collection ... marks an-

other peculiar twist in a protean career, another of the seemingly willful swerves from his natural predispositions that discomfit his admirers almost as much as his detractors." Ultimately, however, Shetley approves of the collection, writing that *Shadow Train* shows Ashbery "if not at his most daring and expansive, certainly at his most masterful...." Later in the same article, he remarks that "*Shadow Train* is a permanent addition to American poetry."

Reviewing the volume for *Commentary,* Robert Richman isn't as kind. Richman claims that *Shadow Train* "parodies the national mood of retrenchment and specifically the new conservatism of form and representation in the arts...." Writing that "the autonomy of language takes on an especially *jejune* cast" in the collection, Richman argues against Ashbery boosters, such as critic Helen Vendler, and suggests that the poet's popularity is undeserved and little more than a con game in which many people willingly participate.

Criticism

Chris Semansky

A widely published poet and fiction writer, Semansky teaches literature at Portland Community College. In the following essay, Semansky argues that Ashbery's "Paradoxes and Oxymorons" is a poem with indeterminate meaning.

Many people resist reading modern poetry because they think it is difficult to understand. They believe there is a hidden or secret meaning that must be ferreted out and that if they do not know the code, they will not understand what the poem is about. That poems are "about" something is an idea that much modern and contemporary poetry itself has questioned. Some recent literary theorists maintain that there is no absolute "aboutness," or theme, to literary texts, that ultimate meaning itself is an impossibility. Indeterminacy, these theorists argue, is the nature of literary texts, for their real meaning can never be known. John Ashbery's difficult and obscure poetry has helped to legitimize (and popularize) the idea of indeterminacy because it is so hard to pin down the subject of his poems. Ironically, his poem "Paradoxes and Oxymorons" literally plays with this very idea. The poem resists interpretation at the same time that it asks to be understood. This is one of its central paradoxes.

Readers are accustomed to poems being about an event, an idea, or an emotion. For example,

William Shakespeare's sonnets are about his love for another person. Robert Frost's poems are about how human beings interact with the natural world. John Ashbery's poems, however, are about nothing in particular, but they often trick readers into believing that they are. In his essay "Indeterminacy," critic and theorist Gerald Graff states that "For many recent theorists the problems of meaning and interpretation ... are not only features of works of literature, but are also what works of literature are *about*. Literary works 'thematize' (or take as their theme) those conflicts that make them indeterminate—conflicts between the claims the works make to tell the truth, represent the world, and present an authoritative picture of things, and the way their status as language and fiction calls these claims into question. In other words ... literary works are ... at some level commentaries on their own indeterminacy." What better way to explain the nature of "Paradoxes and Oxymorons"?

The poem begins by making a declarative statement: "This poem is concerned with language on a very plain level." Readers might feel uncomfortable having a poem tell them what it is about, but this is the way that Ashbery lures readers into the poem, makes them participate in its unfolding. In this way, readers themselves become a necessary part of the poem's meaning. The poem could not exist without them. The poet puts a twist on the old philosophical question, "If a tree fell in the woods and no one was there to hear it, would it make a sound?" Ashbery asks, "If there were no reader, would there still be a poem?" His answer would be a resounding "No," for the poem is about language's interaction with the reader. Meaning emerges from that interaction. It is not a static thing, sitting there full of meaning and just waiting to be discovered.

William Carlos Williams, a twentieth-century American poet who argued for the primacy of the image in poetry, once said, "No ideas but in things." By this he meant that in poetry, meaning itself should come out of concrete descriptions of the empirical world and that description should be sufficient. Abstractions should be avoided at all costs. Ashbery is also interested in the "thingness" of poetry, but things for him can include abstract thoughts or phrases, things that cannot be seen, touched, tasted, heard, or felt. His material is language itself. He uses it like a painter would use color or line or light. The words themselves don't necessarily have to "add up" to any definitive or final meaning; rather, he plays meanings off one another as if he were composing a musical score.

> *Ashbery asks, 'If there were no reader, would there still be a poem?' His answer would be a resounding 'No.'"*

In his study of Ashbery's poetry, *John Ashbery: An Introduction to the Poetry,* David Shapiro writes that for Ashbery "Poetry does not reflect reality; it constitutes reality.... Ashbery's poetry may seem to be a reflection upon a reflection upon a reflection, but it is actually a creation upon a creation.... One reads his surface only misguidedly if one thinks to commit merely the *orthodoxy* of paraphrase upon it." By this, Shapiro means that individual poems of Ashbery's do not lend themselves to paraphrase or summary and that a reader attempting to do so with his poems is foolish and missing the point. The "heresy of the paraphrase" is actually a phrase initially coined by a literary critic in the 1940s to suggest that *all* poetry is by its very nature "unparaphrasable." The reasoning here is that poetry exists precisely *because* there is no other form of expression to convey the complexities of feeling, thought, and experience that a poem can contain. Once one begins to paraphrase a poem, the poem automatically becomes something else.

The abundance of criticism on individual poems and the very idea that a poem can be reduced to "what it really means" is more a product of the institution of literary criticism and the place of criticism in the university system than a characteristic of poetry itself. It is the institution of criticism and the university system that categorizes writing into genres, traditions, periods, schools, movements, and the like, and it is precisely this categorization that Ashbery's work defies. Critics don't know what to do with him. They cannot agree upon a tradition in which to place him nor upon a movement or school to stamp above his name. In her introduction to an anthology of essays on Ashbery, *The Tribe of John Ashbery and Contemporary Poetry,* Ashbery scholar Susan Schultz writes that "There is a meditative Ashbery, a formalist Ashbery, a comic Ashbery, a late-Romantic Ashbery, a Language poet

What Do I Read Next?

- "Paradoxes and Oxymorons" appears in Ashbery's 1981 collection *Shadow Train,* which collects fifty poems, each consisting of four quatrains.

- In his interview with John Tranter in a 1986 issue of *Scripsi,* an Australian magazine, Ashbery discusses his own poetry and its relation to language.

- Bob Perleman's 1996 book *The Marginalization of Poetry* discusses the politics of much contemporary experimental poetry, including Ashbery's.

- Early criticism on Ashbery often labeled him a Language writer. Language writers is a name given to a group of like-minded writers, most of whom are from the West Coast and most of whom experiment with language and see poetry as a vehicle for criticism and theory as much as self-expression. *The L=A=N=G=U=A=G=E Book,* edited by Bruce Andrews and Charles Bernstein and published in 1984, collects essays from this group of writers.

- A number of essays in the 1990 anthology *Poetry After Modernism* criticize Ashbery's poetry for its obscurity and abstraction. Robert McDowell edited the collection.

Ashbery.... No poet since Whitman has tapped into so many distinctly American voices and, at the same time, so preserved his utterance against the jangle of influences." The difficulty that readers have with individual Ashbery poems, then, extends to the difficulties that established institutions have in figuring out what to make of his writing.

Instead of having something to say, Ashbery's poems often have nothing to say, but insist on saying it. Instead of building up to a statement, they start off with possibility and gradually empty themselves of meaning. They seduce but often do not consummate their seduction. Look at the teasing nature of the second and third stanzas:

The poem is sad because it wants to be yours, and
  cannot.
What's a plain level? It is that and other things,
Bringing a system of them into play. Play?
Well, actually, yes, but I consider play to be
A deeper outside thing, a dreamed role-pattern,
As in the division of grace these long August days
Without proof. Open-ended. And before you know
It gets lost in the steam and chatter of typewriters.

The tactic of making a statement and then questioning that statement and then answering that question is common enough in Ashbery's poems. It also forces readers to question their own way of reading and meaning-making and to question the trust that they have placed in the speaker. For Ashbery never really "answers" questions he puts forward; in fact, he evades answers. Readers frequently wind up scratching their heads, wondering if they're missing something. Ashbery plays with readers' expectations, their expectations of what comes next, their expectations of what a poem is. To fully appreciate Ashbery's poetry, readers would do well to adopt the mindset of someone listening to jazz. Having no expectations, only the desire to play and be played by the poem, is the mindset to bring to his poems. If readers expect to glean some deep moral or metaphysical insight into the human condition from his poems, they will be disappointed and frustrated. John Shoptaw, author of *On the Outside Looking Out: John Ashbery's Poetry,* identifies some of the cultural and literary allusions that Ashbery's poem piles up in "playing" the reader:

If infinitely many monkeys are set before typewriters, the statistical paradox goes, they will sooner or later produce Shakespeare's plays. Ashbery's poem "has been played" like a record or a trick. But perhaps it is the reader's trick as well. In the communications system, the ideal reader now resembles the Divine Paradox: "I think you exist," the poet asserts, "and then you aren't there." In his final paradox, "the poem is you," varying the dedication "the poem is yours," Ashbery yields himself to the reader, who nevertheless continues to "miss" him.

Allusions are indirect references to other ideas and texts. Readers aren't always aware of allusions when reading poems, Ashbery's or others, but these allusions work on us at a deeper level. There is also nothing necessarily intentional about allusions. That is, Ashbery may or may not be aware of what he is alluding to when he writes his poems. He may or may not be alluding to the monkey paradox, or the Divine Paradox, that Shoptaw sees. What the reader is left with at the end of "Paradoxes and Oxymorons" and, for that matter, many of Ashbery's poems, is the idea that language knows more than the reader does.

Source: Chris Semansky, in an essay for *Poetry for Students,* Gale Group, 2001.

John Pipkin

Pipkin is a scholar in the fields of British and American Literature. In this essay, he discusses the issues of meaning and interpretation in "Paradoxes and Oxymorons."

"Paradoxes and Oxymorons" is a poem about language. To be more specific, it is a poem concerned with how words come to have meaning and with the roles that poets and readers play in creating and determining that meaning.

"Paradoxes and Oxymorons" is a good example of a postmodern poem. Postmodernism is a broad and sometimes confusing term that includes many different styles, themes, and perspectives. As a general historical term, postmodernism refers to art and literature of the late twentieth century. Stylistically and thematically, postmodernism is often characterized by an awareness that there is no such thing as absolute meaning, and some postmodern works of art raise the question of whether or not art or poetry even exist. In addition, many postmodern poems look beneath the surface of language to point out inconsistencies or contradictions that seem to defeat the purpose of poetic language in the first place.

Ashbery's poem encourages the reader to consider such postmodern issues. The poem's title itself seems to suggest that the poem will be addressing issues of language, meaning, and contradiction. A "paradox" is a phrase that may at first appear absurd or contradictory, but it is one that, upon further consideration, actually makes sense. This is slightly different from an oxymoron, which is a phrase that contains an obvious contradiction for the purpose of making a point or teaching a lesson. By choosing this title, could Ashbery be suggesting that all of language is nothing more than a collection of oxymorons and paradoxes. Is every use of language a contradiction, or something other than what it at first seems to be?

The poem begins with two statements, which present the reader with impossible choices: (1) "This poem is concerned with language on a very plain level." Is this statement true? If the reader accepts this as true, then the second statement presents an impossible command. (2) "Look at it talking to you." How can you "look" at a poem "talking"? And for that matter, do words on a page actually speak? Already, by the second statement of the poem, there is a puzzling contradiction. And

the complexity of this contradiction undermines the first line of the poem, which claimed that it was "concerned with language on a very *plain* level." A reader who accepted the first line as absolutely true has already been tricked. Clearly, the poem is not concerned with *plain* language.

But does this mean that the reader must declare the first sentence a lie? What if there really is no such thing as *plain* language to begin with? Or better yet, what if what we accept to be plain language is really no different from other forms of language, riddled with contradictions and inconsistencies?

The rest of the opening stanza looks at a different kind of inconsistency. "You look out a window / Or pretend to fidget. You have it but you don't have it. / You miss it, it misses you. You miss each other." Here, Ashbery's poem describes the uncomfortable process that a reader goes through when trying to decipher a poem like this one. We yearn for distraction, look out a window, or pretend to fidget because we don't want to admit what we don't understand. Meaning comes to us in bits and pieces. Some of these we catch and some we miss. But Ashbery describes this process as a two-way street. The meaning of the poem does not reside in the poem itself or in the reader's interpretation of it but somewhere in between. Meaning is the result of the poem and the reader reaching out to each other. "You miss each other." If a poem seems to be meaningless, who has failed: the reader, the poem, or both?

To understand what Ashbery is talking about in the second stanza, it is helpful to know a little bit about a literary theory known as deconstruction. In the late 1960s, the French linguistic theorist Jacques Derrida used the term deconstruction to refer to a very complex philosophical method for showing how language has no permanent meaning. Deconstructive critics argue that the meanings of words come from the way that they are used and from the way that they are related to a network or system of other words and statements. Derrida referred to the changing relationships between words as play. Thus, according to deconstruction, linguistic meaning comes from the play between words and statements and can never be nailed down permanently.

This is a disturbing idea because it suggests that we can never really know or prove what anyone is trying to say. In the second stanza of "Paradoxes and Oxymorons," Ashbery reflects on the implications of these ideas. "The poem is sad because it wants to be yours, and cannot be. / What's a plain level? It is that and other things, / Bringing a system of them into play." Ashbery suggests that poems, like poets, want to be understood but that they cannot be understood because of the limitations of language. Thus, language itself is both a means of expression as well as an obstacle to expression. An interesting paradox!

Here Ashbery also asks the question that the first stanza overlooks: "What's a plain level?" A poem cannot exist on a plain level because language is always working on more than one level at the same time. Words and phrases always have more than one meaning. They are always both "that and other things." By using language, Ahsbery's poem cannot express a specific meaning without bringing into play an entire system of words, including those that are not on the page. The meaning of the poem is dependent upon the system of words outside of the poem itself, perhaps in the mind of the reader as well.

The third stanza continues the reflection on the idea of "play" started at the end of the second stanza. "Play? / Well, actually, yes, but I consider play to be / A deeper outside thing, a dreamed role-pattern, / As in the division of grace these long August days / Without proof. Open-ended." Ashbery compares different perspectives on play here. When he thinks of play, he does not think immediately of words but rather of the carefree, meaningless games of warm summer days.

The third stanza concludes by returning to the anxiety that readers and writers feel when confronted by the shifting meaning of language. The sheer joy of "open-ended" play disappears under the desire to nail down specific meanings. "It gets lost in the steam and chatter of typewriters." In the final stanza, Ashbery reflects on having just completed the poem. The false promise of being able to communicate, of being able to say something on a plain level, teased him into writing this poem: "I think you exist only / To tease me into doing it, on your level, and then you aren't there / Or have adopted a different attitude." But as soon as he finishes the poem, he realizes that the *plain level* has again disappeared and the meaning of his words have already shifted. The final stanza then encourages the reader to reflect once more on the relationship between the poet, the reader, and the poem: "The poem is you." If the purpose of poetry is to communicate meaning and if words only have meaning in the act of being "played" or of being read, then how do we define a poem? Is a reader in the act of interpretation actually a part of the poem itself?

According to deconstruction, meaning cannot be proven or nailed down. It is something that is constantly in flux, constantly changing and shifting. This does not mean that Ashbery's poem is meaningless. Its meaning, however, does not take the form that many readers may be accustomed to searching for in a poem. Instead, the meaning of this poem lies in reflecting on the process of interpretation, in that shadowy ground between the reader and the words themselves. What Ashbery's poem does is to force the reader to ask questions about reading, to raise issues about writing, and to think about the purpose and function of poetry.

Source: John Pipkin, in an essay for *Poetry for Students,* Gale Group, 2001.

Sources

Ashbery, John, "Capital Gains," *in New York,* September 3, 1979, p. 56.

———, *Selected Poems,* Penguin, 1985.

Fields, Kenneth, "More Than Language Means," in *Southern Review,* 1979, pp. 196–204.

Graff, Gerald, "Indeterminacy," in *Critical Terms for Literary Study,* edited by Frank Lentricchia and Thomas McLaughlin, University of Chicago Press, 1990.

Lehman, David, ed., *Beyond Amazement: New Essays on John Ashbery,* Cornell University Press, 1980.

———, ed., *John Ashbery,* Cornell University Press, 1979.

Perleman, Bob, *The Marginalization of Poetry: Language Writing and Literary History,* Princeton University Press, 1996.

Richman, Robert, "Our 'Most Important' Living Poet," in *Commentary,* July 1982, pp. 62–8.

Schultz, Susan, *The Tribe of John: Ashbery and Contemporary Poetry,* University of Alabama Press, 1995.

Shapiro, David, *John Ashbery: An Introduction to the Poetry,* Columbia University Press, 1979.

Shetley, Vernon, "Language on a Very Plain Level," in *Poetry,* July 1982, pp. 236–41.

Shoptaw, John, Biographical entry on John Ashbery in *American Writers: A Collection of Literary Biographies,* edited by Lea Baechler and A. Walton Litz, Charles Scribner's Sons, 1991.

———, *On the Outside Looking Out: John Ashbery's Poetry,* Harvard University Press, 1994.

For Further Reading

Ashbery, John, *Self-Portrait in a Convex Mirror,* Viking Press, 1975.

Ashbery won the Pulitzer Prize, the National Book Award, and the National Book Critics Circle Award for this book, which cemented his reputation as a leading American poet.

Glover, Michael, "A Blue Rinse for the Language," in *The Independent,* November 13, 1999.

This Michael Glover interview with Ashbery is refreshing and personal. Ashbery discusses critical reception of his poetry and expresses bemusement at how his life has turned out.

Kermani, David K., *John Ashbery: A Comprehensive Bibliography,* Garland Publishing, Inc. 1976.

This bibliography lists Ashbery's art criticism, catalogues, translations, and other miscellaneous writings, most of which have not yet made it into book form.

Lehman, David, *The Last Avant-Garde: The Making of the New York School of Poets,* Anchor Books, 1999.

Ashbery is considered a poet from the "New York School" of poets, a loose group of writers including Ashbery, Frank O'Hara, Kenneth Koch, and James Schuyler. Lehman claims that the four constituted the last true avant-garde movement in American poetry.

McClatchey, J. D., ed., *Poets on Painters: Essays on the Art of Painting by Twentieth-Century Poets,* University of California Press, 1990.

Ashbery is an art critic as well as a poet. This collection presents reviews and essays by well-known poets on painters.

Shapiro, David, *John Ashbery: An Introduction to the Poetry,* Columbia University Press, 1979.

Shapiro's book is one of the first full-length studies of Ashbery's work. It is quirky and at times difficult reading but well worth the effort.

To a Child Running With Outstretched Arms in Canyon de Chelly

N. Scott Momaday

1976

First published in the 1976 collection *The Gourd Dancer,* the brief poem "To a Child Running with Outstretched Arms in Canyon de Chelly" contains many of the thematic and stylistic qualities of Momaday's poetry. The poem is set in New Mexico's Canyon De Chelly, where the poet lived briefly as a child. As his childhood home, as well as the site of ancient Anazasi cliff dwellings, and of the Navajo tribe's 1864 defeat and forced removal at the hands of the American military, the setting allows Momaday to explore his own Indian heritage. In addition, the poem serves as a joyous reminder of the intense and intimate feelings of belonging—a sense of place—which humans can experience in the natural world. Focusing on images of the canyon's tremendous natural beauty, coupled with the beauty and innocence of a small child, the poem blends two worlds—the human and the non-human—and brings a human presence back into the canyon to "embrace / The spirit of this place."

Author Biography

N. Scott Momaday was born in 1934 in Lawton, Oklahoma, to Alfred Morris Momaday, a Kiowa Indian, and Mayme Natachee Scott, who was part Cherokee. As an infant Momaday was named Tsoaitalee, or "Rock Tree Boy," after a 200-foot volcanic butte in Wyoming (known commonly as Devil's Tower) that is sacred to the Kiowas. As a youngster Momaday lived on several Navaho reser-

N. Scott Momaday

vations and at the Jemez Pueblo in New Mexico, where his parents were teachers. He attended Augusta Military Academy in Virginia his last year of high school to take college prepartory classes that were unavailable at his local school. Momaday then studied at the University of New Mexico; it was there that he began writing poetry. After graduating with a degree in political science, Momaday spent a year teaching on the Jicarilla Apache reservation in Dulce, New Mexico. He returned to academic pursuits after being awarded a creative writing fellowship at Stanford University. He earned his master's degree in 1960 and his doctorate in 1963. Momaday's first published book, *The Complete Poems of Frederick Goddard Tuckerman* (1965), was originally his doctoral dissertation. In 1968 Momady published *House Made of Dawn,* the Pulitzer Prize-winning novel for which he is most famous. Although he has published nonfiction and novels, Momaday considers himself a poet foremost and has published several books of verse. His talent also extends to drawing and painting, and these works have been exhibited in various galleries.

Poem Text

You are small and intense
In your excitement, whole,
Embodied in delight.
The backdrop is immense;

The sand drifts break and roll   5
Through cleavages of light
And shadow. You embrace
The spirit of this place.

Poem Summary

Lines 1–3:

In the poem's opening lines as well as in its title (an important piece of information, especially in a poem as short as this), Momaday both addresses and describes a child at play in the canyon. Perhaps the "small and intense" child may be the poet recalling himself as a young boy as he ran in Canyon De Chelly, or perhaps the poem is addressed to one of Momaday's four daughters. The language of these initial lines conjures up a sense of child-like joy: words such as "intense," and "excitement," and phrases such as "embodied in delight" capture both the sense of wonder and the limitless possibilities of childhood.

Line 4:

Here, the "backdrop" to which Momaday refers is both physical and historical. On a physical level, the canyon walls and other natural scenery form a natural backdrop which seems to dwarf the figure of the small child at play among them. But the Canyon de Chelly also provides a backdrop of history. The canyon was the home of the ancient Anazasi culture, whose cliff dwellings and rock paintings still grace the canyon walls. Centuries later, in 1864, the canyon was the site of the final battle between Navajo Indians and a military force lead by Kit Carson—a confrontation which resulted in the Navajos' forced removal from their home region. The rhyme scheme of the first and fourth lines of the opening stanza brings the child and the canyon's "backdrop" into immediate contrast; the child is "intense," the canyon's backdrop "immense."

Lines 5–6:

Here, a physical description of a portion of the canyon's landscape is used as a metaphor for the passage of time. The image of sifting sand, long used as a means of portraying the movement of history, is paired with description of another landscape feature which comes to stand for time's passing. The "cleavages of light / And shadow" reflected on the canyon's jagged walls may be seen to represent the passing of

Media Adaptations

- PBS Home Video has a videocassette of their 1992 documentary *Momaday: Voice of the West* available. It is part two of the five-part Western Writers series.

- Narrated by Momaday, the videocassette *White Man's Way,* which examines a government program for schooling Indian children in the late nineteenth and early twentieth centuries, is available from the Native American Public Broadcasting Consortium.

- An audiocassette titled *The Indian Oral Tradition: Peter Nabokov Interviews N. Scott Momaday* was released in 1969 by Pacifica Tape Library.

- Momaday is featured on a videotape titled *More Than Bows and Arrows: The legacy of the American Indians,* released by Camera One in 1994.

- *N. Scott Momaday Reads Two Poems and Two Novel Excerpts* is a 1983 audiocassette available from American Audio Prose Library.

- *N. Scott Momaday: A Film by Matteo Bellinelli* is available on cassette. It was released in 1995 by Films for the Sciences and Humanities.

- Momaday's vast knowledge of his land was used as a source for Ken Burns' eight-part documentary for the Public Broadcasting System. This series, called *The West,* is carried by many public libraries.

- At http://www.achievement.org/frames.html readers can find the transcript of an interview conducted with Momaday on June 28, 1996, in Sun Valley, Idaho (see N. Scott Momaday, Ph.D., Pulitzer Prize for Fiction link).

- CBS News Audio Resource Library and Encyclopedia Americana co-produced an audiocassette called *Traditional Arts and the Future of the American Indian* with Momaday looking at contemporary Indian life as well as cultural heritage and ending with a reading of some of his poems.

---

the many days ("light") and nights ("shadow") since the Navajo last occupied the canyon.

Lines 7–8:

The final lines return to the image of the "child running with outstretched arms" presented in the poem's title. Momaday's final phrase "You embrace / The spirit of this place," with its emphasis on the rhyme of "embrace" and "place," may signal the joyous return, after more than a century, of the Indian people to the canyon. A sense of belonging to a "place," the poem seems to suggest, involves much more than the physical landscape; it must also take into account the "backdrop" of one's regional and cultural history.

Themes

Return to Nature

The child described in this poem is, presumably, too young to have gotten very far from na-

ture in his or her short life and, therefore, could not have very far to go to return to nature. Still, as a representative of humanity, the child can be viewed as establishing a new bond with the natural surroundings of the canyon. The point of this poem is to draw a parallel between the child and the canyon. The child is "embodied in delight," and the canyon is lit "through cleavages of light / And shadow." The child is small and the canyon immense. The casual reader of these descriptions might see the child and the canyon presented as opposites, but there is nothing in the descriptions that would prevent these two main characters from coming together in the end.

Focusing on the child's excitement, Momaday invites his readers to see the canyon through the child's eyes, to appreciate the canyon's natural wonders as if seeing them for the first time. The canyon is a place of uneven and changing beauty, shown in its hilly floor and shifting patterns of light. Moving through the canyon provides a look at nature that is constantly new and fresh. Combining the changing surroundings with the child's point of view can return readers to the sense of wonder they once knew. For an adult reader who has, in the process of becoming mature, lost enthusiasm for the surprises nature has to offer, the child's perspective can offer a renewal. The child might not be returning to the canyon, but readers who think they have seen all there is to see can experience a vicarious return to nature while reading this poem.

Guilt and Innocence

The child's relative innocence is established in the way that he or she runs freely with arms outstretched, neither afraid nor self-conscious. The Canyon de Chelly, on the other hand, is a place half-shrouded in erratic, mysterious shadows. The very fact that the canyon has existed for tens of thousands of years and that the child has existed for just a few years says much about their disparate levels of experience. Experience is often used as a contrast of innocence: the innocent are often inexperienced.

There is much guilt traditionally associated with the Canyon de Chelly. The walls of the canyon are covered in places with pictographs, the paintings that were put there by the inhabitants who occupied the area hundreds of years ago. For the past three hundred years, since before America's War of Independence from England, the Navajo have lived in the canyon. The Navajos and the Anasazi who lived there before them have been victims of countless crimes by the Spanish, Mexican and American governments. The Navajo were assaulted, relocated, enslaved and robbed; before the area was protected by National Monument status in 1931, poachers, sometimes thinking to benefit the world's body of archeological knowledge, came and stole the architectural treasures that represented the link between the canyon's present and the past civilizations who lived within it.

The contrast between child-like innocence and the ruthless history of abuse of the indigenous people who inhabit the Canyon de Chelly is implied in the difference between the title, which pictures the child's arms outstretched, and the last line, which shows the child's arms in an embrace. The former gesture is one of naive innocence, while the latter shows an acceptance of the truth that is within the canyon's spirit, regardless of the shadows that darken its past.

Freedom

This poem starts by picturing the child making one of the most open and free gestures possi-

Topics for Further Study

- Observe someone who does not know you are watching them and write a poem about what you see. Use the same rhyme scheme as Momaday uses (*abca bcdd*).

- Compare the ideas expressed in this poem to those expressed in William Wordsworth's "My Heart Leaps Up." What do the two poems tell you about youth? About nature? Does the fact that they were published 175 years apart affect how you understand their meaning, or not?

- What is the "spirit" of the canyon that the poem mentions in the final line? What specific words does the speaker use to make you understand that spirit?

ble, running with outstretched arms. The gesture shows no fear nor restraint upon the child's unbridled excitement. However, the child is not presented as running in an open space but between the high stone walls of the canyon, an environment that might suggest confinement. What allows the Canyon de Chelly to represent freedom, not limitation, in this poem is the immensity mentioned in the fourth line. The backdrop to this child is immense in the sense that the canyon is wide enough to allow an ample view of the sky and of the rocks and of houses at the base of the walls. The child's "backdrop" is also immense in a cultural and historical sense. The physical or cultural background *could* suggest a narrowing of the child's possibilities, inhibiting her or his freedom; instead, the child's excitement and delight indicate a great freedom rather than the confinement that a canyon might suggest.

Coming of Age

Many poems about children offer an observation regarding one of the basic truths about childhood: that childhood fades speedily as the child evolves into adulthood. In the child's running, Momaday seems to emphasize the child's propulsion into the future. Unaware of the adulthood toward which he or she rushes, the child is, as the poem's second line puts it, whole in his or her excitement. The child is not just filled with delight but *is* delight. On the other hand, the description of the Canyon de Chelly suggests that the canyon bears weightier matters in its spirit. The interplay of light and shadow implies the complexity of adult life that is still beyond the child.

What makes this a coming of age poem is the way that the child changes from being self-contained to looking to the larger scope of things. The canyon is immense, well beyond a child's grasp, but the child embraces the spirit of the canyon. The child shows an awakening self-awareness, as well as the recognition of a possible relationship with the canyon. The poem shows the first step in the process of coming of age, the realization that there is something desirable in maturity.

Style

Like many of Momaday's poems, "To a Child Running with Outstretched Arms in Canyon de Chelly" is written in syllabic verse, meaning that the poem's lines are constructed using a given number of syllables, without regard to stress. In this case, each line of the poem contains six syllables. The poem's eight lines are divided into four-line stanzas called quatrains. Momaday employs a rhyme scheme of *abca bcdd,* meaning that the first line and fourth line, the second line and fifth line, etc., end in words that rhyme. This pattern of rhyme provides a symmetry within the two stanzas, but more importantly, it creates a bridge between them. The carryover of rhyme from the first stanza to the second links the subject of the first stanza (the child) to the subject of the second (the landscape of the canyon), setting the stage for their merging in the poem's two final lines.

Historical Context

Canyon de Chelly National Monument

The Canyon de Chelly is located in northeast Arizona, near where that state intersects with Utah, Colorado, and New Mexico. It runs thirty miles long on the Navajo Reservation. The red sandstone walls of the canyon are steep and high, rising to one thousand feet in claustrophobic narrowness in places. Though not the most scenic canyon in the area, the dwellings, paintings, and artifacts of the

primitive people who lived there from the fifth century through the fifteenth century, all before the time that Columbus brought European culture to this continent, gives Canyon de Chelly special significance.

The Anasazi, the Basketmakers, whose civilization dates from the first century A.D., are the oldest recorded inhabitants of the canyon. They are the ancestors of the Pueblo tribes of the Southwest. Anasazi culture was vast and complex. Many of their paintings can be found on the walls of Canyon de Chelly, as well as in other places throughout Arizona and New Mexico. They were hunters and farmers, known for weaving baskets in intricate patterns of black and white. They lived in caves within the walls of the canyon and cultivated crops in the wide areas where the sun could reach the fertile soil on the base of the canyon. The stream that still runs along the canyon floor has seldom run dry, summer or winter, and seldom has irrigation been a problem for the Anasazi. Still today large jars for storing grain, left by the Anasazi, sit among the rocks of the cliffs. Among the oldest dwellings open to the public that were left by the Anasazi are the White House Ruins, a group of stone houses deep in the canyon at the base of a five-hundred-foot cliff. These ruins were occupied from about 1060 to 1275 A.D. and are among the oldest existing dwellings to be found in North America.

There are Navajo dwellings in the canyon dating from the 1700s. The Navajo word for Canyon, *tseyi,* was difficult for the Spanish, who had controlled the area since the mid-1600s, so they pronounced the word "shay-ee," which they spelled Chelly. Navajo people still live there today. In fact, it is the only national monument in which people are an essential part of the ecosystem.

Ruth Underhill, a Navajo historian, tells the story of one branch of Canyon de Chelly that is called the Canyon of the Dead, or Canyon del Muerto. In the winter of 1804–1805, a party of Spaniards rode into the canyon to capture Navajos to work as slaves in the houses of Mexico, which included the area that we now call New Mexico. In retaliation, the Navajo sometimes captured Spanish children and made them tend to their sheep. In the winter of 1804–1805, there had been a period of peace between the two sides for some time when a Spanish raiding party led by Lieutenant Narbona arrived. The Navajo men had gone away on their own raiding party, and the women and children, left behind, were hidden in a cave high above the canyon behind a natural rock parapet that shielded them from sight from below. The Spaniards would have

Compare & Contrast

- **1976:** Office work is revolutionized by the introduction of the Wang computer, which allows secretaries to type information that appears on a cathode ray tube, then edit it, then print it with a printer using a typewriter-style "daisy wheel."

  Today: After a generation that has grown up with typing skills in order to operate computers, Voice Recognition Software is becoming increasingly sophisticated, threatening to make keyboards obsolete.

- **1976:** Citizens Band radios, previously a tool for truckers and cowboys, becomes a fad for the middle class. 11.3 million radios are sold, allowing strangers all over the country to talk to one another via code names, or "handles."

  Today: Cellular phones offer the same ability to call someone from the road; computer chat rooms offer the same anonymity in conversations.

- **1976:** After a ten-year moratorium on capital punishment, the Supreme Court finds that the death penalty does not constitute cruel and unusual punishment, allowing states to begin executions again.

  Today: With improved DNA testing and other evidence, eighty-seven people who were condemned to be executed have been proven innocent. The idea of another moratorium is being debated again.

- **1976:** The Church Report, prepared by a committee led by Congressman Frank Church, shocks America with news of abuses of power by the Central Intelligence Agency, including illegal spying on American citizens and involvement in assassinations of the leaders of foreign countries. Congress votes on legislation to limit the CIA's activities.

  1993: A bomb at the parking garage of the World Trade Center in New York kills six people and forces 100,000 to evacuate the premises. The conviction of Muslim fundamentalists the following year makes it clear that America faces terrorist attacks from outside.

  Today: The powers of the CIA have been expanded, but skeptics still point to the Church Report as a warning that power can easily be abused.

- **1976:** Four new nuclear reactors start producing electricity in the United States.

  1979: Two hundred thousand citizens of Three Mile Island, Pennsylvania, have to evacuate their homes when damage to the nuclear reactor core threatens a nuclear meltdown.

  1986: An explosion at the Chernobyl nuclear plant in the Soviet Union releases radiation that travels in the atmosphere, measured as far away as Scotland. Authorities estimate that as many as 20,000 people will have their lives shortened by exposure to radiation.

  Today: The number of nuclear power plants in the United States is decreasing as old ones are decommissioned and no new ones built, but they are still responsible for three times as much electricity as in 1976.

- **1976:** Genetech is formed as a commercial company to find ways to profit from the use of genetic engineering.

  Today: Genetically altered medicines are common, and products with recombinant DNA can be found in the produce section of any grocery.

---

had no clue that anyone was in the canyon except that one woman, who was rumored to have been a former slave of the Spanish, leaned over the wall and taunted them as they rode away, saying, "There go the men without eyes!" She was heard, and the search party slaughtered everybody. For years the cave, called Massacre Cave, was left with skeletons piled high upon the floor of the Canyon del Muerto.

The White House ruin that rests in the Canyon de Chelly is all that remains of an Anasazi pueblo once located there.

The Navajo

Through linguistic similarities, archeologists can tell that the Navajo are related to tribes that are mostly concentrated in the northern regions of Canada. At some time, possibly over the course of centuries, they wandered southward, ending up in the Four Corners area of northeast Arizona in the sixteenth century. Here they raised crops and were a peaceful people until the eighteenth and nineteenth centuries when Spanish raiders came up through Mexico, making a series of attacks on the Navajo to take their land and to carry their people off into slavery. The one positive influence of their interaction with the Spaniards was that from them they learned to raise livestock, such as horses, sheep and goats, which were easier to tend in the dry, rocky area of Arizona than were plants.

In the middle of the 1800s, the United States government took over the Mexican influence in the area. When the war fought between the United States and Mexico from 1846 to 1848 ended, the Rio Grande River was established as Mexico's northernmost border. In 1846 the Navajo signed their first treaty with the United States government, but the treaty was broken by 1849 when raids erupted between the Navajos and the United States. The fighting finally ended in 1863 when the federal government waged an all-out military assault, led by Kit Carson, and the Navajo eventually surrendered. Carson convinced them that the only way they could escape extinction was to go to Fort Sumner in New Mexico, a migration which was to become known in Navajo history as the Long Walk, a turning point in the history of the tribe.

Nearly 8,000 Navajo set out by foot to Fort Sumner. Many died on the way, and many more died in the terrible conditions that awaited them there. The soil was tough and barren, and the water was alkaline and hardly fit to drink. Other aggressive tribes picked fights with the Navajo. Finally, in 1868, the Navajo leaders signed a new treaty with the United States government and were allowed to return to a reservation that was just a small fraction of their original land in size.

The Navajo have prospered since returning to their land. The 1990 census lists them as the second largest tribe in America with a population of 21,198. They have expanded their land area and now use it for farming, livestock, and a flourishing tourist trade.

Critical Overview

Known primarily as one of America's most prominent Native American writers, much of the critical attention which Momaday has received has dealt with his place in the tradition of Native American literature. Barbara Strelke, in her essay entitled "N. Scott Momaday: Racial Memory and Individual Imagination," finds Momaday's writing significantly enriched by Indian artistic traditions. "Much of the beauty of the work," Strelke writes, "rests on the Indian tradition of art, song, and poetry. Concrete nature imagery is a characteristic of Native American poetry and Momaday's concise haiku-like passages are 'Indian' in their care for detail and their economy in style." In his analysis of Momaday's collection *The Gourd Dancer,* entitled "Beautyway: The Poetry of N. Scott Momaday," Kenneth C. Mason also stresses the poet's Indian background as the basis for one of his most important themes. Mason states that "[t]hrough his skill and the power of his rhetoric Momaday is able to make the themes that emerge distinctly his own: death and time, the beauty of the land, and his Indian heritage." "To a Child Running with Outstretched Arms in Canyon de Chelly" is discussed briefly by Matthias Schubnell in his study, *N. Scott Momaday: The Cultural and Literary Background.* Arguing that the poem takes its sense of joy from Momaday's return to the historic homeland of the Navajo, Schubnell finds that the poem can be seen as "a projection of Momaday's own wonder and delight into the figure of the child," and that "[t]he idea of 'spirit of place' is related to aesthetic and historical considerations in this poem."

Criticism

David Kelly

Kelly is a writer and teacher of creative writing. In the following essay, he explores how the minimalist techniques that Momaday uses in "To a Child Running With Outstretched Arms in Canyon de Chelly" help make its overall point.

In "To A Child Running With Outstretched Arms in Canyon de Chelly," N. Scott Momaday attempts, as writers always should, to give readers a full experience using a minimum number of words. The poem identifies a real place, that people could go to, walk through, and imagine a child running through as they study the walls. The last line refers to "the spirit of this place." Readers sometimes feel

> *Writers should love their tools; readers can tell if they don't."*

that they might be missing out on some important aspect when they find out that the poem has a real-life point of reference. Knowing the canyon and its history helps a little, and readers who know the history of the Anasazi and the Navajo who have lived there might understand the aforementioned "spirit" better than those who don't, but prior understanding is not required or even much of a benefit. This poem is not asking readers to come to it with a knowledge of the Canyon de Chelly, it is *telling* readers what the canyon is like: the canyon is like a child with outstretched arms, running.

Within the compact space of these eight short lines, Momaday has packed a world of information about geography, Native American history, and children, using each as a catalyst for understanding the others. The poem would not be able to give up any more information if it were twice or three times or ten times as long. This is the principle behind minimalist poetry and behind minimalist art in general: capturing readers' full attention to each detail by giving little that will distract them.

Momaday's poem looks like a little rectangle, a brick of words, but readers should not mistake its apparent utility for a lack of artistry. It is one of the most basic of artistic points, though often forgotten, that poetry exists to give some defined shape to the words that an author chooses to use to capture ideas. The words are, without a doubt, important, and a poet who does not radiate a love for the various ways meanings interlock cannot hope to keep hold of any reader who might happen by his or her work. But the poet's love of wordplay is no more than the essayist's, the novelist's, and maybe even the journalist's. Writers should love their tools; readers can tell if they don't. Poets, in addition to caring about what their words amount to, care about how they are arranged on the page. N. Scott Momaday has written in many genres and has garnered critical acclaim for almost every style he has used. He knows when to express his ideas in quantity and when to express them with style. The striking thing about "To a Child Running" is that it makes its firm style practically inconspicuous.

What Do I Read Next?

- Momaday's anthology, *In The Presence of the Sun: Stories and Poems, 1961–1991,* includes other works that were published along with "To a Child Running With Outstretched Arms in Canyon de Chelly," such as "The Gourd Dancer" and many other fascinating pieces.

- Momaday's poem "Old Songs Made New" is just one of the pieces by Native Americans included in the 2000 anthology *Song With the Heart of a Bear: Fusions of Native and American Poetry, 1890–1999.*

- Campbell Grant has written a book full of photographs that give readers a sense of the wonders that inspired this poem. The book, *Canyon de Chelly: Its People and Rock Art,* was first published in 1978 by the University of Arizona Press and is still available.

- Navajo author Lucy Tapahonso grew up on Navajo land in Shiprock, New Mexico, in the 1950s and 1960s. Her 1987 book of poetry, *A Breeze Swept Through,* captures the flavor of modern reservation life.

- The anthology *Growing Up Native American* collects works from noted Indian authors of the past two centuries who write about their childhoods. Included are Leslie Marmon Silko, Black Elk, and Louise Erdrich.

- Besides being a poet, N. Scott Momaday is famous for writing in all fields. His first book, the novel *House Made of Dawn,* won the Pulitzer Prize for 1969.

- One of the most famous and influential books in Native-American literature is *Black Elk Speaks,* first published in 1932 and revised in the late 1960s. Black Elk was a witness at the Battle of Little Big Horn in 1876 and the massacre at Wounded Knee, South Dakota, in 1890. Since Black Elk did not read or write English, his story was written for *Black Elk Speaks* by John G. Neuhardt.

- Leslie Marmon Silko is one of the most famous Native American authors writing today. Her 1997 book *Yellow Woman and a Beauty of the Spirit: Essays on Native American Life Today* expresses anger and hope and defines what life is like among the Pueblo tribes of the Southwest now.

- Many readers have gotten a sense of what life is like on the Navajo reservation today by reading the detective mysteries of Tony Hillerman, including *A Thief of Time, Coyote Waits,* and *The Fallen Man.*

With a long, epic poem, readers can marvel at the poet's "grand scheme." The talent on display is much more impressive when the scale is large, and thinking about the poet's achievement is like ruminating over how architects fit the pyramids together to last. Even while considering a medium-sized poem, one can get lost in considering the myriad choices that the author has gone through. If the poem has a traditional structure, then the author can be assumed to have shaken and reworked all of the ideas and the words used for them to make the thoughts fit the prescribed boundaries. If the poem is in free verse, without rhyme or a set rhythm scheme, then an even greater question arises about how the author knew the right place to end each line.

More elusive, though, and more fascinating, is the poem, like this one, that lasts just a few lines and then is over, exerting its distinct style quickly and unforgettably. Like an eighteenth-century minimalist painter, the poet of the short form forces audiences to stop, stare, squint, and come back several times if there is to be any hope of taking in all of the implications that are presented. Momaday is working with just two simple items here—the child and the canyon—and to make readers consider the full implications of each, he has to convince them, consciously or not, that this piece is well thought-out. He wins confidence from readers by exerting control. The lines all have six syllables, and the stanzas both have four lines. It is hard to feel that this is a poem that just fell out onto the page the way that it popped into the author's head, and so readers sit up and take notice of every word.

When Momaday was a student at Stanford, his mentor, the esteemed poet Yvor Winters, encouraged him toward formal poetry, including syllabic poetry, which uses the same number of syllables in each line regardless of the rhythm formed by degrees of accentuation. In "To a Child Running," syllable-counting offers just enough control to keep readers focused. With the readers' minds engaged, Momaday is able to open up the possibilities that result from loving word play. For instance, in a longer poem, a word like "immense," as a description of the backdrop, might be lost like just another cobblestone in the pavement; "cleavages" might just seem like a clever, but not a particularly poignant, way of describing the erratic pattern of sunbeams in a canyon; and the use of the word "this" in the last line might not draw so much attention to itself. In a longer poem, the four-line stanzas would just be taken for granted, and the poem would not be able to fold back upon itself, springing back to the "you" with which it started so quickly and so powerfully. A longer poem would also disperse Momaday's use of rhyme across a greater area, diluting its effect.

The poem's use of rhyme is somewhat like its use of rhythm but even less formal, helping to tie the whole together and to assure readers of the author's control but popping up as a surprise when it appears. There are rhymes, but there is not an overall rhyme scheme. "Immense" at the end of the first stanza refers back to "intense" at the end of the first line. "Excitement," in line two, is echoed with "delight," in line three. The long "o" sound, as well as their places at the ends of a line and a sentence, bind together "roll" and "shadow." The most conspicuous use of rhyme comes at the end of the poem, where the last two lines form a rhyming couplet, "embrace" fitting neatly against "place," leaving readers with a greater sense of formality when they finish than the poem actually has. Throughout the poem, rhymes pop up occasionally, not unlike the way that coincidences pop up in real life, but in these final lines, there can be no mistake that the poet is manipulating his words to give a small snapshot of the large world.

Momaday is not really doing anything too new here. The model for minimalist poetry has to be Japanese haiku, whose practitioners have produced thousands of meaningful variations within one simple design. Staying within one form, haiku writers avoid the worry of teasing audiences to guess how they came up with any sort of new style. It could be argued that Japanese society was conducive to such a delicate and formal way of thought that could produce and appreciate such focus, especially in the Edo period (1600–1868) when the greatest haiku writers of them all lived. The Japanese patience and openness to subtle experiences is evident in other traditional art forms, including horticulture and Kabuki theater. This sort of immersion into the miniature is not a common part of American culture.

For an American poet, it is particularly unnatural to produce a short, tight poem, to aim for the pureness of artistry that a little piece entails. America is a country based on expansion, on working around rules, not within them. The belief in unlimited expansion, which started with the settlers' move westward across the continent, continues today with the exploration of space and the growth of the stock market, which for some people confirm the hope that the best thing is to keep on the move, producing more and more. All people see things differently, but the general mood that defines this country has always been set by a belief in freedom rather than in self-control. In the arts, especially, intellectual boundaries are seen as extraneous rules to be broken, more than as challenges. American art of the nineteenth century was defined by its attempts to imitate European standards. In the twentieth century, when America developed a unique identity, structure became a thing defined by internal rules, not by such externals as meter and rhyme.

Historically, the link between the ancient haiku form and what Momaday does with predominantly free verse is probably the imagist movement, which flared up quickly at the beginning of the twentieth century and burned away just as fast, leaving a lasting impression on all of American poetry. Imagist poetry, which descended from the French symbolists of the 1800s, was concerned with, as the name implies, imagery. Japanese haiku had a marked influence in the way that it allowed images to speak for themselves without being explained. As a literary movement, imagism opposed the confining use of structured forms. Because they tried to get objects to speak for themselves, imagist poems are often brief, like William Carlos Williams' "The Red Wheelbarrow," which is sixteen words, or Ezra Pound's "In a Station of the Metro," which is only two lines. There are examples of all lengths that represent this school of thought, though. In his book *The Imagist Poem: Modern Poetry in Miniature*, William Pratt defines the imagist poem as "a moment of revealed truth, rather than a structure of consecutive events or thoughts. The plot or argument of older poetry is replaced by a single, dominant image, or a quick succession of images: its effect is meant to be instantaneous rather than cumulative." This certainly applies to the way that "To A Child Running" works its effect, although Momaday, writing sixty years after the imagist movement was at its prime, worked under newer rules that were not so strict about avoiding structure.

Imagism's influence is still felt in almost all of contemporary American poetry. The American tradition of freedom is nicely served by the imagists' movement against poetic rules; the emphasis on concrete imagery has come to be accepted as being what is poetic about a poem. As such, Momaday's poem is a pure example of a late-twentieth-century American poem.

Momaday, unfortunately, is not usually one of the first people thought of when lists of American poets are compiled because he is usually hidden at the front of the folder reserved for the sub-category of Native Americans. This kind of stereotyping in the arts is a disservice to Americans, who need their country's talent revealed, not hidden. It is a source of annoyance to Momaday, who has said that he would rather be thought of as a writer *and* as an Indian, but not narrowly defined as an Indian writer. "I don't know what that means, exactly," he told Dagmar Weiler in a 1988 interview, regarding the subject of being an Indian writer, "and I don't identify with it at all." People reading "To A Child Running With Outstretched Arms in Canyon de Chelly" may feel that they need to understand the people who have lived there in order to catch the poem's entire spectrum, and this may be true, but such background knowledge is not absolutely necessary. Just as one does not need to know, when looking at a miniature model, whether the thing that it represents actually exists to marvel at the artist's ability to create any form of reality on such a small scale, neither does one need to know the Canyon de Chelly or its history to grasp the power of what happens when this child and the canyon become one.

Source: David Kelly, in an essay for *Poetry for Students,* Gale Group, 2001.

Joyce Hart

Hart, a former college professor, has lived with Native Americans and studied their traditional ceremonies. In the following essay, she discusses reader-response theory in reference to the poem, "To a Child Running with Outstretched Arms in Canyon de Chelly."

There is no one right way to interpret a poem any more than there is one right way to view a sunset. The experience of the sunset, as of a poem, will be different for each individual who witnesses it. To passively accept someone else's interpretation is like viewing a sunset with eyes closed while listening to another person describe it. That being said, a poem can be enhanced by examining different factors that might be hidden behind the words and images, thus broadening the knowledge base of the reader. In respect to N. Scott Momaday, it is particularly important to look also at his perspective on culture and the art of storytelling in order to experience a different way of looking at literature and the world.

Momaday's "To a Child Running with Outstretched Arms in Canyon de Chelly" is a poem whose subtle details could easily be overlooked. The entire poem consists of eight lines that together hold thirty-five words. Each word is short, and each image is simple, at least at first sight. It is what the words imply that imbues them with special consequence. In other words, it is significance that gives even the simplest image depth. For instance, someone from the city asked to go into the country to see a sunset might reply, "What is so important about a sunset? It's no big deal. The sun sets every day." But even for the most cynical person, if that particular sunset meant the end of a love affair, or maybe the beginning of a new one, it would give the sunset a special significance; and it would become a big deal.

So what might be the significance behind Momaday's poem? Is it possible to guess what Momaday was thinking? Of course it is, but is that the reason poems are read—to guess what the author means? That might be part of the reason. Poems, like all art forms, are a way of sharing experience, communicating ideas, and sharing emotions. But when it comes to interpretation, just what is being interpreted? Is it what the author means, or is it what the reader feels? Or is it a combination of both? According to a type of literary criticism called reader-response theory, the meaning of a poem exists somewhere in the transaction between the reader and the text, not from the text alone. In other words, the interpretation of a poem is based both upon the images that the author portrays and upon the intellectual and emotional reaction that those images cause in the reader.

On the first reading of "To a Child Running with Outstretched Arms in Canyon de Chelly," the images might appear to be a recollection of Momaday's childhood. Momaday used to live in the area around Canyon de Chelly, and in his writings he refers to this canyon as one of his favorite places. He might have thought of the poem while sitting on the rim of the canyon walls. Maybe he saw a child running deep down inside the canyon. The child might have reminded Momaday of when he was young, living in the country, free from the responsibilities of adulthood, free to run with excitement. The child's outstretched arms could have signified openness and innocence to Momaday.

In the use of the word *intense,* Momaday might have wanted to express the concept that in childhood everything seems intense. Children's minds are fresh. Each experience is new and whole, uninterrupted by layers of habits that tend to dull the adult mind that has witnessed bright, summer days so many times before. The child, for Momaday, might represent not only a child filled with delight but, even more importantly, a child who embodies the whole concept of delightfulness. In relationship to the child, the backdrop of the high, rugged, ancient walls of the canyon are immense; and it is the immensity of the great walled canyon that intensifies the child's smallness.

Those are the images that Momaday uses in the first stanza of this poem. These images appear rather obvious and are easily interpreted in a fairly straightforward manner. But something changes in the second stanza that makes continuing this simple interpretation a little more quizzical. At the end of the first stanza, Momaday switches his focus from the child to the natural setting. In the first few lines of the second stanza, he continues the same line of vision as he looks at the hills, noticing the shadow play of light and darkness in the drifting sand. What could Momaday be seeing? What do the sand drifts and the shadows mean?

He uses the word *break* in reference to the sand drifts. In the next line, he uses the word *cleavage.* These are rather harsh words in some sense of their definitions, but both words are also somewhat ambiguous. The poem says that the sand drifts "break and roll." The word *roll* softens the "breaking" part of the image. Ocean waves break and roll, gently and smoothly. And the word *cleavage* has two opposite meanings: one, to cut away; and another, to cling to. Or maybe, as some interpretations have suggested, Momaday uses both the drifting sands and the light and shadow to represent the passage of time. This makes sense especially in respect to the last line of the poem.

In the last line, Momaday returns his gaze and speaks directly to the child. He tells the child, "You

... the interpretation of a poem is based both upon the images that the author portrays and upon the intellectual and emotional reaction that those images cause in the reader."

embrace the spirit of this place." Is that why the child's arms are outstretched? Is the child trying to wrap his arms around the trees, the rocks, the memories, the history and the spirit of Canyon de Chelly? Or does Momaday want to convey a different meaning of the word *embrace,* such as "to encompass"? Or does he use the word *embrace* to suggest that the child understands? And what is there to understand about the spirit of this place? What is the spirit of Canyon de Chelly?

The spirit of Canyon de Chelly is, like poetry itself, different things to different people. To some, it is a national monument in Arizona. It is a canyon with sheer walls that rise up a spectacular thousand feet to scenic overlooks. It is a quiet, beautiful place for tourists to hike, a place to spend a summer vacation.

To another group of people, Canyon de Chelly is an archeological site, where at one time in 1902 a man named Charles Day built a trading post and hunted the grounds, looking for ancient, Native American artifacts, which he then sold to museums. More recently the United States government has protected the area, and now, to a group of legitimate scientists, Canyon de Chelly is a place where they can uncover history.

To the Navajo people, Canyon de Chelly is home. It is on the valley floor of this canyon that the Navajo people farm the land and raise sheep and goats. The Navajo people have lived in Canyon de Chelly for over three hundred years, except for a dramatic period of six years between 1862 and 1868 when they were rounded up by Colonel Kit Carson and forced to leave the canyon. Carson then marched them on what has been referred to as the Long Walk, a four-hundred-mile walk to the

Bosque Redondo in New Mexico. Many Navajo people died. It is estimated that twelve thousand Navajos began the Long Walk. Six years later only seven thousand Navajos made the Long Walk back home.

Prior to the Navajos, the Anasazi (a Navajo word for "ancient ones") lived in Canyon de Chelly. They lived in and around the canyon area for a period of about two thousand years. The ruin of their culture and their dwellings is the reason the archeologists are there. It is also the reason that the canyon has been designated as a national monument.

Now, the questions that remain might go something like this: Is Momaday's poem referring to all of these various definitions of the canyon? When he talks about the spirit of this place, is he referring to the spirits of all of these people and to all of their well-intentioned as well as ill-intentioned acts? Does this child who is running represent the Native American culture as well as the white culture? Is Momaday thinking about the ancient Anasazi as well as the modern tourists? Or is it none of this? Or is it more than this? And where are the answers to all these questions?

In an interview in the *Journal of Ethnic Studies,* Momaday says that most of us have come to expect answers. He then adds that "many things are not given us, and for the Western man this jars a little bit because we want to know. We expect to be told. We don't expect loose ends in a story. But in Indian tradition, it's not that way at all. There are always loose ends." Despite his belief in loose ends, Momaday does offer some suggestions on how to find answers. In his book *The Man Made of Words,* he says, "Stories are pools of reflection in which we see ourselves through the prism of the imagination." Momaday's thoughts reflect a sentiment that is closely related to reader-response theory—if there are answers to be found, they are to be found somewhere inside the reader.

Since one of the major images of this poem is centered on the landscape, it is important to understand how Momaday looks at the earth:

> "Very old in the Native American worldview is the conviction that the earth is vital, that there is a spiritual dimension to it, a dimension in which man rightly exists.... In the natural order man invests himself in the landscape and at the same time incorporates the landscape into his own most fundamental experience. This trust is sacred.... The Native American is someone who thinks of himself, imagines himself in a particular way. By virtue of his experience, his idea of himself comprehends his relationship to the land."

This passage suggests Momaday's belief that man and the landscape are one. This concept, he claims, is more apparent, or more real, to Native Americans because they have lived on the same region for so many thousands of years. They are connected to the ancient ones through stories that have been handed down to each succeeding generation, and therefore their connection to the ancient ones and to their homeland is strong. Many Native Americans are aware of their lineage, knowing their ancestors' names six or more generations back. Momaday has said that he is always surprised and disappointed to find out that many non-Native Americans know very little about their ancestry. He also questions the effects of the technological revolution, which has uprooted people from the soil. "We have become disoriented," he says, and "[have] suffered a kind of psychic dislocation of ourselves in time and space. We may be perfectly sure of where we are in relation to the supermarket … but [it is doubtful] that any of us knows where he is in relation to the stars …"

Momaday's connection to the land is sacred, and he has specifically referred to Canyon de Chelly as one of the sacred places on earth: "If you would know the earth for what it really is," he says, "learn it through its sacred places." When asked to define *sacred,* he responded, "Sacred transcends definition. The mind does not comprehend it … It is … to be recognized and acknowledged in the heart and soul. Those who seek to study or understand the sacred in academic terms are misled … It is beyond the mechanics of analysis."

Momaday also says that poetry is the crown of literature. Maybe in some ways poetry is sacred. Maybe poetry is meant to stimulate the imagination and is meant to be recognized, not through rational thought, but through the heart and soul. Maybe the purpose of Momaday's poem is to pose questions without giving answers, leaving spaces, like the spaces in Canyon de Chelly, for the imagination to run as freely as the child running with outstretched arms. And then again, maybe it's not. Finally, Momaday says: "We are what we imagine ourselves to be." Maybe the same holds true for Momaday's poetry.

Source: Joyce Hart, in an essay for *Poetry for Students,* Gale Group, 2001.

Sources

Bosque Redondo—Destination of the Long Walk, www. zianet.com/snm/redondo.htm (1998).

Canyon de Chelly, www.navajoland.com/cdc/ (1998, 1999).

Canyon de Chelly National Monument: Archaelogical Investigations Site Report, www.desertusa.com/ind1/du_cdc_arc.html (October 1997).

Mason, Kenneth C., "Beautyway: The Poetry of N. Scott Momaday," in *South Dakota Review,* Vol. XCIII, No. 2, Summer, 1980, pp. 61–83.

Momaday, N. Scott, *The Man Made of Words,* St. Martin's Press, 1997, pp. 39, 114, 169.

———, Dagmar Weiler, "M. Scott Momaday: Story Teller," in *Journal of Ethnic Studies,* Vol. 16, No. 1, Spring, 1988, pp. 118–26.

N. Scott Momaday, Ph.D. Interview, www.achievement.org/autodoc/page/mom0int-5 (June 28, 1996).

Pratt, William, *The Imagist Poem: Modern Poetry in Miniature,* Penguin Books, 1973, p. 29.

Schubnell, Matthias, "The Aboriginal Poems," in *N. Scott Momaday: The Cultural and Literary Background,* University of Oklahoma Press, 1985, pp. 218–39.

Strelke, Barbara, "N. Scott Momaday: Racial Memory and Individual Imagination," in *Literature of the American Indians: A Gathering of Indian Memories, Symbolic Contexts, and Literary Criticism,* edited by Abraham Chapman, New Amerian Library, 1975, pp. 348–57.

Thornton, Russell, *American Indian Holocaust and Survival: A Population History Since 1942,* University of Oklahoma Press, 1987.

Underhill, Ruth, *Here Come the Navajo!,* Bureau of Indian Affairs, 1953.

For Further Reading

Anderson, Scott Edward, "A Review of *In the Presence of the Sun: Stories and Poems, 1961–1991,*" in *Bloomsbury Review,* Volume 13, No. 7, July–August, 1993. pp. 14, 22.

Scott gives an overview of thirty years of Momaday's career, finding that the later poetry does not live up to the early promise.

Bolton, Jonathan W., and Claire M. Wilson, *American Indian Lives: Scholars, Writers and Professionals,* Facts on File, 1994.

One chapter of this book is devoted to Momaday, but the surrounding context, about Native American intellectuals throughout history, is equally fascinating.

Momaday, N. Scott, *The Names,* Harper & Row, 1976.

This is not a memoir in the sense that we are used to, since Momaday goes back to several generations before he was born for part of the story. We learn about the culture as well as the man.

Schubnell, Matthias, *N. Scott Momaday: The Cultural and Literary Background,* University of Oklahoma Press, 1985.

This is one of the most concise intellectual studies of Momaday and the influences from which he developed.

Simonelli, Jean, and Charles D. Winters, *Crossing Between Worlds: The Navajos of the Canyon de Chelly,* School of American Research Press, 1997.

Simonelli, an anthropologist, presents her research on this particular area with photographs by Winters.

Wilson, Hunter, Jr., *Canyon de Chelly in Pictures: The Continuing Story,* K. C. Publications, 1999.

Although something of a travel guide, the illustrations in this book give readers of the poem a good sense of what the canyon is like.

Woodard, Charles L., *Ancestral Voices: Conversations with N. Scott Momaday,* University of Nebraska Press, 1989.

Momaday is an articulate speaker, especially with questions to prompt him, so this volume provides a good sense of his way of seeing the world.

Tonight I Can Write

Pablo Neruda

1924

"Tonight I Can Write" was published in 1924 in a collection of poems by Pablo Neruda titled *Veinte poemas de amor y una cancion desesperada.* The collection was translated into English in 1969 by W. S. Merwin as *Twenty Love Poems and a Song of Despair.* Although some reviewers were shocked by the explicit sexuality in the poems, the collection became a best seller and was translated into several languages. Marjorie Agosin writes in her article on Neruda, "One of the reasons that *Twenty Love Poems* draws the reader so powerfully is the sobriety of expression and the economy of the images." René de Costa in his article on Neruda notes that all the poems in this collection contain "a highly charged confessional intimacy that challenged and charmed the sensibility of its reader, creating in the process a contemporary *stil nuovo* which continues to resonate in the language of love." The poems chart a love story from the initial infatuation to the release of passion, and finally to a separation. "Tonight I Can Write," the penultimate poem in the poetic sequence, expresses the pain the speaker feels after losing his lover. The bittersweet sentiment recalls their passionate relationship and his recognition that "love is so short, forgetting is so long."

Author Biography

Pablo Neruda was born Ricardo Eliezer Neftali Reyes y Basoalto on July 12, 1904, in the agri-

Pablo Neruda

Tonight I can write the saddest lines.

Write, for example, 'The night is starry
and the stars are blue and shiver in the distance.'

The night wind revolves in the sky and sings.

Tonight I can write the saddest lines.   5
I loved her, and sometimes she loved me too.

Through nights like this one I held her in my arms.
I kissed her again and again under the endless sky.

She loved me, sometimes I loved her too.
How could one not have loved her great still eyes.   10

Tonight I can write the saddest lines.
To think that I do not have her. To feel that I have
        lost her.

To hear the immense night, still more immense
        without her.
And the verse falls to the soul like dew to the
        pasture.

What does it matter that my love could not keep   15
        her.
The night is starry and she is not with me.

This is all. In the distance someone is singing. In
        the distance.
My soul is not satisfied that it has lost her.

My sight tries to find her as though to bring her
        closer.
My heart looks for her, and she is not with me.   20

The same night whitening the same trees.
We, of that time, are no longer the same.

I no longer love her, that's certain, but how I loved
        her.
My voice tried to find the wind to touch her
        hearing.

Another's. She will be another's. As she was   25
        before my kisses.
Her voice, her bright body. Her infinite eyes.

I no longer love her, that's certain, but maybe I
        love her.
Love is so short, forgetting is so long.

Because through nights like this one I held her in
        my arms
my soul is not satisfied that it has lost her.   30

Though this be the last pain that she makes me
        suffer
and these the last verses that I write for her.

Lines 1–4:

The theme of distance is introduced in the
opening line. When the speaker informs the reader,

cultural region of Parral, Chile. His father Jose del
Carmen Reyes Morales, a railroad worker, soon
relocated his family to Temuco, a frontier settlement in southern Chile. As a teenager he received
encouragement from one of his teachers, the poet
Gabriela Mistral, who would later win a Nobel
Prize. Manuel Duran and Margery Safir in *Earth
Tones: The Poetry of Pablo Neruda* note, "It is almost inconceivable that two such gifted poets
should find each other in such an unlikely spot.
Mistral recognized the young Neftali's talent and
encouraged it by giving the boy books and the support he lacked at home." This support helped him
find the confidence to write poetry and at fourteen
to change his name legally to Pablo Neruda. During high school he published poems in local papers and won literary competitions. In the early
1920s he attended Instituto Pedagogico in Santiago, Chile, and in 1926, the University of Chile.
His first collection of poetry, *La cancion de la fi-
esta,* was published in Chile in 1921. He followed
that volume with two more: *Crepusculario* in 1923
and *Veinte poemas de amor y una cancion desesperada* in 1924. The latter collection, which includes his poem "Tonight I Can Write," became a
popular success in Latin America and was translated in 1969 as *Twenty Love Poems and a Song
of Despair.*

Media Adaptations

- All of the poems in *Twenty Love Poems and a Song of Despair* were released on cassette by Viking Penguin in 1996.

"Tonight I can write the saddest lines," he suggests that he could not previously. We later learn that his overwhelming sorrow over a lost lover has prevented him from writing about their relationship and its demise. The speaker's constant juxtaposition of past and present illustrate his inability to come to terms with his present isolated state. Neruda's language here, as in the rest of the poem, is simple and to the point, suggesting the sincerity of the speaker's emotions. The sense of distance is again addressed in the second and third lines as he notes the stars shivering "in the distance." These lines also contain images of nature, which will become a central link to his memories and to his present state. The speaker contemplates the natural world, focusing on those aspects of it that remind him of his lost love and the cosmic nature of their relationship. He begins writing at night, a time when darkness will match his mood. The night sky filled with stars offers him no comfort since they "are blue and shiver." Their distance from him reinforces the fact that he is alone. However, he can appreciate the night wind that "sings" as his verses will, describing the woman he loved.

Lines 5–10:

Neruda repeats the first line in the fifth and follows it with a declaration of the speaker's love for an unnamed woman. The staggered repetitions Neruda employs throughout the poem provide thematic unity. The speaker introduces the first detail of their relationship and points to a possible reason for its demise when he admits "sometimes she loved me too." He then reminisces about being with her in "nights like this one." The juxtaposition of nights from the past with this night reveals the change that has taken place, reinforcing his sense of aloneness. In this section, Neruda links the speaker's lover with nature, a technique he will use

throughout the poem to describe the sensual nature of their relationship. In the eighth line, the speaker remembers kissing his love "again and again under the endless sky"—a sky as endless as, he had hoped, their relationship would be. An ironic reversal of line six occurs in line nine when the speaker states, "She loved me, sometimes I loved her too." The speaker may be offering a cynical statement of the fickle nature of love at this point. However, the eloquent, bittersweet lines that follow suggest that in this line he is trying to distance himself from the memory of his love for her and so ease his suffering. Immediately, in the next line he contradicts himself when he admits, "How could one not have loved her great still eyes." The poem's contradictions create a tension that reflects the speaker's desperate attempts to forget the past.

Lines 11–14:

In line eleven Neruda again repeats his opening line, which becomes a plaintive refrain. The repetition of that line shows how the speaker is struggling to maintain distance, to convince himself that enough time has passed for him to have the strength to think about his lost love. But these lines are "the saddest." He cannot yet escape the pain of remembering. It becomes almost unbearable "to think that I do not have her. To feel that I have lost her." His loneliness is reinforced by "the immense night, still more immense without her." Yet the poetry that he creates helps replenish his soul, "like dew to the pasture."

Lines 15–18:

In line fifteen the speaker refuses to analyze their relationship. What is important to him is that "the night is starry and she is not with me" as she used to be on similar starry nights. "This is all" that is now central to him. When the speaker hears someone singing in the distance and repeats "in the distance," he reinforces the fact that he is alone. No one is singing to him. As a result, he admits "my soul is not satisfied."

Lines 19–26:

In these lines the speaker expresses his longing to reunite with his love. His sight and his heart try to find her, but he notes, "she is not with me." He again remembers that this night is so similar to the ones they shared together. Yet he understands that they "are no longer the same." He declares that he no longer loves her, "that's certain," in an effort to relieve his pain, and admits he loved her greatly in the past. Again linking their relationship to nature, he explains that he had "tried to find the wind to touch her hearing" but failed. Now he must face the fact that "she will be another's." He remembers her "bright" body that he knows will be touched by another and her "infinite eyes" that will look upon a new lover.

Lines 27–32:

The speaker reiterates, "I no longer love her, that's certain," but immediately contradicts himself, uncovering his efforts at self deception when he admits, "but maybe I love her." With a world-weary tone of resignation, he concludes, "love is so short, forgetting is so long." His poem has become a painful exercise in forgetting. In line twenty-nine he explains that because this night is so similar to the nights in his memory when he held her in his arms, he cannot forget. Thus he repeats, "my soul is not satisfied." In the final two lines, however, the speaker is determined to erase the memory of her and so ease his pain, insisting that his verses (this poem) will be "the last verses that I write for her."

Themes

Memory and Reminiscence

"Tonight I Can Write" is a poem about memories of a lost love and the pain they can cause. Throughout the poem the speaker recalls the details of a relationship that is now broken. He continually juxtaposes images of the passion he felt for the woman he loved with the loneliness he experiences in the present. He is now at some distance from the relationship and so acknowledges, "tonight I can write the saddest lines," suggesting that the pain he suffered after losing his lover had previously prevented any reminiscences or descriptions of it. While the pain he experienced had blocked his creative energies in the past, he is now able to write about their relationship and find some comfort in "the verse [that] falls to the soul like dew to the pasture."

Love and Passion

Throughout the poem, the speaker expresses his great love for a woman with whom he had a passionate romance. He remembers physical details: "her great still eyes," "her voice, her bright body," "her infinite eyes." He also remembers kissing her "again and again under the endless sky" admitting "how I loved her." His love for her is still evident even though he states twice "I no longer

Topics for Further Study

- Take a walk in a natural setting: the woods, the beach, a park. Write a poem about what you see. Does your mood in any way affect your descriptions?

- Research theories of remembering and forgetting. How does your research relate to the speaker in "Tonight I Can Write" ?

- Compare and contrast the statements on despair in W. H. Auden's "Funeral Blues" and Neruda's "Song of Despair." How does the style in each reflect the theme?

love her, that's certain." The remembrance of their love is still too painful to allow him to admit the depth of his love for her, especially when he thinks, "Another's. She will be another's. As she was before my kisses," imagining her "bright body" under someone else's caress.

Physical and Spiritual

Neruda employs nature imagery to suggest the speaker's conception of the spiritual nature of his relationship with his lover. When he describes them kissing "again and again under the endless sky," he describes his physical relationship with her in cosmic terms. He also uses this type of imagery to describe his lover, creating a connection between her and nature. "Traditionally," states René de Costa in *The Poetry of Pablo Neruda*, "love poetry has equated woman with nature. Neruda took this established mode of comparison and raised it to a cosmic level, making woman into a veritable force of the universe." The speaker compares his lover's "great still" and "infinite eyes" to the "endless sky." He also uses nature to communicate his love for her. His voice tries "to find the wind to touch her hearing."

Alienation and Loneliness

The speaker juxtaposes memories of his passionate relationship with his lover with his present state of alienation and loneliness without her. The speaker employs the imagery of nature to reflect his internal state. He writes his "saddest lines" on a night that is similar to the nights he spent with his lover. Yet the darkness and the stars that "shiver at a distance" in this night suggest his loneliness. The "immense night" becomes "still more immense without her," especially when he notes, "to think that I do not have her. To feel that I have lost her." He compounds his suffering when he remembers "nights like this one" when he held her in his arms.

The speaker expresses his loneliness when he notes that he hears someone in the distance singing and repeats, "in the distance." No one now sings for him. He admits, "my sight tries to find her as though to bring her closer," and "my heart looks for her, and she is not with me." As a result, his "soul is not satisfied. In an effort to assuage the loneliness he feels, he tries to convince himself, "I no longer love her, that's certain," but then later acknowledges, "maybe I love her." With a world-weary tone of resignation, he concludes, "love is so short, forgetting is so long." Determined to end his sense of alienation and loneliness, the speaker insists that these will be "the last verses that I write for her."

Style

Style

Readers responded positively to Neruda's innovative, simple, direct language and sparse imagery in "Tonight I Can Write." In her book on Neruda, Agosin writes that the poem, along with others in the collection, "marks a clear transition from the era of Spanish-American modernism to that of surrealism, with its often disconnected images and metaphors, which will dominate Neruda's next phase." The poem does not contain a regular meter. Neruda suppresses rhyme but attains rhythm through a mixture of consonance and assonance. Often one line will appear by itself, calling attention to content over form. Duran and Safir in their book, *Earth Tones: The Poetry of Pablo Neruda*, determine "Tonight I Can Write" to be a "constructive" poem, in that it is "organized around experiences in which real human beings, Neruda himself and the women he loved, provide a stabilizing platform upon which [the poem] is built."

Symbolism

Neruda uses nature imagery in "Tonight I Can Write" when he describes his lost love and their relationship. When the speaker describes the "end-less sky" and his love's "infinite eyes," he suggests that their relationship achieved a cosmic level. Neruda also uses images of nature to illustrate the speaker's state of mind. When he writes of the stars that are "blue and shiver in the distance" he suggests the distance that has formed between the lovers and the coldness of the speaker's isolation.

Historical Context

Latin American Literature

After World War I, Latin American writers began to gain international recognition. As a result, these writers started to shift the focus in their works from regional preoccupations to more universal themes. They also experimented with new literary forms. Modernism, especially had an impact on Latin American poets. Love, the family, and social protest became popular subjects, especially with the Uruguayans Delmira Agustini and Juana de Ibarbourou and the Chileans Mistral and Neruda.

Marisol and Marisombra

Neruda has admitted that the poems in *Twenty Love Poems and a Song of Despair* were inspired by his relationships with two women during his student years in Santiago. Two distinct women emerge in the poems in this collection—a mysterious girl in a beret and another young woman. Although he does not identify the women by name in the poems, later in an interview he referred to them as Marisol and Marisombra. The posthumous publication of his letters in 1974 revealed the girl in the beret to be Albertina Azocar, the sister of his close friend Ruben Azocar.

Literary Censorship

Chiles leading publisher refused to publish *Twenty Love Poems and a Song of Despair* because of its blatant eroticism. When the collection was eventually published, many readers were scandalized by the sexually explicit imagery. Political and literary censorship has existed in some form since the beginning of civilization. Censorship has existed in the United States since the colonial period, but over the years the emphasis has shifted from political to literary. Prior to 1930, literary classics like James Joyces' *Ulysses* were not allowed entry into the United States on grounds of obscenity. Other works, like D. H. Lawrence's *Lady Chatterleys Lover,* Henry Miller's *Tropic of Cancer,* and John Cleland's *Fanny Hill,* won admittance into the United States only after court fights. In 1957 the

Compare & Contrast

- **1924:** The first airplanes to circle the globe arrive in California after flying 30,000 miles in five months.

  1996: The National Aeronautics and Space Administration (NASA) announces that Mars may have supported life-forms. The report cites evidence gained from an analysis of a meteorite found in Antarctica in 1984.

- **1924:** The United States Congress passes the Johnson-Reed Act, which removes restrictions on immigration from Canada and Latin America. As a result, by the end of the year, immi-

gration numbers from these areas break previous records.

1996: Mexico and the United States sign several pacts including the Migrants' Rights pact, which grants rights to legal and illegal Mexicans in the United States.

- **1924:** The United States Congress recognizes Native Americans as U.S. citizens.

  1996: The South African government makes its final transition from apartheid to democracy with the adoption of a new constitution. President F. W. de Klerk resigns.

Supreme Court began a series of decisions that would relax restrictions on obscene literature. In 1973, however, the Supreme Court granted individual states the right to determine what was obscene.

Critical Overview

"Tonight I Can Write" was published in 1924 in a collection of Pablo Neruda's poetry, *Veinte poemas de amor y una cancion desesperada* and translated into English in 1969 by Merwin as *Twenty Love Poems and a Song of Despair*. Although Chile's leading publisher turned down the collection, arguing that the poems were too erotic, the public response was overwhelmingly positive. Over the years, the collection has been translated into several languages. *Twenty Love Poems and a Song of Despair* established his reputation as a promising new poet. In his article "Pablo Neruda: Overview," de Costa notes that the book was a *"succès de scandale"* when it first appeared in 1924. Judged to be shamelessly erotic and faulted for its bold departure in form and style from the genteel tradition of Hispanic lyricism the book went on to become something of a bestseller, and remains so today." Robert Clemens remarks in the *Saturday Review* that the collection "established [Neruda] at the outset as a frank, sensuous spokesman for love."

George D. Schade in his article on Neruda praises the author's prodigious literary achievements and notes that none of his work has compared "in immediate popularity and continuing success with his first significant book, *Twenty Love Poems and a Song of Despair.*

Criticism

Wendy Perkins

Wendy Perkins is an Associate Professor of English at Prince George's Community College in Maryland. In the following essay, she examines Neruda's use of nature imagery in "Tonight I Can Write" to illustrate the poem's dominant themes.

Nature has played a large role in literature, especially poetry, since the Medieval age. Poets employ the images of nature for several purposes: to express childlike delight in the sense of freedom it affords, as a background to or reflection of human actions or emotions, to express a sense of the infinite, to symbolize the human spirit, or to describe nature for its own sake. References to a sense of awe in the face of an often hostile nature appear in the Medieval age in *Beowulf* while Chaucer tended to create idyllic natural settings for his tales. The Elizabethans' pastorals and sonnets used images in

In the speaker's lyrical evocations of his relationship with the woman he has loved and lost, he and the woman become almost indistinguishable from nature. The lovers' passion and despair thus transcend the human and achieve the cosmic."

nature to provide appropriate settings to dramatic situations and human emotions. Neoclassicists employed descriptions of natural settings as a basis for philosophical reflections. Nature became the primary subject for the Romantic poets like Wordsworth and Coleridge who turned to the natural world as a respite from society and culture and as a more appropriate guide to spiritual concerns. Often, these poets found a wilder, more disordered natural world than did their predecessors, which became a more apt setting for their ruminations on the wilder, more disordered nature of human experience. Chilean poet Pablo Neruda adopted a Romantic vision in the twentieth century in "Tonight I Can Write" in his use of nature as reflection of the spiritual and emotional. Yet in this poem, Neruda's use of nature becomes more complex. In the speaker's lyrical evocations of his relationship with the woman he has loved and lost, he and the woman become almost indistinguishable from nature. The lovers' passion and despair thus transcend the human and achieve the cosmic.

Manuel Duran and Margery Safir in their *Earth Tones: The Poetry of Pablo Neruda* note that in all the poetry in Neruda's *Twenty Love Poems and a Song of Despair* "nature does not enter for itself alone, but rather nature and woman are seen as two aspects of the same reality. The beauty and strength—and mystery, at times terror—of nature and the beauty, strength, and mystery of woman are but mirrors of one another. In *Twenty Poems* nostalgia, love of nature, and love of woman are united

in a single strand and nowhere do we find the detached contemplation of nature itself." Marjorie Agosin, in her book on Neruda, comments, "The image of the woman takes on a transcendental importance in [*Twenty Poems*], for she is associated with the elements and the earth. She is the earth mother, a notion established by the romantic poets of the last century, but which Neruda makes more immediate and secular … Woman, who plays with the world and resembles that world elevated to a cosmic level, is cast in images of the surrounding natural landscape—sky, water, earth." In "Tonight I Can Write" the speaker fuses the spiritual beauty of nature with that of the woman he loved. Her "great still" and "infinite eyes," that no one could help but love, become the "immense night." The natural setting also blends with the delight they experienced in each other. Their passion shone like the "starry night." The speaker notes, "Through nights like this one I held her in my arms. / I kissed her again and again under the endless sky." The sky was as endless as their passion. Her mystery, however, is also reflected in natural images. She and the stars are distant on the night the speaker gains the strength to remember and to express through verse his passionate love for her and the pain he has suffered without her. In this monologue, the woman is absent and their love distant, which makes the sincerity of his emotion more poignant. The speaker seems unsure about why the relationship failed. All he has is a sense that "sometimes" she loved him too.

Neruda also fuses images of nature with the speaker's emotional state in the poem's present. The dark night matches the dark night of his soul as he thinks about "nights like this one" when he held her in his arms. He hears "the immense night, still more immense without her." The juxtaposition of past and present nights reveals the change that has taken place, reinforcing his sense of aloneness. He admits tonight is "the same night whitening the same trees," yet "we, of that time, are no longer the same." Neruda embraces the entirety of nature when he focuses attention on the night sky. When the speaker laments, "the night is starry and she is not with me," sky and earth merge, encompassing his loneliness. The speaker and the stars "shiver in the distance" that separates them from the loved one. Also "in the distance some one is singing. In the distance" not to him. Yet ironically it is that distance that allows the speaker the strength to return finally to the past and express his memories of it, for only now can he write "the saddest lines." In his juxtapositions of past and present, his struggle with his emotions and sense of isolation sometimes becomes overwhelming, as when he acknowledges, "my soul is not satisfied that it has lost her." Agosin comments that in *Twenty Poems* "dialogue does not exist, for this is a collection of monologues where desperation, alienation, and the obsessive need to obliterate loneliness constantly seep through." Neruda's language in "Tonight I Can Write" is direct and concise, suggesting the sincerity of the speaker's emotions. He hopes that the act of remembering and envisioning their love through the poem will alleviate his sense of alienation. "The night wind revolves in the sky and sings" as he hopes his poem will. Later he admits that his "verse falls to the soul like dew to the pasture." He concludes, however, "my voice tried to find the wind to touch her hearing" but could not.

On this night the speaker expresses his sorrow over his inability to hold onto his relationship with his lover. He declares, "My sight tries to find her as though to bring her closer. / My heart looks for her, and she is not with me." In an effort to cope with his loneliness, he tries repeatedly to convince himself that he no longer loves her; "that's certain." But his sensuous descriptions of the night and his love belie his efforts. Ultimately he admits on this night, remembering "nights like this one" when he held her in his arms, "love is so short, forgetting is so long."

Agosin describes *Twenty Poems* as "a book celebrating the unforgettable sentiment of first love, which examines afresh the first stirrings of happiness and lucklessness. Even after the shipwreck, the amorous sentiment survives through the power of language that is integrated with nature." In "Tonight I Can Write" Neruda fuses the images of nature with "the unforgettable sentiment of first love" and so creates a moving, lyrical evocation of its passion and agony.

Source: Wendy Perkins, in an essay for *Poetry for Students,* Gale Group, 2001.

Dean Rader

Rader has published widely in the field of American and Latin American art and literature. In this essay, Rader explores the ways in which Neruda's famous poem both exemplifies and eludes classification as a modernist text.

There may be no more beloved poem in all of Latin America than Pablo Neruda's beguiling poem "Tonight I Can Write." Written when Neruda was in his very early twenties, the poem perfectly captures the paradoxical emotions of recently lost love.

> *The poem succeeds because it, like love, like human emotion, cannot be quantified, classified or confined poem. In other words, "Tonight I Can Write" reflects High Modernist principles while simultaneously transgressing them."*

On some level, this poem absolutely resists interpretation and analysis—it is so simple, so direct, so honest, that there is very little to unpack. Indeed, few students have difficulty understanding the poem, and few critics have made it the focus of their critical attention. The poem's language is accessible, and unlike many modernist texts, it explores emotions that every reader can relate to. Instead of offering a reading of the poem itself, this essay will discuss the ways in which Neruda's poem is profoundly unique for the era in which it was written. "Tonight I Can Write" both embodies many characteristics of modernism, the literary movement of which it is part, and eschews the typical conventions of the modernist poem. The fact that Neruda's poem both participates in and refuses to participate in expected conventions of modernist aesthetics, grounds it in the temporal milieu of an era yet imbues it with a sense of timelessness. At once, the text feels shockingly unpoetic *and* overwhelming so. The "confusion" in the poem, its paradoxical nature, mirrors the confusion within the speaker of the poem and his own paradoxical stances on the woman who has left him. The poem succeeds because it, like love, like human emotion, cannot be quantified, classified or confined poem. In other words, "Tonight I Can Write" reflects High Modernist principles while simultaneously transgressing them.

To be sure, Neruda's poem offers up for examination many of the most important characteristics underpinning the modernist lyric poem. For instance, the very genesis of the poem itself is utterly modernist in that the poem arises out of absence. One of

What Do I Read Next?

- Emily Dickinson's "After great pain, a formal feeling comes" (*The Poems of Emily Dickinson,* 1929) focuses on the acceptance of grief.

- "Funeral Blues" by W. H. Auden, published in 1940 in his *Another Time,* presents a portrait of the suffering experienced after the death of a loved one.

- "The Song of Despair" is another poem by Neruda, published with "Tonight I Can Write" in *Twenty Love Poems and a Song of Despair,* that expresses the speakers memories of a past relationship and pain over its dissolution.

- Edna St. Vincent Millay wrote "What lips my lips have kissed, and where, and why" in 1923. In this poem, published in her *Collected Poems* that same year, the speaker laments the loss of past lovers and the resulting state of emptiness.

---

the classic motifs of modernism is the presence of absence; that is, the realization that absence can become a palpable presence. Rainer Maria Rilke's "Archaic Torso of Apollo," Wallace Stevens' "Snow Man," William Carlos Williams' "This Is Just To Say," and T. S. Eliot's "The Hollow Men" all create a landscape in which the absence of a head or plums or life itself morphs into a disturbing presence. In Neruda's poem, the text's very presence is contingent on the absence of the woman in question. If she and the poet were still together, there would be no need for such a poem. Indeed, Neruda spends the entire poem reminding us of the woman's absence. As is the case in the poems mentioned above, the poem ultimately becomes a proxy for what is missing; thus, the poem becomes a stand-in, the presence needed to fill the void. But, at the same time, we are always aware that, in fact, there is a void.

If modernist writers feel anything, it's alienation; hence, alienation has come to be one of the key concepts associated with modernism. Because of the increased urbanization of the west, the advent of telephones and radio, the residual frag-

mentation following World War I and the popularity of Freudian, Darwinian and Nietzschean thought, individuals, particularly artists, felt themselves alienated from the rest of society. In works like James Joyce's *Ulysses,* Eliot's "The Love Song of J. Alfred Prufrock," Robert Frost's "Stopping By Woods On A Snowy Evening," H. D.'s "Eurydice," Stevens's "Sunday Morning," Franz Kafka's *The Trial,* and Yeats' "The Second Coming," an individual muses over his or her estrangement from either another person or society at large. In "Tonight I Can Write," Neruda establishes the ubiquitous alienation of the individual, a trope he will elaborate on in his *Residencia en la Tierra* books. Not only is the speaker alienated from his love, but so is he divorced from nature, which is itself inscribed with her absence: "To hear the immense night still more immense without her … The night is starry and she is not with me." Though the writer doesn't seem to enjoy experiencing feelings of alienation, almost always it is the genesis for art. The writer uses his text as a means of connection and exchange otherwise unavailable to him. Neruda's poem is no different here, though he uses the medium of poetry to convince himself that his isolation is not only temporary but an occasion to write the "saddest" lines possible.

One last way in which "Tonight I Can Write" embodies some basic tenets of modernism is through its autotelism (the belief that a work of art is an end in itself or its own justification). For better or worse, many modernist texts do not signify outside themselves. They are their own ends. Postmodern critics often criticize modernism because work produced during this period tends to apotheosize art and ignore the world and its problems. When Gabriel in Joyce's short story "The Dead" claims that literature is above politics, he defines the view of a generation of writers. Later in his life, Neruda will completely reverse his stance, but in these early poems, the alpha and omega of poetry is the poem itself. Political concerns, cultural criticisms, economic warnings do not enter the poems at all. For many, there was no world outside of the text; indeed, for the speaker of the poem, there is no world outside of his emotional sphere. The obsessions, anxieties and desires of the individual almost always take precedence over the concerns of society, and while "Tonight I Can Write" does engage common private emotions, it does not necessarily engage larger public interests.

More interesting than exploring how "Tonight I Can Write" recoups modernism is examining how it eludes it. One refreshing distinction of the poem lies in its sincerity. High Modernism is not known for its honesty. On the contrary, most modernist poetic texts feature a prominent persona and emphasize a distanced irony or a diminished emotional landscape. Not so with Neruda. According to René de Costa, this attribute lends the poem a salient uniqueness: "The poem's effectiveness, the reader's empathy with the sincerity of the poetic voice, derives from the fact that this is a composition unlike any other." Compare, for example, the voice of J. Alfred Prufrock with the voice of the speaker of this poem. Both poems attend to complex emotions surrounding romance and love, but Neruda's is clearly more vulnerable. The distance between the poetic persona and the author is indistinguishable in Neruda (even more so than in a poet like Walt Whitman), whereas for Eliot, Pound and even Stevens and Williams, that is simply not the case.

Without question, Neruda was ahead of his time. In fact, in this poem and in others, he predicts certain aspects of postmodernism, most notably questions of textuality and referentiality. "Tonight I Can Write" is utterly aware of itself as a poem. It refers to its own poem-ness, it's own composition. It repeatedly refers to itself as a poem in progress, not a finished piece. For the New Critics, the ideal poem is a "well-wrought urn," an object d'art that is isolated, untouchable, perfect, flawless. Rarely will one find a modernist poem that not only mentions its own textuality but celebrates it. In other words, while we are reading this poem, we are always aware that we are reading a poem, unlike "Prufrock," which is a kind of confession, or "In the Station of the Metro," which works like a photograph. For Neruda, the poem is never a product, always a process.

Perhaps the most important way in which "Tonight I Can Write" averts the modernist impulse lies in its form. As mentioned above, the desired poem for most High Modernists and most New Critics is one that is clearly "made." In poems by Pound or Stevens or Eliot or Hart Crane, one encounters some very difficult language and archaic allusions. Often, the tone is lofty, reverent, even scholarly. Such is the case in Eliot's "The Wasteland" or Pound's "Hugh Selwyn Mauberly." But in Neruda's poem, his language is downright conversational. The poem is contradictory, and at times the speaker seems unsure of his emotions. In fact, the poem feels more like a journal entry than a finished art object. "Neruda has employed here a rhetoric that is not conventionally poetic," argues de Costa. He goes on to contextualize Neruda's text with preconceived notions of what a good poem might be: "The stag-

gered repetitions, the poetic syntax, the irregularity of the temporal exposition are distinctive features to be sure, but features not normally found in 'good poetry.'" For de Costa, Neruda's determination to write against poetic tradition gives the poem it's appeal. Some readers would agree. To express such common and such strong emotions without succumbing to cliché or sentiment or cloying language is an amazing achievement.

There may be no more poignant statement on lost love than "Tonight I Can Write," and, paradoxically, there may be no more accessible statement either. However, this paradox should not deter the reader; in fact, this paradox simply reflects the motif of contradictions inherent in human relationships and, for that matter, in all good poetry.

Source: Dean Rader, in an essay for *Poetry for Students*, Gale Group, 2001.

Cliff Saunders

Saunders teaches writing and literature in the Myrtle Beach, South Carolina area and has published six chapbooks of poetry. In the following essay, Saunders contends that "Tonight I Can Write" is a powerful lament for a lost lover that gains strength because of Pablo Neruda's ability to control his vivid imagination and express his turbulent emotional state with the utmost sincerity, simplicity, honesty, and directness.

Pablo Neruda's "Puedo Escribir Los Versos" ("Tonight I Can Write") has long stood the test of time as arguably the best poem in *Veinte Poemas de Amor y una Cancion Desesperada* (*Twenty Love Poems and a Song of Despair*) (1924), which has been called "one of the finest books of verse in the Spanish language." For English readers, moreover, the 1969 translation of this poem by W. S. Merwin, one of America's foremost poet-translators of the past fifty years, comes as an added boon, for Merwin captures beautifully—and faithfully—the poem's musical and emotional nuances. In Merwin's translation, one experiences the full cathartic brunt of Neruda's complex, and even contradictory, feelings toward the loved one that he "could not keep."

As the culmination of a score of poems that alternate between unbridled joy and overpowering sadness, "Tonight I Can Write" (known hereafter in this essay as "Poem XX," per Neruda's numerical sequencing) struggles to express the inexpressible, to articulate, in the most sincere and direct way possible, Neruda's lyrical cry of the heart over the fact that he and his lover are no longer to-

> *Indeed, such a raw, naked cry of sadness and loss, the kind that informs "Poem XX," can only achieve its full effect with rigorous attention toward eliminating any surface pyrotechnics that may please the reader's eye but interfere with the poem's passionate outcry."*

gether. Deeply personal yet piercingly universal, "Poem XX" derives much of its power from the naked, unadorned simplicity of expression that propels the poem forward. The poem is less ornate in imagery than those preceding it in the *Twenty Love Poems* sequence, almost as if Neruda understood implicitly that the denser, more heavily metaphorical and descriptive language of the preceding poems would no longer suffice in verbalizing the raw, intense emotional state he found himself in at the time of the composition of "Poem XX." In essence, "Poem XX" cuts to the core of the matter in a way no other poem in *Twenty Love Poems* does.

Operating in a "less is more" vein, "Poem XX" actually derives more emotional power from its earthy directness and sparseness of descriptive adjectives than a more elaborate verbal treatment would have. As noted by Manuel Duran and Margery Safir in *Earth Tones,* their probing exploration of Neruda and his poetry, "[v]ery few words in *Twenty Poems* would not be found on a list of the two thousand most frequently used words in the Spanish language," and this observation is particularly true of "Poem XX," with its emphasis on such simple yet highly connotative nouns as "night," "wind," "soul," and "love." Neruda, in this poem, seems to be striving for an absolute purity of expression in which words fall "to the soul like dew to the pasture," to quote one of the poem's more powerful figures of speech. In a desire to approximate the crystalline purity of dewdrops on grass, Neruda keeps the nouns short, sweet, and

largely free of adjectives and other modifiers. "The adjective is the enemy of the noun," wrote Voltaire, and though Neruda may not have been aware of this quote at the time, subconsciously he seems to have composed "Poem XX" with the goal of paring down the language to the bare essentials. Indeed, such a raw, naked cry of sadness and loss, the kind that informs "Poem XX," can only achieve its full effect with rigorous attention toward eliminating any surface pyrotechnics that may please the reader's eye but interfere with the poem's passionate outcry.

Be that as it may, Neruda does not suppress his powerful imagination entirely in "Poem XX," although it is relatively subdued here when compared to the other poems in the collection. Vivid imagery and scintillant figures of speech are still on display in "Poem XX," albeit in a less densely packed arrangement. Aside from the aforementioned brilliant simile in line 14, there are a number of striking metaphors throughout the poem, all of which synthesize Neruda's heightened emotional state with the natural world. Almost immediately, in lines 2–3, the reader encounters a wonderfully ambiguous and resonant image: "'The night is shattered / and the blue stars shiver in the distance.'" The first half of the image, "The night is shattered," suggests a dual intent on Neruda's part. On the one hand, this image could mean that Neruda himself "is shattered" because the awful realization that he and his lover have parted ways permanently has pierced him like a dart. On the other hand, the image could imply that the dark cloud, so to speak, that had hung over him like a black hole ever since the parting of ways has finally dissipated, and now he can see clearly enough to articulate the full depth of his anguish. It could mean, in fact, that he has reached a state of such intense clarity that he can actually see "blue stars shiver in the distance." Along with its striking beauty, this second half of the image communicates the deep chill he feels now in relation to the loss of his lover. That the stars are "blue" is significant, for the color blue connotes not only sadness (i.e., "since my baby left, I've been so blue") but extreme coldness, such as when lips turn blue in the winter wind. And as if these distant, blue stars aren't cold enough already, they're *shivering*. This verb not only adds to the sense of biting coldness (the kind that can numb the human heart when it is broken) but also personifies that deep chill in such a way that the reader can feel it and identify with it. Neruda here is inferring that his sadness is so immense that it is causing distant stars to freeze. One could say that he is grossly overstating the intensity of his emotional state, but try telling that to someone who has lost a lover.

This powerful image is immediately followed by another key figure of speech: "The night wind revolves in the sky and sings." Often in poetry, mention of the night wind signifies a dark, turbulent time in the speaker's soul, and sure enough, that the night wind is in motion in "Poem XX" connotes a certain turbulence. However, this night wind is not howling but singing, which definitely undercuts the usual associations that the night wind delivers in poetry. Here, perhaps, Neruda is implying that since the night has been "shattered," and, to quote a popular song in America, he "can see clearly now," the speaker (as represented by the night wind) can finally give lyrical voice to the tempestuous state of his soul, can sing that soul into rejuvenation. This interpretation is bolstered by the placement of the next line ("Tonight I can write the saddest lines"), which repeats the poem's opening statement and reinforces the idea that the poet is finally able to begin the process of healing his anguish. Like the night wind, the speaker has in a sense been going around in circles and getting nowhere, but now he is ready to sing of the loss of his lover in an attempt (perhaps a doomed one) to exorcise her memory so he can move on with his life. This notion is further reinforced later in the poem, when the speaker says in line 24: "My voice tried to find the wind to touch her hearing." In other words, although he has finally broken through his pain enough to articulate that pain, the one whom he really wants to hear his lament, his lost lover, no longer wants to listen.

Yet another vivid image, line 21's "The same night whitening the same trees," is the most perplexing of all in "Poem XX." On the surface, this line strikes one as utterly irrational; after all, how can night, with its deep blackness, whiten anything? The only time when night can whiten trees is during an overnight snowfall, and while this suggestion seems in keeping with the earlier image of blue stars shivering in the distance, it doesn't really fit into the context of the poem, given that a night when one can see blue stars in the sky couldn't be the same night when snowfall is obscuring the stars from one's vision. The image is a tough one to crack, and after much pondering, some readers might still find it somewhat impenetrable. The only explanation that makes even the slightest sense is that the speaker can see so clearly now—after a time of great darkness, presumably—that pitch-black trees look as bright to him as do "the blue stars shiver[ing] in the distance." In other

words, with absolute clarity, he can now see his way through the dark woods that had surrounded him in the wake of the rift between the loved one and himself. Yet even this explanation of the image seems inadequate, and chances are that Neruda himself had no rational understanding of its implications. Sometimes an image just *feels* right, and ultimately a poet must trust this intuitive feeling. Fortunately for us, Neruda learned to trust his intuitive side at a very young age (he would have been no older than twenty when he wrote "Poem XX"), and this was an early indication of his budding genius.

The poem's figures of speech (what few there are) resonate deeply in the reader's psyche, but ultimately what impresses one about the poem is the undaunted honesty and lyrical intensity of Neruda's voice as he struggles for closure in a situation where closure is difficult, if not impossible. Neruda's stirring combination of colloquial simplicity and use of repetition in key lines such as "Tonight I can write the saddest lines," "The night is shattered," and "I no longer love her, that's certain" helps create an impassioned sincerity and haunting mood not easily forgotten by the reader. While it is true, as noted by René de Costa in *The Poetry of Pablo Neruda,* that ""Poem XX" closes a series of unsuccessful attempts to communicate with the loved one," we, as readers, should be thankful that Neruda at least made the attempt. For although he may not have succeeded in reaching the ears of his former lover, he has very much succeeded in reaching ours. Given the lyrical honesty of Neruda's poetic voice, how could we *not* listen?

Source: Cliff Saunders, in an essay for *Poetry for Students,* Gale Group, 2001.

Marisa Anne Pagnattaro

Pagnattaro has a J.D. and Ph.D. in English and is a freelance writer and a Terry Teaching Fellow in the Terry College of Business at the University of Georgia. In the following essay, Pagnattaro explores Neruda's early love poetry and the loss he expresses in "Tonight I Can Write."

Neruda is well known for his love poetry, yet a lesser known fact is that Neruda, as a young boy, was so painfully shy that he feigned indifference to girls. Fearing that he might somehow embarrass himself, Neruda lived his early years as what he called a kind of "deaf-mute." In his *Memoirs,* Neruda elaborates saying that

instead of going after girls, since I knew I would stutter or turn red in front of them, I preferred to pass them up and go on my way, showing a total lack of interest I was very far from feeling. They were all a deep mystery to me. I would have liked to burn at the stake in that secret fire, to drown in the depth of that inscrutable well, but I lacked the courage to throw myself into the fire or the water. And since I could find no one to give me a push, I walked along the fascinating edge, without even a side glance, much less a smile.

Neruda sought refuge in poetry, publishing his first book, *Crepusculario,* in 1923. Because of its traditional meter, fellow Chilean poet Marjorie Agosin observes that this book "follows the patterns set by Chilean romantic poetry of the last century, mixed with traces of modernism—that Spanish-American literary current that swept the continent from 1888 to 1916 and that was the first original literary movement originating in Spanish America." In this early collection, Neruda frequently used Alexandrine meter (lines consisting of six iambic feet), as he began to explore the fleeting quality of love and the loneliness that the absence of love can produce. Having invested a great deal emotionally and financially in the book, Neruda was elated when *Crepusculario* was first published.

The joy of publication, however, was soon undercut by Neruda's deep poetic anxiety about the direction of his verse. He apparently felt constrained by traditional forms, yet was apprehensive about breaking free of the kind of verse which was readily accepted. Neruda took short trips to the southern part of Chile attempting to renew his creative powers. In his *Memoirs* he describes "a strange experience":

> I had returned home to Temuco. It was past midnight. Before going to bed, I opened the windows in my room. The sky dazzled me. The entire sky was alive, swarming with a lively multitude of stars. The night looked freshly washed and the Antarctic stars were spreading out in formation over my head. I became star-drunk, celestially, cosmically drunk. I rushed to my table and wrote, with heart beating high, as if I were taking dictation … it was smooth going, as if I were swimming in my very own waters.

Neruda tells of how he then "locked the door on a rhetoric" that he "could never go on with, and deliberately toned down" his style and expression.

The result was *Veinte poemas de amor y una cancion desperada* (*Twenty Love Poems and a Song of Despair*), published in 1924. This is one of his best-known and most translated works. In this collection, Neruda begins to develop his own voice, leaving behind the regular rhyme and measured verses. The result is astonishing. As Agosin notes, "Neruda's simplicity, sparse imagery, and above all, unabashed expression of amorous state-

ments were innovations that immediately commanded the attention of the reading public." By Neruda's own description, this is "a painful book of pastoral poems filled with [his] most tormented adolescent passions, mingled with the devastating nature of the southern part of [his] country." Neruda elaborated in his *Memoirs,* saying that the collection captured his love affair with the city of Santiago, the "student-crowded streets," the University of Chile and the "honeysuckle fragrance of requited love."

Indeed, because of the amorous and erotic nature of the poems, Neruda was often asked what woman inspired his *Twenty Love Poems.* In his *Memoirs* he acknowledged that this is a difficult question to answer, then gave the following explanation:

> The two women who weave in and out of these melancholy and passionate poems correspond, let's say, to Marisol and Marisombra: Sea and Sun, Sea and Shadow. Marisol is love in the enchanted countryside, with stars in bold relief at night, and dark eyes like the wet sky of Temuco. She appears with all her joyfulness and her lively beauty on almost every page, surrounded by the waters of the port and by a half-moon over the mountains. Marisombra is the student in the city. Gray beret, very gentle eyes, the ever-present honeysuckle fragrance of my foot-loose and fancy-free school days, the physical peace of the passionate meetings in the city's hideaways.

Despite this explanation, many of Neruda's readers are not satisfied. There is ongoing voyeuristic speculation about the specific identity of the women who might be the subject of these poems. Exposing the actual women, however, is not necessary to understand the universal sense of passion and loss which permeates the verse.

"Tonight I Can Write" is the twentieth love poem in *Twenty Love Poems and a Song of Despair.* The preceding poems are often lavish and sensual often comparing the female body to a lush landscape and the vastness of the natural world. "Tonight I Can Write," however, marks what has often been described as a "shipwreck" in the couple's relationship. The entire poem is a deeply felt elegy for lost love. The first line of the poem begins by repeating the title and adding the characterization "the saddest lines." This suggests a meditative creative place in which the poet can channel his painful resignation into verse. The next three-line stanza sets forth examples of such lines: " 'The night is shattered / and the blue stars shiver in the distance.' / The night wind revolves in the sky and sings." The romance is destroyed utterly and the speaker seems to be both isolated from and taunted by the natural world.

The remainder of the poem consists of fourteen two-line stanzas. In these lines, readers learn that their love was both requited and unrequited: "I loved her, and she sometimes loved me too" and "She loved me, sometimes I loved her too." Despite this ambivalence, the affair was passionate. He says "I kissed her again and again under the endless sky." He feels the immensity of loss, and admitting his "love could not keep her." Unable to accept the loss, he says, "My sight searches for her as though to go to her. / My heart looks for her, and she is not with me." He is trying to come to terms with the end of their relationship. Attempting to convince himself that he is over his lover, he twice repeats the line "I no longer love her, that's certain." Each time, however, his assertion is undercut by his acknowledgment of the extent of his romantic entanglement. He first says "but how I loved her," then later backpedals pondering "but maybe I love her."

The speaker is tormented by the thought of his lover in the arms of another:

> Another's. She will be another's. As she was
> before my kisses.
> Her voice. Her bright body. Her infinite eyes.

The difficult process of moving on is underscored: "Love is so short, forgetting so long." This is a long, lonely night which reminds him of other nights when he held her in his arms, one in which his "soul is not satisfied that it has lost her."

In the final stanza, Neruda enjambs the two lines: "Though this be the last pain that she makes me suffer / and these the last verses that I write for her." The result is to connect unequivocally the pain the speaker feels with the creative impetus for the poem, suggesting that the production of the poem will somehow eradicate the pain. Yet, readers who have experienced the pain of lost love know better; there is a lingering sense of torment in these last lines.

Moreover, because "Tonight I Can Write" is followed by "The Song of Despair," there is a clear indication that the pain continues. Here the speaker is left with the surging memory of his lover in a deep lament expressed in terms of coastal, sea imagery. Great anguish is expressed for the woman he has lost. He implores "Oh flesh, my own flesh, woman whom I have loved and lost, / I summon you in the moist hour, I raise my song to you." He continues, "Deserted like the wharves at dawn. / Only the tremulous shadow twists in my hands."

In the somewhat ambiguous concluding line, "It is the hour of departure. Oh abandoned one!" the poet seems to simultaneously grieve for himself and the woman. Their once passionate relationship is over.

Throughout his career, Neruda sought to write poetry which would be accessible. He believed that "A poet can write for a university or a labor union, for skilled workers and professionals." As he also stressed in his *Memoirs,* he saw poetry as a "deep inner calling in man … Today's social poet is still a member of the earliest order of priests. In the old days he made his pact with the darkness, and now he must interpret the light." Neruda does, indeed, shed light on the darkest moments of the soul.

Source: Marisa Anne Pagnattaro, in an essay for *Poetry for Students,* Gale Group, 2001.

Sources

Agosin, Marjorie, "Chapter 2: Love Poetry," in *Twaynes World Authors Series Online,* G. K. Hall Co., 1999.

———, *Pablo Neruda,* translated by Lorraine Roses, Twayne Publishers, 1986.

Clemens, Robert, Review in *Saturday Review,* July 9, 1966.

de Costa, René, "Pablo Neruda: Overview," in *Reference Guide to World Literature,* 2d ed., edited by Lesley Henderson, St. James Press, 1995.

Duran, Manuel, and Margery Safir, *Earth Tones: The Poetry of Pablo Neruda,* Indiana University Press, 1981.

Neruda, Pablo, *Memoirs,* translated by Hardie St. Martin, Farrar, Straus and Giroux, 1976.

"Pablo Neruda," in *Twentieth Century Authors,* First Supplement, edited by Stanley J. Kunitz, H. W. Wilson Company, 1967, p. 709.

Schade, George D., "Pablo Neruda," in *Latin American Writers,* Vol. 3, Scribners, 1989.

For Further Reading

Bencivenga, Jim, Review in *The Christian Science Monitor,* April 22, 1999, p. 21.
    This reviewer finds Nerudas poems in *Twenty Love Poems and a Song of Despair* to be focused on a speaker who is like "Narcissus turning away from his image in the pool only to find it wherever he looks."

Review in *Publishers Weekly,* Vol. 240, No. 45, November 8, 1993, p. 59.
    This reviewer states that in *Twenty Love Poems and a Song of Despair* "Neruda charts the oceanic movements of passion, repeatedly summoning imagery of the sea and weather."

A Valediction: Forbidding Mourning

John Donne

1633

"A Valediction: Forbidding Mourning" shows many features associated with seventeenth-century metaphysical poetry in general, and with Donne's work in particular. Donne's contemporary, the English writer Izaak Walton, tells us the poem dates from 1611, when Donne, about to travel to France and Germany, wrote for his wife this valediction, or farewell speech. Like most poetry of Donne's time, it did not appear in print during the poet's lifetime. The poem was first published in 1633, two years after Donne's death, in a collection of his poems called *Songs and Sonnets*. Even during his life, however, Donne's poetry became well known because it circulated privately in manuscript and handwritten copies among literate Londoners.

The poem tenderly comforts the speaker's lover at their temporary parting, asking that they separate calmly and quietly, without tears or protests. The speaker justifies the desirability of such calmness by developing the ways in which the two share a holy love, both sexual and spiritual in nature. Donne's celebration of earthly love in this way has often been referred to as the "religion of love," a key feature of many other famous Donne poems, such as "The Canonization" and *The Ecstasy*. Donne treats their love as sacred, elevated above that of ordinary earthly lovers. He argues that because of the confidence their love gives them, they are strong enough to endure a temporary separation. In fact, he discovers ways of suggesting, through metaphysical conceit, that the two of them either possess a single soul and so can never really

be divided, or have twin souls permanently connected to each other. A metaphysical conceit is an extended metaphor or simile in which the poet draws an ingenious comparison between two very unlike objects. "A Valediction: Forbidding Mourning" ends with one of Donne's most famous metaphysical conceits, in which he argues for the lovers' closeness by comparing their two souls to the feet of a drawing compass—a simile that would not typically occur to a poet writing about his love!

Author Biography

Donne was born in London in 1572. His family was of Roman Catholic faith (his mother was a relative of the Catholic martyr Sir Thomas More), and he grew up experiencing the religious discrimination of the Anglican majority in England against Catholics. It has been speculated that it was this very discrimination that prevented Donne from completing his studies at Oxford University. After leaving Oxford, he studied law in London and received his degree in 1596. Seeking adventure, Donne sailed with the English expeditions against the Spanish, and his experiences inspired the poems "The Storm," "The Calm," and "The Burnt Ship." The following year, Donne returned to London and became secretary to Sir Thomas Egerton. In December, 1601, he clandestinely married Egerton's sixteen-year-old niece Ann More. When the news became public, More's father unsuccessfully endeavored to annul the marriage, but did succeed in imprisoning Donne for a short period of time. In 1602 Donne was released and, now unemployed, spent the next thirteen years trying to gain financial security for his family. Eventually, he converted from Roman Catholicism to Anglicism, and was enlisted by Sir Thomas Morton to aid him in writing anti-Catholic pamphlets. In 1610 he published his first work, *Pseudo-Martyr*, which attempted to induce English Catholics to repudiate their allegiance to Rome (home of the Catholic Church) and take an oath of allegiance to the British crown. From 1611 to 1612 Donne accompanied Sir Robert Drury to France on a long diplomatic mission, during which he composed some of his most acclaimed verse letters, funeral poems, holy sonnets and love poems, in particular "A Valediction: Forbidding Mourning." Returning to England in 1612, Donne considered becoming an Anglican minister, but hesitated because of self-doubt. He was finally ordained in early 1615 and quickly be-

John Donne

came one of the most respected clergymen of his time. He was elected dean of St. Paul's in 1621 and devoted the majority of his life to writing sermons and other religious works until his death in 1631.

Poem Text

As virtuous men pass mildly away,
    And whisper to their souls to go,
Whilst some of their sad friends do say,
    The breath goes now, and some say, No:

So let us melt, and make no noise,   5
    No tear-floods, nor sigh-tempests move;
'Twere profanation of our joys
    To tell the laity our love.

Moving of th' earth brings harms and fears,
    Men reckon what it did, and meant;   10
But trepidation of the spheres,
    Though greater far, is innocent.

Dull sublunary lovers' love
    (Whose soul is sense) cannot admit
Absence, because it doth remove   15
    Those things which elemented it.

But we, by a love so much refined
    That ourselves know not what it is,

Inter-assurèd of the mind,
　　Care less eyes, lips and hands to miss.　　　20

Our two souls therefore, which are one,
　　Though I must go, endure not yet
A breach, but an expansion,
　　Like gold to airy thinness beat.

If they be two, they are two so　　　　　　25
　　As stiff twin compasses are two;
Thy soul, the fix'd foot, makes no show
　　To move, but doth, if th' other do.

And though it in the center sit,
　　Yet, when the other far doth roam,　　　30
It leans, and hearkens after it,
　　And grows erect, as that comes home.

Such wilt thou be to me, who must,
　　Like th' other foot, obliquely run;
Thy firmness makes my circle just,　　　35
　　And makes me end where I begun.

Poem Summary

Lines 1–4:

The beginning of the poem causes some readers difficulty because the first two stanzas consist of a metaphysical conceit, but we do not know that until the second stanza. We should not read the word "as," which begins the poem, to mean "while," although that might be our instinct. Instead, "as" here means "in the way that"; it introduces an extended simile comparing the death of virtuous men to the separation of the two lovers. This first stanza describes how virtuous men die. Because they have led good lives, death does not terrify them, and so they die "mildly," even encouraging their souls to depart their bodies. In fact their death is so quiet that their friends gathered around the deathbed disagree on whether they are still alive and breathing.

Lines 5–6:

The speaker now reveals that he is addressing his love, from whom he must separate. The poem itself will prove to be the "Valediction"—the farewell—of the title. He also reveals that he has been using a simile, and that the lovers' separation should resemble the quiet way virtuous men die. This example of metaphysical conceit might seem a bizarre comparison to make—dying men with the separation of lovers—but the key comparison is the quietness of the two events. He might also be suggesting that their separation, though only temporary, will be like a small death to him. Still, he asks

his love that they part quietly and "melt" instead of split: the image of melting together suggests they might still be connected in liquified form, an idea the poem returns to later. He also asks her not to indulge in the overdramatic and clichéd anguish of conventional separating lovers.

Lines 7–8:

These lines suggest why he wants a quiet separation: the joys the two of them share, both spiritual and sexual, are holy to him. To complain loudly with tears or sighs would be to broadcast their love to those he calls the "laity." Through this metaphor, he suggests that ordinary people resemble "laypeople" who do not understand the holiness and mystery of their love. The speaker thus implies that the two of them are like priests in a "religion of love." Therefore, for her to make loud protests about his departure would be to "profane" the joy of their holy union by revealing it to the uninitiated and unworthy. The wish to be let alone, to be able to love privately, is especially characteristic of Donne. Several other of his poems similarly covet privacy, such as "The Canonization" and *"The Sun Rising."* This celebration of the private world of two lovers contrasts strongly with the conventions of Renaissance love poetry, in which the lover wishes to broadcast his love to the world.

Lines 9–12:

This stanza contrasts dramatic upheavals on earth with those in heaven. Earthquakes cause great destruction and create great wonder and confusion among human beings. In contrast, "trepidation of the spheres," a trembling or vibration of the whole universe, is far more significant in its scope, but also "innocent"—we cannot see or feel it because it is a heavenly event. Donne here uses the old-fashioned Ptolemaic model of the cosmos, in which each planet, the sun, the fixed stars, and a *primum mobile,* or "prime mover," occupied a crystalline sphere surrounding the earth, at the center. The contrast between heavenly and earthly vibrations anticipates a contrast to be developed in lines 13–20, between earthly lovers directed by sex and lovers who, like them, depend on their spiritual union.

Line 11:

In ancient and medieval astronomy, trepidation of the spheres referred to the vibration of the outermost sphere of the Ptolemaic universe, causing each sphere within to move accordingly.

Lines 13–16:

The speaker moves from his contrast of earthly with heavenly events to a contrast of earthly love with the experience he and his lover share. In this stanza he develops why earthly lovers cannot endure separation from each other. The "soul" or essence of such ordinary, "sublunary" lovers is "sense": that is, their love is based on the five senses and so consists of sexual attraction. Therefore, when such lovers separate, they remove from each other the very basis of their love, which changes and fades like the moon.

Lines 17–20:

The speaker continues to reassure his love by developing the qualities that make the love they share capable of enduring a separation. In contrast with sublunary lovers, their love is not based solely on sensual gratification. In fact, it is a love so pure that even they themselves cannot define it. But because they feel confident in each's feelings for the other, their physical separation—the absence of eyes, lips, and hands—causes them less anxiety.

Lines 21–24:

The speaker begins drawing conclusions about the relationship between his soul and his love's. The "therefore" sounds like the conclusion of a logical argument, and he has in fact been attempting to persuade his love not to mourn during his absence. Because they are "inter-assured of the mind," he suggests their closeness by saying their two souls actually have combined to form one soul. When he leaves on his journey, that one soul will not tear in two; instead, it is flexible enough that it will actually expand. He uses gold as a simile to clarify this expansion. Although the preciousness of gold suggests the preciousness of their love, the key property of gold here is its malleability. Gold can be made to expand greatly because it can be hammered into an extraordinarily thin, "airy" sheet. Donne therefore uses a simile that works emotionally, since gold is valuable, but also scientifically, since the malleability of gold corresponds to the flexibility and expansiveness of their love. Their love will not snap but expand, keeping them bound together during their separation.

Lines 25–28:

The speaker now admits that he and his love may have two separate souls rather than one. He then develops the connectedness of their two souls in one of Donne's most famous and most ingenious metaphysical conceits, an extended simile in which the speaker compares the lovers' two souls to the feet of a drafting compass. He compares her soul to the compass' "fixed foot" and his to the other

Media Adaptations

- An audiocassette titled *The Love Poems of John Donne* (narrated by Richard Burton) was released in June 1998 by Caedmon Audio Cassette.

- Penguin Audiobooks published the audiocassette *John Donne Poems* in April 1999.

- Vanessa and Corin Redgrave narrate Hodder/Headline Audiobooks' June 1999 release of the audiocassette *John Donne: Poets for Pleasure.*

- An audiocassette titled *John Donne: Selected Poems* was release by Blackstone Audio Books in August 1997.

- In 1987, Spoken Arts released an audiocassette of Donne's works titled *Treasury of John Donne.*

foot. Like the compass, their two souls are joined at the top, reminding us that their love is a spiritual union "interassured of the mind."

Lines 29–32:

The speaker now develops the compass conceit. Although his love's soul is the fixed foot and his soul will roam in his travels, her soul will continually incline faithfully towards him, since their two souls are joined, and will return to its proper, upright position when his foot of the compass returns home to her. At this point in the poem, Donne engages in a number of puns that suggest the completeness of the love of these two people. Although the speaker has been emphasizing the spiritual purity of their love, his assertion that the compass "grows erect" reminds us that their union is important and satisfying to them sexually as well as spiritually. Line 26, with its earlier description of the "stiff twin compasses," may also hint at the man's erection. The speaker may be indulging in further punning by describing how the compass, when closing, "comes home," a common expression for "reaching the target," which might suggest sexual intercourse.

Lines 33–36:

The speaker concludes the conceit—and the poem—by reasserting that his love's fidelity and spiritual firmness will allow him to carry out his journey and return home happily. His running "obliquely" literally describes the angle of the open compass and also suggests the indirect, circuitous route of his journeys. In this final stanza, Donne may have included additional sexual puns to underscore the happy future reunion of the lovers. In the spiritual terms of the compass conceit her firmness enables him to complete his circle, or journey; in sexual terms, his firmness would make her circle just. And in making the speaker "end where I begun," Donne may be suggesting that the speaker will finish his journey by returning to her womb as her lover, just as he originally began his life by leaving his mother's womb. The possibility of Donne's having included these sexual puns shows the richness of his language and the muliplicity of meanings available to readers of his work. It also suggests a vision of human love as healthily integrating both the spiritual and sexual aspects of our nature.

Themes

Death

Death, a theme not uncommon to Donne's writing, is a significant theme in "A Valediction: Forbidding Mourning." In the poem's opening stanza, Donne makes mention of "virtuous men pass[ing] mildly away." He uses this notion of death as a metaphor for his impending departure on a journey that will take him away from his wife for an extended period of time.

Love

Known for his love poetry, it is not unusual that love is an integral theme to "A Valediction: Forbidding Mourning." After likening his departure to death, Donne reminds his wife that an outpouring of sadness and emotion over his leaving would profane their love for one another. He uses the love of "dull sublunary lovers' love," or love that is decidedly ordinary and even immature, to contrast the "refined" love that Donne and his wife share. Their love goes beyond the physical; it is a spiritual love that transcends the material world and the limitations of their own bodies. Donne goes on to say that his love for his wife can only expand over distance, and that it is her love that will hearken his return to her.

Topics for Further Study

- Read William Butler Yeats' "The Second Coming." What would the speaker of Yeats' poem say about the images that Donne uses?

- Compare the ideas expressed in this poem to those expressed in William Wordsworth's "My Heart Leaps Up." What do the two poems tell you about youth? About nature? Does the fact that they were published 175 years apart affect how you understand their meaning, or not?

- Do you agree with the ideas in the fourth stanza? Explain what you think of those who "cannot admit absence."

Religious Faith

Piety is almost always present in the poetry of Donne, and "A Valediction: Forbidding Mourning" is no exception. In likening his departure to the deaths of "virtuous men," he is making reference to the fact that pious men who are secure in their faith do not fear death. Rather, they embrace it, because they know that eternal life awaits them, and they will be welcomed by the arm of their Lord. The "sad friends" that surround these dying men are upset at their loss, but they too are aware that this passing isn't an entirely sad situation, as the men are going to a better place, heaven. Further, the mens' security in their faith is also used as a metaphor for Donne's security in his relationship with his beloved wife.

Science

Science is a theme that is prevalent throughout Donne's valediction, whether it be present in references to mathematical tools, such as a drawing compass, which was invented by Galileo only two years earlier, or to a circle and its infinite, perfect qualities. Science, too, is present as he references the "moving of th' earth," and that such movements, i.e., earthquakes, strike fear into the hearts of men. He also uses science to the spheres, meaning the Ptolemaic spheres in which the celestial bodies moved. Science plays a role, too, as

Donne mentions that his love will expand "like gold to airy thinness beat," referencing both a precious metal and its physical properties.

Style

Donne constructs "A Valediction: Forbidding Mourning" in nine four-line stanzas, called quatrains, using a four-beat, iambic tetrameter line. The rhyme scheme for each stanza is an alternating *abab,* and each stanza is grammatically self-contained. This simple form is uncharacteristic for Donne, who often invented elaborate stanzaic forms and rhyme schemes. Its simplicity, however, permits the reader more readily to follow the speaker's complicated argument.

The first two stanzas argue that the speaker and his love should separate quietly—as quietly as righteous men go to their deaths—because their love is sacred and should not be profaned by public emotional displays. The next three stanzas consider the holy nature of their love, contrasting it with ordinary lovers who base their relationship solely on sexual attraction. The final four stanzas imaginatively consider the ways in which the lovers' souls will remain joined even during their physical separation.

Historical Context

King James I of England

James I ruled England from 1603 to 1625. His mother, Mary, Queen of Scots, was forced to abdicate the throne of Scotland in 1567, and James, born just a year earlier in 1566, was named king in her place. Too young to rule, he didn't formally act as king until 1581. At the time, there was much strife between the Catholics and the Protestants in Scotland, and, in fact, James was kidnapped in 1582 by a group of Protestant nobles and gained his freedom a year later by escaping.

He went on to form an alliance with his cousin Queen Elizabeth I of England, and upon her death, he inherited the English throne, thus uniting the crowns of England and Scotland. During his reign, relations with the Roman Catholics in England were strained at best, leading to the Gunpowder Plot in 1605, which was a plot on behalf of Roman Catholics to blow up Parliament due to the government's harsh penal laws enacted against Roman Catholics. In spite of efforts to quell the tensions, James wound up escalating the feud between Catholics and Protestants by forming an alliance with France and going to war against Spain, a Catholic nation.

Donne soon became involved in the monarch's life after James I read Donne's prose work of 1610, *Pseudo-Martyr,* in which Donne stated that Catholics could pledge their allegiance to the king without breaching their religious loyalty. This won Donne the attention and favor of James I, who believed Donne would be a strong addition to his church. Thus he put considerable pressure on Donne to become an Anglican priest. James I even went so far as to seeing that Donne received no further offers of patronage in order to force the financially unstable poet to acquiesce. In 1615, James I got his wish when Donne took holy orders and went on to become a prosperous emissary of the Church of England. James I conferred the deanship of Saint Paul's on Donne in 1621. Famous for his King James version of the Bible, James I died in 1625 and was succeeded by his son, Charles I.

Metaphysical Poetry

Metaphysical poetry was borne in large part out of the works of Donne. Marked by metaphor and conceit—juxtaposing unrelated thoughts in a manner that spurs a reader to consider the poem's thesis—metaphysical poetry is more concerned with analyzing feeling as opposed to its predecessor, Elizabethan poetry, which was much more literal and focused more on the physicality of its subject rather than emotion and thought. Other Metaphysical poets include Abraham Cowley, Richard Crashaw, and Andrew Marvell. Although Metaphysical poetry fell out of favor by the eighteenth and nineteenth centuries, it enjoyed a revival in appreciation in the early part of the twentieth century, in great part due to poets Rupert Brooke and T. S. Eliot, the latter of whom penned a very influential essay in 1921 titled "The Metaphysical Poets."

Baroque

Baroque was the predominant influence in the seventeenth century, during which Donne wrote. Baroque encompasses styles of architecture and art as well as literature. Baroque art is often marked by strong contrasts of light and dark (known as *chiaroscuro*) as well as an air of realism and religious influences. Although Donne falls within the boundaries of the late Renaissance, which overlap with the dawn of the Baroque era, he is more often viewed as a Baroque poet, because the nature of his poetry differs sharply from that of his immediate predecessors and several contemporaries.

Compare & Contrast

- **1607:** The first permanent English settlement in what is now the state of Virginia in the United States is established in Jamestown.

  Today: The United States, which was formally established after winning its independence from England and organizing its formal government through the Constitution in the late eighteenth century, has grown into one of the most powerful nations in the world.

- **1633:** Galileo Galilei is ordered by the Inquisition to stand trial in Rome for "grave suspicion of heresy," as he has discussed in his writing Copernicus's theories, which the church deemed heretical. He is convicted and sentenced to life in prison, and his book *Dialogue* is ordered to be burned.

  Today: Copernicus's theories have long been accepted and in 1992, a papal commission, brought together at Pope John Paul II's request in 1979, finally acknowledged the Vatican's error in condemning Galileo.

Baroque writers as other artists were strongly influenced by recent scientific discoveries, such as Copernicus's discovery that Earth was not, in fact, the center of the universe. The literature of the times, then, specifically drama and poetry, became less literal and more dramatic, imaginative, and metaphorical as well somewhat rhetorical in nature.

Science and the Age of Discovery

The Renaissance ushered in an age of discovery that was marked by an increase in interest not only in man but also in the world around him. Explorers such as Christopher Columbus and Ponce de Leon explored the Americas and ushered in an era of colonization that was to last for hundreds of years. Scientists also made great discoveries in the latter part of the Renaissance, including Copernicus's monumental discovery that the Sun, not the Earth, was at the universe's center.

Later, Italian physicist and astronomer Galileo Galilei (1564–1642) invented the mathematical compass (which figures centrally in Donne's "Valediction: Forbidding Mourning") and built a telescope of twenty-times magnification that allowed him to view mountains and craters on the moon. His work marked a turn in scientific method: precise measurement would begin to prevail over popular belief. Galileo's work was done at almost the same time as that of Johanes Kepler (1571–1630), a German astronomer and natural philosopher, who formulated his now-famous laws about planetary motion. Kepler also created a system of infinitesimals that was the forerunner to calculus. Interestingly, although it cannot be confirmed wholly by scholars and historians, Donne is said to have visited Kepler in 1619 during a trip to the Austrian town of Linz.

Critical Overview

Some decades after Donne's death, his poetry's metaphysical style and extravagant wit came under attack from important English Neoclassical writers. These included Restoration poet and critic John Dryden, whose 1693 essay "A Discourse Concerning the Original and Progress of Satire" considered Donne's ingenuity "unnatural," and the eighteenth-century critic Samuel Johnson, who in his *Lives of the Poets* first applied the word "metaphysical" to the work of Donne and his followers, but in a derogatory way. Johnson went so far, in fact, as to say of the famous conceit comparing the lovers with a pair of compasses, that "it may be doubted whether absurdity or ingenuity has the better claim." In the early twentieth century, however, modernist writers "rediscovered" Donne's poetry and praised its integration of intellect and emotion, as well as its rhythmic invention. In a 1953 piece reprinted in his *Essays of Four Decades,* American poet and critic Allen Tate has given a detailed explication of several of the poem's most perplexing passages. He concentrates on the opening simile of the dying virtuous man for the lovers' separation, explaining how the figure works in both religious and sexual terms. "The structure of the poem," he argues, "turns on the pun 'to die': orgasmic ecstasy as the literal analogue to spiritual ecstasy; physical union as the analogue to spiritual." To "melt and make no noise," then, means "Let us pass through the body, let us 'die' in both senses, *and* the loss of physical self will prevent the noisy grief of 'sublunary lovers' at parting." In a 1967 essay collected in his *Prefaces to the Experience of Literature,* Lionel Trilling finds in the poem an authoritative voice, reinforced by Donne's avoidance of strict meter. Rhythmically, this "bold freedom leads us to feel that it is saying something 'actual' rather than 'poetic,'" and this feeling of sincerity makes convincing such unlikely devices as the compasses conceit. Helen Gardner also notes the authority of the poem's voice, and further suggests that the desire "to make no noise," uncharacteristic of what a husband would tell a wife, illuminates the heart of the poem, the secret and holy world of love the two lovers share.

Criticism

Caroline M. Levchuck

Levchuck, a writer and editor, has published articles on literature along with nonfiction essays and children's books. In this essay, she focuses on Donne's "A Valediction: Forbidding Mourning" as the portrait of the mature spiritual connection Donne shared with his wife, Ann More.

John Donne's "A Valediction: Forbidding Mourning," a poem written upon the occasion of Donne parting from his wife for an extended period, is a shining example of the mature, spiritual relationship that Donne had with his wife. Certainly, sexual love was often a theme in Donne's poetry and Donne had had a reputation as being something of a rake before falling in love with his wife, Ann More. In reading this selection it seems that it was because of his love relationship with Ann, that Donne experienced a love that knew no bounds; physical separation could not quell it. While certain scholars believe that Donne's poems do not actually document his personal experience, this work, which was written for a genuine occasion and was never published in his lifetime, might be interpreted as a personal testimony to not only Donne's sadness over his departure but to the depth of his feelings for and faith in his wife.

> *His flesh doesn't burn for his wife; his heart and mind do, and so does his soul."*

In the poem's opening lines, Donne likens his faith in his and his wife's connection to that of virtuous mens' confidence in their relationship to God. While others may fear death, the truly pious will journey to the hereafter with quiet resignation and even a bit of optimism. Likening religious devotion and faith to love, especially romantic or sexual love, is a theme that is often seen in other works of the era, particularly in Gianlorenzo Bernini's marble sculpture *Ecstasy of St. Theresa,* in which St. Theresa is overwhelmed with ecstasy because of her devotion to her lord. Religious faith, then, is more often than not unshakable, and this conceit on Donne's part in comparing the sanctity of his marriage to deep-rooted, religious faith exalts his and Ann's bond to something even beyond the romantic or the sexual; it is exemplary of the true, spiritual bond that existed between them.

Donne asserts that shedding tears over their parting would profane the sanctity of their love. Whereas Donne's poetic predecessors often wrote of the physicality of a lover or the urgency with which one desires to see one's lover (i.e., William Shakespeare's famous line from *Romeo and Juliet:* "Parting is such sweet sorrow"), Donne insists that public displays would be vulgar and inappropriate in light of the unique tie he and Ann share. Further, he insists the such actions would "tell the laity our love," thus making public their sorrows to the laypeople would be inconsistent with the private nature of their mature association and would fly in the face of its sacred nature.

As Donne continues on, he speaks further of the calm that should surround his taking leave of his beloved, insisting that it should be as unapparent as the planets revolving in the skies. This movement of the planets, he points out, is certainly more powerful than something ordinary, such as an earthquake, an image that he likens to an obvious outpouring of emotion. In associating his and his wife's love to a heavenly yet silent act, Donne is once more elevating their relationship to a supra-

What Do I Read Next?

- Andre Marvell's *"To His Coy Mistress,"* published first in 1650, is a poem of seduction in which a man attempts to persuade a woman to go to bed with him as they are racing against time and haven't the luxury of falling in love at a leisured pace. The suitor argues persuasively to the object of his lusty affections.

- John Donne's "The Ecstasy," published in 1633, describes two lovers lying next to one another and gazing deep into each other's eyes while their souls move out of their bodies and intertwine to become one, more-perfect, soul. The narrator of the poem also admits, though, that such a union of souls should also be expressed physically, thus pointing out that their bodies are actually somewhat necessary to their love.

- George Herbert's famous religious poem "Easter Wings" (1634) is written in such a manner that its lines, rich with metaphysical imagery, mimic the form about which he writes.

- Richard Crashaw's *"Epitaph upon Husband and Wife, who died and were buried together"* (c. 1646) speaks of the eternal bond that a married couple will share in death. He refers to the bond as everlasting now that it has been sealed by their departure from this world.

---

earthly status. The use of such a metaphor casts the relationship in a light that makes it appear that few could truly grasp the gravity of Donne and Ann's entire relationship, as they would not be fully aware of all its machinations. This air of privacy is not dissimilar to the private nature of deep religious devotion. Faith and some of its more important activities, such as confession and prayer, are highly intimate acts; faith itself is also an internal process, and the truly pious are not always obvious about the depth of their beliefs.

This elevated state to which he ascribes his and Ann's bond is contrasted in the next stanza with the love of "dull sublunary lovers," meaning the love of ordinary lovers in most of society. This common love, "whose soul is sense," cannot withstand absence, as physicality is the very thing upon which such precarious, immature love is cemented. By contrast, Donne posits that he and his wife share a "refined" love that is almost indefinable. It is "inter-assured of the mind," which again points to an affection that is much more spiritual in nature rather than being dependent upon proximity of an individual's beloved. Donne insists that he "care less, eyes, lips, and hands to miss." His flesh doesn't burn for his wife; his heart and mind do, and so does his soul.

Donne has found in his wife his soul-mate. He reminds her that their two souls "are one." This proclamation is again indicative of the divine connection the two share. And, again, flying in the face of the constraints of ordinary love that demands closeness and abhors absence, Donne makes another grand statement, urging his wife to "endure not yet / a breach, but an expansion, / like gold to airy thinness beat." This statement calls to mind the adage, "Absence makes the heart grow fonder." Donne is telling Ann that their love will grow to cover whatever physical distance separates them. The distance will not cause a rift in their love; rather, their devotion will actually increase in area as a result of the division. The reference to gold, a precious metal, also belies his view of their relationship as something precious and rare.

The last three stanzas of the poem contain one of Donne's most famous metaphysical conceits. He likens himself and his wife to the two feet of a mathematical compass. The compass in itself calls to mind sturdiness (because of its composition) as well as accuracy, precision, and certainty. It is also an instrument whose function depends on two parts working in tandem. Confidence and teamwork are clearly the hallmarks of a mature love relationship. Fiery feeling alone will not accomplish anything. A mature relationship requires strength too. Ann, as the "fixed foot," provides strength to Donne who, as the other foot that moves about, must roam far. He points out though, that it is Ann who "leans and hearkens" after him. This supports his claim that their love will expand to fill the space between them. Donne references Ann's "firmness," which belies, again, his confidence in her feelings toward him. It is this firmness, he states, that "makes [his] circle just." Circles are an image not uncommon to Donne's poetry and symbolize not only perfection but infinity. The notion of the infinite, something that is without end, cements the notion of Donne's elevated affection for his wife.

The mature tone of this poem is in sharp contrast to some of Donne's other works, written presumably in his younger days. In "Song," for example, Donne writes of the impossibility of finding a woman who is both beautiful and faithful. He likens the task to catching a falling star or impregnating a plant. This cynicism can be taken as evidence of the fact that Donne had not yet experienced love that transformed his soul and his poetry.

Even though Donne wrote of a deep love that transcends physical proximity, he did believe in the physical side of romance. In fact, many of Donne's poems are actually quite suggestive in nature. His poem "The Ecstasy" discusses the commingling of two lovers' souls, leading to the formation of one perfect soul. Despite this, though, the poem ends on a note in which Donne acknowledges that the cerebral is still ideally manifested in the physical.

The sacred nature of Donne's relationship may also be contrasted with the poetry of his contemporary Andrew Marvell. Marvell's famous poem "To His Coy Mistress" is a thinly veiled seduction from a suitor urging his intended that they haven't the time to indulge in forming a deep-rooted bond; he believes they should act on their physical urges rather than form an alliance of the mind and soul. For Donne and Ann, however, physical possession, while the reward of the relationship, is not necessarily a factor integral to the immediate viability of the relationship.

There is a certain degree of irony surrounding "A Valediction: Forbidding Mourning" in that Donne's beloved wife Ann died after giving birth to the couple's twelfth child while Donne was on one of his many business excursions. Legend has it that Donne was dining with friends while an apparition of his wife appeared to him. Shortly thereafter he was notified that she had fallen desperately ill. Certainly, this is evidence of their devotion and the exceptional connection that they shared, even to critics who may claim that his poetry is not a direct reflection of his personal emotional experiences.

Source: Caroline M. Levchuck, in an essay for *Poetry for Students,* Gale Group, 2001.

Jennifer Bussey

Bussey holds a Master's degree in interdisciplinary studies and a Bachelor's degree in English literature. She is an independent writer specializing in literature. In the following essay, she provides an overview of imagery in Donne's poem, demonstrating how each image contributes to the poem's overall meaning. Donne's use of metaphysical conceit is explained and identified.

> *The poem, though intricate, is accessible precisely because of the array of interconnected images presented throughout."*

John Donne wrote "A Valediction: Forbidding Mourning" in 1611 as he was preparing for one of his frequent journeys away from his wife, Ann. Donne's deep love for his wife is evident in the poem, which explains that the couple should not be sorrowful when they are apart from each other because their love binds them together, regardless of distance.

Donne and his young wife had been married for ten years at the time the poem was written. She was the niece of Donne's employer; when he eloped with her in 1601, he ruined his career prospects. As a result, Donne had considerable difficulty finding work, and the couple struggled to provide for their ever-growing family. (Ann died in 1617 while giving birth to their twelfth child.) The background to this poem is significant because it gives the reader an understanding of the kind of love Donne and his wife shared; it was a love that kept the marriage strong and vibrant in the face of hardship.

As a Metaphysical poet, Donne expressed love in a particular way. Many of the characteristics typical of Metaphysical poetry are found in "A Valediction: Forbidding Mourning." These include intellectual descriptions of emotions; unusual and often startling comparisons; a preoccupation with love, death, and religion; simple diction; images taken from everyday life; and the formulation of an argument.

Besides being a beautiful love poem, "A Valediction: Forbidding Mourning" endures because it contains classic illustrations of the *metaphysical conceit.* This term refers to a technique used by metaphysical poets in which commonplace objects or ideas are used to create analogies, offering insight into something important or profound. Modern students are sometimes misled by the word *conceit,* because in contemporary language it means "arrogance"; but at the time the term was coined, it meant "concept." The metaphysical conceit is especially effective when the reader is almost immediately able to identify with the poet's meaning, despite the unexpected nature of the comparison. Today, discussion of the metaphysical conceit inevitably refers to "A Valediction: Forbidding Mourning" because of Donne's skilled use of unexpected imagery. In fact, of all the imagery in the poem, only one example does not represent the metaphysical conceit.

The poem addresses the moment when the lovers are preparing to bid each other farewell. Although the separation will be only temporary, it is a potentially emotional scene, and the speaker is explaining why there is no need for tears or sorrow. The speaker's task is a difficult one, and his argument is carried by the poem's unusual imagery. With the very first word of the poem, "as," Donne conveys the importance of simile and analogy in the poem. To some readers, the opening word, "as," is confusing because it can be read as meaning "while," when it actually means "like." The stanza compares the dying of virtuous men to the speaker's upcoming separation from his beloved. This is an odd analogy (and is, therefore, an example of the metaphysical conceit), but Donne's purpose is to explain that the virtuous accept both death and separation calmly and without fear ("As virtuous men pass mildly' away, / And whisper to their souls to go.") To emphasize the quietude of virtuous men's deaths, Donne adds that death comes so imperceptibly that friends cannot tell if the last breath has actually gone ("Whilst some of their sad friends do say / The breath goes now, and some say, No.") This stanza's serene tone contrasts with much of Donne's poetry, which often opens with great drama and passion. A few examples include: "For God's sake hold your tongue, and let me love," "Kind pity chokes my spleen; brave scorn forbids," and "Batter my heart, three-personed God." Readers familiar with Donne's work as a whole will make special note that the calm entrance into this poem in itself has meaning, as Donne is setting the tone for his argument as well as for the lovers' parting.

In the second stanza, Donne introduces imagery of molten gold ("So let us melt, and make no noise"), to which he will later return. He then draws on extreme weather conditions as imagery for emotional outpouring. The analogy is not flattering because he is discouraging this behavior; the poet suggests that dramatic "tear-floods" and "sigh-tempests" are profane and unfitting for these lovers. He adds that onlookers ("the laity") are unworthy

of witnessing the lovers' expressions of their feelings. Donne's mention of onlookers recalls the first stanza, where the poet comments that the dying men's friends are assessing him. In both images, the persons experiencing the events possess understanding that outsiders do not. The grieving friends do not know that the dying man is unafraid and tranquil about death, nor do they know if he has yet died. The public will not know what the lovers are feeling nor the depths of their love, as they face separation.

In the third stanza, Donne introduces one of the classic images of the metaphysical conceit—the Ptolemaic universe. He begins by extending the weather imagery from the previous stanza: "Moving of th' earth brings harms and fears, / Men reckon what it did and meant." Referring to dramatic thunderstorms and natural disasters, Donne observes that these forces are destructive and terrifying, and they leave people confused about their meaning. The next lines indirectly compare the couple's love to a force greater than natural disasters, and yet harmless, by introducing Ptolemy's astronomical theories. (The comparison is indirect because the poet does not allude to the lovers at all in this stanza.) Donne writes, "But trepidation of the spheres, / Though greater far, is innocent." Ptolemy theorized that the earth was the center of the universe, and that the other celestial bodies orbited it. What his complex mathematical "proof" of his theory could not explain, Ptolemy accounted for by describing heavenly trembling that supposedly brought about unexplained phenomena of celestial events, such as equinoxes. Donne's phrase "trepidation of the spheres" is a reference to Ptolemy's "trembling." Donne notes that these mighty tremblings in the universe do not harm anyone, despite their magnitude and force. The indirect parallel is that the inner trembling that the lovers feel at the prospect of being apart is powerful yet causes no real harm. Another element of the Ptolemaic universe is astrology, a belief that the stars foretell the future of individuals and nations. By extension, the speaker may be suggesting that his love is destined, as it is "written in the stars."

Donne uses gold imagery in the sixth stanza, which carries meaning on many levels. This image is the only one in the poem that is not an example of the metaphysical conceit because it is not unexpected. Poets (especially in the Renaissance) had long used gold imagery in their verse. Donne writes, "Our two souls therefore, which are one, / Though I must go, endure not yet / A breach, but an expansion, / Like gold to airy thinness beat."

Being bright, luminous, durable, and valuable, gold is obviously analogous to the type of love the poet describes in this poem. Donne, however, takes the imagery a step further. Describing the malleability of gold, the poet compares gold's ability to change shape and to extend with the lovers' ability to bend to circumstance yet keep each other spiritually close by virtue of their deep bond. Gold's qualities are expressed in two ways: it can be melted and merged, as suggested in line twenty-one, and it can be hammered and elongated. This analogy is well crafted because it works from every angle: both gold and love can be melted and merged; both can be "hammered" and yet remain strong and essentially unchanged.

In the seventh, eighth, and ninth stanzas, Donne develops the compass imagery that has become almost synonymous with the term "metaphysical conceit" in contemporary literary discourse. The image is first presented in the seventh stanza: "If they be two, they are two so / As stiff twin compasses are two; / Thy soul, the fixed foot, makes no show / To move, but doth, if th' other do." Here Donne is referring to a compass used in geometry (not a directional compass) and explains that his beloved is the stationary leg in the center, while he is the outer leg that must travel. This idea is carried into the eighth stanza, where the poet adds, "And though it in the center sit, / Yet when the other far doth roam, / It leans and hearkens after it, / And grows erect, as that comes home." With his depiction of the lovers as two legs of a compass, the poet seems to contradict the earlier claim that their souls have become one ("Our two souls therefore, which are one.") The separate analogies maintain their integrity, however, because the compass is a unit, and its two legs only represent physical separation; they are not structurally separate. The compass' behavior (leaning, straightening) conveys that the two legs are connected.

If the reader pictures a compass being used to draw a circle, Donne's imagery makes perfect sense. The center leg remains still, but leans toward the moving leg, and when the outside leg is brought back in to the center, they both stand up straight again. The poet's lover is the one left behind, like the compass leg in the center, while the speaker is traveling, like the outer leg. The beloved left behind will certainly miss the other, as Donne acknowledges when he notes, "Yet when the other far doth roam, / It leans and hearkens after it." When the travels come to an end, and the lovers are reunited, they both stand tall and remain steadfastly side by side, as the two legs of a closed compass.

In the final stanza, Donne concludes, "Such wilt thou be to me, who must / Like th' other foot, obliquely run; / Thy firmness makes my circle just, / And makes me end where I begun." Making full use of the compass metaphor, the speaker explains that while he is away, the steadfastness of his distant lover keeps him true. The image of the circle in line thirty-five carries multiple meanings and is particularly appropriate with the compass metaphor. Circles traditionally symbolize infinity, perfection, balance, symmetry, and cycles. This is the reason that rings are important in wedding ceremonies. In addition, the circle with a dot in the center (like the one left by the center leg after a circle has been drawn with a compass) was the alchemist's symbol for gold. Again, Donne establishes unity and integration by tying the various images together throughout the poem. The allusion to the circle signifies that the lovers will be together forever in perfect love. Since compasses create circles, the image of the compass legs separating, drawing a circle (where the beginning meets the end), and then coming back together thoroughly illustrates the lover's journey that "makes me end where I begun."

Through the progression of the poem, the poet has built a complex, yet flowing and beautiful, argument for why the lovers should not be saddened or worried about their upcoming separation. Donne's method is unique and a wonderful tool for understanding the Metaphysical poets. The poem, though intricate, is accessible precisely because of the array of interconnected images presented throughout. Although the images may not at first seem to be related, Donne's poetic genius becomes apparent as the thoughtful reader pieces the images together.

Source: Jennifer Bussey, in an essay for *Poetry for Students,* Gale Group, 2001.

John Pipkin

Pipkin is a scholar in the fields of British and American literature. In this essay, he discusses the use of simile and metaphysical wit in "A Valediction: Forbidding Mourning."

A valediction is a speech or a poem of farewell, one that often carries with it some sense of foreboding or uncertainty about the events to come. Although the title "A Valediction Forbidding Mourning" might seem to suggest a dark, brooding theme, John Donne's poem is actually a love poem, and as such it is a fine example of sixteenth-century Metaphysical wit. The Metaphysical school of poets (whose members included Donne, George Her-

> *... his soul and his wife's soul are like the two legs of a compass, permanently fixed by a pivot at one end.... Just as a compass has a fixed point, one leg that rotates on the same spot, so does Donne's soul have a fixed point: his wife."*

bert, and Andrew Marvell, among others) were formally given this name by the critic and essayist Samuel Johnson (perhaps best known for his *Dictionary of the English Language* of 1775), who criticized them for introducing metaphysics or a kind of abstract logic into their poetry.

The term *wit* originally meant intelligence, but in the hands of the Metaphysical poets, *wit* came to signify a clever or ingenious use of reason to compare and contrast highly dissimilar things in order to develop a persuasive argument. In "A Valediction: Forbidding Mourning," for example, Donne is speaking to his wife, Anne, before leaving on a long journey, and he attempts to comfort her by drawing an unlikely comparison between their love for each other and the way that virtuous men behave at the moment of death.

The first stanza describes a deathbed scene, but it is important to notice that the opening word "as" establishes a conditional statement that is dependent upon the second stanza to complete its meaning. The first two stanzas should be read as a single sentence. "As" is a clue that this poem is really not about the way that "virtuos men passe mildly away," but is concerned with using this image as simile for something else. A simile is a type of metaphor in which a writer makes the reader look at something differently by comparing it to something else. In this opening stanza, Donne describes how virtuous men, who have led good and honest lives on earth, do not put up a struggle on their deathbeds. In fact, a virtuous man allows his soul to depart so quietly that the friends gathered around

the bed disagree over whether the man has actually died. A man of virtue has no reason to fear death or the departure of his soul, because he can be certain of his soul's reward in the afterlife. Donne uses this scene of spiritual confidence and composure as an example of how he wants his wife to behave when he leaves for his journey.

Donne urges his wife to remain silent about their love, especially at this particular moment of his departure. "Melt" is a popular image for physical love, and the speaker elevates this love to a spiritual level by suggesting that speaking about this love and their "joyes" would profane it. The final line further elevates their love to a religious experience and refers to those who do not know of their love as the "layetie," in other words, the people who are unordained in the sacrament of their love. It is important to remember that marriage also functions as a type of sacrament, and therefore only a husband and wife can truly know and understand the love that they themselves feel for each other. Donne argues that any attempt to display this love to the "layetie" through "tears" or "sighs" would be an insult to the sacrament itself.

Once he has elevated his physical love to a spiritual level, Donne uses the third and forth stanza to compare this love to those mundane love affairs that are only physical and therefore at the mercy of earthly change. His logical argument is that only "dull" lovers mourn the physical absence of each other, because their love is sublunary (literally beneath the moon or earth-bound). "Elemented" refers to physical objects that are composed of any or all of the four elements (earth, air, water, fire). As a result, lovers who cannot "admit" (or tolerate) the physical absence or departure, cannot do so precisely because physical proximity is all that their love was based on in the first place. Such an earthly love is made only of physical elements and when any of these elements are absent, that love is in danger. But Donne argues that his love is not dependent on such elements. His own love is of a far superior kind, a spiritual love, and there is no reason for his wife to be upset over his physical departure.

In the sixth stanza, Donne clarifies this argument, stating that "our two soules … are one" and he expands his argument in this stanza by introducing the first of two new similes to describe how his leaving is actually a good thing. Using the kind of logic for which the metaphysical poets are famous, Donne argues that if their souls are one, then his leaving does not signify a "breach" or division, but rather an expansion or a stretching. The simile that he uses here is that of a piece of gold that has been hammered into a thin sheet in order to be used to decorate a much larger surface area than it ever could have as a solid lump.

In addition to comparing their love to a thin sheet of gold that becomes more beautiful and brilliant as its ends are spread farther apart, Donne also develops a more complicated comparison in the final three stanzas, and this simile is one of his most well-known. He offers his wife an alternative to thinking about their souls as one and the same. Basically, in stanza seven he is telling her that if she wants to think about their souls as two separate entities, then here is how she should consider them. "If they be two," he says, then his soul and his wife's soul are like the two legs of a compass, permanently fixed by a pivot at one end. (The kind of compass to which Donne is referring here is the two-legged device used for drawing circles and, appropriately for this poem, for measuring distances on a map.) Though the bottom of the legs can move far apart, they cannot be separated at the top.

Just as a compass has a fixed point, one leg that rotates on the same spot, so does Donne's soul have a fixed point: his wife. When Donne travels (when his soul "far doth rome") his wife remains fixed in place, but like the center leg of a compass, she "leans" in the direction of his travels and "hearkens" after him. In other words, her thoughts, affections, and, perhaps, letters are directed toward him wherever he might be, and it is this that defines his course and draws him back to her. And just like the two legs of a compass, when he returns home they stand together, straight and upright.

In the final stanza, the concluding image that Donne offers to his wife is one of reassurance. He underscores and clarifies the simile of the compass by saying outright: "such wilt thou be to me." No matter how far he roams, the path of his travels will always lead him back to where he started, just as a compass, anchored by the center foot, completes the circle it is drawing by returning to the point where it began.

It is important to recognize that Donne employs his metaphysical wit to develop not just one but a series of arguments to console his wife on the eve of his departure. He tries to convince her first that spiritual love cannot be affected by physical distance. Then he tries to show her that since their souls are one, distance will only increase their love and make it more beautiful, like gold that is hammered and spread out into a thin sheet. And finally, if these first two arguments are unsatisfying, Donne

argues that he and his wife, though separate, function like the legs of a compass. In each case, the similes Donne uses force the reader to see the logic behind comparisons that may at first seem unlikely or far-fetched.

Source: John Pipkin, in an essay for *Poetry for Students,* Gale Group, 2001.

Sources

Bernstein, Jeremy, "Dr. Donne & Sir Edmund Gosse," in *New Criterion,* March, 1998, p. 16.

Dryden, John, "A Discourse Concerning the Original and Progress of Satire," in *Essays of John Dryden,* Vol. II, edited by W. P. Ker, Oxford at the Clarendon Press, 1900, pp. 15–114.

Eliot, T. S., "The Metaphysical Poets," in *Times Literary Supplement,* Vol. 20, October, 1921, pp. 669–670. Reprinted in *Selected Essays,* Harcourt Brace, 1950.

Gardner, Helen, Introduction to *The Elegies and the Songs and Sonnets by John Donne,* Oxford at the Clarendon Press, 1965, pp. xvii–xlxii.

Johnson, Samuel, "Cowley," in *Lives of the English Poets,* Vol I, 1906, reprint by Oxford University Press, 1955–56, pp. 1–53.

McCoy, Kathleen and Judith A. V. Harlan, "John Donne," in *English Literature to 1985,* HarperCollins Publishers, 1992.

Tate, Allen, "The Point of Dying: Donne's 'Virtuous Men,'" in *Essays of Four Decades,* Swallow Press Inc., 1968, pp. 247–52.

Trilling, Lionel, "John Donne: A Valediction, Forbidding Mourning," in *Prefaces to the Experience of Literature,* Harcourt Brace Jovanovich, 1979, pp. 188–93.

Warnke, Frank J., "John Donne," *Twayne's English Authors Series Online,* G. K. Hall & Co., 1999. Previously published in print by Twayne Publishers.

For Further Reading

Bald, R. C., *John Donne: A Life,* edited by Wesley Milgate, Oxford University Press, 1970.
    Considered the definitive biography of Donne's life and time.

Carey, John, *John Donne: Life, Mind, and Art,* Oxford University Press, 1981.
    A study of Donne's works that takes into consideration the poet's life and his religious beliefs, with an emphasis on his Catholic roots.

Ferry, Anne, *All in War with Time: Love Poetry of Shakespeare, Donne, Jonson, Marvell,* Harvard University Press, 1975.
    A study of the love poetry of Donne and several of his contemporaries.

The War Against the Trees

Stanley Kunitz

1958

"The War Against the Trees" is included in Stanley Kunitz's third volume of poetry *Selected Poems, 1928–1958*. Though *Selected Poems* was rejected by eight publishers—three of whom did not read the manuscript—the collection won the 1959 Pulitzer Prize. In the Author's Note to *Selected Poems,* Kunitz writes that the poems are not arranged chronologically but "in groups that bear some relevance to the themes, the arguments, that have preoccupied me since I began to write." The grouping that contains "The War Against the Trees," entitled "The Terrible Threshold," is likely so-named because the poems in it describe various ways in which humanity and the earth are on the brink of catastrophic change. It is the last poem in the section. Perhaps the reason "The War Against the Trees" appears in many anthologies is partially due to its obvious sympathies with environmental causes.

"The War Against the Trees" describes bulldozers toppling and digging out plants and large trees on a parcel of lawn recently purchased by an oil company. The poet mourns the loss of the past, of nature, and the absence of human concern for the "war's" victims, the plants and animals. Before Rachel Carson's *Silent Spring* helped inspire the environmental movement, "The War Against the Trees" recognized the local attack on a plot of land as part of a larger, undeclared war on nature. In an interview with Kunitz, critic Selden Rodman asserts that "The War Against the Trees" was an early ecological statement. Kunitz agreed, quipping that

"one of the measures of art is the amount of wilderness it contains."

Author Biography

Born in Worcester, Massachusetts, in 1905, Stanley Jasspon Kunitz was the youngest of three children of Russian-Jewish parents. Six weeks before Kunitz's birth, his father, a thirty-nine-year-old dress manufacturer, killed himself in a park by ingesting carbolic acid. Kunitz's mother kept the family going by supporting herself as a supervising seamstress and married again when Kunitz was eight. But her new husband died just one year later. In high school, Kunitz was captain of the debating team, founder of a literary magazine (in which he printed his first poem), and class valedictorian. During these years, Kunitz worked summers at the *Worcester Telegram* as a cub reporter. After high school, he attended Harvard, where he won the Lloyd McKim Garrison Medal for Poetry in 1926. That same year he graduated *summa cum laude*. He completed a master's degree at Harvard in 1927, and expected to teach there, but was not hired because he was Jewish.

After Harvard, Kunitz published poems in *Poetry, Commonweal, The New Republic, The Nation,* and *Dial.* He also returned to the *Worcester Telegram,* for which he covered the Sacco-Vanzetti case. Kunitz became convinced the defendants—poor Italian immigrants accused of a payroll robbery and murder—would never receive justice from a judge who labeled them "anarchistic bastards." Kunitz fought to save Sacco and Vanzetti from what he thought to be a miscarriage of justice, but in August, 1927, both men were electrocuted. Kunitz moved to New York City where he unsuccessfully attempted to find a publisher for Vanzetti's death-row letters. Shortly after, he began work at the H. W. Wilson Company, a publishing house, whom he was with from 1928 until the 1970s. At Wilson, Kunitz edited the house journal, the *Wilson Bulletin for Librarians,* and wrote a monthly column. More importantly, Kunitz edited nine respected biographical dictionaries.

In 1943, at age thirty-seven, Kunitz was drafted. Because of his objection to bearing arms, the military designated him a nonaffiliated pacifist. He hoped to be assigned to the Medical Corps, but spent much of the war ill and humiliated from digging latrines and KP ("kitchen patrol") duty. At the

Stanley Kunitz

same time, his second book of poems, *Passport to the War* (1944) was published. During his service, Kunitz received a letter from Bennington College asking him to teach at the end of the war. His friend, Bennington poet and teacher, Theodore Roethke, had suffered a nervous breakdown and insisted on Kunitz replacing him. At war's end, Kunitz received a Guggenheim Fellowship and in the fall of 1946 began teaching at Bennington, the first of many part-time positions at distinguished colleges and universities. In 1958 "The War Against the Trees" appeared in *Selected Poems, 1928–1958.* This same year, Kunitz divorced his second wife and married his third, won the Harriet Monroe Award and a Ford Foundation grant, and was appointed poet-in-residence at Brandeis University. In 1959, Kunitz won the Pulitzer Prize for *Selected Poems* and the National Institute of Arts and Letters award.

Poem Text

The man who sold his lawn to standard oil
Joked with his neighbors come to watch the show
While the bulldozers, drunk with gasoline,
Tested the virtue of the soil
Under the branchy sky   5
By overthowing first the privet-row.

Forsythia-forays and hydrangea-raids
Were but preliminaries to a war
Against the great-grandfathers of the town,
So freshly lopped and maimed.   10
They struck and struck again,
And with each elm a century went down.

All day the hireling engines charged the trees,
Subverting them by hacking underground
In grub-dominions, where dark summer's mole   15
Rampages through his halls,
Till a northern seizure shook
Those crowns, forcing the giants to their knees.

I saw the ghosts of children at their games
Racing beyond their childhood in the shade,   20
And while the green world turned its death-foxed
        page

And a red wagon wheeled,
I watched them disappear
Into the suburbs of their grievous age.

Ripped from the craters much too big for hearts 25
The club-roots bared their amputated coils,
Raw gorgons matted blind, whose pocks and scars
Cried Moon! On a corner lot
One witness-moment, caught
In the rear-view mirrors of the passing cars.   30

Media Adaptations

- The audiocassette tape, *Stanley Kunitz* (1991), introduced by the poet Galway Kinnell, is available from The Academy of American Poets Tapes Program, 584 Broadway, Suite 1208, New York, NY 10012–3250. The Academy of American Poets, http://www.he.net/susannah/academy.htm

- Stanley Kunitz reads his poems "King of the River" (1970) and "The Quarrel" (1979) on the *The Atlantic Review*'s website, Atlantic Unbound, http://www.theatlantic.com/unbound/poetry/antholog/aaindx.htm

- An audiocassette tape of Kunitz, *The Only Dance,* (1981) is available from Watershed Tapes, (Watershed Online), http://www.watershed.winnipeg.mb.ca/

Poem Summary

Stanza 1:

The poem opens with a man and his neighbors watching bulldozers tear up the man's lawn. The man is joking with the neighbors, and the event is referred to as a "show." The man's upbeat behavior suggests that he has sold the land for a good price. "Branchy sky" indicates that this parcel of "lawn" has quite a few trees on it, as the branches seem as much a part of the sky as of the tree. Contributing to the carnival-like atmosphere is the personification of the bulldozers as sloppy males on a date, who, "drunk with gasoline," force themselves on the woman, as they test the "virtue of the soil." This last phrase is also ironic since the bulldozers are not concerned with the soil's quality, as farmers are, but with what lies beneath the soil.

Stanza 2:

Stanza two begins full mobilization of the language of war ("forays" and "raids"). The bulldozers-as-tanks, having taken out what would be the first line of defense, the privet-row, now take out the second line—forsythias and hydrangeas. But the real "enemy" lies ahead. Bulldozers head for the hard-to-root-out trees, analogous to a nest of machine guns protected by lines of surrounding troops. The trees themselves are monuments of a civilization, and every time an elm fell "a century went down." In a familiar metaphor the trees are also likened to human bodies, as they are described as having been "lopped and maimed." This is akin to the trees' beheading, or the hacking of limbs from their torsos (trunk), an occurrence in human-to-human war. The offensiveness of the acts is heightened because the trees are humanized, referred to as the "great-grandfathers of the town."

Stanza 3:

The war continues as bulldozers and Caterpillars ("hireling engines") dig up tree after tree. The limbs and tops have already been hacked away and the roots are the last to go. The speaker remarks that undermining the trees also destroys the habitat of soil grubs and moles, a destruction of beings and ecology. Then, as in the previous stanza, trees are again linked to humans: they are kings when standing (they have "crowns"), and subservient subjects when felled (on their "knees," as if begging). The final personification is the death throes or tremblings the trees suffer before dying, their "seizures." That is, their leafy tops ("northern") can be seen to shake before the trees topple and fall.

Stanza 4:

From the effect of bulldozers on trees and land, Kunitz now moves to the larger picture affected by both the presence and absence of trees. He imagines children of the past ("ghosts") playing in the trees' shade, growing up alongside the trees. The poet also imagines nature ("the green world") with a book, perhaps its own biography or photo album, turning another worn ("foxed") page, perhaps reading about or viewing another slaughter in its own history. At stanza's end, the children disappear into "their grievous age," which could indicate either crippling old age and death or the era in which the children live, the 1950s, when suburban developments flourished. The word "suburbs," short for suburban, indicates a kind of environment where trees are cut down and substituted with housing developments. It can also represent a place where people sometimes grow "grievously" into old age because they become isolated and preoccupied only with raising children and maintaining property. This is the suburbs as the breeding place of sameness and mediocrity, to some, a living death.

Stanza 5:

In the last stanza, the trees are down and uprooted, leaving behind craters "too big for hearts," the phrase pointing to the inability of humans to love, care, or protect trees. From being maimed in root and branch, the killing field is now complete—roots are now "amputated" from the soil, exposed for all to see. The poet compares the huge snarls of roots to gorgons, mythological female creatures with snakes for hair who turned those looking at them into stone.

With this vision of a pock-marked landscape, the poet imagines the cornered lot as a cratered moon, a dead landscape. But others do not necessarily see the scene as the poet does. They see it like the joking neighbor at the beginning, or like drivers glancing for a "witness-moment" in their rearview mirrors, giving the scene no more than a passing or backward glance on their way to other scenes and concerns more important, or more subject to their control. By the final line and word, the poem has come full circle: from producers of oil (Standard Oil) clearing the land at the beginning of the poem, to consumers of oil driving over cleared and paved land at poem's end. For only a moment, drivers might have the opportunity to link their own practice to the unsightly mess on the corner lot.

Themes

Growth and Development

"The War Against the Trees" recounts the bulldozing of a plot of wooded land recently purchased by an oil company and the effect of this destruction on the town and speaker. Throughout the 1950s, an average of three thousand acres of farmland were bulldozed per day for tract housing. Such development was partially enabled by preexisting roads allowing commutes to and from outlying areas. In the fifties, exploding suburban development (houses and stores), caused, in turn, construction of newer and larger roads to accommodate the ever-rising numbers of cars that transformed the United States into an oil-dependant nation. And finally, in this chain reaction, increasing oil consumption led to the bulldozing of more land (as in "The War Against the Trees") to look for oil and provide to the consumer. While Kunitz does not tell readers exactly what purpose the poem's cleared land will serve, he does write that the bulldozers operate at the behest of Standard Oil, one of the largest oil companies in the world. Against this background, the poem supplies a foreground. Whether slated for offices or drilling operations, the land is eradicated of its flora and denuded of its fauna for the sake of what is usually called growth and development. While *growth* and *development* are usually considered positive terms, Kunitz paints the practices behind those words with a more critical brush. "The bulldozers, drunk with gasoline" ready land for more oil production (whether through drilling or administration of delivery systems) thereby enabling mobility. Greater mobility, in turn, leads to more bulldozing of land for roads, development, and oil production. This cycle from production to consumption, commonly referred to as "growth and development," Kunitz calls "war."

War and Peace

If the poet refers to growth and development as a war against nature, it appears he thinks there are more battalions of soldiers than the one driving the bulldozers. Another regiment works for the oil company and still another drives cars (Kunitz seems to have left out only road and store builders). Growth and development are usually considered peacetime activities, but Kunitz construes them as acts of war. Human activity can be divided into two major categories, wartime and peacetime. People already know that war kills, not just people, but plants and animals as well. But in "The War Against the Trees," readers are asked to consider

Topics for Further Study

- Research the history of American environmentalism from 1892 (the beginning of the Sierra Club), to 1962 (the publication of Rachel Carson's *Silent Spring*). What themes and questions do you see recurring?

- Paying special attention to Standard Oil, research the history of the oil industry in the United States during the 1950s. Prepare a report describing who benefitted from the industry's actions, and who suffered.

- Gather photos of 1950s suburbia from your parents, friends, and photo books. Sort them according to topics such as "Conformity," "Affluence," "The American Lawn," "Suburban American Architecture," etc. Write an essay investigating the values that these images embody, and compare those values to your own. Are they the same, different?

- Investigate the Ozone activist Ken Saro-Wiwa, hanged by the Nigerian government on November 10, 1995, for alleged murders. Saro-Wiwa led the protest against Shell Oil's polluting of Nigerian operations and their support by the Nigerian government. Present your findings to your class.

that peace also kills, that peace is also war, less against masses of humanity, but more against masses of plants and animals. The result, as Kunitz sees it, is a devastated battlefield replete with craters, a moonscape devoid of life—human, animal, and vegetable.

Memory and Reminiscence

When the poem's "corner lot" is bulldozed, plants are killed and animals destroyed and exiled ("the green world turned its death-foxed page"). Something else is killed as well: The past. In the third stanza Kunitz seems to recall a childhood filled with trees, where children played and grew up in the shade. Now he sees an aging process he terms "grievous," partially because it occurs in a figurative or real suburb with little flora and fauna, and no wilderness. This denuded space is also metaphorically the space of memory, now wiped clean of fond reminiscence, scoured of nostalgia called upon during the often difficult process of growing old, of being what is often termed, "replaced." If the trees are killed off, the past will be too, and, Kunitz thinks, will no more be a "place" to revisit. The only thing left will be a future devoid of plants and animals and refilled with a very human culture of growth and development. Neither of these terms, the poem suggests, should be confused with progress.

Style

"The War Against the Trees" consists of a total of thirty lines organized into five stanzas of six lines each. In each stanza, at least two lines rhyme. Rhyme is always masculine, that is, monosyllabic, as in show/row, town/down, and scars/cars. These rhyming lines are further unified by having approximately the same number of syllables and accents, and generally, the same rhythm, either iambic tetrameter or pentameter. Finally, these lines are united by their appearance on the page, by extending farther than the stanza's other lines. Together, these similarities constitute a "major pair." In addition to the major pairs, there are also minor pairs, "minor" because if the lines rhyme, as in lines 1 and 4 (oil/soil), they do not share the same number of syllables. The rhyme in the minor pairs is sometimes a form of off-rhyme or assonance, as in stanza two's "raids" / "maimed" / "again."

By assigning human attributes to inanimate things, Kunitz personifies both technology, as in the bulldozers, and nature, as in the trees and plants. The nineteenth-century art critic John Ruskin took a dim view of making human the inhuman and termed this literary device "pathetic fallacy." Ruskin believed the primary criterion of art and literature is truth, and saw in personification a form of literally lying about the appearance of things. Ruskin's criticism, however, is dismissed by many, and the use of personification, in all genres of literature, continues.

Historical Context

When World War II ended in 1945, some ten million American soldiers were discharged from the armed forces. To shelter them, housing develop-

Compare & Contrast

- **1958:** *The Affluent Society,* by Harvard economics professor John Kenneth Galbraith, decries the overemphasis on consumer goods in the U.S. economy and the use of advertising to create artificial demand for such goods. More of the nation's wealth should be allocated to the public, says Galbraith.

  1999: *The Overspent American: Why We Want What We Don't Need* by Juliet Schor shows how keeping up with the Joneses has evolved from keeping pace with one's neighbors and those in a similar social strata, to keeping up with coworkers who earn five times one's own salary, or television characters with a lifestyle unattainable for the average person.

- **1958:** "The torrent of foreign oil robs Texas of her oil market" and costs the state $1 million per day, says the chairman of the Texas Railroad Commission which controls production in the state. The Commission reduces Texas oil wells to eight producing days per month.

  2000: Truckers march on Washington demanding that the federal government lower oil prices. With American pressure, the organization of oil producing nations, OPEC, agrees to step up oil production in order to lower prices.

- **1958:** The median U.S. family income is $5,087, up from $3,187 in 1948 (half of all families have incomes below the median, half above), but prices have climbed along with incomes.

  Today: The median family income adjusted for inflation is $42,000.

---

ments were built outside the city. Though suburbs existed in America before the fifties, they were nothing like those to come. The most infamous and influential plan for suburbia was Levittown, located on Long Island, New York. On July 3, 1950, William J. Levitt appeared on the cover of *Time* magazine in front of a row of identical boxlike houses on freshly bulldozed land. The caption read: "House Builder Levitt. For Sale: A New Way of Life." First on Long Island, then near Philadelphia, and in New Jersey, Levitt helped model the suburbia of the 1950s. In October 1947, the first Levittown home was purchased, just one of many mass-produced, affordable, look-alike houses characterizing 1950s suburbia. These developments helped foment middle-class migration to the suburbs and the need for more and larger high-speed roads to handle high-powered cars. Not only were houses nearly identical, but lots as well, with a tree planted every twenty-eight feet (two-and-a-half trees per home). In the beginning, Levitt included a free television set and a washing machine as incentives to buy. Homeowners could not build fences, lawns had to be mowed at least once a week, and laundry could be hung on rotary racks only, not on lines, and never on weekends. Despite such restrictions, 1.4 million housing units were built in 1950. The rate continued throughout the decade, an average of three thousand acres of farmland bulldozed per day for tract housing. By 1952, Long Island's Levittown population was ten thousand, and Pennsylvania's Levittown could accommodate seventeen thousand families.

"The War Against the Trees," while commonly appearing in modern poetry anthologies, is nearly absent from criticism. It seems that only Selden Rodman finds the poem worthy of comment, asking Kunitz in an interview whether "The War Against the Trees" wasn't "a primer of ecology." Rodman's observation is not surprising given the interview took place in 1971, not long after the sanctioning of environmentalism with the first Earth Day in April 1970. More remarkable, however, is that "The War Against the Trees" (1958) was published well before what by some accounts was the inspiration for America's modern environmental movement—the publication of Rachel Carson's *Silent Spring* in 1962.

Although critics have ignored "The War Against the Trees," they have not ignored *Selected Poems,* the volume in which it appears. In 1958, poet and critic David Wagoner wrote that the eighty-five poems in *Selected Poems* "exhibit a simultaneously delightful and frightening mind. Its ways are intricate, surprising, and clear; but they occasionally lead so deep or so far forward that the reader performing Pound's 'dance along the intellect' discovers himself in a country where he is his own most dangerous enemy, where he is forced to choose sides at the bottom of his own mind." In the case of "The War Against the Trees," that choice might refer to the tough one between nature and development. Nine years later, Jean H. Hagstrum remarked that "the latest poems (which include "The War Against the Trees") make the old metaphysical boldness even bolder and intensify the already unparaphrasable imagistic intensity. At the same time, the long colloquial line of 1944 has now become a marvel of flexible strength. Suffusing these familiar effects is a golden romanticism ... " Had Hagstrum specifically addressed the case of "The War Against the Trees," she might have supplied one more adjective to describe that "golden romanticism": A *frustrated* golden romanticism. Robert Weisburg picks up the issue of Kunitz's romanticism in his "Stanley Kunitz: The Stubborn Middle Way": "Kunitz, in fact, is a devout Romantic in his adherence to the natural world as his model for human experience, though he has successfully transformed nature from Wordsworthian harmony and sublimity to the modern disfigurement he must deal with, especially by dealing more with man's body than with earth's body." This is less true of "The War Against the Trees," where the human heart is too small to save the "earth's body" from desertification, disfigurement, and death. But Weisburg is certainly correct, in terms of "The War Against the Trees," when he writes that harmony between humans and nature is non-existent. Not just non-existent, but as fallen as if Adam and Eve had themselves driven the bulldozers.

Criticism

Chris Semansky

Semansky's most recent collection of poems, Blindsided, *has been published by 26 Books of Portland, Oregon and nominated for an Oregon book award. In the following essay, Semansky examines Kunitz's "The War Against the Trees," pay-*

ing close attention to the complexity of the poet's word choice.

"The War Against the Trees" appears in several popular classroom anthologies of poetry, yet little about the poem exists in the biographical literature about Kunitz, or in the substantial criticism focused on his *Selected Poems* (1958), the volume in which "The War Against the Trees" appears. Perhaps this is because the poem seems self-evident. Or, from a different angle, so fragile that vigorous investigation would "break" it. While these arguments are not without their virtues (as is true for many poems), "The War Against the Trees" is neither so simple that deeper analysis cannot reveal its complexity, nor so fragile it cannot be shaken up without shattering its message. A close reading of the poem, with special attention paid to Kunitz's word choice, will help to unpack its complexity.

In the first line of "The War Against the Trees," "standard oil," a proper noun, is not capitalized. The effect is to diminish the company's real value, the poet, careful to avoid showing respect for a company bulldozing a parcel of land home to trees, flowers, and a vibrant underground ecology. The man who has sold the corner property is, Kunitz writes, "joking" with others watching the "show." "Laughed" is not employed because the word would seem a direct response to the "show," and would connote direct joy in the destruction, a kind of sadism. "Joking," however, indicates a response less evil, an unconcern about, or ignorance of, the fuller meanings of this destruction. To these neighbors (or at least the man who sold the property), it is as if these trees and flowers were inanimate objects or mere things. This is not bloodsport, but a celebration of *action,* of noise and movement of bulldozers, the crash of big trees. The tone of this "celebration" is underscored by the description of the bulldozers, which are "drunk with gasoline." Drunkenness personifies these machines, possibly prompting readers to think of drunken males in cars on a destructive spree, and then to bring readers back to the watching neighbors—are they drunk as well? Whatever the case, these neighbors would likely have been just as satisfied having attended a demolition derby or monster truck rally. This is a scene no one except the poet understands as a killing field. Instead, this seems a harmless arena to an audience as oblivious to the killing as are the bulldozers.

In "The War Against the Trees," personification works both ways—to vilify and dignify. In the second stanza, personification is employed not only to vilify bulldozers, but to dignify plants. Kunitz casts the plants as under attack by the bulldozers-as-tanks. Unfortunately, the metaphor begins to backfire if taking tall trees seems like taking an enemy bunker of big guns or missile launchers. But Kunitz prevents such thoughts from proceeding when he calls the trees "great-grandfathers," "lopped and maimed." This directs the comparison away from trees as enemies to trees as human-like victims, especially through the attribute of having severed limbs. Bulldozers represented as cars full of drunk males or tanks, and trees characterized as old men with severed limbs not only portrays this happening as an unfair fight, but as a destruction of the past (grandfathers) by the present (youth), a theme revisited in the poem's fourth stanza.

The third stanza's "hireling engines," might conjure up an image of mercenaries (a further personification of bulldozers) hired by Standard Oil to "pacify" the site, eradicate from this corner lot any obstacles to development making it "safe" for business. "Hacking" is a verb describing a repulsive act, building empathy for the trees by casting them as living victims. Kunitz's sensitivity extends not only to plants, but to what are usually disliked and unconsidered ground-dwellers, moles and grubs. Kunitz, however, dignifies the moles as human, as possessors of homes with "halls" under attack from humans and their machines. Grubs are exalted by having "dominions" making it not just grub homes suffering an attack, but grub communities and lands. From the ground's smallest and most hidden creatures, Kunitz fast cuts to the largest and sometimes most visible, the "giants" of the sky: trees. These giant grandfathers, king-or queen-like with their crowns, are now humbled, forced to their "knees" in submission to the new, self-crowned kings of the wood, humans. This exaltation of plants and "lower" animals is the kind of sensibility describable as *biophilia,* care for all that lives. Kunitz, however, goes further by dignifying plants and animals, and, at the same time, vilifying humans. Or more precisely, vilifying a specified set of human actions.

If personification is Kunitz's tool to enliven and vilify machines, and, in addition, extra-enliven and dignify nature, a rather opposite technique is employed on people, one depicting them as not fully alive. If, in the first stanza, the neighbors can be said to be "dead" to the import of the events in front of them, the fourth stanza is inhabited by "ghosts of children." The word "shade" enhances the real and figurative deaths in this scene. Shade describes not only the shade of trees but, in a long

What Do I Read Next?

- Arguably the most important book of the modern environmental movement, Rachel Carson's *Silent Spring* (1962), won eight awards from conservation and women's groups and became a national bestseller.

- Bill McKibben, in *The End of Nature* (1989), wrote about air and weather as Rachel Carson had about soil, plants, and insects in *Silent Spring,* both warning of irreversible damage if humanity keeps up the increasing pace of production and consumption.

- *Nature* is one of the more complex words in the English language. To tackle the history of the transformation of ideas of nature from early Greeks to modern Americans, Clarence Glacken's *Traces on the Rhodian Shore: Nature and Culture in Western Thought from Ancient Times to the End of the Eighteenth Century* (1967) is an indispensable resource.

- What Clarence Glacken did for the concept of nature in 1967, Max Oelschlaeger did for the concept of wilderness in his *The Idea of Wilderness* (1991). Oelschlaeger's scope extends from prehistory to the age of ecology.

- Derek Wall's anthology, *Green History* (1994), covers environmental writings by philosophers, writers, and scientists, including authors from Plato to D. H. Lawrence, Sappho to Leo Tolstoy.

literary tradition, the state of a person after death, as in the phrase describing the afterworld, "land of the shades." Children playing in the shade of trees, "racing beyond their childhood," says Kunitz, disappear into "grievous old age," die and become shades. Kunitz seems to say that an absence of tree-shade—which describes many a sparsely-arbored, fifties suburb—hastens people into the "suburbs" of human old age, and finally, the "suburbs" of death (life as urban), a final move to the land of shades. Such a claim might be explained this way:

> *If personification is Kunitz's tool to enliven and vilify machines, and, in addition, extra-enliven and dignify nature, a rather opposite technique is employed on people, one depicting them as not fully alive.*

eradication of trees and plants helps kill off memories of what was, pushes humans increasingly into hope for an unknown and suspect future, hastens time and therefore, the approach of death. Nostalgia and cognizance, on the other hand, work to slow time, to make aging less grievous, less, if you will, suburban. "Suburbs," then, not only describes a place outside the "urb(an)," but a purgatory on the edge of life, an anteroom to the land of the shades.

In stanza four, "the green world," or nature, is again personified—nature turns the page of an old book, its own biography. Nature has a long tradition of comparison to a book, one that with the *Book of God* comprised the two-volume set of the *Book of Life*. Nature turning the pages of its own book is a kind of objectification (nature as book), personification, and deification (nature as a kind of god or demiurge) rolled into one. The particular page nature turns is "death-foxed," not just yellowed or brown with age, but possibly inhabited by images of nature's losses like a page of deceased relatives in a family photo album. If the picture conjured up from Kunitz's description is of nature sadly turning the pages of its own history, mourning its losses at the hand of its own children (humanity), the reader's response might be one similar to Christ crucified: empathy for a god under attack from its own, from those who know not what they do.

As one might expect from the title, "The War Against the Trees," the poem's last stanza brings readers back to those victims of "war," those "great-grandfathers of the town / So freshly lopped and maimed," those "giants" brought "to their knees" in a "seizure" of death. In this last stanza,

the trees are toppled, their roots exposed. The craters left behind are "too big for hearts," these giants being larger in size and in sensitivity than the humans killing them. Kunitz calls the exposed roots, "club-roots" which is also the name for a plant disease caused by a slime mold. Symptoms of the disease include large malformed roots. Because this definition does not fit well with these toppled, healthy elms, club-root is probably a play on *club foot,* defined as "a congenitally deformed or distorted foot." Add this personification of tree roots to the word, "amputated," that follows, and readers are not only presented with murdered bodies, but deformed corpses. The image of club-roots radically morphs with the word, "gorgons," female monsters with snakes for hair who turn those looking at them to stone. "Gorgons" is a somewhat imperfect attribution because the word might provoke a conflation of trees with monsters rather than tree corpses as monstrous. Apart from this quibble, "gorgons" is effective because the exposure, *the sight,* of "club-roots" indicates that the once-green earth is being desertified into a treeless, stony moonscape. These gorgons, however, are different from the blindness-causing gorgons of myth since the club-roots do not *cause* blindness, but *are* blind, another injury to these sympathy-provoking trees already "maimed," "lopped," "amputated," and brought "to their knees."

In the last stanza's fourth line, the blindness metaphor is mixed with an aural component when the gorgon roots cry "Moon," a kind of synesthesia where a sight (and site) is so offensive it "cries out" to be heard. Yet Kunitz seems doubtful anyone else hears the trees crying out, even if "caught / in the rear-view mirrors of passing cars." More likely it is that upon seeing the site, drivers will not view it as a slaughter, like the poet. Or, if they do, Kunitz thinks they will be too busy to give it much thought. And if a driver should stop her car and ask Mr. Kunitz (is he not one of the witnesses?) who it is that's bulldozing the land, he just might answer, "All of us."

Source: Chris Semansky, in an essay for *Poetry for Students,* Gale Group, 2001.

Jonathan N. Barron

Barron is an associate professor of English at the University of Southern Mississippi. He has co-edited Jewish American Poetry *(University Press of New England) and* Roads Not Taken: Rereading Robert Frost *(University of Missouri Press), as well as a forthcoming collection of essays on the poetic movement,* New Formalism. *Beginning in 2001, he will be the editor-in-chief of* The Robert Frost Review. *In the following essay he examines the structure of Kunitz's "The War Against The Trees."*

In "The War Against the Trees," Kunitz weaves together two ancient poetic forms using metrical lines that depend in every stanza on at least one set of rhymes. First, he engages the ancient pastoral tradition that depends on the opposition between mechanized civilization and the agrarian life of farms, and pastures. Second, he sets his pastoral poem into a prophetic context: he uses his poem as an occasion to charge his readers with moral, even theologically based fervor about a grave injustice, a terrible transgression.

The pastoral element of the poem is the most readily noticed. Generally speaking, a pastoral poem is any poem that takes nature as its occasion. In fact, however, the genre of pastoral poetry is a bit more complex and nuanced. Recently, a scholar of pastoral poetry, Paul Alpers, declared that people, not nature, make a poem pastoral. While the poem must contain nature, it must do more than merely describe the flora and fauna. According to Alpers, ever since the ancient Greeks first set pastoral verse to parchment it has been the case that "we will have a far truer idea of pastoral if we take its representative anecdote to be herdsmen and their lives, rather than landscape or idealized nature." To Alpers, this means that pastoral poetry always concerns and explores a relationship between people and nature, not just nature all by itself. Further, as a poetic type, pastoral poetry defines itself by asking what the nature of that human relationship to nature might be. Because it does this, he says, pastoral poetry inevitably contains social and ethical themes. According to Alpers, one can recognize a pastoral poem by its formal structure. That structure, he says, depends on the following plot: a person in nature addresses some natural object which, in turn, raises serious questions about both the relation between individuals and nature, and individuals and social institutions.

Meanwhile, not too far from ancient Greece, the Hebrews developed a literary form which is now part of the Hebrew Bible, the various books of the Prophets. Eventually, prophecy, as a literary form, took root in America during the seventeenth century when the Puritans, who envisioned themselves to be the new Israelites creating a New Jerusalem in a new England, saw it as their mission to write a new Bible for a new Canaan. In the works of their new bible the Puritans developed a literary form, the jeremiad, modeled on the Book

> *What makes the poem, 'The War Against the Trees,' so exciting, unusual and interesting, then, is the way it blends the pastoral tradition of the classical age with the jeremiad, the New England version of the Hebrew Prophets."*

of Jeremiah from the Hebrew Bible. As the literary scholar Sargent Bush explains "the jeremiad" is "a sermon form that served both to admonish and to encourage."

Of the many poets of his generation born in the first decades of the twentieth century, Kunitz was in an ideal position to blend the Hebrew, Puritan jeremiad with the classical Greek and Roman pastoral. Born into a Jewish family in New England, he grew up with the Hebrew Bible and the Prophets as well as with the Puritan inflected literature of New England. Born and educated in Massachusetts, and a student of literature both undergraduate and graduate at Harvard, he expected to teach at Harvard as well. But after achieving his master's degree in 1927, he was told, in his words, "that Anglo-Saxons would resent being taught English by a Jew, even a Jew with a *summa cum laude.*" Despite this setback, he went on to edit at least seventeen reference books on literature that were standard material on the subject throughout the 1930s and early 1940s. In effect, he was as knowledgeable about the western pastoral and classical tradition as any poet of his generation.

What makes the poem, "The War Against the Trees," so exciting, unusual and interesting, then, is the way it blends the pastoral tradition of the classical age with the jeremiad, the New England version of the Hebrew Prophets. This blending of poetic types produces a work of unusual and striking force. Part of this force is due to the variations on these forms that Kunitz makes. For example, rather than taking place among shepherds in a pasture, the poem occurs in a settled town. But the pastoral structure is retained because the poem is an address to nature, in this case a group of elm trees that are so ancient they literally have witnessed the events of a century. The ethical, social aspect of Kunitz's modern pastoral is that these modern shepherds, neighbors in a small town, must consider the consequences and meaning of ripping these trees out of the soil. To destroy something so old, is it not a kind of betrayal of one's own roots? One's own past?

To ask that question, however, is to engage not only a pastoral convention but also a convention far more common to the Puritan jeremiad. When Kunitz laments the "war against the trees" he does not just set a series of questions about the proper relationship to nature in motion, he also begins an angry, admonishing, even scolding jeremiad of his own. The pastoral scene becomes, in effect, a platform for Kunitz's own prophecy of a hopeless, even catastrophic future.

What is that future? What is the transgression Kunitz means to have us notice? It is the new rise of suburbs. The post-World War II phenomenon of the suburb made possible by a new automobile culture was quite literally changing the very idea of the landscape all over America. In his poem, Kunitz renders this transformation into the language of a visionary war of biblical proportions. In this prophecy, the evil ones are not philistines but suburbanites and the evil god is not Moloch but oil. By contrast, the heroes are the mighty elms, the "giants" who wear "crowns." The suburb, in other words, is more than just an idea about the proper relationship between people and nature. It is, says Kunitz's poem, a profoundly unethical, potentially immoral attitude towards nature itself because it sees nature only as decoration, a mere appendage to commercial life. By contrast, the century old elms give the lie to such a shallow relationship. Ultimately, the poem, in good jeremiad fashion, urges a return to a more symbiotic relationship with nature. It condemns the suburban transformation as an unholy model of dominance where nature is merely so much land to develop for cash.

Kunitz's attack on the suburb implies that the small town is a kind of American pastoral. This idea asserts itself most strongly at the poem's conclusion when he connects the elms to the town's own historical sense of itself. To destroy the elms in the name of suburbanization, he says, is to destroy one's own history. The jeremiad is meant to be a warning to the town: Kunitz all but says that

to sell its land to an oil company is to sell its soul, its past, its roots. This warning has an angry edge to it because, as the poem indicates, this very attack itself will likely have no power or influence in modern American life. Kunitz is aware that nothing will stop suburbanization and it is this pessimism, this anger, that defines the poem's tone. Kunitz's angry critique of a society that has given up any respect or interest in the integrity of nature becomes the ethical, and social heart and soul of the poem.

Turning now to the poem itself, one discovers that it depends on a strict sense of form. In five, six line, metrical stanzas it develops its story through the use of symbolism, metaphor, complex imagery, and literary allusion. Every stanza also contains at least one pair of rhymes. It is as if Kunitz, by appealing to form in this way, were saying, through the use this formal style, that some traditions must not be lost, must be preserved. Although his subject is modern, the selling of land and the bulldozing of trees, the structure is ancient (pastoral and jeremiad), and the form (meter and rhyme) is, if not ancient, at least several centuries old. Both the forms and structure of this poem make it traditional, dependent on the past, and as ancient and noble as the very trees it means to defend and champion! By contrasting these old forms and styles to a modern subject, in other words, Kunitz highlights his own position; he becomes a man in tune with nature and, as such, he opposes nature's dominance in the name of the modern suburbs.

The first stanza establishes the anecdote, the scene that will drive what follows. Note that in this stanza the war depicted is between machine and nature: people are, in this instance, mere commentators even though they are responsible for the event itself. Ultimately, though, the larger economic system, suburbanization, is the real culprit here: "The man who sold his lawn to standard oil / Joked with his neighbors come to watch the show." Here, the man sells his bit of earth to an oil company. But why shouldn't he? No doubt he made a great deal of money off the sale and can enjoy his new profit by trading a few jokes with his neighbors. Presumably, the scene is a small town somewhere in the United States. But what is "the show"? It is "bulldozers, drunk with gasoline" who "test the virtue of the soil." Here, the gendered imagery makes the case against such a sale plain. The bulldozers become drunken male warriors who test the female virtue of what one famous scholar of American culture called the Virgin Land (Henry Nash

Smith). Innocent, female earth, in other words, will be raped by the machines of suburbanization.

The next stanza makes even more plain that the culprit is neither the man who sold the land nor necessarily even the bulldozers. Rather, it shows that suburbanization, the transformation of America from a place of cities, farms, and towns, to a place where the majority of citizens will live in suburbs has begun. This point is made in the opening lines of the second stanza:

> Forsythia-forays and hydrangea-raids
> Were but the preliminaries to a war
> Against the great-grandfathers of the town

In these lines, Kunitz explains that the bulldozers are, in the fact, the last battle, in a much older war against nature. For not only has the earth been raped but even the plants have been transformed as more and more decorative flowers replace the grandfathers, the trees, the real indigenous ecosystem. The typical yard even of the town was but the first "foray" and "raid" against nature that would be concluded when the great-grandfather trees are felled. Kunitz here says that no one ought to be surprised for he, like a prophet, could have predicted upon first seeing the silly hydrangea and forsythia that soon bulldozers would "lop" and "maim" these trees. To emphasize his view that the bulldozers merely conclude a centuries long "war against the trees," the poem's second stanza ends by declaring that, as each elm tree falls, "a century went down."

As he begins his third stanza the poem that began as a pastoral enters into high jeremiad gear. The stanza asks just how important a tree is? What is its value? Mere cash to be cashed in? Or is its value to be measured in terms of its history? Kunitz gives us nature's view of this calamity by turning his gaze to the moles underground who are the panicked first witnesses to this final battle of the war. In so doing, Kunitz suggests that the trees are fundamental to this place, to its ecosystem, to its very identity as a place. They can be said to embody history. This has profound implications for people since it assumes that insofar as one belongs to a particular place the flora and fauna of that place are, as it were, one's relatives. To kill off the trees, then, is to kill off one's own history, a part not only of the town but of one's self as well.

The third stanza's powerful description of the felling of the elms, Kunitz gives us the perspective of the mole "rampaging" through "his halls" as the trees are uprooted. In effect, this third stanza transforms the landscape into a kind of epic battle. The

trees, understood as giants, are "forced to their knees," and their citizens, like this mole, flee in terror. That Kunitz sets the poem underground in this stanza indicates, through the metaphor, "underground," just how fundamental these elms are to this place. Words such as "deep" and "roots" are often used as metaphors to indicate a connection to a place. In this poem, real roots actually do run deep and they are with great labor and with mighty machines eradicated nonetheless. In other words, by going underground Kunitz emphasizes the metaphorical, even symbolic meaning of the trees suggesting through the metaphor that they are the very definition of this place's history. To attack them is to attack one's own past.

The reading explains why the next stanza returns to the human realm as a lost place of mere ghosts. It begins, "I saw the ghosts of children at their games / Racing beyond their childhood in the shade." Here, Kunitz connects the trees to the children of this town. He connects the trees to the children's experience and, in so doing, he links the trees both to the town's past (the children) and to its future, since these same children will grow up to run the town itself. The prophetic admonition here is Kunitz's implication that, by cutting the trees, the town is effectively cutting off its own roots, its own childhood, its own history. The stanza concludes:

> And while the green world turned its death-foxed
>   page
> And a red wagon wheeled,
> I watched them disappear
> Into the suburbs of their grievous age.

These lines only increase the prophetic anger of the poem's theme. "The green world" is a traditional poetic figure, a trope, for the pastoral ideal of a bucolic natural pasture of shepherds at home with their flocks. Imagining the passage of time as a book turning its pages, Kunitz tells us that the next page, our present commercial civilization, is "death-foxed." The new postwar suburban age belongs to a "grievous" time when the kings, the elms, will lose their crowns to drunken machines and laughing neighbors. The trees, and the children who knew them, will be nothing but ghosts, forgotten to history.

One could argue that this stanza implies that the suburbs made the bulldozers necessary. The suburbs, we are told, create a mentality, a "grievous age," that disconnects the human from the natural by removing people ever more completely from the great-grandfathers of their past. The poem's concluding stanza, therefore, angrily blasts

The children, who played in the past, enter a future which is the present for the narrator. The bulldozers, which work in the present, move into an unknown future. The narrator stands in the present, examining the past as it moves into the future—a paradox of the past, present and future all occurring at once."

the world of automobiles. The suburb as a place entirely dependent on cars becomes, in this poem, a final human victory over the great-grandfathers, and over the last gasp of the pastoral ideal, the lost American town. In the first three lines of the last stanza, Kunitz returns to the classical age, specifically to Greek myth, when he says that the trees, with their roots sticking up in the air, look like gorgons, those fantastically ugly women with snakes for hair: one look at a gorgon and one would turn to stone. In Greek mythology Perseus kills Medusa, one of the three gorgon sisters, but, in Kunitz's poem, Perseus is no hero and the Medusa is no monster. Indeed, just as Perseus could only look at the gorgon he was to kill through the mirror of the shield Athena gave him, so the unnamed victor of these gorgons, can only look at them in mirrors as well. Ironically, even sarcastically, the mirror this present day Perseus uses is not a shield granted to the conquering hero by a goddess but rather it is merely "the rear-view mirrors of the passing cars." All those who drive, in other words, are, in part, responsible for the death of these great-grandfathers. The poem, as is true for jeremiads generally, implicates its readers. It says that we, in our blindness and our greed, have transformed our heritage, our history, our own past into modern day gorgons. In the final stanza of this poem, then, Kunitz offers us a portrait of the automobile age: a time of disconnection, loss, the end of the pastoral ideal.

That Kunitz's poem has the force of a prophecy must have struck readers of the book in which it appeared, his third. For it won the Pulitzer Prize for the best book of poetry in 1958. Whatever politicians might have us believe, poets, at any rate, as well as their readers welcome such civilized calls to account for our transgressions.

Source: Jonathan N. Barron, in an essay for *Poetry for Students,* Gale Group, 2001.

Carl Mowery

Mowery holds a Ph.D. from Southern Illinois University, Carbondale, in Rhetoric and Composition and American Literature. He has written numerous essays for the Gale Group. In the following, Mowery examines the theme of life and death and Kunitz's special use of language.

Kunitz was born in the industrial town of Worchester, Massachusetts in 1905. He was raised by his mother; his father had died before his birth. He was subjected to anti-Semitism as a youth. (Worchester is built on seven hills, each of which was inhabited by a different ethnic group. At that time these groups remained apart and oftentimes were antagonistic to the others.) In an interview with Leslie Kelen he said, "I was curious about the world of possibilities beyond those other alien hills (in Worchester)." Later in another interview he said, "In my youth, as might be expected, I had little knowledge of the world to draw on. But I had fallen in love with language and was excited by ideas." To Leslie Kelen he also remarked, "I'm not a nature poet, but I am a poet of the natural world." Kunitz's five stanza poem reveals his love of nature and shows his fascination with special forms of language in order to present his ideas. The poem takes a look at the modern world's relentless quest for oil at the expense of the environment. In it, the narrator stands to the side and watches and comments on the changes occurring before him.

In *Touch Melt,* published in 1995 in *The Later Poems: New and Selected,* the question is asked, "What makes the engine go?" The answer is: "Desire, desire, desire." It is "desire" for oil-consuming machines that pushes the oil company to seek more sources of oil. A new and "grievous age" makes unquenchable and immediate demands for more oil. The consequence of this desire is that the future has become dependent on oil, just as the past has been. And so to satisfy the future, the present now destroys the past.

Kunitz once said, "I know … that I am living and dying at once." This acceptance of life and death simultaneously is a major theme in his poetry. In this poem the theme of death in life is reintroduced as the theme of past and future. The future informs the past, just as the past determines the future. In Kunitz's poem the future will destroy the past upon which it will be built. As the bulldozers and other machines test "the virtue of the soil" and remove the greenery, they leave a cratered moon-like world. The forsythia, hydrangeas, and privet hedge all fall to the power of the machines, as one part of the natural world is uprooted and destroyed in order to find another. With the felling of each "great-grandfather" the link between the past and the future is reduced. The ancient trees, representatives of the past, yield to the machines that now bring them "to their knees."

Ironically, this attack on trees is also an attack on the primal origin of oil itself: the prehistoric accumulation of forest material which under pressure and over time is turned into oil. These trees would not be turned into oil, but they are descendants of those trees from ages past. The oil is used by the past-driven machine to destroy the present-day trees to gain access to more prehistoric oil deposits that will be needed to fuel future machines in their quest for more oil! And the cycle continues without end. In this search for oil the needs of the future destroy two pasts: the oil itself and the memories of the past. The cycle brings to mind the ancient imagery of a snake eating its own tail until nothing exists except the memory of the snake. But in this poem, even the memory disappears.

In the headlong quest for new sources, the oil-seeking Standard Oil Company attacks the landscape, laying low everything in its path. This is the environmental equivalent to General Sherman's march to the sea during the American Civil War and it is reported using warlike imagery and phrases. The attack on the "lawn" and the neighborhood soil is as frantic as the children's games. This event brings to mind the phrase often repeated during the Vietnam war: We had to destroy the village, in order to save it. In this poem, the neighborhood is destroyed in order to provide it with the oil it will need in order to survive in the oil-dependant future. The image left on that "corner lot" is one fleeting rear-view mirror glimpse, the "witness-moment" of the cratered moonscape (a bombed landscape image) disappearing into the distance.

The ghostly images of playing children soon disappear because those memories depend on the existence of the old trees under which they played their games "in the shade." The children's frantic play, as they go "racing beyond their childhood"

into a future of their own, is replaced by the frantic destruction of the gasoline-drunken machines as they charge into their own future. But each enters a different future. The children, who played in the past, enter a future which is the present for the narrator. The bulldozers, which work in the present, move into an unknown future. The narrator stands in the present, examining the past as it moves into the future—a paradox of the past, present and future all occurring at once.

An important poetic construction comes into play in the poem: the use of hyphenated words. In each stanza Kunitz uses a specially crafted word to create new meanings. "Forsythia-forays and hydrangea-raids" in stanza two create new images of plants and flowers with the war being waged on them by the machines. These new words combine the tender innocence of flowering shrubs with the brutality of war. The word "witness-moment" combines the instant of glancing into a rear-view mirror with the intensity of witnessing an event. It is more than just a casual seeing of the event because to witness carries a stronger involvement with it. It means to attest or to affirm an event to be true.

In the fourth stanza, "death-foxed" is Kunitz's manufactured word that combines several meanings into one. An old meaning for "foxed" is intoxicated. Another correlation with the word death-foxed is the old word death-bird, a carrion eater. The combination of these meanings at this point creates a new meaning: being intoxicated with the death of the "green world" in the recently devoured neighborhood.

The passing moment of defoliation is also witnessed by others. Some see it through the rear-view mirrors of their gasoline consuming cars. In the fleeting "witness-moment" the driver sees the past, literally the scenery behind him, but continues on the road to the future. In so doing the driver fulfills his part in the course of events according to Picard as the road ahead, his future, soon becomes the road in the mirror, his past.

The red wagon, a non-oil-dependent vehicle, is important to the narrator, because it combines the images of cheerful child's play and the non-oil-dependant children (as in Kunitz's youth). But these are soon replaced by the oil-powered machines that eat at the greenery of the neighborhood and the automobiles that carry witnesses past it.

The machines wage their impersonal war and bring the tree "giants to their knees." There are no people are involved in the attacks. Only machines attack the trees and only the trees suffer from the attack. The implication that the machines have taken over the world in an insatiable attempt to quench their thirst for oil products is conveyed by the narrator's inaction. The humans (the narrator and the watching neighbors) are passive observers. The drivers of passing cars are also detached as they witness the events as a reflected image in a rear-view mirror.

The boldly stated environmental concern addressed in this poem is especially poignant because it was published in 1958 (in Selected Poems, 1928–1958), when environmentalism was a little-known concept. The result of his far-reaching vision is this well-crafted little poem. The "intellectual courage that insists on the truth" as he saw it allowed him to raise the issues in his poem. "If I hadn't had an urgent impulse, if the poem didn't seem to me terribly important," Kunitz said, "I never wanted to write it and didn't." Kunitz grappled with images that have become all too commonplace. But many trees and landscapes have been sacrificed since this poem first appeared. He once revealed in the *New York Times:* "The deepest thing I know is that I am living and dying at once, and my conviction is to report that dialogue. It is a rather terrifying thought that is at the root of much of my poetry." That combination of life and death, as present and past, is at the heart of this poem.

Source: Carl Mowery, in an essay for *Poetry for Students,* Gale Group, 2001.

Sources

Alpers, Paul, "What Is Pastoral?" in *Columbia Literary History of the United States,* edited by Emory Elliott, et al., Columbia, 1988.

Bush, Sargent, "Sermons and Theological Writings," in *Columbia Literary History of the United States,* edited by Emory Elliott, et al., Columbia, 1988.

Hagstrum, Jean H., "The Poetry of Stanley Kunitz: An Introductory Essay," in *Poets in Progress,* Northwestern University Press, 1967, pp. 38–58.

Hanault, Marie, *Stanley Kunitz,* Twayne, 1980.

Kelen, Leslie, "Stanley Kunitz, An Interview with a Poet," in *The American Poetry Review,* March–April, 1998, Vol. 27, No. 2, p. 49.

Kunitz, Stanley, *Selected Poems, 1928–1958,* Little, Brown, 1958.

Orr, Gregory, *Stanley Kunitz: An Introduction to the Poetry,* Columbia University Press, 1985.

Rodman, Selden, "Tongues of Fallen Angels," in *Interviews and Encounters with Stanley Kunitz,* edited by Stanley Moss, Sheep Meadow Press, 1993, p. 24.

Wagoner, David, "The Thirty Years' War," in *Poetry,* Vol. 93, No. 3, December, 1958, pp. 174–78.

Weisburg, Robert, "Stanley Kunitz: The Stubborn Middle Way," in *Modern Poetry Studies,* Vol. 6, No. 1, pp. 49–73.

For Further Reading

Brantley, Robin, "A Touch of the Poet," in *New York Times Magazine,* September 7, 1945, pp. 80–83.
 A commentary on and description of Kunitz's gardens at his homes in New York City and Provincetown.

Kunitz, Stanley, "Creative Writing Workshop," in *Education,* Vol. 73, November, 1952, pp. 152–56.
 This is a valuable account of the poet's teaching aims and methods.

———, *Passing Through: The Later Poems, New and Selected,* W. W. Norton, 1997.
 Kunitz's ninth book of poetry includes works from three collections published since 1971 as well as nine poems written since 1985.

Mercier, Vivian, Review of *Selected Poems,* in *Commonweal,* Vol. 69, February 13, 1959, p. 523.
 Mercier comments on the capacity of Kunitz's later poems to speak more directly to readers. She attributes this to the wisdom that comes with age.

Rupp, Rebecca, *Red Oaks and Black Birches,* Storey Communications, 1990.
 In this unusual but rewarding book Rupp provides a cultural history of trees, touching on their symbolic as well as their literal importance.

The Weight of Sweetness

"The Weight of Sweetness" is the fourth poem in Li-Young Lee's first collection of poems, *Rose*. It follows his most-anthologized poem in the collection, "Persimmons," which, like "The Weight of Sweetness," uses fruit as a central metaphor for exploring the poet's relationship to his past. In "The Weight of Sweetness." Lee takes twenty-nine lines to meditate on the relationship between memory and loss, mourning his dead father while remembering his father's tenderness.

Many of Lee's poems are about his father, Richard K. Y. Lee, a highly accomplished man who was personal physician to the Chinese leader Mao Tse-tung before he emigrated to Indonesia to found a college. An intellectual and a deeply religious man, Richard Lee had a profound impact on his son's life, an impact that the younger Lee continues to grapple with in his poetry. "Sweetness" is used in this poem as a metaphor which encompasses "song, wisdom, sadness, and joy," and Lee suggests that loss necessarily has to include some measure of all of these.

The poem begins in the abstract, then becomes gradually more concrete as Lee develops his metaphor of sweetness, using peaches as the vehicle for his comparison. He then moves on to a childhood anecdote in which he and his father lug bags of peaches through the wind and rain. The final image is one of separation of father and son, which echoes Lee's present tense exploration of loss and memory. In searching for the meaning of

Li-Young Lee

1986

sweetness, Lee is also searching for a clearer sense of his own identity in relation to his father. This search is developed in many other poems in *Rose*, in particular "Mneomic" and "Eating Together." "The Weight of Sweetness" itself is rarely mentioned in reviews or criticism of Lee's poetry.

Author Biography

Li-Young Lee's poetry has often been praised for its tenderness and passion. A relentless examination of his past and his emotional vulnerability characterize his poetry. Born in Jakarta, Indonesia, in 1957 to Richard K. Y. Lee and Joice Yuan Jiaying, Lee was raised among the social unrest and political turbulence of Indonesia in the late 1950s. His mother is the granddaughter of China's provisional president, Yuan Shikai, elected in 1912 during the country's transition from monarchy to republic. His Chinese father was once Mao Tsetung's personal physician, and when anti-Chinese rioting erupted in Jakarta in 1959, the elder Lee was imprisoned for nineteen months for sedition. Lee's memories and stories of this time appear in his memoir, *The Winged Seed.*

An educator and a minister as well as a physician, Lee's father instilled a love of literature in his children, reciting poems from the Tang Dynasty and reading the King James Bible to them. The figure of Richard Lee appears prominently in Lee's writing. He is a distant, almost godlike presence that the poet Lee struggles to comprehend in his descriptions and stories. Richard Lee, who became a Presbyterian minister in the United States, died in 1980 in the small Pennsylvania town in which he and the family settled.

Lee's formal education began in the United States where, after graduating from high school in Vandergrift, Pennsylvania, he attended the Universities of Pittsburgh (1975–1979) and Arizona (1979–1980); and the State University of New York at Brockport (1980–1981).

In 1986 Lee's first collection of poems, *Rose,* received New York University's Delmore Schwartz Memorial Poetry Award, and in 1990 he published another collection, *The City in Which I Love You,* which received the Lamont Poetry Selection of the Academy of American Poets. Among other awards, Lee has received a Ludwig Vogelstein Foundation fellowship, a writer's award from the Mrs. Giles Whiting Foundation, and a fellowship from the Guggenheim Foundation. Lee's poems appear frequently in anthologies of Asian-American literature, and he is widely considered one of the most talented young Asian-American writers in the United States. Poet Gerald Stern has likened Lee's poetry to that of John Keats and Rainer Maria Rilke; Lee himself has named writers such as Robert Frost, Emily Dickinson, Walt Whitman, Li Bai, Tu Fu, Su Tung Po, and Yang Wan Li as influences.

Poem Text

No easy thing to bear, the weight of sweetness.

Song, wisdom, sadness, joy: sweetness
equals three of any of these gravities.

See a peach bend
the branch and strain the stem until   5
it snaps.
Hold the peach, try the weight, sweetness
and death so round and snug
in your palm.
And, so, there is   10
    the weight of memory:

Windblown, a rain-soaked
bough shakes, showering
the man and the boy.
They shiver in delight,   15
and the father lifts from his son's cheek
one green leaf
    fallen like a kiss.

The good boy hugs a bag of peaches
his father has entrusted   20
to him.
Now he follows
his father, who carries a bagful in each arm.
See the look on the boy's face
as his father moves   25
faster and farther ahead, while his own steps
flag, and his arms grow weak, as he labors
under the weight
of peaches.

Poem Summary

Lines 1–3:

The title of the poem "The Weight of Sweetness" is a phrase readers might expect to find as a title for a surrealist poem. By using one sensory experience (gravity) to evoke another (taste), Lee creates a paradox of sorts which his poem works to resolve. The first line, a fragment, alerts us to the tone of the poem. The speaker is having a difficult time enduring sweetness, which the reader understands here as a synonym for tenderness. This line is also an understatement, as readers can infer that the weight of sweetness is no doubt almost unbearable for the speaker. The next two lines are presented as a multiple choice item one might expect to find on a college entrance test, but here the speaker provides the answer as well. Gravity is the force which both literally and metaphorically weighs things down. By saying that it takes three of the items listed to equal sweetness, Lee underscores the complex nature of sweetness.

Lines 4–11:

The poet's voice in these lines is directive. He is instructing readers on how to look. His use of enjambed lines, that is, lines whose syntax and meaning spills onto the next line, metaphorically embodies the very thing he describes: the bending and snapping of a peach from its branch. By using a peach to symbolize sweetness, Lee is piling up associations with the term and making it more palpable, more sensuous. Peaches, like song, wisdom, sadness, and joy, all abstractions, are also subject to the laws of gravity. By directing readers to "Hold the peach," Lee wants them to participate bodily, as well as intellectually, in the idea of sweetness his poem explores. The peach is literally sweet in taste, but because it has been snapped from its branch it is also dead. In comparing the peach in "your palm" to "the weight of memory," the speaker seeks to show how both are sweet, even though the memory may be of something or someone dead. This is the lesson that these lines offer.

Lines 12–18:

Syntactically completing the sentence from the preceding stanza, these seven lines describe a moment between a boy and his father that readers understand is the speaker talking about an experience from his past. It is meant to illustrate the poet's comparison of sweetness to the weight of memory. The scene is sensuous, as father and son are showered with wet leaves from a windblown branch. The description of the father picking a leaf, "fallen like a kiss," from his son's cheek shows readers the father's love for the son. That the poet remembers this incident shows the son's love for his father.

Lines 19–29:

Continuing with the anecdote about the father and the son, the poet describes the boy now as "good," meaning that he meets his father's approval. That he "hugs" the bag of peaches shows that he values that approval. The varying lengths of these lines suggest the way that memory ebbs and flows.

Media Adaptations

- Lee appears with Bill Moyers in the Public Broadcasting System series *The Power of the Word*.

- W. W. Norton has a website from which you can listen to Lee read his poem "Persimmons": http://www.wwnorton.com/sounds/lee.ram

Readers again are enjoined to "See," this time the expression on the boy's face, as if in a close up. But the poet does not describe the expression. Instead readers are left to imagine it as the boy watches his father outpace him, and his own body grows weak from the peaches. This image encapsulates Lee's central metaphor, for it yokes together the sensuous (peaches) and the abstract (the weight of memory), the past and the present, and presence (the speaker's grief) and absence (his dead father). The fact that his father has "entrusted" the peaches to his son speaks to the son's burden of responsibility, the responsibility of carrying the memory of his father's own sweetness into the future.

Themes

Identity: Search for Self

In meditating on the idea of sweetness, which for Lee means tenderness plus grief, the speaker of "The Weight of Sweetness" examines his own emotional relationship to the past and to his father, hoping that such an examination will better help him integrate the memory of his father into his own life. The capacity to integrate the past, especially loss, into one's life successfully is often the mark of someone with a strong sense of identity.

Human beings often experience a sweep of emotions after losing a loved one, from denial to anger to grief and, finally, to acceptance; but after enough time has passed these emotions frequently settle into a kind of bittersweet nostalgia in which they mourn for the loved one yet simultaneously

Topics for Further Study

- Compare and contrast Lee's use of the peach as a metaphor in "The Weight of Sweetness" with his use of the persimmon in "Persimmons," also found in *Rose.*

- Write a short essay about someone you love whom you have lost, then write a poem about that same person. What did you leave out of the poem that you included in the essay? Which piece is more truthful to your emotions?

- How is the father character in "The Weight of Sweetness" mythical and how is he real? Write descriptions of one of your parents as a mythical figure and as a real person, then explain the difference between the two.

---

remember the happiness shared with that person. The inability to find peace with one's losses often marks a self still searching for its own identity, for a satisfactory way of being in the world, of understanding one's personal relationship to the past. In the first eleven lines of the poem readers see the speaker struggling to intellectually understand the meaning of sweetness and the "weight of memory." After attempting to list what sweetness contains by naming a range of other emotions and emotive words that go into it, Lee settles on the image of a peach, picked from its branch, as the symbol of sweetness, the thing that will metaphorically carry the weight of Lee's bittersweet grief. The peach is simultaneously alive (it retains its color, flavor, and texture) and dead (it is no longer a part of the tree), just as memory of a loved one contains death and life.

Whereas the speaker uses meditation in the first half of the poem to understand the meaning of his feelings, he uses memory in the second half of the poem. In a fairly straightforward story, the speaker recounts a particularly tender moment with his father. In this recounting the speaker tells a story about his past in which he has been given the burden of experiencing his father's tenderness, exemplified in his father's lifting the leaf from his face. The speaker lingers over this gesture just as the boy

labors under the weight of peaches, itself synonymous with the weight of sweetness. At the end of the story, which is also the end of the poem, it is unclear whether the speaker understands his own feelings any better, or how to make sense of the loss of his father any more. Readers are left with the sense that Lee will continue to tell stories about his father, and in that telling continue to grapple with how he fits into that story.

Love

"The Weight of Sweetness" explores the love between a father and his son. It is a love that continues after death, and one which needs to be understood in relation to death. Lee suggests in this poem that the person who dies lives on not only in the memory of those left behind but also in their everyday lives. Symbolically, and in effect, the son becomes the father whom the son is mourning. Death is part of a cycle from which life begins. This idea is illustrated in the poem's last stanza, when the father "entrusts" his son with a bag of peaches. The peaches themselves signify both sweetness and responsibility, the duty a son has to follow in the footsteps of his father, carrying on his life as it were, while also forging his own. It is the difficulty of doing both at once to which this poems speaks. The "weight of sweetness" is at once a burden, a duty, and a joy for the son.

Style

"The Weight of Sweetness" proceeds from abstract statements to concrete images. Abstractions are ideas, and are rooted in the intellect. Concrete images are things which can be seen: blue hair, spilled milk, etc. Lee begins his poems by making connections among abstractions such as wisdom, sadness, joy, gravity, and sweetness. He then uses concrete imagery such as peaches to illustrate these connections. The connections themselves are made by way of metaphor. Metaphors make comparisons between unlike things, underscoring their similarities. For example, "the weight of memory" is like the "weight / of peaches" in that they are both heavy, the former emotionally so, the latter physically. They are also both "sweet," one figuratively and one literally. Lee employs enjambment along with a mixture of short and long lines to visually suggest the ways in which memory and emotion interact, how one thing or idea reminds the speaker of something else, and so on. Enjambment is an-

Compare & Contrast

- **1945:** Sukarno, with Mohammad Hatta, proclaims independence from the Netherlands for Indonesia on August 17, two days after the Japanese surrender.

  1953: President Dwight Eisenhower draws the attention of U.S. politicians to Indonesia. In a speech to a governors' conference, he says that Washington should continue to foot the bill for the French war in Indochina because "if we lost all that, how would the free world hold the rich empire of Indonesia?"

  1958: A CIA pilot, Allen Lawrence Pope, is shot down over Sumatra while flying with an Indonesian right-wing rebel force.

  1959–1965: The United States pumps $64 million in military aid to the right-wing Indonesian generals.

  1963: Sukarno proclaims himself president for life.

  1975: The Indonesian military government invades East Timor—with the blessing of U.S. President Gerald Ford and Secretary of State Henry Kissinger—and tries to crush the liberation movement there.

  Today: Twenty years and 200,000 deaths later, the struggle in East Timor continues.

- **1967:** 45-year-old Suharto, an army commander and anti-communist, wrests power from President Sukarno, who is put under house arrest. Suharto promptly orders a purge of leftist sympathizers and communists, mostly ethnic Chinese. Some 500,000 Indonesians are killed.

  1998: President Suharto resigns after the collapse of Indonesia's economy and massive popular protests and riots.

---

other word for run-on lines. In the lines "See a peach bend / the branch and strain the stem until / it snaps," the sentence spills over onto succeeding lines until the thought is complete. The use of alternating long and short lines creates a kind of stop and start rhythm for the poem, causing readers to stop and try to see what Lee is describing. The run-on lines compel readers to continue reading, while the line length often slow readers down.

Historical Context

The image at the end of "The Weight of Sweetness" is the father moving away from the son, both metaphorically and literally, as the son is weighed down by a bag of peaches. Lee has always been obsessed with walking, the idea of steps and the image of feet. No doubt this stems from his family's own wanderings.

After escaping from Indonesia in 1959, the Lees journeyed through various parts of Asia, including Hong Kong, Macau, and Japan, before coming to the United States in 1964. In *The Winged Seed,* Lee describes the effect of all this travelling on his own feet and his father's: "By the time we got to America, my feet were tired. My father put down our suitcase, untied my shoes, and rubbed my feet, one at a time with such deep turns of his wrist. I heard the water in him through my soles. Since then I have listened for him in my steps, And have not found him…. My father's feet were ulcerous, as was his body, diseased. And water denied him days at a time, administered in a prison cell in Indonesia, ruined his kidneys, and changed the way he lay or sat or knelt or got up to walk the whole way down the stairs." His father's imprisonment in Indonesia was a result of Indonesian's dictator President Sukarno's campaign against ethnic Chinese. Richard Lee would speak to people as they went about their daily chores on the banks of the Solo River, and the Indonesian War Administration accused him of being a spy and charged him with sedition. Sukarno himself was ousted from power in 1967 by General Suharto, an anti-communist who assumed the Indonesian presidency in 1967 after helping to quell an uprising.

The late 1980s and early 1990s in America saw a renewed interest in men's issues, particularly issues involving fathers and sons. Poet Robert Bly helped fan this interest with articles and books such as *Iron John* (1992), which turns the Brothers Grimm's fairy tale of the wild man and his foster son into a metaphor for an archetypal initiation into manhood. Bly's central claim is that modern men suffer because their culture fails to connect boys with older male mentors. Another central text of the 1990s men's movement is Sam Keen's 1992 *A Fire in the Belly,* a guide of sorts for men helping them to analyze the myths, roles, and stereotypes of contemporary men and to conceptualize their own personal ideals of heroism and strength. In the 1970s a new male image had emerged: the sensitive male, a result, Bly claims, of the social and cultural ascendancy of women. But for society at large, at least in the West, the traditional male who confidently and often aggressively asserts his desires remains the model after which most men shape themselves. For men *and* women traditional male behavior remains the measuring stick for "true" masculinity. Bly blames the industrial revolution for disconnecting father from son, as fathers no longer initiate their sons into the "true nature" of manhood, either by cultural rights or by working alongside them. Boys are now raised by women, who cannot provide a model for male behavior. All men are victims in Bly's view, even (and especially) those who believe they are not.

Critical Overview

The collection in which "The Weight of Sweetness" appears, *Rose,* received New York University's Delmore Schwartz Memorial Poetry Award, and reviews of the collection were favorable. In the foreword poet Gerald Stern writes, "What characterizes Lee's poetry is a certain humility, a kind of cunning, a love of plain speech, a search for wisdom and understanding—but more like a sad than desperate search—a willingness to let the sublime enter his field of concentration and take over, a devotion to language, a belief in its holiness, a pursuit of certain Chinese ideas."

About Lee's father, the subject of "The Weight of Sweetness" and many of Lee's poems, Stern says "This is not a quaint and literary father-figure he is writing and thinking about. It is a real father, an

extraordinary and heroic figure.... What makes him work as a mythical figure in Lee's poems is that it is a real human being, however converted in Lee's mind, that Lee is searching for."

Writing in *Dictionary of Literary Biography,* Ruth Hsu says of *Rose* that "Lee's writing often displays this capacity to call up and interweave, always from the simplest objects, painful or happy memories, musings about his father or the past, and to make the association of object and profound yearnings seem natural." The "musings about his father" dominate the book. In fact, the father is the magnet around which all of Lee's other memories coalesce.

Reviewing the book for *Prairie Schooner,* Roger Mitchell writes: "I don't think Lee set out to write a book about the loss of his father ... but the dead father enters almost all of these poems like a half-bidden ghost. So close is the father that Lee asks at the end of 'Ash, Snow, or Moonlight,' 'Is this my father's house or mine?'" Mitchell identifies tenderness as the primary feature of Lee's poetry, saying, "Lee has committed himself to tenderness the way other poets have committed themselves to reality, the imagination, nature, or some other enveloping generalization."

Criticism

Chris Semansky

A widely published poet, fiction writer, and critic, Semansky teaches literature and writing at Portland Community College. In the following essay Semansky examines the idea of "sweetness" in Li-Young Lee's poem "The Weight of Sweetness."

Much of Lee's poetry concerns his father, a powerful, if enigmatic, presence in Lee's life. A physician, founder of an Indonesian university, and Presbyterian minister, Richard K. Y. Lee died in 1980, and Lee's two poetry collections, *Rose* (1986) and *The City in Which I Love You,* (1990) and his prose memoir, *The Winged Seed* (1995), can be read both as elegies for his father and ongoing attempts to fully integrate his father into the story of his life. Lee's poem from *Rose,* "The Weight of Sweetness," captures the tone of the son's complex feelings about his father's loss. Into the idea of sweetness, Lee injects the bittersweetness of nostalgia. His poem is a recipe for the lingering grief he still feels.

Lee begins the poem with a rather banal statement: "No easy thing to bear, the weight of sweetness." The strangeness in this statement is the way in which sweetness, which could mean either tenderness or a kind of taste, is described in terms of its weight. In the next lines, however, readers learn that Lee is being metaphoric:

> Song, wisdom, sadness, joy: sweetness
> equals three of any of these gravities.

Sweetness, for Lee, is an emotionally complex and powerful idea, as it contains a range of ingredients we don't normally think about when we think about sweetness. Lee's continued description of these abstract ingredients in terms of weight, or gravity, is difficult, but possible to comprehend. Song, conventionally associated with celebration, can have gravity if it is a lament or dirge. The weight of wisdom might be the responsibility to act or that such knowledge brings with it. Sadness is the easiest of these terms to understand in terms of weight, as feelings of sadness are often associated with slowness and heaviness. How is joy a gravity, though? This last term is confusing, but then the speaker does say that "sweetness / equals [only] three of any of these gravities."

These first lines are reflective. They ask readers to think, rather than feel, to participate in ruminating about abstractions with the writer. The next stanza develops this thinking using imagery:

> See a peach bend
> the branch and strain the stem until
> it snaps.
> Hold the peach, try the weight, sweetness
> and death so round and snug
> in your palm.
> And, so, there is
> the weight of memory:

The images are a tool for the speaker, allowing him to *show* readers his thoughts rather than tell them. Showing rather than telling has more emotional impact because images are more connected to our bodies than are abstract ideas. When readers can see, feel, or hear something being described, their emotions are set to work and they become more involved with the text. The voice is instructive, as if providing directions on the process of making something. A ripe peach falling from its branch is like "the weight of memory." Both are sweet, both are heavy. The speaker encourages readers to "try the weight" just as recipe directions might encourage one to "taste" or "sample." The "your" here, however, is as much another part of the speaker, an imagined self, as it is the reader. This is made more apparent in the next stanza when the speaker provides an illustration of "the weight of memory" in terms of an anecdote.

> *Sweetness, for Lee, is an emotionally complex and powerful idea, as it contains a range of ingredients we don't normally think about when we think about sweetness."*

> Windblown, a rain-soaked
> bough shakes, showering
> the man and the boy.
> They shiver in delight,
> and the father lifts from his son's cheek
> one green leaf
> fallen like a kiss.

Memories are often stirred by the senses. Smells, taste, touch, sounds, sights often unlock memories of events buried deep in our minds. This poem has a similar trajectory, as it moves from the image, the sensation of holding a peach and imagining its sweetness, to how it, though ripe, is off the branch and dead. In this case, the memory itself is also a sensual one. This detail is important for the poem because the line between the past and the present is so fluid, past events evoking the present just as the present evokes the past. The oscillation between the two creates a kind of static moment, embodied in an image, which stands for the weight of sweetness itself. Lee finishes his anecdote:

> The good boy lugs a bag of peaches
> his father has entrusted
> to him.
> Now he follows
> his father, who carries a bagful in each arm.
> See the look on the boy's face
> as his father moves
> farther and farther ahead, while his own steps
> flag, and his arms grow weak, as he labors
> under the weight
> of peaches.

The transmission of peaches from father to son underscores the bond between the two. If we understand peaches as a symbolic image for sweetness, and sweetness as embodying song, wisdom, sadness, and joy, we can read the gesture as one of the father passing on instructions for how to live, how to be in the world, to his son, who eagerly accepts them. Readers are instructed once again to

What Do I Read Next?

- Lee's collection *Rose,* published in 1986, includes "The Weight of Sweetness." These poems, many of which explore the poet's relationship to his father, are full of nostalgia and tenderness. Of particular interest are the poems "Eating Alone," "Persimmons," and "Always a Rose."

- In his interview with Tod Marshall in the *Kenyon Review*'s Winter 2000 issue, Lee discusses his family background and the challenges he faced learning English.

"See," meaning to imagine the look on the face of a boy who is scurrying, unsuccessfully, to catch up to his father. We can imagine the look of awe and reverence on the boy's face as his father recedes into the distance. In this case the father is moving into the future, towards death, as the boy is weighed down by all he has been given by his father.

In the foreword to *Rose,* Gerald Stern argues that what makes Lee's father work as a mythical figure in his poems is that he is also a flesh-and-blood human being. "If the father does become mythical," Stern says, "it is partly because of his dramatic, even tragic, life, and it is partly because Lee touches powerful emotional psychic layers in his search." But Lee himself admits to an impulse towards the mythic when he composes. In an interview with Tod Marshall, Lee says this about poetry: "Poetry comes out of a need to somehow—in language—connect with universe mind, and somehow when I read poetry—and maybe all poetry is quest, a poetry of longing—when I read poetry, I feel I'm in the presence of universe mind; that is, a mind I would describe as a 360-degree seeing; it is manifold in consciousness, so that a line of poetry says one thing, but it also says many other things. That manifold quality of intention and consciousness: that feels to me like universe. So that's why I read poetry, and that's why I write it, to hear that voice, which is the voice of the universe."

This "voice of the universe," then, as heard in "The Weight of Sweetness," is a voice which urges readers to experience loss not merely as the diminution of their own world but as a phenomenon that expands their world as well, in the song that comes from celebrating the dead, the wisdom that comes from knowing how to sing that song, and the sadness that comes when the song ends, which it always does. Lee's poem about his father is universal because everyone has experienced loss and everyone has memories of that loss. Indeed loss, for Lee, is at the center of the universe. In an interview with Tod Marshall, Lee says, asserting that the invisible should be more important to poets than the visible: "I can't help but live with this constant feeling, this knowledge, that everything we're seeing is fading away. So where is ground? What is materiality? I can't assume the material world." Readers can "see" the fading image of the father walking ahead of the son in "The Weight of Sweetness" in these words. Lee considers the *mind* the ground upon which all humans walk. And for Lee, whose poems are laced with images of feet and walking, walking implies time. But it is an Eastern concept of time for Lee, one which turns the past and the future on their respective heads. About time, Lee states in the interview: "in the West we usually think of the future as lying ahead of us and we walk forward into it, leaving the past behind. But it's probably the other way around for an eastern mind. The Chinese word for the day after tomorrow is *hou,* meaning behind, and the word denoting the day before yesterday is actually *chien,* meaning in front of. So, you see … that to a Chinese mind, tomorrow, the future, is behind me, while the past lies in front of me. Therefore, we go backing up into the future, into the unknown, the what's-about-to-be, and everything that lies before our eyes is past, over already." The final image of "The Weight of Sweetness" illustrates this idea. For the speaker, the future is also behind him, in the image of his father, whom he runs toward, even as his father moves ahead into death.

Source: Chris Semansky, in an essay for *Poetry for Students,* Gale Group, 2001.

Sharon Kraus

Kraus's book of poems, Generation, *was published by Alice James Books in 1997; individual poems have appeared in* The Georgia Review, Tri-Quarterly, *and elsewhere. She teaches creative writing, literature, and other courses at Queens College, CUNY (Flushing, NY). In this essay, Kraus suggests that "The Weight of Sweetness" relies on a tone of restraint and unusual narrative development to render emotional complexity.*

"The Weight of Sweetness" is from Lee's *Rose,* an elegaic book largely about an Asian-American son's relationship with his father and loss of that father. The power of "The Weight of Sweetness" lies in its formal grace: the poem's control of pacing and careful development allow its delicate treatment of a father-son relationship to emerge fully and without sentimentality. The poet structures this poem, surprisingly, by moving from the abstract to the concrete—"surprisingly" because so many contemporary poems move the way a fable does, from the concrete narrative or image to the abstract meaning that can be extracted from it.

"No easy thing to bear, the weight of sweetness," is an unexpected and provocative thought, because we tend to think of things in dichotomies, such as pleasure / pain or joy / sadness. Sweetness, surely, is relief from the bitter pains of life. It should surely be light to carry; it should be one of the rewards of the great American Dream. But, in "The Weight of Sweetness," Lee invites us into complexity and to see from an unexpected perspective where even the sweetness of life is a weight that must be carried. Sweetness here has its own *gravitas,* and as an active ingredient in the well-lived life, it conveys a solemnity we more commonly associate with the archetypal themes of poets— love, death, pain, renewal, or lack of renewal. Oddly enough, we can more easily accept that pain should have a role in life's fullness, since pain is a challenge we have to rise to, is the shock that can sometimes create wisdom or effect change. And the "sweetness" of the poem is a weighty burden—a peach, a sack of peaches, a fallen leaf that must be "lift[ed]" as though it were massive, a tender gesture that might seem fleeting but accrues great significance for the poet. Once Lee says that sweetness too, is heavy, ponderous, and a burden to carry, it seems obvious, and we believe we knew it all along.

Lee's poem is powerful in part because it knits these philosophical considerations with personal narrative. The first turn of the poem is simple and direct: from the abstraction, sweetness, comes the illustration, the peach. Indeed, throughout *Rose,* Lee likes to illustrate his thoughts with simple objects of conventional beauty—the persimmon, blossoms, irises, hair. His twist is to show the conventional image of beauty revealing an unconventional thought process. The peach, replete with sweetness, snaps the stem, causing fracture, separation, pain, bruising: "Hold ... / death so round and snug / in your palm." How, Lee suggests, could sweetness be any less than the other mysteries of

> *Lee's poem is powerful in part because it knits these philosophical considerations with personal narrative. The first turn of the poem is simple and direct: from the abstraction, sweetness, comes the illustration, the peach.*

life, double-edged, as destructive and dangerous as it is pleasurable?

Indeed, when the poem then turns from peaches in general ("See a peach bend") to a specific memory involving peaches (the poet-speaker and his father) we see that sweetness and pain are inextricable and require each other. Some biographical information about the poet and his father may help illuminate the relationship that the poem allows us to glimpse. Lee's father was, for a time, personal physician to Mao Tse-tung; when in Indonesia, where Lee was born, he taught medicine, Shakespeare, and philosophy at the university level until jailed by then-President Sukarno for his "Western leanings." The poet views his father as "a man of huge intellectual and artistic talents." He was, as the poet reports, a kind man and a gentle one, but perhaps someone hard to emulate, someone so kind the need to please him was so much stronger. He also was strict and stern, and demanded that his children succeed by the terms he set for them: that they learn seven languages, for example. Li-Young Lee has said, in an interview with the journalist Bill Moyers, he feels that "Nothing I do is going to be good enough for him." And yet, the poet confesses, he still finds himself trying to please the father.

Thus, the gesture that the father in the poem makes, of taking the errant peach leaf from the son's cheek, is tender and protective, yet has an underside that the poem's last stanza explores. Notice that Lee does not have the father or the son speak, nor does he describe a facial expression, and it is by this, perhaps, that he maintains a personal yet impersonal touch. As the poem prepares for the final turn, the boy is "the good boy": the article "the" implies that someone (possibly the father, possibly the wistful speaker) has referred to him this way. And we are given the poem's key word: "entrusted." The son in the poem holds the weight of the peaches that the father has entrusted to him—the legacy a child holds which will one day be all that exists of the parent. The pain of the sweetness of the relationship, like the pain of the peach severed from the branch, is that the father will inevitably recede from this son, do what the son will. Thus the poem points to mortality. It also may be pointing to an individual relationship where the son feels he will never live up to the father's high expectations of him: "his own steps / flag, and his arms grow weak." Does the father recede because he is more capable (in the poem, he carries twice the burden of peaches that the speaker carries)—characterized by Lee as having "huge … talents" and therefore admired by the poet? Or does he recede because time pulls him away, as it simultaneously holds fast to the son, dragging at his feet and keeping him, emotionally, fixed in this scene?

The poem leaves these questions unresolved; perhaps they are not resolvable for the poet, as they are not resolvable for many of us. We are now invited to "See the look on the boy's face," but of course the invitation is really to invent the disappointment, despair, longing, whatever that look will be for us, and so the poet cleverly invites us in to the place of the son, deprived of the thing most longed for, lost, and at the same time still possessed.

Without resorting to clichés, Lee places sweetness—perhaps he means human joy—in the cycle of life. If the peach is to come into existence and be sweet, it must also fall from the bough and create rupture and pain. The very act of loving parents means accepting the inevitable pain of their loss when they die. The act of loving a parent may also entail acknowledging one's own differences from that parent, and setting them aside. The poet-critic Roger Mitchell has said that Lee's poems in *Rose* are characterized by their "commit[ment] to tenderness"; Mitchell suggests that the poems are narrowed in scope by the poet's will to be tender. However, a close reading of "The Weight of Sweetness" suggests, rather, the largeness of Lee's scope. Here is a poet who deftly and delicately shows us how fleeting and even provisional tenderness is. America has given us many descriptions of the dysfunctional family, as is only right as we work to examine, assess, and heal our wounds. Lee reminds us that sweet relationships deserve as close attention.

Source: Sharon Kraus, in an essay for *Poetry for Students,* Gale Group, 2001.

Katrinka Moore

Moore teaches writing at Long Island University in Brooklyn, New York, and is a poet whose work appears in anthologies and literary journals. In this essay, she examines Lee's use of imagery and narrative as he explores memory in "The Weight of Sweetness."

"The Weight of Sweetness" is a poem about a son and his father. It is a poem about a particular memory, and also the idea of memory. The principal words are sent out and then return, bringing new meaning with them—sweetness, weight, peaches, father and son. The peaches symbolize sweetness—the taste of the fruit and the semi-sweet memory the speaker has of picking peaches with his father. Weight is seriousness, gravity, a force of attraction. There is the weight of memory itself, the specific memory of the father, and the weight of the father himself—all seen in a peach:

> Hold the peach, try the weight, sweetness
> and death so round and snug
> in your palm.

It seems that the speaker, as a grown man, picks a peach and holds it in his hand, which reminds him of an outing he took with his father when he was a child. Holding the peach, he remembers that day, but he also feels the weight of the peach on his palm, as if he is weighing the fruit to see how heavy it is. To weigh also means to evaluate, to consider, to measure. He may be weighing the memory along with the peach. Is it good? Is it bad? It is more complicated than either good or bad: "No easy thing to bear, the weight of sweetness."

What is sweetness, according to Lee in this poem? Choose three from this list: "Song, wisdom, sadness, joy." These are the elements that make memory sweet, but it is not an unalloyed sweetness. There is sadness in each grouping, whether with song, wisdom, or joy. Take away sadness and there is still wisdom, which must include sadness in this context. What wisdom does the speaker have? He knows that the peach represents not only something sweet, but death. He has, after all, just pulled the peach from its stem.

The speaker pulls the peach from its stem, and knows that he has grown up and left his father. But what he remembers is his father leaving him behind. They are picking peaches, and the father gives the son a bag of peaches to carry home. The "father has entrusted" the bag to the boy; it seems a sacred trust to be allowed to carry the sweet fruit. The father, being powerful, "carries a bagful in each arm." Even with only one bag, the boy is unable to keep up. He gets tired, "his arms grow weak," and he cannot live up to his father's expectations. Meanwhile, the father, without looking back, "moves / faster and farther ahead." When the speaker says that the child "labors / under the weight / of peaches," he refers not only to the heaviness of the bag but to the weight of wanting to please his father, who is both loving and demanding.

The speaker pulls the peach from its stem, and remembers a tender moment with his father. They are picking peaches together, and they "shiver with delight" in the wind, the tree leaves shaking rain drops onto them. Father and son love each other; the "father lifts from his son's cheek / one green leaf / fallen like a kiss." They are together, just the two of them, fulfilling a task for the family.

The speaker pulls a peach from its stem and holds it, weighing its meaning. His father has died and left him behind. The memories are sweet, containing both sadness and joy, wisdom and song.

Lee directs the image of peaches to lead to both the memory and its meaning. As the critic Zhou Xiaojing writes in *Melus Review,* the poet often uses a technique in which he "relies on a central image as the organizing principle for both the subject matter and structure of the poem." In "The Weight of Sweetness," this central image is the peach, which guides the speaker to not only remember the event but to consider its meaning. Xiaojing goes on to discuss Lee's strategy of incorporating "narrative as the material for meditation … and the shifting point of departure for transition or development within the poem." Thus, the peach inspires the narrative of the childhood memory, which inspires the speaker's meditation on his father and on the idea of memory, with its measure of sweetness and sadness. The images and the narrative are woven together throughout the poem, though the poet does not bring the reader to a conclusion or solution. The remembered story has no definite ending; it is primarily a memory of a feeling.

Lee is certainly an American poet. The discussion of self and family and the free verse structure are common in contemporary American poetry. However, like many Americans, Lee possesses a bi-cultural view of living in the world. He gained knowledge of his Chinese heritage from his family, though he has lived most of his life in the United States. His father, who was a doctor and a scholar, taught him Chinese classical poems and

> *He thinks of his father, and he thinks of the act of memory. Both thoughts carry the burden of sadness as well as the pleasure of remembering something happy."*

read to him from the Bible. It would be a mistake to identify Lee with only one side of his background, as Xiaojing explains, since it is a "misconception that a pure and fixed Chinese culture has been inherited and maintained by Chinese immigrants and their descendants in America." However, as poet and teacher Gerald Stern writes in the foreword to *Rose,* in which "Weight of Sweetness" appears, Lee's poetry is characterized by "a pursuit of certain Chinese ideas, or Chinese memories, without any self-conscious ethnocentricity."

Lee draws on his Chinese lineage in "Weight of Sweetness," whether deliberately or not. For example, his images are often complementary, showing two sides of the same characteristic, rather than the traditional Western oppositional approach. In his description of the peach—"sweetness / and death so round and snug / in your palm"—he could be explaining the nature of Yin and Yang, a Chinese philosophical idea. The term Yin originally meant the northern, or shaded, slope of a mountain; Yang referred to the sunny southern slope. Yin and Yang correspond to soft and hard, negative and positive, passive and active, but they are considered complementary parts of a whole, not opposites. Thus, when Lee views the peach as both "sweetness and death," he is not being contradictory but expressing a view of the balance of nature that comes from ancient Chinese thought.

This view extends throughout the poem. The memory brings both joy and sadness; the poem is both song, indicating lightheartedness, and something of gravity, or seriousness. Likewise, the relationship of the father and son is neither purely amicable nor adversarial. It has given the son both delight and sorrow, which are complementary aspects of love. In the Yin and Yang of the speaker's memory of his father, both happiness and sadness exist in harmony.

In the introduction of *Li Po and Tu Fu,* a collection of poems by two eighth-century Chinese poets, Arthur Cooper discusses aspects of Yin and Yang as they relate to poetry. Any healthy living being (and this includes rocks, earth, and sky as well as living things) "is made up of both elements harmoniously balanced, even though one of them may in some way be in the lead." It does not follow, therefore, that the Yin and Yang must be of equal amounts to create harmony in a person or thing. Some poets are more identified with Yin; these tend to write more intuitively, less directly. Yang-identified poets, on the other hand, are considered more pro-active and intellectual. While these divisions are speculative only, Lee seems likely to be classified with the Yin poets, because of his indirect way of expressing his purpose. Naturally, though, even a Yin poet contains Yang as well.

Stephen Mitchell, in his translation of the *Tao te Ching,* a fifth-century B.C. book of Chinese philosophy, explains that the contradictions that appear in the uniting of Yin and Yang are "paradoxical on the surface only." A follower of the philosophy of *Tao te Ching,* or Tao, would see the power in "non-doing" as opposed to doing something. That is, he or she would not feel the necessity of reconciling the surface differences of what may appear to be a contradictory situation. Thus Lee, in writing about his memory of his father, accepts both the "delight" and the regret that remembering entails.

Lee weaves his imagery and narrative together with his intuitive understanding based on Chinese thought. His approach makes it possible for him to tell a story without an ending, and to meditate on the subject and object of memory at the same time. He thinks of his father, and he thinks of the act of memory. Both thoughts carry the burden of sadness as well as the pleasure of remembering something happy. In Lee's world view, these contrasting images are not impossible to reconcile, but are the complex, essential—and beautiful—elements of existence.

Source: Katrinka Moore, in an essay for *Poetry for Students,* Gale Group, 2001.

Sources

Cooper, Arthur, *Li Po and Tu Fu,* Penguin Books, 1973.

Hsu, Ruth Y., and Li-Young Lee, *Dictionary of Literary Biography,* Volume 165: *American Poets since World War II,* fourth series, edited by Joseph Conte, Gale, 1996, pp. 139–46.

Lee, Li-Young, *The City in Which I Love You,* BOA Editions, 1990.

———, *Rose,* BOA Editions, 1986.

———, *The Winged Seed: A Remembrance,* Simon & Schuster, 1995.

Lo, Benjamin Pang Jeng, et al., *The Essence of T'ai Chi Ch'uan, The Literary Tradition,* North Atlantic Books, 1979.

Marshall, Tod, "To Witness the Invisible: An Interview with Li-Young Lee," in *Kenyon Review,* Winter, 2000, pp. 129–48.

Mitchell, Roger, Review of *Rose,* in *Prairie Schooner,* No. 63, Fall, 1989, pp. 129–39.

Mitchell, Stephen, *A New English Version of Tao Te Ching,* HarperPerennial, 1991.

Moyers, Bill, "Interview with Li-Young Lee," in *The Language of Life: A Festival of Poets,* Doubleday, 1995, pp. 257–69.

Neff, David, "Remembering the Man Who Forgot Nothing," in *Christianity Today,* September, 1988, p. 63.

Pinsker, Sanford, Review of *Rose,* in *Literary Review,* Winter, 1989, pp. 256–62.

Stern, Gerald, "Foreword" to *Rose,* by Li-Young Lee, BOA Editions, 1986.

Wong, Sau-Ling Cynthia, *Reading Asian-American Literature: From Necessity to Extravagance,* Princeton University Press, 1993.

Xiaojing, Zhou, "Inheritance and Invention in Li-Young Lee's Poetry," in *MELUS,* Spring, 1996, p. 113.

For Further Reading

Baumli, Francis, ed., *Men Freeing Men: Exploding the Myth of the Traditional Male,* New Atlantis Press, 1991.

This collection of short essays explores a variety of men's social roles, paying particular attention to how men negotiate gendered behavior and social expectations of maleness.

Lee, Li-Young, *The Winged Seed: A Remembrance,* Simon & Schuster, 1995.

Part prose poem, part memoir, *The Winged Seed* presents memories of Lee's family in Indonesia in a dreamy, poetic prose. Readers feels as if they're seeing Lee's descriptions as if through gauze.

Miller, Matt, "Poetry: Asian-American Li-Young Lee Lights Up His Family's Murky Past," in *Far Eastern Economic Review,* May 30, 1996. pp. 34–37.

American poet Li-Young Lee's work addresses his family's past and the challenges he faced in learning English. He was born in Indonesia, but his family was forced to leave because of a crackdown on ethnic Chinese. He is uncertain about the history of his father and his family, and this uncertainty colors his work.

Glossary of Literary Terms

A

Abstract: Used as a noun, the term refers to a short summary or outline of a longer work. As an adjective applied to writing or literary works, abstract refers to words or phrases that name things not knowable through the five senses.

Accent: The emphasis or stress placed on a syllable in poetry. Traditional poetry commonly uses patterns of accented and unaccented syllables (known as feet) that create distinct rhythms. Much modern poetry uses less formal arrangements that create a sense of freedom and spontaneity.

Aestheticism: A literary and artistic movement of the nineteenth century. Followers of the movement believed that art should not be mixed with social, political, or moral teaching. The statement "art for art's sake" is a good summary of aestheticism. The movement had its roots in France, but it gained widespread importance in England in the last half of the nineteenth century, where it helped change the Victorian practice of including moral lessons in literature.

Affective Fallacy: An error in judging the merits or faults of a work of literature. The "error" results from stressing the importance of the work's effect upon the reader—that is, how it makes a reader "feel" emotionally, what it does as a literary work—instead of stressing its inner qualities as a created object, or what it "is."

Age of Johnson: The period in English literature between 1750 and 1798, named after the most

prominent literary figure of the age, Samuel Johnson. Works written during this time are noted for their emphasis on "sensibility," or emotional quality. These works formed a transition between the rational works of the Age of Reason, or Neoclassical period, and the emphasis on individual feelings and responses of the Romantic period.

Age of Reason: See *Neoclassicism*

Age of Sensibility: See *Age of Johnson*

Agrarians: A group of Southern American writers of the 1930s and 1940s who fostered an economic and cultural program for the South based on agriculture, in opposition to the industrial society of the North. The term can refer to any group that promotes the value of farm life and agricultural society.

Alexandrine Meter: See *Meter*

Allegory: A narrative technique in which characters representing things or abstract ideas are used to convey a message or teach a lesson. Allegory is typically used to teach moral, ethical, or religious lessons but is sometimes used for satiric or political purposes.

Alliteration: A poetic device where the first consonant sounds or any vowel sounds in words or syllables are repeated.

Allusion: A reference to a familiar literary or historical person or event, used to make an idea more easily understood.

Amerind Literature: The writing and oral traditions of Native Americans. Native American literature was originally passed on by word of mouth, so it consisted largely of stories and events that were easily memorized. Amerind prose is often rhythmic like poetry because it was recited to the beat of a ceremonial drum.

Analogy: A comparison of two things made to explain something unfamiliar through its similarities to something familiar, or to prove one point based on the acceptedness of another. Similes and metaphors are types of analogies.

Anapest: See *Foot*

Angry Young Men: A group of British writers of the 1950s whose work expressed bitterness and disillusionment with society. Common to their work is an antihero who rebels against a corrupt social order and strives for personal integrity.

Anthropomorphism: The presentation of animals or objects in human shape or with human characteristics. The term is derived from the Greek word for "human form."

Antimasque: See *Masque*

Antithesis: The antithesis of something is its direct opposite. In literature, the use of antithesis as a figure of speech results in two statements that show a contrast through the balancing of two opposite ideas. Technically, it is the second portion of the statement that is defined as the "antithesis"; the first portion is the "thesis."

Apocrypha: Writings tentatively attributed to an author but not proven or universally accepted to be their works. The term was originally applied to certain books of the Bible that were not considered inspired and so were not included in the "sacred canon."

Apollonian and Dionysian: The two impulses believed to guide authors of dramatic tragedy. The Apollonian impulse is named after Apollo, the Greek god of light and beauty and the symbol of intellectual order. The Dionysian impulse is named after Dionysus, the Greek god of wine and the symbol of the unrestrained forces of nature. The Apollonian impulse is to create a rational, harmonious world, while the Dionysian is to express the irrational forces of personality.

Apostrophe: A statement, question, or request addressed to an inanimate object or concept or to a nonexistent or absent person.

Archetype: The word archetype is commonly used to describe an original pattern or model from which all other things of the same kind are made. This term was introduced to literary criticism from the psychology of Carl Jung. It expresses Jung's theory that behind every person's "unconscious," or repressed memories of the past, lies the "collective unconscious" of the human race: memories of the countless typical experiences of our ancestors. These memories are said to prompt illogical associations that trigger powerful emotions in the reader. Often, the emotional process is primitive, even primordial. Archetypes are the literary images that grow out of the "collective unconscious." They appear in literature as incidents and plots that repeat basic patterns of life. They may also appear as stereotyped characters.

Argument: The argument of a work is the author's subject matter or principal idea.

Art for Art's Sake: See *Aestheticism*

Assonance: The repetition of similar vowel sounds in poetry.

Audience: The people for whom a piece of literature is written. Authors usually write with a certain audience in mind, for example, children, members of a religious or ethnic group, or colleagues in a professional field. The term "audience" also applies to the people who gather to see or hear any performance, including plays, poetry readings, speeches, and concerts.

Automatic Writing: Writing carried out without a preconceived plan in an effort to capture every random thought. Authors who engage in automatic writing typically do not revise their work, preferring instead to preserve the revealed truth and beauty of spontaneous expression.

Avant-garde: A French term meaning "vanguard." It is used in literary criticism to describe new writing that rejects traditional approaches to literature in favor of innovations in style or content.

B

Ballad: A short poem that tells a simple story and has a repeated refrain. Ballads were originally intended to be sung. Early ballads, known as folk ballads, were passed down through generations, so their authors are often unknown. Later ballads composed by known authors are called literary ballads.

Baroque: A term used in literary criticism to describe literature that is complex or ornate in style or diction. Baroque works typically express tension, anxiety, and violent emotion. The term "Baroque Age" designates a period in Western European literature beginning in the late sixteenth century and ending about one hundred years later.

Works of this period often mirror the qualities of works more generally associated with the label "baroque" and sometimes feature elaborate conceits.

Baroque Age: See *Baroque*

Baroque Period: See *Baroque*

Beat Generation: See *Beat Movement*

Beat Movement: A period featuring a group of American poets and novelists of the 1950s and 1960s—including Jack Kerouac, Allen Ginsberg, Gregory Corso, William S. Burroughs, and Lawrence Ferlinghetti—who rejected established social and literary values. Using such techniques as stream-of-consciousness writing and jazz-influenced free verse and focusing on unusual or abnormal states of mind—generated by religious ecstasy or the use of drugs—the Beat writers aimed to create works that were unconventional in both form and subject matter.

Beat Poets: See *Beat Movement*

Beats, The: See *Beat Movement*

Belles-lettres: A French term meaning "fine letters" or "beautiful writing." It is often used as a synonym for literature, typically referring to imaginative and artistic rather than scientific or expository writing. Current usage sometimes restricts the meaning to light or humorous writing and appreciative essays about literature.

Black Aesthetic Movement: A period of artistic and literary development among African Americans in the 1960s and early 1970s. This was the first major African American artistic movement since the Harlem Renaissance and was closely paralleled by the civil rights and black power movements. The black aesthetic writers attempted to produce works of art that would be meaningful to the black masses. Key figures in black aesthetics included one of its founders, poet and playwright Amiri Baraka, formerly known as LeRoi Jones; poet and essayist Haki R. Madhubuti, formerly Don L. Lee; poet and playwright Sonia Sanchez; and dramatist Ed Bullins.

Black Arts Movement: See *Black Aesthetic Movement*

Black Comedy: See *Black Humor*

Black Humor: Writing that places grotesque elements side by side with humorous ones in an attempt to shock the reader, forcing him or her to laugh at the horrifying reality of a disordered world.

Black Mountain School: Black Mountain College and three of its instructors—Robert Creeley, Robert Duncan, and Charles Olson—were all influential in projective verse. Today poets working in projective verse are referred to as members of the Black Mountain school.

Blank Verse: Loosely, any unrhymed poetry, but more generally, unrhymed iambic pentameter verse (composed of lines of five two-syllable feet with the first syllable accented, the second unaccented). Blank verse has been used by poets since the Renaissance for its flexibility and its graceful, dignified tone.

Bloomsbury Group: A group of English writers, artists, and intellectuals who held informal artistic and philosophical discussions in Bloomsbury, a district of London, from around 1907 to the early 1930s. The Bloomsbury Group held no uniform philosophical beliefs but did commonly express an aversion to moral prudery and a desire for greater social tolerance.

Bon Mot: A French term meaning "good word." A *bon mot* is a witty remark or clever observation.

Breath Verse: See *Projective Verse*

Burlesque: Any literary work that uses exaggeration to make its subject appear ridiculous, either by treating a trivial subject with profound seriousness or by treating a dignified subject frivolously. The word "burlesque" may also be used as an adjective, as in "burlesque show," to mean "striptease act."

C

Cadence: The natural rhythm of language caused by the alternation of accented and unaccented syllables. Much modern poetry—notably free verse—deliberately manipulates cadence to create complex rhythmic effects.

Caesura: A pause in a line of poetry, usually occurring near the middle. It typically corresponds to a break in the natural rhythm or sense of the line but is sometimes shifted to create special meanings or rhythmic effects.

Canzone: A short Italian or Provencal lyric poem, commonly about love and often set to music. The *canzone* has no set form but typically contains five or six stanzas made up of seven to twenty lines of eleven syllables each. A shorter, five- to ten-line "envoy," or concluding stanza, completes the poem.

Carpe Diem: A Latin term meaning "seize the day." This is a traditional theme of poetry, especially lyrics. A *carpe diem* poem advises the reader or the person it addresses to live for today and enjoy the pleasures of the moment.

Catharsis: The release or purging of unwanted emotions—specifically fear and pity—brought about by exposure to art. The term was first used by the Greek philosopher Aristotle in his *Poetics* to refer to the desired effect of tragedy on spectators.

Celtic Renaissance: A period of Irish literary and cultural history at the end of the nineteenth century. Followers of the movement aimed to create a romantic vision of Celtic myth and legend. The most significant works of the Celtic Renaissance typically present a dreamy, unreal world, usually in reaction against the reality of contemporary problems.

Celtic Twilight: See *Celtic Renaissance*

Character: Broadly speaking, a person in a literary work. The actions of characters are what constitute the plot of a story, novel, or poem. There are numerous types of characters, ranging from simple, stereotypical figures to intricate, multifaceted ones. In the techniques of anthropomorphism and personification, animals—and even places or things—can assume aspects of character. "Characterization" is the process by which an author creates vivid, believable characters in a work of art. This may be done in a variety of ways, including (1) direct description of the character by the narrator; (2) the direct presentation of the speech, thoughts, or actions of the character; and (3) the responses of other characters to the character. The term "character" also refers to a form originated by the ancient Greek writer Theophrastus that later became popular in the seventeenth and eighteenth centuries. It is a short essay or sketch of a person who prominently displays a specific attribute or quality, such as miserliness or ambition.

Characterization: See *Character*

Classical: In its strictest definition in literary criticism, classicism refers to works of ancient Greek or Roman literature. The term may also be used to describe a literary work of recognized importance (a "classic") from any time period or literature that exhibits the traits of classicism.

Classicism: A term used in literary criticism to describe critical doctrines that have their roots in ancient Greek and Roman literature, philosophy, and art. Works associated with classicism typically exhibit restraint on the part of the author, unity of design and purpose, clarity, simplicity, logical organization, and respect for tradition.

Colloquialism: A word, phrase, or form of pronunciation that is acceptable in casual conversation but not in formal, written communication. It is considered more acceptable than slang.

Complaint: A lyric poem, popular in the Renaissance, in which the speaker expresses sorrow about his or her condition. Typically, the speaker's sadness is caused by an unresponsive lover, but some complaints cite other sources of unhappiness, such as poverty or fate.

Conceit: A clever and fanciful metaphor, usually expressed through elaborate and extended comparison, that presents a striking parallel between two seemingly dissimilar things—for example, elaborately comparing a beautiful woman to an object like a garden or the sun. The conceit was a popular device throughout the Elizabethan Age and Baroque Age and was the principal technique of the seventeenth-century English metaphysical poets. This usage of the word conceit is unrelated to the best-known definition of conceit as an arrogant attitude or behavior.

Concrete: Concrete is the opposite of abstract, and refers to a thing that actually exists or a description that allows the reader to experience an object or concept with the senses.

Concrete Poetry: Poetry in which visual elements play a large part in the poetic effect. Punctuation marks, letters, or words are arranged on a page to form a visual design: a cross, for example, or a bumblebee.

Confessional Poetry: A form of poetry in which the poet reveals very personal, intimate, sometimes shocking information about himself or herself.

Connotation: The impression that a word gives beyond its defined meaning. Connotations may be universally understood or may be significant only to a certain group.

Consonance: Consonance occurs in poetry when words appearing at the ends of two or more verses have similar final consonant sounds but have final vowel sounds that differ, as with "stuff" and "off."

Convention: Any widely accepted literary device, style, or form.

Corrido: A Mexican ballad.

Couplet: Two lines of poetry with the same rhyme and meter, often expressing a complete and self-contained thought.

Criticism: The systematic study and evaluation of literary works, usually based on a specific method or set of principles. An important part of literary studies since ancient times, the practice of criticism has given rise to numerous theories, methods, and "schools," sometimes producing conflicting, even contradictory, interpretations of literature in general as well as of individual works. Even such basic issues as what constitutes a poem or a novel have been the subject of much criticism over the centuries.

D

Dactyl: See *Foot*

Dadaism: A protest movement in art and literature founded by Tristan Tzara in 1916. Followers of the movement expressed their outrage at the destruction brought about by World War I by revolting against numerous forms of social convention. The Dadaists presented works marked by calculated madness and flamboyant nonsense. They stressed total freedom of expression, commonly through primitive displays of emotion and illogical, often senseless, poetry. The movement ended shortly after the war, when it was replaced by surrealism.

Decadent: See *Decadents*

Decadents: The followers of a nineteenth-century literary movement that had its beginnings in French aestheticism. Decadent literature displays a fascination with perverse and morbid states; a search for novelty and sensation—the "new thrill"; a preoccupation with mysticism; and a belief in the senselessness of human existence. The movement is closely associated with the doctrine Art for Art's Sake. The term "decadence" is sometimes used to denote a decline in the quality of art or literature following a period of greatness.

Deconstruction: A method of literary criticism developed by Jacques Derrida and characterized by multiple conflicting interpretations of a given work. Deconstructionists consider the impact of the language of a work and suggest that the true meaning of the work is not necessarily the meaning that the author intended.

Deduction: The process of reaching a conclusion through reasoning from general premises to a specific premise.

Denotation: The definition of a word, apart from the impressions or feelings it creates in the reader.

Diction: The selection and arrangement of words in a literary work. Either or both may vary depending on the desired effect. There are four general types of diction: "formal," used in scholarly or lofty writing; "informal," used in relaxed but educated conversation; "colloquial," used in everyday speech; and "slang," containing newly coined words and other terms not accepted in formal usage.

Didactic: A term used to describe works of literature that aim to teach some moral, religious, political, or practical lesson. Although didactic elements are often found in artistically pleasing works, the term "didactic" usually refers to literature in which the message is more important than the form. The term may also be used to criticize a work that the critic finds "overly didactic," that is, heavy-handed in its delivery of a lesson.

Dimeter: See *Meter*

Dionysian: See *Apollonian and Dionysian*

Discordia concours: A Latin phrase meaning "discord in harmony." The term was coined by the eighteenth-century English writer Samuel Johnson to describe "a combination of dissimilar images or discovery of occult resemblances in things apparently unlike." Johnson created the expression by reversing a phrase by the Latin poet Horace.

Dissonance: A combination of harsh or jarring sounds, especially in poetry. Although such combinations may be accidental, poets sometimes intentionally make them to achieve particular effects. Dissonance is also sometimes used to refer to close but not identical rhymes. When this is the case, the word functions as a synonym for consonance.

Double Entendre: A corruption of a French phrase meaning "double meaning." The term is used to indicate a word or phrase that is deliberately ambiguous, especially when one of the meanings is risque or improper.

Draft: Any preliminary version of a written work. An author may write dozens of drafts which are revised to form the final work, or he or she may write only one, with few or no revisions.

Dramatic Monologue: See *Monologue*

Dramatic Poetry: Any lyric work that employs elements of drama such as dialogue, conflict, or characterization, but excluding works that are intended for stage presentation.

Dream Allegory: See *Dream Vision*

Dream Vision: A literary convention, chiefly of the Middle Ages. In a dream vision a story is presented as a literal dream of the narrator. This device was commonly used to teach moral and religious lessons.

E

Eclogue: In classical literature, a poem featuring rural themes and structured as a dialogue among shepherds. Eclogues often took specific poetic forms, such as elegies or love poems. Some were written as the soliloquy of a shepherd. In later centuries, "eclogue" came to refer to any poem that was in the pastoral tradition or that had a dialogue or monologue structure.

Edwardian: Describes cultural conventions identified with the period of the reign of Edward VII of England (1901–1910). Writers of the Edwardian Age typically displayed a strong reaction against the propriety and conservatism of the Victorian Age. Their work often exhibits distrust of authority in religion, politics, and art and expresses strong doubts about the soundness of conventional values.

Edwardian Age: See *Edwardian*

Electra Complex: A daughter's amorous obsession with her father.

Elegy: A lyric poem that laments the death of a person or the eventual death of all people. In a conventional elegy, set in a classical world, the poet and subject are spoken of as shepherds. In modern criticism, the word elegy is often used to refer to a poem that is melancholy or mournfully contemplative.

Elizabethan Age: A period of great economic growth, religious controversy, and nationalism closely associated with the reign of Elizabeth I of England (1558–1603). The Elizabethan Age is considered a part of the general renaissance—that is, the flowering of arts and literature—that took place in Europe during the fourteenth through sixteenth centuries. The era is considered the golden age of English literature. The most important dramas in English and a great deal of lyric poetry were produced during this period, and modern English criticism began around this time.

Empathy: A sense of shared experience, including emotional and physical feelings, with someone or something other than oneself. Empathy is often used to describe the response of a reader to a literary character.

English Sonnet: See *Sonnet*

Enjambment: The running over of the sense and structure of a line of verse or a couplet into the following verse or couplet.

Enlightenment, The: An eighteenth-century philosophical movement. It began in France but had a wide impact throughout Europe and America. Thinkers of the Enlightenment valued reason and believed that both the individual and society could achieve a state of perfection. Corresponding to this essentially humanist vision was a resistance to religious authority.

Epic: A long narrative poem about the adventures of a hero of great historic or legendary importance. The setting is vast and the action is often given cosmic significance through the intervention of supernatural forces such as gods, angels, or demons. Epics are typically written in a classical style of grand simplicity with elaborate metaphors and allusions that enhance the symbolic importance of a hero's adventures.

Epic Simile: See *Homeric Simile*

Epigram: A saying that makes the speaker's point quickly and concisely.

Epilogue: A concluding statement or section of a literary work. In dramas, particularly those of the seventeenth and eighteenth centuries, the epilogue is a closing speech, often in verse, delivered by an actor at the end of a play and spoken directly to the audience.

Epiphany: A sudden revelation of truth inspired by a seemingly trivial incident.

Epitaph: An inscription on a tomb or tombstone, or a verse written on the occasion of a person's death. Epitaphs may be serious or humorous.

Epithalamion: A song or poem written to honor and commemorate a marriage ceremony.

Epithalamium: See *Epithalamion*

Epithet: A word or phrase, often disparaging or abusive, that expresses a character trait of someone or something.

Erziehungsroman: See *Bildungsroman*

Essay: A prose composition with a focused subject of discussion. The term was coined by Michel de Montaigne to describe his 1580 collection of brief, informal reflections on himself and on various topics relating to human nature. An essay can also be a long, systematic discourse.

Existentialism: A predominantly twentieth-century philosophy concerned with the nature and perception of human existence. There are two major strains of existentialist thought: atheistic and Christian. Followers of atheistic existentialism believe that the individual is alone in a godless universe and that the basic human condition is one of suffering and loneliness. Nevertheless, because there are no fixed values, individuals can create their own characters—indeed, they can shape themselves—through the exercise of free will. The atheistic strain culminates in and is popularly associated with the works of Jean-Paul Sartre. The Christian existentialists, on the other hand, believe that only in God may people find freedom from life's anguish. The two strains hold certain beliefs in common: that existence cannot be fully understood or described through empirical effort; that anguish is a universal element of life; that individuals must bear responsibility for their actions; and that there is no common standard of behavior or perception for religious and ethical matters.

Expatriates: See *Expatriatism*

Expatriatism: The practice of leaving one's country to live for an extended period in another country.

Exposition: Writing intended to explain the nature of an idea, thing, or theme. Expository writing is often combined with description, narration, or argument. In dramatic writing, the exposition is the introductory material which presents the characters, setting, and tone of the play.

Expressionism: An indistinct literary term, originally used to describe an early twentieth-century school of German painting. The term applies to almost any mode of unconventional, highly subjective writing that distorts reality in some way.

Extended Monologue: See *Monologue*

F

Feet: See *Foot*

Feminine Rhyme: See *Rhyme*

Fiction: Any story that is the product of imagination rather than a documentation of fact. Characters and events in such narratives may be based in real life but their ultimate form and configuration is a creation of the author.

Figurative Language: A technique in writing in which the author temporarily interrupts the order, construction, or meaning of the writing for a particular effect. This interruption takes the form of one or more figures of speech such as hyperbole, irony, or simile. Figurative language is the opposite of literal language, in which every word is truthful, accurate, and free of exaggeration or embellishment.

Figures of Speech: Writing that differs from customary conventions for construction, meaning, order, or significance for the purpose of a special meaning or effect. There are two major types of figures of speech: rhetorical figures, which do not make changes in the meaning of the words; and tropes, which do.

Fin de siecle: A French term meaning "end of the century." The term is used to denote the last decade of the nineteenth century, a transition period when

writers and other artists abandoned old conventions and looked for new techniques and objectives.

First Person: See *Point of View*

Folk Ballad: See *Ballad*

Folklore: Traditions and myths preserved in a culture or group of people. Typically, these are passed on by word of mouth in various forms—such as legends, songs, and proverbs—or preserved in customs and ceremonies. This term was first used by W. J. Thoms in 1846.

Folktale: A story originating in oral tradition. Folktales fall into a variety of categories, including legends, ghost stories, fairy tales, fables, and anecdotes based on historical figures and events.

Foot: The smallest unit of rhythm in a line of poetry. In English-language poetry, a foot is typically one accented syllable combined with one or two unaccented syllables.

Form: The pattern or construction of a work which identifies its genre and distinguishes it from other genres.

Formalism: In literary criticism, the belief that literature should follow prescribed rules of construction, such as those that govern the sonnet form.

Fourteener Meter: See *Meter*

Free Verse: Poetry that lacks regular metrical and rhyme patterns but that tries to capture the cadences of everyday speech. The form allows a poet to exploit a variety of rhythmical effects within a single poem.

Futurism: A flamboyant literary and artistic movement that developed in France, Italy, and Russia from 1908 through the 1920s. Futurist theater and poetry abandoned traditional literary forms. In their place, followers of the movement attempted to achieve total freedom of expression through bizarre imagery and deformed or newly invented words. The Futurists were self-consciously modern artists who attempted to incorporate the appearances and sounds of modern life into their work.

G

Genre: A category of literary work. In critical theory, genre may refer to both the content of a given work—tragedy, comedy, pastoral—and to its form, such as poetry, novel, or drama.

Genteel Tradition: A term coined by critic George Santayana to describe the literary practice of certain late nineteenth-century American writers, especially New Englanders. Followers of the Genteel

Tradition emphasized conventionality in social, religious, moral, and literary standards.

Georgian Age: See *Georgian Poets*

Georgian Period: See *Georgian Poets*

Georgian Poets: A loose grouping of English poets during the years 1912–1922. The Georgians reacted against certain literary schools and practices, especially Victorian wordiness, turn-of-the-century aestheticism, and contemporary urban realism. In their place, the Georgians embraced the nineteenth-century poetic practices of William Wordsworth and the other Lake Poets.

Georgic: A poem about farming and the farmer's way of life, named from Virgil's *Georgics*.

Gilded Age: A period in American history during the 1870s characterized by political corruption and materialism. A number of important novels of social and political criticism were written during this time.

Gothic: See *Gothicism*

Gothicism: In literary criticism, works characterized by a taste for the medieval or morbidly attractive. A gothic novel prominently features elements of horror, the supernatural, gloom, and violence: clanking chains, terror, charnel houses, ghosts, medieval castles, and mysteriously slamming doors. The term "gothic novel" is also applied to novels that lack elements of the traditional Gothic setting but that create a similar atmosphere of terror or dread.

Graveyard School: A group of eighteenth-century English poets who wrote long, picturesque meditations on death. Their works were designed to cause the reader to ponder immortality.

Great Chain of Being: The belief that all things and creatures in nature are organized in a hierarchy from inanimate objects at the bottom to God at the top. This system of belief was popular in the seventeenth and eighteenth centuries.

Grotesque: In literary criticism, the subject matter of a work or a style of expression characterized by exaggeration, deformity, freakishness, and disorder. The grotesque often includes an element of comic absurdity.

H

Haiku: The shortest form of Japanese poetry, constructed in three lines of five, seven, and five syllables respectively. The message of a *haiku* poem usually centers on some aspect of spirituality and provokes an emotional response in the reader.

Half Rhyme: See *Consonance*

Harlem Renaissance: The Harlem Renaissance of the 1920s is generally considered the first significant movement of black writers and artists in the United States. During this period, new and established black writers published more fiction and poetry than ever before, the first influential black literary journals were established, and black authors and artists received their first widespread recognition and serious critical appraisal. Among the major writers associated with this period are Claude McKay, Jean Toomer, Countee Cullen, Langston Hughes, Arna Bontemps, Nella Larsen, and Zora Neale Hurston.

Hellenism: Imitation of ancient Greek thought or styles. Also, an approach to life that focuses on the growth and development of the intellect. "Hellenism" is sometimes used to refer to the belief that reason can be applied to examine all human experience.

Heptameter: See *Meter*

Hero/Heroine: The principal sympathetic character (male or female) in a literary work. Heroes and heroines typically exhibit admirable traits: idealism, courage, and integrity, for example.

Heroic Couplet: A rhyming couplet written in iambic pentameter (a verse with five iambic feet).

Heroic Line: The meter and length of a line of verse in epic or heroic poetry. This varies by language and time period.

Heroine: See *Hero/Heroine*

Hexameter: See *Meter*

Historical Criticism: The study of a work based on its impact on the world of the time period in which it was written.

Hokku: See *Haiku*

Holocaust: See *Holocaust Literature*

Holocaust Literature: Literature influenced by or written about the Holocaust of World War II. Such literature includes true stories of survival in concentration camps, escape, and life after the war, as well as fictional works and poetry.

Homeric Simile: An elaborate, detailed comparison written as a simile many lines in length.

Horatian Satire: See *Satire*

Humanism: A philosophy that places faith in the dignity of humankind and rejects the medieval perception of the individual as a weak, fallen creature. "Humanists" typically believe in the perfectibility of human nature and view reason and education as the means to that end.

Humors: Mentions of the humors refer to the ancient Greek theory that a person's health and personality were determined by the balance of four basic fluids in the body: blood, phlegm, yellow bile, and black bile. A dominance of any fluid would cause extremes in behavior. An excess of blood created a sanguine person who was joyful, aggressive, and passionate; a phlegmatic person was shy, fearful, and sluggish; too much yellow bile led to a choleric temperament characterized by impatience, anger, bitterness, and stubbornness; and excessive black bile created melancholy, a state of laziness, gluttony, and lack of motivation.

Humours: See *Humors*

Hyperbole: In literary criticism, deliberate exaggeration used to achieve an effect.

I

Iamb: See *Foot*

Idiom: A word construction or verbal expression closely associated with a given language.

Image: A concrete representation of an object or sensory experience. Typically, such a representation helps evoke the feelings associated with the object or experience itself. Images are either "literal" or "figurative." Literal images are especially concrete and involve little or no extension of the obvious meaning of the words used to express them. Figurative images do not follow the literal meaning of the words exactly. Images in literature are usually visual, but the term "image" can also refer to the representation of any sensory experience.

Imagery: The array of images in a literary work. Also, figurative language.

Imagism: An English and American poetry movement that flourished between 1908 and 1917. The Imagists used precise, clearly presented images in their works. They also used common, everyday speech and aimed for conciseness, concrete imagery, and the creation of new rhythms.

In medias res: A Latin term meaning "in the middle of things." It refers to the technique of beginning a story at its midpoint and then using various flashback devices to reveal previous action.

Induction: The process of reaching a conclusion by reasoning from specific premises to form a general premise. Also, an introductory portion of a work of literature, especially a play.

Intentional Fallacy: The belief that judgments of a literary work based solely on an author's stated or implied intentions are false and misleading. Critics who believe in the concept of the intentional fallacy typically argue that the work itself is sufficient matter for interpretation, even though they may concede that an author's statement of purpose can be useful.

Interior Monologue: A narrative technique in which characters' thoughts are revealed in a way that appears to be uncontrolled by the author. The interior monologue typically aims to reveal the inner self of a character. It portrays emotional experiences as they occur at both a conscious and unconscious level. Images are often used to represent sensations or emotions.

Internal Rhyme: Rhyme that occurs within a single line of verse.

Irish Literary Renaissance: A late nineteenth- and early twentieth-century movement in Irish literature. Members of the movement aimed to reduce the influence of British culture in Ireland and create an Irish national literature.

Irony: In literary criticism, the effect of language in which the intended meaning is the opposite of what is stated.

Italian Sonnet: See *Sonnet*

J

Jacobean Age: The period of the reign of James I of England (1603–1625). The early literature of this period reflected the worldview of the Elizabethan Age, but a darker, more cynical attitude steadily grew in the art and literature of the Jacobean Age. This was an important time for English drama and poetry.

Jargon: Language that is used or understood only by a select group of people. Jargon may refer to terminology used in a certain profession, such as computer jargon, or it may refer to any nonsensical language that is not understood by most people.

Journalism: Writing intended for publication in a newspaper or magazine, or for broadcast on a radio or television program featuring news, sports, entertainment, or other timely material.

K

Knickerbocker Group: A somewhat indistinct group of New York writers of the first half of the nineteenth century. Members of the group were linked only by location and a common theme: New York life.

Kunstlerroman: See *Bildungsroman*

L

Lais: See *Lay*

Lake Poets: See *Lake School*

Lake School: These poets all lived in the Lake District of England at the turn of the nineteenth century. As a group, they followed no single "school" of thought or literary practice, although their works were uniformly disparaged by the *Edinburgh Review*.

Lay: A song or simple narrative poem. The form originated in medieval France. Early French *lais* were often based on the Celtic legends and other tales sung by Breton minstrels—thus the name of the "Breton lay." In fourteenth-century England, the term "lay" was used to describe short narratives written in imitation of the Breton lays.

Leitmotiv: See *Motif*

Literal Language: An author uses literal language when he or she writes without exaggerating or embellishing the subject matter and without any tools of figurative language.

Literary Ballad: See *Ballad*

Literature: Literature is broadly defined as any written or spoken material, but the term most often refers to creative works.

Lost Generation: A term first used by Gertrude Stein to describe the post-World War I generation of American writers: men and women haunted by a sense of betrayal and emptiness brought about by the destructiveness of the war.

Lyric Poetry: A poem expressing the subjective feelings and personal emotions of the poet. Such poetry is melodic, since it was originally accompanied by a lyre in recitals. Most Western poetry in the twentieth century may be classified as lyrical.

M

Mannerism: Exaggerated, artificial adherence to a literary manner or style. Also, a popular style of the visual arts of late sixteenth-century Europe that was marked by elongation of the human form and by intentional spatial distortion. Literary works that are self-consciously high-toned and artistic are often said to be "mannered."

Masculine Rhyme: See *Rhyme*

Measure: The foot, verse, or time sequence used in a literary work, especially a poem. Measure is often used somewhat incorrectly as a synonym for meter.

Metaphor: A figure of speech that expresses an idea through the image of another object. Metaphors suggest the essence of the first object by identifying it with certain qualities of the second object.

Metaphysical Conceit: See *Conceit*

Metaphysical Poetry: The body of poetry produced by a group of seventeenth-century English writers called the "Metaphysical Poets." The group includes John Donne and Andrew Marvell. The Metaphysical Poets made use of everyday speech, intellectual analysis, and unique imagery. They aimed to portray the ordinary conflicts and contradictions of life. Their poems often took the form of an argument, and many of them emphasize physical and religious love as well as the fleeting nature of life. Elaborate conceits are typical in metaphysical poetry.

Metaphysical Poets: See *Metaphysical Poetry*

Meter: In literary criticism, the repetition of sound patterns that creates a rhythm in poetry. The patterns are based on the number of syllables and the presence and absence of accents. The unit of rhythm in a line is called a foot. Types of meter are classified according to the number of feet in a line. These are the standard English lines: Monometer, one foot; Dimeter, two feet; Trimeter, three feet; Tetrameter, four feet; Pentameter, five feet; Hexameter, six feet (also called the Alexandrine); Heptameter, seven feet (also called the "Fourteener" when the feet are iambic).

Modernism: Modern literary practices. Also, the principles of a literary school that lasted from roughly the beginning of the twentieth century until the end of World War II. Modernism is defined by its rejection of the literary conventions of the nineteenth century and by its opposition to conventional morality, taste, traditions, and economic values.

Monologue: A composition, written or oral, by a single individual. More specifically, a speech given by a single individual in a drama or other public entertainment. It has no set length, although it is usually several or more lines long.

Monometer: See *Meter*

Mood: The prevailing emotions of a work or of the author in his or her creation of the work. The mood of a work is not always what might be expected based on its subject matter.

Motif: A theme, character type, image, metaphor, or other verbal element that recurs throughout a single work of literature or occurs in a number of different works over a period of time.

Motiv: See *Motif*

Muckrakers: An early twentieth-century group of American writers. Typically, their works exposed the wrongdoings of big business and government in the United States.

Muses: Nine Greek mythological goddesses, the daughters of Zeus and Mnemosyne (Memory). Each muse patronized a specific area of the liberal arts and sciences. Calliope presided over epic poetry, Clio over history, Erato over love poetry, Euterpe over music or lyric poetry, Melpomene over tragedy, Polyhymnia over hymns to the gods, Terpsichore over dance, Thalia over comedy, and Urania over astronomy. Poets and writers traditionally made appeals to the Muses for inspiration in their work.

Myth: An anonymous tale emerging from the traditional beliefs of a culture or social unit. Myths use supernatural explanations for natural phenomena. They may also explain cosmic issues like creation and death. Collections of myths, known as mythologies, are common to all cultures and nations, but the best-known myths belong to the Norse, Roman, and Greek mythologies.

N

Narration: The telling of a series of events, real or invented. A narration may be either a simple narrative, in which the events are recounted chronologically, or a narrative with a plot, in which the account is given in a style reflecting the author's artistic concept of the story. Narration is sometimes used as a synonym for "storyline."

Narrative: A verse or prose accounting of an event or sequence of events, real or invented. The term is also used as an adjective in the sense "method of narration." For example, in literary criticism, the expression "narrative technique" usually refers to the way the author structures and presents his or her story.

Narrative Poetry: A nondramatic poem in which the author tells a story. Such poems may be of any length or level of complexity.

Narrator: The teller of a story. The narrator may be the author or a character in the story through whom the author speaks.

Naturalism: A literary movement of the late nineteenth and early twentieth centuries. The movement's major theorist, French novelist Emile Zola,

envisioned a type of fiction that would examine human life with the objectivity of scientific inquiry. The Naturalists typically viewed human beings as either the products of "biological determinism," ruled by hereditary instincts and engaged in an endless struggle for survival, or as the products of "socioeconomic determinism," ruled by social and economic forces beyond their control. In their works, the Naturalists generally ignored the highest levels of society and focused on degradation: poverty, alcoholism, prostitution, insanity, and disease.

Negritude: A literary movement based on the concept of a shared cultural bond on the part of black Africans, wherever they may be in the world. It traces its origins to the former French colonies of Africa and the Caribbean. Negritude poets, novelists, and essayists generally stress four points in their writings: One, black alienation from traditional African culture can lead to feelings of inferiority. Two, European colonialism and Western education should be resisted. Three, black Africans should seek to affirm and define their own identity. Four, African culture can and should be reclaimed. Many Negritude writers also claim that blacks can make unique contributions to the world, based on a heightened appreciation of nature, rhythm, and human emotions—aspects of life they say are not so highly valued in the materialistic and rationalistic West.

Negro Renaissance: See *Harlem Renaissance*

Neoclassical Period: See *Neoclassicism*

Neoclassicism: In literary criticism, this term refers to the revival of the attitudes and styles of expression of classical literature. It is generally used to describe a period in European history beginning in the late seventeenth century and lasting until about 1800. In its purest form, Neoclassicism marked a return to order, proportion, restraint, logic, accuracy, and decorum. In England, where Neoclassicism perhaps was most popular, it reflected the influence of seventeenth-century French writers, especially dramatists. Neoclassical writers typically reacted against the intensity and enthusiasm of the Renaissance period. They wrote works that appealed to the intellect, using elevated language and classical literary forms such as satire and the ode. Neoclassical works were often governed by the classical goal of instruction.

Neoclassicists: See *Neoclassicism*

New Criticism: A movement in literary criticism, dating from the late 1920s, that stressed close textual analysis in the interpretation of works of literature. The New Critics saw little merit in historical and biographical analysis. Rather, they aimed to examine the text alone, free from the question of how external events—biographical or otherwise—may have helped shape it.

New Journalism: A type of writing in which the journalist presents factual information in a form usually used in fiction. New journalism emphasizes description, narration, and character development to bring readers closer to the human element of the story, and is often used in personality profiles and in-depth feature articles. It is not compatible with "straight" or "hard" newswriting, which is generally composed in a brief, fact-based style.

New Journalists: See *New Journalism*

New Negro Movement: See *Harlem Renaissance*

Noble Savage: The idea that primitive man is noble and good but becomes evil and corrupted as he becomes civilized. The concept of the noble savage originated in the Renaissance period but is more closely identified with such later writers as Jean-Jacques Rousseau and Aphra Behn.

O

Objective Correlative: An outward set of objects, a situation, or a chain of events corresponding to an inward experience and evoking this experience in the reader. The term frequently appears in modern criticism in discussions of authors' intended effects on the emotional responses of readers.

Objectivity: A quality in writing characterized by the absence of the author's opinion or feeling about the subject matter. Objectivity is an important factor in criticism.

Occasional Verse: Poetry written on the occasion of a significant historical or personal event. *Vers de societe* is sometimes called occasional verse although it is of a less serious nature.

Octave: A poem or stanza composed of eight lines. The term octave most often represents the first eight lines of a Petrarchan sonnet.

Ode: Name given to an extended lyric poem characterized by exalted emotion and dignified style. An ode usually concerns a single, serious theme. Most odes, but not all, are addressed to an object or individual. Odes are distinguished from other lyric poetic forms by their complex rhythmic and stanzaic patterns.

Oedipus Complex: A son's amorous obsession with his mother. The phrase is derived from the story of the ancient Theban hero Oedipus, who un-

knowingly killed his father and married his mother.

Omniscience: See *Point of View*

Onomatopoeia: The use of words whose sounds express or suggest their meaning. In its simplest sense, onomatopoeia may be represented by words that mimic the sounds they denote such as "hiss" or "meow." At a more subtle level, the pattern and rhythm of sounds and rhymes of a line or poem may be onomatopoeic.

Oral Tradition: See *Oral Transmission*

Oral Transmission: A process by which songs, ballads, folklore, and other material are transmitted by word of mouth. The tradition of oral transmission predates the written record systems of literate society. Oral transmission preserves material sometimes over generations, although often with variations. Memory plays a large part in the recitation and preservation of orally transmitted material.

Ottava Rima: An eight-line stanza of poetry composed in iambic pentameter (a five-foot line in which each foot consists of an unaccented syllable followed by an accented syllable), following the *abababcc* rhyme scheme.

Oxymoron: A phrase combining two contradictory terms. Oxymorons may be intentional or unintentional.

P

Pantheism: The idea that all things are both a manifestation or revelation of God and a part of God at the same time. Pantheism was a common attitude in the early societies of Egypt, India, and Greece—the term derives from the Greek *pan* meaning "all" and *theos* meaning "deity." It later became a significant part of the Christian faith.

Parable: A story intended to teach a moral lesson or answer an ethical question.

Paradox: A statement that appears illogical or contradictory at first, but may actually point to an underlying truth.

Parallelism: A method of comparison of two ideas in which each is developed in the same grammatical structure.

Parnassianism: A mid nineteenth-century movement in French literature. Followers of the movement stressed adherence to well-defined artistic forms as a reaction against the often chaotic expression of the artist's ego that dominated the work of the Romantics. The Parnassians also rejected the moral, ethical, and social themes exhibited in the works of French Romantics such as Victor Hugo. The aesthetic doctrines of the Parnassians strongly influenced the later symbolist and decadent movements.

Parody: In literary criticism, this term refers to an imitation of a serious literary work or the signature style of a particular author in a ridiculous manner. A typical parody adopts the style of the original and applies it to an inappropriate subject for humorous effect. Parody is a form of satire and could be considered the literary equivalent of a caricature or cartoon.

Pastoral: A term derived from the Latin word "pastor," meaning shepherd. A pastoral is a literary composition on a rural theme. The conventions of the pastoral were originated by the third-century Greek poet Theocritus, who wrote about the experiences, love affairs, and pastimes of Sicilian shepherds. In a pastoral, characters and language of a courtly nature are often placed in a simple setting. The term pastoral is also used to classify dramas, elegies, and lyrics that exhibit the use of country settings and shepherd characters.

Pathetic Fallacy: A term coined by English critic John Ruskin to identify writing that falsely endows nonhuman things with human intentions and feelings, such as "angry clouds" and "sad trees."

Pen Name: See *Pseudonym*

Pentameter: See *Meter*

Persona: A Latin term meaning "mask." *Personae* are the characters in a fictional work of literature. The *persona* generally functions as a mask through which the author tells a story in a voice other than his or her own. A *persona* is usually either a character in a story who acts as a narrator or an "implied author," a voice created by the author to act as the narrator for himself or herself.

Personae: See *Persona*

Personal Point of View: See *Point of View*

Personification: A figure of speech that gives human qualities to abstract ideas, animals, and inanimate objects.

Petrarchan Sonnet: See *Sonnet*

Phenomenology: A method of literary criticism based on the belief that things have no existence outside of human consciousness or awareness. Proponents of this theory believe that art is a process that takes place in the mind of the observer as he or she contemplates an object rather than a quality of the object itself.

Plagiarism: Claiming another person's written material as one's own. Plagiarism can take the form of direct, word-for-word copying or the theft of the substance or idea of the work.

Platonic Criticism: A form of criticism that stresses an artistic work's usefulness as an agent of social engineering rather than any quality or value of the work itself.

Platonism: The embracing of the doctrines of the philosopher Plato, popular among the poets of the Renaissance and the Romantic period. Platonism is more flexible than Aristotelian Criticism and places more emphasis on the supernatural and unknown aspects of life.

Plot: In literary criticism, this term refers to the pattern of events in a narrative or drama. In its simplest sense, the plot guides the author in composing the work and helps the reader follow the work. Typically, plots exhibit causality and unity and have a beginning, a middle, and an end. Sometimes, however, a plot may consist of a series of disconnected events, in which case it is known as an "episodic plot."

Poem: In its broadest sense, a composition utilizing rhyme, meter, concrete detail, and expressive language to create a literary experience with emotional and aesthetic appeal.

Poet: An author who writes poetry or verse. The term is also used to refer to an artist or writer who has an exceptional gift for expression, imagination, and energy in the making of art in any form.

Poete maudit: A term derived from Paul Verlaine's *Les poetes maudits* (*The Accursed Poets*), a collection of essays on the French symbolist writers Stephane Mallarme, Arthur Rimbaud, and Tristan Corbiere. In the sense intended by Verlaine, the poet is "accursed" for choosing to explore extremes of human experience outside of middle-class society.

Poetic Fallacy: See *Pathetic Fallacy*

Poetic Justice: An outcome in a literary work, not necessarily a poem, in which the good are rewarded and the evil are punished, especially in ways that particularly fit their virtues or crimes.

Poetic License: Distortions of fact and literary convention made by a writer—not always a poet—for the sake of the effect gained. Poetic license is closely related to the concept of "artistic freedom."

Poetics: This term has two closely related meanings. It denotes (1) an aesthetic theory in literary criticism about the essence of poetry or (2) rules prescribing the proper methods, content, style, or diction of poetry. The term poetics may also refer to theories about literature in general, not just poetry.

Poetry: In its broadest sense, writing that aims to present ideas and evoke an emotional experience in the reader through the use of meter, imagery, connotative and concrete words, and a carefully constructed structure based on rhythmic patterns. Poetry typically relies on words and expressions that have several layers of meaning. It also makes use of the effects of regular rhythm on the ear and may make a strong appeal to the senses through the use of imagery.

Point of View: The narrative perspective from which a literary work is presented to the reader. There are four traditional points of view. The "third person omniscient" gives the reader a "godlike" perspective, unrestricted by time or place, from which to see actions and look into the minds of characters. This allows the author to comment openly on characters and events in the work. The "third-person" point of view presents the events of the story from outside of any single character's perception, much like the omniscient point of view, but the reader must understand the action as it takes place and without any special insight into characters' minds or motivations. The "first person" or "personal" point of view relates events as they are perceived by a single character. The main character "tells" the story and may offer opinions about the action and characters which differ from those of the author. Much less common than omniscient, third person, and first person is the "second-person" point of view, wherein the author tells the story as if it is happening to the reader.

Polemic: A work in which the author takes a stand on a controversial subject, such as abortion or religion. Such works are often extremely argumentative or provocative.

Pornography: Writing intended to provoke feelings of lust in the reader. Such works are often condemned by critics and teachers, but those which can be shown to have literary value are viewed less harshly.

Post-Aesthetic Movement: An artistic response made by African Americans to the black aesthetic movement of the 1960s and early 1970s. Writers since that time have adopted a somewhat different tone in their work, with less emphasis placed on the disparity between black and white in the United States. In the words of post-aesthetic authors such as Toni Morrison, John Edgar Wideman, and Kristin Hunter, African Americans are portrayed as

looking inward for answers to their own questions, rather than always looking to the outside world.

Postmodernism: Writing from the 1960s forward characterized by experimentation and continuing to apply some of the fundamentals of modernism, which included existentialism and alienation. Postmodernists have gone a step further in the rejection of tradition begun with the modernists by also rejecting traditional forms, preferring the antinovel over the novel and the antihero over the hero.

Pre-Raphaelites: A circle of writers and artists in mid nineteenth-century England. Valuing the pre-Renaissance artistic qualities of religious symbolism, lavish pictorialism, and natural sensuousness, the Pre-Raphaelites cultivated a sense of mystery and melancholy that influenced later writers associated with the Symbolist and Decadent movements.

Primitivism: The belief that primitive peoples were nobler and less flawed than civilized peoples because they had not been subjected to the corrupt influence of society.

Projective Verse: A form of free verse in which the poet's breathing pattern determines the lines of the poem. Poets who advocate projective verse are against all formal structures in writing, including meter and form.

Prologue: An introductory section of a literary work. It often contains information establishing the situation of the characters or presents information about the setting, time period, or action. In drama, the prologue is spoken by a chorus or by one of the principal characters.

Prose: A literary medium that attempts to mirror the language of everyday speech. It is distinguished from poetry by its use of unmetered, unrhymed language consisting of logically related sentences. Prose is usually grouped into paragraphs that form a cohesive whole such as an essay or a novel.

Prosopopoeia: See *Personification*

Protagonist: The central character of a story who serves as a focus for its themes and incidents and as the principal rationale for its development. The protagonist is sometimes referred to in discussions of modern literature as the hero or antihero.

Proverb: A brief, sage saying that expresses a truth about life in a striking manner.

Pseudonym: A name assumed by a writer, most often intended to prevent his or her identification as the author of a work. Two or more authors may work together under one pseudonym, or an author may use a different name for each genre he or she publishes in. Some publishing companies maintain "house pseudonyms," under which any number of authors may write installations in a series. Some authors also choose a pseudonym over their real names the way an actor may use a stage name.

Pun: A play on words that have similar sounds but different meanings.

Pure Poetry: poetry written without instructional intent or moral purpose that aims only to please a reader by its imagery or musical flow. The term pure poetry is used as the antonym of the term "didacticism."

Q

Quatrain: A four-line stanza of a poem or an entire poem consisting of four lines.

R

Realism: A nineteenth-century European literary movement that sought to portray familiar characters, situations, and settings in a realistic manner. This was done primarily by using an objective narrative point of view and through the buildup of accurate detail. The standard for success of any realistic work depends on how faithfully it transfers common experience into fictional forms. The realistic method may be altered or extended, as in stream of consciousness writing, to record highly subjective experience.

Refrain: A phrase repeated at intervals throughout a poem. A refrain may appear at the end of each stanza or at less regular intervals. It may be altered slightly at each appearance.

Renaissance: The period in European history that marked the end of the Middle Ages. It began in Italy in the late fourteenth century. In broad terms, it is usually seen as spanning the fourteenth, fifteenth, and sixteenth centuries, although it did not reach Great Britain, for example, until the 1480s or so. The Renaissance saw an awakening in almost every sphere of human activity, especially science, philosophy, and the arts. The period is best defined by the emergence of a general philosophy that emphasized the importance of the intellect, the individual, and world affairs. It contrasts strongly with the medieval worldview, characterized by the dominant concerns of faith, the social collective, and spiritual salvation.

Repartee: Conversation featuring snappy retorts and witticisms.

Restoration: See *Restoration Age*

Restoration Age: A period in English literature beginning with the crowning of Charles II in 1660 and running to about 1700. The era, which was characterized by a reaction against Puritanism, was the first great age of the comedy of manners. The finest literature of the era is typically witty and urbane, and often lewd.

Rhetoric: In literary criticism, this term denotes the art of ethical persuasion. In its strictest sense, rhetoric adheres to various principles developed since classical times for arranging facts and ideas in a clear, persuasive, appealing manner. The term is also used to refer to effective prose in general and theories of or methods for composing effective prose.

Rhetorical Question: A question intended to provoke thought, but not an expressed answer, in the reader. It is most commonly used in oratory and other persuasive genres.

Rhyme: When used as a noun in literary criticism, this term generally refers to a poem in which words sound identical or very similar and appear in parallel positions in two or more lines. Rhymes are classified into different types according to where they fall in a line or stanza or according to the degree of similarity they exhibit in their spellings and sounds. Some major types of rhyme are "masculine" rhyme, "feminine" rhyme, and "triple" rhyme. In a masculine rhyme, the rhyming sound falls in a single accented syllable, as with "heat" and "eat." Feminine rhyme is a rhyme of two syllables, one stressed and one unstressed, as with "merry" and "tarry." Triple rhyme matches the sound of the accented syllable and the two unaccented syllables that follow: "narrative" and "declarative."

Rhyme Royal: A stanza of seven lines composed in iambic pentameter and rhymed *ababbcc.* The name is said to be a tribute to King James I of Scotland, who made much use of the form in his poetry.

Rhyme Scheme: See *Rhyme*

Rhythm: A regular pattern of sound, time intervals, or events occurring in writing, most often and most discernably in poetry. Regular, reliable rhythm is known to be soothing to humans, while interrupted, unpredictable, or rapidly changing rhythm is disturbing. These effects are known to authors, who use them to produce a desired reaction in the reader.

Rococo: A style of European architecture that flourished in the eighteenth century, especially in

France. The most notable features of *rococo* are its extensive use of ornamentation and its themes of lightness, gaiety, and intimacy. In literary criticism, the term is often used disparagingly to refer to a decadent or overly ornamental style.

Romance:

Romantic Age: See *Romanticism*

Romanticism: This term has two widely accepted meanings. In historical criticism, it refers to a European intellectual and artistic movement of the late eighteenth and early nineteenth centuries that sought greater freedom of personal expression than that allowed by the strict rules of literary form and logic of the eighteenth-century Neoclassicists. The Romantics preferred emotional and imaginative expression to rational analysis. They considered the individual to be at the center of all experience and so placed him or her at the center of their art. The Romantics believed that the creative imagination reveals nobler truths—unique feelings and attitudes—than those that could be discovered by logic or by scientific examination. Both the natural world and the state of childhood were important sources for revelations of "eternal truths." "Romanticism" is also used as a general term to refer to a type of sensibility found in all periods of literary history and usually considered to be in opposition to the principles of classicism. In this sense, Romanticism signifies any work or philosophy in which the exotic or dreamlike figure strongly, or that is devoted to individualistic expression, self-analysis, or a pursuit of a higher realm of knowledge than can be discovered by human reason.

Romantics: See *Romanticism*

Russian Symbolism: A Russian poetic movement, derived from French symbolism, that flourished between 1894 and 1910. While some Russian Symbolists continued in the French tradition, stressing aestheticism and the importance of suggestion above didactic intent, others saw their craft as a form of mystical worship, and themselves as mediators between the supernatural and the mundane.

S

Satire: A work that uses ridicule, humor, and wit to criticize and provoke change in human nature and institutions. There are two major types of satire: "formal" or "direct" satire speaks directly to the reader or to a character in the work; "indirect" satire relies upon the ridiculous behavior of its characters to make its point. Formal satire is further divided into two manners: the "Horatian," which

ridicules gently, and the "Juvenalian," which derides its subjects harshly and bitterly.

Scansion: The analysis or "scanning" of a poem to determine its meter and often its rhyme scheme. The most common system of scansion uses accents (slanted lines drawn above syllables) to show stressed syllables, breves (curved lines drawn above syllables) to show unstressed syllables, and vertical lines to separate each foot.

Second Person: See *Point of View*

Semiotics: The study of how literary forms and conventions affect the meaning of language.

Sestet: Any six-line poem or stanza.

Setting: The time, place, and culture in which the action of a narrative takes place. The elements of setting may include geographic location, characters' physical and mental environments, prevailing cultural attitudes, or the historical time in which the action takes place.

Shakespearean Sonnet: See *Sonnet*

Signifying Monkey: A popular trickster figure in black folklore, with hundreds of tales about this character documented since the nineteenth century.

Simile: A comparison, usually using "like" or "as," of two essentially dissimilar things, as in "coffee as cold as ice" or "He sounded like a broken record."

Slang: A type of informal verbal communication that is generally unacceptable for formal writing. Slang words and phrases are often colorful exaggerations used to emphasize the speaker's point; they may also be shortened versions of an often-used word or phrase.

Slant Rhyme: See *Consonance*

Slave Narrative: Autobiographical accounts of American slave life as told by escaped slaves. These works first appeared during the abolition movement of the 1830s through the 1850s.

Social Realism: See *Socialist Realism*

Socialist Realism: The Socialist Realism school of literary theory was proposed by Maxim Gorky and established as a dogma by the first Soviet Congress of Writers. It demanded adherence to a communist worldview in works of literature. Its doctrines required an objective viewpoint comprehensible to the working classes and themes of social struggle featuring strong proletarian heroes.

Soliloquy: A monologue in a drama used to give the audience information and to develop the speaker's character. It is typically a projection of the speaker's innermost thoughts. Usually delivered while the speaker is alone on stage, a solilo-quy is intended to present an illusion of unspoken reflection.

Sonnet: A fourteen-line poem, usually composed in iambic pentameter, employing one of several rhyme schemes. There are three major types of son-nets, upon which all other variations of the form are based: the "Petrarchan" or "Italian" sonnet, the "Shakespearean" or "English" sonnet, and the "Spenserian" sonnet. A Petrarchan sonnet consists of an octave rhymed *abbaabba* and a "sestet" rhymed either *cdecde, cdccdc,* or *cdedce.* The oc-tave poses a question or problem, relates a narra-tive, or puts forth a proposition; the sestet presents a solution to the problem, comments upon the nar-rative, or applies the proposition put forth in the octave. The Shakespearean sonnet is divided into three quatrains and a couplet rhymed *abab cdcd efef gg.* The couplet provides an epigrammatic comment on the narrative or problem put forth in the quatrains. The Spenserian sonnet uses three quatrains and a couplet like the Shakespearean, but links their three rhyme schemes in this way: *abab bcbc cdcd ee.* The Spenserian sonnet develops its theme in two parts like the Petrarchan, its final six lines resolving a problem, analyzing a narrative, or applying a proposition put forth in its first eight lines.

Spenserian Sonnet: See *Sonnet*

Spenserian Stanza: A nine-line stanza having eight verses in iambic pentameter, its ninth verse in iambic hexameter, and the rhyme scheme *abab-bcbcc.*

Spondee: In poetry meter, a foot consisting of two long or stressed syllables occurring together. This form is quite rare in English verse, and is usually composed of two monosyllabic words.

Sprung Rhythm: Versification using a specific number of accented syllables per line but disre-garding the number of unaccented syllables that fall in each line, producing an irregular rhythm in the poem.

Stanza: A subdivision of a poem consisting of lines grouped together, often in recurring patterns of rhyme, line length, and meter. Stanzas may also serve as units of thought in a poem much like para-graphs in prose.

Stereotype: A stereotype was originally the name for a duplication made during the printing process; this led to its modern definition as a person or thing that is (or is assumed to be) the same as all others of its type.

Stream of Consciousness: A narrative technique for rendering the inward experience of a character. This technique is designed to give the impression of an ever-changing series of thoughts, emotions, images, and memories in the spontaneous and seemingly illogical order that they occur in life.

Structuralism: A twentieth-century movement in literary criticism that examines how literary texts arrive at their meanings, rather than the meanings themselves. There are two major types of struc-turalist analysis: one examines the way patterns of linguistic structures unify a specific text and em-phasize certain elements of that text, and the other interprets the way literary forms and conventions affect the meaning of language itself.

Structure: The form taken by a piece of literature. The structure may be made obvious for ease of un-derstanding, as in nonfiction works, or may ob-scured for artistic purposes, as in some poetry or seemingly "unstructured" prose.

Sturm und Drang: A German term meaning "storm and stress." It refers to a German literary movement of the 1770s and 1780s that reacted against the order and rationalism of the enlighten-ment, focusing instead on the intense experience of extraordinary individuals.

Style: A writer's distinctive manner of arranging words to suit his or her ideas and purpose in writ-ing. The unique imprint of the author's personality upon his or her writing, style is the product of an author's way of arranging ideas and his or her use of diction, different sentence structures, rhythm, figures of speech, rhetorical principles, and other elements of composition.

Subject: The person, event, or theme at the center of a work of literature. A work may have one or more subjects of each type, with shorter works tending to have fewer and longer works tending to have more.

Subjectivity: Writing that expresses the author's personal feelings about his subject, and which may or may not include factual information about the subject.

Surrealism: A term introduced to criticism by Guillaume Apollinaire and later adopted by Andre Breton. It refers to a French literary and artistic movement founded in the 1920s. The Surrealists sought to express unconscious thoughts and feel-ings in their works. The best-known technique used for achieving this aim was automatic writing—tran-scriptions of spontaneous outpourings from the un-conscious. The Surrealists proposed to unify the contrary levels of conscious and unconscious, dream and reality, objectivity and subjectivity into a new level of "super-realism."

Suspense: A literary device in which the author maintains the audience's attention through the buildup of events, the outcome of which will soon be revealed.

Syllogism: A method of presenting a logical argument. In its most basic form, the syllogism consists of a major premise, a minor premise, and a conclusion.

Symbol: Something that suggests or stands for something else without losing its original identity. In literature, symbols combine their literal meaning with the suggestion of an abstract concept. Literary symbols are of two types: those that carry complex associations of meaning no matter what their contexts, and those that derive their suggestive meaning from their functions in specific literary works.

Symbolism: This term has two widely accepted meanings. In historical criticism, it denotes an early modernist literary movement initiated in France during the nineteenth century that reacted against the prevailing standards of realism. Writers in this movement aimed to evoke, indirectly and symbolically, an order of being beyond the material world of the five senses. Poetic expression of personal emotion figured strongly in the movement, typically by means of a private set of symbols uniquely identifiable with the individual poet. The principal aim of the Symbolists was to express in words the highly complex feelings that grew out of everyday contact with the world. In a broader sense, the term "symbolism" refers to the use of one object to represent another.

Symbolist: See *Symbolism*

Symbolist Movement: See *Symbolism*

Sympathetic Fallacy: See *Affective Fallacy*

T

Tanka: A form of Japanese poetry similar to *haiku*. A *tanka* is five lines long, with the lines containing five, seven, five, seven, and seven syllables respectively.

Terza Rima: A three-line stanza form in poetry in which the rhymes are made on the last word of each line in the following manner: the first and third lines of the first stanza, then the second line of the first stanza and the first and third lines of the second stanza, and so on with the middle line of any

stanza rhyming with the first and third lines of the following stanza.

Tetrameter: See *Meter*

Textual Criticism: A branch of literary criticism that seeks to establish the authoritative text of a literary work. Textual critics typically compare all known manuscripts or printings of a single work in order to assess the meanings of differences and revisions. This procedure allows them to arrive at a definitive version that (supposedly) corresponds to the author's original intention.

Theme: The main point of a work of literature. The term is used interchangeably with thesis.

Thesis: A thesis is both an essay and the point argued in the essay. Thesis novels and thesis plays share the quality of containing a thesis which is supported through the action of the story.

Third Person: See *Point of View*

Tone: The author's attitude toward his or her audience may be deduced from the tone of the work. A formal tone may create distance or convey politeness, while an informal tone may encourage a friendly, intimate, or intrusive feeling in the reader. The author's attitude toward his or her subject matter may also be deduced from the tone of the words he or she uses in discussing it.

Tragedy: A drama in prose or poetry about a noble, courageous hero of excellent character who, because of some tragic character flaw or *hamartia*, brings ruin upon him- or herself. Tragedy treats its subjects in a dignified and serious manner, using poetic language to help evoke pity and fear and bring about catharsis, a purging of these emotions. The tragic form was practiced extensively by the ancient Greeks. In the Middle Ages, when classical works were virtually unknown, tragedy came to denote any works about the fall of persons from exalted to low conditions due to any reason: fate, vice, weakness, etc. According to the classical definition of tragedy, such works present the "pathetic"—that which evokes pity—rather than the tragic. The classical form of tragedy was revived in the sixteenth century; it flourished especially on the Elizabethan stage. In modern times, dramatists have attempted to adapt the form to the needs of modern society by drawing their heroes from the ranks of ordinary men and women and defining the nobility of these heroes in terms of spirit rather than exalted social standing.

Tragic Flaw: In a tragedy, the quality within the hero or heroine which leads to his or her downfall.

Transcendentalism: An American philosophical and religious movement, based in New England from around 1835 until the Civil War. Transcendentalism was a form of American romanticism that had its roots abroad in the works of Thomas Carlyle, Samuel Coleridge, and Johann Wolfgang von Goethe. The Transcendentalists stressed the importance of intuition and subjective experience in communication with God. They rejected religious dogma and texts in favor of mysticism and scientific naturalism. They pursued truths that lie beyond the "colorless" realms perceived by reason and the senses and were active social reformers in public education, women's rights, and the abolition of slavery.

Trickster: A character or figure common in Native American and African literature who uses his ingenuity to defeat enemies and escape difficult situations. Tricksters are most often animals, such as the spider, hare, or coyote, although they may take the form of humans as well.

Trimeter: See *Meter*

Triple Rhyme: See *Rhyme*

Trochee: See *Foot*

U

Understatement: See *Irony*

Unities: Strict rules of dramatic structure, formulated by Italian and French critics of the Renaissance and based loosely on the principles of drama discussed by Aristotle in his *Poetics*. Foremost among these rules were the three unities of action, time, and place that compelled a dramatist to: (1) construct a single plot with a beginning, middle, and end that details the causal relationships of action and character; (2) restrict the action to the events of a single day; and (3) limit the scene to a single place or city. The unities were observed faithfully by continental European writers until the Romantic Age, but they were never regularly observed in English drama. Modern dramatists are typically more concerned with a unity of impression or emotional effect than with any of the classical unities.

Urban Realism: A branch of realist writing that attempts to accurately reflect the often harsh facts of modern urban existence.

Utopia: A fictional perfect place, such as "paradise" or "heaven."

Utopian: See *Utopia*

Utopianism: See *Utopia*

V

Verisimilitude: Literally, the appearance of truth. In literary criticism, the term refers to aspects of a work of literature that seem true to the reader.

Vers de societe: See *Occasional Verse*

Vers libre: See *Free Verse*

Verse: A line of metered language, a line of a poem, or any work written in verse.

Versification: The writing of verse. Versification may also refer to the meter, rhyme, and other mechanical components of a poem.

Victorian: Refers broadly to the reign of Queen Victoria of England (1837–1901) and to anything with qualities typical of that era. For example, the qualities of smug narrowmindedness, bourgeois materialism, faith in social progress, and priggish morality are often considered Victorian. This stereotype is contradicted by such dramatic intellectual developments as the theories of Charles Darwin, Karl Marx, and Sigmund Freud (which stirred strong debates in England) and the critical attitudes of serious Victorian writers like Charles Dickens and George Eliot. In literature, the Victorian Period was the great age of the English novel, and the latter part of the era saw the rise of movements such as decadence and symbolism.

Victorian Age: See *Victorian*

Victorian Period: See *Victorian*

W

Weltanschauung: A German term referring to a person's worldview or philosophy.

Weltschmerz: A German term meaning "world pain." It describes a sense of anguish about the nature of existence, usually associated with a melancholy, pessimistic attitude.

Z

Zarzuela: A type of Spanish operetta.

Zeitgeist: A German term meaning "spirit of the time." It refers to the moral and intellectual trends of a given era.

Cumulative Author/Title Index

Cumulative Nationality/Ethnicity Index

Acoma Pueblo

Ortiz, Simon
    Hunger in New York City: V4

African American

Angelou, Maya
    Harlem Hopscotch: V2
    On the Pulse of Morning: V3
Baraka, Amiri
    In Memory of Radio: V9
Brooks, Gwendolyn
    The Bean Eaters: V2
    The Sonnet-Ballad: V1
    Strong Men, Riding Horses: V4
    We Real Cool: V6
Clifton, Lucille
    Miss Rosie: V1
Cullen, Countee
    Any Human to Another: V3
Dove, Rita
    This Life: V1
Hayden, Robert
    Those Winter Sundays: V1
Hughes, Langston
    Harlem: V1
    Mother to Son: V3
    The Negro Speaks of Rivers: V10
    Theme for English B: V6
Johnson, James Weldon
    The Creation: V1
Komunyakaa, Yusef
    Facing It: V5
Madgett, Naomi Long
    Alabama Centennial: V10
McElroy, Colleen
    A Pièd: V3

Randall, Dudley
    Ballad of Birmingham: V5
Reed, Ishmael
    Beware: Do Not Read This Poem:
        V6

American

Angelou, Maya
    Harlem Hopscotch: V2
    On the Pulse of Morning: V3
Ashbery, John
    Paradoxes and Oxymorons: V11
Auden, W. H.
    As I Walked Out One Evening: V4
    Musée des Beaux Arts: V1
    The Unknown Citizen: V3
Bishop, Elizabeth
    Brazil, January 1, 1502: V6
Blumenthal, Michael
    Inventors: V7
Bly, Robert
    Come with Me: V6
Bradstreet, Anne
    To My Dear and Loving Husband:
        V6
Brooks, Gwendolyn
    The Bean Eaters: V2
    The Sonnet-Ballad: V1
    Strong Men, Riding Horses: V4
    We Real Cool: V6
Clifton, Lucille
    Miss Rosie: V1
Crane, Stephen
    War Is Kind: V9
Cullen, Countee
    Any Human to Another: V3

cummings, e. e.
    l(a: V1
    old age sticks: V3
Dickey, James
    The Heaven of Animals: V6
    The Hospital Window: V11
Dickinson, Emily
    *Because I Could Not Stop for
        Death*: V2
    The Bustle in a House: V10
    *"Hope" Is the Thing with
        Feathers*: V3
    *I Heard a Fly Buzz—When I
        Died—*: V5
    *My Life Closed Twice Before Its
        Close*: V8
    A Narrow Fellow in the Grass:
        V11
    *The Soul Selects Her Own
        Society*: V1
    There's a Certain Slant of Light:
        V6
    This Is My Letter to the World: V4
Dove, Rita
    This Life: V1
Dugan, Alan
    How We Heard the Name: V10
Eliot, T. S.
    Journey of the Magi: V7
    *The Love Song of J. Alfred
        Prufrock*: V1
Emerson, Ralph Waldo
    Concord Hymn: V4
Frost, Robert
    The Death of the Hired Man: V4
    Fire and Ice: V7
    Mending Wall: V5
    Nothing Gold Can Stay: V3

Subject/Theme Index

***Boldface** denotes dicussion in *Themes* section.

A

Absurdity
  Jabberwocky: 90–91, 93–97, 99–106
Adventure and Exploration
  Beowulf: 2, 4, 6–7
Africa
  Go Down, Moses: 43–47, 51–55
  Jabberwocky: 96, 99
Alien Lands
  The Milkfish Gatherers: 116
Alienation
  Beowulf: 4–6
  Tonight I Can Write: 194
Alienation and Loneliness
  Beowulf: 4
  Island of the Three Marias: 82
  Tonight I Can Write: 189
Allegory
  Jabberwocky: 94, 97, 100
Alliteration
  Beowulf: 10–11
  The Hospital Window: 64
  Jabberwocky: 93–95, 97
  The Milkfish Gatherers: 118
  A Narrow Fellow in the Grass: 133–134
American Northeast
  Overture to a Dance of Locomotives: 141, 144, 147, 149–150, 156–157
  The War Against the Trees: 223

American Southwest
  To a Child Running With Outstretched Arms in Canyon de Chelly: 172, 176, 178
Anger
  The Hospital Window: 57, 61–62, 66–67
  The War Against the Trees: 223–225
Appearances and Reality
  Beowulf: 5
  A Narrow Fellow in the Grass: 129
  Paradoxes and Oxymorons: 164
Art and Experience
  Chocolates: 19
Arthurian Legend
  The Eagle: 40
Artists and Society
  Chocolates: 19
Asia
  The Milkfish Gatherers: 110, 112–114, 116–122
  The Weight of Sweetness: 229, 233
Atonement
  Island of the Three Marias: 82
Avant-Garde
  Overture to a Dance of Locomotives: 156

B

Ballad
  Jabberwocky: 90, 94–95, 97, 100
Beauty
  Go Down, Moses: 44–45, 47

Overture to a Dance of Locomotives: 142–143, 145–148
  To a Child Running With Outstretched Arms in Canyon de Chelly: 172, 174, 179

C

Central America
  Island of the Three Marias: 83–84
Christianity
  The Hospital Window: 72–74
  Island of the Three Marias: 84–86
City Life
  Overture to a Dance of Locomotives: 156–157
Classicism
  The War Against the Trees: 223, 226
Coming of Age
  To a Child Running With Outstretched Arms in Canyon de Chelly: 175
Communism
  Beowulf: 6–7
Courage
  Beowulf: 1, 4
  Go Down, Moses: 43–45
Courage and Community
  Go Down, Moses: 45
Crime and Criminals
  The Eagle: 30, 32–35
  Island of the Three Marias: 78, 80–83
Cubism
  Overture to a Dance of Locomotives: 148–149, 154

Subject/Theme Index

Cumulative Index of
First Lines

Cumulative Index of
Last Lines

A

a man then suddenly stops running (Island of Three Marias) V11:80

a space in the lives of their friends (Beware: Do Not Read This Poem) V6:3

A terrible beauty is born (Easter 1916) V5:91

About my big, new, automatically defrosting refrigerator with the built-in electric eye (Reactionary Essay on Applied Science) V9:199

Across the expedient and wicked stones (Auto Wreck) V3:31

Ah, dear father, graybeard, lonely old courage-teacher, what America did you have when Charon quit poling his ferry and you got out on a smoking bank and stood watching the boat disappear on the black waters of Lethe? (A Supermarket in California) V5:261

All losses are restored and sorrows end (Sonnet 30) V4:192

Amen. Amen (The Creation) V1:20

Anasazi (Anasazi) V9:3

and all beyond saving by children (Ethics) V8:88

And all we need of hell (My Life Closed Twice Before Its Close) V8:127

and changed, back to the class ("Trouble with Math in a One-Room Country School") V9:238

And Death shall be no more: Death, thou shalt die (Holy Sonnet 10) V2:103

And drunk the milk of Paradise (Kubla Khan) V5:172

And gallop terribly against each other's bodies (Autumn Begins in Martins Ferry, Ohio) V8:17

And his own Word (The Phoenix) V10:226

And life for me ain't been no crystal stair (Mother to Son) V3:179

And like a thunderbolt he falls (The Eagle) V11:30

And makes me end where I begun (A Valediction: Forbidding Mourning) V11:202

And miles to go before I sleep (Stopping by Woods on a Snowy Evening) V1:272

And not waving but drowning (Not Waving but Drowning) V3:216

And oh, 'tis true, 'tis true (When I Was One-and-Twenty) V4:268

and retreating, always retreating, behind it (Brazil, January 1, 1502) V6:16

And settled upon his eyes in a black soot ("More Light! More Light!") V6:120

And so live ever—or else swoon to death (Bright Star! Would I Were Steadfast as Thou Art) V9:44

and strange and loud was the dingoes' cry (Drought Year) V8:78

And that has made all the difference (The Road Not Taken) V2:195

And the deep river ran on (As I Walked Out One Evening) V4:16

And the midnight message of Paul Revere (Paul Revere's Ride) V2:180

And the mome raths outgrabe (Jabberwocky) V11:91

and these the last verses that I write for her (Tonight I Can Write) V11:187

And those roads in South Dakota that feel around in the darkness ... (Come with Me) V6:31

and to know she will stay in the field till you die? (Landscape with Tractor) V10:183

and two blankets embroidered with smallpox (Meeting the British) V7:138

And would suffice (Fire and Ice) V7:57

And Zero at the Bone— (A Narrow Fellow in the Grass) V11:127

As any She belied with false compare (Sonnet 130) V1:248

As far as Cho-fu-Sa (The River-Merchant's Wife: A Letter) V8:165

As the contagion of those molten eyes (For An Assyrian Frieze) V9:120

As they lean over the beans in their rented back room that is full of beads and receipts and dolls and

U

W

Y